Grantees of Arms
Named in Docquets and Patents
Volume 1 (A to J)
1687 – 1898
Alphabetically arranged by
Joseph Foster Hon. M.A. Oxon.
Edited by
W. Harry Rylands F.S.A

First Published in 1916
A facsimile copy produced and privately printed by
The Armorial Register Limited 2017

First Published in 2017
by
The Armorial Register Limited
All rights reserved

ISBN: 978-0-9957246-0-0

British Library Cataloguing-in-Publication Data
A catalogue record of this book is available on request from the British
Library

THE

Publications

OF

The Harleian Society.

ESTABLISHED A.D. MDCCCLXIX.

Volume LXVIII.

FOR THE YEAR MDCCCCXVI.

Grantees of Arms

NAMED IN

DOCQUETS AND PATENTS

BETWEEN THE YEARS

1687 AND 1898,

PRESERVED IN

VARIOUS MANUSCRIPTS,

COLLECTED AND

ALPHABETICALLY ARRANGED BY

THE LATE JOSEPH FOSTER, HON. M.A. OXON.,

AND CONTAINED IN THE ADDITIONAL

MS. No. 37,149, IN THE BRITISH MUSEUM.

EDITED BY

W. HARRY RYLANDS, F.S.A.

LONDON.

1916.

LONDON :
PRINTED BY ROWORTH AND COMPANY LIMITED,
NEWTON STREET, W.C. 2.

Preface.

THIS Volume contains the first half of another of the Manuscripts compiled by the late Joseph Foster and purchased by the Authorities of the British Museum, from Josslyn Foster, 14th Oct., 1905.

It bears the Press-mark, Add. MS. 37,149, and contains a continuation of the Names of Grantees of Arms, commenced in the volume already printed by the Society. It must, however, be clearly pointed out that, whereas in the first volume there were always the Harleian and other MSS. to refer to, in this case it is not so. The Volume contains almost entirely references to the Grant Books preserved at the Heralds' College; and, of course, it follows that, even had time allowed, to check any of the information given in it was naturally impossible. Every care has been taken to give the references correctly. Unfortunately, however, the numbers of the volumes are wrongly given by Foster in Arabic numerals, and badly-written figures often lead to error; I have restored the Roman numerals.

Foster commenced by filling in a certain portion of the date to each Patent; this has been continued, as also the references to printed books where a copy of the Grant referred to will be found.

It seems certain that Foster added items of information, after his first index slips had been made, with the object of identifying the person mentioned. It seems most probable that many if not all the later additions are enclosed in round brackets, and it will be noticed that some of the Grantees are marked with a rank they did not obtain until after the date of the Patent of Arms.

It must also be pointed out that the references to Berry, Berry's Supplement, and Berry's Appendix must not be taken as giving in every instance the date of the Patent, &c. Therefore it is sometimes difficult, on turning to Berry's *Encyclopædia Heraldica*, to identify the Arms intended, particularly when the date of the Patent is after that of the publication of Berry's volumes.

In using the book it is also necessary to remember that Foster very often uses the words "before" and "after" when expressing a change of name, simply as describing the position of the two or more names referred to. To take one instance, he writes "Fitzgerald after Dalton," but Dalton was the name really added. It would have been clearer to have written "Fitzgerald to Dalton-Fitzgerald"; to have altered all the instances in which this error occurs would have taken more time than was at my disposal.

Foster gives a list of the volumes of Grants with dates attached, and it will be found printed on page vii, together with some additions by myself, in order to bring the list up to the date required. In the case of the last volume referred to, LXXI, it must be noticed that no folios are given in the manuscript, so I have printed the year for this volume, 18 . . ., although, at the same time, it may be assumed that it contains some portions of the years 1899 and 1900.

I hope, in Part 2 of this Volume, to print another list I have been compiling, giving more complete information about the dates.

From a comparison of the dates given in this list, as well as notes from printed books and my own collections, it has been possible to add, here and there, dates to the Patents. These, and all other additions, have been placed in square brackets, except simple connecting words, and in some instances the names of the counties.

It must be remembered that one of Foster's failings was an infatuation for brevity, quite regardless, it seems to me, of any clearness of expression. This, together with the indifferent and confused writing, has led to some difficulties. Many of them were overcome by the interest as well as the care and trouble given by Miss Drucker, the transcriber.

My thanks I also gladly give to my brother, J. Paul Rylands, Esq., F.S.A., and to the Secretary, W. Bruce Bannerman, Esq., F.S.A., for kind assistance.

I must also mention how much I have benefited by the consideration and advice of the printers, Messrs. Roworth & Co., who have throughout freely given me the advantage of their skill and experience.

W. HARRY RYLANDS.

Dates at which the Various Grant Books commence and from which
dates can be approximately assigned to each Grant, 18th-Century entries
ending with Grants [Vol.] XX.

1.—1637 ⎫ Hodge-podge,	31.— 1 May 1818.
2.—1639 ⎬ *see* end of MS. and	32.— 5 Jan. 1820.
3.—1664 ⎭ the earlier index.	33.—31 Aug. 1821.
4.—1687.	34.—27 Feb. 1823.
5.—10 Feb. 1699-1700.	35.—22 Aug. 1824.
6.—31 Oct. 1711.	36.— 3 April 1826.
7.— June 1720.	37.— 4 Jan. 1828.
8.— 1727.	38.— 6 Aug. 1829.
9.—15 Dec. 1740.	39.—27 Jan. 1832.
10.—31 Jan. 1755.	40.—17 Sept. 1833.
11.— 2 Jan. 1764.	41.—19 May 1835.
12.— Jan. 1770.	42.—23 Nov. 1836.
13.—20 Sept. 1774.	43.—30 April 1838.
14.—31 Oct. 1777.	44.—21 May 1839.
15.—16 Jan. 1782.	45.—21 Sept. 1840.
16.—10 Feb. 1785.	46.— 1 Mar. 1842.
17.—13 May 1788.	47.—17 Nov. 1843.
18.—27 Feb. 1792.	48.— 8 July 1845.
19.— 4 Feb. 1795.	49.— Mar. 1848.
20.— 2 Aug. 1797.	50.—13 June 1851.
21.—31 Mar. 1800.	51.—14 Feb. 1854.
22.— 5 Nov. 1802.	52.—12 April 1856.
23.— 8 May 1804-6.	53.—13 Aug. 1858.
24.—(10 July 1804)	54.— July 1860.
Aug. 1806-8.	55.—15 Jan. 1863.
25.—20 Sept. 1808.	56.—25 Aug. 1865.
26.—20 June 1810.	57.—28 April 1868.
27.—29 Aug. 1811.	58.—18 May 1871.
28.— 8 Jan. 1814.	59.— June 1874-7.
29.— June 1815.	60.— April 1880.
30.—22 Aug. 1816.	Ends 1877-80.

Foster's List ends here; the following has been compiled from the
Patents entered in the MS., and is simply a tentative list of the years
to be found in the Volumes :—

61.—1880-1882.	67.—1892-1894.
62.—1882-1884.	68.—1894-1895.
63.—1884 (?)-1887.	69.—1895-1897.
64.—1887-1888.	70.—1897-1899.
65.—1889-1890.	71.—1899-1900 (?)
66.—1890-1892.	

Grantees of Arms, 1687—1898.

ADDITIONS AND CORRECTIONS.

PAGE

2. Acland (Fuller) before Hood, *for* LIX *read* XLIX.

3. Addington, Henry, *read* Viscount Sidmouth, 12 Jan. 1805; and *for* [1805] *read* [1804].

4. Albert, Courtail, *should be* COURTAIL.

5. Allan, Robert Henry, *for* XXXVII *read* XXXVIII.
Allanson, *after* late Winn *read* 1777; and *for* 1777 *read* [1777].

6. Amherst after Tyssen, *after* Quarterly Arms *for* 188 . . *read* [1867].

8. Antrim, Earl of, *for* McDonald *read* McDonnell.

11. Ashe-a'Court, *after* Bart. *read* [4 July 1795].
Ashton, Baron, *after* or 1896 *add* [1895].

12. Atkins, Michael, *after* 1748-9 *add* [174$\frac{8}{9}$].

15. Baddeford, *after* 1703-4 *add* [170$\frac{3}{4}$].

16. Baker (s. of Sir William), *for* 1802 ? *read* 1803 ?

19. Barkworth, *after* 1894 *add* [1879] (? an error here).
Barnard, Gilbert Vane, *after* 1724-5 *add* [172$\frac{4}{5}$].

22. Baskerville before Mynors, *after* Mynors *read* [3 July 1817]; and this name is out of its place.

24. Baynton, Rear-Adm., *for* fol. 44 *read* Vol. XLIV, fol. . . . .

26. Beckford to Pitt-Rivers, *dele* the ? after [1828].
Bendall, *after* 1692-3 *add* [169$\frac{2}{3}$].

29. Benson, Robert, *after* 1880 *add* [1841] (? an error here).

30. Berkeley, Adm., fol. 238 [? 1813, fol. 338].

32. Bickerton, Rear-Adm., Vol. XXIII [? Vol. XXIX].

33. Bigg to Gulston, 1823 is Vol. XXIV; Vol. XX, fol. 189, is 1798.
Yeatman-Biggs, 1878 is Vol. LX; Vol. LXII, fol. 159, is 1883.
Bingley, Baron, Robert Benson, *read* BENSON; and *after* 1713-14 *add* [171$\frac{3}{4}$].

34. Birt, William Morlais, 1896 is Vol. LXIX; Vol. LXV, fol. 69, is 1889.
Blach, *for* 1819 *read* 1809.
Blackburn, John, M.A., 1803 is Vol. XXII; Vol. XXXVI, fol. 129, is 1826.

35. Blackett, Elizabeth, *after* 1729-30 *add* [17$\frac{29}{30}$].

38. Bonovrier, *after* 1737-8 *add* [173$\frac{7}{8}$].

39. Borthwick, Sir Algernon, *read* afterwards [1895] Baron Glenesk, Scotland [Bart.], 1887, Vol. LXIV, fol. 46.
Bosanquet, Samuel, *after* 1786-7 *add* [1787].

40. Bosville before Macdonald, *for* 11 April 1814 *read* 16 Sept. 1824.
Boughey quartered by Lingard, *after* 1868 *add* [1871].

41. Bourke, Michael, *after* 1737 *add* [1757].
Bowen, Sir George Fergusson, 1880, Vol. LXI, fol. 23 [? 1860, LIV, fol. 23].

43. Boynton, Adriana, Lady, *after* 1723-24 *add* [172$\frac{3}{4}$].
Brace, *after* K.C.B. *add* [1834], and *for* [1834] *read* [1836].

44. Braybrooke to Griffin, *for* [1798] *read* [1797].

48. Brooke, Sir Thomas, *read after* Thomas [Bart., 1899].
Brookfield, *after* 1872 *add* [1877].

51. Browne, John, of Salperton, *erase* [? 80].
Bruce after Wright [1 Feb. 1867], and *after* U.S. Minister *add* [1867].

52. Brunner, *after* Bart. *read* 1895, and *after* Lanc. *add* [1847 ?].

PAGE

52. Brydges, Samuel Egerton, *after* Kent *add* [27 Dec.].
53. Buller-Elphinstone, *for* XXIV *read* XXXIV.
54. Bulwer before Lytton, Bart., *after* Lytton *read* [10 Feb. 1844]; and *after* Norf. *add* [1843].
57. Bushman, *for* 178¾ *read* 1783-4 [1784].
58. Button, *after* 1768 or 1769 *add* [1768].
59. Cadogan, William, Baron, *for* [1718] *read* [1716].
   Caldwell, Adm., *for* 180 . ., *read* [1820].
61. Campbell, Sir Archibald, Vol. XXXVIII is 1831 [? Vol. XXXV]; *after* Vol. XXXIX, which is 1833, *add* [?].
   Campbell to Campbell-Wyndham, *add* 1844; and *for* 1844, *after* Wilts., *read* [1843].
62. Carbonnel ? Cardonnel.
   Carew ? *to read* Carew after Hallowell [1828 ?], Vol. XXXVII, fol. 176, Vice-Adm. Sir Benjamin, K.C.B. [1815], of co. Surrey [G.C.B. 6 June 1831]. Supporters, [Vol. XXXVIII, fol. . . . .].
66. Causton (both entries), *after* 1699-1700, *add* [$\frac{1632}{1700}$].
   Cave-Orme, *for* fol. 92 *read* [1894] 292.
68. Chamier, *after* 1815 *add* [1851].
69. Chapple, *after* 1702 *add* [1782].
   Chatteris, *after* 1826 *add* [1831].
70. Cheeke, *after* 1707 *add* [1700].
71. Child, Sir Francis, *after* 1700-1701 *add* [170$\frac{0}{1}$].
   Chisman, formerly Muilman, *after* 1772 or 3 *add* [1772].
   Cholmley, late Strickland, *after* LII *add* [LV, for 1865].
73. Clare, Earl of, *after* Supporters *add* [1799, Baron FitzGibbon, created 24 Sept. 1799].
   Clarke, Charles, *dele* [Edward] and [22 Oct. 1600], which refer to the patent to Edward Clarke, of Ardington, Berks.; Berry gives Arms "Granted to Charles Clarke, of Ockley, Surrey," without a date. *Instead of* [22 Oct. 1600] *insert* [1755].
   Clarke after Price, *for* 1786 *read* 1787.
76. Clifton, Sir Robert, *after* fol. 47 *add* [? 470].
   Clinton, Maj.-Gen. Sir Henry, *for* [1815] *read* [1813].
   Clinton, Maj.-Gen. Sir William, *add* [Henry].
   Clive after Windsor, [? Windsor after Clive, 8 Nov. 1855], *for* 1885 *read* 1851 and *add* after it [1855].
77. Coape before Sherbrooke, *for* [180 . .] *read* [1810].
79. Cole, late Loggin, *after* Loggin *add* [1802].
80. Collingwood, Baron [20 Nov. ? 1805] and *after* Supporters *add* [1806].
81. Colpoys, Vice-Adm., *read* after K.B. [14 Feb. 1798], and *after* Supporters *add* [1798].
   Colville, Maj.-Gen., *after* G.C.B. *read* [7 April 1815] and *after* Supporters *add* [1817]. He was made G.C.H. in 1816.
   Colyear-Dawkins, *for* XXXI *read* XLI and *add* before it [1836].
   Combermere, Lieut.-Gen., *add* at the end [*see* Cotton].
82. Congleton, Baron [18 Aug. 1841], and *after* Arms *add* [1842].
   Conway, *for* Lord *read* Baron [17 Mar. 170⅔], and *after* Supporters *add* [170⅔].
83. Cook, Sir Francis [Bart., 1886], *after* Surrey *for* 186 . ., *read* [1870].
85. Copeland, *after* 1836 *add* [1819], and *for* fol. 238 *read* 283. 1836 (fol. 283) would be Vol. XLI.
86. Cotton, *after* Baron *add* Combermere, and the same *after* Viscount; *after* Supporters *for* 18 . . . ., *read* [1830]. Should the Vol. number be XXVIII for 1814 or Vol. XXXVI, fol. 180, for 1827 ?
87. Cotton after Stapleton [Stapleton before Cotton, 21 Nov. 1827], *after* [1827] *add* [1829] for Vol. XXXVII, fol. 254. ? Should it be Vol. XXXVI ?
   Coulthart, *after* Nov. 1846 *add* [Vol. XLVIII, fol. . . .], and *place* Vol. LIII, fol. 57, *after* [and 17 Jan. 1859].

PAGE
89. Cranley, *for* Lord *read* Baron.
Cranworth, Baron, *for* 184 . . ., *read* [1851].
91. Croft, Sir John, *for* Coaling *read* Cowling, and *add* within the brackets, *before* 22 March, the word Arms.
Cromwell to Frankland, [1806], and *for* 18 . . ., *read* [1806].
92. Crossley, Sir Francis, Bart., *for* 18 . . ., *read* [1851] and *dele* [? LV.].
95. Dacre to Assey, *after* 1723-4 *add* [1836].
Dalton to Norcliffe, *after* Norcliffe *read* [Aug. 1807], and *after* York *add* [1808].
97. Dartinequinave, *after* 1720 *add* [1710 ?].
Davenport-Handley, *for* Hansley *read* Handley; *after* Aug. *add* [May]; *after* 1881 *add* [1851], and *add* at the end the sentence ("Genealogist, VII, p. 23, and Berry's Suppl.") from Davenport-Bromley.
98. Davie, John, *after* 1699-1700 *add* [$\frac{1699}{1700}$].
102. De Coussmaker, *for* [1799] *read* [1779].
103. Denison, late Beckett, *add after* Edmund [Bart., 8 Sept. 1813] and *add after* Nottingham [1816].
Denison, now Beckett, *for* Edmond *read* Edmund.
105. De Wallmoden, *for* 1750 *read* 1740, and *add* before the Vol. number [$17\frac{33}{8}$].
107. Dinevor, Baroness, *enter* the year [1782] *after* (Rice).
Dipple, Mary, *after* IV *add* [VIII].
108. Don, Gen. Sir George, Vol. XXXVII, fol. 51, is 1828; Vol. XXXII, fol. 51, would be 1820.
109. Dottin, *read* of English; 1817 is Vol. XXX; Vol. XXXVI, fol. 107, is 1826.
110. Downe, Viscount Henry, *for* [1687] *read* [1698].
111. Drummond, Baron, *read* [26 Oct. 1797] *after* and, and *add* [1798] *after* Supporters.
Ducie (Moreton, late Reynolds), *after* ? fol. 63 *add* [? 163].
112. Dudley, Lord, *after* Lord enter the date [19 Nov. 1740], and *add* [1748] *after* Supporters.
Dugdale, Sir John, *after* (Match) *add* [1688].
Dugdale, Adam, third line of this entry, *for* 1833, Vol. XXIX, *read* 1833, Vol. XXXIX.
113. Duncan (Beveridge), *after* 1813 *add* [1799].
115. Dyson, Henry, *after* 1824 *add* [1825].
116. Eckersall, *after* 1765 *add* [1766].
121. Ellis after Joyner, *for* 1813 ? *read* 1817 ?
Elphin, *add* [*see* Tilson].
Elsley, William, *for* Vol. VII *read* Vol. VIII.
122. Engleheart, *for* [1821] *read* [1820].
English, P. J., *after* or 81 *add* [181].
125. Eyre, late Archer-Houblon, *for* 18 . . . *read* 1831; and *after* fol. 336 *for* 1831 *read see* [1819].
126. Farnaby, Sir Charles, *read* after fol. 98 (from the entry next above), [$170\frac{3}{4}$, Charles, of Kippington, Gwillim, p. 171].
127. Faudel-Phillips (last line), *for* [? 1897] *read* [1898].
128. Fielden, *after* 1856 *add* [1836].
Fell, *for* 1722 *read* 1772.
129. Fenwick(-Clennell), ..., *for* XLI *read* LXI.
Ferrers, Baroness, *for* [1778] *read* [1779].
Ferris, *for* XXXVII *read* XXVII.
Fetherston, late Dilke, *for* XXIX *read* XXXIX.
130. Feversham, Lord, *for* Fevesham *read* Feversham.
131. Fish, *for* 18$\frac{10}{13}$ *read* 1810-12.
Fisher, Joseph, *after* 1730 *add* [1720].
137. Fountain, formerly Price, *after* 1874 *add* [1870].
139. Freeman, now Thomas, *for* XV *read* XVI.
Freeman, J. R., *for* XLV *read* LXV.

PAGE
141. Gabriel, *for* [1866-67] *read* [1867].
      Gage, Rokewode-, Sir Edward, *for* [1866] *read* [1867].
143. Gardner, John, of St. Olave's, Southwark, *after* 170⅔ *add* [172⅔].
146. Giddy to Gilbert, *add* [1816] *before* Vol. XXX; and *place* 1818 *before* fol. 360.
      Gilbert, late Giddy, *after* 1817-18 *add* [1816]; and *before* fol. 360 *add* [1818].
154. Graves, Richard, *for* Vol. VII *read* Vol. [? VIII].
157. Gray [Baron Grey], Egerton *should be* EGERTON.
      Grey, Gen. Sir Henry George, *for* 182 . ., *read* [1831].
159. Grosvenor, Erle-Drax, *read* Grosvenor to Erle-Drax-Grosvenor; and *add*
      [*see* Burke under Drax].
160. Gull, Sir William, *after* Vol. LVIII *read* [1871]; and *enter* Augmentation,
      17 Sept. 1872 *before* fol. 146.
165. Hamilton, Lieut.-Gen. Sir John, *for* [1814] *read* [1815].
      Hamilton, Major Sir James John, *for* [1835 or 36] *read* [1836].
166. Hammond, *after* Baron *read* [5 Mar. 1874].
167. Harbord, Sir William Morden, *for* 17 . . *read* [Supporters, ? 1744].
168. Hare, late Leigh, *after* 1814-15 *add* [1814].
171. Harrison William, F.S.A., *for* [1858] *read* [1859-60].
      Harrison, William John, *for* [1790] *read* [1791 ?].
172. Harrop after Hulton, *after* Hulton *read* [8 Dec. 1866]; and *after* co. Lanc.
      add [1866].
173. Harvey, John Springett, *dele* [?] *after* XXII.
174. Havelock, ..., of Guisborough, *for* [?] *read* [1817].
175. Hayes, John Macnamara, *for* [?] *read* [1796].
176. Heard, Isaac, *after* Norroy *for* [1776] *read* [1774]; and *after* Clarenceux
      for [1776] Vol. XIII *read* [1780] Vol. XIV.
177. Hele after Selby, *for* [1790] *read* [1791].
179. Herschell, Baron, *dele* [1886] and [?] at the end.
180. Hesketh-Fleetwood, *to read* fols. 2 and [1831] 258.
181. Heywood (Bart.), *dele* [?] *after* Vol. XL.
183. Hillary, Sir William, *for* [1806 ?] *read* [1807].
184. Hislop, after 1813, *for* [?] *read* [1822].
      Hoar to Harland, Sir Charles, Bart. [1808]; assumed the name of Harland
      26 May 1802, died 1810 (*see* Burke's Commoners, III, p. 194). The
      reference given, Vol. XXXV, fol. 226, is 1827; 1802 would be Vol. XXI.
187. Hollester, Luke, *for* [1780 ?] *read* [1781].
      Holloway, John, of Westham, *after* 1725 *add* [172⅘].
      Holmes, John, s. of James Edward, *for* [1780] *read* [1781].
189. Hopson, late Ongley, *after* 1824 *add* [1825] and *dele* [?].
190. Horton, Anne, *after* 1725 *add* [1726] and *dele* [? 333].
191. Howard, Charles, *after* 1756 *add* [1755].
192. Howard, Thomas, *after* 1833-35 *add* [1834].
193. Hubbuck, *for* Vol. LXX, *read* Vol. LX.
194. Hughes-Le Fleming, *after* 1861 *add* [1862].
195. Humphrey, Alfred Paget, *dele* [? 1897].
197. Hutchinson, Robert, *for* [1861] *read* [1862].
199. Ironside after Bax, *for* [1866] *read* [1867].
202. James after Grevis, *after* 1817 *add* [1818].
      Jarrett, James, *after* 1696, *add* [1697].
203. Jenkinson, Baron Hawkesbury, *after* [23 July 1796] *add* [1797].
204. Jervoise after Purefoy, ..., M.A., *for* [1791] *read* [1795 ?].
205. Joddrell, late Bower, *after* 1775 *add* [1774].
      Johnson, Elizabeth, Vol. XLIII, fol. 45, is 1838; 12 Feb. 174½ is Vol. IX, fol. 45.
      Johnson, ..., formerly wife of Edward Hughes Ball, *for* [1818] *read* [1819].
207. Jones, of co. Radnor, *for* [1824] *read* [1808].
208. Jones, Samuel Thomas, *for* [1861] *read* [1862].
      Jones, Lieut.-Gen. Sir Harry David, *for* [1861] *read* [1862].
209. Juxon to Hesketh, *enclose* 5 May 1761 in square brackets.

𝔄 fairly ℭomplete and 𝔘nique 𝔄lphabetical 𝔏ist

OF

𝔓ersonal 𝔊rants of 𝔄rms

ON RECORD AT THE

ℭollege of 𝔄rms, 1687—1898.

With reference to the Grant Books at the Heralds' College, printed books
and MSS. in British Museum, incorporated by J. F.

AS CONTAINED IN ADDITIONAL MS. 37,149.

By J. FOSTER, Hon. M.A., Oxon, 1898.

(Refer also to Brit. Museum Add. MSS. 14,830 and 14,831, and Add. MS. 35,336,
by Townley, Bluemantle, since incorporated 1898.)

---

* Indicates special limitations to relatives of the Grantees other than descendants.

A

ABBEY, Henry, of Fairlee, Brighton, co. Sussex, Vol. LXXI, fol. . . . .
ABBOT, of Sudbury, co. Suff. (see UPCHER), 1774-77,* Vol. XIII, fol. 269.
  ,, Henry Alexis, s. of Jasper, of Bengal and London and Angora, 1802-4,*
    Vol. XXII, fol. 377.
  ,, Charles, Baron Colchester, of co. Essex and co. Sussex. Arms, 1817, Vol.
    XXX, fol. 194. Supporters, Vol. XXX, fol. 196.
ABBOTT, Charles, of Queen's Square and the Inner Temple, London, of the precincts
    of Canterbury, 181 . ., Vol. XXVI, fol. 92 (see MATSELL). 182 . ., Vol.
    XXXVI, fol. 252, Baron Tenterden, 1827. Supporters, 18 . . .*
  ,, Vernon and Christopher, brothers, of Highbury Cottage, Newland, co. Glouc.,
    and sisters Anne and Clementina, 18 . . .,* Vol. XXVI, fol. 87.
  ,, John, of Braemar House, Lancaster Gate, London, 1882,* Vol. LXII,
    fol. 10. (Berry's Suppl.)
ABDY, Thomas Neville, of Albyns, co. Essex, 1848-51, Vol. XLIX, fol. 238.
A'BECKETT, A. W., of 33, Eccleston Square, London, 1888, Vol. LXIV, fol. 221.
  ,, W. A. Callendar, of Melbourne, Victoria, 1888, Vol. LXIV, fol. 221.
  ,, W. A. Callendar, of Penleigh House, Westbury, co. Wilts. ? MILLS escutcheon
    of pretence. 1891, Vol. LXVIII, fol. 161.
ABEL, Sir Frederick Augustus, Bart. [1893], of London, 1883,* Vol. LXII, fol. 132.
ABERCROMBIE, Lieut.-Gen. Sir John [K.C.B. 1815, G.C.B. 1815]. Supporters,
    1815-17, Vol. XXIX, fol. 37.
  ,, Sir Ralph, Commr-in-Chief, Ireland [Maj.-Gen. Sir Ralph, K.B., 22 July
    1795]. Supporters, 1797-180 . ., Vol. XX, fol. 80.

A

ABERCROMBIE [General] Sir Robert, Comm^r-in-Chief, India [K.B. 1792].
Supporters, 179 . ., Vol. XX, fol. 143.
,, Baroness. Supporters, 1800-2, Vol. XXI, fol. 248.   Augmentation, Vol.
XXI, fol. 253
ABERDEIN to HARVEY, John, of Covent Garden, London, and Isle of Grenada.
Match, 17 . . .,* Vol. XVII, fol. 428.
[ABERGAVENNY,Wales, Borough of, 27 March 1901. (Geneal. Mag.,Vol.V, p. 157.)]
ABINGDON, Countess (VENABLES Arms), 17 . . ., Vol. VIII, fol. 16.
ABINGER, James, Baron, of Surrey and Norwich, co. Norf., and his descendants,
1835,* Vol. XL, fol. 334.
ABNEY before HASTINGS, of Willesley Hall, co. Derby, Bart.   Quarterly Arms,
1823-24, Vol. XXXIV, fol. 216.
ABRAHAM, John, of Grassendale, in Liverpool, 1876, Vol. LIX, fol. 274.
ACCRINGTON, co. Lanc., Borough of, 1897, Vol. LX, fol. 309.
ACKERS, B. St. John, of Prinknash Park and Huntley Manor, co. Glouc., 1885,
Vol. LXIII, fol. 97.
ACKROYD, see AKROYD, 1875.
ACLAND after PALMER, Sir John, Bart., of Petherton Park, co. Somerset, Newhouse
and Columb John, co. Devon.   Quarterly Arms, 1818, Vol. XXXI, fol. 144.
ACLAND (PALMER) after FULLER, Bart., Sir Peregrine, of Catsfield, co. Sussex.
Quarterly Arms, 1834, Vol. XL, fol. 237.
ACLAND (PALMER after FULLER, Bart., Sir Peregrine, of Catsfield, co. Sussex).
Match with GROVE, 185 . ., Vol. L, fol. 297.
ACLAND (FULLER) before HOOD, Sir Alexander, B.P., Capt. R. H. Guards, of
Wootton and Fairfield, co. Somerset.   Quarterly Arms, 1849, Vol. LIX,
fol. 215.
ACLAND to TROYTE, Arthur Henry Dyke, of Huntsham and Killerton, co. Devon,
Puckington, co. Somerset.   Quarterly Arms, 1852, Vol. L, fol. 197.
A'COURT before HOLMES, William Henry Ashe, of Westover, Isle of Wight.
Quarterly Arms, 1833,* Vol. XL, fol. 13.
,, before REPINGTON, Edward Henry, of Amington Hall, co. Warw.
Quarterly Arms, 1847, Vol. XLVIII, fol. 356.   (Berry's Suppl.)
,, before REPINGTON, Lieut.-Gen. Charles Ashe, C.B., 1855, Vol. LI, fol. 356.
(Berry's Suppl.)
A'COURT, HOLMES to HOLMES-A'COURT, for issue of William, 2nd Baron Heytes-
bury, 1860,* Vol. LIV, fol. 14-15.
ACTON, John s. of William, of Beach, near Macclesfield, co. Chester, 17 . . .,*
Vol. X, fol. 200.
,, Edward William, of Acton Scott, Shropshire.   Match with STACKHOUSE and
GREGORY, 1813, Vol. XXVIII, fol. 24^b.
ACTON after DALBERG, 8th Bart., Sir John E. E., of Aldenham Hall, Shropshire.
Quarterly, Supporters, 183 . ., Vol. XL, fol. 216.
ACTON after WOOD, Augustus, of Acton Scott, Shropsh., 1874, Vol. LIX, fol. 26.
(Berry's Suppl.)
ACWORTH, Abraham, s. of John, of Westminster [7 July], 1748,* Vol. IX,
fol. 230 [Misc. G. et H., 4th S., I, p. 212].
ADAM, John William, s. of William, of Crutched Friars, London, and Scotland,
1799, Vol. XXI, fol. 196.
,, James, of Burblethwaite, co. Lanc., 1810,* Vol. XXVI, fol. 214.
ADAMS, Robert, of Shropshire and Cavendish Square, London, Govr of the Coast
of Malabar, 15 May 1732,* Vol. VIII, fol. 148.
ADAMS to ANSON, George, of Orgreave, co. Staff., 1773, Vol. XII, fol. 238.
,, to ANSON [1773 ?] George, Viscount Anson.   Crest, 1804, Vol. XXIII,
fol. 344.   Match with SAMBROOKE, Vol. XXIII, fol. 343.
ADAMS, William, M.P., and brother Samuel and three sisters, of Bowden and
Totnes, co. Devon, 1806, Vol. XXIV, fol. 88 (WYNELL and PARKIN
[quarterings ?], 183 . ., Vol. XXXIX, fol. 119).   Quarterings to
descendants of William Dacre Adams, 1832-3, Vol. XXXIX, fol. 119.

ADAMS to HYETT, William Henry (minor), of Gloucester and Painswick, co. Glouc., 1813, Vol. XXVII, fol. 343.

ADAMS now RAWSON (wife) and Sir William, of Belmont House, co. Wicklow. Quarterly Arms, 1824, Vol. XXXV, fols. 146-48.

ADAMS late CUFFE, Thomas, of Middleton Hall, co. Carmarthen, and to brothers Edward and Alfred, 1843, Vol. XLVI, fol. 132.

ADAMS, Joseph Harrison, of Chadwell Court, Sheriff Hales, co. Staff., and of Newport, Shropsh., J.P. co. Staff., and his only brother Thomas Harper Adams, of Anceller House, Edgmond, Shropsh., 1856,* Vol. LII, fol. 170.

„ Thomas, of Sible Hedingham, co. Essex, Lincoln's Inn Fields, London, and Nottingham, 1858,* Vol. LIII, fol. 54.

„ William Cokayne, M.A., Rector of Dummer Grange, Hampshire, of Thorpe, co. Surrey, Bushey Grove, co. Hertf., and Chastleton, co. Oxf. Quartering, March 1869, Vol. LVII, fol. 71, 73. (Berry's Suppl.)

„ George, St. John's Coll., Oxf., Rector of Farndon, co. Northampton, of Chastleton, co. Oxf. CRANAGE Quartering, 18 . . ., Vol. LVII, fol. 84.

ADAMS to COKAYNE, George Edward, of Putney and Thorpe, co. Surrey, and Rushton Hall, co. Northampton, 187 . ., Vol. LVIII, fol. 252.

ADAMS, Francis Ottiwell, of John Street, Berkeley Square, 187 . ., Vol. LVIII, fol. 280. (Berry's Suppl.)

„ James Williams, Chaplain B.C.S., 1882, Vol. LXI, fol. 317. (Berry's Suppl.)

ADAMSON, Laur. W., of Whitley by Newcastle-upon-Tyne, co. Northumb., 1885, Vol. LXIII, fol. 105.

ADCOCK to HALL, Thomas, of Workington and Carlisle, co. Cumberl., 1835, Vol. XLI, fol. 343 ; crest for issue, Vol. XLI, fol. 344.

ADDENBROOKE late HOMFRAY, John A., of Wollaston Hall, co. Worc., 20 [29] April 1795, Vol. XIX, fol. 34. [See Her. of Worc., I, pp. 6, 295.]

ADDERLEY, Baron (Norton). Supporters, 1885, Vol. LXIII, fol. 17. [Sir Charles Bowyer Adderley created Baron Norton, 16 April 1878.]

ADDINGTON, Henry, Viscount Sidmouth. Arms and Supporters [1805], Vol. XXIII, fol. 94.

„ Baron. See HUBBARD. Supporters and Arms, 1887, Vol. LXIV, fols. 107, 109.

ADDISON, Edward, s. of Charles, of London, 1786, Vol. XVI, fol. 389.

ADDISON before FOUNTAINE, William, B.A., of Middleton St. George, co. Durham, and Leeds, co. York. Quarterly Arms, 180 . ., Vol. XXI, fol. 72.

ADDISON, John Romains, student at Edinb. Univ., of Newark House, Maidstone, co. Kent, 1830, Vol. XXXVIII, fol. 141.

„ Samuel, J.P., s. of Samuel, of Charnes Old Hall, Eccleshill, co. Staff., 1837, Vol. XLIII, fol. 66.

A'DEANE late TUCKER, John, of Ashcott, n^r Napier, Hawkes Bay, New Zealand, and Alderley, co. Glouc., 1827, Vol. XXXV, fol. 36 ; 186 . ., Vol. LVI, fol. . . . . .

ADEY to WILLETT, John Willett, of Merley Place, co. Dorset, 1795,* Vol. XIX, fol. 19.

ADLAM, William, of Bristol, 184 . ..,* Vol. XLVI, fol. 50.

AFFLECK, Sir Robert, Bart., co. Suff., 1880,* Vol. LXI, fol. 7.

AFFLECK to DANBY, George, of Swinton Park, co. York, 1880, Vol. LXI, fol. 21.

AGAR to ELLIS, Henry Welbore, Viscount Clifden and Baron Mendip, 1804, Vol. XXII, fol. 367.

AGAR before ROBARTES, Thomas James, of Llanhydrock, co. Cornw., 1822, Vol. XXXIII, fol. 192.

„ before ROBARTES (Thomas James), Baron Robartes. Supporters, 1869, Vol. LVII, fol. 206.

AGLAND . . . . Match with WICKEY and DENNETT (see DENNETT). 178 . ., Vol. XV, fol. 213.

AGNEW, Sir William, Bart., of London and co. Lanc., 1895, Vol. LXVIII, fol. 282.

DE AGUILAR, Diego, of Alderman's Walk, London, Baron H. R. E. (*see* Berry, Aguilar, 95), 1756, Vol. X, fol. 52.

AIKENHEAD, Robert, of Otterington Hall, South Otterington, co. York, 1894, Vol. LXVIII, fol. 118.

AIREY, Major H. P., of New South Wales, 2nd s. of the late Capt. Henry Cookson Airey, dec^d, 1894,* Vol. LXVIII, fol. 95.

　„　Gen. Sir Richard, G.C.B. (F.M. and Baron). Arms and Supporters, 1874, Vol. LIX, fol. 5 ; s. Sir George, Vol. LIX, fol. 7.

AITCHISON, Gen. Sir John [K.C.B. 1859], G.C.B. [1867]. Supporters, 186 . ., Vol. LVI, fol. 260.

AKERMAN, Isaac, of St. Bennet, Gracechurch Street, London, and Battersea, co. Surrey, 1761,* Vol. X, fol. 382. (Burke.)

AKERS before DOUGLAS, Aretas, of Chilston Park, Maidstone, co. Kent, and Baads, Edinburgh, 1875, Vol. LIX, fol. 110.

AKROYD, Edward, of Bankfield, Halifax, and Denton Park, Otley, co. York, 185 . ., Vol. LI, fol. 209.

ACKROYD after RAWSON, John William, of The Grange, Dean Park, co. Bedf., and Undercliff and Otley, Bradford, co. York, 1875, Vol. LIX, fol. 171.

ALAVOINE, Peter, s. of Peter and Lewis (brother of Peter), Old Artillery Yard, Liberty Tower, London, and Mary Magdalene Alavoine, widow (*see* DELAMERE), Dec. 1852, Vols. IX, fol. 424, 460.

ALBERT, Sophia Nancy, wife of Charles Courtail (late BRADLEY), St. James' Palace, London. Crest to her brothers, Hugh Lewis and William John, 5 July 1806,* Vol. XXIII, fol. 400.

ALCESTER, Baron [Admiral Sir Frederick Beauchamp Paget] (Seymour) [K.C.B. 1877, G.C.B. 1881]. Supporters, 1882, Vol. LXI, fol. 393.

ALCOCK-BECK late TOWERS, William, of Esthwaite Lodge, Hawkeshead, and Sawcey Beek, co. Lancashire. Arms, 1856, Vol. LII, fol. 31.

ALDAM, William, of Frickley Hall and Warmsworth, co. York, 184 . ., Vol. XLVIII, fol. 52.

ALDAM to WARDE-ALDAM, William Wright, Warde-Aldam, of Frickley Hall and Warmsworth, and Hooton Pagnell, co. York, 18 . . ., Vol. LX. fol. 165. (Berry's Suppl.)

ALDENHAM, Henry Hucks Gibbs, Baron, co. Hertf. Supporters, 1896, Vol. LXIX, fol. 120.

ALDERSON, Rev. Christopher, Rector of Oddington, co. Glouc., 24 April 1780, Vol. XIV, fol. 211.

ALDERSON late HARKER, Christopher, of Carsdale and Askrigg, co. York, and Homerton, co. Midd., 11 Mar. 1811, Vol. XXVI, fol. 190.

ALDRIDGE, John, of King's Clere, Hampshire, 1772,* Vol. XII, fol. 125. (Burke.)

　„　Robert, s. of John, of Cork and New Lodge, co. Sussex, 1820, Vol. XXXII, fol. 191.

ALDRIDGE before BUSHBY, Robert, of Cork, and Rochester, co. Kent, 1820, Vol. XXXII, fol. 193.

　„　John, s. of William, of Sackville Street [? Dublin], and Romsey, Hampshire, 1820,* Vol. XXXII, fol. 323.

ALDRIDGE to BLISS, Henry, s. of James, of Notting Hill, London, gent., and Brandon Park, co. Suff. (now DE BARRETO), 184 . ., Vol. XLVII, fol. 347.

ALDWELL, Rev. Basil S., of St. Luke's, Portsea, Hampsh., Vol. LXXI, fol. . . . .

ALDWORTH to NEVILLE, Richard Neville, Baron Braybrooke, of Billingbere, co. Berks., 1792, Vol. XX, fol. 47.

ALERS before HANKEY, William, of London and Hackney, co. Middx., 1815, Vol. XXIX, fol. 216.

ALEXANDER, William, M.D., of Halifax, co. York., 3 March 1808, Vol. XXII, fol. 84.

ALFORD, Rev. Josiah George, Stoke Bishop Vicarage, Bristol, 189 . ., Vol. LXXI, fol. . . . .

ALINGTON to PYE, Henry, of Louth and Swinhope, co. Linc., 182 . ., Vol.
XXXVII, fol. 203.

ALISON (see ROME), of Dornoch, nr. Arran, Scotland. Match with ROME, 177 . .,
Vol. XII, fol. 207.

ALLAN late MURRAY, Thomas, of Fowey, co. Cornw., 7 June 1800,* Vol. XXI,
fol. 27.

„ Richard, s. of Richard (s. of Michael), of Malton, Whitby and Helmsley,
co. York, 181 . .. Vol. XXX, fol. 322.

„ Lieut.-Col. Sir Alexander (Bart. 1819), M.P., of Kingsgate, co. Kent,
and Musselborough, Edinburghshire (d. 1820 s.p.), 18 . . ., Vol. XXXI,
fol. 230.

„ Robert Henry, s. of Robert s. of Robert, of Blackwall Grange, co. Durham,
and Yarm, co. York, 1830, Vol. XXXVII, fol. 233.

ALLAN before FRASER, Patrick, of Hawkesbury Hall, Foleshill, co. Warw. (s. of
Robert, of Arbroath), and Hospitalfield, St. Vigeans, Forfar., Scotland.
Quarterly (died 1890), 1851, Vol. L, fol. 19.

ALLAN after HAVELOCK, Major-Gen. Sir Henry, M.B., C.B., co. Durham, 1880,
Vol. LXI, fol. 377.

ALLANSON, late WINN, George, Bart., co. York, 1777, Vol. XIII, fol. 291.

ALLAWAY, Stephen, of Pencraig Court, co. Heref., and Watford House, Watford,
185 . ., Vol. L, fol. 205. (Berry's Suppl.)

ALLCARD, William, of Warrington, co. Lanc., J.P., and of Burton Closes, par. of
Bakewell, co. Derby., 18 . . .,* Vol. XLIX, fol. 129.

ALLCARD late COURTIN, Henry Julius, of Hermosa West, Teignmouth, co. Devon,
186 . .,* Vol. LV, fol. 48.

ALLCROFT, John Derby, of Stokesay Castle, Onibury, Shropsh., and his descendants, 1870, Vol. LVII, fol. 212. (Berry's Suppl.)

„ John Derby, of Lancaster Gate, London. Quartering, 1878, Vol. LX,
fol. 175.

ALLEN (see WEBB), of Upton, Berks. Match with WEBB, 17 . . ., Vol. XI,
fol. 190.

„ Match with FERRIS. See FERRIS.

ALLEN before WILKIE, John, of Hetton, par. of Chatton and Wooler, co. North-
umber^ld. Quarterly Arms, 181 . .,* Vol. XXVII, fol. 220.

ALLEN, ..., of Sheffield and Chapel Allerton, co. Yorks. Match MIDDLETON
and CARVER, 182 . ., Vol. XXXIII, fol. 220.

„ . . . ., of Sheffield and Chapel Ailerton, co. York. Match (? WALSH and
FREEMAN), 182 . ., Vol. XXXIV, fol. 5.

ALLEN late POMFRET, Ralph (reputed son of Allen), of Sawbridgeworth, co. Hertf.,
and Newhouse, Little Hallingbury, co. Essex, 182 . .,* Vol. XXXIV.,
fol. 206.

ALLEN after HOGGE, Fountaine, Capt. 2nd Life Guards, of Lyndhurst, Hampsh.,
and King's Lynn, Norf., 1857,* Vol. LII, fol. 243.

ALLEN to GREENLY, Charles William, s. of Henry, of Titley Court, co. Heref.
[10 Mar. 1865], Vol. LV, fol. 302.

ALLEN to TOURNAY [1870], Henry Tournay (died 24 Aug. 1871), 18 . . .,
Vol. LVII, fol. 232.

„ to TOURNAY [1871], William Brockhill, of Saltwood, co. Kent, 18 . .,
Vol. LVII, fol. 232.

ALLEN, George, Surbiton House, Englefield Green, co. Surrey, 1896,* Vol. LXIX,
fol. 138.

ALLENBY, S. Hynman, of Gainsgate Hall, co. Linc., and Long Sutton, co. Camb.,
1893,* Vol. LXVII, fol. 227.

„ -Montgomery, S. H., of Gainsgate Hall, co. Linc., and Long Sutton,
co. Camb., 1893,* Vol. LXVII, fol. 298.

ALLGOOD, Lancelot, M.P., of co. Northumberld. (and of Budleigh Salterton,
co. Devon). Confirmation of arms and grant of crest, 1750, Vol. IX,
fol. 405.

ALLHUSEN, Christian A. H., of Elswick Hall, co. Northumberld., 187 . ., Vol. LVIII, fol. 40. (Berry's Suppl.)

ALLISTON, Frederick Pratt, of Kamesburgh, Beckenham, co. Kent, 187 . ., Vol. LXIX, fol. 263.

ALLNUTT, John, of Clapham Common, co. Surrey, 186 . .,* Vol. LIV, fol. 108.

ALLOTT, Rev. Robert, of St. John's Coll., Camb., and Vicar of South Kirkby, co. York, 9 June 1729, Vol. VIII, fol. 34ᵇ (see Berry).

ALLPRESS, W. D'A., of Little St. James' Street, Westminster, 1896,* Vol. LXIX, fol. 69 (sic).

ALSOP, Robert, Alderm. and Sheriff of London, 29 Mar. 1738, Vol. VIII, fol. 234 (see Berry).

ALLSOP before LOWDHAM, Lewis, of Lincoln's Inn, London, and of Nottinghamsh. and Leic. Quarterly Arms, 182 . .,* Vol. XXXV, fol. 160.

   „   Henry, of Hindlip, co. Worc., and Elizabeth TONGUE, his wife, 1880, Vol. LX, fol. 366.

ALSTON, William Charles (s. of James, s. of James), Lieut.-Col. E.I.C.S., of Dirleton, Edinb., 181 . .,* Vol. XXVI, fol. 169.

ALT, Henry, Minister for Hessia, London, 6 Nov. 1749,* Vol. IX, fol. 207.

ALTHAM late COOK, William S. (Major). Quarterly Arms, 1862, Vol. LIV, fol. 268.

ALVANLEY, Baron [22 May 1801] ([Sir Richard Pepper] Arden). Supporters, 180 . ., Vol. XXI, fol. 215.

AMBROSE, William Henry, of 45, St. James' Square, Notting Hill, and Stock Exchange, London, 1882,* Vol. LXI, fol. 345. (Berry's Suppl.)

AMCOTTS late EMERSON, of Wharton, Kettlethorpe, co. Linc., and East Retford, co. Nottingham, 1777, Vol. XIII, fol. 299.

AMCOTTS before INGILBY, Bart., William, of Ripley Castle, co. York. Quarterly Arms, 1822, Vol. XXXIII, fols. 180, 182 ; 185 . ., Vol. LI, fols. 104, 106.

AMCOTTS after CRACROFT, Weston, of Hackthorne and Kettlethorpe, co. Linc. Quarterly Arms, 1857, Vol. LII, fol. 277.

AMES to LYDE, Lionel, of Lincoln's Inn, London ; Shirehampton, co. Glouc. ; and Ayot St. Lawrence, co. Hertf., 1806, Vol. XXIII, fol. 348. Match.

AMES, Henry Metcalfe, of Linden, Long Horsley, co. Northumberld., and Hyde, co. Hertf., 20 April 1874, Vol. LVIII, fol. 331. (Genealogist, I, p. 206.)

AMES to LYDE, Lionel N. F., of Hyde, co. Herts., and Thornham Hall, Brancester, co. Norf. Quarterly Arms, 1874, Vol. LVIII, fols. 349, 355.

AMHERST, Sir Jeffry, K.B. [1761]. Supporters, 17 . . ., Vol. X, fol. 324.

   „ ([William] Pitt) [2nd] Baron [1797]. Supporters, 17 . . ., Vol. XX, fol. 88.

AMHERST after TYSSEN, co. Norf. Quarterly Arms, 188 . ., Vol. LVI, fols. 180, 186, 273, 278, 280.

TYSSEN-AMHERST, William Amhurst Tyssen, formerly Tyssen-Amhurst and before that Daniel-Tyssen. (See TYSSEN.) Quarterly Arms, 186 . ., Vol. LV, fol. 62.

AMHURST, Baron, of Hackney. Supporters, 1892, Vol. LXVII, fol. 89. *See also* DANIEL and TYSSEN.

AMORY after HEATHCOAT, (Sir) John, of Knightshayes, co. Devon. Quarterly Arms, 1874, Vol. LVIII, fol. 312.

[AMPHLETT, Edward Greenhill, of Union Place, Worthing, co. Sussex, and Horseley, Tipton, co. Staff., eldest s. of Edward Amphlett, late of Horseley and Queen's Gate Terrace, Kensington, London, decd., 23 Feb. 1903. Crisp, Notes, V, p. 43.]

AMPHLETT late DUNN, Charles, of Earls Croome, co. Warwick, and Four Ashes, co. Staff., 185 . ., Vol. LI, fol. 255.

AMPTHILL, Baron. Supporters, 1881, Vol. LXI, fol. 193.

AMSON, John, of Evershaw, Sheriff of Cheshire, 3 April 1711,* Vol. V., fol. 415, and Add. MS. 14,831, fol. 67 (see Berry).

AMYAND to CORNEWALL, Sir George, Bart., of co. Hereford. Quarterly Arms, 1771, Vol. XII, fols. 93, 94 (see Berry).

ANBUREY, Sir Thomas, Knt., C.B., Lieut.-Col. R.E., 182 . .,* Vol. XXXVII, fol. 394.

ANCASTER and KESTEVEN, [2nd] Duke of, daus. married GREATHED and MATHEW (and ? [dau. of 3rd Duke mar.] Baron Gwydir, 182 . ., Vol. XXXVII, fol. 356), 181 . ., Vol. XXXI, fols. 222, 292.

ANDERSON, James, of Hollam, Hampsh., and Linlithgow, 26 Jan. 1789,* Vol. XVII, fol. 61.

ANDERSON before PELHAM, Baron Yarborough [1794], Vol. XVIII, fol. 402.

ANDERSON, Sir John William, Bart.. Lord Mayor of London, 17 May 1798. Vol. XX, fol. 148.

„ Andrew, Col. H.E.I.C.S., 21 Mar. 1808,* Vol. XXIV, fol. 378.

ANDERSON to SETON, James, LL.D., of Mounie, Aberdeen, and West Ham, co. Essex. Match, 181 . ., Vol. XXVI, fol. 381.

ANDERSON, Major Robert (and his wife Anne, nat. dau. of WRIGHT, impaled), London, and Dunbar, Scotland. Arms of WRIGHT only, 181 . .,* Vol. XXVII, fol. 224.

ANDERSON to BEWICKE, Calverley Bewicke, of Close Hill, co. Northumberl[d], 1815, Vol. XXIX, fol. 202.

ANDERSON, Alexander, Lieut.-Col., C.B., K.T.S., of Portugal, 182 . ., Vol. XXXVI, fol. 327.

„ Mathew, s. of William (M.A., Camb.), of Sonning, co. Berks., and Herne Hill, co. Kent, 184 . ., Vol. XLVII, fol. 170.

„ Thomas, s. of John, of London, Jasmond [? Jesmond House, co. Northumberl[d]], and St. Petersburg, 185 . ., Vol. LI, fol. 92 (see Burke).

„ George, of Little Harle Tower, Newcastle-upon-Tyne, co. Northumb., 1883,* Vol. LXII, fol. 93. (Berry's Suppl.)

„ James Henry, of Russetings, Bournemouth, Hampsh., 1889,* Vol. LXV, fol. 69.

„ Mrs. Hannah, widow of Thomas Scott Anderson and daughter of James, LOWTHORPE, 10, Norfolk Crescent, Hyde Park, London, 1891,* Vol. LXVI, fol. 33.

„ W . . . ., Rimswell, Norton, co. Northumberl[d], 1892, Vol. LXVII, fol. 57.

„ William, arms for, of Thornaby-on-Tees, co. York. Mayor of Thornaby, 1893,* Vol. LXVII, fol. 116.

ANDERTON, Wilfrid Francis, of Haighton House, nr. Preston, co. Lanc., 183 . ., Vol. XLI, fol. 168.

„ Arthur Wellesley Gill, of Southport, co. Lanc., 189 . ., Vol. LXVI, fol. 334 ; mar. the dau. of J. P. ANDERTON, 18 . . ., Vol. LXV, fol. 279.

„ James Parkinson, M.R.C.S., of Brondyffryn, co. Denbigh, 1890,* Vol. LXV, fol. 279.

ANDREW after HARRISON, Thomas, of Moss Side, Finchley, co. Middx. Quarterly Arms, 1796,* Vol. XIX, fol. 221.

ANDREW, George, J.P., of Greenhill, Compstall, co. Chester, 186 . ., Vol. LIV., fol. 26.

„ Christopher Thomas, of Menkee and Tregarden, St. Mabyn, co. Cornw., 18 . , Vol. LVII, fol. 177.

ANDREWS, Jonathan, Knt., of Kempton Park, nr. Ipswich (see Berry) [Kimpton Park, co. Middx. (Burke)], 2 Sept. 1704, Vol. V, fol. 163.

„ Henry, of Holborn, London, 22 Oct. 1729,* Vol. VIII, fol. 42[b].

„ . . . ., of Bulmer, co. Essex, 17 . .,* Vol. XI, fol. 244. Match with WRIGHT. See WRIGHT.

ANDREWS to WOODWARD, of Great Comberton, co. Worc., and Butlers Marston, co. Worc., and Chalmerton, co. Northampton. (Match.) 179 . ., Vol. XIX, fol. 289 (of London, &c., 182 . ., Vol. XXXII, fol. 176, and 185 . ., Vol. L, fols. 276, 278. See also ATKINS.

ANDREWS, Amy, dau. of WOODWARD, and widow of Thomas Andrews, 182 . ., Vol. XXXII, fol. 176.

ANDREWS to WOODWARD, Anne Catherine, 185 . ., Vol. L, fol. 278.

ANDREWS, Joshua, of Bartley House, Ealing, co. Middx., and Winterbourne Gunner, co. Wilts., 13 Dec. 1808*, Vol. XXV, fol. 58.

ANDREWS, late HUNT, Elizabeth Anne, widow of Charles Henry Hunt, of Coldicote, co. Worc., and Shaw Place, co. Berks., 182 . .,* Vol. XXXIII, fol. 246

ANDREWS, Biggs, Q.C., of Mildenhall and the Middle Temple, London, 183 . .,* Vol. XLIV, fol. 233.

ANGELL, late BROWN, Benedict John, of Waxlow House, Hayes; [? and] Studley, co. Wilts.; and Binfield, co. Berks. Match, 18 Aug. 1800,* Vol. XXI, fol. 245.

ANGERSTEIN, John, s. of John Julius, of Woodlands, Greenwich, and co. Norf., 182 . ., Vol. XXXVI, fol. 243.

ANNAND, Adam (Alexander ?), (B.A., Oxf.), of Bushey Park, Aberdeen (arms to wife, dau. of BENNETT, escutcheon of pretence), 181 . .,* Vol. XXVII, fols. 422, 426.

ANNE to TASBURGH, Michael, of Burghwallis, co. York, and Bodney, co. Norfolk, 20 June 1810, Vol. XXVI, fol. 1.

„ E. L. Swinburne, of Doncaster, co. York, 1884, Vol. LXII, fol. 194., (Berry's Suppl.)

ANNESLEY late MACLEOD, Arthur, late Capt., s. of Maj.-Gen., of Arley Castle, co. Staff. Quarterly Arms, 1844, Vol. XLVII., fol. 281.

ANNESLEY, William Gore, 2nd s. of Francis Charles, Commander, R.N., 189 . ., Vol. LXXI, fol. . . . . .

ANSLEY, John (L. Mayor of London, 1808 ?), of Walthamstow, co. Essex, and of Hunslet, Leeds, co. York, 24 Aug. 1798, Vol. XX, fol. 205.

ANSON late ADAMS, George, of Orgreave, co. Staff., 1773, Vol. XII, fol. 238.

„ Baron (Anson), George. Supporters, Confirmation of Arms and Crest, 1747, Vol. IX, fols. 213, 215.

„ Thomas Anson, Viscount, 21 Mar. 1806. Supporters, Vol. XXIII, fols. 344, 346.

„ Sir George, K.C.B. Supporters, 17 Sept. 1833, Vol. XL, fol. 1.

ANSON-HORTON, Mrs, of Catton House, co. Derby (died 27 Jan. 1899), 1888, Vol. LXIV, fol. 246.

ANSTEY before CALVERT, Arthur (Anstey), of Lincoln's Inn, London, and Bath, co. Somerset, 181 . ., Vol. XXXI, fol. 382.

ANSTIS, Sir John, Garter King of Arms, of London and co. Cornw. Quarterly Arms, SMITH and CADLIP quarterings, 17 . . .,* Vol. IX, fol. 108.

ANSTRUTHER to LESLIE, William, of London and Scotland. (Match.) 14 Nov. 1799,* Vol. XX, fol. 396.

ANSTRUTHER after LLOYD, James Hamilton, of Hintlesham Hall, co. Suff., 183 . ., Vol. XLII, fol. 146.

ANTHONY, ..., of Hackney, co. Middx. Match with WILTS (which see), 17 . . .,* Vol. XI, fol. 358.

„ William, of Harrias, Beaconsfield, co. Bucks., 20 Feb. 1804,* Vol. XXII, fol. 373.

ANTHONY before WILLSON, George Lindsay, of Westbourne Terrace, London, 18 . . .,* Vol. LIII, fol. 23.

ANTONIE after LEE, William, of Colworth House, co. Bedf. (LEE formerly FIOTT.) 182 . .,* Vol. XXX, fol. 145. [See Burke.]

ANTRIM, Countess of, 1817, Vol. XXX, fol. 215.

„ Earl of, KERR to McDONALD. Quarterly Arms, 1835, Vol. XLI, fol. 345; 1855, Vol. LI, fol. 347.

APPACK, Thomas, s. of John Jacob, of Stamford Hill and Brecon, 182 . .,* Vol. XXXV, fol. 359.

[APPLEGARTH, Mary Ann (Mrs. George GWILT), 22 Feb. 1826 (Her. and Geneal., II, 80n.]

APPLEYARD to BOYNTON, Boynton, of Rawcliffe, Snaith, co. York, 23 April 1701, Vol. V, fol. 37, and Add. MS. 14,831, fol. 75.

APSLEY, Baron [1771] (Bathurst). Supporters, 17 . . ., Vol. XII, fol. 60.
ARCEDUKNE, Chaloner, of Harley Street, London, 178 . .,* Vol. XVI, fol 281.
ARCHBOLD after PEARS [1870] of Furham Hall and Gallowgate, Newcastle-upon-
Tyne, co. Northumb. Quarterly Arms, 18 . .,* LVII, fol. 238.
ARCHDALL before GRATWICKE, George, D.D., of Emmanuel College, Camb.,
Canon of Norwich, of Ham, Angmering, co. Sussex. Quarterly Arms,
186 . .,* Vol. LV. fol. 44.
ARCHER, Baron [1747] (Thomas Archer). Supporters, change, 17 . . ., Vol. IX,
fols. 197-8.
  „   Thomas, of Chelmsford, co. Essex, 182 . .,* Vol. XXXII, fol. 44.
ARCHER (HOUBLON before NEWTON), Susannah, widow of Houblon, of
Coopersale House, co. Essex ; Welford, co. Berks ; and Highlow,
co. Derby. Quarterly Arms, 1819,* Vol. XXXI, fols. 348, 350.
ARCHER HOUBLON to EYRE, Charles, of co. Berks., Essex and Derby, 18 . . .,
Vol. XXXVIII, fol. 326 ; 183 . ., Vol. XXXIX, fol. 4.
ARCHER HOUBLON, Lieut.-Col. George Bramston, of co. Essex and Berks., 1892,
Vol. LXVI, fol. 248.
ARCHER-BURTON, Lancelot, of Harlow, co. Essex, 1834,* Vol. XLI, fol. 144.
ARCHER, quartering to Elizabeth WALMSLEY, widow, of Feversham, co. Kent.
Quarterly Arms, 184 . .,* Vol. XLVIII, fol. 294.
ARCHIBALD, Sir Thomas D., Justice of the Queen's Bench, of Bickley, co. Surrey,
and Halifax, Nova Scotia, s. of Samuel George William, M. R. Nova
Scotia. To his descendants, 1872, Vol. LVIII, fol. 175.
ARDEN [Richard Pepper], Baron ALVANLEY [of Alvanley, 22 May 1801],
co. Chester. Supporters, 180 . ., Vol. XXI, fol. 215.
  „   Joseph, of Rickmansworth, co. Hertford, 184 . ., Vol. XLVII, fol. 158.
  „   Richard Edward, of Sunbury Park, co. Middlesex, 184 . ., Vol. XLVII,
      · fol. 229.
ARDERNE, D.D., s. of D. Jones, of Warborne, co. Hampshire, 1888, Vol. LXIV,
fol. 248.
ARDING, A. C., late WELLS, of Braziers Park, Checkendon, co. Oxford, 1890,
Vol. LXV, fol. 271.
ARDLEY, Isaac, of St. Bride's, London, and Colchester, co. Essex, 10 Oct., 1732,*
Vol. VIII, fol. 153a.
ARGYLL, Duchess of (Baroness HAMILTON [4 May 1776]). Supporters, 17 . . .,
Vol. XIII, fol. 281.
ARKWRIGHT, Sir Richard, of Willersley, co. Derby, Knt. [29 Jan.], 17[87],
Vol. XVI, fol. 215. [Misc. G. et II., 4th S., I, p. 113].
ARMITAGE, Sir Elkannah, Knt., of the Priory, Pendleton and Newton, co. Lanc.,
18 . . ., Vol. XLIX, fol. 144.
  „   Benjamin, of Egremont, co. Chester, and Liverpool, 185 . .,* Vol L,
      fol. 367.
  „   Harriet, of 34, Cambridge Square, London, widow of Thomas Rhodes
      Armitage (s. of James), of Noan, nr. Thurles, co. Tipperary, Ireland,
      1898, Vol. LXX, fol. 120.
ARMITAGE to WORMALD, of Cookridge Hall and Sawley Hall, co. York. Quarterly
Arms, 187 . .,* Vol. LVIII, fol. 53.
ARMITSTEAD, Rev. John, of Middlewich, co. Chester (s. of John, of Horton,
co. York), to descendants of his grandfather, 1799.* Vol. XIX, fol. 402.
  „   (Richard Lewthwaite, impalement, Rector of Moresby (1813) and Minister
      of St. James, Whitehaven. Match, 181 . ., Vol. XXIX, fol. 352.)
ARMSTRONG late BROWN, Thomas, of Ovington, co. Hampshire. Match, 1773,*
Vol. XII, fol. 275.
ARMSTRONG before MARTINEZ, William Joseph, of Gloucester Lodge, Regent's
Park, London, s. of William Henry, 183 . .,* Vol. XLIII, fols. (138), 201.
ARMSTRONG, Sir William George, Knt., C.B., of Jesmond, Berwick-on-Tweed,
co. Northumb., 185 . ., Vol. LIII, fol. 162. Baron Armstrong, supporters,
1887, Vol. LXIV, fol. 84.

ARMSTRONG after WRIGHT, William Jones, J.P., of Killylea House, co. Armagh [20 Feb. 1868], Vol. LVI, fol. 339.

ARMSTRONG-LUSBRUGTON-TULLOCH, W.C., of London and Rodmersham, co. Kent, 1884,* Vol. LXII, fol. 321.

ARMSTRONG, William Henry, of London, father of William Joseph Armstrong MARTINEZ, 183 . .,* Vol. XLIII, fol. 138.

ARMYTAGE to WENTWORTH, of Hickleton and Woolley, co. York, 17 . . ., Vol. XVII, fol. 111.

ARMYTAGE late GREEN, Joseph, of Thickhollings, Almondbury and Green House, co. York, 21 April 1808, Vol. XXIV, fol. 400.

ARNALL. See THOMPSON.

ARNISON, Major W. B., of Penrith, co. Cumberld., 18 . . ., Vol. LVII, fol. 102. (Berry's Suppl.)

ARNO to ANGUS to HAYWARD, Catherine Margaret, widow of Joseph (dau. of Walter WILKINS), of Tiverton, co. Devon, and of Walsworth Hall, co. Glouc. Crest to male issue, 181 . ., Vol. XXVI, fol. 294.

ARNOLD, George, of Ashby St. Leger, co. Northampton. (See COAPE, 1867.*) 3 June 1725, Vol. VII, fol. 308.

ARNOLD late SARGENT, George Arnold, of Halsted Place, co. Kent, 1777, Vol. XIII, fol. 287.

ARNOLD to HAUGHTON, Henry (s. of the above), of Halsted Place, co. Kent, mar. with LANGSTON, 17 . .,* Vol. XX., fol. 84.

ARNOLD before BAINBRIGGE, William, of Uttoxeter and Woodseat, co. Staff., 184 . ., Vol. XLVIII, fol. 8.

ARNOLD, Henry Fraser James (formerly COAPE), of Wolvey Hall, Hinckley. Arms of Arnold, 1898,* Vol. LXX, fol. 162.

ARNOTT, Rev. Samuel Brazier, M.A., of St. John's Coll., Oxf. (died 25 Feb. 1876), 184 . ., Vol. XLVIII, fol. 78.

ARTHUR, Sir George, Knt., K.C.H. (afterwards Bart.), of Plymouth,co.Devon, Col. and Lieut.-Gov'' of Upper Canada, 183 . ., Vol. XLII, fol. 269. Match with BETTINGTON, 184 . .,* Vol. XLVII, fol. 248. See BETTINGTON.

  „ Francis Robert, of Whitwell Hall, co. Derby, and Victoria, &c., 185 . .,* Vol. LII, fol. 217.

ARTINDALE, Thomas Frederick, of Green Hill, Burnley, co. Lanc., 186 . ., Vol. LV, fol. 326. (Berry's Suppl.)

ARUNDEL late BRAZIER, Sir John, Knt., of Huntingdon, Alderman (Bishop's MSS.), 27 Feb. 1801,* Vol. XXI, fol. 125.

  „ late JAGO, Francis Vyvyan, of Landulph, &c., co. Cornw., 181 . ., Vol. XXVIII, fol. 280.

ARUNDEL after HARRIS, William Arundell, of Lifton Park and Hayne, co. Devon, and Heneage, Trengwainton, &c., co. Cornw. Quarterly Arms [8 and 11 May], 1829, Vol. XXXVII, fols. 399, 401. (R. C. Fam., III, p. 166.)

ARUNDELL late MONCKTON, Viscount Galway. Arms of Arundell and Supporters, 177 . ., Vol. XII, fol. 8. [Created Viscount Galway and Baron Killard, 1727.]

ARUNDELL, William George Monckton, 13 April, 1826, Vol. XXXV, fol. 371. (R. C. Fam. III, 165.)

  „ James, of Exeter and Thorverton, co. Devon, 22 July 1820,* Vol. XXXII, fol. 105. (R. C. Fam., III, p. 163.)

ARUNDELL after HUNTER, William Francis, of Helston and Marazion, co. Cornwall, and Barjarg Tower, &c., Dumfries [15 March 1825], Vol. XXXV, fol. 98. (R. C. Fam., III, p. 164.)

ARUNDELL to SAUNDERS, Frederick William, of Cheriton Fitzpaine and Lifton, co. Devon, 1873,* Vol. LVIII, fol. 260.

ASHCROFT, James, of Grange House, Oakhill Park, West Derby, co. Lanc., 1880,* Vol. LXI, fol. 73. (Berry's Suppl.)

ASGILL, Sir Charles, Bart., of London, afterwards of Fawley in Hampshire (extinct 1823), 1761, Vol. XXXII, fol. 215.

ASHBOURNE, Baron (GILSON). Supporters, 1885, Vol. LXIII, fol. 151.

ASHBURNHAM, Baron [1689 [John Ashburnham, of Ashburnham], co. Sussex. Supporters, 16 . ., Vol. IV, fol. 45. Baron Ashburnham, 30 May 1689.]

ASHBURTON, Baron ([John] DUNNING), co. Devon. Arms and Supporters [1782], Vol. XV, fol. 47.

„ Baroness ([Elizabeth] BARING), co. Devon. Arms and Supporters [1782], Vol. XV, fol. 47.

ASHBURY, John, of London, 186 . .,* Vol. LV, fol. 220. (? James Lloyd Ashbury, M.P., Brighton, 1874.)

ASHBY late LATHOM, Mary Elizabeth, widow of Lathom, of Quenby Hall, co. Liec. Crest to male issue, 180 . ., Vol. XXIV, fol. 222.

„ late MADDOCK, George A., of Naseby, co. Northampt., and Shropshire. Quarterly Arms, 1857, Vol. LII, fol. 252.

„ late BERNARD, Nicholas M. H. A., of Quenby, co. Northampton, and Bickley, co. Kent, 1871, Vol. LVIII, fol. 32. (Berry's Suppl.)

ASHCOMBE, Baron (George CUBITT). (See CUBITT.) Supporters, 1892, Vol. LXVII, fol. 87.

ASHE-A'COURT (late A'COURT), Sr William Pierce, Bart., of Heytesbury, co. Wilts., and Rodden, co. Somerset, 1795, Vol. XIX, fol. 119.

ASHENHURST, ..., of Ashenhurst, co. Derby, 17 . . ., Vol. VI, fol. 71. (See REVELL.)

ASHFORD, ..., of Ashford, co. Devon. Quartering to SANFORD, 177 . ., Vol. XIV, fol. 149.

ASHFORDBY to TRENCHARD, Rev. John, of Staunton Fitzherbert, co. Wilts., co. Berks. and Somerset. Quartering, 180 . ., Vol. XXII, fols. 55, 57.

ASHPINSHAM to Rev. John STAUNTON, LL.D. (Elizabeth Brough, wife of), of Calverton and Staunton. Escutcheon of Pretence for wife, 1807,* Vol. XXIV, fol. 217.

ASHTON, Nicholas, s. of John (of Ashton-in-Makerfield, co. Lanc.), and Liverpool. A Crest, 1 Jan., 1763,* Vol. X, fol. 460.

„ Thomas, of Hyde and Werneth, co. Lanc., and Cheshire, 184 . ., Vol. XLVII, fol. 374.

„ Thomas, M.D., of Manchester and Gorton, co. Lanc., 185 . .,* Vol. LI, fol. 412.

ASHTON after MACKENZIE, Arundell Mackenzie, of Bredbury, Stockport, co. Chester, and Folkestone, co. Kent. Quarterly Arms, and two Crests, 1879, Vol. LX, fol. 324. (Berry's Suppl.)

ASHTON, Baron [1895] (James WILLIAMSON), of co. Lanc. Supporters, 189 . ., Vol. LXIX, fol. 9. WILLIAMSON arms, 1895 or 1896, Vol. LXVIII, fol. 302.

ASHTON. See BURCHARDT-ASHTON.

ASHWORTH, Edward, of Staghills, Newchurch, co. Lanc., 189 . ., Vol. LXIX, fol. 34. (Berry's Suppl.)

„ G. B., of Birtenshaw, Tenton, co. Lanc., 1890,* Vol. LXVI, fol. 9.

„ Margaret, dau. of John, of Bolton, co. Lanc., and wife of John WHITTAKER. (See WHITTAKER). 1897, Vol. LXX, fol. 32.

ASKEW, Adam, of Newcastle-upon-Tyne, co. Northumb., and Lacra, &c., co. Cumberld., 9 May, 1760, Vol. X, fol. 232.

ASKEW-ROBERTSON, Watson, of Pallingsburn House, Cornhill, co. Northumberld., 1892, Vol. LXVI, fol. 262.

ASPINALL, John, s. of Alexander, of Preston, co. Lanc., 6 Dec. 1748,* Vol. IX, fol. 279.

ASPINWALL (and OLDFIELD, his wife), James Leigh, s. of James, of Pildon, co. Essex, 186 . ., Vol. LIV, fol. 338.

ASPLAND, Lindsey Middleton, LL.D., of the Middle Temple, London, and his brother, Arthur Palmer Aspland, &c., 187 . ., Vol. LVIII, fol. 68.

ASSAY, Charles Chaston, s. of John, of Beccles, co. Suffolk, 1818, Vol. XXXI, fol. 123.

Assey (formerly Dacre), Charles William, of Carlisle, co. Cumberld., 183 . .,
    Vol. XLI, fol. 337.
Assheton-Smith after Duff, George William, of the Isle of Wight and
    Carmarthen, Wales, 186 . ., Vol. LIV, fol. 190.
Assheton, Ralph, 40 quarterings. Crisp, Vol. I, fol. 71.
Astbury, John, s. of William, s. of William, of Newcastle-under-Lyme, co. Staff.,
    181 . ., Vol. XXXI, fol. 370.
Astell, William, A. S. S., Director, and of London, merchant, of Everton,
    co. Bedf., and Moggerhanger, co. Huntingdon, 21 April 1717, Vol. VI,
    fol. 295, and Add. MS. 14,830, fol. 171.
Astell late Thornton, William, of Everton, co. Bedf., and Moggerhanger, .
    co. Huntingdon, 1777, Vol. XIII, fol. 285 ; Match, 1807, Vol. XXIV,
    fol. 290.
Astell, William Thornton, 1777, Vol. XIII, fol. 285.
Astley to Gough, Richard, of Oldstone Hall, co. Leic., and Perry Hall, co. Staff.,
    1815, Vol. XXIX, fol. 200.
Astley-Corbett, Sir F. E. G., Bart., of co. Norf. and Shropshire, 1890,
    Vol. LXV, fol. 236.
Aston, Elizabeth, dau. of Richard, of Wadley, co. Berks. Match with Warren,
    17 . . ., Vol. XVIII, fol. 363. (? See Masemore.)
Aston to Pudsey, Thomas Peach, of Seisdon and Trysull, co. Staff., 1807,
    Vol. XXIV, fol. 203 (and Vol. XLVIII, fol. 269, John) (both
    died s.p.).
Aston before Pudsey, George Pudsey, of Seisdon and Trysull, and of Newton
    Stottesdon, co. Shropshire, 1861, Vol. LIV, fol. 232.
Aston, Henry Charles, s. of Henry Hervey, of Aston Hall, co. Chester, 181 . .,
    Vol. XXVIII, fol. 202.
Atcherley late Jones, David F., of Marton, Shropshire, and Eymman, co.
    Flint, 1834, Vol. XL, fol. 105.
Atherton, Sir William, Q.C., M.P., Bencher of the Inner Temple, of Wakefield,
    co. York, 185 . ., Vol. LI, fol. 229.
Atherton (see Byrom late Fox), of Kersall and Manchester, co. Lanc., 18 . . .,
    Vol. LVII, fol. 327.
Athill, Charles Harold, Richmond Herald, 1891,* Vol. LXVI, fol. 84.
Athorpe late Middleton, John Carver, of Dinnington and Leam, co. Derby,
    182 . ., Vol. XXXIII, fol. 222.
Atkey, Frederick Walter, of Chichester, co. Sussex, 187 . ., Vol. LVIII,
    fol. 246. (Berry's Suppl.)
Atkins, Abraham, of London and Clapham, May 1729, Vol. VIII, fol. 49.
Atkins late Martin, Edwin, of the Priory, nr. Reading, and Kingston Lisle,
    co. Berks., and Clapham, 31 Mar. 1792, Vol. XVIII, fol. 15.
Atkins, Michael, s. of Michael, of Bruton, co. Somerset, and Bristol, co. Glouc.,
    14 Mar. 1748-9, Vol. IX, fol. 302.
Atkins before Bowyer, William, of Stoke House, Surrey, and Denham, co.
    Bucks., 183 . ., Vol. LXI, fol. 142.
Atkins to Woodward, widow, of Bulters Marston, co. Warw., and St. Lawrence,
    Jersey. (See also Andrews to Woodward.) 185 . ., Vol. L, fol. 276.
Atkin-Roberts, Major J. Roberts, of Glassenbury and Cranbrook, co. Kent,
    1882,* Vol. LXII, fols. 25, 58. (Berry's Suppl.)
Atkins, Frederick Thomas, of Madras, Banker, 1883, Vol. LXII, fol. 77.
    (Berry's Suppl.)
Atkinson, Samuel (s. of Richard, minister, Kessingland, co. Suff.), Commiss^r
    of Transports, 30 Nov. 1708,* Vol. V, fol. 308 ; Add. MS. 14,831,
    fol. 21.
Atkinson to Savile, Christopher Hale, of Norf., and Enfield, co. Middx.,
    25 Oct. 1798, Vol. XX, fol. 241.
Atkinson, Michael, of Temple Sowerby, co. Westmorld. Arms of Mackworth,
    his wife, to her and descendants, 28 June 1806, Vol. XXIII, fol. 385.

ATKINSON to HARLE, Thomas, of Long Witton and Morpeth, co. Northumberld., 16 April 1808, Vol. XXIV, fol. 387.

ATKINSON, William Waltham, of Gray's Inn, London, and Burton, &c., co. Westmorld., 181 . ., Vol. XXVI, fol. 64.

ATKINSON late RUTHERFORD, spinster, of Angerton, co. Northumberld., 1827, Vol. XXXVI, fol. 367.

ATKINSON late PURVES, Robert Aulty, of Angerton, co. Northumberld., 1828, Vol. XXXVII, fol. 146 (? 182 . ., Vol. XXXVI. fol. 246).

ATKINSON late BRASFORD, James Henry H. (s. of Lieut.-Gen. Sir Thomas), of Angerton, co. Northumberld., 1840, Vol. XLIV, fol. 214, and Ralph, 1871, Vol. LVIII, fol. 84.

ATKINSON to LACON, Walter Lacon, of Newport and Linley, Shropshire, 182 . ., Vol. XXXVII, fol. 344.

ATKINSON (see GORTON), of Great Horton and Toug, co. York, 183 . ., Vol. XLI, fol. 360. (? John Frank Atkinson, of Micklegate House, Pontefract, co. York.)

ATKINSON after WILSON, George Christian (late Capt.), of Long Benton, co. Northumberld., 186 . ., Vol. LIV, fol. 92.

ATKINSON late WILKINSON, John Jepson, of Skellow and Hunslet, co. York, 186 . ., Vol. LIV, fol. 176.

ATKINSON before GRIMSHAW, Richard, Vicar of Cockerham, &c., co. Lanc., 1878, Vol. LX, fol. 92.

ATKINSON, Mrs. Buddle (Clara), of Wooley Grange, Bradford-on-Avon, co. Wilts., 1882, Vol. LXII, fol. 4. (Berry's Suppl.)

„ Hon. Nicholas, Justice in British Guiana, 1890, Vol. LXV, fol. 325.

ATTLAY, Stephen Oakeley, of Cheshunt House, co. Hertfordsh., and Jamaica, 1 Mar. 1787, Vol. XVI, fol. 227.

ATTREE, Frederick W. Town, Lieut., R. E., of Middleton, Wirksworth, co. Derby (s. of Francis Town Attree), 1877, Vol. LX, fol. 8. (Berry's Suppl.)

ATTWOOD, George R., of Glenthorne, Twickenham, co. Middlesex, 1887, Vol. LXIV, fol. 36.

„ T. A. Carless, of Malvern Wells, co. Worc., 1887. Vol. LXIV, fol. 36 ; and 1895,* Vol. LXVIII, fol. 322.

AUBERT, Alexander, of London and Dauphiny, France. Quarterly Arms, 1779, Vol. XIV, fol. 112 (see Berry).

„ John Daniel, of Raunds, co. Northampt., and Montpellier, France, 182 . ., Vol. XXXVII, fol. 320.

AUBERTIN, Peter, M.A., of Yew Sands, Banstead, co. Surrey, Rector of Chipstead, co. Surrey, 183 . ., Vol. XLII, fol. 320.

AUBREY formerly TOZER, Henry Pinson, of Broadhempstow, co. Devon, and Clehonger, co. Heref., 1813, Vol. XXVII, fol. 403.

AUBREY late RICKETTS, Charles Aubrey, of Dorton, co. Bucks. Quarterly Arms, 1874, Vol. LIX, fol. 32.

AUCHMUTY, Maj.-Gen. Sir Samuel, K.B. [1812], of New York. Arms, 181 . ., Vol. XXVI, fol. 438. Supporters, 181 . ., Vol. XXVI, fol. 445. Supporters, Gen. Sir Samuel Benjamin, G.C.B. [1861].

AUFRERE, George, of Chelsea, co. Middx., 30 June, 1795, Vol. XIX, fol. 111.

AUGERAUD, William, of Addison Road, Kensington, London, 1893, Vol. LXVII, fol. 109.

AUST, George Chelsea (and LOWE, quarterly), of Corsham, co. Wilts. Match, 180 . ., Vol. XXII, fol. 330. (See LOWE.)

AUSTEN to KNIGHT, Edward, of Godmersham Park, co. Kent, and Chawton, Hampsh., 1812, Vol. XXVII, fol. 181.

AUSTEN before LEIGH, James Edward, of Scarletts, Wargrave, co. Berks., 183 . ., Vol. XLII, fol. 42.

AUSTEN to TREFFRY, Joseph Thomas Place, of Fowey, co. Cornwall, 1836, Vol. XLII, fol. 292.

AUSTIN, John, of Clapton, co. Glouc., 17 . . .,* Vol. XVI, fol. 223. (*See* trick in J[oseph] F[oster]'s MS. amongst grants 13.)

„ George, reputed s. of Anthony, Lieut.-Col. Militia, co. Glouc., 8 Mar. 1800,° Vol. XX, fol. 453.

AUSTIN after BROCAS, Bernard (reputed s. of Brocas), of Beaurepaire, in Hampshire and co. Berks, 182 . ., Vol. XXXIII, fol. 324.

AUSTIN, William Piercy, D.D., Oxf., Bp. of Guiana. 1842, Vol. XLVI, fol. 138.

„ Sir J., Bart., of Red Hill, Castleford, co. York, 1894, Vol. LXVIII, fol. 63.

AUSTIN-CARTMELL, James, 18 . . ., Vol. LXV, fol. 5.

AVELAND, Baron [1856], Vol. LII, fol. 85 (Earl of Ancaster [1892]), 186 . ., Vol. LVII, fol. 286 ; 187 . ., Vol. LVIII, fols. 112, 114.

AVELING to NAIRN, William, of Barnet Place, West Hoathley, co. Sussex. Quarterly Arms, 183 . ., Vol. XL, fol. 239.

AWDRY, Thomas, of Salisbury, 1st s. of Sir John Wither Awdry, 189 . ., Vol. LXXI, fol. . . .

AYERST (late DE LASAUX), Robert Gunsley, of Ashford and Speldhurst, co. Kent, 181 . ., Vol. XXVII, fol. 153.

AYERST, Elizabeth, wife of Henry WINCHESTER, of Hawkhurst, co. Kent, 182 . ., Vol. XXXVI, fols. 99, 100.

ATLESBURY after WALKER, John Henry, s. of John Walker, of Packwood, co. Warw.; of Marpool Hall, co. Devon. Quarterly Arms, 185 . ., Vol. LII, fol. 295.

AYLESBURY-ROBERTS, Wilson, of Packwood, co. Warw. Quarterly Arms, 1774, Vol. XII, fol. 297.

AYLMER before WHITWORTH, Baron. Quartering, 182 . ., Vol. XXXV, fol. 307.

AYNSLEY late MIDFORD, of Little Harle Tower, co. Northumbld. Crest, 1793, Vol. XVIII, fol. 224.

„ late MURRAY, Lord Charles and Aynsley (his wife). Quarterly Arms, 24 June 1793, Vol. XVIII, fol. 226. (Berry's Add.)

AYNSWORTH, ..., of Long Whatton, co. Leic. Match with WILDE, 17 . . ., Vol. IX, fol. 87. (*See* WILDE.)

AYSCOUGH, ... *See* ASKEW, 17 . . ., Vol. X, fol. 232.

„ George Edward, 11 June, 1772, Vol. XII, fol. 189.

AYTON to LEE, Richard, of Lombard Street, London, 1773, Vol. XII, fol. 239.

B

BABINGTON, ... (*see* BIGLAND), of Keddington and Heaton, co. Northumberl⁴, co. Oxf. and Shropshire. Match with ERRINGTON, 17 . . ., Vol. X, fol. 215.

BACCHUS, William Ernest, of Hornton Grounds, Banbury, co. Oxford, 1897, Vol. LXX, fol. 30.

BACHE to BOOTH, William Charles, of Twemlow Hall, co. Chester. (Crest.) 181 . ., Vol. XXVI, fols. 388, 390.

BACHE, Thomas, of Coventry, co. Warwick [28 July 1828], Vol. XXXVII, fol. 156. (Crisp, Fragm. Geneal., V, p. 62.)

BACK, William Henry, of Norwich, co. Norf., 180 . ., Vol. XXV, fol. 186. (Crisp, VI, p. 118.)

BACKHOUSE, J. E., of The Rookery, Middleton Tyas, Richmond, co. York, 1891,* Vol. LXVI, fol. 172.

BACON, John (s. of William, s. of John), F.R.S., of Newton Cap, co. Durham, and Staward Peel, co. Northumb., 1752, Vol. IX, fol. 413.

BACON (late BUSHBY), Anthony Bacon, of the Middle Temple, London, and Cyfartha, co. Glamorgan, 17 . . ., Vol. XVIII, fol. 183.

BACON before HICKMAN, Bart., arms of BACON and PROCTOR quarterly, 182 . ., Vol. XXXVI, fol. 29.

BACON, Edward, of Sutton Bonnington, co. Nottingham, 17 . . ., Vol. VIII, fol. 42.
„ Rev. Thomas, M.A., Rector of Wiggonholt, co. Sussex, 1874, Vol. LIX, fol. 61. (Berry's Suppl.)
„ Captain Kenrick Vernlam, of Hole, Farnham, Vol. LXXI, fol. . . . . .
„ William Bacon (formerly FORSTER), of Newton Cap, co. Durham, 1800, Vol. XXI, fol. 213.
BADCOCK, Henry, of Taunton, co. Somerset, 184 . ., Vol. XLVII, fol. 59.
BADDELEY, William Clinton, C.B., Lieut.-Col., Beng., Eng., 182 . ., Vol. XXXVI, fol. 364.
BADDEFORD, William, B.Med., of Dartmouth, co. Devon, 24 Mar. 1703-4, Vol. V, fol. 148, and Add. MS. 14,831, fol. 35.
BADGER, ..., wife of WETHERED, of Fritwell, co. Oxf., 17 . ., Vol. VIII, fol. 247.
BAGGALLAY, Richard, of Lambeth, co. Surrey, 184 . ., Vol. XLVI, fol. 171.
BAGGE (to LEE-WARNER), William Wilson, Edward, Arthur and Thomas, 4 sons of Charles Elsden Bagge, M.D., and his wife, Ann Lee-Warner, of Quebec House, East Dereham, co. Norf. Match, 1814, Vol. XXVIII, fol. 124.
BAGGE, ..., Bart. [1867], of Stradsett Hall, Downham, co. Norfolk, 185 . ., Vol. LI, fol. 107.
BAGHOTT late WATHEN, Paul and Anne, of Lyppiat Park, King's Stanley, Naunton, Dumbleton and Prestbury, co. Glouc. Quarterly Arms. Match, 1815, Vol. XXVIII, fol. 381.
BAGHOTT-DE LA BERE (late EDWARDS), Rev. John, Vicar of Prestbury, Bristol and King's Stanley, co. Glouc., [31 May] 1879, Vol. LX, fol. 277. [Baghott and De la Bere quarterly.] (Berry's Suppl.)
BAGNALL, Thomas, of West Bromwich, co. Staff., 184 . ., Vol. XLVII, fol. 394.
BAGNALL-WILD late KIRBY, of Cambridge and the Inner Temple, London, and Costocks, co. Nottingham, 18 . ., Vol. LVII, fol. 88.
BAGOT, Baron [1780]. Supporters, 17 . . ., Vol. XIV, fol. 259.
BAGOT afterwards CHESTER, Charles, of co. Bucks., 186 . ., Vol. LV, fol. 38.
BAGSHAWE late DARLING, Sir William Chambers, Knt., of Coatshill Craven and Oakes, co. Derby, and Glauford Bridge, co. Linc. Wife's Arms impaled, 181 . ., Vol. XXIX, fol. 79.
BAGSTER, William, of St. Albans, Chichester, and the Isle of Wight, 17 . . ., Vol. XVII, fol. 258.
BAIGRIE, Col. Robert, C.B., of Midgarty, Sutherland, Scotland, s. of John Sutherland Baigrie, 1876, Vol. LIX, fol. 206. (Berry's Suppl.)
BAILEY [Joseph], Bart. [1852], of Brecon, and co. Suffolk, 185 . ., Vol. L, fol. 166.
„ . . . . of Heigham, Norwich, 185 . ., Vol. LII, fol. 119.
„ Capt. James Alderson, of Regency Square, Brighton, co. Sussex, 18 . ., Vol. LVII, fol. 80.
„ John Eglington, of Stretford, co. Lanc., 1878, Vol. LX, fol. 171.
„ Sir William Henry, of Sale Hall, Ashton-upon-Mersey, co. Chester, 1898, Vol. LXX, fol. 82.
„ James, M.P., of Shotgrove, Newport, co. Essex, 1898, Vol. LXX, fol. 96.
BAILLIE after CROOKSHANKS, Samuel (Scotland ?). Quarterly Arms, 17 . . ., Vol. XIV, fol. 213.
BAILLIE late REID, John, of Jamaica, 17 . . ., Vol. XVIII, fol. 85 (John, 181 . ., Vol. XXIX, fol. 71).
BAILLIE, John, of Roehampton, co. Surrey ; St. James, co. Cornwall ; Minard, par. of St. Anne's, co. Middx. ; and Jamaica, 181 . ., Vol. XXIX, fol. 71.
BAIN, William Richard, M.A., of Flempton-with-Hengrave, co. Suffolk, 186 . ., Vol. LV, fol. 244.
BAINBRIDGE, George (s. of John), of Carlebury, co. Durham, 180 . ., Vol. XXII, fol. 445.
„ Cuthbert Bainbridge, of Leazes House, Wolsingham, co. Durham, 1886, Vol. LXIII, fol. 289.
BAINBRIGGE before LE HUNT, co. Derby. Quarterly Arms, 183 . ., Vol. XXXIX, fol. 199.

BAINES, ..., Capt., R.N., of Penzance, co. Cornwall, and Layham, co. Suff. Quarterly Arms. Match, 180 . ., Vol. XXII, fol. 412.

BAINES to EMMITT, of Sausthorpe, co. Linc.. 182 . ., Vol. XXXVI, fol. 135.

BAINES to SIKES, Francis, of Chauntry House, Newark, co. Nottingham, 185 . ., Vol. LII, fol. 301.

BAIRD, David, Maj.-Gen., Sir [K.B. 1809, G.C.B. 1815], Bart. 1809, with remainder over (died s.p.). Augmentation, 1804, Vol. XXIII, fol. 52. Supporters, fol. 54.

BAIRD late FORSTER, John, of Newcastle-upon-Tyne and Alnwick, Northumb., 182 . ., Vol. XXXII, fols. 231, 233 ; William, fol. 233.

BAKER, Daniel, of Hatton Garden, London, 16 . ., Vol. III, fol. 105.

„ John, of the City of London, 15 Jan. 1702, Vol. V, fol. 89, and Add. MS. 14,830, fol. 137 (see Misc. G. et H., 3rd S., II., p. 65).

„ Judith and Elizabeth, d. and the heirs of Thomas, of London, mercht., 23 Dec. 1720, Vol. VII, fol. 45, and Add. MS. 14,830, fol. 136.

„ Vice-Admiral Hercules, M.P., of the Port of Hythe, co. Kent ? (1722 until his death 1 Nov. 1744), 21 Jan. 1720, Vol. VII, fol. 1a.

BAKER before BERE, Montague, of Timberscourt, co. Somerset, 7 Feb. 1776, Vol. XIII, fol. 166.

BAKER late ELSLEY, Thomas Baker, of Mayfield, co. Sussex, and Cambridge, 17 . . ., Vol. XVIII, fol. 285 (see HILLIER KIRBY, 181 . ., Vol. XXVI).

BAKER, Robert, grandson of James, of Upper Dunstable House, co. Surrey, Nicholashayne, Culmstock, co. Devon ; Bucklaw, par. of Durston, co. Somerset, 17 . . ., Vol. XIX, fol. 255.

„ (s. of Sir William), of Bayfordbury, co. Hertf. [13 May 1802 ?], Vol. XXII, fol. 193.

BAKER to TATHWELL, of Stamford, co. Linc., and Lyme, co. Dorset, 180 . ., Vol. XXIII, fol. 24.

BAKER, Richard, of Bridgnorth, Shropshire. Match with GUEST and BOULTON, 181 . ., Vol. XXVII, fol. 235.

„ William (s. of William), of Fenton, Stoke-upon-Trent, co. Staff. Match with BOURNE, 181 . ., Vol. XXIX, fol. 286. (Pratt.)

BAKER late LITTLEHALES, Bart., of Ranstone, Iwerne Courtney, co. Dorset ; Moulsey, co. Surrey, 181 . ., Vol. XXX, fol. 101.

BAKER to WATSON, Richard, of Ebberston, Pickering, and Old Malton Abbey, co. York, 181 . ., Vol. XXX, fol. 310.

„ Addison John (Creswell) and REED his wife, of Woodhorne and Cresswell, co. Northumb., 18 . . ., Vol. XLIV, fols. 361, 389.

„ Richard, of Westbrook, Cottesmore, and Langham Hall, co. Rutland, 17 . . ., Vol. XLV, fol. 19.

BAKER late TOWER, Henry John, of Elemore Hall, co. Durham, 1844, Vol. XLVII, fol. 119.

BAKER late WINGFIELD, William, Q.C., of Orsett Hall, co. Essex, 1849, Vol. XLIX, fol. 264.

BAKER, William, of Derby, 185 . ., Vol. L, fol. 435.

„ John, s. of Richard Chaffey, Bart., of Lopen, Ilminster, co. Somerset, and Morialta, Adelaide, South Australia, 186 . ., Vol. LIV, fol. 154.

„ Maj.-Gen. Sir William Erskine, K.C.B. [1 Feb. 1870], of Presteign, Radnor, 187 . ., Vol. LVIII, fol. 42.

„ Thomas, of Skerton House, Manchester (and Alfred Baker, of Birmingham), 187 . ., Vol. LVIII, fol. 269. (Berry's Suppl.)

BAKER to RHODES, Frederick Edward, of Loventon, co. Devon, and Ticehurst, co. Sussex, 1879, Vol. LX, fol. 235.

BAKER, L. J., of Ottershaw Park, Chertsey, co. Surrey, and Queen's Gate, London, 1889, Vol. LXV, fol. 283.

„ Sir S. White, of Sandford Orleigh, Highweek, co. Devon, 1886,* Vol. LXIII, fol. 215.

„ Sir George, Bart., of Loventon, Devon, 1879, Vol. LX, fol. 218.

BALACK, Hanway to HANWAY, of the Middle Temple. 7 Sept., 1775, Vol. XIII, fol. 123.

BALDERS, ..., Lieut.-Col., C.B., of West Barsham, co. Norf., 184 . .. Vol. XLVIII, fol. 400.

BALDOCK, ... of Petham, Whitstable, Greenwich and Bleane, co. Kent, 181 . ., Vol. XXVII, fol. 273.

„ . . . ., of Buxted, co. Sussex, 184 . ., Vol. XLVI, fol. 374.

BALDWIN now RIGBYE, ... of Harrock Hall, co. Lanc., 17 . . ., Vol. XVI, fol. 297 ; 179 . ., Vol. XIX, fol. 264.

„ . . . ., of Grose Hall, Camberwell : Richmond, co. Surrey, 182 . ., Vol. XXXIV, fol. 172.

BALDWIN to CHILDE, ..., of Kinlet, Shropsh., and Aqualate, co. Staff., 18 . ., Vol. XLIX, fol. 175.

BALL, Alexander John, Capt., R.N. (s. of Robert), of Ebworth and Stonehouse, co. Glouc., 180 . ., Vol. XXI, fol. 184.

„ Edward ? Hughes, of Bishops Hall, co. Essex, 181 . ., Vol. XXXI, fol. 160.

BALL-HUGHES, Edward, 181 . ., Vol. XXXI, fol. 329. See JOHNSON.

BALL (Edward) before HUGHES. Edward Hughes Ball, 181 . ., Vol. XXXI, fol. 160, to be Edward Ball-Hughes, 181 . ., Vol. XXXI, fol. 239, of Upper Brook Street, London. Quarterly Arms, 181 . .. Vol. XXXI, fol. 239.

BALL, Thomas, of Harrow. (?)

BALLANTINE to DYKES, Joseph, of Dovenby Hall and Ward Hall, co. Cumberld. (Ballantine late Dykes, Match), 18 . . ., Vol. XX, fol. 450.

BALLANTYNE-DYKES-BALLANTYNE, Lawson, 24 June, 1773, Vol. XII, fol. 251.

DYKES-BALLANTYNE-DYKES, Joseph, 17 . . ., Vol. XX, fol. 450.

BALLARD, ..., of Ludlow, Shropsh., 182 . ., Vol. XXXII, fol. 53.

BALLOWE, Henry, Dep.-Chamberlain of the Exchqr, Westminster (s. of Henry, of Norwich) [and to the issue of Augustine Ballow, brother of Henry], 28 July 1709,* Vol. V, fol. 376, and Add. MS. 14,830, fol. 151.

BALLY, William Ford, F.R.C.S., of Downing, co. Somerset, 185 . ., Vol. LI, fol. 168.

BALSTON, ..., Commander, E.I.C.S., of Corse Hill, Radipole, co. Dorset, and Martinstown, co. Somerset, 182 . ., Vol. XXXVI, fol. 81.

„ T., ? M. B., of Chart Place, Sutton, co. Kent, 1894, Vol. LXVIII, fol. 37.

BALTIMORE, Baron (Calvert), Ireland, 17 . . ., Vol. XVI, fol. 11 [?].

BAMFORD, late HESKETH, Robert } of Gwyrch, co. Denbigh ; Bamford Hall, co. Lanc. ; and Newton, co. Chester, 180 . ., Vol. XXIII, fol. 379 ; 180 . .,Vol. XXV,fol. 377. Arms to descendants by late wife, 180 . ., Vol. XXV, fol. 382.

BAMFORD, before HESKETH, Robert

BAMFORD, Charles ?, of Green Bank, Birkenhead, co. Chester, and Wednesbury, co. Staff., 187 . ., Vol. LVIII, fol. 134. (Berry's Suppl.)

BAMPFYLDE, ..., co. Devon. Match with WARRE and TYNDALE. Quarterly with WARRE (see WARRE), 181 . ., Vol. XXX, fol. 157.

BAMPTON, Henry, M.A., Camb., of Marine Parade, Dover, co. Kent, 186 . ., Vol. LVII, fol. 328.

BANCE, John (s. of John), of Challow, Berks., and of London, Mercht., 23 Oct. 1721,* Vol. VII, fol. 71, and Add. MS. 14,830, fol. 152.

BANCROFT, Peter, see William Bancroft HARRISON, 1897, Vol. LXIX, fol. 283.

„ Sir Squire, of 18 Berkeley Square, London, 1897, Vol. LXX, fol. 52.

BANISTER, ..., of Westerham, co. Kent. Match with LOVELL, rather SORELL (see SORELL), 181 . ., Vol. XXVII, fol. 15.

BANKES (late HOLME), Meyrick, of Winstanley and Upholland, co. Lanc., 180 . ., Vol. XXII, fol. 320.

BANKES, Frances, d. of Alderm. Sir Henry Bankes and wife of Sir Brownlow CUST, Bart., 177 . ., Vol. XIII, fol. 295.

BANKES, M⁗ E. S. L., of Winstanley House, Wigan. co. Lanc., 1882, Vol. LXI, fol. 288.

BANKHEAD, ..., Minister to Mexican Republic, 184 . ., Vol. XLVII, fol. 17.

BANKS, Rev. Frederick, M.A., Magd. Hall. Oxf., of Kenilworth, co. Warw., and Hadley, Shropsh., 185 . ., Vol. L, fol. 232.

,, Sir Joseph, K.B. and Bart., P.R.S. Supporters, 179 . ., Vol. XIX, fol. 178. [K.B. 1 July 1795, G.C.B. 2 Jan. 1815.]

BANKS, George, of Loversall and Doncaster, co. York, 182 . ., Vol. XXXVI, fol. 331.

., James Falconer B., B.A., co. Glouc. (see SHARPE), 185 . ., Vol. LI, fols. 25-27.

,, Sir Edward, Knt., of Royal Terrace, Adelphi, London, 182 . ., Vol. XXXVII, fol. 355.

,, William, J.P., of Highmore House, Wigton, co. Cumberld., 186 . ., Vol. LIV, fol. 264.

BANNER, Richard, Attorney of London, and brother Samuel, of Birmingham, 27 Sept. 1700, Vol. V, fol. 10, and Add. MS. 14,830, fol. 168, and Guillim, p. 396.

BANNING, Charles Barber [Greaves-Banning] (and WHITLOW his wife), of Liverpool. [Greaves] Quarterly with Banning [6 Nov. 1865], Vol. LVI, fol. 32.

GREAVES-BANNING, Louisa Sophia (d. of Richard WHITLOW). [Greaves] Quarterly with WHITLOW, 1865, Vol. LVI, fol. 48.

BANNISTER, John, of Bidlington, Steyning, co. Sussex, 181 . ., Vol. XXIX, fol. 457.

BARATTY, John Bartholomew, of The Grissons, Switzerland, and of London, 17 . . ., Vol. IX, fol. 448.

BARBENSON, Thomas Nicholas, Queen's Procureur, Isle of Alderney, 186 . ., Vol. LV, fol. 98. (Berry's Suppl.)

BARBER, ..., (of London, 16 . . ., Vol. II, fol. 653).

,, John, of the City of London and East Sheen, co. Surrey, 25 Oct. 1720, Vol. VII, fol. 23, and Add. MS. 14,830, fol. 172.

BARBER, of Whickham, Hampsh., and Clapham Rise, co. Surrey, 185 . ., Vol. LI, fol. 392.

BARBER to BARBER-STARKEY, William Joseph (arms), of Hutton Hall, co. York, and Quorndon, co. Derby, 187 . ., Vol. LVIII, fol. 204. (Berry's Suppl.)

BARBOUR, George, of Bolesworth Castle, Malpas, co. Chester, 1886,* Vol. LXIII, fol. 237.

BARCHARD, John, of Wandsworth, co. Surrey, 17 . . ., Vol. XVIII, fol. 262.

,, ..., of Ashcombe, St. Anne's, Lewes, co. Sussex, 184 . ., Vol. XLVII, fol. 351.

BARGRAVE after TOURNAY, Robert T., of Eastry, co. Kent, 1800, Vol. XXI, fol. 74. (Berry.)

BARHAM, 1st Baron [1805] ([Sir Charles] MIDDLETON [Bart. 1781]), Admiral [1787], of co. Kent. Arms and Supporters, [1805], Vol. XXIII, fol. 157.

,, Baroness, of co. Kent. Supporters, Earls of MIDDLETON with destinations, 181 . ., Vol. XXIX, fol. 381.

BARING, Baroness Ashburton, of Larkbear, co. Devon, 17 . . ., Vol. XV. fol. 47.

,, Sir Francis, Bart., of Beddington, co. Surrey, and Larkbere, co. Devon, impaled with his wife (HERRING), 17 . . ., Vol. XVIII, fol. 230.

BARING before GOULD, of Lew Trenchard and Larkbere, co. Devon, 17 . . ., Vol. XIX, fol. 121. (Crisp, XIX, p. 121.)

BARING-GOULD (Flora Maria Marsden DAVIES, wife of Francis Baring-Gould), of Merrow Grange, Guildford, co. Surrey. Arms for DAVIES, 1897, Vol. LXIX, fol. 215.

BARKER, ..., of Debenham, co. Suff. Match with SUTTON, 176 . ., Vol. XI, fol. 220.

,, Sir Robert, Knt., 1774, Vol. XIII, fol. 56.

BARKER late RAYMOND, John, of Fairford Park, co. Glouc., 17 . . ., Vol. XVII, fol. 99.

BARKER now HETHERSETT, Lieut.-Gen., of Shropham and Thetford, co. Norf. Match, 180 . ., Vol. XXII, fol. 393.

BARKER to HALL (2 sons and 4 daus.), of Weston Colville, co. Camb. (reputed sons and daus. of John Hall), 181 . ., Vol. XXIX, fols. 234-244.

BARKER, ..., of Oldham, co. Lanc., 182 . ., Vol. XXXV, fol. 332.

„ Francis Edge, of Chester, and Llandir, co. Denbigh, 182 . ., Vol. XXXVI, fol. 104.

„ . . . ., of Lanedelph, co. Staff., 182 . ., Vol. XXXVII, fol. 27.

„ Robert and George, sons of Robert, of Goldings Hill, Loughton, co. Essex, mar. with DOBBET, 182 . ., Vol. XXXVIII, fol. 21.

BARKER (late CRAGG), Richard Barker, reputed s., of Ruddington, co. Nottingham, 17 . . ., Vol. XL, fol. 5.

BARKER before MILL, Rev. John, M.A., Vicar of King Sombourne, Hampsh., and Bury House, Eling, Hampsh., 19 May 1835, Vol. XLI, fol. 1.

BARKER, Richard, of Fitzroy Square, London. 184 . ., Vol. XLVII, fol. 131.

„ Thomas, ..., of Roslyn Hall, Sydney, N.S.W., and of Dunmow, co. Essex, 185 . ., Vol. LII, fol. 200.

BARKER after DARLING, James, of Halnaker House, Boxgrove, co. Sussex, and Stockton, co. Durham, 186 . ., Vol. LIV, fol. 68 [?].

BARKER, John Daye, of Broughton Lodge, Cartmel, co. Lanc., and Cadogan Square, London, 1884,* Vol. LXII, fol. 196.

„ George Rickard, of Hemsley Hall, Hemsley, co. Norf., 1889, Vol. LXV, fol. 91.

„ Christopher Dove (s. of Thomas), of Radnor House, Great Malvern, co. Worc., 1897, Vol. LXIX, fol. 303.

„ Evan Barker, James JONES, 189 . ., Vol. LXXI, fol. . . . .

BARKWORTH, A., B[arkworth] Wilson, of Kingston-upon-Hull, and Milton-in-Walton, co. York, 1894, Vol. LX, fol. 232.

BARLEE (late BUCKLE), William, of Worlingworth and Wrentham, co. Suff., and Ditchingham, co. Norf., 181 . ., Vol. XXVI, fol. 348. Match, fol. 346.

BARLEE to DAVY (widow of Barlee), of The Grove, Yoxford, and Wrentham, co. Suff., 185 . ., Vol. L, fol. 133.

BARLOW, Thomas, of Sheffield, co. York, 1691, Vol. IV, fol. 88. (See Berry.)

BARLOW late OWEN, Hugh, of Lawrenny, co. Pembroke. 1789, Vol. XVII, fol. 113.

BARLOW after OWEN, Sir William, Bart., of Lawrenny, co. Pembroke, 1845, XLVII, fol. 204.

BARLOW (late BREDALL), Thomas Anthony, of Barlow, co. Lanc. Match, 1799. Vol. XX, fol. 402.

BARLOW, Sir George II. [ilario], B. C. S. and London, Gov.-Genl. of Bengal, 180 . ., Vol. XXII, fol. 280. Supporters [K.B. 1806, G.C.B. 1815], Vol. XXIV, fol. 79.

BARLOW to MASTERMAN, of Settrington, co. York, and Millbrook, co. Hertf., 182 . ., Vol. XXXIV, fol. 45.

BARLOW to HOY, of Medenbury House, Hampsh., and Walthamstow, co. Essex, 182 . ., Vol. XXXVII, fols. 241, 318.

BARLOW, ..., of Woolwich, co. Kent, late Prof. of Mathematics at the Military Acad., 18 . ., Vol. XLIX, fol. 414.

„ John (s. of James), of Upton House and Hardwick Grange, Manchester. 18 . ., Vol. XLIX, fol. 464.

BARNARD, Gilbert Vane, Baron Barnard, of co. Durham. Supporters, 27 Sep. 1724-5, Vol. VII, fol. 261, and Harl. MS. 6832, fol. 256.

BARNARD before BOLDERS, of Lewyns, South Cave, co. York, 17 . . . Vol. XII, fol. 7.

BARNARD, Benjamin, of Park Gate House, co. Surrey, and Newbury, Berks., 182 . ., Vol. XXXVII, fol. 174.

„ Joseph, of Notcliffe House, and Whitefield Court, Deerhurst, co. Glouc., 184 . ., Vol. XLVIII, fol. 315.

BARNARD, Baron WILLOUGHBY DE BROKE, grandson [of Thomas Barnard], Rector of Withersfield, co. Suff., 185 . ., Vol. L, fols. 332, 334.

„   John, of St. Mark's, Kensington, co. Middx., 185 . ., Vol. LII, fol. 14. (Berry's Suppl.)

BARNARD-BOLDERO, Edward Gee, of Case Castle and South Cave, co. York, 18 . . ., Vol. LX, fol. 42.

BARNARD, G. W. G., Solicitor, of Norwich, 1888,ᵉ Vol. LXIV, fol. 244.

BARNATO, B. J., of Park Lane, London, 1895, Vol. LXIX, fol. 3.

BARNE, George, Mayor of Tiverton, co. Devon, 182 . ., Vol. XXXVII, fol. 196.

BARNEBY to HIGGINSON, of Saltmarsh and Brockhampton, co. Heref., 182 . ., Vol. XXXV, fol. 264 ; 182 . ., Vol. XXXIV, fol. 142.

BARNED after LEWIS, Israel, of Gloucester Terrace and Great Ormond Street, London, 185 . ., Vol. LII, fol. 383.

BARNED.   *See* LEWIS, Israel. Roy. Lic., 24 July 1858.

BARNES, Richard, of Reigate, co. Surrey, 180 . ., Vol. XXIV, fol. 186.

„   William (of Ch. Coll., Camb.), Rector of Richmond, co. York, 1823, Vol. XXXIV, fol. 116.

„   Richard Knowles, Capt., R.N., of Thurlby and Stamford, co. Linc., 183 . ., Vol. XLIII, fol. 304.

„   Miss, of Smyth Hall, co. Essex, 18 . . ., Vol. XLIX, fol. 406.

BARNES after PEMBERTON, of Smyth Hall, Havering-atte-Bower, co. Essex, 18 . ., Vol. XLIX, fol. 411.

BARNES, ..., Mayor of Manchester, 185 . ., Vol. L, fol. 149.

„   William Black, of Popes Wood House, Binfield, Berks., 186 . ., Vol. LIV, fol. 314.

„   Richard, of Canonbury Park, co. Middx., and Lombard Street, London, and Jamaica, 186 . ., Vol. LV, fol. 58.

„   Rev. G., Vicar of St. Barnabas, Bethnal Green, and Grove Road, Bow, London, 1889,ᵉ Vol. LXV, fol. 143.

„   Alfred (s. of John Gorell Barnes), of Ashgate Lodge, Chesterfield, co. Derby, 1897, Vol. LXIX, fol. 319.

BARNET, Martha, only dau. and heir of Jacob Barnet, of London, mar. with ROLLS (*see* Lord LLANGATTOCK), 183 . ., Vol. XLII, fol. 288.

BARN(E)WELL (late HERRING), Charles B., of Norwich, and Beeston-next-Mileham, co. Norf., 17 . . ., Vol. XXXVI, fols. 17 and 13.

BARN(E)WELL (after TURNER), Frederick Henry, M.A., F.R.S., of Mileham, co. Norf., and Bury St. Edmunds, Brockley, Lawshall and Stanningfield, co. Suff., 1826, Vol. XXXVI, fol. 51. [Add MS. 37,150.]

BARNS, Col. James Stevenson, C.B., of Kirkhill, Ayrshire. Augmentation, 181 . ., Vol. XXIX, fol. 422.

BARNSTON (*see* OWEN), of Churton, co. Chester. Match with OWEN, 17 . . ., Vol. XVII, fol. 205.

BARON, Rev. John, M.A., Queen's Coll., Oxf., of Upton Scudamore, Wilts, and Brill and Boarstall, Bucks., 186 . ., Vol. LVI, fol. 140.

„   John, of Heywood and Larkhill, Burnley, co. Lanc., 1881,ᵉ Vol. LXI, fol. 171. (Berry's Suppl.).

BARRAN, Sir John, Bart., of Chapel Allerton Hall, nr. Leeds, co. York, 1895, Vol. LXVIII, fol. 152.

BARRATT (*see* LAYLAND), 1898, Vol. LXX, fol. 208.

BARRETT, Capt. Samuel (s. of Edmund), of Cinnamon Hill, Isle of Jamaica, 17 . ., Vol. XVIII, fol. 121.

BARRETT-BARRETT, Edward and bro. Samuel (late MOULTON), of Cinnamon Hill, Isle of Jamaica, and New York, 17 . .. Vol. XX, fol. 110 ; Ed. M. B. [Edward Moulton Barrett], of Hope End [co. Heref. ?], 181 . ., Vol. XXIX, fol. 25.

BARRETT-LENNARD late THOMAS, of co. Essex, 180 . ., Vol. XXI, fol. 200.

BARRETT, George Rogers (and brother), of Stockwell, co. Essex, and co. Surrey, 181 . ., Vol. XXVI, fol. 366.

BARRETT, Susannah, of London, wife of Sir Justinian ISHAM, Bart., and dau. of Edmondson BERRY, azure, two barrulets or between three doves or, 9 Jan. 1773, Vol. XII, fol. 222.

BARRETTO, Joseph, of Calcutta, 1813, Vol. XXVII, fol. 211. (Berry's Suppl.)

BARRIE, Rear-Adm. Sir Robert, K.C.B. [1840], of Swarthdale, co. Lanc., 18 . ., Vol. XLIV, fol. 397.

BARRITT, Thomas Hercy, of Jamaica, 28 Oct. 1768, Vol. XI, fol. 312.

BARRINGTON, Sir V. H. B. K., 188 . ., Vol. LXIII, fol. 10 ; 179 . ., Vol. XIX, fol. 29.

BARROW, Richard, Rector of Barnoldby-le-Beck, co. Linc. ; Southwell and South Wheatley, co. Nottingham ; and Howgill, co. York, 1815, Vol. XXIX, fol. 67.

BARROW heretofore CORDOZA, of Madras and London, 182 . ., Vol. XXXVII, fol. 225.

BARROW, Simon, of Lansdown Grove, Bath, co. Somerset, 182 . ., Vol. XXXVII, fol. 284.

  ,, [Sir John], Bart. [1835]. 2nd Sec. Admiralty, of Ulverstone, co. Lanc., 183 . ., Vol. XL, fol. 323.

  ,, Alfred, of London and Antwerp. 183 . ., Vol. XLI, fol. 186.

  ,, George Martin, of St. John's Green [?], Writtle, co. Essex, 1877, Vol. LX, fol. 64.

BARROWBY, William, M.D., of Knaresborough, co. York, and Aldermanbury, London, 17 May 1732, Vol. VIII, fol. 137b.

BARRS, Alfred (s. of George), of High Harcourt and Rowley Regis, co. Staff., 1876, Vol. LIX, fol. 290. (Berry's Suppl.)

BARRS before HADEN, Alfred Haden, of High Harcourt and Rowley Regis, co. Staff., 1877, Vol. LIX, fol. 304. (Berry's Suppl.)

BARRY late NEALE, Pendock, of Tollerton Hall and Mansfield Woodhouse, co. Nott., 1811, Vol. XXVI, fol. 358. Crest, fol. 360.

BARRY after OTTER, of Clarges Street, London, 187 . ., Vol. LVIII, fol. 235. (Berry's Suppl.)

BARRY, Charles, of Parliament Mansions, Victoria Street, Westminster, s. of the late Sir Charles, 1898, Vol. LXX, fol. 84.

  ,, Francis Tress (Bart.), of St. Leonard Hill, Clewer, Windsor, Berks., 1899, Vol. LXX, fol. 332.

[BARRYMORE, Earl of, David BARRY, Viscount BARRY, &c., 28 Feb. 1627-8. (Crisp, Fragm. Geneal., X, p. 84.)]

BARSTOW, John J. Jackson, of Thornton, co. York, and Weston-super-Mare, co. Somerset, 1896, Vol. LXIX, fol. 118.

BARTHOLOMEW, David Ewan, C.B., Post-Capt., R.N., of London, 181 . ., Vol. XXIX, fol. 248.

BARTLETT, Thomas, of Holwell House, Cranborne, co. Dorset, and Harnham, Wilts. Match, 17 . . ., Vol. XVIII, fol. 301.

BARTLETT after STUCKEY, Barnaby John, of Weston House, Branscombe, co. Devon. Quarterly Arms, 180 . ., Vol. XXV, fol. 357.

BARTLETT, Sir Ellis A., of 6, Grosvenor Street, London, and Grange House, Eastbourne, co. Sussex, 1881, Vol. LXI, fols. 115, 117.

  ,, William L. A. BURDETT-COUTTS, of Piccadilly, London, 188 . ., Vol. LXI, fols. 115, 117, 326.

  ,, John Adams, of Pembroke Place, Liverpool, 1880,² Vol. LXI, fol. 35. (Crisp, I, p. 65 ; VI, p. 27.)

  ,, John A., Solicitor, Lynton, Wavertree, co. Lanc. Quarterings, 189 . ., Vol. LXVI, fol. 29. (Crisp, I. p. 65 ; VI, p. 27.)

  ,, Rev. J. M. (de L.), of the Manor House, Ludbrooke, Ermington, co. Devon, 1894, Vol. LXVIII, fol. 122.

BARTON (late METCALFE), Henry, of the Chancery Office, London. Match with TURTON, 17 . . ., Vol. XIX, fol. 141.

BARTON, ..., Dep. Compts. and King's Clerk of copper coinage, 182 . ., Vol. XXXVII, fol. 41.

BARTON, ..., of Stapleton Park, co. York, and Swinton, co. Lanc., 183 . .,
Vol. XLIII, fol. 227.
„ Charles, s. of Charles, D.D., Dean of Bocking, of Holbrooke House, Charlton
Musgrave, co. Somerset, and Monks Eleigh, co. Suff., 18 . . ., Vol. XLIX,
fol. 110.
„ Everard William, of Warstone House, Kidderminster, co. Worc., 1886,*
Vol. LXIII, fol. 261. (Crisp, I, p. 90.)
BARUH-LOUSADA, Emanuel, of London and Jamaica, 28 Jan. 1777, Vol. XIII,
fol. 255.
BARWICK. . . . ., see STATTER, of Holt Lodge, co. Norf. Match with STATTER,
181 . ., Vol. XXVI, fol. 328.
BASKERVILLE before MYNORS (formerly Rickards), Thomas Peter, of Poulton
House, Wilts., and co. Heref., and Aberdeen Court, co. Radnor, (1787),
Vol. XVI, fol. 305 ; Thomas, 1818, Vol. XXX, fol. 301. Match with
POWELL.
BASELEY to WADE, of Scotts House, Boldon, co. Durham, 182 . ., Vol. XXXII,
fol. 281.
BASHALL, ..., of Farington Lodge, Penwortham and Walton-le-Dale, co. Lanc.,
184 . ., Vol. XLVII, fol. 290.
BASHFORD, Col. W. C. L., of Brunswick Square, Brighton, co. Sussex, 1886,*
Vol. LXIII, fol. 315.
BASKERVILLE, Col. Thomas, B. M. MYNORS, of Poulton House, Wilts., Clyro
Court and Evenglode, co. Radnor, and Treago, co. Heref., 18 . . .,
Vol. XXX, fol. 301. POWELL quartering, 1837, Vol. XLII, fol. 77.
BASKERVILLE late VIVEASH, Henry, of Madras C.S., of Calne and Wooley
Bradford, Wilts, 183 . ., Vol. XLII, fol. 334.
BASS, Sir M. I., Bart., of Glen Quoick, Inverness. Supporters, as Baron BURTON,
1882°, Vol. LXI, fol. 273.
„ Baron BURTON, of Glen Quoick, Inverness, 1887, Vol. LXIII, fol. 322.
BASSET, Baron de Dunstanville [1796], co. Cornwall. Escutcheon of Pretence
for wife. Supporters, 17 . . ., Vol. XIX, fol. 365.
BASSET late DAVIE, of Watermouth, Beninharbor and Heauton Court, co. Devon.
Quarterly, 180 . ., Vol. XXII, fol. 173.
„ late BRUCE, William W. J. Bruce, Major in the Army, of Beaupré, co.
Glamorgan, 186 . ., Vol. LVI, fol. 57.
BASSET, Charles Henry, of Pilton House, Barnstaple, co. Devon, 1880, Vol. LXI,
fol. 79. (Berry's Suppl.)
BASSETT, A. B., F.R.S., Bar.-at-Law, of Berks., 1891, Vol. LXVI, fol. 55.
BASTARD, Edmund P., M.P. Devon, Kitley, co. Devon, 182 . ., Vol. XXXII,
fol. 307.
BATE-DUDLEY, Henry, of Bradwell Lodge, co. Essex, and Kilscoran House, co.
Wexford, and Sloane Street, London, 180 . ., Vol. XXIII, fol. 318.
„ Capt. Thomas, of Kilsterton, co. Flint, 1890,* Vol. LXVI, fol. 11 ; Add.
MS. 14,831, fol. 171. (Crisp, IV, p. 173.)
BATEMAN, Sr James, Knt., of Haesbroke, Flanders, and of London, Mercht,
Vol. V, fol. 254. 10 Oct. 1707. Harl. Soc., VIII, p. 463 [Le Neve's
Book of Knights].
„ Thomas, s. of Mathew, s. of Thomas, of Whitechapel (to descendants
of his father), 24 June 1707, Vol. V, fol. 226 ; Add. MS. 14,831,
fol. 170.
„ Robson (late HOLLAND), Richard, of Hartfield, co. Huntingdon, and Orchard
Street, London, 17 . . ., Vol. XVIII, fol. 13.
„ James, of Tolson House, Kendal, and Staveley, co. Westmorld, and Islington
House, co. Lanc., and Knypersley Hall, co. Staff., 180 . ., Vol. XXV,
fol. 395.
BATEMAN (late HUDSON), Thomas, of the Middle Temple, London, and Hipper-
holme, co. York, and Halton Park, co. Lanc., 181 . ., Vol. XXXI,
fol. 80.

BATEMAN late BUCKLEY, of Guilsborough, co. Northampton, 182 . ., Vol. XXXVI, fol. 373.

BATEMAN before HANBURY (Baron Bateman [1837]), of co. Heref. and Northampton, 183 . ., Vol. XLIII, fol. 58.

BATEMAN, John Foster, of Moor Park, Farnham, co. Surrey, 1881, Vol. LXI, fol. 176. (Berry's Suppl.)

BATES, see CLAYTON, of Newbottle, co. Durham. Clayton formerly BRACK. Match, 181 . ., Vol. XXVIII, fol. 187.

„ William R., of Creerist, Holyhead, and Liverpool, 183 . ., Vol. XLI, fol. 138.

„ Rev. J. E. ELLIOT-, Rector of Whatton, 1880, Vol. LXI, fol. 96.

„ Sir Edward, Bart., of Manydown Park, Basingstoke, Hampsh., and Castle Holywell, co. Flint, 1880,* Vol. LXI, fol. 5.

BATESON before HARVEY, Sir Robert, of Garstang, co. Lanc., and London. Quarterly Arms, 1788, Vol. XVII, fol. 15.

„ Thomas, of Liverpool, and Forton, co. Lanc., 1808, Vol. XXV, fol. 203.

BATESON before YARBURGH, George William, of Heslington Hall, co. York, 1876, Vol. LIX, fol. 204.

BATH, Earl of [1742] (PULTENEY). Supporters, 17 . . ., Vol. IX, fol. 67.

„ Baroness, 17 . . ., Vol. XVIII, fol. 203.

„ Henry James, J.P., of Alltyferin, Llanywad, co. Carmarthen, and Swansea, co. Glamorgan, 1868, Vol. LVII, fol. 17. (Berry's Suppl.)

BATHURST, Baron [1712], of Wilts. Supporters, 17 . . ., Vol. VI, fol. 105.

„ Baron [Apsley, 1771], of Apsley, Wilts. Supporters, 17 . . ., Vol. XII, fol. 60.

BATHURST before HERVEY, of Clarendon Park, Wilts. Match with ELWILL, 18 . . ., Vol. XXI, fol. 329.

BATHURST after HERVEY, of Clarendon Park, Wilts., Surrey and Hampsh., 182 . ., Vol. XXXVII, fol. 197.

BATHURST late BRAGGE, Charles, of Lydney Park, co. Glouc., 180 . ., Vol. XXII, fol. 424.

BATLEY to BEYNON, Rev. Edward T., of Carshalton, Surrey. Quarterly Arms, 1805, Vol. XXIII, fol. 230. (Berry's Suppl.)

BATSON, Capt. Thomas, of Highworth, Wilts., and Bourton-on-the-Hill, co. Glouc., 24 Dec. 1702, Vol. V, fol. 85. (Berry.)

„ Thomas, late DAVIS, 24 Dec. 1702, Vol. V, fol. 85. (Berry.)

BATT, Christopher, of Kensington, co. Middx. (s. of William, of New Sarum, Wilts.), to descendants of his father, 21 June, 1717, Vol. VI, fol. 305 ; Add. MS. 14,831, fol. 140.

„ . . . ., of Longfield, co. Kent, 183 . ., Vol. XLIV, fol. 198.

BATTEN-POOLL, Robert Pooll Henry, of Finsbury and Road Manor, co. Somerset, s. of Joseph Langford, 1871, Vol. LVIII, fol. 12. (Berry's Suppl.)

BATTERSBY after HARFORD, Abraham, of Blaze Castle, co. Glouc., 181 . ., Vol. XXIX, fol. 97.

BATTERSBY, Worsley, of Onslow Gardens, London, and Liverpool, co. Lanc., 1881, Vol. LXI, fol. 164. (Berry's Suppl.)

BATTERSEA, Baron [1892] (FLOWER), 189 . ., Vol. LXVII, fol. 111.

BATTIE-WRIGHTSON, W. H., of Cusworth Park, Sprotborough, York, 1892, Vol. LXVII, fol. 97.

BATTINE, Col. William, (C.B.), R.A., 183 . ., Vol. XLIV, fol. 67.

BAVERSTOCK, ..., of Windsor, Berks., and Alton, Hampshire, 181 . ., Vol. XXXI, fol. 20.

BAX-IRONSIDE, M. Henry, C.B., of Houghton-le-Spring, co. Durham, and Twyford, co. Hertf. Quarterly Arms, 188 . ., Vol. LVI, fols. 221, 223.

BAX, Alfred Ridley (s. of Daniel), of Ivy Bank, Haverstock Hill, London, 1899, Vol. LXX, fol. 308.

BAXENDALE, Joseph William, of Hursley Park, Southampton, 1897, Vol. LXIX, fol. 321.

BAXTER, Robert, s. of Nicholas Posthumous, of Atherstone, co. Warw., 17 . .,
     Vol. XIV, fol. 326.
,,   Henry, of Elmhirst, co. York, and Worc. Coll., Oxf., 185 . ., Vol. LI,
     fol. 176.
,,   Richard, Bar.-at-Law, of Lincoln's Inn, and Leinster Gardens, London,
     1877, Vol. LX, fol. 68. (Berry's Suppl.)
,,   Henry, of Lincoln's Inn, London, and The Tower, Rainhill, co. Lanc., 1879,
     Vol. LX, fol. 287. (Berry's Suppl.)
BAYARD after CAMPBELL, Francis, reputed s. of Bayard, Richmond, co. Surrey,
     and Cornwall Terrace, London, 186 . ., Vol. LIV, fol. 34.
BAYFORD, John (s. of David), of Arches Court, Canterbury, and Lewes, co. Sussex,
     180 . ., Vol. XXII, fol. 323.
BAYLEY, Isaac (to gt.[?] Daniel), of Market Harborough, co. Leic.; Chesterton,
     co. Huntingd. ; and Willow Hall, Whittlesey, co. Camb., 1782, Vol. XV,
     fol. 113.
BAYLEY before WORTHINGTON, of Sharston Hall, Northenden, co. Chester, 186 . .,
     Vol. LV, fol. 154.
BAYLIS, Robert, Alderm. and Sheriff of London, 2 June 1725, Vol. VII, fol. 310.
     (Burke.)
,,   Thomas, of New Mills, Stroud, co. Glouc., 1755, Vol. X, fol. 14 (see Berry
     and Burke).
,,   of Manchester, 182 . ., Vol. XXXIV, fol. 52.
BAYLY, Barbara (see BEAN), of Lincoln's Inn, London, 1788, Vol. XVII, fol. 89.
BAYLY before WALLIS, Lieut.-Col., of Plas Newyth, co. Anglesey, and London,
     18 . ., Vol. XXI, fol. 81.
BAYLY, William, First Master, R.N. Acad., Portsmouth, 180 . ., Vol. XXIII,
     fol. 404.
BAYLY late DARK, William Henry, of Market Lavington, Wilts., and Portsea,
     Hampsh., 180 . ., Vol. XXV, fol. 240. Match.
BAYNES, Bart. [1801], of Harefield Place, co. Middx., 18 . . ., Vol. XXI, fol. 139.
,,   (see CATOR), Maj.-Gen. (CATOR Arms), 181 . ., Vol. XXX, fol. 403.
,,   of Blackburn, co. Lanc., 185 . ., Vol. LIII, fol. 245.
BAYNING, Viscountess (MURRAY), Berks. Supporters [1674], Vol. III, fol. 6.
,,   Baron [1797]. Supporters, 179 . ., Vol. XX, fol. 32.
BAYNTUN before SANDYS, of Great Misenden Park, co. Glouc. ; Chadlington Hall,
     co. Oxf.; Knowle House, Frogmore ; and Bowringsleigh House, co. Devon,
     180 . ., Vol. XXV, fol. 252.
BAYNTON [BAYNTUN], Rear-Adm. Sir Henry William, K.C.B. [1815], 181 . .,
     Vol. XXIX, fol. 331. (A mission to serve at Trafalgar.) Supporters,
     fol. 44, G.C.B. [1839].
BAZALGETTE, Evelyn, Q.C., of Wimbledon, co. Surrey, and to his nephew Sir
     Joseph, 1878, Vol. LX, fol. 190. (Berry's Suppl.)
BAZELY, John, Capt., R.N. (s. of John), of Dover, co. Kent [6 Aug.] 1784,
     Vol. XV, fol. 353. [Misc. G. et H., 4th S., III, p. 274 ; Genealogist,
     XXV, p. 119.]
BAZETT, Henry, s. of John, of the Island of St. Helena, 1786, Vol. XVI, fol. 87.
BAZLEY, Thomas, Bart. [1869], of Tolmers, co. Hertf., and Hatherop House,
     co. Glouc., 186 . ., Vol. LVII, fol. 169.
BEACH after HICKS, of Beverstone Castle, co. Glouc., and Netheravon, Wilts.,
     17 . . ., Vol. XVII, fol. 264.
BEACH, Thomas (s. of Thomas), of West Ashton, Wilts., and Clarendon, Island of
     Jamaica, 17 . . ., Vol. XVII, fol. 308.
BEACH late HICKS-BEACH, of Oakley Hall, Hampsh. ; Beverstone Castle, co.
     Glouc., and Netheravon, Wilts., 183 . ., Vol. XLII, fol. 281.
BEACHCROFT, Sir Robert, 13 Sept. 1700, Vol. V, fol. 3.
,, ..., brother of Sir Robert, Lord Mayor of London, 1712 (5 of them)
     [? five brothers]. Sheriff-Elect, Nov. 12, 1717, Vol. VI, fol. 348.
     [See below.]

BEACHCROFT to TURVER, and issue male of Samuel and Joseph (brothers of Sir Robert Beachcroft, Knt., Alderm. and sometime Lord Mayor of London), 12 Nov. 1717, Vol. VI, fol. 348, and Add. MS. 14,831, fol. 173.

BEACONSFIELD, Viscountess [1868], Vol. LVII, fol. . . . ., [Mary Ann Disraeli], [Countess, 1876], Vol. LIX. fols. 270-273.

„ Earl of, Benjamin D'ISRAELI. Arms and Supporters, 1876, Vol. LIX, fol. 270.

BEADNELL, John, J.P. (s. of John), of Cynhuifa and Castell-y-dail, co. Montgomery, and of Lincoln's Inn, 1863, Vol. LV, fol. 8.

BEADON, Richard, of Fitzhead, co. Somerset, s. of Bp. of Bath and Wells, 1824, Vol. XXXIV, fol. 328.

BEAKER (see HUNTLY), of Nettleton, Wilts., 185 . ., Vol. L, fol. 412

BEAL . . . . to BOUNELL, James, of Spring Gardens, St. Martin's, co. Middx., 16 Oct. 1774, Vol. XIII, fol. 21.

BEALE, ..., of Swindon, co. Glouc., 184 . ., Vol. XLVII, fol. 211.

„ Mary, wife of John BROWNE, of Salperton, co. Glouc. Beale and ROBBINS quarterly [2 Mar. 1779], Vol. XIV, fol. 80.

BEAMES, John, of Lincoln's Inn, London, 182 . ., Vol. XXXV, fols. 90, 91.

„ William, of Cearns Road, Oxton, co. Chester, 1881, Vol. LXI, fol. 128. (Berry's Suppl.)

BEAN, John, of Lidlington, co. Sussex (sister Barbara BAYLY), 178 . ., Vol. XVII, fol. 89.

BEANE, Elizabeth, wife of Sir John PARSONS, of Epsom, co. Surrey, Alderm. of London, 17 . . ., Vol. V, fol. 172.

BEARSLEY, Peter, s. of John, of the City of London (? of Coventry, see Burke), 1750, Vol. IX, fol. 308.

BEATY before POWNALL alias COLYEAR, M.A., Camb., of Brighton, co. Sussex, 1834, Vol. XL, fol. 319.

BEAUCHAMP [William Lygon], Baron [1806], of co. Worc. Arms and Supporters, 180 . ., Vol. XXIII, fol. 332.

BEAUCHAMP after FARTHING, of Tetton House, Kingston, co. Somerset, 182 . ., Vol. XXXII, fol. 88.

BEAUCHANT, Stephen Usticke, of Falmouth, co. Cornw., 185 . ., Vol. L, fol. 119.

BEAUCHANT to NOWELL-USTICKE, [1852], Vol. L, fol. 131.

BEAUMONT, Thomas Richard (Diana WENTWORTH [wife of and] nat. dau. of Sir Thomas Wentworth BLACKETT [Bart.]). Arms of WENTWORTH (differenced) to wife, 1810, Vol. XXV, fol. 392.

„ Richard Henry (died s.p. 1857), of Whitley Beaumont, co. York, and Mytton Hall, co. Lanc., 1827, Vol. XXXVI, fol. 277.

BEAUMONT, late McCUMMING, Lieut.-Col. Richard Henry John, 185 . ., Vol. LII, fol. 219 (see Burke's Auth. Arms).

BEAUMONT, Lewis Anthony, Capt. R.N., 3, Sloane Gardens, Chelsea, and 37, Montagu Square, London, 1889, Vol LXV, fol. 152.

„ Baron. Supporters, 1896, Vol. LXIX, fol. 154.

BEAVIS, Mrs., of Clifton and Bristol, co. Glouc., 1892, Vol. LXVII, fol. 10.

BEAUVOIR (DE) after BENYON (late POWLETT-WRIGHT), Richard, of Englefield House, Berks., and Gilden Hall, co. Essex, 1822, Vol. XXXIII, fol. 261.

BEAUVOIR (DE) [Mary] late BROWNE (wid. of Vice-Adm. McDougall), of Connaught Place, London, and Johnstown, co. Dublin, 182 . ., Vol. XXXVI, fol. 270.

BEAVER, Hugh (s. of Robert of Mass.), of The Temple, Manchester, and Glyngarth and Maes-y-Llwyn, co. Anglesey, 1836, Vol. XLI, fol. 49.

BEAZLEY, Frank Charles (s. of James), of Fernhill, Woodchurch, co. Chester, 1898, Vol. LXX, fol. 202.

BEBB, John, of Marylebone, London, 180 . ., Vol. XXI, fol. 84.

BEBB, late LAWRELL, Horatio, of Donnington Grove, Berks., and Gloucester Street, London, and Frimley, co. Surrey, 18 . . ., Vol. XLIX, fol. 338. Roy. Lic. 3 June, 1850 (see Burke).

BECHER, *see* LEECE, of Howbury, co. Bedf. Match with LEWIS and CLERKE, 17 . . ., Vol. XX, fol. 334.

BECK, to CHURCH, William, of Hatfield, co. Hertf., and Temple Bar, London (Church his godfather), 17 . . ., Vol. XVII, fol. 109.

BECK, James (s. of James), of London and Bombay, 18 . . ., Vol. XXI, fol. 57.
„ . . . . ., of Hawkshead, co. Lanc., 181 . ., Vol. XXX, fol. 266.
„ Henry, Surgeon, of Creeting St. Mary, co. Suff., 183 . ., Vol. XLI, fol. 122.
„ . . . ., of Woodside, Croydon, co. Surrey, and Charlton, co. Kent, 186 . ., Vol. LV, fol. 240.
„ P. A., of Ashorne Hill, co. Warw., 1888, Vol. LXIV, fol. 318. (Berry's Suppl.)

BECKETT before TURNER, Thomas, and brother William Beckett, of Wootton-under-Wood, Bucks., and Little Pagnell and Penleigh, Westbury, Wilts. Quarterly Arms, Match, 180 . ., Vol. XXV, fols. 61, 65. (Turner crest, fol. 65.)
„ John, of Leeds and Barnsley, co. York, and Somerley Park, co. Linc., 181 . ., Vol. XXVII, fol. 356.

BECKETT to DENISON, Edmund, of Carlton, co. Nottingham, 181 . ., Vol. XXX, fol. 9, and Beckett late Denison, 187 . ., Vol. LVIII, fol. 164.

BECKETT before TURNER (? Thomas), of Wantage, Berks., and Littleton, P[annell ?], and Penleight, Wilts., 183 . ., Vol. XLIV, fol. 30.

BECKETT late DENISON, Sr Edmund, Bart., co. York and Lincolnshire, 187 . ., Vol. LVIII, fol. 164.

BECKETT, Oliver, of Queen's Square, London, s. of Thomas, s. of Oliver, of Parkside, co. Lanc., 3 July 1777, Vol. XIII, fol. . . . . (Misc. G. et H., New S., II, p. 192.)

BECKLEY, ..., of Lymyngton, Hampsh. Match with HOWE and JONES, 180 . ., Vol. XXV, fol. 5.

BECKFORD to PITT-RIVERS, Baron Rivers, co. Dorset and Hampsh. [1828 ?], Vol. XXXVII, fol. 229.

BECKFORD (and GORDON, wife), William, of Fonthill-Gifford, Wilts., and the Island of Jamaica. Arms, 1791, Vol. XVII, fol. 414.

BECKFORD, William. Quartering HERRING. Match, 1793, Vol. XVIII, fol. 163.

BECKFORD and HAMILTON, William. Match and augmentation, 1799, Vol. XX, fol. 283. Crest, 180 . ., Vol. XXV, fol. 387.

BECKFORD, Clarence, of Victoria Street, Westminster, Solicitor, 1895, Vol. LXVIII, fol. 272.
„ William, of Fonthill Gifford, Wilts. 2nd Crest, augmentation, 20 Mar. 1810, Vol. XXV, fol. 387. (Berry.)

BECKMAN, Diederick, of London, 8 July 1761, Vol. X, fol. 401.

BECKWITH, (*see* PARKER), of Aldborough, co. York, Bart., mar. with Parker, 17 . . ., Vol. XII, fol. 182.

BECKWITH, Lieut.-Gen. Sir George, K.B. [1809, G.C.B. 1815], Gov. of Barbados. ? Arms and Supporters, 181 . ., Vol. XXVII, fols. 428, 434. Crest of augmentation, 181 . ., Vol. XXVIII, fol. 260.

BECQUET, "a Fleming," Cabinet Sec. to the Duchess of Bavaria. Arms of Thomas BECKET, Archbp. of Canterbury, 16 . . ., Vol. IV, fol. 208.

BEDDINGTON, A. H., of Cornwall Terrace, Regent's Park, London, 1888, Vol. LXIV, fol. 259.
„ Hyam L., of Cornwall Terrace, Regent's Park, London, 1890, Vol. LXV, fol. 232.
„ S. H., of 21, Hyde Park Square, London, 1890, Vol. LXV, fol. 275.

BEDFORD to KENYON, of Highfield-within-Pemberton and Wigan, co. Lanc., 182 . ., Vol. XXXIV, fol. 308.

BEDFORD, John, of Oughtsbridge and Birley House, co. York, [19 Nov.] 1878, Vol. LX, fol. 194. (Berry's Suppl.) [Misc. G. et H., New. S., III, p. 189.]

BEDFORD to EDWARDS [*sic*].

BEDINGFELD after PASTON, Bart., of Norfolk [1830], Vol. XXXVIII, fol. 81.

BEDINGFELD to PASTON-BISSHOPP BEDINGFELD, 184 . ., Vol. XLV, fol. 169.

BEDINGFELD, R. S. Paston Bisshopp, co. Norf., 1887, Vol. LXIV, fol. 126.

BEDWARD, Mary Wisdom (dau. of George, of Jamaica), wife of John WEDDERBURN, of Clapham, co. Surrey, 1797-1800, Vol. XX, fol. . . . . .

BEECH, R. J., of Brandon Hall, Wolston, co. Warw., 1894,° Vol. LXVII, fol. 294.

BEECHAM, Joseph, of Ewanville, Huyton, co. Lanc., 1891, Vol. LXVI, fol. 138.

BEECHING, J. P. G., of Whitton, co. Middx., 1893,° Vol. LXVII, fol. 229.

BEECHEY, Sir William (Knt.), R.A., of Craven Hill, Bayswater, London, 182 . ., Vol. XXXVII, fols. 302-3.

BEEVOR, Thomas, of Hethel, nr. Norwich, co. Norf., 25 May 1761, Vol. X, fol. 342. (1761, Berry.)

„ (see INGRAM), of Wakefield. Match with BRADLEY, 178 . ., Vol. XVI, fol. 147.

BEEVOR to LOMBE, of the Middle Temple, and Great Melton, co. Norf., Edward, 181 . ., Vol. XXX, fol. 225 ; Charles, 185 . ., Vol. L, fol. 139 ; Edward, 184 . ., Vol. XLVIII. fol. 380.

BEGBIE, Peter (s. of Alexander), of Hendon, co. Middx., and Stenton, Haddington, Scotland. Match with AINSLIE ; and to sisters and to descendants of his brother Alexander, decd., 180 . ., Vol. XXIV, fol. 313.

BEHRENS, Sir Jacob, of Springfield House, Bradford, co. York, 1883, Vol. LXII, fol. 54. (Berry's Suppl.)

BEILBY, to HERBERT (D.D.), of Kingston-upon Hull, co. York, and Tinterne, co. Monmouth. Quarterly Arms, 17 . . ., Vol. XX, fol 92.

BELASYSE late [? before] WYNN, Lady Charlotte, wife of Thomas Edward, of Newburgh Hall, co. York. Quarterly Arms, 180 . ., Vol. XXII, fol. 74.

BELASYSE before COYTMORE (heretofore WYNN), William, of Coytmore, co. Carnarvon, and Newburgh Priory, co. York, 1832, Vol. XXXIX, fol. 319.

BELDAM-JOHNS (late NASH-WOODHAM), Frederick Meadows, of Bishop Stortford, co. Hertf., and Shepreth, co. Camb., 1867, Vol. LVI, fol. 232.

BELEY, Charles Allen Evans, of St John's Hill, Battersea, co. Surrey, and Bootle, co. Lanc., 185 . ., Vol. LII, fol. 17. (Berry's Suppl.)

BELITHA, William, Sheriff Surrey, of Kingston-upon-Thames, co. Surrey, 10 July, 1730, Vol. VIII, fol. 85.

BELL, Henry Nugent, Student of the Inner Temple. Augmentation of Earl of HUNTINGDON. Crest, 182 . ., Vol. XXXIII, fol. 35. (Author of the Huntingdon peerage and his son, 1820.)

„ James, and Alicia Christian, d. and h. of John, of London, 1807, Vol. XXIV, fol. 220.

„ Adam, of Deptford, co. Kent, and Berwick-on-Tweed, co. Northumberland, 182 . ., Vol. XXVI, fol. 136.

BELL (died s.p. 1875), late MACBEAN, Frederick, of Magd. Coll., Oxf., ; Peter Tavey, co. Devon ; and Thirsk, co. York, 185 . ., Vol. L, fol. 121.

BELL . . . . (late SMITH), Reginald, of Thirsk Hall, co. York, s. of Henry, of Easton Maudit, co. Northampton, 1878, Vol. LX, fol. 76. (Berry's Suppl.)

BELL, ..., of Elm Lawn, Kingston, co. Surrey, 186 . ., Vol. LVII, fol. 111.

„ C. L., of Woolsington, co. Northumberland, 1890, Vol. LXVI, fol. 1.

„ C. W., of Bronsill, co. Hereford, 1891, Vol. LXVI, fol. 63.

„ G. R., Commander, R.N., of Selby House, Croxteth, Liverpool, 1892,° Vol. LXVI, fol. 318.

„ Sir J. Lowthian, Bart., of Rounton Grange, Northallerton, co. York, 1884,° Vol. LXII, fol. 178.

„ Alderm. John C., of Portland Place, London, 1896, Vol. LXIX, fol. 193.

„ Thomas, of Windsor Terrace, Newcastle-upon-Tyne, 1889,° Vol. LXV, fol. 141.

„ James, of Leicester, 3rd s. of William, D. of Med., 189 . .? Vol. LXXI, fol. . . . . .

SPENCER-BELL, James, Vol. LVII, fol. 111.
BELL, William Abraham, B. of Med., Camb., s. of William, of London, D. of Med., 189 . .? Vol. LXXI, fol. . . . .
BELLAERS, James, of Stamford and Uffington, co. Linc., and Stamford Baron, co. Northampton, 30 April 1776, Vol. XIII, fol. 189. [Genealogist, New S., XXII, p. 156.]
BELLAIRS, James, (Vol. XV, fol. 26. Quartering WALFORD). Crest and quartering, 17 . . ., Vol. XVI, fols. 16, 129.
,, [or BELLAERS, Abel WALFORD, of Stamford, co. Linc., alteration and quartering WALFORD, 9 Mar. 1782. Alteration of crest, 7 April 1785. Alteration in arms, quarterings BELLAERS, LEA, FOOTE, and WALFORD, 16 May 1786. (Genealogist, N. S., XXII, p. 157)].
BELLAIRS to STEVENSON, of Haverfordwest, co. Pembroke, and Stamford, co. Linc., 184 . ., Vol. XLVII, fol. 229.
BELLAS to BELLASIS, ..., D.D., of Yattendon, and Basildon, Berks., and Long Marton, co. Westmorland. HARVEY quartering LYBBE on escutcheon of pretence, 179 . ., Vol. XVIII, fol. 73. (See Burke and Crisp, II, p. 57.)
BELLAS before GREENOUGH, of Bedford Square, London, and Cambridge. Quarterly, 179 . ., Vol. XIX, fol. 11.
,, to GREENOUGH. Quartering, 179 . ., Vol. XIX, fol. 11.
BELLASIS, Edward, Bluemantle Pursuivant of Arms. VIAL quartering, 18 . . ., Vol. LX, fol. . . . .
BELLASIS after OLIVER, Lieut., 20th Hussars. Quarterly, 18 . . ., Vol. LX, fol. 224.
,, (see also BELLAS), 179 . ., Vol. XVIII, fol. 73.
BELLENDEN, William, of Ramridge, Hampsh. KER and GAWLER quarterly. (4th Duke of ROXBURGHE, died s.p. 1806), 1804, Vol. XXIII, fol. 96.
BELLI, John, of Southampton, 181 . ., Vol. XXVI, fol. 88.
,, Lieut.-Col., B.S.C. [Bombay Staff Corps ?], 182 . ., Vol. XXXII, fol. 26.
BELLOTT, ..., of Bochim, co. Cornw. Match with HAWKINS. Crest to HAWKINS, Bart. (see HAWKINS), 17 . . ., Vol. XVIII, fol. 244.
BELOE, William, B.D., F.S.A., of All Hallows, London Wall, London, and Prebendary of St. Paul's, and of Lincoln and Earlham, co. Norf., 180 . ., Vol. XXIII, fol. 220.
BELPER, Baron [1856] (Edward STRUTT), of co. Derby. Arms and Supporters, 185 . ., Vol. LII, fols. 74, 76.
BELTZ, George Frederick, John Philip, and Samuel, of London and Jamaica. Quarterly with GUTTRIDGE, 1804, Vol. XXII, fol. 405.
BELWARD after MOYSE, of Caius [Coll., Camb. ?], South Town, co. Suff., 181 . ., Vol. XXVII, fol. 337.
BEMPDÉ after VANDEN, late JOHNSTONE (Richard), of Hackness Hall, co. Yorks, and Westerhall, Annandale, Dumfries, 17 . . ., Vol. XIX, fol. 56.
,, after VANDEN to JOHNSTONE, Richard, 17 . . ., Vol. XIX, fol. 59.
BENCE (late SPARROW), Rev. Bence, of Thorington Hall, Bence, co. Suff. Match with SPARROW and GOLDING, 180 . ., Vol. XXIII, fol. 32.
BENCE, George Wright, M.A., Incumb. of Bishopston Marshfield, co. Glouc., 186 . ., Vol. LIV, fol 328.
BENDALL, Hopefor, of Mile End, co. Middx. [8 Feb.], 1692-3, Vol. IV, fol. 130. Harl. MS. 1085, fol. 57 (see Berry).
BENDY, see HODGETTS. Match with Hodgetts, 17 . . ., Vol. XI, fol. 308.
BENET, Sir John, Knt., created Baron OSSULSTON [1682], co. Northumberland and co. Surrey, 16 . . ., Vol. IV, fol. 182.
BENET after PYE (and LEGH, his wife), William Bathurst and Elizabeth Legh, of Salthrop, Wroughton, Wilts., 180 . ., Vol. XXI, fol. 427.
BENETT late FANE, Vere, of Pytt House, Warminster, Wilts., 185 . ., Vol. LII, fol. 221.
BENETT before STANFORD (his wife) Vere, of Preston Park, co. Sussex, 18 . . ., Vol. LVII, fol. 74.

BENFIELD, Paul, of Woodhall Park, co. Hertf., and Cumberland Street, Marylebone, co. Middx., 182 . ., Vol. XXXVI, fols. 55, 56.

BENGOUGH, George, of The Ridge, nr. Wootton-under-Edge, co. Glouc., 184 . ., Vol. XLVI, fol. 95.

BENN to WALSH and FOWKE, wife of, of Warfield, Berks., and London, 17 . . ., Vol. XIX, fol. 81.

BENN, Thomas, of Clifton-upon-Dunsmore, co. Warw., decᵈ, to widow and descendants, 181 . ., Vol. XXXI, fol. 218.

  ,, Joseph, of Melbourne Place, Bradford, co. York, 1887, Vol. LXIV, fol. 48.

BENNET, ... of Lincoln's Inn, London, 16 . . ., Vol. IV, fol. 22. Match.

  ,, Thomas, s. of Christopher, s. of John, all of Steeple Ashton, Wilts., 21 Mar. 1700, Vol. V, fol. 33 : Add. MS. 14,831, fol. 70 (see Burke).

  ,, Henry, of St. Nyott, co. Cornw., 17 . . ., Vol. IX, fol. 138.

BENNET late RICHARDS, William Benett, Major in Army, of Laleston House and St. Andrews, co. Glamorgan, 186 . ., Vol. LVI, fol. 298.

BENNETT (after BURLTON), Anthony, s. of Anthony, of Donhead, Wilts. Quarterly, 17 . . ., Vol. XVI, fol. 379.

BENNETT, Edmond (s. of James), of Great Yarmouth, co. Norf., and Ovan, co. Kilkenny. 18 . . ., Vol. XXI, fol. 121.

  ,, James, of North Cadbury House, co. Somerset, 181 . ., Vol. XXVII, fol. 169.

  ,, ..., of Sloane Street, London, 182 . ., Vol. XXXVII, fol. 308.

  ,, ..., of Eccleston Square, London, 184 . ., Vol. XLVIII, fol. 171.

  ,, Mrs. Ann Buswell, of Carisbrook Villa, Lambeth, co. Surrey, 1880, Vol. LXI, fol. 83.

  ,, Sir Henry (1st s. of William), of Westlands, Grimsby, and Thorpe Hall, Lower Elkington, co. Linc.. 1895, Vol. LXVIII, fol. 160.

JACKSON-BENNETT, John Charles, late Lieut., 1st West India Regt. (see Burke).

BENNITT, Capt. William, of Dudley, co. Worc., and Stourton, co. Staff., 184 . ., Vol. XLIX, fol. 258.

BENSLEY, William (after Bart.), of St. Mary le Bone, co. Middx. (E. I. Co.), and Robert Bensley, of Knightsbridge, only surviving son of James Bensley, uncle of the said William Bensley [3 June 1801], Vol. XXI, fol. 180. [Crisp, Fragm. Geneal., X, p. 32.]

BENSON, Robert, Baron [1713] of Bingley. Arms, 17 . . ., Vol. VI, fol. 122. Supporters, fol. 123.

  ,, Moses, of Kingston, Jamaica, Liverpool and Ulverston, co. Lanc., 17 . . ., Vol. XVII. fol. 11.

  ,, Thomas Starling, of Sanderstead Court, co. Surrey, and North Cray Park, co. Kent, 182 . ., Vol. XXXVII, fol. 187.

  ,, Robert, of Lodge House, Liverpool, and Stang End, Hawkshead, co. Lanc., 1880, Vol. XLV, fol. 189.

  ,, Robson (Colonel), s. of Thomas, of Perrymead Court, Widcombe, co. Somerset, and Chigwell, co. Essex, 18 . . ., Vol. LX, fol. 342. (Berry's Suppl.)

  ,, Edmund White, D.D., Bp. of Truro, 1877, Vol. LIX, fol. 341 (see Crisp, V, p. 122).

BENT, John Major, of The Lodge, Wexham, Bucks., J.P., and of Jacobstowe, Highbray, and Sandford, co. Devon, 184 . ., Vol. XLVIII, fol. 207.

BENTHAM, Maj.-Gen. William, of Coppul, co. Lanc., 181 . ., Vol. XXVII, fol. 92.

BENTINCK [William], Earl of PORTLAND [1689]. Supporters, 16 . . ., Vol. IV, fol. 49.

BENTINCK after CAVENDISH [1801, 3rd] Duke [of Portland], 180 . ., Vol. XXI, fol. 237.

BENTINCK, Lord William Cavendish, Lieut.-Gen., K.B. [1813]. Supporters, 181 . ., Vol. XXVIII, fol. 39.

BENTLEY (after GORDON), of Bentley Naish, co. Worc., and Little Kington, co. Warw., 5 June 1777, Vol. XIII, fol. 301.

  ,, after FORBES, Thomas, of Clifton, 182 . ., Vol. XXXIII, fol. 172.

BENTLEY, Edward, of Ely Place, London, 18 July 1834, Vol. XL, fol. 212.
      (Misc. G. et H., New S., III, p. 122 ; Crisp, I, p. 141.)
   „   James-Kersey, of Hadleigh and Boxford, co. Suff., and Scarborough,
          co. York, 183 . ., Vol. XLI, fol. 258.
BENTLEY (FORBES) late CALLAND, George, of Glyncollen, co. Glamorgan, 185 . .,
      Vol. LI, fol. 57.
BENWELL, Joseph, and wife Elizabeth BURCH, of Battersea, co. Surrey. Impaled
      Arms, 180 . ., Vol. XXIV, fol. 459.
BENYON, Richard, of Englefield House, Berks., and Gidea Hall, co. Essex,
      and co. Huntingdon, 182 . ., Vol. XXXIII, fols. 260, 261.
BENYON before DE BEAUVOIR, Richard, of Englefield House, Berks. (died s.p.
      1854).
BENYON, late FELLOWES, Richard, of Ramsey Abbey, co. Huntingdon, 1854,
      Vol. LI, fol. 215.
BENYON, formerly FELLOWES, James Herbert, of Englefield House, Berks.,
      s. of James Fellowes, of Knyeton House, co. Dorset, esq. Arms
      exemplified, Benyon and Fellowes, quarterly 1897, Vol. LXX, fol. 50.
BENYON before (? after) WINSON, William Henry, of Cwersyllt, Wrexham,
      186 . ., Vol. LVI, fol. 214.
BERE (after BAKER), Montagu, of Timberscourt, co. Somerset, 7 Feb. 1776,
      Vol. XIII, fol. 166.
BERENS (formerly McLOUGHLIN), Rev. Randolph Humphrey, of Sidcup Place,
      Chislehurst, co. Kent, 1885, Vol. LXIII, fol. 117.
BERESFORD, Rev. Tyryngham, of Long Leadenham, co. Linc. Match, 17 . . .,
      Vol. XVII, fol. 118.
   „   Maj.-Gen. Sir William Carr, K.B. [1810]. Supporters, 1811, Vol. XXVI,
          fols. 273, 278.
   „   John Poo, Post-Capt., R.N., M.P. Arms with distinctions. Match, 181 . .,
          Vol. XXVII, fol. 33.
BERESFORD before PEIRSE, Henry William, of Bedale Hall, co. York, 1851,
      Vol. L, fol. 60.
BERGER, Lewis C., of Hackney, London, and 17, Ashburton Road, Southsea,
      Hampsh., 1886,° Vol. LXIII, fol. 231.
BERGNE before COUPLAND, Richard, of Skellingthorpe, co. Linc., and Streatham,
      co. Surrey [24 Feb. 1868], Vol. LVI, fol. 337 (see Burke).
BERIDGE, B. J. H. (formerly SPARROW), of Gosfield Place, co. Essex, 188 . .,
      Vol. LXI, fol. 327 ; 1895, Vol. LXVIII, fol. 247.
BERKELEY to PORTMAN, grant and exemplification, 17 . . .., Vol. VIII, fol. 12.
BERKELEY, Baron Botetourt [1764], of Stoke, co. Glouc. Supporters, 176 . .,
      Vol. XI, fol. 17.
   „   Adm. Sir George Cranfield, K.B. [1813]. Supporters, Vol. XXVII, fol. 238.
BERKELEY before CALCOTT, Capt. George, of Caynham Court, Shropsh., and
      Writtle, co. Essex, 182 . ., Vol. XXXVI, fol. 153.
BERKELEY, late TOMKYNS, Rector of Great Horwood, Bucks., and of Catheridge
      Court, co. Worc., 183 . ., Vol. XXXIX, fol. 190.
BERKIN, Meackham, Rev. William, D.C.L., Canon of Llandaff, of St. Fagans,
      co. Glamorgan, Llantilio Pertholey, co. Monmouth, 180 . ., Vol. XXII,
      fol. 108.
[BERMONDSEY, Borough of, London, 25 Mar. 1901. (Geneal. Mag., V, p. 249.)]
BERNAL, Ralph, of Lincoln's Inn, London, from Seville in Andalusia, Spain,
      181 . ., Vol. XXX, fol. 252.
   „   Osborne, Ralph, of Newtown Anner, co. Tipperary, 184 . ., Vol. XLVII,
          fol. 206.
BERNARD, Scrope, and Harriet MORLAND, wife of (Morland quartering, with
      escutcheon of pretence), of Nether Winchendon, Bucks., and Brightwell,
      Berks., 1789, Vol. XVII, fol. 118.
BERNARD before MORLAND, Scrope, of Nether Winchendon, Bucks. (Bart.),
      181 . ., Vol. XXVI, fol. 271.

BERNARD, late CAMPLIN, George, of Combe Flory and Crocombe Court, co. Somerset, 181 . ., Vol. XXVI, fol. 363. Match, fol. 312.

BERNARD, Fanny, late GRAY (natural dau. of Gen.), of Heton Lodge, nr. Leeds, co. York, 181 . ., Vol. XXXI, fol. 374.

BERRIMAN, ... Quartering to RUMBOLD (Bart.), co. Hertf. and London, 17 . . ., Vol. XIV, fol. 145.

BERRY to FERGUSON, William, of Austin Friars, London, and Raith, Scotland, 17 . . ., Vol. XV, fol. 11.

BERRY, Capt. Sir Edward, Knt., of London, s. of Edward, 17 . . ., Vol. XX, fol. 293.

„ Henry, of Eskold House, Rothwell, co. York, 189 . ., Vol. LXXI, fol. . . . . .

BERTIE (VENABLES), Lord NORREYS, of co. Essex. Quarterly with WILLOUGHBY, 16 . . ., Vol. III, fol. 333.

BERTIE, Earl of ABINGDON. Match, 17 . . ., Vol. VIII, fol. 16.

BERTIE, late HOAR, Capt. Thomas, R.N., of Essex, Vice-Adm., to continue name and arms, 17 . . ., Vol. XVI, fol. 409.

„ late LICHIGARAY, of Low Layton, co. Essex, widow of Thomas, 182 . ., Vol. XXXIV, fol. 39.

„ late DOWNMAN, of Low Layton, co. Essex, reputed son of Thomas, 182 . ., Vol. XXXIV, fol. 158.

„ late CODWISE, of Low Layton, co. Essex, reputed dau. of Thomas, 183 . ., Vol. XXXIX, fol. 115.

BERTIE of [s. ?] BERTIE, by consent of the Earl of LINDSEY, &c., 18 . . ., Vol. XXVII, fol. 141.

„ Susan Priscilla, wife of Lieut.-Gen. Banastre TARLETON, M.P. (natural dau. of the Duke of ANCASTER and KESTEVEN), of co. Lanc. Arms to Bertie (he died s.p.), 18 . . ., Vol. XXIII, fol. 5.

BERTIE before GREATHEED, Anne Caroline, of co. Essex and Warw., 181 . ., Vol. XXXI, fols. 222, 224.

BERTIE (GREATHEED) before PERCIE (Hon. Charles), of Guys Cliff, co. Warw. (mar. Anne Caroline Bertie), 182 . ., Vol. XXXV, fol. 392.

BERTIE-MATHEW, Brownlow, 181 . ., Vol. XXXI, fol. 296.

BERTRAND, late D'ANGLEBERMES, of the Island of Dominica, 182 . ., Vol. XXXII, fol. 179.

BERWICK, Baron [1784] (Noel HILL), of Shropsh. Supporters, 178 . ., Vol. XV, fol. 309.

BESANT, Sir Walter, of Frognal End, Hampstead, London, 1896,ᵒ Vol. LXIX, fol. 128.

BESSEMER, Sir Henry, of Denmark Hill, co. Surrey, 1880, Vol. LXI, fol. 47. (Berry's Suppl.)

BESLEY, E. H., [of] Wood [co. Devon ?], 188 . ., Vol. LXV, fol. 315.

„ Mrs. David FINCH-NATHAN, 189 . ., Vol. LXVIII, fol. 43.

BEST, Mawdistley, Sheriff, 1730 ?, of Boxley, co. Kent, 26 July or 18 Dec. 1742, Vol. IX, fol. 76.

„ [Sir William Draper Best], Baron WYNFORD [1829], of co. Dorset. Arms and Supporters, 182 . ., Vol. XXXVII, fols. 388, 389.

„ [Sarah, wife of James RUSSELL, of Handsworth, co. Staff., 29 May 1835. (Misc. G. et H., New S., IV, p. 18.)]

„ of Vallendens, Brinstead, Hampsh., and London, 184 . ., Vol. XLVI, fol. 281.

BEST, now NORCLIFFE (widow of ROBINSON), co. York, 186 . ., Vol. LIV, fols. 272, 273.

BEST to HADEN-BEST, George Alfred, of Haden Hill, Rowley Regis, co. Staff., and Withymore House, Dudley, co. Worc., 1879, Vol. LX, fol. 322.

BESWICKE-ROYDS, Clement, R.N., of Pyke House, Rochdale, co. Lanc., 186 . ., Vol. XXXII (? LVII), fol. 155. (Roy. Lic. 19 July 1869. Crisp, III, p. 12.)

BETCHINOE, Mary, Duchess of ROXBURGHE. Match with SMITH, 180 . ., Vol. XXIII, fol. 99.

BETHELL, late CODRINGTON, Christopher, of Dodington, co. Glouc., 17 . . ., Vol. XX, fol. 68. *See* CODRINGTON, Bart.

    „   late CODRINGTON, of Swindon Hall, co. York, 17 . . ., Vol. XX, fol. 125. *See* CODRINGTON, Bart.

BETHELL, Sir Richard, Baron WESTBURY [1861], co. Glouc. Arms and Supporters, 186 . ., Vol. LIV, fols. 170-2.

BETHUNE, late SHARPE, Lieut.-Col. Alexander, of Blebo, co. Fife, 181 . ., Vol. XXIX, fol. 196.

BETHUNE, Walter D. P. Patton, of Clayton Priory, co. Surrey, 188 . ., Vol. LXI, fol. 366 ; 188 . ., Vol. LXII, fol. 60.

BETTESWORTH before TREVANION, John F. Purnel, of Carhair, co. Cornw., and Luton, co. Bedf., 180 . ., Vol. XXI, fol. 304. Bettesworth before Trevanion, fol. 306.

BETTINGTON, ... of Barrow House, nr. Bristol, of Indian C.S., 184 . ., Vol. XLVII, fol. 248.

BETTS, ..., of Bevoir Mount, South Stoneham, Hampsh., 185 . ., Vol. LI, fol. 112.

BEVAN, William, J.P., Pen-y-coed, co. Carmarthen, and to his brothers Theophilus and Thomas, D.D., [1 June] 1695,* Vol. IV, fol. 198 (*see* Burke).

    „   Thomas (s. of Richard, of Carmarthen), of Ashted, co. Surrey, 183 . ., Vol. XLIII, fol. 2 ; 20 Sept. 1774, Vol. XIII, fol. 2.

    „   Robert Cooper Lee, of Fosbury, Wilts. ; Trent Park, co. Middx. ; and Belmont, co. Hertf., 185 . ., Vol. LII, fol. 20. (Fosbury, co. Wilts., and Trent Park, co. Middx. Quartering LEE, 185 . ., Vol. LII, fol. 192.)

    „   Thomas (s. of Thomas), of Stone Park, Stone-next-Dartford, co. Kent, 1878, Vol. LX, fol. 133. (Berry's Suppl.)

BEVERIDGE-DUNCAN, James, of Blackheath, co. Kent, and Damside, co. Perth, 17 . . ., Vol. XX, fol. 344.

BEWES, Thomas, of St. Neots, co. Cornw., 25 April 1726, Vol. VII, fol. 444.

BEWICKE-CAPLEY, R. C. A., of Sprotborough, Doncaster, co. York, 1893, Vol. LXVI, fol. 340.

BEWICKE-CAPLEY, late ANDERSON, Calverley Berwicke, of Close Hall, co. Northumberland, 181 . ., Vol. XXIX, fol. 202.

BEYNON, late BATLEY, Rev. Edmund Turner (Beynon, wife of), of Carshalton, co. Surrey. Quarterly Arms, 1805, Vol. XXIII, fol. 230 (*see* Berry's Suppl.)

BEYNON after CROWTHER, Richard William Barnardiston Crowther, Capt., 1st Regiment of Foot, of Shires Oaks, Chelsham, co. Surrey, 1874, Vol. LIX, fol. 69. (Berry's Suppl.)

BEYNON, Rev. Samuel, of Lodsworth Vicarage, Petworth, co. Surrey, 1879, Vol. LX, fol. 303.

BIANDOS (DE)-SCARISBRICK, Marquis de Castega, of Scarisbrick Hall, co. Lanc., Vol. LVIII, fol. 264. (Berry's Suppl.)

BIBBY-HESKETH. *See* HESKETH.

BICHNER, ..., of Soho Square, London, 182 . ., Vol. XXXV, fol. 34.

BICKERSTETH, Henry, Baron [1836], of Langdale, co. Westmorland. Arms and Supporters, 183 . ., Vol. XLI, fols. 412-414.

    „   Robert, M.A., Rector St. Giles, co. Middx., Canon of Salisbury, and of Kirkby Lonsdale, co. Westmorland, to descendants of his grandfather Henry, 185 . ., Vol. LII, fol. 125.

BICKERTON, Rear-Adm. Sir Richard, Bart., of Upwood, co. Huntingdon. Augmentation and Supporters. [K.C.B. 1815], 180 . ., Vol. XXIII, fols. 198, 200.

BICKNELL, Algernon S., of 23, Onslow Gardens, London, 1884, Vol. LXII, fol. 266.

    „   Algernon S., of 23, Onslow Gardens, London, 1894, Vol. LXVIII, fol. 39.

BIDDULPH to MYDDELTON, Myddelton wife, of Crofton Hall, M.P., co. Worc., and of Chirk Castle, co. Denbigh. Quarterly Arms, 180 . ., Vol. XXIII, fol. 8.

BIDDULPH after WRIGHT, of Walton, nr. Linton, co. Camb., and Burton Park, co. Sussex, 183 . ., Vol. XLI, fol. 194.

BIDGOOD, John, M.D., and Humphrey, of Fulford, Tiverton, co Devon, 1690, Vol IV, fol. 62.

BIDGOOD, late SLOANE (? STONE), Henry Fisher, of Rockbeare, co. Devon, and Island of Tobago. 1822, Vol. XXXIII, fol. 336 (see Burke).

BIGG before WITHER, Lovelace, of Manydown, Hampsh., and Chilton Follyatt, Wilts. Quarterly (LOVELACE). 178 . .. Vol. XVII, fol. 167.

BIGG to GULSTON, Frederick, of Wydiall, co. Hertf., and Claudon, co. Surrey, 1823, Vol. XX. fol. 189.

YEATMAN-BIGGS, Capt. Arthur Godolphin (see YEATMAN), 1878, Vol. LXII, fol. 159. (Berry's Suppl.)

BIGHAM, John C., Q.C., of Palace Gate, London, 1896, Vol. LXIX, fol. 180.

BIGLAND, Ralph, Somerset Herald, of Heaton, co. Northumberland ; Frocester, co. Glouc. ; Bigland, co. Lanc. ; and Bigland Hall, co. Westmorland. Quarterly, WILKINS and WOOD, 21 Feb. 1760, Vol. X, fol. 215.

BIGLAND (late OWEN), Ralph (Richmond Herald), nephew of Ralph Bigland, Clarenceaux King of Arms, London and Lancashire, 17 . . ., Vol. XIII, fol. 23.

BIGLAND, Richard (s. of Garter K. of Arms), of Frocester, co. Glouc., 179 . ., Vol. XIX, fols. 211, 215.

BIGNELL, William, of Allhallows, Barking, and Salisbury, Wilts., 1764, Vol. XI, fol. 41.

„ Attorney-at-Law, of Banbury and Deddington, co. Oxf., 182 . ., Vol. XXXIII, fol. 69.

BILKE, Edward and Mary, Middleton his wife, and Samuel his eldest brother, of Axminster, co. Devon, Newington Butts and Stamford Street, co. Surrey, 181 . ., Vol. XXVIII, fol. 43.

BILLAMORE, ..., widow of Capt., 182 . ., Vol. XXXII, fols. 5, 12.

BILLIAT, Joseph, of Aisthorp Hall, co. Linc., 189 . ., Vol. LXXI, fol. . . . .

BILLINGHURST to WOODROFFE, William, of Godalming and Poyle-Seale, co. Surrey, 17 . . ., Vol. XVII, fol. 268.

„ to WOODROFFE, Lieut.-Col. (? George), of Godalming and Poyle-Seale, co. Surrey, 182 . ., Vol. XXXV, fol. 35 (sic).

BILLINGTON, John, of Univ. Coll., Oxf., and Kent, 182 . ., Vol. XXXII, fol. 47.

„ . . . ., of Cockerham, co. Lanc., 17 . . ., Vol. XIV, fol. 358. See BRADSHAW.

BINDON, Earl of [1706] (Henry HOWARD). Supporters, 170 . ., Vol. V, fol. 188.

BINGHAM, Miss Catherine (d. of Daniel), of Northaw, co. Hertf., 1890, Vol. LXV, fol. 186.

„ Oswald SMITH-, of Thornbury, Heston, co. Middx., and Lea Green, Cliffe, co. Kent, 189 . ., Vol. LXVII, fol. 253 ; 189 . ., Vol. LXVIII. fol. 201 [? 101, see SMITH].

BINGLEY, Baron, Robert Benson. Supporters, 20 Jan. 1713-4, Vol. VI, fols. 122, 133.

„ . . . ., co. Lanc. Supporters, 176 . .. Vol. X, fol. 414. [? George Fox Lane, M.P. for York, created Baron Bingley in 1762.]

„ . . . ., of Bolton, West Riding, co. York, 17 . . ., Vol. XXXVIII, fol. 319.

„ Thomas Henry, B.A., of Whitley Hall, Ecclesfield, co. York, 1878, Vol. LX, fol. 171. (Berry's Suppl.)

BINKS, Maj.-Gen. William, of Plymouth, 182 . ., Vol. XXXII, fol. 343.

BINNEY, James, Bar.-at-Law, of Manchester, 1891, Vol. LXVI, fol. 184.

BINNS, Edward Knowles, Solicitor, of Sheffield, co. York, 1883, Vol. LXII, fol. 143. (Berry's Suppl.)

BINSTEED to FARRANT, of Northstead House, Chelmsford, co. Essex, 17 . . .. Vol. XIX, fol. 97.

BIRCH, Samuel (late NEW), of the Middle Temple, London, and Bedminster, co. Somerset, and his wife Susanna. Vol. XX, fol. 421.

„ Sir Joseph, Bart., of Hazles, Huyton, and Liverpool, co. Lanc., 18 . . ., Vol. XXI, fol. 148.

BIRCH before REYNARDSON, Lieut.-Col. and Dep. Q.M.-Gen., of Holywell, co. Line., 18 . . ., Vol. XXVII, fol. 80.

„ before WOLFE, of Woodhall, Arkesden, co. Essex, 182 . ., Vol. XXXVI, fols. 309-311.

„ before WOLFE, Thomas Birch Wolfe, of Woodhall, Arkesden, co. Essex, 185 . ., Vol. LIII, fol. 202. Rev. William, M.A., Rector of Hardwicke, co. Camb., 186 . ., Vol. LV, fol. 250.

BIRCH, William Jarvis, of Croydon, co. Surrey, 183 . ., Vol. XL, fol. 290.

BIRCH after NEWELL, John William, Asst of the Parliaments, of Henley Park, co. Oxf., and St. Leonard's Hill, Berks., 184 . ., XLVIII, fol. 312.

BIRCH, George (s. of Moses), of Barton-under-Needwood, co. Staff., 184 . ., XLIX, fol. 165.

BIRD, Edward, of Westminster (s. of Thomas, late of Brimslowe, Shropsh., and Westminster), and to the descendants of his brother Thomas, deceased, 16 Sept. 1723, Vol. VII, fol. 213 ; Add. MS. 14,831, fol. 169. (Berry and Burke.)

„ John, of Coventry, co. Warw., 2 Aug., 1742, Vol. IX, fol. 70.

„ C. H., of Crookhey, Cockerham, co. Cumberland, 1890,* Vol. LXV, fol. 267.

BIRKBECK, Sir Edward, Bart., and his brothers, of co. Norf., 1886,* Vol. LXIII, fol. 205.

BIRKENHEAD, The Borough of, co. Chester, [28 Aug.] 1878, Vol. LX, fol. 146.

[BIRKENHEAD, Sir John, LL.D., Master of Requests, &c., 22 Aug. 1649. (Harl. Soc., VIII, Le Neve's Knts., p. 162.)]

BIRLEY, William (s. of John), of Kirkham, co. Lanc., 1848, Vol. XLIX, fol. 9.

[BIRMINGHAM UNIVERSITY, 27 Aug. 1900. (Geneal. Mag., IV, p. 512.)]

BIRT (and STAYNER, his wife), of Sussex Gardens, London, 1844, Vol. XLVII, fols. 135, 136.

„ William Morlais, of Hallington, Catford Hill, co. Surrey, 1896, Vol. LXV, fol. 69.

BISCHOFFSHEIM, of Cornwall Terrace, London, naturalized Brit. subject, 185 . ., Vol. LIII, fol. 357.

BISCOE, Anne, late EARLE (widow of Timothy Hare Earle), of Holton Park, co. Oxf., and Swallowfield, Berks., 1829, Vol. XXXVIII, fols. 79, 80.

BISCOE, late TYNDALE, William Earle, of Holton Park, co. Oxf., 1866, Vol. LVI, fol. 125. (6 July, Burke.)

BISHOP, Charles, of Canterbury, 17 . . ., Vol. XVII, fol. 250.

„ James (s. of William), of Hampstead et Grimston and Leicester, co. Leic., 180 . ., Vol. XXV, fol. 319.

„ Edward, of Essequibo, in Guiana, and Island of Barbados, 181 . ., Vol. XXXI, fol. 260.

„ C. J., of St. Helens, co. Lanc., 1890, Vol. LXVI, fol. 5.

BISSE before CHALLONER, Lieut.-Col., of Portnall Place, Egham, co. Surrey, 182 . ., Vol. XXXVIII, fol. 367 ; 183 . ., Vol. XXXIX, fol. 6.

BLACH (see BLATCH), of London. Match with WHITE, 1819, Vol. XXV, fol. 69.

BLACK, Charles Christopher, of the Inner Temple, London (Trin. Coll., Camb.), 183 . ., Vol. XL, fol. 44.

„ . . . . ., C.B., Judge, Vice-Admiralty Court, Quebec, Canada, 186 . ., Vol. LV, fol. 92.

BLACKBURN, John, of London, Mercht., only surviving s. of John, late of Wigton, co. Cumberland, decd., 178 . ., Vol. XV, fol. 361 [dat. 27 Aug. 1784].

„ John, F.R.S., of Orford and Hale, co. Lanc. Quartering, GREEVE and ASPINWALL, 180 . ., Vol. XXII, fol. 187.

„ John, M.A., of John's Coll., Camb., Incumbt of Attercliffe-cum-Darnall, co. York, 1803, Vol. XXXVI, fol. 129.

BLACKBURNE before MAZE, William Ireland, of Spring Hill, Boughton, co. Chester: Prestwich and Eccles, co. Lanc.; 185.., Vol. LI, fol. 401, 186.., Vol. LVII, fol. 204.

BLACKET, Elizabeth, nat. dau. of Sir Walter, Bart. (a minor), of Hexham, co. Northumberland, 9 June 1729, Vol. VIII, fol. 32[b].

BLACKETT, Elizabeth, wife of Walter (formerly CALVERLEY), of Newcastle-upon-Tyne, co. Northumb. Coat of, 9 June 1729, Vol. VIII, fol. 32[b], relinquished for another granted 26 Feb. 1729-30, Vol. VIII, fol. 71[h].

„ Sir Thomas, late WENTWORTH, Bart., of Bretton Hall, co. York (see BEAUMONT) (died s.p.l. 1792), 18..., Vol. XXV, fol. 392.

BLACKETT before ORD, ..., B.A., of Whitfield, co. Northumberland, Rector of Wolsingham, co. Durham, 185.., Vol. LI, fol. 406.

BLACKFORD (BLACHFORD), William Henry, Lieut.-Gen., B.S.C. [Bombay Staff Corps?], of Ham, co. Surrey, 182.., Vol. XXXVII, fol. 145 (see Burke).

BLACKMAN, James, s. of James, of Ramsbury, Wilts., impaled with WOOLDREDGE, 17..., Vol. XX, fol. 368.

„ George, of Durdens, Epsom, co. Surrey, 1803, Vol. XXII, fol. 223.

BLACKMAN to HARNAGE, George, Bart., of Shropsh., s. of John Lucie Blackman, of London, 1821, Vol. XXXIII, fol. 88.

BLACKMORE, Thomas, of London, 24 Sept. 1701, Vol. V, fol. 48 (see Burke and Berry).

[BLACKPOOL, co. Lanc., Borough of, 10 June 1899. (Geneal. Mag., III, p. 235.)]

BLACKWALL, John. Arms confirmed, 1764 (see Burke).

BLADES, John, of Brockwell Hall, co. Surrey, and Ludgate Hill, London, 181.., Vol. XXVII, fol. 71.

BLAGDEN to HALE, John, of Alderley, co. Glouc., 17..., Vol. XV, fol. 387.

BLAGRAVE, Thomas, of Reading and Purley, Berks., 13 or 31 Aug. 17..., Vol. VIII, fol. 113.

BLAGROVE, late BRADSHAW, of Abshott, Hampsh.; Ankerwyke House, Bucks.; Lifton, co. Devon; and Woodmans, King's Langley, co. Hertf., 1840, Vol. XLV, fol. 51.

BLAGROVE to BRADSHAW, of Abshott, &c., as above, 1856, Vol. LII, fol. 98.

BLAGROVE (late COARE), Henry John, of Orange Valley, St. Anne's, Jamaica, and Ankerwyke House, Bucks., 184.., Vol. XLVI, fol. 191.

BLAIR afterwards STOFFORD, of Wigton, Scotland, with design "of Penningham," 184.., Vol. XLVI, fol. 59.

BLAKE-DELAVAL, Sir Francis [Blake], K.B. [1761], of Northumberland. Supporters, 17..., Vol. X, fol. 333.

„ Sir Francis, Bart., s. of Robert, of Twisel Castle, co. Northumberland, and co. Galway, 17..., Vol. XIV, fol. 67.

BLAKE to HARWARD, of Hayne House, Plymtree and Brampton, and Grove Cottage, Steignton, co. Devon. Match, 181.., Vol. XXIX, fol. 366.

BLAKE, late NORMAN, Silas Wood, of Venne, Upton, co. Somerset, 183.., Vol. XXXIX, fol. 210.

BLAKE after JEX, William, of Swanton Abbots, and Scotton, co. Norf., 1837, Vol. XLII, fols. 168, 170, 180.

BLAKE before HUMPHREY, Robert, of Watfield and Wroxham, co. Norf., 184.., Vol. XLVIII, fol. 369.

BLAKE-HUMFREY to HUMFREY-MASON, of Necton Hall and Heggard Hall, Horstead, co. Norf., 18.., Vol. LX, fol. 258.

BLAKE, William, of Bathwick, co. Somerset, 186.., Vol. LV, fol. 72.

BLAKELOCK, ..., of Gimingham, co. Norf., 184.., Vol. XLVII, fol. 131.

BLAKELY, ..., of Thorpe Hamlet, Norwich, and Goswold Hall, co. Suff., 181.., Vol. XLVI, fol. 326.

BLAKEMORE after BOOKER, T., of The Leys, Gancrew, co. Hereford, and Velindia House, Whitchurch, co. Glamorgan, 185.., Vol. LI, fol. 325.

BLAKENEY, Sir William, K.B. [K.B. 1756, Baron Blakeney 1756]. Supporters, 17..,[c] Vol. X, fol. 74.

BLAND, late CRUMPE, Nathaniel, of Randall Park, Letherhead, co. Surrey, and
    Limerick, Ireland. Match, 181 . ., Vol. XXVI, fol. 344.
BLAND, ..., of Montagu Place, London, 182 . ., Vol. XXXV, fol. 407.
  ,, ..., of Liverpool, 186 . ., Vol. LVI, fol. 79.
BLANDY, John, of Letcombe-Bassett, Berks., 14 Nov. 1720, Vol. VII,
    fol. 33.
BLANDY (late WALKER), Adam, of Kingston-Bagpuze, Berks., 17 . ., Vol. XVIII,
    fol. 31.
BLANE, Gilbert, M.D., of Culverlands, Burghfield, Blanefield and Kirk-Oswald,
    co. Ayr. Augmentation, 1811, Vol. XXVII, fol. 101.
BLAQUIERE, Sir John, K.B. [1774], of Austin Friars, London, 28 Sept. 1774,
    Vol. XIII, fol. 13. Supporters, fol. 19 ; John Peter, 17 . ., Vol. IX,
    fol. 469.
BLATCH, Thomas, of London, s. of Thomas White, and brothers and sister Martha
    Blatch, 1809, Vol. XXV, fol. 69.
BLATHWAYT (late CRANE), James, of Lillieput and Dyrham Park, co. Glouc.
    Match, 181 . ., Vol. XXX, fol. 147.
BLAXLAND, John, s. of John, of Luddenham, co. Kent, s. of John, of Allen
    Court, Minster, co. Kent, and to descendants of his grandfather, 16 Nov.
    1730,* Vol. VIII, fol 99 ; Add. MS. 14,831, fol. 91.
BLAXTON, ..., late Lieut., R.N. Match, 18 . . .,* Vol. XXX, fol. 221.
BLAYDS, Francis, of Leeds, 6 June 1761, Vol. X, fol. 379 (see Berry).
BLAYDS (late CALVERLEY), John, of Leeds and Oulton, co. Lanc. [Oulton Hall,
    co. York], 1807, Vol. XXIV, fol. 174 [see Burke].
BLEAMIRE, William, G.I., of Penrith, co. Cumberland, and Clifton, co. West-
    morland, 4 April 1775, Vol. XIII, fol. 86.
BLEGBOROUGH, ..., of Woodlands, Streatham, and Bridge Street, Blackfriars,
    London, 184 . ., Vol. XLVIII, fol 340.
BLENCOWE before SHUCKBURGH, Charles, Vicar of Marston St. Laurence, co.
    Northampton, and Bourton-on-Dunsmore, co. Warw., 1848, Vol. XLIX,
    fol. 69. (See also SHUCKBURGH late WOOD.)
BLENMAN, Jonathan, Attorney-General of Barbados, and of Croscombe, co.
    Somerset, to descendants of his father Thomas, 10 Oct. 1739,* Vol. VIII,
    fol. 260 ; Add. MS. 14,831, fol. 119.
BLEWITT, Reginald James, M.P., of Llantarnam Abbey, co. Monmouth, 183 . .,
    Vol. XLIV, fol. 178.
BLICK, Thomas (s. of Thomas), of Swanburn, Bucks., 27 Feb. 1800, Vol. XX,
    fol. 448.
BLICKE, Sir Charles, Knt., Surgeon, of Caroon Park, St. Mary, Lambeth, co. Surrey,
    1809, Vol. XXVI, fol. 309.
  ,,   Charles Tufton, eq. fil. [?] (Crest), of Carroon Park, St. Mary, Lambeth,
    co. Surrey (died s. p.), 1819, Vol. XXXI, fol. 366.
BLIGH, Adm. Sir Richard Rodney, G.C.B. [1820]. Arms and Supporters, 182 . .,
    Vol. XXXII, fols. 135-139.
BLISS, Henry, late ALDRIDGE, of Brandon Park, co. Suff. (now DE BARRETO),
    184 . ., Vol. XLVII, fol. 347.
  ,,   Henry, 4th s. of Jonathan, Q.C., of the Inner Temple, London, and New
    Brunswick, 186 . ., Vol. LV, fol. 60.
BLOCK, Samuel Richard, of Kentish Town, co. Middx., 182 . ., Vol. XXXVIII,
    fol. 32.
BLOMEFIELD, Maj.-Gen. Thomas, of Shooter's Hill, co. Kent, and Attleborough,
    co. Norf., 180 . ., Vol. XXIV, fol. 331.
BLOMEFIELD, late MASON, Major George, of Necton and Swaffham, co. Norf.,
    Vol. XLII, fol. 5 ; 187 . ., Vol. LVIII, fol. 48.
  ,,   late JENYNS, Rev. Leonard, M.A., of Belmont, Bath, Bottesham Hall,
    Camb., and Swaffham, co. Norf., 1871, Vol. LVIII, fol. 48 (see
    Burke's Suppl.).
BLOMFIELD, Elizabeth, of Colchester, co. Essex, 1797, Vol. XX, fol. 228.

BLOUNT, John Darall, of Calchill, co. Kent, and Mapledurham, co. Oxf., 188 . ., Vol. LXI, fol. 267.

BLOXSOME, ..., D.L., Rangers, Dursley, co. Glouc., 184 . ., XLIX, fol. 192.

BLUMBERG, Ludwig Alexander, and Victor George (naturalized), Palace Gardens, London, 185 . ., Vol. L, fol. 159. (Berry's Suppl.)

BLUNDELL, late PEPPARD, Nicholas, of Little Crosby, co. Lanc., 1772, Vol. XII, fol. 141.

BLUNDELL (before HOLLINGSHEAD), Henry, of Liverpool and Chorley, co. Lanc., 180 . ., Vol. XXII, fol. 34.

BLUNDELL, late WELD, Thomas, of Ince Blundell Hall, co. Lanc., and Lulworth Castle, co. Dorset, 184 . ., Vol. XLVI, fol. 278.

BLUNT (see HELSHAM-BROWN), of Kilkenny, 182 . ., Vol. XXXVI, fol. 63.

„ Robert, Vicar of Belton and Loughborough, co. Leic., 1850, Vol. L., fol. 294.

BLUNT to DALBY, 185 . ., Vol. L, fol. 309.

BLYTH, William, Mayor of Norwich, 20 June 1723, Vol. VII, fol. 195.

„ Benjamin, M.A. of Mag. Coll., Oxf., of Richmond, co. Surrey, 185 . ., Vol. LIII, fol. 111.

„ Sir J., Bart., of Blythwood, Stansted, Mount Fitchett, co. Essex, 1895,* Vol. LXVIII, fol. 259.

BLYTHSWOOD, Baron [Bart. 1880, Baron Blythswood 1892], Archibald CAMPBELL, of Blythswood House, co. Renfrew, 1893, Vol. LXVII, fol. 161.

BOAK, Jacob, of St. Andrew under Shaft, London, 180 . ., Vol. XXIII, fol. 206.

BOARDMAN alias BOWMAN (see COATES), Charles (nat. s. of Bowman), of Roehampton, co. Surrey, and the Temple, 17 . . ., Vol. XX, fol. 251.

BOARDMAN to HAYDOCK (minor), of Datchett, Bucks., 181 . ., Vol. XXVIII, fol. 428.

BOARDMAN, William, of Faringdon House, Penwortham, co. Lanc., 184 . ., Vol. XLVI, fol. 163.

BOARDMAN. See BRINCKMAN, Bart.

BOASE, Henry, and his brothers Arthur, Richard and William, of Penzance and Madron, co. Cornw., and Tiverton, co. Devon, 180 . ., Vol. XXV, fol. 326.

BOATES, William, of Liverpool, co. Lanc., 17 . . ., Vol. XVI, fol. 285.

BOCONNOC, Baron of [1784], (Thomas Pitt), of co. Cornw. [See CAMELFORD.] Supporters, 17 . . ., Vol. XV, fol. 259.

BODDINGTON, Henry, of Pownall Hall, Wilmslow, co. Chester, 1890,* Vol. LXV, fol. 225.

BODEN, Marshall, of Burton Crescent, London, 183 . ., Vol. XL, fol. 214 (see Burke).

„ . . . ., of Whalley Grange, Withington, co. Lanc., 185 . ., Vol. LIII, fol. 90.

BODHAM-WHETHAM, J. W., of Kirklington Hall, co. Nottingham, 1885, Vol. LXIII, fol. 12.

„ -WHETHAM, A. T., of Kirklington Hall, co. Nottingham, 1885, Vol. LXIII, fol. 12.

„ -WHETHAM, Capt., of Kirklington Hall, co. Nottingham, 1885, Vol. LXIII, fol. 12.

BODICOTE, Thomas, of London, 3 Aug. 1720, Vol. VI, fol. 442. (Fragm. Geneal., Crisp, V, p. 55.)

BODY, Charles Ash, of Ashbourne, Sydenham Rise, co. Kent, 1898, Vol. LXX, fol. 112.

BOEHM, Sir J. E., Bart., of Surrey, 1889, Vol. LXV, fol. 67.

BOEVEY-(CRAWLEY), Thomas, of Flaxley Abbey, co. Glouc. Arms of Crawley, with Boevey in chief, 1789, Vol. XVII, fol. 127.

BOGER, Admiral Richard, of St. Gerran's, co. Cornw., and Elburton, Plymstock, co. Devon, 181 . ., Vol. XXX, fol. 297.

„ Rev. Edmund, M.A., Queen Eliz. Grammar School, Southwark, 1893,* Vol. LXVII, fol. 149.

BOGLE, (?) Capt. John, of Woodside, Tor-Mohun, co. Devon, 186 . ., Vol. LVII, fol. 131. (Berry's Suppl.)

BOILEAU before POLLEN, of Little Bookham, co. Surrey, 182 . ., Vol. XXXII, fol. 383.

BOLCKOW, Henry William Ferdinand, M.P. for Middlesbrough, naturalized by Act of Parliament, Arms Registered to [see Burke].

BOLD after PATTEN, of Bold and Bank Hall, Warrington, co. Lanc. Exemplified quarterly, 181 . ., Vol. XXVIII, fol. 91.

BOLD before HOGHTON, of Walton Hall, co. Lanc., 182 . ., Vol. XXXV, fol. 138.

BOLDEN, formerly LEONARD, John, of Hyning, co. Lanc. [no reference].

BOLDERO-BARNARD, Edward Gee, of Cave Castle, co. York, 1877, Vol. LX, fol. 42.

BOLDING, John Frederick and George Frederick, sons of Thomas of Birmingham, 189 . ., Vol. LXXI, fol. . . . .

BOLINGBROKE, Viscount (ST. JOHN), [Bart. 1611, Visc. Bolingbroke and Baron St. John of Lidiard Tregoze, 1712]. Supporters, 17 . . ., Vol. VI, fol. 64.

BOLITHO, ..., of Chyandour, nr. Penzance, co. Cornw., 1811, Vol. XXVII, fol. 22.

„ Thomas, of The Coombe, Madron, Penzance, co. Cornw., 1852, Vol. L, fol. 104.

BOLLAND, ..., of Clapham, co. Surrey, and Masham, co. York, 181 . ., Vol. XXX, fol. 257.

BOLSOVER, Baroness. Supporters, decd., mother of the Duke of PORTLAND, 1880, Vol. LXI, fol. 46.

BOLTON, ..., of Coddenham and Hollesley, co. Suff., 180 . ., Vol. XXII, fol. 209.

„ Capt., s. of Col., C.B., of Sligo, 184 . ., Vol. XLIX, fol. 479.

„ Henry Hargreaves, J.P., of Newchurch-in-Rossendale, co. Lanc., 18 . . ., Vol. LXXI, fol. . . . .

„ Mary Katherine (Lady THURLOW), eldest dau. of Sir Richard Bolton, of St. Martin's-in-the-Fields, co. Middx., 181 . ., Vol. XXVII, fol. 327.

BOMBAY, Presidency of. Arms, 1877, Vol. LX, fol. 34. Supporters, fol. 37.

BOND, Jane, wife of Henry (dau. of GODFREY), of Bury St. Edmunds, co. Suff., 22 Nov. 1732, Vol. VIII, fol. 159ᵇ.

BOND to HOPKINS, of Hackney and London, 20 Jan. 1773, Vol. XII, fol. 220.

BONHAM, Sir Samuel George, K.C.B. [1850], Gov. and Com.-in-Chief, of Hong Kong [1874], of Great Warley, Essex, 185 . ., Vol. L, fol. 242.

BONNELL, John, of London, 1691, Vol. IV, fol. 82.

BONNELL, late BEALE, James, of Spring Gardens, St. Martin's, co. Middx., 6 Oct. 1774, Vol. XIII, fol. 21.

BONNELL after HARVEY, Mary Ann (Spinster), of Pelling Place, Old Windsor, Berks., 184 . ., Vol. XLV, fol. 146 (see Burke).

BONNER to WARWICK, of Warwick Hall, co. Cumberland, and Callerton, co. Northumberland, 17 . ., Vol. XVII, fol. 434.

BONNET, Benjamin, of the City of London, and Die, Dauphiny, France, 1751, Vol. IX, fol. 387 (see Burke and Berry).

BONNOR, George (s. of Benjamin), of Queen's Gate Terrace, London, and Fairlawn, Walton-on-Thames, co. Surrey, 1878, Vol. LX, fol. 167. (Berry's Suppl.)

BONOVRIER, Peter, and his grandfather Isaac, of St. Catherine's Cree, London, and St. Tonge, France, 23 Feb. 1737-8, Vol. VIII, fol. 232.

BONSALL after HUGHES, James Frederick, of Aberystwith and Glanrheidd-Capel, Bangor, co. Cardigan, and Perrow, co. Worc., 18 . ., Vol. LX, fol. 239.

BONSOR, Joseph, of Polesden Place, Great Bookham, co. Surrey, 1823, Vol. XXXIV, fol. 38.

BOODE, ..., of Bryanston Square, London, 182 . ., Vol. XXXIV, fol. 353.

BOOKER to GREGOR, of Trewarthericke and Creed, co. Cornw., 182 . ., Vol. XXXVI, fol. 19.

BOOKER, Thomas William, of The Leys, Ganerew and Tedstone de la mere, co. Hereford; Velindia House, Whitchurch, co. Glamorgan; and Dudley, co. Worc., 185 . ., Vol. LI, fols. 321, 325.

BOOKER, Josias (Lieut.-Col.), s. of Josias of Liverpool, co. Lanc., 186.., Vol. LV, fol. 214. Widow, quarterly escutcheon of pretence, 186.., Vol. LVI, fol. 262.

BOON, Robert, B.D., Rector of Ufford-with-Bainton, co. Northampton; Stokerston, co. Leic., and Gretton, co. Northampton, 1837, Vol. XLII, fol. 265.

BOORD, Sir J. W., Bart., of Wakehurst Place, Ardingley, co. Sussex, 1896, Vol. LXIX, fol. 30.

BOORMAN (and MARTYR), Thomas Hugh, of East Peckham, co. Kent, and Lamberhurst, co. Sussex, 182.., Vol. XXXVII, fol. 415.

BOOTH, late CALVERT, Thomas, of Warlaby, co. York, 1783, Vol. XV, fol. 129.

BOOTH (late GRIFFETH), Walter, Capt., R.N., of Twemlow Hall, co. Chester, 1792, Vol. XVIII, fol. 17.

,. (late BACHE), William Charles, of Twemlow Hall and Birmingham, 1811, Vol. XXVI, fol. 388. Crest, fol. 390.

BOOTH (late GORE), Robert Newcomen, Bart., of Salford, co. Lanc., and Lissadel, co. Sligo, [30 Aug. 1804] Vol. XXIII, fol. 119.

BOOTH, Sir Felix, Bart., of Portland Place, London, [27 Mar.] 1835, Vol. XL, fol. 317 (see Burke).

„ Rev. Caleb (s. of William, of Itchingswell, Hampsh.), Minister of St. Peter's, Melbourne, 185.., Vol. LIII, fol. 216.

HAWORTH-BOOTH, Lieut.-Col., Yorkshire, by Roy. Lic., 1869.

BOOTLE, Elizabeth (dau. of TAYLOR), of Lathom House, co. Lanc., 1814, Vol. XXVIII, fol. 178.

BOOTLE before WILBRAHAM, of Lathom House, co. Lanc., and Rode House, co. Chester, [8 Dec. 1814] Vol. XXVIII, fol. 215.

BORINGDON, Baron [1784] (PARKER), of co. Devon. Supporters, 17..., Vol. XV, fol. 305.

BORLASE-WARREN (before) VENABLES VERNON, Hon. W. J. W. (s. of the Baron of KINDERTON), of Stapleford Hall, co. Warw., 185.., Vol. LI, fol. 414.

BOROUGH to ROBERTS-GAWEN, of Chetwynd Park, Shropsh., 187.., Vol. LIX, fol. 108.

BORRER, William (s. of William), of Barrow Hill, Henfield, and Pakyns, Hurstpierpoint, co. Sussex, 1849, Vol. XLIX, fol. 210.

BORRETT, William, of the Inner Temple, Solicitor to Treasury,
„ John, of the Inner Temple, Prothonotary of the Common Pleas,
sons of Edward, late of Kirkby Lonsdale, co. Westmorld., 10 July 1707, Vol. V, fol. 244, and Add. MS. 14,830, fol. 101.

BORRON, William Geddes, of Glasgow, Mercht., &c., confirmed 20 July 1868, by G. Burnett, Lyon K. of Arms. (Misc. G. et H., New S., I, p. 356.)

BORROW, John, of the Town of Derby, High Sheriff of the County and J.P. (1st s. of Humphrey, late of Gotham, co. Nottingham, decd.), and unto his younger brother Samuel, of Mansfield, 2 Oct. 1702, Vol. V, fol. 81, and Add. MS. 14,831, fol. 187.

BORTHWICK before GILCHRIST, ..., co. Surrey. Quarterly Arms, Vol. XXIV, fol. 9.

BORTHWICK, Sir Algernon, afterwards Baron GLENESK, Scotland [1895], 1887, Vol. LXIV, fol. 46.

BORTON, Gen. Sir Arthur, K.C.B., Gov. of Malta, s. of John Drew, Rector of Blofield, co. Norf., to descdts. of his father, 1880, Vol. LX, fol. 373. (Berry's Suppl.)

BORWICK, Robert Hudson, of Berkeley Square, London, impaling JOHNSTON, 1893, Vol. LXVII, fol. 141. ?

„ Joseph Cooksey, of Gwynne House, Woodford, co. Essex, 1893, Vol. LXVII, fol. 141. ?

BOSANQUET, Samuel, s. of Samuel, of London, 1786-87, Vol. XVI, fol. 258.

BOSANQUET after SMITH, Horace James, of Broxbourne, co. Hertf., 1866, Vol. LVI, fol. 154. (Crisp and Berry's Suppl.)

BOSCAWEN-ROSE, Viscount FALMOUTH [1720], of co. Cornw. Supporters, 172 . ., Vol. VII, fol. 3.

BOSSLEY (see DAINTRY), J. S. (Vicar of Chesterfield, co. Derby, 181 . ., Vol. XXVI, fol. 281.

BOSTOCK, Robert, of Otford and Chevening, co. Kent, and Bostock, co. Chester, 6 Oct. 1733, Vol. VIII, fol. 181. (Berry's Suppl.)

BOSTOCK to RICH. Rev. Charles, LL.D., of Waverley Abbey, co. Surrey, 17 . . ., Vol. XVII, fol. 382.

BOSTOCK, Robert, of Otford, co. Kent, s. of Samuel, and to his nephew Robert, s. and h. of Samuel, his elder brother, 6 Oct. 1733. (Misc. G. et H., New S., IV, p. 92.)

BOSTON, Baron [1761], (Sir William IRBY, Bart.), of co. Linc. Supporters, 17 . . ., Vol. X, fol. 301.

BOSVILLE, late MACDONALD, Lieut.-Col., of Gunthwaite and Thorpe, co. York, s. of Baron SLATE, in Ireland, 181 . ., Vol. XXVIII, fols. 82, 85.

BOSVILLE before MACDONALD [Godfrey, 3rd Baron], Macdonald, Major Gen., Ireland, and co. York [? Roy. Lic., 11 April 1814], 182 . ., Vol. XXXV, fol. 11. (James William, fol. 228.)

BOSWALL (with designation "of Blackadder") after HOUSTON, Bart. [1836], of Blackadder, co. Berwick, [? 1847] Vol. XLVIII, fol. 281.

BOTELER after CASBERD, William John, R.N., of Taplow, Bucks., and Landaugh Castle and Penmark, co. Glamorgan, 186 . ., Vol. LVI, fol. 182.

BOTETOURT, Baron [1764] (BERKELEY), of co. Glouc. Supporters, 176 . ., Vol. XI, fol. 17.

BOTFIELD after GARNETT, Rev. William Botfield, M.A., of Deaker Hill, Shifnal, Shropsh.; Houghton Hall, Bunbury, and Tilston, co. Chester, 30 Oct. 1863, Vol. LV, fol. 130.

BOTT, James, s. of Michael of Birmingham (Sophia Bott, widow). (See JELF.) 180 . ., Vol. XXV, fol. 180.

BOTTOMLEY, Samuel, of Wade House, Shelf, Halifax, co. York, 184 . ., Vol. XLIX, fol. 430. (See CAUTLEY.)

BOUCHER, late CRABB, of Shedfield, Droxford House, Hampsh., and Marlboro' Mount (Middx.), Jamaica, 183 . ., Vol. XLII, fol. 195.

BOUGHEY, late FLETCHER, of Aqualate Hall, Newcastle, Betley and Audley, co. Staff., 180 . ., Vol. XXIII, fol. 167.

BOUGHEY (quartered by LINGARD, of Audlem, co. Chester, 1868, Vol. LVII, fols. 311, 313.)

BOUGHEY (see LINGARD-MONK and JENNINGS). (Genealogist, Vol. V, p. 144.)

BOUGHTON before ROUSE, of Rouse Lench, co. Worc., and Downton Hall, Shropsh., and Lawford, co. Warw., 17 . ., Vol. XVII, fol. 352.

BOUGHTON, George Charles Braithwaite (late BRAITHWAITE), (and for his wife DAVIS impaled), of Poston Court, co. Heref., 17 . ., Vol. XX, fol. 207.

BOUGHTON-LEIGH after WARD, of Brownsover Hall, co. Warw., and Guilsboro, co. Northampton, 183 . ., Vol. XXXIX, fols. 63-67.

BOUGHTON-ROUSE before KNIGHT, of Downton Castle, co. Hereford, and Downton Hall, Shropsh., 185 . ., Vol. LII, fol. 172.

BOULCOTT, John, of Forest House, West Ham, co. Essex, 180 . ., Vol. XXV, fol. 247.

BOULDERSON, Capt., of Boswarren, co. Cornw., 182 . ., Vol. XXXV, fol. 43.

BOULT, ..., of Liverpool, 186 . ., Vol. LIV, fol. 322.

BOULTER, Dr. Hugh (Bp. of Bristol), co. Glouc., 4 April, 1720, Vol. VI, fol. 397 (see Burke and Misc. G. et H., II, p. 252).

BOULTON late CRABB, Henry and brother Richard, of Ipsley, co. Warw., and London, 17 . . ., Vol. IX, fol. 182.

BOULTON (and ROBINSON, late wife), Matthew, of Handsworth, co. Staff. Arms to descendants of his late wife, 17 . . ., Vol. XVIII, fol. 297.

BOULTON, of Bridgnorth, Shropsh. Match with BAKER, 181 . ., Vol. XXVII, fol. 235.

BOULTON, co. Staff., 184. ., Vol. XLVIII, fol. 106.

„ Samuel Bagster, of Copped Hall, Totteridge, co. Hertf., 1897, Vol. LXX, fol. 65.

„ James, Solicitor, 21a, Northampton Square, and Great Marlborough Street, London, 1898, Vol. LXX, fol. 280.

BOURKE, Michael, of St. Andrew, Holborn, London, 1737, Vol. X, fol. 120 (*see* Berry).

BOURNE, Ralph, s. of James Fenton, of Stoke-upon-Trent and Spot Grange, Stone, co. Staff., mar. with PRATT and BAKER, 1815, Vol. XXIX, fol. 286.

„ (Sir) James, of Hackinsall, co. Lanc., 1848, Vol. XLVIII. fol. 407. (Crisp. III, p. 148 ; Berry's Suppl.)

BOURNE-MAY, James William Seaburne, of Hackinsall, Stalmine, co. Lanc., 1897, Vol. LXIX, fol. 245.

BOUSFIELD, ..., wife of John R. Vaizey [Bousfield ?], of Newington, co. Surrey, 187 . ., Vol. LIX, fols. 326-8.

BOUSTEAD, ..., of Cumrenton, co. Cumberland, and London. Paymaster, Ceylon Rifle Brigade, 184 . ., Vol. XLIX, fol. 394.

BOUTCHER, Emmanuel, of Oxford Square, London, 185 . ., Vol. LII, fol. 135.

BOUVERIE, Visct. FOLKESTONE [1747], co. Kent. Supporters, 17 . . ., Vol. IX, fol. 200 (*see* Berry).

BOUVERIE-CAMPBELL-WYNDHAM, P. A. P., of Yateley, Hampsh., 1891, Vol. LXVI, fols. 112, 113.

BOUWENS, Lambart Henry (s. of Theodore), of Fingest Grove, Bucks., 1898, Vol. LXX, fol. 172.

BOVEY, Charles, of Warden Abbey, co. Bedf., and Stowe, co. Camb., Vol. VI, fol. 43, and Add. MS. 14,830, fol. 2, 21 June 1712 (*see* Burke).

BOW (wife of William Nicholas Darnell, B.D.), of Thurloxton, co. Somerset, 18 . . ., Vol. XXXVIII, fols. 229, 230.

BOWATER, Maj.-Gen. Sir Edward, of Hampton Court, K.H., 1844 (*see* Burke).

BOWDEN, ..., of Stroud Green, Croydon, co. Surrey : Kingston-upon-Hull, co. York, 183 . ., Vol. XLIII, fol. 24.

BOWDON, Richard Catlow (J. P. B. or Henry), of Southgate House, Clown, and Beighton Fields, Barlbrough, co. Derby, 1810 Vol. XLVI, fol. 27.

BOWDON-BUTLER, John Butler, of Pleasington Hall, co. Lanc. [to quarter Butler, 21 Jan. 1841], 184 . ., Vol. XLV, fol. 53. [Misc. G. et H., New S., II, p. 525.]

BOWEN, Thomas, Treasury Clerk, London, 1 Nov. 1729, Vol. VIII, fol. 44.

„ Sir George Fergusson, G.C.M.G. [1860], of London. Supporters, 1880 [?], Vol. LXI, fol. 23.

BOWER, to JODRELL, John, of Manchester, co. Lanc., 5 April 1775, Vol. XIII, fol. 89.

BOWER after JODRELL, (Phillips), of Henbury, co. Chester, 186 . ., Vol. LVII, fol. 68.

BOWER, John, of Middlethorpe Hall and Broxholm, co. York, 1836, Vol. XLII, fol. 38 ; 185 . ., Vol. LIII, fol. . . . .

„ J., Bower, of Carlton Lodge, Teignmouth, co. Devon, 1881, Vol. LXI, fol. 130. (Berry's Suppl.)

BOWERBANK and DE JERSEY, wife of, Lamonby, co. Cumberland, and London. 1801, Vol. XXI, fol. 271.

BOWERS, Thomas, Bp. of Chichester, co. Sussex, 1722, Vol. VII, fol. 96.

BOWES after FOORD, Timothy Fysh, of Wold Cott and Barnhey, co. York, and co. Linc., 20 Oct. 1812, Vol. XXVII, fol. 139, and for his wife, 182 . ., Vol. XXXII, fol. 211.

BOWES-FOORD to FOORD-BOWES, Col. Barnard, co. York, 1809, Vol. XXV, fol. 128. Market Deeping, co. Linc. (*see* JOHNSON in Baronets).

BOWES, Barnard FOORD- (formerly TROLLOPE), of Sidmouth, co. Devon, and Cowlam, co. York, 1861, Vol. LIV, fol. . . . .

Bowes, John, reputed son of Bowes, Earl of Strathmore, co. Durham, 183 . ., Vol. XXXIX, fol. 160.

Bowker before Jebb, Robert, of Manchester, co. Lanc. Match, 178 . ., Vol. XVI, fol. 308.

Bowlby, E. S., of Gilston Park, Harlow, co. Hertf., 1888,* Vol. LXIV, fol. 185.

Bowler, Lieut., E.I.C.S., Madras. Match, Rainier (see Rainier), 181 . ., Vol. XXVI, fol. 152.

Bowles, Carington, of St. Gregory, London, 17 . . ., Vol. XV, fol. 9.

., John (s. of John), of the Inner Temple, London, to the descendants of his father, 1796,* Vol. XIX, fol. 293 (see Burke and Berry).

Bowles after Rushout, s. of Baron Northwick, co. Essex and Shropsh. Quarterly Arms, 181 . ., Vol. XXX, fol. 236.

Bowles (late Treacher), Henry C., of Myddleton House, Enfield, co. Middx., 1852, Vol. L, fol. 144.

Bowles to Shakespear, of Langley Priory, co. Leic., 185 . ., Vol. LIII, fol. 40.

Bowling, Thomas, of Ramsgate, co. Kent, 1892, Vol. LXVII, fol. 75.

Bowlt to Sharp, Rev., of Clare Hill, South Mimms, co. Middx., and co. Durham, 181 . ., Vol. XXX, fol. 339.

Bowman, William (s. of John, s. of Robert), of Stainton and Stanwix, co. Cumberland, 17 . . ., Vol. XIV, fol. 229.

Bowman, formerly Coates, otherwise Boardman, of Tanfield Court, Temple, London, rep. s. of William Bowman, of Roehampton, co. Surrey. Arms of Bowman only, 11 Dec. 1798, Vol. XX, fol. 251. (Crisp, Fragm. Geneal., V, p. 54.)

Bowman [Seymour, of Salisbury, Wilts., 16 Feb. 1696. (Guillim, p. 331)].

„ Sir William, Bart., of London, 1883,* Vol. LXII, fol. 164.

„ Alfred John, Bar.-at-Law, of the Inner Temple, London, s. of John, of Tunbridge Wells, 189 . ., Vol. LXXI, fol. . . . .

Bown to Winston, of Thavies Inn, London, 17 . . ., Vol. XIX, fol. 139.

Bownas, William, of Westmorland. Quartering with Strickland, 180 . ., Vol. XXIV, fol. 301.

Bowring, John Charles, of Forest Farm, Winkfield, Berks., and Claremont, Exeter, s. of Sir John, 1877, Vol. LX, fol. 52. (Crisp, VI, p. 1, and Berry's Suppl.)

Bowser or Bowzer, Richard (s. of Richard), of St. John's, Southwark, and co. York, 17 . . ., Vol. XIX, fol. 444.

Bowser, Lieut.-Col., of Kirkby Thore, co. Westmorland, and London, 180 . ., Vol. XXII, fol. 357 Lieut.-Gen. Sir Thomas, K.C.B. [1827], of Kirkby Thore, co. Westmorland. Augmentation, 182 . ., Vol. XXXVI, fol. 161.

Bowyer, William, of Comb End, Elkstone, and Minchinhampton, co. Glouc., 17 . . ., Vol. XVIII, fol. 155.

Bowyer after Atkins, Henry, of Stoke House, Cobham, co. Surrey, and Denham, Bucks., 1835, Vol. XLI, fol. 142.

Bowyer before Smyth, Sir Edward, Bart., of co. Essex and co. Norf., 1839, Vol. XLIV, fol. 140.

Boyce, Robert Henry. ? by Ulster K. of Arms.

„ Rev. William Woolcombe, M.A., s. of Henry Charles ?, of Prestbury, 189 . ., Vol. LXXI, fol. . . . .

Boycott after Morse, John Hall, of Sennowe, Sprowston Hall and Mount Ida, Bagthorpe, co. Norf., 1844, Vol. XLVII, fol. 175 (see Burke).

Boyd, Lieut.-Gen. Sir Robert, K.B. [1785]. Supporters, 178 . ., Vol. XVI, fol. 139.

„ Ven Archdeacon William Boyd, the original grantee, 1882,* Vol. LXI, fol. 370 (Berry's Suppl.), and Edward F. (dead), of Moor House, West Rainton, co. Durham; George F., of Whitby, co. Northumberland; Robert F., co. Northumberland; Hugh F., co. Northumberland; William, of North House, Long Benton, Northumberland; Rev. Charles T., of Colombo, Ceylon.

Boyle, Baron [1711 ?], of Carleton, co. York, 17 . . ., Vol. VI, fol. 196.

BOYLES, Rear-Adm. Charles. (*See* HAWKER.) 181 . ., Vol. XXVII, fol. 347.

BOYMAN (late PIZZEY), Richard Boyman, of Hastings, co. Sussex, and London, 181 . ., Vol. XXXI, fol. 214.

BOYNTON, late APPLEYARD, of Boynton, co. Nottingham, 23 April 1701, Vol. V, fol. 37, and Add. MS. 14,831, fol. 75.

BOYNTON, Adriana, Lady (*see* SYKES), 21 Mar. 1723-4, Vol. VII, fol. 253.

., Adriana, Lady, co. Nottingham, 17 . . ., Vol. IX, fol. 174.

BOYS (*see* REYNOLDS), Phys[n], Royal Naval Hospital, Haslar, Hampsh. Match with REYNOLDS, 180 . ., Vol. XXV, fol. 276.

BRABAZON, late SHARPE, William John, of Oatlands, co. Sussex (grandson of the Irish Bart.), 1841, Vol. XLV, fol. 167.

„ late SHARPE, Brabazon Park, co. Mayo, and of Lincoln's Inn, London, 1847, Vol. XLVIII, fol. 367.

BRABAZON after MOORE, Rev. William John, of New Lodge, co. Hertf. (M.A., St. John's Coll., Camb.), Vicar of Sarat, 1845, Vol. XLVII fol. 420.

„ [after MOORE], Major John [Arthur Henry], of New Lodge, co. Hertf., [1868], Vol. LVII, fol. 3.

BRABOURNE, Baron [Edward Knatchbull-Hughesson], of co. Kent. Supporters, 1880,[*] Vol. LXI, fol. 33.

BRACE, Rear-Adm. Sir Edward, K.C.B., of Sutton and Stagbatch, co. Hereford, and Hertf., Catisfield Lodge, Hampsh., [1834] Vol. XLI, fol. 314. Crest for his descendants, fol. 316. (Crisp, VI, p. 88.)

BRACEBRIDGE, now LUDFORD, to NEWDICATE, ..., D.C.L., of Ansley Hall and Arbury, co. Warw., and Haresfield, co. Middx., 180 . ., Vol. XXIV, fol. 454.

BRACK to CLAYTON (Spr.), of Newcastle-upon-Tyne, co. Northumberland. Match with BATES, 181 . ., Vol. XXVIII, fol. 187.

BRACKENRIDGE, George Charles, of Ireland [no reference].

BRADBURY to RYE, ..., of Norton, co. Sussex. 17 . ., Vol. XIX, fol. 36.

BRADBURY, ..., of Manchester, 183 . ., Vol. XLIV, fol. 148.

„ Augustus Henry (s. of Charles, decd.), of Grosvenor Street, Edinburgh, and Hobart Town, Tasmania, 1875, Vol. LIX, fol. 74.

„ T. H., Bradley, Huddersfield, co. York, 1889,[*] Vol. LXV, fol. 154.

BRADDICK, of Boughton Mount, Boughton Monchelsey, co. Kent, 183 . ., Vol. XLII, fol. 245.

BRADDYLL, late GALE, Wilson, of Bardsea Noll, co. Lanc., 20 Sept. 1776, Vol. XIII, fol. 231.

BRADDYLL after RICHMOND-GALE, Thomas, of Conishead Priory, co. Lanc., and Cleator Noll and Highhead Castle, co. Cumberland, 181 . ., Vol. XXXI, fol. 352.

BRADFIELD after SANDERS, James Bradfield (a minor), of Stoke Ferry, co. Norf., 1815, Vol. XXVIII, fol. 416.

BRADFORD, Baron (BRIDGMAN) [1794], co. Staff. and Warw. Supporters and Ancient Crest, 179 . ., Vol. XVIII, fol. 385.

BRADFORD to ATKINSON, James Henry H., of Angerston, co. Northumberland, 18 . ., Vol. XLIV, fol. 214.

., to ATKINSON, Ralph, co. Northumberland, 187 . ., Vol. LVIII, fol. 84.

BRADLEY, Charles, of Halesowen, Shropsh., 180 . ., Vol. XXIII, fol. 396.

„ Courtail Charles (and ALBERT, his wife), of Halesowen and Burwash, co. Sussex, 180 . ., Vol. XXIII, fol. 400 [*see* Albert].

„ James, late MELLOR, M.D. (reputed son of Bradley, of co. York), of Clifton Cottage, Huddersfield, co. York, 183 . ., Vol. XXXIX, fol. 346.

DYNE-BRADLEY, Andrew Harves, of Gore Court, co. Kent. ? Name only. 1800. (*see* Burke).

BRADLY to SAYER, of Sandwich, co. Kent, 185 . ., Vol. L, fol. 386.

BRADNEY, Ellen, dau. and co-h. of Thomas, of Pem, co. Staff. Arms only. 17 . . ., Vol. XV, fol. 142.

BRADNEY, Joseph Alfred Bradney, of Bawdrip, co. Somerset, and of Llanfiliangel Ystern Llanern, co. Monmouth, 1883, Vol. LXII, fol. 64. (Crisp, I, p. 1.)

BRADSHAW after FLETCHER, William Bradshaw, of Halton Hall and Highfield, co. Lanc. (Match with BILLINGTON), 17 . . ., Vol. XIV, fol. 358.

   ,, after CAVENDISH, of Dovebridge, co. Derby. and Cork, Ireland. (*See* Baron WATERPARK.) 17 . ., Vol. XVII, fol. 292.

BRADSHAW to GREAVES, of Nettleworth Hall, co. Nottingham, 182 . ., Vol. XXXV, fol. 92.

BRADSHAW (formerly BLAGROVE, originally Bradshaw), of Ankerwyke House, Bucks., 184 . . ., Vol. XLV, fol. 51 ; and 185 . ., Vol. LII, fol. 98.

BRADSHAW to HARTHONTHWAITE, of Lower Lee, Over Wyersdale, co. Lanc., 186 . ., Vol. LVII, fol. 157.

BRAE, Thomas, of Bengal, 184 . ., Vol. XLVI, fol. 83.

BRAGGE, to BATHURST, Charles, co. Glouc., 180 . ., Vol. XXII, fol. 424.

BRAHAM, John, of Tavistock Square, London, [2nd Sept. 1817], Vol. XXX, fol. 294. (Berry.)

BRAIKENRIDGE, George Weare, of Broomwell House, Brislington, co. Somerset, 182 . ., Vol. XXXVIII, fol. 48.

BRAILSFORD, Thomas, of East Barkwich, co. Linc., 182 . ., Vol. XXXV, fol. 256.

BRAIN, Samuel Arthur (s. of Samuel), of Roxburgh, Penarth, co. Glouc., 1898, Vol. LXX, fol. 211.

BRATHWAITE to OXLEY, Christopher, of Ripon, co. York., 15 May 1775, Vol. XIII, fol. 100.

BRAMWELL, Baron of the Court of Exchequer, of London, 185 . ., Vol. LII, fol. 23.

   ,, Sir Frederick Joseph, Bart., of London, 1889, Vol. LXIV, fol. 309.

BRAND, Ellis, of Wherstead, nr. Ipswich, co. Suff., 29 June 1741, Vol. IX, fol. 31.

   ,, Rev. John, of London, 17 . . ., Vol. XVI, fol. 169.

BRAND to TREVOR, Henry, of co. Hertf., 182 . ., Vol. XXXV, fol. 100.

   ,,   ,,   Baron DACRE, Thomas, of co. Hertf., [12 April 1851] Vol. XLIX, fol. 470.

BRANDER (late SPICKER), John, of Christchurch, Hampsh., 17 . . ., Vol. XVI, fol. 231.

BRANDFORD, William, of St. Nicholas, Cole Abbey, London, and Barbados, 1757, Vol. X, fol. 88 (*see* Berry).

BRANDRAM, Samuel, of Weston-upon-Trent, co. Derby, and London, 17 . . ., Vol. XIX, fol. 42.

BRANDRETH (late GIBBS), Humphry (of Ampthill, co. Bedf.), of Houghton House, Houghton Regis, co. Bedf., 184 . ., Vol. XLVIII, fol. 209.

BRANIGAN, Henry, of Jamaica and London, 181 . ., Vol. XXIX, fol. 237.

BRANKSTON, ..., of Blackheath, co. Kent ; Wooler, co. Northumberland ; and Mickletield Green, co. Hertf., 186 . ., Vol. LIV, fol. 216.

BRANTON before DAY, of Rickmansworth, co. Hertf., 182 . ., Vol. XXXVII, fol. 37 (*sic*).

BRASSEY, Baron, of co. Sussex. Supporters, 1886, Vol. LXIII, fol. 309.

BRATHWAITE to BOUGHTON, and his wife, DAVIS, of co. Hereford, 17 . . ., Vol. XX, fol. 207.

BRATT to SMITH, ..., of London, 182 . ., Vol. XXXVII, fol. 211.

BRAUND, Samuel, of Devon House, Prospect, South Australia, 1895, Vol. LXVIII, fol. 314.

BRAWSTON to STANE, Rev. John, of Skreens and Forest Hall, co. Essex. Quarterly Arms, 17 . . ., Vol. XXI, fol. 192.

BRAY (Baroness BRIDPORT), Maria Sophia, d. and h. of Thomas, of Edmonton, co. Middx. BRAY and SADLEIR quarterly (died *s*. p. 1831), 17 . . ., Vol. XIX, fol. 282.

BRAYBROOKE, Baron [1788], ALDWORTH to NEVILLE, Berks., 179 . ., Vol. XX, fol. 47.

   ,, Baron NEVILLE, ..., Berks. Supporters, 179 . ., Vol. XX, fol. 50.

BRAYBROOKE to GRIFFIN, Berks., [1798] Vol. XX, fol. 52.

BRAZIER to ARUNDEL, Sir John, Knt., Alderm. of co. Huntingdon, 27 Feb. 1801, Vol. XXI, fol. 125. (Bishop's MSS.)

BREACH to RAYMOND, of London, 180 . ., Vol. XXV, fols. 12 and 14.

BREDALL to BARLOW, of Barlow, co. Lanc. (Match), 17 . . ., Vol. XX, fol. 402.

BREE to STAPYLTON, Martin, of Marks Tey, co. Essex, and Myton Hall, co. York. (Match), 181 . ., Vol. XXX, fol. 393.

BREEDON after SYMONDS, Rev. John, Fellow, St. John's Coll., Oxf., and of Bere Court, nr. Pangbourne, Berks., 1783, Vol. XV, fol. 127.

BREEKS, ..., of Eden Gate and Hilbrook Hall, Westmorland, 186 . ., Vol. LIV, fol. 296.

BREMER (James John GORDON), Post-Capt., R.N., C.B., of Plymouth, co. Devon. Allusion to services, 181 . ., Vol. XXX, fol. 120 (see Burke).

BRENT, Timothy, and Eleanor, and Elizabeth, of Richmond, London, and co. Kent, 180 . ., Vol. XXIV, fol. 249.

BRENT, late (now) HODGKINSON, William, of London, and Brompton, co. Kent, and sister ROSSEAU, 180 . ., Vol. XXIV, fol. 269.

BRENTON, Jahleel, Post-Capt., R.N. (Bart.), of Rhode Island, N. America, and Halifax, Nova Scotia, 3 Nov. 1812, Vol. XXVII, fol. 112.

BRERETON, late TRELAWNY, Charles, of Clifton, Bristol, co. Glouc., 1800, Vol. XXI, fol. 50.

BRETHERTON, widow of Bartholomew Joseph, of Rainhill, co. Lanc., 186 . ., Vol. LVI, fol. 342.

  „ William, of Runshaw Hall, Leyland, co. Lanc. (died 1890), 1881, Vol. LXI, fol. 113.

BRETON to WOLSTENHOLME, of Forty Hall, Enfield, co. Middx.; Holly Hill, Hartfield, co. Surrey; and Norton, co. Northampton. (Match), 180 . ., Vol. XXIV, fol. 166.

BRETT, Lord ESHER, William Baliol, co. Hertf., 1887,* Vol. LXIII, fols. 338, 340.

BRETTELL-VAUGHAN after EDWARDS, of Berway, par. of Brainfield and Ludlow, Shropsh., [1850] Vol. XLIX, fol. 343. [Her. of Worc., I, p. 272n.]

BRETTINGHAM, Robert William, of Grosvenor Place, London, 17 . . ., Vol. XXI, fol. 229.

BREWERTON to HIRONS, of Wardington, co. Oxf., and North Arson [? Aston], 182 . ., Vol. XXXVI, fol. 268.

BREWIN, ..., of Loughborough, co. Leic., 183 . ., Vol. XXXIX, fol. 357.

BREWSTER (and DARLEY, of co. York), of Cold Green, co. Hertf., and co. York. Match with Darley, 17 . . ., Vol. XX, fol. 177.

  „ (and DARLEY, of co. York), of co. Hertf. Quarterly to Darley, 180 . ., Vol. XXV, fol. 264.

BREWSTER (see BACON), of Lucker, Northumberland. Match with FORSTER, 180 . ., Vol. XXI, fol. 213.

BRICE, now KINGSMILL, of Belfast, Ireland, 17 . . ., Vol. XVI, fol. 313.

  „ „ Adm. [Sir Robert, Bart. 1800], and CORRY, his late wife, of Stomanton, Hampsh., 180 . ., Vol. XXI, fol. 93.

BRICE, Arthur John Montefiore, 2nd s. of Thomas L. Montefiore, M.A., Rector (see MONTEFIORE), 185 . ., Vol. LI, fol. 43.

BRICKDALE, John (s. of John), of St. Michael's, Bristol, co. Glouc., 1765, Vol. XI, fol. 166. (Crest to BROMLEY, fol. 276, to Thomas, see next entry) (see Berry : Brickdale, co. Lanc., and Knowle, Bedminster, co. Somerset).

  „ ? Thomas, of Clifton, Bristol (different Crest of BROMLEY), 17 May 1768, Vol. XI, fol. 276 (see Edmondson and Berry).

BRICKDALE after FORTESCUE, John, of West Monckton and Coomble Flory, co. Somerset; Newland, co. Glouc.; and Dawlish, co. Devon, 186 . ., Vol. LIV, fol. 106.

BRICKWOOD, John, s. of J[ohn ?], of Wansford, co. Huntingdon, and Thornham, co. Northampton, 17 . . ., Vol. XV, fol. 5.

BRIDGE, ..., of Puddletrenthide and Isle of Purbeck, co. Dorset, and Andover, Hampsh., 1810, Vol. XXVI, fol. 36.

BRIDGEMAN (*see* Baron BRADFORD), of co. Staff., 17 . . ., Vol. XVIII. fol. 385.
BRIDGEN, Edward, of London (s. of William, of Bridgnorth, Shropsh.), 15 May 1725, Vol. VII, fol. 280, and Add. MS. 14,830, fol. 194.
BRIDGES, Rev. Brook and Sir Brook, Bart., of Danbury, co. Essex ; Bedford Row, London ; and Wallington House, Surrey. [Assumed the Christian name of Brook ? between 1785 and 1788], 17 . . ., Vol. XVI, fol. 354.
  „ George, of London (s. of George, of Leeds), 180 . ., Vol. XXII, fol. 251.
  „ Sir B. W., Bart., of Goodneston, co. Kent. FOWLER quartering. 183 . ., Vol. XL, fol. 191.
BRIDPORT, Baroness (*see* BRAY), 179 . ., Vol. XIX, fol. 282.
BRIDSON, Thomas R., of Bridge House, Bolton-le-Moors, co. Lanc., 1893,* Vol. LXVII, fol. 163.
BRIERLEY, John Swallow, s. of Joseph, of Huddersfield, co. York, 189 . ., Vol. LXXI, fol . . . .
BRIGGS, Sir Humphry, Bart., of Haughton, Shropsh., 16 . . ., Vol. III, fol. 192.
  „ (*see* BROOKE), of Haughton, Shropsh., 17 . . ., Vol. XVI. fol. 41.
  „ Rawon (s. of John), of Halifax, co. York, 1825, Vol. XXXV, fol. 280.
  „ Bart., of Barbados, 1871, Vol. LVIII, fol. . . . . (*see* Burke).
BRIGHT, Lowbridge, s. of Robert, s. of Henry, of Brocksbury, co. Hereford, and the City of Bristol. [Confirmation of Grant, 24 June 1779.] Vol. XIV, fol. 169. (Crisp, II, p. 16.) [Notes, IV, p. 5.]
  „ , ..., of Cadley, co. Devon. Quarterly to SWEETLAND, 180 . ., Vol. XXV, fol. 46.
BRIGHTON, co. Sussex, Corporation of, 14 April 1897, Vol. LXIX, fol. 251.
BRINCKMAN, Bart., Sir Theodore Henry (3 brothers, formerly BROADHEAD), co. York. and Berks., 184 . ., Vol. XLVI, fol. 380 (*see* BROADHEAD) ; 17 . . ., Vol. VIII, fol. 154ᵇ.
BRINDLEY, ..., of Chell House, Woolstanton, and Compton, Kinfare, co. Staff., 182 . ., Vol. XXXVII, fol. 208.
BRINE, James, B.D., of St. John's Coll., Oxf., and of Blandford, co. Dorset (grandson of the Admiral ?), 1860, Vol. LIV, fol. 18. (Crisp, IV, p. 17.)
BRINE to KNAPTON, Augustus James, M.A., Oxf., and of Boldre, Hampsh., 1860, Vol. LIV, fol. 46.
BRINKLEY, John (Bp. of Cloyne), of Woodbridge, co. Suff., [1826] Vol. XXXVI, fols. 157-8.
BRINTON, William, M.D., of London and Kidderminster, co. Worc., 186 . ., Vol. LV, fol. 14.
BRISBANE after MACDOUGALL, Lieut.-Gen. Sir Thomas, K.C.B., co. Roxburgh, 182 . ., Vol. XXXVI, fol. 83.
BRISCOE (*see* MAGNALL), of Little Lever, Bolton, co. Lanc., mar. with MAGNALL, 17 . . ., Vol. XI, fol. 61.
BRISE (*see* John Ruggles BRISE), 1827, Vol. XXXVI, fol. . . . . ?
BRISTOW after COLLYER, William, of Crawley, Hampsh., and Farnham and Beddington, co. Surrey (1st s. of Andrew), 1859, Vol. LIII, fol. 84.
  „ after COLLYER (s. of Andrew, of Beddington), Hampsh. and co. Surrey. Roy. Lic., 15 Jan. 1859, Vol. LIII, fol. 316.
BRITTON, Philip William Poole CARLYON- [of Hanham Court, Hanham Abbotts, co. Glouc., and Bitton House, Enfield], co. Middx. [and Lincoln's Inn Fields, London (Capt., Roy. Inniskilling Fusiliers)]. Quarterly Arms. [19 June 1897] Vol. LXIX, fols. 195, 289. (Crisp, II, p. 77.) [Notes, IV, p. 70.]
  „ . . . ., of Britton House, Enfield, co. Middx., 1892,* Vol. LXVII, fol. 39.
BROADBENT, Sir W. H., Bart., of Longwood, co. York, and London, 1893,* Vol. LXVII, fol. 199.
BROADE, Francis (Philip), after STANIER (a minor), Francis STANIER-PHILIP-BROADE, of Madeley Manor, Newcastle-under-Lyme, co. Staff., 185 . ., Vol. LII, fol. 372.

BROADHEAD, Henry, of Monk Bretton, co. York, 3 sons, Theodore Henry, John Richard and Charles, s. of G. BRINCKMAN [see Brinckman], 22 Dec. 1732, Vol. VIII. fol. 154ᵇ.

BROADHURST, ..., of Foston and Duffield, co. Derby, 180 . ., Vol. XXV, fol. 218.

BROADLEY, John Henry, F.S.A., and Mary Sophia, of Kirk Ella and Ferriby, co. York, 181 . ., Vol. XXXI, fol. 16.

BROADLEY before HARRISON, William Henry, of Ripon, and Welton House, co. York, 1865, Vol. LV, fol. 312.

BROADMEAD, Philip, of Milverton, co. Somerset, 184 . ., Vol. XLVII, fol. 110.

BROADNAX, ... (goldsmith, of London. Seal with Arms and Crest), 16 . . ., Vol. III, fol. 103.

BROADNAX to MAY and MAY to KNIGHT (Thomas), of co. Kent, 17 . . ., Vol. VIII, fol. 241ᵇ.

BROADRICK, Rev. George, of Broxholme, Doncaster, co. York, and Jesus Coll., Camb., 181 . ., Vol. XXVI, fol. 379.

BROADWOOD, James Tschudi, of Lyne, Newdigate, co. Surrey and Essex (s. of John, of Reeve-Hall, co. Essex), 1824, Vol. XXXIV, fol. 298.

BROCAS, formerly AUSTEN, Barnard, natural son of Brocas of Wokefield, Berks., and Beaurepaire, Hampsh., 182 . ., Vol. XXXIII, fol. 324.

BROCK before HOLLINSHEAD, of Stockport, co. Chester, and Chorley and Wigan, co. Lanc., 180 . ., Vol. XXII, fols. 21 and 359.

BROCK after CLUTTON (minor), Col. Thomas, of Davenham, co. Chester, and Kinnerley Castle, co. Hereford. (Match), 1809, Vol. XXVI, fol. 77.

„ Maj.-Gen. Sir Isaac, K.B. [1812] (of Guernsey). Arms, 181 . ., Vol. XXVII, fol. 200. Supporters, 15 Feb. 1813, fol. 203 (see Burke).

BROCKDEN, ..., of Barbados. (Match with HEYSHAM), 172 . ., Vol. VII, fol. 158.

BROCKET, late CHAMBERLAYNE, of Staines, Rye, co. Sussex, and of the Middle Temple, London, 183 . ., Vol. XL, fol. 206.

BROCKET, Mrs., of Spain's Hall, Wellingdale Spain, co. Essex, 1896, Vol. LXIX, fol. 79.

BROCKHOLES after FITZHERBERT, William, of Claughton, co. Lanc., and Swinnerton, co. Staff., 4th s. of Basil, 1782 ?, Vol. XV, fol. 185.

„ after FITZHERBERT, William Joseph, of Claughton, co. Lanc., and co. Staff., 1875, Vol. LIX, fol. 158.

BROCKLEBANK (late FISHER), Sir Thomas, Bart., of Stansfield, nr. Liverpool, co. Lanc., and Keeble Court, co. Cumberland, 184 . ., Vol. XLVIII, fol. 61.

BROCKLEBANK, Ralph, of Childwall Hall, Liverpool, co. Lanc. (d. 1892), 1884, Vol. LXII, fol. 299. (Berry's Suppl.)

BROCKLEHURST, Thomas Unett, s. of Thomas, and to descendants of his uncle John, decd., of Henbury Park, co. Chester ; The Fence and Hardsfield, &c., 1879,* Vol. LX, fol. 285. (Berry's Suppl.)

„ Robert St. Clare, of West Derby, co. Lanc., 1883, Vol. LXII, fol. 166.

BROCKSOPP, Edward, of North Winfield, Haslam, Chesterfield, and Ashdown, co. Derby, 180 . ., Vol. XXIV, fol. 201.

BRODBELT, Francis Rigby, M.D., of Bath Easton, co. Somerset, and Jamaica, 182 . ., Vol. XXXIV, fol. 3.

BRODHURST, late NICHOLLS, Major-Gen., E.I.C.S., of co. Chester, and Drayton Lodge, Shropsh., 180 . ., Vol. XXV, fol. 244.

„ (late JENKS), Thomas (a minor), of Cheddington, Bucks., s. of the Rector of Albury, co. Hertf., 1813, Vol. XXVII, fol. 366.

BRODIE, Benjamin Collins (Bart.), Serg. Surgeon to Queen Victoria, of Wilts., 183 . ., Vol. XL, fol. 299.

BRODRIBB, F. C., of Wyalcah, Toowoomba, Queensland, 1892,* Vol. LXVI, fol. 251.

BROGRAVE, late RYE, ..., of Worstead Hall, co. Norf., and co. Somerset, of St. Alban Hall, Oxford, 1830, Vol. XXXVIII, fol. 271.

BROKE, Philip Bowes Vere, Bart., Post-Capt., R.N., Commander of the "Shannon," of co. Suff. Crest of augmentation, [1 Mar.] 1814,* Vol. XXVIII, fol. 15. (Geneal. Mag., 1, p. 67.)

BROKE before VERE, Lieut.-Col. Sir Chas., K.C.B., of Thorpe, next Norwich, co. Norf., and Henley Hall, co. Suff., 1822, Vol. XXXIII, fol. 272.

„ before MIDDLETON, Sir George [Nathaniel, 3rd] Bart., co. Suff. (died s. p. 1887, [aged ?] XL), [17 July] 1860, Vol. LIV, fol. 3.

BROMHEAD, Brig.-Gen. [Gonville], of Thurlby and Bassingham, co. Linc., 180 . ., Vol. XXIII, fol. 286.

BROMILOW, David, of Bittesworth Hall, Lutterworth, co. Leic., 1885, Vol. LXIII, fol. 25.

BROMLEY, Henry, Baron MONTFORT [9 May 1741], co. Camb. and co. Worc. Change of Arms and Crest. Supporters, 174 . ., Vol. IX, fol. 23.

[BROMLEY. See CHESTER.]

BROMLEY, late SMITH, Sir George, Bart., of East Stoke, co. Nottingham [7 Feb. 1778], Vol. XIV, fol. 25.

BROMLEY after DAVENPORT, Rev. Walter, of Wootton Hall, Ullarton, co. Staff. ; Capesthorne, co. Chester ; Bagginton Hall, co. Warw., 182 . ., Vol. XXXIII, fol. 379.

BROMLEY before DAVENPORT, William Bromley, of co. Chester, Staff., and Warw., 186 . .. Vol. LVI, fol. 324.

BROMLEY-WILSON, Maurice, of Dallam Tower, Milnethorpe, co. Westmorland, 1897, Vol. LXIX, fol. 300.

BROOK, Richard, of London, Dep. Alderm. of the Ward of Cheap, 1825, Vol. XXXV, fol. 121. (Berry.)

BROOKE and of WARWICK, Earl (GREVILLE), co. Warw. Crest, 17 . . ., Vol. X, fol. 223.

BROOKE, Rev. John, of Haughton, Shifnal and Blakeland, Shropsh., 1785, Vol. XVI, fol. 41 ; George, fol. 334.

BROOKE, late TOWNSEND, G. B. B., of Haughton and Chester, Shropsh., 1797, Vol. XIX, fol. 377.

BROOKE, John Charles, Somerset Herald, of London ; Wakefield and Dodsworth, co. York, 17 . . ., Vol. XVIII, fol. 312.

BROOKE after SHAWE, Rev. John K., of Eltham and West Malling, co. Kent (died s.p. 1840). (Match), 17 . . ., Vol. XIX, fol. 349.

BROOKE-DE CAPELL, late SUPPLE, Richard, of Great Oakley, co. Northampton, and Aghadore, Innakelly, co. Cork, 17 . . ., Vol. XX, fol. 70.

BROOKE after HOWARD, Richard, of Castle Howard, co. Wicklow, Ireland ; Roskelton, Queen's Co., and Colebrooke, co. Fermanagh, 183 . ., Vol. XL, fol. 303.

BROOKE, late REEVE, John (the younger), of Great Walsingham and Wighton, co. Norf., 1840, Vol. XLIV, fol. 204.

BROOKE, Sir James, K.C.B. [1848], Rajah, of Sarawak, 184 . ., Vol. XLIX, fol. 76.

„ (Sir) Thomas, of Almondbury and Armitage Bridge, co. York [Bart. 1899], 187 . ., Vol. LVIII, fol. 14. (Crisp, I, p. 73.)

BROOKE to OSBALDESTON, Humphrey, of Hunmanby, co. York, 17 . ., Vol. XII, fol. 46.

BROOKE, Charles A. Luxmoore, of Ashbrook Hall, co. Chester, and Witherdon, co. Devon, 18 . . ., Vol. LXIV, fol. 64.

BROOKER (see BOSTOCK), ..., of Brasted, co. Kent. (Match), 17 . ., Vol. VIII, fol. 181.

BROOKES before KEMP, George, of Goodyers, Hendon, co. Middx., 188 . ., Vol. XLIV, fol. 162.

BROOKFIELD, Arthur Montagu, Lieut., 13th Hussars (s. of William Henry), of Somerfield-with-Hamby, co. Linc., and Thurlow Place, co. Kent, 1872, Vol. LX, fol. 62. (Berry's Suppl.)

BROOKING, ..., of East Worthele, co. Devon, 183 . ., Vol. XLIII, fol. 204.

BROOKS, Thomas (s. of Robert), of Kingham, co. Oxf., and London, 17 . . ., Vol. XVI, fol. 165.
  ,, William Cunliffe (Bart.), of Barber Hall, co. Lanc., 28 April 1868, Vol. LVII, fol. 1.
  ,, J. B. Close, of Birtles Hall, co. Chester, 1889, Vol. LXV, fol. 15.
  ,, Samuel Burd, of Beckenham, co. Kent, 18 . . ., Vol. LXV, fol. 17.
BROOKSBANKE, Joseph and John, of Elland, Halifax, co. York (E. Marshal's Warrant, 12 July), Grant, 27 July 1703, Vol. V, fol. 126. Stowe MS. 714, fol. 137ᵇ.
  ,, William Lyon, of Bromley and Sydenham Hill, co. Kent, s. of Robert Collinson Brooksbanke, 1875, Vol. LIX, fol. 167. (Berry's Suppl.)
BROOMHEAD, John S., afterwards COLTON-FOX, of Todwick Grange, co. York, 1894, Vol. LXVIII, fol. 47.
  ,, -COLTON-FOX, B. P., of Sheffield, co. York, and Wales, 1890, Vol. LXV, fol. 337.
BROUGH to WATSON, Robert, of Melton, and the Manor House, Swanland, co. York, 185 . ., Vol. LI, fol. 40.
BROUGHAM to LAMPLUGH, Peter, of Dovenby, co. Cumberland, 17 . . ., Vol. XV, fol. 148.
BROUGHAM and VAUX, Henry, Baron, of Brougham, co. Westmorland [1830]. Arms, 18 . . ., Vol. XXXVIII, fol. 189, and Supporters, 18 . . ., Vol. XXXVIII, fol. 191.
BROUGHTON, ..., of Old Woman's Island, and Bombay. Quarterly to JONES, 181 . ., Vol. XXX, fol. 129.
BROUGHTON to PICKUP (reputed son of PICUP), of Springhill, Accrington, co. Lanc., 185 . ., Vol. LI, fol. 374.
BROUGHTON-ADDERLEY, H. J., of Barlaston Hall, co. Staff., 1887, Vol. LXIII, fol. 320.
BROUNCKER, ..., of Beveridge, co. Dorset, and Island of St. Christophers, 183 . ., Vol. XLII, fol. 161.
BROWELL, William, Post-Capt., R.N., co. Kent, Lieut.-Gov. of Greenwich Hospital, 1830, Vol. XXXVIII, fol. 209.
BROWN to ARMSTRONG, Thomas, of Hampsh., 1773, Vol. XII, fol. 275.
  ,, Sir William Augustus, Bart., of Westminster, London. (Match with BRICE), 1784, Vol. XV, fol. 381.
BROWN (late MAXWELL), Lieut.-Gen. Edward Maxwell, Hanover Square, London, 17 . . ., Vol. XVI, fol. 203.
BROWN, James, of Stoke Newington, co. Middx. Quarterly Arms. (Match), 31 Mar. 1789, Vol. XVII, fol. 185. (Genealogist, I, p. 220.)
BROWN to ANGELL, Benedict John, of Berks., co. Middx., and Wilts., 180 . ., Vol. XXI, fol. 245.
BROWN, late CANDLER, Edward, Combe Hill, co. Somerset, and London, 1804, Vol. XXII, fol. 288.
BROWN, George, of Stockton, co. Durham, and Deighton and Thornaby, co. York, 1805, Vol. XXIII, fol. 163. See 185 . ., Vol. LI, fol. 23 ?
  ,, Thomas, of Woolsmore, co. Hertf., 1761. (Edmondson.)
  ,, (. .) Ralph Wylde, of Caughley Hall, Shropsh., 1788, Vol. XVI, fol. 319.
BROWN (late ROBISON), William, of Everton, Walton-on-the-Hill, co. Lanc., 180 . ., Vol. XXV, fol. 449.
BROWN (see BILKE), of Honiton, co. Devon, 181 . ., Vol. XXVIII, fol. 43.
  ,, James, of Harehill Grove, Leeds, co. York. (Match with RHODES?), 18 . . .,° Vol. XXX, fol. 270. [Some of this entry seems to be crossed out.]
GRAVER-BROWNE, John Turner, of Morley Hall, co. Norf., 1815, Vol. XXVIII, fol. 320.
BROWN to DIXON, of Long Benton, co. Northumberland, 1825, Vol. XXXV, fol. 266 (died s. p., 1859).
BROWN after HELSHAM, Edward, of Comb Hill, co. Somerset, and Aghcniuve, Callan, co. Kilkenny, 1826, Vol. XXXVI, fol. 63.

BROWN, after CANDLER, William, of Comb Hill, co. Somerset, and Agheninve, Callan, co. Kilkenny, 16 July 1857, Vol. LII, fol. 238.

BROWN (and DUNCAN), William W. (s. of James), of Leeds, Chapel Allerton, and Hare Hills Grove, co. York, 18 . . .,* Vol. XXXIX, fol. 207.

BROWN, John, of Lea Castle, Wolverleigh, co. Worc., and The Cottage, Manchester, 183 . ., Vol. XXXIX, fol. 243.

BROWN before WESTHEAD, Joshua Proctor, of co. Worc., and Chester Terrace, Regent's Park, London, 18 . . ., Vol. XLIX, fol. 281.

BROWN, Sir William, Bart. [of Liverpool, co. Lanc.], s. of Alexander, of co. Lanc., and Baltimore, U.S.A., 183 . ., Vol. XLII, fol. 211 [Bart. 24 Jan. 1863].

BROWN, late "MAYOR" (? Peter), of Wood Plumpton, St. Michael, co. Lanc., 184 . ., Vol. XLV, fol. 299.

BROWN, ..., of Ebbw Vale, Bedwelty, co. Monmouth, 185 . ., Vol. L, fol. 438.

BROWN after GILPIN, George, of Sedbury, Gilling, co. York, and Stockton, co. Durham, 185 . ., Vol. LI, fol. 23.

„ after CORNISH, Charles Brown, of Sandford, co. Devon, 1863, Vol. LV, fol. 134.

BROWN to DREWITT, Thomas, of Jarrow, co. Durham; Colerne, Wilts.; and New Grove, Stepney, 1867, Vol. LVI, fol. 311.

BROWN, Sir John, Knt., of Endcliffe, Sheffield, co. York, 186 . ., Vol. LVII, fol. 25. (Berry's Suppl.)

BROWN to TROTTER [William], ..., wife of, [only dau. of George] WELBANK, of Horton Place, Epsom, co. Surrey, and Penshurst, co. Kent [Brown and Trotter quarterly, 1868 ?], 1869, Vol. LVII, fol. 98.

BROWN before GREAVES, Richard Edward, of Woodthorpe Hall, co. York (for Greaves), 1877, Vol. LIX, fol. 346.

BROWN, Alfred, of Durban, Natal, 1896,* Vol. LXIX, fol. 166.

„ . . . ., C.B., of Dowlands, Hordle, Hampsh. (see FICKLIN), 1889, Vol. LXV, fol. 60.

„ Sir William Roger, of Highfield, Hilperton, Wilts., 1888, Vol. LXIV, fol. 261.

„ Mrs. Haigh, of Westfield Terrace, Wakefield, co. York, 1887,* Vol. LXIV, fol. 118.

„ Robert, of Hull, co. York (see DAUNTESEY), 18 . . ., Vol. LX, fol. 137.

„ Sir Charles Gage, K.C.M.G. [1897], s. of Charles, Comm. R.N., of Portsmouth, 189 . ., Vol. LXXI, fol. . . . . .

BROWNE, Thomas, of London, merchant (s. of Philip, late of Norwich), to descendants of his father Philip, 6 May, 1724, Vol. VII, fol. 491 ; Add. MS. 14,830, fol. 127. [Crisp, Fragm. Geneal., XIII, p. 19.]

„ Thomas, late Lancaster Herald, since Norroy King of Arms, of Snelston, co. Derby, and co. Hertf., and to his brothers Henry and John, s. John, s. William, and a different crest, of Woolsmire, co. Hertf., 1761, Vol. X, fol. 394 (see Berry and Berry's Suppl.).

„ Isaac Hawkins (Preb. of Lichfield), of Badger, Shropsh., and of Lincoln's Inn, and to the descendants of his grandfather William, M.P., 14 May 1779, Vol. XIV, fol. 129 (see Berry). [Misc. G. et H., New S., III, p. 41.]

BROWNE before WYLDE, Ralph, of Shropsh. (BARROW Match.) 1788, Vol. XVI, fol. 319.

BROWNE, late EATON (B.A.), Richard, of co. Norf., 1798, Vol. XX, fol. 227.

„ late EATON, Rev. Richard, of Elsing, co. Norf., 27 Feb. 1845, Vol. XLVII, fol. 306, and 179 . ., Vol. XX, fol. 227 (see Burke, p. 135).

BROWNE before MILL, George Gaeni, of Bath, and Cariaçou, West Indies, 180 . ., Vol. XXII, fol. 298.

BROWNE after GRAVER, John Turner (a minor), of Wymondham, co. Norf., and Tacolnestone [?], 181 . ., Vol. XXVIII, fol. 320.

BROWNE, Wade (s. of Wade), of Moortown, and Trinity Coll., Camb., and Leeds, co. York, 1823, Vol. XXXIV, fol. 180.

BROWNE (late JONES), Thomas B., of Mellington Hall, co. Montgomery, 182 . ., Vol. XXXIV, fol. 182.

BROWNE, now PHILLIPS, natural sons of Maj.-Gen., of Hampsh., 1, William Edward, Gov. of Penang; 2, Major-Gen. Sir Charles, Knt., of Lyndhurst, Hampsh., 182 . ., Vol. XXXV, fols. 295, 297.

BROWNE to DE BEAUVOIR, Bart., Ireland, 182 . ., Vol. XXXVI, fol. 270.

BROWNE (GRANT) before SHERIDAN, R. B., of Frampton, co. Dorset. Browne and Grant quarterly, 1836, Vol. XLI, fol. 226.

BROWNE before CAVE, brothers Sir John Robert, Bart., co. Derby and Warw.: William Asteley. co. Derby and Warw. : Thomas and Wilmot, co. Derby and Warw. ; Rev⁴ Edward Sacheverell, co. Staff. and Warw., 183 . ., Vol. XLIII, fol. 306.

BROWNE after STAPLES, Richard Thomas, of Launton, co. Oxf., and Norwood, co. Surrey, 184 . ., Vol. XLVI, fol. 270.

BROWNE, William James (and Mary DIXON his wife), of Hampton Wick, co. Middx. ; Ilford, Wilts. ; and Port Gawlor, South Australia, Vol. LII, fol. 363.

  ,, John, of Boston, co. Linc. (1728-40), 28 June 1733, Vol. VIII, fol. 168.

  ., Mrs. Du Moulin, 188 . ., Vol. LXIII, fol. 157.

  ,, John, of Salperton, co. Glouc., 17 . . ., Vol. XIV, fol. 79, and for Mary BEALE his wife, of Temple Guiting, quartering ROBBINS, [2 Mar. 1779] Vol. XIV, fol. 181 [? 80].

BROWNELL, Robert Christian, of Mile End, co. Middx.. and Richmond, co. Surrey, 1775, Vol. XIII, fol. 76.

BROWNFIELD, William, of Chatterley House, Stoke-upon-Trent, co. Staff., 1854, Vol. LI, fol. 173.

BROWNING, ..., of Stamford, co. Surrey. (Match with ANNAND.), 181 . ., Vol. XXVII, fol. 426.

BROWNJOHN, ..., of Shaw, Melksham, Wilts., 18 . . ., Vol. LIII, fol. 345.

BROWNLOW [Baron, of Belton, co. Linc., 1776] (Cust, Bart.). Supporters, 177 . .,* Vol. XIII, fol. 213, and for his wife, Frances BANKS, Lady Brownlow, fol. 201.

BROWNRIGG (see UPCHER), of Willisham Hall, co. Suff. (Match), 17 . . ., Vol. XIII, fol. 269.

BROWNRIGG, Maj.-Gen. Robert Brownrigg, of co. Cumberland, and Wingfield, co. Wicklow, 1802, Vol. XXII, fol. 7.

  ,, Lieut.-Gen. Sir Robert, Bart., G.C.B. [1815]. Supporters, 181 . ., Vol. XXIX, fol. 348 (and ? Augmentation, 23 Mar. 1822).

BROWNSWORD, John, of Whitechapel, co. Middx., 1747, Vol. IX, fols. 291 and 305 (see Berry).

BRUCE, Baron [of Tottenham, Wilts., 1746] (BRUDENELL), of co. Northampton, Supporters, 17 . . ., Vol. IX, fol. 336.

BRUCE, late KNIGHT, John, of Duffryn, Wales. (Match), 180 . ., Vol. XXIII, fol. 241.

BRUCE after TYNDALL, Onesiphorous, of Lincoln's Inn (s. of Thomas Tyndall), of Grange Hill and Falkland Fife and Bristol and Lincoln's Inn, London, 18 . . ., Vol. XXXVIII ; Bruce, fol. 233 ; Bruce Tyndall Bruce, fol. 238.

BRUCE to PRYCE (son of KNIGHT), John, of Duffrayn, co. Glamorgan, 1837, Vol. XLII, fols. 185, 187. 188.

BRUCE after KNIGHT, Sir James Lewis, of Duffrayn, co. Glamorgan, and co. Devon, and ? of Fairlinch, co. Devon. 183 . ., Vol. XLII, fol. 190.

BRUCE, Edward Jackson, Lieut. R.H.A., 1854, Vol. LI, fol. 149.

BRUCE to BASSETT, Major (74th and 94th Regts.), of Beaupré, co. Glouc.. and Wales, 1865, Vol. LVI, fol. 57.

BRUCE after WRIGHT, Sir Frederick William Adolphus, G.C.B. [1865], of Hampsh., U.S. Minister [1 Feb. 1867], Vol. LVI, fol. 258.

BRUCE, Sir George Barclay, of Boundary Road, London, 1892,* Vol. LXVII, fol. 51.

BRUCE, Mr. Justice Gainsford, of London, 1892, Vol. LXVII, fol. 51.
BRUDENELL, Baron Bruce, of co. Northampton.   Supporters, 17 . . ., Vol. IX,
        fol. 336.
    „   Baron [1780], James Brudenell, of [Deene] co. Northampton [d. s.p. 1811].
        Supporters, 17 . . ., Vol. XIV, fol. 251.
BRUERE, William (son of George James, Gov. of Bermuda), of Ashted, co.
        Surrey, and to the descendants of his grandfather George, 14 May 1803,
        Vol. XXII, fol. 183 (see Burke). (Misc. G. et H., II, p. 20.)
BRUGES after LUDLOW, William Heald, of Seend, Melksham, Wilts., 1835, Vol.
        XL, fol. 368.
BRULEY, Joseph (s. of James), of Liverpool, co. Lanc., and the Island of Tortola,
        180 . ., Vol. XXIII, fol. 112.
BRUNE, late PRIDEAUX, Rev. Charles, of Place, co. Cornw., and Plumber,
        co. Dorset. (Match), 1799, Vol. XX, fol. 346.
    „   late PRIDEAUX, of Place, co. Cornw., and Plumber, of co. Dorset. (Match),
        18 . . ., Vol. XXV, fol. 388.
BRUNNER, Sir J. T., Bart., of co. Chester and Lanc., 1895, Vol. XLVIII, fol. 243.
BRYAN, ..., co. Camb. (Match with BYATT), 172 . ., Vol. VIII, fol. 97ᵇ.
    „   Thomas, of Cadogan Place, London, 180 . ., Vol. XXIV, fol. 347 (and
        MORRIS, his wife), Thomas, of London, 181 . ., Vol. XXX, fol. 99.
    „   Edward Langdon, M.D., of Clifton, Bristol, co. Glouc., and Kensington
        Park Gardens, London, 186 . ., Vol. LV, fol. 336.
BRYDGES-CHANDOS (TEMPLE-NUGENT) GRENVILLE, late TEMPLE NUGENT
        GREVILLE, Earl Temple, Bucks., 18 . . ., Vol. XXI, fol. 54.
BRYDGES, John, of the Middle Temple, London, 1814, Vol. XXVIII, fol. 247.
    „   Samuel Egerton, of Denton Court and Wootton Court, co. Kent, 1814,
        Vol. XXVIII, fol. 273.
BRYDGES after JONES, Bart., of Harford, co. Radnor, and co. Somerset, 182 . .,
        Vol. XXXVI, fol. 133.
BRYMER, Col. Alexander, of Bathwick, co. Somerset, Col. Comdt. Mil. and
        Deputy-Paymʳ-Gen. of Nova Scotia, 181 . ., Vol. XXVIII, fol. 49.
BUCHAN, J. J., a Colonel of Volunteers, of Tinhaven, Studley Park, co. Kent ;
        nr. Melbourne, Australia, 1891, Vol. LXVI, fol. 146.
BUCHANAN, Sir Andrew, G.C.B. [1866], P.C. [1863], Scotland, 186 . ., Vol. LVI,
        fol. 172. Ambass. to Russia. Supporters, 18 . . ., Vol. LX, fol. 283.
    „   W. F., of Clareinnis, Sydney, N. South Wales, 1895, Vol. LXVIII, fol. 220.
BUCHER to RODBARD (natural s. of Rodbard), of Merriott, co. Somerset, 17 . . .,
        Vol. XVIII, fol. 207.
BUCK, George (grandfather George), of Affeton and Daddon and Bideford [ancestor
        came from Ireland], co. Devon [12 Aug. 1780], Vol. XIV, fol. 243.
        (Crisp, II, p. 148) [and Notes, IV, p. 129].
BUCK to STUCLEY, Sir George, Bart., of Hartland Abbey and Affeton Castle,
        co. Devon, [27 July 1858] Vol. LII, fol. 381.
    „   to DAUNTESEY, John, of Agecroft Hall, Eccles, co. Lanc. [1863], Vol. LV,
        fol. 132.
BUCKBY to BATEMAN, of Guilsbourgh, co. Northampton, 182 . ., Vol. XXXVI,
        fol. 373.
BUCKBY, Henry Baynbrigg, of Lincoln's Inn, London, and Grantchester, co.
        Camb., 1 April, 1738, Vol. VIII, fol. 236.
BUCKINGHAM, Sir Owen, Knt., Lord Mayor of London, 15 Dec. 1708, Vol. V,
        fol. 318 (see Burke (15 Dec.), Berry and Add. MS. 14,831, fol. 28).
BUCKLE to PUNCHON, of Killingworth Cottage, Long Benton, co. Northumberland,
        182 . ., Vol. XXXIV, fol. 124.
BUCKLE. See BARLEE.
BUCKLEY, Edmund, of Ardwick, co. Lanc., the father of Edmund and Joseph,
        1863, Vol. LV, fol. 152.
BUCKLEY, formerly PECK (nat. son of Buckley), Edmund, of Dinas Mawddy,
        co. Merioneth and Lanc., 1863, Vol. LV, fol. 164.

BUCKLEY, Joseph, M.A., Vicar of Tor Moham, co. Devon, Rector of Sopworth, Wilts., and co. Lanc., 186 . ., Vol. LV, fol. 166.

„ H. Burton, Q.C., of Lincoln's Inn, London, 1894,* Vol. LXVIII, fol. 24.

BUCKNALL, Thomas Skip, of London. Quarterly with SKIPP (DYOT on a Canton), 10 Feb. 1785, Vol. XVI, fol 3.

BUCKNALL, late GRIMSTON, William Okley, co. Hertf. (left an only dau., 17 . . ., Vol. XVII, fol. 286). 179 . ., Vol. XIX, fol. 361 (17 . . ., Vol. XVII, fol. 286, escutcheon of pretence for Viscount Grimston).

BUCKNALL (late GRIMSTON), Rev. Harbottle, M.A., of Halston, co. Kent; Oxhey, co. Hertf. ; Pebmarsh, co. Essex ; d. unmarried, 181 . ., Vol. XXVIII, fol. 134.

„ late ESTCOURT, James Bucknall, of Estcourt, co. Glouc., and Oxhey, co. Hertf. (died s. p. 1855), 1823, Vol. XXXIV, fol. 49.

BUCKNALL-ESTCOURT to SOTHERAN, T. H. S., Bowden Park and Laycock, Wilts., and Kirkling Hall, co. Nottingham, 1839, Vol. XLIV, fol. 48.

„ -ESTCOURT to SOTHERAN-ESTCOURT, T. H. S., of Newnton House, Wilts., and Darrington Hall, co. York, 187 . ., Vol. LIX, fol. 198.

BUCKNER, John, LL.D., Bishop of Chichester, 180 . ., Vol. XXIII, fol. 80 (see Berry's Suppl.).

BUCKWORTH-HERNE-SOAME, Bart., Haydon House, co. Essex, and Broxbourne, co. Hertf., 180 . ., Vol. XXIV, fols. 97, 99.

BUCKWORTH, now SHAKERLEY, Somerford Park, co. Chester, 183 . ., Vol. XLIII, fol. 112.

BUDDICOM, Ellen (dau. of the Rev. Robert Pedder Buddicom, Principal of St. Bees Coll., co. Cumberland), widow of the Rev. John SANDARS, 1897, Vol. LXIX, fol. 279.

BUDGETT, John Payne, of Henleage Park, Westbury-on-Trym, co. Glouc., 18 . . ., Vol. LIII, fol. 285.

„ James Smith, of Stoke Park, Stoke, co. Surrey, and co. Glouc., s. of Samuel, of Kingswood Hill, Bilton, decd., 1880, Vol. LX, fol. 340. (Berry's Suppl.)

BUDWORTH to PALMER, of Palmerston, co. Mayo, Ireland, and Oxford Street, London, 181 . ., Vol. XXVIII, fol. 379.

BUGGIN. See UNDERWOOD.

BULKELEY after WARREN, Thomas James, Baron, of Beaumoris, Wales [20 Sept. 1802], Vol. XXI, fol. 441.

„ after WILLIAMS, Sir Richard, Bart., of co. Anglesey and Carnarvon, Wales, [26 June 1827] Vol. XXXVI, fol. 147. (Burke.)

BULKELEY before OWEN (formerly HATCHETT), of Tedsmore and Ellesmere, Shropsh., and Llguldocdd, co. Montgomery, 18 . . ., Vol. XLIX, fol. 47.

„ before OWEN (formerly HATCHETT), of Coedane, co. Anglesey, and Tedsmore and Ellesmere, Shropsh., 18 . . ., Vol. XLIX, fol. 84.

BULL, M.R.C.S., of Oxford, 182 . ., Vol. XXXII, fol. 166.

BULLEN (afterwards Adm. Sir), Charles, C.B. and Post-Capt., R.N., of Charmouth and Weymouth, co. Dorset. Alteration to Trafalgar Medal, 1818, Vol. XXX, fol. 318.

BULLEN, now TATCHELL, John, of Stoke-under-Hambdon, Stoke Abbott and Charmouth, co. Dorset, 1824, Vol. XXXIV, fol. 342.

BULLEN after TATCHELL, John, of Sydling House, Stoke Abbott and Charmouth, co. Dorset, 1852, Vol. L, fol. 146.

„ after SYMES, John, of Charmouth, co. Dorset, 1868, Vol. LVII, fol. 51.

BULLEN, C. W. Dunbar, of Toft Monks, co. Norf., and Woburn Carrowdock, co. Down, 1892, Vol. LXVI, fol. 255.

BULLER, Rear-Adm. Sir Edward, Bart., M.P., of Trenant, Wiveliscombe, co. Cornw. (Augmentation), 18 . . .,* Vol. XXV, fol. 369.

BULLER-ELPHINSTONE (15th Baron Elphinstone), James Drummond Buller-Elphinstone, of Scotland, 1824, Vol. XXIV, fol. 286-7.

BULLER-MANNINGHAM, Edward, of Dilborne Hall, co. Staff., 186 . . ., Vol. LVI, fol. 71.

BULLIN to LEYLAND, Richard, Harbreck House, Walton Hill and Knowsley, co. Lanc., 182 . ., Vol. XXXVI, fol. 283.

BULLOCK, late WATSON, Jonathan J. C., Major of Militia, of Faulkborne House, co. Essex, 180 . ., Vol. XXV, fol. 328.

BULLOCK, of North Coker House, co. Somerset, 185 . ., Vol. L, fol. 100.

BULLOCK after TROYTE, of North Coker House, co. Somerset, and Huntsham, co. Devon, 185 . ., Vol. L, fol. 256.

BULLOCK to HALL, William Henry, of Mestley and Six Mile Bottom, co. Camb., 187 . ., Vol. LVIII, fol. 142.

BULLOCK, Mary Ann, widow of Sir Henry FETHERSTONHAUGH, Bart. (who died s.p. 1846), 18 . . ., Vol. XLIX, fol. . . . .

BULMAN, ... of Cox Lodge, nr. Newcastle-upon-Tyne, co. Northumberland, 180 . ., Vol. XXIII, fol. 142.

BULMER, William, of Lemington, Newburn, co. Northumberland, and Kingston-upon-Hull, co. York, 180 . ., Vol. XXXIV, fol. 294.

BULWER before LYTTON (Arms of Lytton [and Bulwer quarterly]), of Knebworth Place, co. Hertf., and Wood Dalling and Heydon, co. Norf. [25 Nov. 1811], Vol. XXVI, fol. 371.

„   before LYTTON, Bart., of co. Hertf. and Norf. [10 Feb. 1844], Vol. XLVII, fol. 61.

BULWER, Sir Henry Earle [K.C.B. 1848], G.C.B. [1851]. Supporters, Lord DALLING and Bulwer, 1888, Vol. LXIV, fol. 253.

„   Lieut.-Col. J. R., Q.C., of 2, Temple Gardens, London, 1890,* Vol. LXV, fol. 244.

BUNBURY after RICHARDSON, [2nd] Bart., of Ireland, [? 20 April 1822] 183 . ., Vol. XXXIX, fol. 113.

BUNBURY, Col. Adolphus Halket Versturme, of Walcot, co. Somerset, 189 . ., Vol. LXXI, fol. . . . .

BUNCOMBE-PAWLETT before THOMPSON, of Rochampton and Waverley Abbey, co. Surrey, and Goathurst, co. Somerset, 181 . ., Vol. XXVIII, fol. 149.

BUND after WILLIS [John William Bund Willis], of Wick House, Wick Episcopi, co. Worc., and Port Philip, New South Wales, 186 . ., Vol. LV, fol. 226. [Quarterly Arms, 5 Aug. 1864], Vol. LV, fol. 226 [Her. of Worc., I, p. 92.]

BUNNY, now HARTOPP, and HURLOCK, his wife, co. Leic., FREEBY and NEWARK quarterly, 17 . . ., Vol. XIX, fol. 249.

BURCH, wife of ROSHER, of Northfleet, co. Kent. Arms for self and husband, 1868, Vol. LVII, fols. 59, 60.

BURCH, Nathaniel G., of Edenwood, Sydenham Hill, co. Kent, 1896, Vol. LXIX, fol. 126.

BURCHARDT-ASHTON, F., of Pole Bostock, Gee Cross, co. Lanc., 1890,* Vol. LXV, fols. 285-311.

„   -ASHTON, A. G., of Gee Cross, Werneth, co. Lanc., 18 . . ., Vol. LXV, fol. 313.

BURD-BROOKS, S., of Heathfield House, Beckenham, co. Kent, 1889, Vol. LXV, fol. 17.

BURDEKIN, S. . . . . ., of Sydney, New South Wales, 1892, Vol. LXVI, fol. 279.

BURDER, Rev. George, of Islington, Coventry, co. Warw., 17 . . ., Vol. XVII, fol. 131.

„   John, of Buckden, co. Huntingdon, 183 . ., Vol. XLI, fol. 293.

„   John, of Buckden, co. Huntingdon. An alteration, 183 . ., Vol. XLII, fol. 260.

BURDETT-COUTTS, Miss (Spr.), of London. Arms quarterly, [14 Sept. 1837] Vol. XLII, fol. 200.

„   -COUTTS, Baroness [9 June 1871]. Supporters, 187 . ., Vol. LVIII, fol. 22.

BURDON to SANDERSON, Richard, of Lincoln's Inn, London, and co. Northumberland, 181 . ., Vol. XXVIII, fol. 427.

BURDON, late DE BUTTS, Augustus Edward, 17th Lancers, of Newcastle-upon-Tyne, co. Northumberland, 1871, Vol. LVIII, fol. 1 (see Burke, Roy. Lic. dated Mar. 1871).

BURDUS, Thomas, Paymaster late Queen's Lottery, J.P., co. Middx., 8 Aug. 1720, Vol. VII, fol. 7 (sic), and Add. MS. 14,830, fol. 95 (see Berry).

BURFOOT, Thomas, s. of Thomas, of the City of London, Merchant, and to the descendants of his father, Thomas Burfoot, of Withyham, co. Kent, deed., [30 Dec.] 1752, Vol. IX, fol. 428 (see Berry). [Misc. G. et H., 2nd S. III, p. 397].

BURGES, late SMITH, John, of Havering-atte-Bower and Eastham, co. Essex, 10 June 1790, Vol. XVII, fol. 223. (Misc. G. et H., 3rd S., III, p. 237.)

BURGES, Sir James Bland, Bart. [1795], Knight Marshal of the Royal Household, of co. Sussex, 17 . . ., Vol. XIX, fol. 207.

BURGES to LAMB, Sir James Bland, Bart., co. Sussex [Lamb and Burges quarterly], [25 Oct. 1821] Vol. XXXIII, fol. 55.

„ to LAMB, Sir James Bland, Bart., co. Sussex, 182 . ., Vol. XXXV, fol. 154.

BURGESS, Thomas, D.D. Oxf., of Winstow, co. Durham, and Odiham, Hampsh., 180 . ., Vol. XXII, fol. 159, afterwards [1825] Bp. of Salisbury.

DE BURGH, late LILL, James Godfrey, of West Drayton and Cotham, co. Middx., and Gaulstown, co. Westmeath, 18 . . ., Vol. XXI, fol. 52.

DE BURGH before CANNING, of Ireland, 3rd s. of the Marquis of Clanricarde, 186 . ., Vol. LIV, fol. 298.

BURGH (formerly COPPINGER), Easter, wife of FYSH, of Berks., 17 . . ., Vol. XIV, fol. 121.

BURGHCLERE, Baron [Herbert Coulston Gardner], co. Essex, 1895, Vol. LXVIII, fols. 309, 310.

BURGOYNE, Lieut.-Gen. Sir John Fox [K.C.B. 1838], G.C.B. [1852], London, (illeg.), 185 . ., Vol. LI, fol. 457.

BURKE after HAVILAND, Thomas William Aston, of Lincoln's Inn, London, and Butler's Court, Beaconsfield, Bucks., 1818, Vol. XXXI, fol. 48.

BURLAND after HARRIS, of Wootton-under-Edge, co. Glouc., and Stoke House, Stoke Gaylard, co. Dorset, 183 . ., Vol. XLI, fol. 77.

BURLTON before BENNETT, Anthony, Wilts., 17 . . ., Vol. XVI, fol. 379.

BURLTON, Rear-Adm. Sir George, K.C.B. [1815], Commander-in-Chief, E. Indies, 18 . . ., Vol. XXIX, fol. 210.

„ Thomas Davies (s. of Thomas), of Eaton Hill, Leominster, co. Hereford, 1898, Vol. LXX, fol. 259.

BURN, late TEASDALE, Joseph, and wife VILLA, of Lincoln's Inn Square, London, and Orton, co. Westmorland, 18 . . ., Vol. XXV, fol. 373.

BURN, Henry John, Lieut., 10th Hussars, 183 . ., Vol. XLIII, fol. 208.

BURNABY, Sir William, Knt. and Bart., of Broughton Hall, co. Oxf., 1767, Vol. XI, fol. 236.

BURNARD, C. F., of Chatworth Lodge, Compton Gifford, co. Devon, 1892, Vol. LXVI, fol. 253.

BURNARD-CHICHESTER, Rev. Arthur Chichester (s. of John Langfield Burnard), Rector of Bedlesmere, co. Kent, 1898, Vol. LXX, fol. 290.

BURNE, Thomas, of Aldstone Moor, co. Cumberland (18 Mar.), 1807, Vol. XXIV, fol. 139.

BURNE-JONES, Sir E. C. B., Bart., of co. Sussex and London, 1894,* Vol. LXVIII, fol. 14.

BURNELL-(PEGGE), late STEADE, Benjamin Broughton, of Beauchief Abbey, co. Derby, and Winkburne, co. Nottingham, 1836, Vol. XLI, fol. 254.

BURNETT to RAMSAY, Bart. [1806], of Balmain and Leys, co. Kincardine, 180 . ., Vol. XXIV, fol. 5.

BURNETT (see MAIR) (Match with MAIR), of Aberdeen, Scotland, 17 . ., Vol. XIII, fol. 26.

BURNETT, Sir Robert, Knt., of Morden Hall, co. Surrey, 180 . ., Vol. XXVI, fol. 369.

BURNEY, Richard Allen (s. of Charles), of Rimpton, co. Somerset, and Barbourne
Lodge, co. Worc. (Match), 180 . ., Vol. XXIV, fol. 253.
„ Col. Henry Edward, of Wavendon Tower, Bucks., s. of Henry, Rector of
Wavendon, 189 . ., Vol. LXXI, fol. . . . .
„ . . . ., of Brunswick Square, London, 182 . ., Vol. XXXIV, fol. 16.
BURNS before LINDOW [1871], Hazell Holme, Ingmell and Cleator, co. Cumberland,
18 . . ., Vol. LVII, fol. 324.
BURNS-HARTOPP, Capt. James, of Scraptoft Hall, nr. Leicester, s. of John William
Burns, of Kilmahew, co. Dumbarton, 1898, Vol. LXX, fol. 231.
BURNYEAT, William, of Millgrove, Moresby, co. Cumberland, 1882, Vol. LXII,
fol. 8. (Berry's Suppl.)
BURR, Lieut.-Gen. Daniel, of Holme Lacy, co. Hereford, and Ramsay, co. Essex,
13 June 1822, Vol. XXXIII, fol. 215 (see Misc. G. et H., New S., III, p. 156).
BURR to HIGFORD, of Aldermaston Court, Berks., 186 . ., Vol. LIV, fol. 1.
BURRA, ..., of Carshalton, co. Surrey, 184 . ., Vol. XLVII, fol. 416.
BURRARD (now NEALE), Bart. [3 April 1769], of Walhampton, Hampsh., and
Shaw House, Melksham, and Cosham, Wilts., 17 . ., Vol. XIX, fol. 29.
BURRARD, Lieut.-General [Sir Harry], of Lymington, Hampsh. [cr. a Baronet
12 Nov. 1807], 180 . ., Vol. XXIV, fol. 327.
„ Rev. George, brother of Sir H. NEALE, Bart., of Hampsh, Chaplain to the
King and the Prince Regent, Vicar of Yarmouth, I. of W., 31 Oct. 1815,
Vol. XXIX, fol. 144.
BURRELL [Sir Peter, Bart.], Baron GWYDYR [1796], of co. Kent and Suff. Crest
and Supporters, 17 . . ., Vol. XIX, fol. 307.
BURRELL to DRUMMOND, [Peter Robert, the 1st] s. of Baron GWYDIR. Quarterly
Arms, [6 Nov. 1807], Vol. XXIV, fol. 310.
BURRELL-DRUMMOND [Peter Robert] to DRUMMOND-WILLOUGHBY, 2nd Baron
GWYDYR, [26 June 1829], Vol. XXXVII, fol. 356.
BURRIDGE, Robert, Merchant, of Tiverton, co. Devon, 8 Mar. 1700, Vol. V,
fol. 42 ; Add. MS. 14,831, fol. 65 (see Berry).
„ William (s. of William), of Portsmouth, Hampsh., and Chard, co. Somerset,
17 . . ., Vol. XXI, fol. 135.
BURROUGHS, late SALUSBURY, Lynch, M.A., Vicar of Offley, co. Hertf. (died
s.p.m.s., 1837), 1804, Vol. XXIII, fol. 30.
BURROUGHS, Sir William, Bart., M.P., of London, Adv.-Gen. of Bengal, 180 . .,
Vol. XXIII, fol. 83.
BURROWS, Sir Cordy, Knt., Highlands, Keymer, and Brighton, co. Sussex, 187 . .,
Vol. LVIII, fol. 208.
„ Sir George, Bart., M.D., of Sussex, [19 Mar. 1874], Vol. LVIII, fol. 302.
„ (Henry William), B.D., Preb. of St. Paul's ; of Long Crendon, Bucks. ; and
Sydenham, co. Oxf., ? s. of Lieut.-Gen. Montagu Burrows, 1877, Vol.
LIX, fol. 310. (Berry's Suppl.)
„ Elizabeth, widow of Walter, of Lambeth, co. Surrey, sole surviving dau. of
Francis MARSHALL, of Lambeth (see Miscell. Marescaliana), 12 July 1785.
BURSLEM, Borough of, co. Staff., 1878, Vol. LX, fol. 183.
BURT to CHAMPNEYS, Rev. Henry William, of Kent, Vol. XIV, fol. 46, and
Thomas Charles Burt, 1778, Vol. XIV, fol. 46 (see Berry's Suppl.).
BURTHOGGE, Richard, of Bowdon, co. Devon, 1688, Vol. IV, fol. 5.
BURT, George, of Purbeck House, Swanage, co. Dorset (died 1894), 1893,
Vol. LXVI, fol. 320.
BURTON, Bartholomew and William, of Norwood, co. Nottingham, Receiver of
Excise Duties, Westminster, 1696, Vol. IV, fol. 228.
BURTON to CONYNGHAM, Baron Conyngham, Francis Pierpont, Ireland, [3 May
1781], Vol. XIV, fols. 316, 318.
BURTON after CHRISTIE, Napier, 3rd Foot Guards, of co. York, wife Mary Burton,
17 . . .,* Vol. XV, fol. 385.
BURTON-PHILLIPSON (late WRIGHT), Charles, of Rayleigh, co. Essex, and Peter-
borough, co. Northampton, 17 . . ., Vol. XVIII, fol. 115.

BURTON (Sir Richard), of Sacket Hill House, Isle of Thanet, co. Kent. (*See* CROFTS.) (Match), 182 . ., Vol. XXVI, fol. 8 (*see* 184 . ., Vol. XLV, fol. 384).

„ Sir Richard, Knt., of Sacketts Hill House, St. Peters, Isle of Thanet, co. Kent, 184 . ., Vol. XLV, fol. 384 (*see* 181 . ., Vol. XXVI, fol. 8).

BURTON, late RAYNOR, William, of The Close, co. Linc., 181 . ., Vol. XXVIII, fol. 308.

„ late CLIFTON, of Buckminster Hall and Billingborough, co. Linc., 182 . ., Vol. XXXII, fol. 313.

BURTON, ..., of Buckminster Hall and Billingborough and Boston, co. Linc., 182 . ., Vol. XXXII, fol. 315.

BURTON-PETERS, Henry, of Hotham Hall and Hollbank, co. York, 18 . . .,° Vol. XXXIII, fol. 370.

BURTON, late ROBINSON, David, of Sunderland, co. Durham ; Cherry Burton and Yarm, co. York, 1828, Vol. XXXVII, fol. 193.

BURTON (ARCHER), Lancelot, of Harlow, co. Essex, 1834, Vol. XLI, fol. 144.

BURTON to NORTH, of Thurland Castle, co. Lanc., 186 . ., Vol. LVI, fol. 266.

BURTON-TYLDESLEY, of Tyldesley, co. Lanc., 186 . ., Vol. LVII, fol. 115. (Berry's Suppl.)

BURTON, William Schoolcroft, of Foggathorpe, Bubwith, co. York ; Childrey, Berks. ; and Walton Hall, Walton, Bucks., 1877, Vol. LIX, fol. 329.

„ Baron (Michael Arthur BASS), co. Derby. Supporters (*see* BASS), 1887, Vol. LXIII, fol. 322.

„ Mrs. Catherine Sophia (Catherine Sophia KINGSFORD), wife of the Rev. Algernon Godfrey Burton, of Longnor Hall, Atcham, Shrewsbury. Burton and CLEAVELAND quarterly, 1898, Vol. LXX, fol. 192.

BURY, Sir Thomas, Knt., of Elston, nr. Exeter, co. Devon, 25 Nov. 1708, Vol. V, fol. 305 (*see* Misc. G. et H., 2nd S., V, p. 49).

BURY, late COLLINS (Brian Bury), M.A., of Linwood Grange, co. Linc., and Bath, co. Somerset, 1800, Vol. XX, fol. 426.

BURY, Borough of, co. Lanc., 1877, Vol. LIX, fol. 321.

BUSFIELD-FERRAND, William, of Harden Grange and Cottingley, Bingley, co. York ; and Morland Hall, co. Westmorland, 18 . . ., Vol. XLIV, fols. 123, 129.

BUSFIELD, Lieut.-Col. William, of Upwood Bingley, co. York, 1886, Vol. LXIII, fol. 299.

„ William, Bart., of Morland Hall, co. Westmorland, 1886, Vol. LXIII, fol. 299. Assumed the name of FERRAND by Roy. Licence, 1890.

BUSHBY to BACON, Anthony Bacon, of the Middle Temple, London, and of Wales, 17 . . ., Vol. XVIII, fol. 183.

BUSHBY, Thomas, and his sisters Margaret, Elizabeth and Martha, of Goring and Arundel, co. Sussex, 181 . ., Vol. XXXI, fol. 30.

BUSHBY after ALDRIDGE, Robert, of Rochester, co. Kent, and Cork, Ireland, 1820, Vol. XXXII, fol. 193.

BUSHBY, Henry Jeffreys, of the Inner Temple, London, and Kirkmichael and Lamphits, co. Dumfries, Scotland, 1861, Vol. LIV, fol. 208.

BUSHBY to DURGATE or DUSGATE, Richard Dusgate or Durgate, of Halkin Street, London, 18 . . ., Vol. LX, fol. 54.

BUSHELL, John and Joseph, of Ormskirk, co. Lanc., 181 . ., Vol. XXVI, fol. 394.

BUSHMAN, Joseph, of London (s. of James of Stratford, co. Essex, decd.), 178$\frac{3}{4}$, Vol. XV, fol. 373. (13 Nov., *see* Burke and Berry.)

BUSSELL to PETTIWARD, of Great Finborough Hall, co. Suff., 185 . ., Vol. LI, fol. 416.

BUTCHER, Robert, s. of Samuel, of Ravenden (Sheriff), co. Bedf., and Ickleford, co. Hertf., Dec. 1769, Vol. XI, fol. 374.

BUTCHER to PEMBERTON, Edward R., of Cardington, co. Bedf., Patron and Rector of Milton, ? co. Nottingham, Vol. XLVI, fol. 141.

BUTLER (late DIGHT), John Butler, of Yeovil, co. Somerset, and Nova Scotia, 17 . . ., Vol. XVIII, fol. 199.

BUTLER before DANVERS, of London, son of Earl of LONDESBOROUGH, 17 . . ., Vol. XIX, fols. 373, 375.

BUTLER, late FOWLER, Richard, of Pendeford Hall and Barton-under-Needwood, co. Staff., 1824, Vol. XXXIV, fol. 275.

BUTLER-CLARKE before SOUTHWELL-WANDESFORD, of Iniscough (?), co. Limerick, Ireland, 1830, Vol. XXXVIII, fol. 111.

BUTLER before CLARKE, Hon. Charles Harward, of Ireland, 1820, Vol. XXXII, fol. 181.

BUTLER-BOWDON, of Pleasington Hall, co. Lanc., 184 . ., Vol. XLV, fol. 53.

BUTLER, of St. John's, Worc., and Ceylon, 184 . ., Vol. XLVII, fol. 146.

„ Philip, of Ewelme, co. Oxf., and Yattalunga, Adelaide, 18 . . ., Vol. LIII, fol. 35.

„ of Warminghurst Park, co. Sussex (see CLOUGH), 18 . . ., Vol. LX, fol. 328.

„ Henry, of Elmore, Chipstead, co. Surrey, 1889,* Vol. LXV, fol. 162.

BUTLER (RAWSON dropped), Hon. H. E., of Nydd Hall, co. York (s. and h. of Viset. MOUNTGARRET), 1891, Vol. LXVI, fol. 137.

BUTLER, William, of Clifton Grove, Bristol, 1898, Vol. LXX, fol. 92.

„ James Evan, M.A., Bar.-at-Law, of the Inner Temple (s. of Samuel), 189 . ., Vol. LXXI, fol. . . . .

BUTT, now EVERETT (reputed son, a minor), of Heytesbeere, Wilts., 181 . ., Vol. XXVI, fol. 205.

BUTT, George Medd, of the Inner Temple, 184 . ., Vol. XLV, fol. 91.

„ William, P. C., B.A., of Trin. Coll., Oxf. ; Purton, Wilts. ; and Arle, co. Glouc., 184 . ., Vol. XLVII, fol. 371.

BUTTER to WARRE, Capt., of Embrook, Wokingham, Berks. Match, 181 . ., Vol. XXVII, fol. 401.

BUTTERFIELD, Elizabeth and Jane, of Clapham, co. Surrey, 1754, Vol. IX, fol. 503.

BUTTERWORTH, Joseph, M.P., of Coventry, co. Warw., 181 . ., Vol. XXIX, fol. 194.

„ Maj.-Gen. William John, C.B., Gov. of Prince of W. Island, 185 . ., Vol. LI, fol. 362.

BUTTERWORTH to FREMAN, of Stifford and East Horndon, co. Essex, 182 . ., Vol. XXXVIII, fol. 353.

BUTTON, John, of Grays Thorock, and Zachariah, of Mucking, co. Essex, sons of Zachariah Button, of Mucking, decd., by Anne, dau. of Thomas JOHNSON, of Mucking, gent., 14 Dec. 1768 or 1769, Vol. XI, fol. 342 (see Berry).

BUXTON, Sir Thomas Fowell, Bart., of co. Essex. Supporters, [1840] Vol. XLIV, fol. 399 ; [30 July 1840] Vol. XLIV, fol. 313.

BYAS, Ann and Thomas, of St. Botolph, Bishopsgate, and Spitalfields, London, 17 . . ., Vol. IX, fol. 486.

BYASS, Robert Nicholas, of Daylesford House, co. Worc., 1875, Vol. LIX, fol. 78.

BYATT, Richard, of Bury St. Edmunds and Bergholt, co. Suff. (s. of Rev. William), 10 or 19 Sept. 1730, Vol. VIII, fol. 97ᵇ (see Burke).

BYFIELD before HIGDEN, George, of Bridge Road, St. Mary, Lambeth ; FASSETT, widow of HIGDON, wife of BYFIELD, 181 . ., Vol. XXX, fol. 11.

BYNG, ..., of Wrotham, co. Kent, 16 . . ., Vol. I, fol. 112.

„ [Adm. George], Viscount TORRINGTON [and Baron Byng, 1721]. Supporters, 172 . ., Vol. VII, fol. 162.

„ Major-Gen. Sir John, K.C.B. [2 Jan. 1815]. Augmentation, 181 . ., Vol. XXIX, fol 124.

„ A. M. Cranmer, of Quendon Hall, co. Essex, 1882, Vol. LXI, fol. 323.

BYRCH, William Dejoras, late Fellow S. S. Coll., Camb., and of France (s. of BIRCH), 11 Aug. 1758, Vol. X, fol. 161 (see Berry).

BYRNE after LEICESTER, ..., of co. Chester and Ireland, Baron DE TABLEY [1826, extinct 1895], 182 . ., Vol. XXXVI, fol. 57.

Byrne, Sir Edmund Widdrington (s. of Edmund), of 33, Lancaster Gate, London, and a Judge of the High Court, 1898, Vol. LXX, fol. 133.

Byrom, late Fox, Edward, of Scarborough, co. York, 2nd s. of Edward Vigor Fox. R. Lic., 29 Dec. 1870, Vol. LVII, fol. 326 (see Burke).

Byron [George Gordon, Baron (the Poet), and Anne Isabella, Baroness Byron, his wife, only child of Sir Ralph Noel (heretofore Sir Ralph Milbanke, Bart.). Arms and Crest of Noel to Baron Byron and the same Arms to the Baroness, 1 Mar. 1822 (Cat. Her. Exhibition, p. 75; Crisp, Fragm. Geneal., II, p. 32)].

Byron, Thomas (s. of Edmund Wells), of Hanover Square and Soho, London, and co. Somerset, 17 . . ., Vol. XVI, fol. 269.

Bythesea, Samuel William, of Staples Hill, Freshford, co. Somerset, and Wick House, Trowbridge, and Chapmans Lade, Wilts., 183 . ., Vol. XL, fol. 243.

C

Cable, Ernest (s. of George), of Calcutta, 189 . ., Vol. LXXI, fol . . . .

Cadell, Thomas, Alderm. of London, and of Bristol, co. Glouc., 180 . . ., Vol. XXI, fol. 319.

Cadman, Rev. William Snape, M.A., Vicar of Boxley, co. Kent, s. of William, Canon of Canterbury, 189 . . ., Vol. LXXI, fol. . . . .

Cadogan, William, Baron [1718], of co. Suff. Supporters, 17 . . ., Vol. VI, fol. 343.

  ,, George, created Baron Oakley [1831]. Supporters, 18 . . ., Vol. XXXVIII, fol. 279.

Cafe, Maj.-Gen. William Martin, V.C., of Sidmouth, co. Devon, 1883,* Vol. LXII, fol. 157.

Cain, William J., of Woodbourne Square, Douglas, Isle of Man, 1897, Vol. LXIX, fol. 203.

Cairns, Baron [1867, Earl Cairns 1878], 1878, Vol. LX, fol. 207.

Calcott after Berkeley, George, of Caynham, Shropsh., and East Writtle, co. Essex, 181 . ., Vol. XXXVI, fol. 153.

Calcraft, Granby Thomas, Richard and Catherine, of Ingress, co. Kent, natural children, 8 Dec. 1770, Vol. XII, fol. 35 (see Berry).

Calcraft, late Lucas, John Charles, of Ingress, co. Kent, 17 . . ., Vol. XVI, fol. 177.

  ,, late Lucas, John Charles, of Ancaster, co. Linc., 1792, Vol. XVIII, fol. 39.

[Calcutta, City of, India, two patents, one for Supporters, 26 Dec. 1896. (Geneal. Mag., IV, p. 233).]

Caldecot, late Jones (Caldecot, wife of), William Lloyd, of Holton-cum-Beckering, co. Linc., 181 . ., Vol. XXVI, fol. 211.

  ,, late Reid, ..., M.D., of co. Linc., 181 . ., Vol. XXVI, fol. 211.

Calder, Rear-Adm., Knt. and Bart., of Southwick, Hampsh., and Parkhouse, co. Kent. Crest, 17 . . ., Vol. XX, fol. 354.

Caldwell, Adm. Sir Benjamin, G.C.B. [20 May 1820], of Ireland. Arms, 180 . ., Vol. XXXII, fol. 119. Supporters, 182 . ., Vol. XXXVII, fol. 45.

  ,, Sir Alexander, G.C.B. [1838], of co. Renfrew, Scotland. Arms, 21 May 1839, Vol. XLIV, fol. 8. Supporters, Vol. XLIV, fol. 15.

  ,, Maj.-Gen. Sir James [Lillyman], K.C., K.C.B. [1837]. 183 . ... Vol. XLII, fol. 233. [G.C.B. 1848]. Supporters, 184 . ., Vol. XLIX, fol. 59.

  ,, ..., of Linley Wood and Newcastle-under-Lyme, co. Staff., 183 . ., Vol. XLIV, fol. 260.

Call, C. W., of Nether Walstead, Lindfield, co. Sussex, 1891,* Vol. LXVI, fol. 61.

Calland, John Forbes, of Glyncollen, co. Glamorgan, Wales, 185 . ., Vol. LI, fol. 55.

CALLAND to FORBES-BENTLEY, George (a minor), by John his father? 185 . .,
    Vol. LI. fol. 57.

CALLANDER, Col. John (s. of Alexander), of Westerton, co. Stirling, and London,
    17 . . ., Vol. XX, fol. 193.

CALLCOTT to EVANS, George, of Maesinela, Llaubeblig, co. Carnarvon, Wales,
    183 . ., Vol. XL, fol. 268.

CALMADY, late EVERITT, Charles Holmes, of Combeshead, co. Cornw., 17 . . .,
    Vol. XVI, fol. 325.

CALMADY-HAMLYN, Mary Sylvia (a minor), grand-dau. of Sir Joseph W. PEASE,
    Bart. Arms for Calmady and Hamlyn, 1898, Vol. LXX, fol. 122.

CALROW, ..., of Wilton Lodge, Preston, co. Lanc., 182 . ., Vol. XXXIV,
    fol. 290.

CALTHORPE, Sir Henry, K.B. [28 May 1744], of Elvetham, Hampsh., 17 . . .,
    Vol. IX, fol. 125.

CALTHORPE after GOUGH, Bart. [1728], of Hampsh., 17 . . ., Vol. XVI, fol. 406.

CALTHORPE, Baron [1796], of Hampsh. Supporters, 179 . ., Vol. XIX,
    fol. 346.

CALTHORPE to GOUGH, late GOUGH-CALTHORPE, of Hampsh. and co. Warw.,
    184 . ., Vol. XLVII, fol. 408.

CALTHROP to COLLINGWOOD, Robert, of Irton and co. Cumberland, and Dissington
    Hall, co. Northumberland, [1868] Vol. LVI, fol. 348.

CALTHROP after HOLLWAY, Henry C., of Stanhoe, co. Norf., 1878, Vol. LX,
    fol. 153. (Berry's Suppl.)

CALVERLEY to BLACKET, Elizabeth, &c. (Sir Walter), of co. York, 17 . . ., Vol.
    VIII, fol. 71ᵇ.

  „ to BLAYDS, John, of Leeds and Oulton, co. York, 180 . ., Vol. XXIV,
    fol. 174.

CALVERLEY-RUDSTON, Trevor W., of Hoyton. co. York, 1887, Vol. LXIII,
    fol. 352.

CALVER(T), John, of St. George's, Colegate, Norwich, co. Norf., 1732, Vol. VIII,
    fol. 152.

CALVERT to BOOTH, Thomas, of Warleby, co. York, 17 . . ., Vol. XV, fol. 129.

CALVERT, Lieut.-Gen. Sir Harry, G.C.B. [2 Jan. 1815], of Albury Hall, co.
    Hertf., 1815, Vol. XXIX, fol. 356. Supporters, fol. 360.

CALVERT, wife of WRIGHT, now VERNEY, of Hall Place, co. Kent, 181 . ., Vol.
    XXVI, fol. 165.

CALVERT to VERNEY, Bart., of Bucks. and co. Hertf., 182 . ., Vol. XXXVI,
    fol. 184.

CALVERT, late JACKSON, Thomas, of Preston, co. Lanc. (B.D. St. John's Coll.,
    Camb.), 181 . ., Vol. XXX, fols. 383-385.

CALVERT after ANSTEY, Arthur, of Lincoln's Inn, London, and Bath, co. Somerset,
    181 . ., Vol. XXXI, fol. 382.

[CAMBERWELL, Borough of, London. 1901 ? (Geneal. Mag., V, p. 251.)]

CAMBRIDGE after PICKARD, M.A., of Warmwell, co. Dorset, and Whitminster
    House, Wheatenhurst, co. Glouc., 184 . ., Vol. XLIX, fol. 45.

CAMDEN, Baron [1765], (PRATT), of co. Sussex, and Wales, 17 . . ., Vol. XI,
    fol. 97.

  „ Earl [1786]. Crest of JEFFREYS, 179 . ., Vol. XX, fol. 361.

CAMELFORD, Lord [Baron of Boconnoe, co. Cornw., 5 Jan. 1784] (Thomas
    PITT). Supporters, 17 . . ., Vol. XV, fol. 259.

CAMERON, Col. and Lieut.-Col., 92nd Highlders., Scotland ? Crest of Augmenta-
    tion, 20 May 1815, Vol. XXIX, fol. 393.

  „ Major-Gen. Sir Alexander, K.C.B. [19 July, 1838], of Scotland, Dep.-Gov. of
    St. Mawes [co. Cornw.], 184 . ., Vol. XLV, fol. 46.

CAMERON before HAMPDEN, of Hampden, Bucks., and Lochiel, co. Inverness,
    186 . ., Vol. LVI, fol. 142.

CAMM to THORNHILL, Christopher, of Thornhill, co. Durham, and Antigua, 180 . .,
    Vol. XXII, fol. 156.

CAMMELL, Charles, of Norton Hall and Brookfield Manor, co. Derby : Ditcham Park, Buriton, Hampsh.; Harting, co. Sussex ; and Hall, co. York, 1877, Vol. LX, fol. 66. (Burke's Suppl.)

CAMMEYER, Charles, of Leytonstone, co. Essex, 181 . ., Vol. XXVII, fol. 296.

CAMMEYER before DOORMAN, Charles, of Leytonstone, co. Essex. Crest for Doorman, 181 . ., Vol. XXVII, fols. 296, 298.

CAMP, Laurence, of London, 23 July 1804. (Berry.)

CAMPBELL, Marchioness GREY. Supporters, 174 . ., Vol. IX, fol. 480.
,, Sir John, K.B. [1725], Viscount GLENORCHY, 174 . ., Vol. IX, fol. 480.
,, ([Alexander] Lord POLWARTH), cr. Baron HUME [14 May 1776]. Supporters, 177 . ., Vol. XIII, fol. 273.
,, [Maj.-Gen.] Sir Archibald, K.B. [30 Sept. 1785], Gov. of Fort St. George, Madras. Supporters, 178 . ., Vol. XVI, fol. 101.
,, ..., of co. York and Lanc. (Match with LESLIE.) Augmentation, 179 . ., Vol. XX, fols. 214. 217.

CAMPBELL, late MACKINNON, ... of Greenock, co. Renfrew : Kilmodan and Ormaig, co. Argyll, Scotland ; and Island of Tobago, 180 . ., Vol. XXIII, fol. 430.

CAMPBELL, Col. [John] Knt. [1815], of Scotland. Augmentation (Russian Order), 181 . .. Vol. XXIX, fol. 372.
,, Col., ..., C.B., of Scotland. Augmentation (Portuguese Order), 181 . . ., Vol. XXIX, fol. 438.

CAMPBELL, late HAMILTON, Catherine Eleanor, widow of Captain Henry Hamilton, of Asknish, co. Argyll, Scotland (died s.p.), 181 . . .., Vol. XXXI, fol. 162.
,, late JEKYLL, Sarah Charlotte, widow of Capt. Nathaniel Jekyll, of Asknish, co. Argyll, Scotland (died s.p.), 183 . .. Vol. XLIII, fol. 110.

CAMPBELL, Adm. Sir George, G.C.B. [1820], of Scotland. Supporters, 182 . .. Vol. XXXII, fol. 131.

CAMPBELL after COCKBURN. Bart., of Scotland. 182 . ., Vol. XXXV, fol. 274.

CAMPBELL, Sir Archibald, Bart., G.C.B. [1826]. Arms, 182 . ., Vol. XXXVIII, fol. 361. Supporters, 183 . ., Vol. XXXIX, fol. 255.
,, Baron (John) [1841], Lord High Chancellor of Ireland, of co. Fife, 184 . .. Vol. XLV, fol. 266. Supporters, 184 . ., Vol. XLV, fol. 268.

CAMPBELL to HARTLEY, Leonard, of Middleton Lodge, co. York, 184 . ., Vol. XLV, fol. 337.

CAMPBELL (M.A., Camb.), of Tivoli Lawn, Cheltenham, co. Glouc., and Guernsey, 184 . ., Vol. XLVII, fol. 8.

CAMPBELL to CAMPBELL-WYNDHAM, Francis, of The College, New Sarum, Wilts., 1844, Vol. XLVII, fol. 95.
,, to CAMPBELL-BAYARD, natural s. of Bayard, of Richmond, co. Surrey, 186 . .. Vol. LIV, fol. 34

CAMPION to COATES, John, of The Heights, Eskdaleside, co. York, 178 . .. Vol. XVII, fol. 238.

CAMPION after COVENTRY, John William, of Oundle, co. Northampton, 183 . ., Vol. XLI, fol. 160.

CAMPION, formerly EASOM, Frank, of The Mount, St. Alkmund, co. Derby, 186 . ., Vol. LVI, fol. 230.

CAMPLEASHON, Hannah, of co. York, wife of Edward MOSLEY, of Newcastle-upon-Tyne, co. Northumberland, 176 . .. Vol. XI, fol. 11.

CAMPLIN to BERNARD, George, of co. Somerset, 181 . ., Vol. XXVI, fol. 363.

[CANADA, Provinces of, 22 May 1867. (Hulme, Flags of the World, p. 81.)]

CANDLER to BROWN, Edward, of co. Somerset, 180 . ., Vol. XXII, fol. 288.
,, (-BROWN, heretofore Candler, of co. Somerset) (see HELSHAM-BROWN), 182 . .. Vol. XXXVI, fol. 63.
,, to CANDLER-BROWNE, of co. Somerset, and Ageniure. Callan, co. Kilkenny, 185 . ., Vol. LII, fol. 238.
,, to SEMPILL, Maria Janet, Baroness Sempill, of Scotland [and her husband, Edward Candler, Roy. Lic.], 1853, Vol. L, fol. 392.

CANKRIEN, John Christopher, of Kirk Ella, Kupon, Hull, co. York, 24 Feb. 1809, Vol. XXV, fol. 136 (*see* Berry's Suppl.).

CANN-LIPPINCOTT (nat. s. of Cann-Lippincott), of Stoke Park, Westbury-on-Taym, co. Glouc., 1831, Vol. XXXVIII, fol. 248.

CANN after SKOULDING, John Frederick, of Gilston, co. Hereford (? Gilston), Wymoudham, 1866, Vol. LVI, fol. 300. 29 Nov. (*see* Burke).

CANNING, ..., of Garvagh, co. Londonderry, Ireland, 18 . . ., Vol. XXI, fol. 43.

„   [Sir Stratford. Supporters, 24 Jan. 1833. (Crisp, Fragm. Geneal., I, p. 64)].

CANNING after GORDON, of Home Lodge, Woodstock, co. Oxf. ; Foxcote, co. Warw. ; and Hartpury, co. Glouc., 184 . ., Vol. XLIX, fol. 246.

CANTERBURY, Archbp. of (GRINDALL), of co. Kent, 181 . ., Vol. XXX, fol. 284.

CANTIS, Valentine, of Canterbury, co. Kent, 4 Nov. 1769, Vol. XI, fol. 366 (*see* Berry).

CANTRELL-HUBERSTEY, A., of Felley Abbey, co. Nottingham, 1893, Vol. LXVII, fol. 237.

„   -HUBERSTEY, Lient.-Col. A., of Felley Abbey, co. Nottingham, 1894, Vol. LXVIII, fols. 16, 126.

[CAPE OF GOOD HOPE (Cape Colony), 29 May 1876. (Geneal. Mag., IV, p. 185.)]

[CAPE TOWN, City of, 29 Dec. 1899. (Geneal. Mag., IV, p. 156.)]

CAPPELL, Rev. Louis, of London, 1883, Vol. LXII, fol. 69. (Berry's Suppl.)

CAPPER, Richard, of Lincoln's Inn, London, 1727, Vol. VIII, fol. 2.

„   Peter, of Birmingham and Rugeley, co. Staff., 176 . ., Vol. XI, fol. 53 (*see* Berry).

„   James, M.A., Vicar of Wilmington and Lullington Ashurst, co. Kent, and Rugeley, co. Staff. Match with SMALLWOOD, 9 July 1804, Vol. XXIII, fol. 65 (*see* Berry).

CAPRON, George, of Oundle, co. Northampton, and London, 182 . ., Vol. XXXVII, fol. 206.

CAPRON to HOLLIST, of Lodsworth, co. Surrey, 183 . ., Vol. XXXIX, fol. 376.

CARBONNEL, William, of London and Normandy. Crest [21 Mar.], 169¾. Match, Vol. IV, fols. 154 and 156. (*See* DE CARDONNEL.) [Guillim, p. 380.]

CARBUTT, Sir E. H., Bart., of Manhurst, co. Surrey, and London, 1892,* Vol. LXVII, fol. 45.

CARD, Andrew [Bar.-at-Law], of Gray's Inn, London, [31 May 1695] Vol. IV, fol. 194. [Guillim, p. 184.]

CARDALL, Rev. William, M.A., of Peter House, co. Camb., 1884, Vol. LXII, fol. 214.

CARDEN, Sir Robert Walter, Bart., of Berks., 1887,* Vol. LXIV, fol. 30.

CARDEW, Cornelius, D.D., Vicar of Ewny Lalant, co. Cornw., 178 . ., Vol. XVI, fol. 211.

CARDIFF, Baron [20 May 1776] (John STUART, called Lord MOUNT STUART [1761]), of Scotland and Wales. Supporters, 177 . ., Vol. XIII, fol. 221.

CARDONNEL, Mansfeldt, of Chirton, co. Northumberland, 8 June 1773, Vol. XII, fol. 255.

CARDOZO, Samuel Nunez, of Hackney, co. Middx., 182 . ., Vol. XXXVII, fol. 222.

CARDOZO, now BARROW, Samuel Nunez, of Hackney, co. Middx., 182 . ., Vol. XXXVII, fol. 255.

CARDWELL, Edward, D.D., of Blackburn, co. Lanc., and Principal of St. Alban Hall, Oxf., 185 . ., Vol. LII, fol. 34.

„   Viscount. Supporters, 1874, Vol. LIX, fol. 40.

CAREW, George Henry (late WARRINGTON), Carew, wife of, of Pontrepant, Shropsh. ; Anthony, co. Cornw. ; Crowcombe Court and Camaton, co. Somerset ; and Carew Castle, co. Pembroke. Arms to wife and issues, 1810, Vol. XXVI, fol. 311. [1811, *see* Burke.]

CAREW after HALLOWELL, Vice-Adm. Sir Benjamin, K.C.B. [1815], of co. Surrey. [G.C.B. 6 June 1831.] Supporters, 182 . ., Vol. XXXVII [XXXVIII ?], fol. 176.

CAREW after HALLOWELL, Charles (minor), s. of Charles, of Beddington, co. Surrey, and Orpington Park, co. Kent, 184 . ., Vol. XLIX, fol. 160.
CAREW, Capt. Charles, R.N., of Beddington, co. Surrey, 183 . ., Vol. XL, fol. 305.
 Supporters by Roy. Lic., 183 . ., Vol. XL, fol. 330.
CAREY, William, Bp. of Exeter, co. Devon, 182 . ., Vol. XXXII, fols. 174, 175.
 „ (Arthur), of De Vere Gardens, London, 1892, Vol. LXVI, fol. 277.
CARFRAE, James Alston, C.E., of Wimbledon Common, co. Surrey, 1869. Lyon Off. Reg. [No. 91].
CARILL-WORSLEY, late LEES, John, of Platt, of Manchester, co. Lanc., 1775, Vol. XIII, fol. 61.
CARILL-WORSLEY after TINDALL, ..., B.A., of Manchester, co. Lanc., 18 . . ., Vol. LX, fol. 161.
CARLETON, Baron [19 Oct. 1714] (Boyle). Supporters, 17 . . ., Vol. VI, fol. 196.
 „ Gen. Sir Guy, K.B. [1776]. Supporters, 177 . ., Vol. XIV, fol. 74.
 „ Baron [1786], Dorchester [Gen. Sir Guy Carleton], K.B. Supporters, 178 . ., Vol. XVI, fol. 177.
CARLETON, late METCALFE, John, of Brough and Appleby, co. Westmorland, 178 . ., Vol. XVII, fol. 410.
 „ late GROOME, Rhoda (Spr.), of Thakeham and Arundel, co. Sussex. (Match), 181 . ., Vol. XXVII, fol. 310.
 „ Hon. Dudley MASSEY-, formerly PIGOTT (-STAINSBY-CONANT), of Greywell Hill, Hampsh., 189 . ., Vol. LXXI, fol. . . . . .
 „ [quartering, 30 April 1714, see VANBRUGH].
 „ Major-Gen. Richard Langford Leir, of Ditcheat Priory, co. Somerset, 189 . ., Vol. LXXI, fol. . . . . .
CARLINGFORD, Baron [Chichester Fortescue]. Supporters, 1874, Vol. LIX, fol. 1.
CARLISLE, Bp. of (see GOODENOUGH), of co. Cumberland, 180 . ., Vol. XXIV, fol. 375.
 „ William Thomas, of Lincoln's Inn, London, and The Elms, Ewell, co. Surrey, 18 . . ., Vol. LX, fol. 90. (Berry's Suppl.)
CARLYON, Thomas, [Rector] of St. Just, co. Cornw., [2nd but eldest surv. s. of Thomas Carlyon, of] Oregrehan, co. Cornw., [15 July 1784] Vol. XV, fol. 337. Crisp, II, pp. 114, 77. [Notes, IV, p. 103.]
 „ Fred. H. Witherden, of Germanswick, co. Cornw., 1894, Vol. LXVIII, fol. 12.
CARLYON (see BRITTON), [19 June] 1897, Vol. LXIX, fols. 195 and 289.
CARMALT, William, of Lanrigg, Brumfield, co. Cumberland, 19 May 1740, Vol. VIII, fol. 271 (see Berry).
CARMARTHEN, Marquis of, of co. York. Crest of GODOLPHIN, 178 . ., Vol. XVI, fol. 71.
CARNAC, late RIVETT, James, of Bombay, 1801, Vol. XXI, fol. 219.
CARNCROSS, Joseph Hugh, Lieut.-Col. R.A., also to brother William, 15 Nov. 1814 (see Burke).
CARNE, late NICHOLL, of Diertlands House, Nash, co. Glouc., 184 . ., Vol. XLVI, fol. 218.
CARPENTER, ..., of Launceston, co. Cornw. Match with MEDLAND, 17 . . ., Vol. VIII, fol. 106.
 „ Lieut.-Col., of Bridport and Cheselbourne, co. Dorset, 18 . . ., Vol. XLIX, fol. 242.
CARPENTER before GARNIER, John, of M'Tavy, in Tavistock, co. Devon, 186 . ., Vol. LV, fol. 242.
CARPENTER, late TALBOT (Earl of SHREWSBURY), co. Staff., 18 . . ., Vol. LVII, fol. 27.
CARR, late HOLWELL [Lady Charlotte Hay], wife of William, of Menheniot, co. Cornw., and Etal, co. Northumberland, 17 . . ., Vol. XX, fol. 257. [Lic. to quarter Carr, 20 Nov. 1798, see Misc. G. et H., New S., 11, p. 417.]

CARR, George (s. of George, of Newcastle-upon-Tyne, co. Northumberland), of
  Camberwell, co. Surrey, 18 . . ., Vol. XXI, fol. 145.
„ (see STATTER), of Newcastle-upon-Tyne, co. Northumberland, and St.
  Petersburg, 181 . ., Vol. XXVI, fol. 328.
„ John, of Askham, Richard Hall, &c., co. York, ex-Lord Mayor of York,
  180 . ., Vol. XXIII, fol. 181.
„ Thomas, D.D., Bp. of Bombay [1837], of co. York. Arms of Sec,
  permission to impale, 183 . ., Vol. XLII, fol. 10.
CARR to STANDISH, of Cocken, co. Durham. and Duxbury Hall, co. Lanc., 184 . .,
  Vol. XLV, fol. 178.
CARR, Lieut.-Col. (s. of the Bp. of Worc.), of Ealing, co. Middx., 185 . .,
  Vol. LI, fol. 259.
CARR-LLOYD (s. of the Bp. of Worc.), of Lancing, co. Sussex, 185 . ., Vol.
  LI, fol. 261.
CARR-ELLISON, Ralph, of Dunston Hill and Hebburn, co. Durham, and Hedgeley,
  co. Northumberland, 1871, Vol. LVII, fol. 320.
„ -ELLISON, J. R., of Dunston Hall, Whickham, co. Durham, and Hedgeley,
  Eglingham, co. Northumberland, 1896,* Vol. LXIX, fol. 42. (Crisp, VI,
  159.)
CARR, Walter Raleigh, of Esholt Heugh, Felton, co. Northumberland, London, and
  co. Warw., s. of Andrew Morton Carr, Bar.-at-Law, s. of Thomas William,
  of Esholt, &c., to descendants of his grandfather, 1878, Vol. LX, fol. 117.
CARR-GOMM, Francis Culling, and his wife Emily [Blanche, dau. of Andrew
  Morton Carr], of London, [9 Mar.] 1878, Vol. LX, fol. 130. [Geneal.
  Mag., IV, p. 244.]
CARR, Rev. Edward, of Holbrook Hall, and Vicar of Derby, 1896°, Vol. LXIX,
  fol. 178.
„ Rev. H. B., of Whickham, co. Durham, 1891,* Vol. LXVI, fol. 225.
„ Rev. Edmund Donald, of Woolstaston, Shropsh., 1896, Vol. LXIX, fol. 152.
CARRE after RIDDELL, Capt., R.N., Cavers and Carniston, co. Roxburgh, 182 . .,
  Vol. XXXVII, fol. 308.
CARRE, ..., Jurat of Guernsey, 183 . ., Vol. XLII, fol. 308.
CARRINGTON, Thomas, of Field Head, Sheffield, co. York, and Holywell House,
  Chesterfield, co. Derby, 187 . ., Vol. LVIII, fol. 323. (Berry's Suppl.)
„ J. B., of Regent Street and Netherall Gardens, London, 1895, Vol.
  LXVIII, fol. 286.
CARROLL, Edward, of Kingston, Island of Jamaica, 181 . ., Vol. XXVI, fol. 163.
CARSAN to PORTER, of South Carolina, N.A., and London. (Match with EWART),
  180 . ., Vol. XXIV, fol. 349.
CARSON, William Somerville, of Seacombe, Cheshire, 1880,° Vol. LXI, fol. 69.
CART, James, of St. Sepulchre's, London ; Dunstable, co. Bedf. ; and Stoke
  Goulding, co. Leic., 26 May 1729, Vol. VIII, fol. 51^b.
„ (see WALKER ?), of Trinity Coll., Camb., M.D. (Match with WALKER),
  177 . ., Vol. XII, fol. 204.
CARTER to HOLE, ..., of Bideford and Ebberley House, Roborough, co. Devon,
  185 . ., Vol. L, fol. 225.
CARTER, late CHURCHILL, Bartholomew, of Upper Todmarton, co. Oxf., 17 . . .,
  Vol. XVII, fol. 169.
„ late LANGHAM, John, of Tevington and Northwold, co. Norf., 181 . .,
  Vol. XXVII, fol. 430.
CARTER, Henry, D.D., of Kendal, co. Westmorland, Dean of Tuam and Rector of
  Ballymore, Ireland, 182 . ., Vol. XXXIII, fol. 250.
„ George W., M.A., of Pembroke Coll., Camb., and Knottingley, co. York,
  1886°, Vol. LXIII, fol. 297.
„ Sir Gilbert T. (died 1897), 1893, Vol. LXVII, fol. 263.
„ John, of Harrogate, co. York, s. of John, 1897, Vol. LXIX, fol. 309.
„ Edward, of Birmingham, s. of Jeremiah, of London, 189 . ., Vol. LXXI,
  fol. . . . .

CARTER, John Robert, s. of John Suffolk-Sandhurst, of Seven Kings, co. Essex, 189 . ., Vol. LXXI, fol. . . . .

CARTERET, Baron, of co. Bedf. Quarterly to GRANVILLE (descendants of Grace, Viscountess Carteret and Countess Granville by George, Baron Carteret), [1 Jan. 171⅘] Vol. VI, fol. 211.

CARTERET before SILVESTER, Philip, C.B., of Yardley House, co. Essex, 2nd Bart., 182 . ., Vol. XXXIII, fol. 136.

DE CARTERET after MALLET, ..., Seigneur de St Ouen and Lieut., Isle of Jersey, 185 . ., Vol. LIII, fol. 155.

CARTIER, George Etienne (afterwards C.B.), Bart. [1868], of Montreal (died s.p. 1873), 18 . ., Vol. LVII, fol. 35. (Berry's Suppl.)

CARTLAND, John Howard, of The Priory, Kings Heath, nr. Birmingham, co. Warw., 1898, Vol. LXX, fol. 247.

CARTLEDGE, Rebecca, widow of William Cartledge, of Woodthorpe, Bashford, co. Nottingham, 186 . ., Vol. LV, fol. 192 (see Reliquary, XV, 231 ; XVI, 50).

CARTMEL, Isaac, of London Road, Carlisle, co. Cumberland, 1837, Vol. LXIV, fol. 62.

CARTMELL, James Austen, Bar.-at-Law, of 14, Onslow Gardens, London, 1889, Vol. LXV, fol. 5.

CARTWRIGHT, late HOGG, Ellis, wife of, of Preston Bagot, co. Warw., and Bank House, Astbury, co. Chester, 181 . ., Vol. XXX, fol. 305.

„ Major Edmund (E.I.C.), 1819, Vol. XXXI, fol. 264.

„ William, of South Tawton and West Teignmouth, co. Devon, 184 . ., Vol. XLV, fol. 241.

CARTWRIGHT, late COBB, Rev. Robert, B.A., of Lydd, co. Kent, and Ixworth Abbey, co. Suff., Rector of Thwaite St. Mary and Ellingham, co. Norf., 1865, Vol. LVI, fol. 107.

„ Sir Henry E., of the Middle Temple, London, and Magherafeldt, London-derry, Ireland, 1888, Vol. LXIV, fol. 142.

CARUS before WILSON, SHEPPHARD wife of, of co. Westmorland. Escutcheon of pretence, 179 . ., Vol. XVIII, fol. 359.

„ before WILSON, of Carterton Hall, co. Westmorland, 179 . ., Vol. XVIII, fol. 195.

CARVER, John, of Morthen Hall, co. York, 17 . . ., Vol. IX, fol. 78.

„ Mary, d. and h. of John (died s.p.), of Morthen Hall, co. York. Quarterly, DUDLEY and WARD (2nd wife of John DUDLEY), 17 . . ., Vol. XVII, fol. 81.

CARVER, now MIDDLETON, Marmaduke, of Leam, Eyam, co. Derby, and Morthen, co. York, 182 . ., Vol. XXXIII, fol. 220.

CARVER (quartered by MIDDLETON, now ATHORPE), John, of Eyam, co. Derby, and Morthen, co. York, 182 . ., Vol. XXXIII, fol. 220.

CARY, John, of Bristol, and brother Richard and kinsman John, of Torre Abbey, co. Devon, 1699, Vol. IV, fol. 326.

CASBERD before BOTELER, William John, of Taplow, Bucks. ; Landough Castle and Penmarth, Wales ; and co. Glouc., 186 . ., Vol. LVI, fol. 182.

CASBURNE, Robert, of Isleham, co. Camb., 18 Oct. 1728, Vol. VIII, fol. 14.

CASE, Jonathan, of Red Hasles, Huyton, co. Lanc., 1771, Vol. XII, fol. 78. (Berry's Suppl.)

CASE to NORWOOD, Rev. Henry, of Alfreton, co. Derby, and Ladebroke, co. Warw., 179 . ., Vol. XVIII, fol. 157.

CASE before NORWOOD, of Alfreton, co. Derby, Norf., Warw., and Suff., 179 . ., Vol. XVIII, fol. 191.

CASEY, Arthur Edwin, B.C.S., of Comerford, 189 . ., Vol. LXXI, fol. . . . . .

CASLON, widow of HANLEY, of Homerton, co. Middx., 17 . . ., Vol. XVII, fol. 65.

CASS, John and Thomas, of Hackney, co. Middx., 1699, Vol. IV, fol. 311 (Crisp, I, 114, and Notes, II, 114).

CASS, Frederick, of Winchmore Hill, co. Middx., 181 . ., Vol. XXXI, fol. 390 (Crisp, I, 114, and Notes, II, 114).
  „ Rev. F. C., of Monken Hadley, Barnet, co. Middx., 1889,* Vol. LXV, fol. 28 (Crisp, I, 114, and Notes, II, 114).
  „ Rev. Charles W., ..., of co. Middx. SUMMERS quartering, 1896, Vol. LXIX, fol. 111 (Crisp, I, 114, and Notes, II, 114).
  „ Bernard Croft, s. of Sir John, of Bradford, 189 . ., Vol. LXVIII, fol. 212.
CASSELS, Larrett Godfrey, 2nd s. of Walter, of Toronto. (Lyon Reg.)
CASTEGA, Marquis of (see SCARISBRICK), of co. Lanc., 187 . ., Vol. LVIII, fol. 264.
CASTELLO, Edward F., of Rue de Bassins, Paris, 1885,* Vol. LXIII, fol. 41.
CASTLEHOW, Rev. William, B.D., of Water Mock, co. Cumberland, 185 . ., Vol. LII, fol. 325.
CASTLEREAGH, Viscount, commonly called Sir Robert STEWART, K.G. [1814], s. of the Earl of LONDONDERRY. Supporters, 1814, Vol. XXVIII, fol. 142.
CATCHMAYD to GWINNETT, William, of co. Monmouth, 178 . ., Vol. XV, fol. 94 ; 179 . ., Vol. XVIII, fol. 232.
CATHERLOUGH, Earl of (Knight), of co. Warw. (Arms), 177 . ., Vol. XII, fol. 142.
CATHROW, James, Somerset Herald [1813], of Hoddesdon, co. Hertf., 181 . ., Vol. XXVIII, fol. 219.
CATHROW before DISNEY, James, Somerset Herald, of Pluckley, co. Kent, 182 . ., Vol. XXXII, fol. 107.
CATO, Thomas E., of Summerhill, Colchester, co. Essex, 1884, Vol. LXII, fol. 186.
CATON, ..., of Woodmancote, co. Sussex ; Binbrooke, co. Linc. ; and Thorpe Abbots, co. Norf., 183 . ., Vol. XLII, fol. 279.
CATOR, John, of Beckenham Place, co. Kent, and Bastwick, co. Norf., 181 . ., Vol. XXX, fol. 403. (Crisp, V, p. 55.)
CATOR to LENNARD, late Capt. R.A., of Wickham Court, co. Kent, 186 . ., Vol. LIV, fol. 226.
CATT to WILLETT, Henry, of Arnold House, Brighton, and Newhaven, co. Sussex, 186 . ., Vol. LV, fol. 78.
  „ to WILLETT, William, of West House, Brighton, co. Sussex, 186 . ., Vol. LV, fol. 80.
CATT, John, of Lewes and Whitehaven, co. Sussex, 186 . ., Vol. LV, fol. 196.
  „ Edmund, of York Place, Brighton, co. Sussex, 186 . ., Vol. LV, fol. 122.
CAUSTON, Mary (widow), Thomas, of Oxted, co Surrey, 26 Feb. 1699-1700, Vol. IV, fol. 333.
  „ Thomas, of co. Surrey. Inscription, Coat of Arms, 26 Feb. 1699-1700, Vol. IV, fol. 331.
CAUTLEY, Lieut.-Col. Sir Proby Thomas, K.C.B. [29 July 1854], of Roydon and Stratford St. Mary, co. Suff., and Moulsoe, Bucks, 185 . ., Vol. LI, fol. 226.
  „ Nathaniel, M.A., Bar.-at-Law., of Shelf Hall, Halifax, co. York (s. of Samuel Bottomley), 189 . ., Vol. LXXI, fol. . . . .
CAVAN, ..., of London, 183 . ., Vol. XLII, fol. 142.
CAVE after OTWAY, ..., of Stamford Hall, co. Leic., and Castle Otway, Ireland, 17 . . ., Vol. XVII, fol. 292.
  „ after BROWNE (see BROWNE), of co. Leic., 183 . ., Vol. XLIII, fol. 306.
CAVE, Belmont, of Hendon, co. Middx. ; Bodicote and Calthorpe Place, Banbury, co. Oxf., 186 . ., Vol. LV, fol. 84.
CAVE-ORME, George Alington (G. A. ROBINSON), of Emanuel Coll., Camb., late of Melbourne, Australia, Bar.-at-Law of the Middle Temple, 1893, Vol. LXVII, fols. 261, 92.
CAVENAGH-MAINWARING, W., of Whitmore Hall, co. Staff., 1893, Vol. LXVII, fol. 127.

CAVENDISH before BRADSHAW, of Dovebridge, co. Derby, 17 . ., Vol. XVII, fol. 292.

  ,, before BENTINCK, of co. Nottingham (Duke of PORTLAND, K.G.), 18 . . ., Vol. XXI, fol. 237.

CAWLEY to FLOYER, ..., of Hints, co. Staff., and Gwersyllt, co. Denbigh, 179 . ., Vol. XVIII, fol. 287.

CAWLEY, Frederick (s. of Thomas), of Brooklands, Prestwich. co. Lanc., 1897, Vol. LXIX, fol. 307.

CAWSTON, George (2nd s. of S. W.), of London, and Cawston Manor House, co. Norf., 189 . ., Vol. LXXI, fol. . . . . .

CAWTHORNE, G. J., of Stretton House, Leamington, co. Warw., 1892, Vol. LXVI, fol. 298.

CAWTHRAY, Henry, Bar.-at-Law, of Toronto, 1883,* Vol. LXII, fol. 102. (Berry's Suppl.)

CAYZER, C. W., of Plymouth, co. Devon, 1891. Vol. LXVI, fol. 178.

CAZALET, Edward (s. of Peter), of Fairlawn, co. Kent, and St. Petersburgh ; and to the descendants of his father, 1874, Vol. LIX, fol. 28. (Berry's Suppl.)

CAZENOVE, Charles (s. of Philip), of 183, Regent Street, London, 1897, Vol. LXIX, fol. 225.

CECIL, Baron, Countess of Exeter, of co. Linc., Sarah (late HOGGINS). wife of, Arms to wife and crest to Thomas Hoggins, father of the Countess, 179 . ., Vol. XVIII, fol. 304.

  ,, Mary, of co. Hertf. Arms of Cecil (differenced) to the reputed dau. of James, Earl of SALISBURY, relict of JACKSON and wife of TAYLOR, High Sheriff of Hertfordshire, 180 . ., Vol. XXV, fol. 443.

CECIL after GASCOYNE, Mary S., of co. Hertf., 184 . ., Vol. XLVI, fol. 52.

CECIL (see JOICEY), 1898, Vol. LXX, fol. 237.

CHAD, George, s. of Robert, of Lincoln's Inn, London, and Thursford, co. Norf., 17 . . .. Vol. X, fol. 153.

CHADD after SCOTT. Joseph S., of Thursford, Pinkney and Colney Hall, co. Norf., 1855, Vol. LI, fol. 388.

CHADWICK, John, of Healey Hall, co. Lanc. (Crest of MAVESYN, co. Staff.), 1 Aug. 1791, Vol. XVII, fol. 386.

  ., Hugo M[avesyn] (minor), of Healey Hall, co. Lanc. Quartering, MAVESYN, co. Staff., 181 . ., Vol. XXVI, fol. 55.

  ,, Elias, of Swinton House, co. Lanc., 183 . ., Vol. XLIII, fol. 223.

  ., Robert, of Salford and Eccles, co. Lanc., 184 . ., Vol. XLVII, fol. 301.

  ., Alfred, s. of William, of Camberwell, London, and Mark's Cross, co. Sussex, 188 . ., Vol. LXXI. fol. . . . . .

CHADWYCK-HEALEY, C. E. H., Bar.-at-Law, of Harley Street, London, 1884, Vol. LXII, fols. 309, 311.

CHAFFERS, Jeremiah, of Liverpool, co. Lanc., 184 . ., Vol. XLVI, fol. 79.

CHAFFEY, ..., of East Stoke, co. Somerset, 184 . ., Vol. XLVIII, fol. 126.

CHAFY, Rev. William, M.A., Rector of Swalecliffe and Vicar of Sturry, co. Kent, 1822, Vol. XXXIII, fol. 331.

  ., William Westwood ?, of Bowes House, Ongar, co. Essex ; Sidley and Brighton, co. Sussex ; and co. Camb., 1868, Vol. LVII, fol. 196.

CHALKE, Alfred Raymond, of Coryton Terrace, Mutley, Plymouth, 1896, Vol. LXIX, fol. 184.

CHALLIS. . . . ., of Enfield, co. Middx., and Alderman of London, 184 . ., Vol. XLVIII, fol. 81.

  ,, Lieut. in the Army, of Exmouth, co. Devon, 185 . ., Vol. LI, fol. 293.

CHALLONER after BISSE, Lieut.-Col. Thomas C., of co. Surrey, 18 . . ., Vol. XXXVIII, fol. 367. Quartering, 1832, Vol. XXXIX, fol. 6.

CHALMERS, widow of Maj.-Gen. Sir John M., K.C.B. [7 April 1815], of co. Surrey. (Augmentation), 181 . ., Vol. XXXI. fol. 199.

  ,, John Henry, of Tor Mohun House, Torquay, co. Devon, 1898, Vol. LXX, fol 278.

CHALONER, Capt. R. G. W., of Gisborough, co. York, 1888, Vol. LXIV, fol. 189.
CHAMBERLAIN, late HUGHES, Thomas Chamberlain, of Wardington, co. Oxf., 179 . ., Vol. XVIII, fol. 276.
CHAMBERLAIN, Consul General to Brazil, 182 . ., Vol. XXXVI, fol. 401.
CHAMBERLAIN to DYNELEY, Richard Dyneley, of co. York, 186 . ., Vol. LIV, fol. 180.
CHAMBERLAIN, R. E. HUGHES-, of Wardington, co. Oxf., 1892, Vol. LXVII, fol. 14.
CHAMBERLAYNE to BROCKET, ..., of the Middle Temple, and of Rye, co. Sussex, 183 . ., Vol. XL, fol. 206.
CHAMBERS, Thomas (London), 20 July 1723, Vol. VII, fol. 203 (see Berry).
　„　Edward Hanover, of co. Cornw. and Jamaica, 1771, Vol. XII, fol. 106. (Berry.)
CHAMBERS, late ROGERMAN, John, of Kingston and St. Elizabeth, Jamaica, 179 . ., Vol. XVIII, fol. 437.
CHAMBERS, ..., of Wardenlaw, co. Durham ; Beech Hill, co. Essex ; Rotherham, co. York ; and Felton Overgrass, Newcastle-on-Tyne, co. Northumberland, 183 . ., Vol. XL, fol. 294.
CHAMBERS after HAMMOND, Robert S. B., of Great Marlow, Bucks., 18 . ., Vol. LIII, fol. 235.
CHAMBERS to HODGETTS, of Instow, co. Devon, and Hagley, co. Worc., 186 . ., Vol. LVI, fol. 248.
CHAMBERS, John, of The Hurst, Tibshelf, co. Derby, 187 . ., Vol. LVII, fol. 141.
　„　Sir George Henry, of Berkeley Square, Bristol, co. Glouc., and Mincing Lane, London, 1883, Vol. LXII, fol. 112. (Berry's Suppl.)
　„　Robert J., of Keppel Street, London (Burke) [no date in Burke].
　„　[Thomas, of London and Derby, 20 July 1723 (Her. and Geneal., VII, p. 488).]
CHAMBRES, late JONES, Rev. Edward, M.A., of Llysmeirchion, Plas Chambres, &c., co. Denbigh, Wales, 181 . ., Vol. XXVII, fol. 405.
CHAMIER (formerly DES CHAMPS), Henry, s. of John, of Richmond, co. Surrey, and Essex, Chief Sec. Governm^t of Madras, 1815, Vol. L, fol. 6.
CHAMPANTE after JOGGETT, ..., of Taunton, co. Somerset, 182 . ., Vol. XXXII, fol. 177.
CHAMPERNOWNE, late HARRINGTON, Arthur, of Powderham, co. Devon, 20 Sept. 1774, Vol. XIII, fol. 9.
CHAMPION, Peter, of St. Columb Major, co. Cornw., 14 Nov. 1720, Vol. VII, fol. 37.
CHAMPNESS, ..., of Fulham, co. Middx., 183 . ., Vol. XL, fol. 41.
CHAMPNEYS, late BURT, Rev. Henry William, of co. Kent, 17 . . ., Vol. XIV, fol. 46 (see Burke's Commoners, III, p. 555).
CHANCE, ..., of Birmingham, J.P., of co. Warw., 184 . ., Vol. XLVII, fol. 359 (Crisp, III, p. 61).
CHANDLER, late GASCOYNE, Rev. George, LL.D., of St. Maries, co. Kent, 179 . ., Vol. XVIII, fol. 237.
CHANDLER, Nun, of Wilby and Woodbridge, co. Suff., 18 . . ., Vol. LVII, fol. 298.
CHANDOS, Duchess of (GARNON, brother of the), of Bucks. GARNON impaled, 179 . ., Vol. XVIII, fol. 343.
　„　Earl TEMPLE, of Stowe, Bucks. Arms of BRYDGES and Chandos, 180 . ., Vol. XXI, fol. 54.
　„　before POLE, of Radborne, co. Derby, 180 . ., Vol. XXIV, fol. 146.
CHANDOS-POLE-GELL, of Barton Fields, Barton Blount, and Hopton, all co. Derby, 186 . ., Vol. LV, fol. 28.
CHANNELL, William Fry, of the Inner Temple, London, and Peckham, co. Surrey (after Baron of the Exchequer), 183 . ., Vol. XLII, fol. 117.
CHAPLIN, Thomas, of Anerley Park, St. Philips, Upper Norwood, co. Surrey, 1898, Vol. LXX, fol. 217.

CHAPMAN (*see* HUNT), of Stainton, co. York. (Match). 16 . . ., Vol. IV, fol. 86.
„ William, of Skegness, co. Linc.. 6 Mar. 170¾, Vol. V, fol. 145 ; and Pedigree,
    2 D. 14 ; Add. MS. 14,831, fol. 36 (*see* Berry).
„ (*see* DAVIS), of Old or Wold, co. Northampton, 181 . ., Vol. XXVII,
    fol. 187.
CHAPMAN to YAPP, s. to Chapman only, Sarah Ann, of Cheltenham, co. Glouc.,
    183 . ., Vol. XLIII, fols. 183, 351.
CHAPMAN, late YAPP, of co. Glouc., 184 . ., Vol. XLVI. fols. 195, 197.
CHAPMAN, Abel, of Woodford, co. Essex, and Whitby, co. York, and Elder
    Brother of the Trinity House. 184 . ., Vol. XLVI, fol. 330.
„ John, of Hill End, Mottram-in-Longdondale, co. Chester, 184 . ., Vol. XLVI,
    fol. 333. (Berry's Suppl.)
„ William, of St. James', Westminster, London, 184 . ., Vol. XLVIII, fol. 297.
CHAPPEL (*see* WESTHEAD), 184 . ., Vol. XLVII, fol. 339.
CHAPPLE (Lady GRANTLEY), and the descendants of Sir William Chapple, Knt.,
    of co. York. Arms exemplified. 28 May 1702, Vol. XV, fol. 51.
„ Frederick, of Liverpool, co. Lanc. 185 . ., Vol. LI, fol. 60.
CHARD, William Wheaton, of Pathe House, Othery, co. Somerset, 18 . . .,
    Vol. XLIV, fol. 403.
CHARGE, Robert, of Low Fields, Kirkby Fleetham, co. York., 181 . ., Vol.
    XXVI, fol. 303.
CHARLESWORTH, Rev. John, M.A., Fellow Trin. Coll., Camb., Minister of
    Ossington, co. Nottingham. 178 . ., Vol. XV, fol. 255.
CHARLETON to MAXWELL, Richard, of Bird Town, co. Donegal, Ireland, 17 . . .,
    Vol. XVII, fol. 189.
CHARLEVILLE, Countess of (COGHILL), of Ireland. (Match with MAINS), 17 . . .,
    Vol. XIV, fol. 171.
NEWPORT-CHARLETT, James Wakeman, 1821 (*see* Burke).
CHARLSWORTH, Joseph, of Lofthouse, Rothwell, co. York, 184 . ., Vol. XLVII,
    fol. 381.
CHARLTON, St. John, of Apley Castle, Shropsh. TAMPSELL quartering, 1779,
    Vol. XIV, fol. 185 (Her. and Geneal., VI, p. 120).
CHARLTON, late LECHMERE, Nicholas, of Ludford, co. Hereford, [13 Jan.] 1785,
    Vol. XV, fol. 389. [Grant of Arms of Charlton, 1 Feb. 1785
    (Genealogist. New S., XXII, p. 155).]
CHARLTON, William John, of Hesleyside, co. Northumberland, 180 . ., Vol. XXII,
    fol. 168.
CHARLTON to MEYRICK, Bart., of Apley Castle, Wellington, Shropsh., and Bush,
    co. Pembroke, 18 . . ., Vol. LIII, fol. 50.
CHARRINGTON, Edward, of Bury's Court, Leigh, co. Surrey (died 1888), 1887,°
    Vol. LXIV, fol. 122.
CHARTER, Wick and Broome, Bishops Lydiard, co. Somerset, 18 . . ., Vol. XLIX,
    fol. 320.
CHARTERS. See GARVIS.
CHASTON (*see* ASSEY), of Beccles, co. Suff., 18 . . ., Vol. XXXI, fol. 123.
CHATHAM, Earl of (PITT), of co. Cornw. and Dorset. Supporters, [4 Aug. 1766]
    Vol. XI, fol. 178.
„ Baroness [of Chatham, co. Kent], of co. Cornw. and Dorset. Supporters,
    [4 Dec. 1761] Vol. X, fol. 405.
CHATTERIS, William (an only son), of Brasenose Coll., Oxf., 1826, Vol. XXXVIII,
    fol. 237.
CHATTO after POTTS, William John, of Torquay, co. Devon ; Main House,
    Roxb. ; Carlton House Terrace and Lincoln's Inn, London, 1864, Vol.
    LV, fol. 216.
CHAUNCEY after SNELL, William, of Edmonton and Newington, co. Middx., 1783,
    Vol. XIV, fol. 306 (*see* Berry's Suppl.).
„ after SNELL, of co. Middx., and Austin Friars, London, 178 . ., Vol. XV,
    fol. 173.

CHAUNCEY. (Match with SNELL), of co. Middx., 181 . .., Vol. XXVI, fol. 182.

CHAVASSE, Capt. Henry, of Glandofer, Colgerran, co. Pembroke, Wales, 1895,* Vol. LXVIII, fol. 276.

CHAWORTH, ..., of Annesley Hall, co. Nottingham, 1 Dec. 1780 (see Berry's Suppl.).

CHAWORTH, late MUSTERS, John George, of Annesley Hall, co. Nottingham, 21 Mar. 1806, Vol. XXIII, fol. 343.

„ (late MUSTERS), of Annesley Hall and Colwick Hall, co. Nottingham, 182 . .., Vol. XXXIV, fol. 362.

CHAWORTH-MUSTERS, J.P., of Annesley Hall, co. Nottingham, 1888, Vol. LXIV, fol. 295.

CHAYTOR, William (afterwards a Bart.), of co. York, and Croft, co. Durham, 18 . . .., Vol. XXXVIII, fol. 330.

CHECKLAND, ..., of Hawkswick, St. Albans, co. Hertf. (and for TAYLOR, his wife), 187 . .., Vol. LVIII, fol. 325.

CHEDWORTH, Baron [12 May 1741] (John HOWE), of co. Glouc. and Wilts. Supporters, 174 . ., Vol. IX, fol. 29.

CHEEK, Edward, of Exeter, co. Devon, and kinsman of Roger, of co. Essex. (Match), 1707, Vol. V, fol. 4. Harl. MS. 6834, fol. 125.

CHEERE, Sir Henry, Knt. and Bart., of London, and St. Margaret's, Westminster, 30 July 1766, Vol. XI, fol. 174. (Berry.)

CHEERE, after MADRYLL, of White Rooting, co. Essex, and Popworth St. Everard, co. Camb., 180 . ., Vol. XXIV, fols. 434-36.

CHEESMENT, John, of Christ Ch., Oxf., 180 . ., Vol. XXII, fol. 165 (see SEVERN ?).

CHEETHAM, Charles, of Rycroft House, Rochdale, co. Lanc., 1882, Vol. LXI, fol. 311. (Berry's Suppl.)

„ Joshua Milnes, of Singleton House, Higher Broughton, co. Lanc., 1883, Vol. LXII, fol. 122. (Berry's Suppl.)

CHELTENHAM, Borough of, co. Glouc., 1877, Vol. LIX, fol. 312.

CHELTENHAM COLLEGE, co. Glouc., 1896, Vol. LXIX, fol. 144.

CHENERY, Charles Dallinger, M.A., T.C.D., of Wilby, co. Suff. (? editor of *The Times*), 18 . ., Vol. LIII, fol. 291.

CHERRY-GARRARD, Maj.-Gen. A., of Durford House, Kintbury, Berks., 1893, Vol. LXVII, fol. 185.

CHESHIRE, late WIDDOWSON, John, of Northwich Hall and Hartford Hall, co. Chester, 181 . ., Vol. XXX, fol. 341.

CHESTER, ..., of Islington and Staple Inn, London, 184 . ., Vol. XLVIII, fol. 423.

[CHESTER, William Bromley, M.P., of Cleve Hill, co. Glouc. Name and Arms of Chester, son of Francis Bromley. Match, 20 April 1765. N. & Q., 12th S., I, p. 455.]

CHESTER to ST. LEGER (Baron BAGOT), John, of co. Leic., Surrey and York (now prisoner at Verdun, in France), 186 . ., Vol. LV, fol. 38.

CHETHAM before STRODE, Thomas, of co. Derby and Southall, West Cranmere, co. Somerset, 1808, Vol. XXVI, fols. 317, 335.

CHETHAM-STRODE, Lieut.-Col. Richard, of co. Somerset, and Mellor Hall and Farden, co. Derby, 1827, Vol. XXXVI, fol. 345.

„ -STRODE, Randle, of co. Derby, Somerset and Westmorland, 1828, Vol. XXXVII, fol. 189.

„ -STRODE, Sir Edward, K.C.B., of Forton Lodge, Gosport, Hampsh., 1845, Vol. XLVII, fol. 406 (all four brothers).

CHETHAM-CHETWODE, after NEWDIGATE-LUDFORD, John, of co. Warw. and Shropsh. (afterwards a Bart.), 1826, Vol. XXXVI, fol. 73. (Berry.)

CHETWYND before STAPYLTON, Hon. Granville Anson, of London and co. York, 178 . ., Vol. XV, fol. 203.

„ before TALBOT, Earl Talbot, of co. Staff. Quarterly Arms, 178 . ., Vol. XVI, fol. 135.

CHEVALL-TOOKE, Charles, of the Middle Temple, London, and Hurston Clays, co. Sussex, 18 . . ., Vol LIII, fol. 82.

CHEW, William, of London, Mercht. (s. of Thomas, of Dunstable, co. Bedf.), to the descendants of his father, 15 Sept. 1703, Vol. V, fol. 132 ; Add MS. 14,831, fol. 57 (see Berry).

CHEYLESMORE, Baron (Henry William EATON), of co. Warw., 1887, Vol. LXIV, fols. 80-82.

CHICHESTER, Bp. of [1722-1724] (Thomas BOWERS), of co. Sussex, 172 . ., Vol. VII, fol. 96.

„ Bp. of [1798-1824] (John BUCKNER), of co. Sussex, 180 . ., Vol. XXIII, fol. 80.

CHICHESTER-CONSTABLE, W. G. R., of Runnamoat, co. Roscommon, Ireland, 1895, Vol. LXVIII, fol. 176.

CHICHESTER, Rev. Arthur Chichester (s. of John Longfield Burnard), Rector of Badlesmere, co. Kent, 189 . ., Vol. LXX, fol. 290.

CHIGNELL, Thomas, of Castlemount, Dover, co. Kent, 1887, Vol. LXIII, fol. 333.

CHILD, Sir Francis, Kt., Lord Mayor of London, 28 Jan. 1700-1701, Vol. V, fol. 21 ; Add. MS. 14,831, fol. 122 ; and Harl. Soc., VIII, p. 425.

„ Theophilus, of London, and Newton, co. Northampton, Reading, &c., s. of John Child and Margaret READ, 20 Feb. 170½, Vol. V, fol. 64.

CHILD before VILLIERS, [George, 5th] Earl of JERSEY, of co. Oxf., [1 Dec. 1819] Vol. XXXI, fol. 394.

CHILD after FIELD, of Yaxley, co. Huntingdon, 182 . ., Vol. XXXIII, fol. 228.

CHILD, of Stanford Street and Clapham Common, co. Surrey, 182 . ., Vol. XXXV, fol. 226.

„ Sir Smith (Bart. [7 Dec. 1868]) (grandson of Adm. [Smith Child]), of co. Suff. ; Glen Lossett, co. Argyll, Scotland ; Newfield, Wolstanton and Stallington Hall, Stone, co. Staff., 186 . ., Vol. LVI, fol. 203.

CHILD after HOOK, Albert Theodore, of Begellay House, co. Pembroke, and Finchley New Road, London, 1872, Vol. LVIII, fol. 160.

CHILDE, late BALDWIN, William Kimlet, of Shropsh., and Aqualate, co. Staff., 18 . . ., Vol. XLIX, fol. 175.

CHILDE before PEMBERTON, ..., late of Millichope and Church Stretton, Shropsh., 18 . . ., Vol. XLIX, fol. 182.

CHINNERY (and TRESILIAN, wife of), William Bassett, of Gelwall, Sewardstone, co. Essex (escutcheon of pretence), 180 . ., Vol. XXI, fol. 39.

CHINNERY-HALDANE, James Robert Alexander, of Greenhill House, Edinburgh, and Flintfield, co. Cork, 1879, Vol. LX, fol. 279. (Berry's Suppl.)

CHISSENHALE-MARSH, W. S., of Gaynes Park, co. Essex, 1895,* Vol. LXVIII, fol. 280 (see Crisp, IV, p. 6).

CHISWELL, Richard, of London, Turkey Mercht. (s. of Richard, of London, decd.), 16 April 1714, Vol. VI, fol. 145 ; Add. MS. 14,831, fol. 103. (Berry.)

CHISWELL, formerly MUILMAN, Richard, of Debden Hall, co. Essex (TRENCH-CHISWELL, formerly Muilman), 10 Dec. 1772 or 3, Vol. XII, fols. 216 and 218. (Berry.)

CHITTY, Sir Thomas, Knt., Lord Mayor of London, [1760] 17 . . ., Vol. X, fol. 359.

CHOLMLEY, late HOPKINS, Fane Henry, wife [of ?] (escutcheon of pretence), of Elmshall, Howsham, co. York, 179 . ., Vol. XVIII, fol. 29.

„ late GRIMES, Robert, of Coton House, co. Warw., and Howsham, co. York (Cholmley and WENTWORTH, quarterly), 185 . ., Vol. LII, fol. 327.

„ late STRICKLAND, Sir George, 7th Bart., of Boynton and Howsham, co. York, 1865, Vol. LII, fol. 341.

CHOLMONDELEY, Earl of, natural dau., wife of LAMBTON, of co. Chester and Durham. Arms to wife of LAMBTON impaled, 181 . ., Vol. XXVII, fol. 258.

CHOLMONDELEY to OWEN, Thomas, of Condone Park, Hodnet, and Moreton Say, Shropsh. ; and Knutsford, co. Chester (died s. p.), 186 . ., Vol. LV, fol. 66.

CHOLWICH after LEAR, Thomas William, of Teignmouth, co. Devon, 1835, Vol. XLI, fol. 130.

CHOWNE, late TILSON, Maj.-Gen., of Watlington Park, co. Oxf., 181 . ., Vol. XXVI, fol. 404.

„ late TILSON, of Goring, co. Oxf., 183 . ., Vol. XLI, fol. 238.

CHRISTIAN (*see* BROWNELL), of Guernsey. (Match with BROWNELL), 177 . ., Vol. XIII, fol. 76.

„ John, of Unerigg and Workington Hall, co. Cumberland, and Milntown, Isle of Man, 13 Mar. 1788, Vol. XVII, fol. 3.

„ Adm. Sir Hugh, K.B. [17 Feb. 1796], of Cleobury, co. Cumberland. Supporters, 179 . ., Vol. XIX, fols. 232 and 236.

CHRISTIAN to CURWEN, of Ewanrigg, co. Cumberland, 17 . . ., Vol. XVII, fol. 207.

„ to HARE, Rev. Edward, of Workington and Onsby, co. Cumberland, and Docking, co. Norf. (*See* BELL.) 17 . . ., Vol. XX, fol. 259.

CHRISTIE before BURTON (wife Mary), NAPIER, of co. York, Lieut. 3rd Foot Guards. Quarterly Arms, 178 . ., Vol. XV, fol. 285.

CHRISTIE to BURTON (NAPIER ?), of Hotbam Hall, co. York. (*See also* Henry BURTON-PETERS.) 182 . ., Vol. XXXIII, fol. 370.

CHRISTIE, Daniel Beat . . . ., Major, E.I.C.S., of Whaplode, co. Linc., 18 . . ., Vol. XXII, fol. 152. (Crisp, II, p. 125.)

„ John, of Hackney Wick House, London, and Scotland (s. of John, of Stirling and Liverpool), 181 . ., Vol. XXVIII, fol. 171.

CHRISTIE, late PLENDERLEATH, William, of Montreal, Canada, and London, 183 . ., Vol. XLI, fol. 295.

CHRISTIE-MILLER, W., of Brooklands, Broomfield, co. Essex, 1890, Vol. LXV, fol. 200.

CHRISTMAS (late SMITH), John Christmas, of Biddlesford, co. Devon, and Waterford, Ireland, 179 . ., Vol. XVIII, fol. 270.

CHRISTOPHER, ..., of Great Coram Street, London, 182 . ., Vol. XXXIV, fol. 212.

CHRISTOPHER, late DUNDAS (Lady Mary, his wife), of Scotland, 183 . ., Vol. XLI, fols. 222-224.

CHRISTY, William Miller, of The Woodbines, Kingston, and Stockwell, co. Surrey, 1855, Vol. LI, fol. 162.

CHRISTY-MILLER, Samuel, of Britwell House, Bucks ; Priors Broomfield, co. Essex ; and Craigentinny, Scotland, 1862, Vol. LIV, fol. 324.

CHURCH, late BECK, William, of Hatfield, co. Hertf., and Temple Bar, London (Church his godfather), 17 . . ., Vol. XVII, fol. 109.

CHURCH, William Henry (s. of William, of East Acton), of Chigwell, co. Essex, and co. Hertf. Personal [Arms ?], 182 . ., Vol. XXXV, fol. 283.

CHURCH after HANDY, Major, of Wells House, Acton, and Holt St. Stephen, St. Albans, co. Hertf. (*See* CHURCH after KING). Personal Arms, 183 . ., Vol. XXXIX, fol. 184.

„ after PEARCE, Lieut.-Col. (late) John (K.H.), of co. Glouc., and ffrywdgrech, co. Brecon, Wales (died s.p.), 184 . ., Vol. XLVIII, fols. 47 and 178.

CHURCH, John Church PEARCE- (a minor), s. of William Pearce, K.H., of Staverton House, co. Glouc., and of ffrywdgrech, co. Brecon, Wales, 184 . ., Vol. XLVIII, fol. 47.

„ Mary, his mother, and her descendants, 184 . ., Vol. XLVIII, fol. 178.

CHURCH, late PHILLIPS, Samuel, of Staverton, co. Glouc., and ffrywdgrech, co. Brecon, Wales. Church and Phillips quarterly, 1869, Vol. LVII, fol. 158.

„ late PHILLIPS, Samuel Church, of Wales. (*See also* CHURCH after PEARCE.) 1869, Vol. LVII, fol. 158 [*see* Burke].

CHURCH after KING, Henry John, of Acton, co. Middx.. and Albury, co. Surrey. (*See* CHURCH after HANDY.) 18 . . ., Vol. XLIX, fol. 112.

CHURCH, Rev. William Montague Higginson, of Hampton, co. Middx., Vicar of Hunstanton, co. Norf., 186 . ., Vol. LIV, fol. 198.

CHURCH, Henry John King, sometime of the Ordnance in the Tower of London, became an Irvingite Apostle ; of Albury, co. Surrey, 184 . ., Vol. XLIX, fol. 107.

CHURCHILL to CARTER, Bartholomew, of co. Oxf., 17 . . . Vol. XVII, fol. 169.

CHURCHILL after SPENCER, [5th] Duke of MARLBOROUGH, of Wilts. [Quarterly Arms and] Supporters, [26 May 1817] Vol. XXX, fol. 286.

CHURCHILL, Col. Chatham Horace. Augmentation for Waterloo, 184 . ., Vol. XLV, fol. 119.

  ,, Baron. Supporters, 1898, Vol. LXX, fol. 282.

CHURCHWARD (DIMOND-), Rev. Marcus D., of Stoke Gabriel, co. Devon (B.A., Ch. Coll., Camb.), 189 . ., Vol. LIII, fol. 150.

CHURTON, John, s. of William, 1875, Vol. LIX, fol. 90. (Berry's Suppl.)

CHUTE (see ALDRIDGE), of The Vine, Hampsh., 177 . ., Vol. XII, fol. 125.

CHUTE after WIGGITT, William Lyde, of the Middle Temple, London ; Crudwell and Hankerton, Wilts. ; and Pickenham, co. Norf., 1827, Vol. XXXVI, fol. 201.

CHUTE-ELLIS, C. E., of Kennington [Kensington ?] Gate, London, 1895, Vol. LXVIII, fol. 326.

CLACK, Richard, of Wallingford, Berks., and Hereford, 13 Nov. 1768, [Vol. XI], fol. 322 (see Berry).

CLANCHY to JOHNSON, Lieut.-Col., of Burleighfield, co. Leic., and Aston-upon-Trent, co. Derby, 185 . ., Vol. L, fol. 10.

CLAPTON, Edward, M.D., of Towercroft, Eltham, co. Kent, and London, s. of Jeremiah, of Stamford, 1879, Vol. LX, fol. 312.

CLARE, Earl of [12 June 1795, John] (FITZGIBBON), of Ireland. Supporters, 17 . . ., Vol. XX, fol. 394.

  ,, Michael Benignus, M.D., of Spanish Town, Jamaica (Ballyshanby, co. Tipperary, Ireland), 182 . ., Vol. XXXII, fol. 221.

  ,, William, of Walton-on-the-Hill, co. Lanc., [28 Dec. 1846] Vol. XLVIII, fol. 224 [see Misc. G. et H., 5th S., II, p. 122].

CLARGES after HARE, Maj.-Gen., C.B., of Colne Saint Dennis, co. Glouc., Vol. XLVII, fol. 143.

CLARIDGE, John, of Pall Mall, London, and Jervaulx Abbey, co. York, 18 . . ., Vol. XXXI, fol. 373.

CLARK, ..., of London. (Match), 16 . . ., Vol. I, fol. 358.

  ,, (see BELLAIRS), of London. (Match with WALFORD), 178 . ., Vol. XV, fol. 26.

  ,, James, ..., Serj[t] of H. M. Chandry, Whitehall, and Constable of Dublin Castle, 26 Jan. 168⅜, Vol. IV, fol. 30.

  ,, William, of Plymouth, co. Devon, 178 . ., Vol. XVI, fol. 249.

  ,, widow of MILLER and wife of GROUT, of co. Essex, 182 . ., Vol. XXXIV, fol. 224.

  ,, James (Sir), M.D., of London, Physician-in-Ordinary to H.M., 1837, Vol. XLII, fol. 224.

  ,, ..., of Trowbridge and Bradford, Wilts., 185 . ., Vol. LII, fol. 206.

  ,, Henry, Vicar of Harmston, co. Linc., 1857, Vol. LII, fol. 379.

  ,, William, s. of William, of Wolverhampton, co. Staff., 186 . ., Vol. LV, fol. 124.

  ,, Sir Andrew, Bart., of London, 1883, Vol. LXII, fol. 118.

  ,, Frederick, of 42[a], Great Cumberland Place, London, 1881, Vol. LXI, fol. 225. (Berry's Suppl.)

CLARK, quartered by David MILLIGAN, 1775, Vol. XIII, fol. 52.

CLARK after GRAHAM, John, of Newcastle-upon-Tyne, co. Northumberland, 178 . ., Vol. XVI, fol. 199.

CLARKE, Charles, [Edward], of Ardington, Berks. ; Newark, co. Nottingham ; and Ockley, co. Surrey, [22 Oct. 1600] Vol. X, fol. 19 (see Berry).

CLARKE after PRICE, of Aldershot, Hampsh., [18 Nov. 1786] Vol. XVI, fol. 241.

CLARKE, (WINCKWORTH, wife of), Richard Henry, of Totnes, co. Devon. and Arms to his wife and descendants (Clarke, of Wapping and Horsley Down, London), 17 . . ., Vol. XVII, fol. 45.

„ wife of OGILVIE, late PERRY, of co. Banff, Scotland, 180 . ., Vol. XXI, fol. 163.

„ Lieut.-Gen. Sir Alured, K.B. [1797]. Arms and Supporters, 180 . ., Vol. XXI, fol. 265.

„ Maj.-Gen. Sir William, Bart. [1803], of Ireland, 180 . ., Vol. XXIV, fol. 37.

CLARKE before JERVOISE, of Woodford, co. Essex, and Idsworth Park, Hampsh., 181 . ., Vol. XXVII, fol. 395.

CLARKE to WHITFIELD, of Rickmansworth Park, co. Hertf.; Malmesbury, Wilts.; and Emanuel Coll., Camb., 181 . ., Vol. XXVIII, fol. 105.

CLARKE, Bart., with HAUGHTON, of Oak Hill, Barnet, co. Hertf., and Jamaica, 182 . ., Vol. XXXIII, fol. 298.

„ Charles M., M.D., Phys. in Ordinary, of Dunham, co. Norf., and Wigginton Lodge, co. Staff., 18 . ., Vol. XXXVIII, fol. 305.

„ of Little Burstead, co. Essex, and Leatherhead, co. Surrey, 183 . . ., Vol. XLIII, fol. 14.

„ Vice-Adm. William, of Belford Hall, co. Northumberland, and Oxf., 1840, Vol. XLIV, fol. 208.

CLARKE- to [before ?] THORNHILL, late Capt. in the Army, William, of Fixby and Riddlesworth, co. York ; Rushton, co. Northampton ; and Swakerleys, Ickenham, co. Middx., [1855] Vol. LI, fol. 422.

CLARKE, David Ross, of Maze Hill, Greenwich, co. Kent, and Erriboll, Durness, co. Sutherland, Scotland. 185 . ., Vol. LIII, fol. 366.

„ John Creemer (M.P.), of Waste Court, par. of St. Helens, Abingdon, Berks. eldest s. of Robert, of St. Giles-in-the-Wood, co. Devon (decd.), 8 Jan. 1876, Vol. LIX, fol. 173. (Berry's Suppl. and Genealogist, II, p. 173.)

„ Alexander Felix, of St. Petersburg, 1895, Vol. LXVIII, fol. 206.

„ Thomas, of Holbeach, co. Linc., and Upper Hamilton Terrace, London, 1885, Vol. LXIII, fols. 134 and 135.

„ Thomas, of Masson House, Matlock Bath, co. Derby, 1890,* Vol. LXV, fol. 329. (Crisp, III, 5.)

„ Sir William John, Bart., of Victoria, Australia (died May 1897), 1882, Vol. LXII, fol. 16.

„ Sarah, dau. of GUEST, 20 May 1732, Vol. VIII, fol. 141.

CLAUGHTON, Thomas, of Middleton Parish, Winwick, co. Lanc., 180 . ., Vol. XXII, fol. 286.

CLAUSON, Julia Burton (widow of Charles), 12, Park Place Villas, London, 1898, Vol. LXX, fol. 233.

CLAVELL, late RICHARDS, William, of Smedmore, and Warmwell, and Knoll, Isle of Purbeck, co. Dorset, 179 . ., Vol. XIX, fol. 359.

„ late RICHARDS, John, M.A., of Smedmore, and Warmwell, and Knoll, Isle of Purbeck, co. Dorset, 181 . ., Vol. XXX, fol. 299.

CLAVERING to SAVAGE, of Elmslay Castle, co. Worc., 179 . ., Vol. XX, fol. 12.

CLAVERING [Rev. John Warren NAPIER., Roy. Lic., 1894. Surname and Arms of Clavering. Genealogist, New S., XXV, p. 125n].

CLAXTON, ..., of co. Glouc., 181 . ., Vol. XXX, fol. 47.

CLAY, Sir William, Bart., M.P., of Fulwell Lodge, co. Middx., 184 . ., Vol. XLV, fol. 250.

„ Charles, of Walton Lodge, Sandal Magna, co. York, 185 . ., Vol. LIII, fol. 360.

CLAY before KER-SEYMER, Harry Ernest, of Hanford, co. Dorset, Sec. of the Embassy at Paris, [5 Jan. 1865 (Burke)] Vol. LV, fol. 276.

CLAY, Charles J., of West House, Newenham, co. Camb., 1896,* Vol. LXIX, fol. 130.

„ Henry, of Piercefield Park, Clepstow, co. Monmouth, 1884,* Vol. LXII, fol. 224.

CLAY, Joseph Travis, of Rastrick, Halifax, co. York, 1884,* Vol. LXII, fol. 328. (Crisp, I, p. 68.)

CLAYFIELD, Michael, of Bristol, co. Glouc. Match with Mary MORGAN (see MORGAN), 180 . ., Vol. XXI, fol. 177.

CLAYFIELD before IRELAND, ..., of Brislington, co. Somerset, 182 . ., Vol. XXXVI, fol. 230.

CLAYTON, late BRACK, Dorothea (Spr.), of co. Northumberland, 181 . ., Vol. XXVIII, fol. 187.

CLAYTON-EAST, [Sir East George], Bart. [17 Aug. 1838], of Hall Place, Berks., [6 April 1829] Vol. XXXVIII, fol. 15.

„ -EAST to GILBERT-EAST, Bart., of Hall Place, Berks., [Arms of East only] [4 April 1839] Vol. XLIII, fol. 361.

CLAYTON after EVERY-CLAYTON, [Edward], Bart. [?], of co. Lanc., 183 . ., Vol. XLI, fol. 107. [Edward Every, of Rowley, near Burnley, co. Lanc., assumed by Roy. Lic., 21 Aug. 1835, the surname of Clayton after Every.]

CLAYTON, ..., of Preston and Lostock Hall, co. Lanc. (see next name), 184 . ., Vol. XLV, fols. 323-325.

CLAYTON to LOWNDES, ..., of Barrington Hall, co. Essex (see last name), 184 . ., Vol. XLV, fol. 325.

CLAYTON, Nathaniel, of Withcall, co. Linc., 1881, Vol. LXI, fol. 134. (Berry's Suppl.)

CLEASBY, Richard, of Craighouse, Brough, co. Westmorland, and co. York, 182 . ., Vol. XXXIV, fol. 336.

CLEAVER, ... (M.A., s. of Bp. of St. Asaph), of Twyford, Bucks., and Carburton, co. Nottingham, 184 . ., Vol. XLVIII, fols. 273, 276.

CLEAVER to PEACH [James Jarvis Cleaver], Rector of Holme Pierrepoint, &c., co. Nottingham. PEACH and CRUGER quarterly, [16 June 1845] Vol. XLVIII, fol. 276. (Misc. G. et H., II, p. 310.)

CLEGG-HILL, [Anne, 2nd] Viscount Hill, of Shropsh. Arms of Clegg, [16 Dec. 1844] Vol. XLVII, fol. 279. [Genealogist, New S., XXII, p. 156.]

„ -HILL, Rowland Clegg, [3rd] Viscount Hill, [17 April] 1875, Vol. LIX, fol. 94.

CLEGG, Harry, of Plas Llanfair, Llanfair, co. Anglesey, Wales, 1893, Vol. LXVI, fol. 338.

CLELAND, John William Henderson, of Roke Manor, Romsey, Hampsh., and co. Perth, Scotland [name and Arms of HENDERSON 1868], Vol. LVII, fol. 92. (Berry's Suppl.)

„ W. H., of Rook's Nest, Banstead, co. Surrey, 1896, Vol. LXIX, fol. 105.

CLEMENTI-SMITH, Rev. A. E., of Chadwick St. Mary Rectory, co. Essex, 1889, Vol. LXV, fol. 43.

CLEMENTS, Rev. James Crooks, of Welwickthorpe, co. York, and London, 184 . ., Vol. XLVI, fol. 110.

CLENNELL, late FENWICK, Thomas F., of Harbottle and Newcastle-upon-Tyne, co. Northumberland. Name and Arms of Clennell only, 6 Aug. 1796, Vol. XIX, fol. 295.

CLENNELL, Thomas (s. of Christopher, fol. 382), of Harbottle, co. Northumberland, 1882, Vol. LXI, fols. 372 and 382.

CLERKE, Joseph (s. of John), of Wethersfield Hall, co. Essex, and the descendants of his father, 25 May 1761, Vol. X, fol. 390. Misc. G. et H., 2nd S., II, p. 324 (see Berry).

„ (see LEECE), of Walford, co. Northampton, 179 . ., Vol. XX, fol. 331.

CLEVELAND, Duke of, of co. Durham, 182 . ., ? Vol. XXXVI, fol. 334 : 186 . ., Vol. LV, fols. 150 and 259.

CLEVLAND (see STEVENS), of Tapley, co. Devon. Match with Stevens, 181 . ., Vol. XXX, fol. 223, and 183 . ., Vol. XXXIX, fol. 146.

CLEVLAND, late SALTREN-WILLETT, of Tapley, co. Devon, 184 . ., Vol. XLVIII, fol. 352.

CLIES, John, s. of John, s. of Francis, of co. Cornw., and Oporto, Lisbon, 17 . . ., Vol. XIV, fol. 340.

CLIFF, William, of Claremont, West Derby, co. Lanc. (*also* CLIFF MCCALLOCK), 1891, Vol. LXVI, fol. 168.

CLIFFE to SYMES, of Ross, co. Wexford, Ireland. Quarterly with Symes, 178 . ., Vol. XVI, fol. 363.

CLIFFORD, George, of Corringham, Landbeach, co. Camb. ; Stow, co. Linc. ; Borscomb, Wilts. ; and CLIFFORD, of Barons, co. Essex, and Amsterdam, 29 Dec. 1740, Vol. IX, fol. 8.

CLIFFORD, late WINCHCOMBE, of Frampton Court, Frampton-on-Severn, co. Glouc., 180 . ., Vol. XXI, fol. 262.

CLIFFORD to CONSTABLE, Sir Thomas Hugh, Bart., of co. York and Staff., 182 . ., Vol. XXXII, fol. 365.

CLIFFORD (Sir Augustus W. J., Knt., afterwards Bart.), Post-Capt., R.N., of London, 183 . ., Vol. XL, fol. 200.

    „   Frederick, Q.C., of 24, Collingham Gardens, Kensington, London, 1897, Vol. LXX, fol. 60.

CLIFT to SELWYN (reputed son), of Congreve, co. Glouc. ; Clarence Square, Cheltenham ; and of Exeter Coll., Oxf., 186 . ., Vol. LIV, fol. 44.

CLIFTON, Sir Robert, K.B. [1725], of co. Nottingham. Supporters, 172 . ., Vol. VII, fol. 47.

CLIFTON, now BURTON, of Buckminster Hall and Boston, co. Linc., Vol. XXXII, fols. 313 and 315.

CLIFTON, widow of TABOR, of London, 185 . ., Vol. L, fol. 265.

CLIFTON, late MARKHAM, Henry Robert, of Clifton Hall, co. Nottingham [Clifton quarterly with Markham], 1869, Vol. LVII, fol. 296.

CLIFTON-DICCONSON, W. C., of Wrightington Hall, co. Lanc., 1881, Vol. LXI, fol. 241.

    „   -DICCONSON, Charles, of Wrightington Hall, co. Lanc., 1890, Vol. LXV, fol. 221.

CLIFTON-HASTINGS-CAMPBELL, Hon. G. T. C., of 82, Cadogan Square, London, 1896, Vol. LXIX, fol. 63.

[CLIFTON COLLEGE, Corporation of, 8 April 1895. (Geneal. Mag., IV, p. 352.)]

CLIMENSON, John, of Croyland, co. Linc., and Trinity Coll., Camb., LL.M., 185 . ., Vol. LIII, fol. 348.

CLINTON, Sir Henry, K.B. [1777]. Supporters, 177 . ., Vol. XIV, fol. 152.

CLINTON-PELHAM. Quarterly Arms, 180 . ., Vol. XXIV, fol. 224.

    „   Maj.-Gen. Sir Henry, K.B. [1815]. Supporters, 181 . ., Vol. XXVIII, fol. 33.

    „   Lieut.-Gen. Sir William, G.C.B. [1815]. Supporters, 181 . ., Vol. XXIX, fol. 53.

CLIFTON-HEPBURN-STUART-FORBES, before TREFUSIS, of co. Devon, 186 . ., Vol. LVI, fol. 303.

CLIPPINGDALE, S. D., M.D., of 36, Holland Park Avenue, London, 1891,* Vol. LXVI, fol. 100.

CLITHEROW after STRACEY, late Lieut.-Col., of Sprowston, co. Norf., and Boston House, Brentford, co. Middx., 186 . ., Vol. LV, fol. 352.

CLIVE to HERBERT, [Edward] Viscount, s. of Earl of Powis, of Shropsh. [Arms of Herbert, 20 Mar. 1807], 1806, Vol. XXIV, fol. 144. [Powisland Club, V, pp. 167 and 168.]

CLIVE after WINDSOR, Baroness, of Shropsh., 1885, Vol. LI, fol. 408.

CLOËTE, Maj.-Gen. Sir Abraham Josias, K.C.B. [1862], (died 1886), of London, 1884,* Vol. LXII, fol. 270.

CLOPTON, late SKRYMSHER, Charles Boothby, of Clopton, Old Stratford, co. Warw., 179 . ., Vol. XVIII, fol. 135.

    „   late INGRAM, Edward, of Barnet, co. Hertf., and Chelsea, co. Middx., 180 . ., Vol. XXI, fol. 186.

    „   late INGRAM, John, of Barnet, co. Hertf., 181 . ., Vol. XXXI, fol. 58.

CLOSE, Thomas, of Nottingham, and Manchester, co. Lanc., 186 . ., Vol. LVII, fol. 179.

CLOSE-BROOKS, J. B., of Birtles Hall, Chelford, co. Chester, 1889, Vol. LXV, fol. 15.

CLOUGH, now TAYLOR, Major E. H., of Beverley, co. York, and Bishop Stortford, co. Hertf., and Trinity Coll., Camb., 180 . ., Vol. XXIV, fol. 267.

CLOUGH (late ELLIS), Thomas Parr Williams, a lunatic, of Liverpool. co. Lanc., and Plas Clough, co. Denbigh, Wales, s. of John William Ellis, 1879, Vol. LX, fol. 328.

CLOUGH, W. O., of Enfield, co. Middx., 1890, Vol. LXV, fol. 263.

CLOVER, George Robert, J.P., of Birkenhead, co. Chester (s. of George Robert), 189 . ., Vol. LXXI, fol. . . . .

CLOWES, William, of Gloucester Terrace, Hyde Park, London, 1881,* Vol. LXI, fol. 207. (Berry's Suppl.)

CLULOW, ... (C.S., Madras), of Echingham, co. Essex, and of Chancery Lane, London, 182 . ., Vol. XXXVII, fol. 237.

CLUTTERBUCK, Thomas, of Watford, co. Hertf., 178 . ., Vol. XVI, fol. 273.

CLUTTON before BROCK (minor), of Cheshire, 181 . ., Vol. XXVI, fol. 77.

CLYDESDALE and DOUGLAS, Marquis of, and Duke of HAMILTON and BRANDON, of Scotland. Supporters, 180 . ., Vol. XXV, fol. 322.

COAPE before SHERBROOKE, Maj.-Gen. Sir John, K.C.B. Quarterly Arms and Supporters, 180 . ., Vol. XXV, fols. 414, 416, 419. [K.B. 16 Sept. 1809, G.C.B. 2 Jan. 1815.]

COAPE to COAPE-ARNOLD, Henry F. J., by Roy. Lic., 1867, Vol. LXX, fol. 162 (see Burke's Landed Gentry, under Arnold).

COATES, late CAMPION, John, of The Heights, Eskdaleside, co. York (and William Coates, his uncle), 17 . ., Vol. XVII, fol. 238.

COATES alias BOARDMAN, Charles, to BOWMAN alias BOARDMAN, of the Temple, London, nat. s. of Bowman, of Roehampton, co. Surrey, 17 . . ., Vol. XX, fol. 251.

COATES, Edward (s. of Saul, s. of John), of Bishopton, Ripon, co. York, 181 . ., Vol. XXVIII, fols. 193 and 194.

COATES to THOMPSON, William, of Addingham, co. York (and Jesus Coll., Camb., 1838), 183 . ., Vol. XLI, fol. 268.

COATES, ..., of Stanton Drew and Stanton Court, co. Somerset, 184 . ., Vol. XLVIII, fol. 22.

„ (? Edward), of Pembridge, co. Hereford, and Colutton, co. Radnor, Wales, 186 . ., Vol. LVI, fol. 91.

COBB to CARTWRIGHT, see 186 . ., Vol. LVI, fol. 107.

COBHAM, Baron [19 Oct. 1714], ([Sir Richard] TEMPLE [4th Bart.]), of Bucks. [Viscount, 23 May 1718]. Supporters, 171 . ., Vol. VI, fol. 201.

„ Viscountess [18 Oct. 1749] ([Hester] GRENVILLE), of Bucks. Supporters, 174 . ., Vol. IX, fol. 329.

COBHAM, late MARTYR (minor), of Shinfield, Berks., and Greenwich, co. Kent, 181 . ., Vol. XXVII, fol. 283.

COCHRANE, Rear.-Adm. Sir Alexander Forrester, K.B. [1806], of Scotland (brother to the Earl of DUNDONALD). Supporters and Augmentation, 180 . ., Vol. XXV, fols. 25 and 27.

„ Lord (Sir) Thomas, K.B. [1809], Post-Capt., R.N., M.P., of Scotland, afterwards 10th Earl, G.C.B. [1847], son of the Earl of DUNDONALD. Supporters, 181 . ., Vol. XXVI, fol. 431.

„ Nathaniel Day, Post-Capt., R.N., 181 . ., Vol. XXVII, fol. 27 } Reputed sons of Hon. (Thomas) Cochrane,

„ James Johnston, Capt., Foot Guards, 181 . ., Vol. XXVII, fol. 29 } son of the Earl of DUNDONALD.

COCK, John, D.D., S.T.P. (St. John's Coll., 1761), Camb. ; (s. of Joseph), of Great Horsley, co. Essex. Quartering with TUER, 1796, Vol. XIX, fol. 165.

Cock to Lamb. . . . ., of Golden Square, London.   Quarterly Arms, 17 . . ., Vol. XX, fol. 129.

Cock, ..., of Tottenham, co. Middx., 182 . ., Vol. XXXIII, fol. 19.
  „   Alfred, Q.C., of 8, Kensington Park Gardens, London, 1894, Vol. LXVIII, fol. 45.

Cockburn, Rear-Adm. Sir George, G.C.B. [1818], of Scotland.   Augmentations, 181 . ., Vol. XXXI, fols. 26 and 75.   Supporters, 182 . ., Vol. XXXII, fol. 59.

Cockburn-Campbell, Bart., Sir Alexander (minor), of Scotland, 182 . ., Vol. XXXV, fol. 274.

Cockburn after Kidney, Sir James, Bart., Inspr.-Gen. Marines (?), of Langton, co. Berwick ; Kinston Hall, co. Northampton ; Little Stratton Hall and Gamley, co. Leic., 1828, Vol. XXXVII, fol. 69.

Cockell, Lieut.-Gen. William, of Leeds. co. York, 181 . ., Vol. XXIX, fol. 63.

Cockerell, ..., of Sezincot, co. Glouc., and Bishop's Hall, co. Somerset. (Match), 181 . ., Vol. XXVI, fol. 88.

Cockerell to Rushout, [6 June 1849, 2nd] Bart., of co. Glouc., 18 . ., Vol. XLIX, fol. 162.

Cocks, Charles, Baron Somers [1784].   Supporters, 178 . ., Vol. XV, fol. 301.

Cocks to Pemberton, Elizabeth and Sally (Sprs.), of Middleton Hall, co. Durham, 18 . . ., Vol. XXI, fol. 399.

Cocks, Countess, Stamford and Warrington, of co. Dorset, 187 . ., Vol. LVIII, fol. 214.

Cockshutt to Twisleton, Josias, of Widdington, co. Essex ; Osbaston and Keyworth, co. Leic. ; and Rawcliffe, co. York, 180 . ., Vol. XXI, fol. 243.

Codd to Walls, ..., of Spilsby and Stainton, co. Linc., 177 . ., Vol. XIV, fol. 21.

Codd, Major, ..., of South Brett, co. Devon, 182 . ., Vol. XXXVII, fol. 265.

Coddington, Sir William, Bart., of Wycollon, Blackburn, co. Lanc., 1896,* Vol. LXIX, fol. 26.

Codrington, ..., of co. Glouc., 16 . . ., Vol. II, fol. 533.

Codrington, late Miller, Jane Charlotte, of Dodington, co. Glouc., nat. d. of Sir William Codrington, F.D. [?], Bart., 179 . ., Vol. XVIII, fol. 33.

Codrington to Bethell, William and Christopher, of Dodington, [1798] Vol. XX, fol. 68, and of Swindon Hall, co. York, 179 . ., Vol. XX, fol. 125.

Codrington, Sir Edward, K.C.B. [1815], of co. Glouc. ?   Arms for wife Jane Hall, 182 . ., Vol. XXXIII, fol. 102.

Codwise to Bertie, of Low Layton, co. Essex, 183 . ., Vol. XXXIX, fol. 115.

Coffin after Pyne, ..., of East Down and Portledge, co. Devon, 179 . ., Vol. XIX, fol. 398.

Coffin, Rear-Adm. Isaac [Greenly], (Bart.) [1804], of Magdelaine Island, N. America, 180 . ., Vol. XXII, fol. 427.

Coffin before Greenly, [1810-11] Vice-Adm. Sir Isaac, Bart., of Titley Court, co. Hereford, 181 . ., Vol. XXVI, fol. 226.

Coffin, Robert Harris, (reputed son of), University Coll., Oxf., s. Thomas Aston of Quebec, Canada, 181 . ., Vol. XXXI, fol. 71.

Coggs, John, Citizen and Goldsmith (and brother Daniel), of London, (William in Harl. MS. 1105, fol. 38) ; 7 Aug. 1703, Vol. V, fol. 92 ; Add. MS. 14,830, fol. 188.   (Berry.)

Coghill, ..., of Bucks.   (Match with Maine), 177 . ., Vol. XIV, fol. 171.

Coghill, late Maine, John, of Bucks.   (Match with Countess Charleville), 17 . . ., Vol. XIV, fol. 171.
  „   late Cramer, Josiah, of Coghill Hall, co. York, and Ireland, 1817, Vol. XXX, fol. 190.

Coham, William H. B., of Dewsland Coham, &c., co. Devon, and Belvidere House, Drumcondra, co. Dublin, 1845, Vol. XLVII, fol. 313.

Cohen, ..., of co. Norf., and London, 18 . . ., Vol. XXXI, fol. 357.

COHEN to PALGRAVE, of Cottishall, co. Norf., and the Inner Temple, London, 182 . ., Vol. XXXV, fol. 217.

COHEN, Samuel, of Parkplace, Brixton, co. Surrey, 183 . ., Vol. XLIII, fol. 146.

COHN, Maurice, of 21, Grosvenor Place, London, 1898, Vol. LXX, fol. 294.

COKAYNE, late ADAMS, George Edward, Lancaster Herald, London (now Clarenceux King of Arms), 1873, Vol. LVIII, fol. 252. (Berry's Suppl.)

COKBURNE after KER, ..., M.A., of Etwall, co. Derby, and Norton-in-Hales and Bellaport, Shropsh., 1833, Vol. XXXIX, fol. 298.

COKE, Sir Thomas, K.B. [1725]. Supporters, 172 . ., Vol. VII, fol. 427.

COLBATCH, Sir John, Knt., of St. Martin's-in-the-Fields, London, 2 Nov. 1716, Vol. VI, fol. 282. (Berry.)

   ,, Dr. John, of [co. Middx. and] Trinity Coll., Camb., Casuistical Professor of Divinity, 2 Nov. 1716, Vol. VI, fol. 282, and Add. MS. 14,830, fol. 190 (Sir John, see above).

COLBORNE after RIDLEY, ..., of Heaton and Blagdon, co. Northumberland, 180 . ., Vol. XXII, fol. 308.

COLBORNE, Sir John, G.C.B. [1838], &c., of co. Devon. Arms, Cross, Clasps and Supporters, 183 . ., Vol. XLIII, fols. 355-59.

COLBORNE and SEATON, Ladies, of co. Devon. Supporters, 18 . . ., Vol. XLIV, fol. 23.

COLBORNE-VEEL, Joseph Veel, of Cowley, Alkerton, Eastington, co. Glouc., and Magdalen Hall, Oxf., 185 . ., Vol. L, fol. 388.

COLBY, Rev. Frederick Thomas, M.A., Fellow of Exeter Coll., Oxf., and of Great Torrington, co. Devon, 186 . ., Vol. LVI, fol. 329. (Crisp, I, p. 4.)

COLCHESTER, Baron [3 June 1817] (ABBOT), of co. Essex and Sussex, 181 . ., Vol. XXX, fol. 194. Arms and Supporters, fol. 196.

COLDRIDGE, ..., of East Budleigh, co. Devon, 185 . ., Vol. L, fol. 425.

COLDWELL to THICKNESSE, ..., M.A., of Wigan, co. Lanc., afterwards Archdeacon and Dean, 18 . . ., Vol. LIII, fol. 136.

COLE, now TUDOR, of Duddington, co. Northampton, 17 . ., Vol. XX, fols. 2 and 316.

COLE, late LOGGIN, William, of Long Marton, co. Glouc.; Besley, co. Worc.; Buckish, co. Devon; Enstone, co. Oxf.; and Chipping Warden, co. Northampton, 180 . ., Vol. XXII, fol. 137.

   ,, late VAN THUYSEN (wife Cole), Thomas Hunt, of Pidley-cum-Fenton, co. Huntingdon, 180 . ., Vol. XXIII, fol. 134.

COLE, John, of Gulval, nr. Penzance, co. Cornw., D.D., Rector of Exeter Coll., Oxf., 181 . ., Vol. XXVII, fol. 7.

   ,, Sir Christopher, Knt. [1812], Capt. R.N. Augmentation, 181 . ., Vol. XXVII, fol. 193.

   ,, Lieut.-Gen. Sir Galbraith Lowry, K.B. [1 Feb. 1813], M.P., of Ireland. Supporters, 181 . ., Vol. XXVIII, fol. 116.

   ,, of Shotton, co. Durham. (Match with ORD and WRIGHT, see), 181 . ., Vol. XXVIII, fol. 251.

COLE to MARSHALL, ..., of Kirkby Moorside and Pickering, co. York, 182 . ., Vol. XXXVII, fol. 251.

COLE, William Cole, Banker, and his brother, John Cole, of Exeter, co. Devon, 8 April 1833, Vol. XXXIX, fol. 284. (Crisp, Notes, I, p. 66.)

   ,, Samuel, D.D., Chaplain of Greenwich Hospital, of co. Cornw., 183 . ., Vol. XLI, fol. 389.

   ,, Sir Christopher, his brother, of co. Cornw. Augmentation, 183 . ., Vol. XLI, fol. 391.

   ,, Rev. George Lamont, M.A., St. John's Coll., Camb., of Wellisford House, Langford Budville, co. Somerset, 185 . ., Vol. LI, fol. 21.

   ,, John, of Rutland Gate and Twickenham, co. Middx., 18 . . ., Vol. LIII, fol. 165.

   ,, C. F., of Flintfield, Caterham, co. Surrey, 1891,* Vol. LXVI, fol. 106. (Crisp, I, p. 12, and Notes).

COLEBROOKE, James, of Southgate, co. Middx., 23 Oct. 1772, Vol. VII, fol. 121
  or 125 ; Add. MS. 14,830, fol. 189.
COLEGRAVE, late MANBY, William, of Downsall and Caine Hall, co. Essex,
  18 . . ., Vol. XXXI, fol. 152.
  „   late MANBY, John William, J.M.L., of Downsall, co. Essex, and Little
      Ellingham, co. Norf., 1868, Vol. LVII, fol. 37.
COLEMAN (widow), of Norwich, co. Norf. (George Lovick Coleman, of Bixley
      Lodge, Norwich ?), 1843, Vol. XLVII, fol. 20.
COLEMAN to PROCTER, of Church Stretton, Shropsh., and Aberhafesp Hall,
      co. Monmouth, Wales, 18 . . ., Vol. LX, fol. 271.
COLEMAN, James Henry, of Napier, New Zealand, 1880,* Vol. LXI, fol. 19.
      (Berry's Suppl.)
COLERIDGE, [Sir] John Duke, of Thorverton and Ottery St. Mary, co. Devon.
      M.A., Ch. Ch., Oxf. [Judge of the Queen's Bench], 182 . ., Vol. XXXIV,
      fol. 370.
  „   Baron [Sir John Duke Coleridge], of Thorverton and Ottery St. Mary,
      co. Devon. Supporters, [10 Jan. 1874] Vol. LVIII, fol. 308.
  „   [Dr. William Hart, D.D., Bishop of Barbados, 1824 to 1841. 1824 (Her. and
      Geneal., V, p. 280)].
COLES, James. and HORSMAN, his wife, of Clapham Common, co. Surrey, 183 . .,
      Vol. XLIV, fols. 293-94.
COLFOX, William, of Westmead, nr. Bridport, co. Dorset, 1898, Vol. LXX, fol. 219.
COLLARD, A. B., of Hamilton Terrace, London, 1889, Vol. LXV, fol. 133.
COLLEDGE, Thomas, F.R.C.P., M.R.C.S., of Cheltenham, co. Glouc., 18 . . ., Vol.
      XXXVIII, fol. 225.
  „   Richard, of Couton, co. Glouc., 186 . . ., Vol. LV, fol. 272.
COLLET, Sir M. W., Bart., co. Kent, 1888, Vol. LXIV, fol. 213.
COLLETON, late GARTH, Charles, of Hurst, Berks., and Haynes Hill and Devizes,
      Wilts., 180 . ., Vol. XXIII, fol. 177.
COLLETT, Sir James, and sisters Susanna and Elizabeth, of London, children of
      Sir James, Knt., Sheriff, 7 May 1711, Vol. V, fol. 418 ; Add. MS. 14,831,
      fol. 5. (Berry.)
COLLIER, Sir Edward, Knt., Post-Capt., R.N. (after Vice-Adm. and K.C.B.), of
      East Wickham Place, co. Kent, and London, 181 . ., Vol. XXVIII,
      fol. 233.
  „   Baron MONKSWELL [1885], Vol. LXIII, fol. 138.
COLLIN, John, of Elton, &c., co. Nottingham, s. of Thomas, s. of Lawrence,
      nephew and heir of Abel, of Nottingham Town, decd., 27 June 1712,
      Vol. VI, fol. 48 ; Add. MS. 14,830, fol. 3. (Berry.)
COLLINGE, Edward, of Woodfield, Werneth, co. Lanc., 1886,* Vol. LXIII,
      fol. 253.
COLLINGS (Lieut.-Col., Guernsey Militia), of Guernsey. (See CARRÉ.) 182 . ., Vol.
      XXXIII, fol. 190.
  „   . . . ., of Guernsey and Rotterdam, 184 . ., Vol. XLV, fol. 195.
  „   Rev. Henry, of St. Michael's Vicarage, Bowes Park, co. Middx., 1884,
      Vol. LXII, fol. 313.
COLLINGWOOD, Baron, Vice-Adm., of Hethpool and Caldburne, co. Northumberland.
      Supporters, [20 Oct 1805] Vol. XXIII, fol. 346.
  „   of Hethpool and Caldburne, co. Northumberland. Augmentation, 180 . .,
      Vol. XXIV, fol. 188.
COLLINGWOOD, late SPENCER-STANHOPE, Edward, of co. York, 181 . ., Vol. XXX,
      fol. 59.
COLLINGWOOD after NEWNHAM, George Lewis, of Hethpool and Caldburne,
      co. Northumberland, 18 . . ., Vol. XXXI, fol. 236.
COLLINGWOOD, late CALTHROP, Robert G., of Dissington, co. Cumberland, 1868,
      Vol. LVI, fol. 348.
COLLINS (see GIDDY), of co. Cornw. (Match with Giddy), 177 . ., Vol. XII,
      fol. 24.

COLLINS to WARD, of Sandhurst, co. Kent, 178 . ., Vol. XV, fol. 175.

„ to BURY (Rev. Brian Bury), M.A., Camb., of co. Linc., and Bath, co. Somerset, 17 . ., Vol. XX, fol. 426.

COLLINS before POORE, George, of Portsmouth, Hampsh., and Grove, Isle of Wight, 181 . ., Vol. XXX, fol. 391.

COLLINS-SPLATT, of Exeter and Brixham, co. Devon, 183 . ., Vol. XXXIX, fol. 359.

COLLINS-TRELAWNEY, Charles, M.A., of Trelawney Ham in Tir, co. Devon, Rector of Timsbury, co. Somerset, 1839, Vol. XLIII, fol. 291.

COLLINS, James Tertius, of Churchfield, Edgbaston, Birmingham, 1898, Vol. LXX, fol. 274.

COLLYER-BRISTOW, William, of Crawley, Hampsh., and of Farnham and Beddington, co. Surrey, 185 . ., Vol. LIII, fols. 69 and 84.

„ -BRISTOW, Andrew, of Farnham and Beddington, co. Surrey, 18 . . ., [Vol. LIII ?], fol. 316.

COLMAN, Jeremiah, of Carshalton Park, co. Surrey, 1884, Vol. LXII, fol. 301. (Berry's Suppl.)

COLMORE after CREGOE, Frind, of Moore End, co. Glouc., 183 . ., Vol. XLI, fols. 180 and 182.

COLONSAY, Lord (MACNEILL), of Scotland. Supporters, [1867] Vol. LVI, fol. 286.

COLPOYS, Vice-Adm. Sir John, K.B. Arms and Supporters, [14 Feb. 1798] Vol. XX, fol. 197.

COLPOYS after GRIFFITH, Rear-Adm., of Raheen, co. Waterford, Ireland, 182 . ., Vol. XXXIII, fol. 31.

COLQUITT to GOODWIN, of Farndon, co. Chester, Capt. of Dragoons, 184 . ., Vol. XLV, fol. 378.

COLVILE (late WEDDERBURN), Alexander and Andrew, of Crombie, co. Fife, and Ochiltree, Scotland, 181 . ., Vol. XXVIII, fol. 151.

COLVILLE, Maj.-Gen. Sir Charles, G.C.B. Supporters, [7 April 1815] Vol. XXX, fol. 177.

COLVIN, ..., of Denoran, Dunnipace, Scotland, and London, Vol. XXXI, fol. 42.

COLYEAR-DAWKINS, [James], of Over-Norton, co. Oxf.; Richmond, co. Surrey, [s. and heir of Henry Dawkins, of] Standlinch, Wilts. [Colyear in the second quarter, 21 Jan. 1836], Vol. XXXI, fol. 188.

COMBE, late MADDISON, of Lincoln's Inn, London, and Earnshill, co. Somerset, 1850, Vol. XLIX, fol. 244.

COMBE, Charles, of Cobham Park, co. Surrey, 1883,* Vol. LXII, fol. 114. (Berry's Suppl.)

COMBER, George, of Knutsford, co. Chester, J.P., Lanc., s. of Edward, of Myddleton Hall, co. Lanc., 189 . ., Vol. LXXI, fol. . . . . .

COMBERMERE, Lieut.-Gen., Baron [17 May 1814], G.C.B. [2 Jan. 1815], of co. Chester. Augmentation, 181 . ., Vol. XXVIII, fol. 347.

COMER, ..., of Fitzhead, co. Somerset, and London, Vol. XLIX, fol. 379.

COMMYNS, now MANNOCK, William (Valentine), of Gifford's Hall, Stoke, co. Suff., 17 . ., Vol. XX, fol. 400.

COMPTON, Sir Spencer, K.B. [1725]. Supporters, 172 . ., Vol. VII, fol. 336.

„ Earl of NORTHAMPTON. (Match with Baroness FERRERS), 177 . ., Vol. XIV, fol. 96.

COMPTON after DOUGLAS [3rd Marquis of NORTHAMPTON], of co. Northampton, and Warw., [5 Jan. 1831] Vol. XXXVIII, fol. 201.

COMPTON, Mary, of co. Northampton, and Warw. Supporters, 18 . ., Vol. LIII, fol. 31.

„ G. W., of Kimberley, South Africa, 1891, Vol. LXVI, fol. 237.

CONANT, Sarah, dau. of John, (WHISTON, late wife of) Sir Nathaniel Conant, Knt., of Mount Nugent, in Bellingham, Bucks. Arms to issue of late wife, 181 . ., Vol. XXVII, fol. 433.

CONANT (-STAINSBY) after PIGOTT, of Archer Lodge, Sherfield-upon-Loddon, Hampsh., 183 . ., Vol. XLI, fol. 158.

CONDER, Edward, of Old Town, Kirkby Lonsdale, co. Westmorland, 1883,* Vol. LXII, fol. 141. (Crisp, I, p. 18.)

CONDUIT, John, of the City of Westminster, 16 Aug. 1717, Vol. VI, fol. 320 ; Add. MS. 14,830, fol. 7 ; and Berry.

CONGLETON, Baron, of co. Chester. PARNELL Arms, [18 Aug. 1841], Vol. XLVI, fol. 30. Supporters, fol. 32.

CONINGSBY, Viscountess, Lady Margaret. Supporters and quarterings, JONES and . . . ., 1716,* Vol. VI, fol. 310.

CONNEMARA, Baron, of Ireland. Supporters, 1889, Vol. LXV, fol. 37.

CONNOR, WOODHAM, wife of, of Nash, co. Hereford, and Enfield, co. Middx., escutcheon of pretence for wife, 179 . . ., Vol. XVIII, fol. 95.

CONRAN { William A., 1. / Henry Arthur, 3. } William, of Jamaica, and Plymouth, co. Devon. { Gerald M., 4. Of Bradbridge House, South Brent, co. Devon, 189 . ., Vol. LXXI, fol. . . . .

CONSTABLE, ..., of Reading, Berks. (*See* George PEMBROKE), 177 . ., Vol. XII, fol. 57.

CONSTABLE, late SHELDON, Edward, of Burton Constable, co. York, 17 . . ., Vol. XVII, fol. 392.

   „ late SHELDON, Francis, of Burton Constable and Wycliffe, co. York, 180 . ., Vol. XXII, fol. 362.

CONSTABLE to STANLEY, Charles II., of Hooton, co. Chester ; Everingham, co. York ; and Tereagles, Carlaverock Castle, co Dumfries, Scotland, 179 . ., Vol. XVIII, fol. 246.

CONSTABLE, ANNE, wife of Sir William CURTIS [Bart., 23 Dec. 1802], of Edmonton and London, 180 . ., Vol. XXII, fol. 49.

CONSTABLE, late CLIFFORD, Sir Thomas Hugh, Bart., of Tixall, co. Staff., and Burton Constable, co. York, [1821] Vol. XXXII, fol. 365.

CONWAY, Lord (SEYMOUR-CONWAY), of co. Warw. Supporters, [17 Mar. 170⅔] Vol. V, fol. 119.

CONWAY (SEYMOUR) after INGRAM, [18 Dec. 1807, 2nd] Marquis of Hertford, of co. Warw. Coat of Ingram, 180 . ., Vol. XXIV, fols. 352 and 354.

CONWY after ROWLEY, of co. Flint, 1896, Vol. LXIX, fol. 29.

CONYBEARE, John, Dean of Christ Ch., Oxf. (and others), and her [his ?] sisters Mary and Anne, 13 April 1733, Vol. VIII, fol. 165.

CONYERS, Col., C.B., of Fulham, London, 18 . . ., Vol. XLIV, fol. 105.

CONYERS, late LANG (Spr.), of Lower Redlands, nr. Reading, Berks., and Calverley Terrace, Tunbridge Wells, co. Sussex, 187 . ., Vol. LVIII, fol. 196.

CONYNGHAM, late BURTON [3 April 1781], Francis Pierpont, Baron Conyngham, of Ireland, 17 . . ., Vol. XIV, fols. 316 and 318.

CONYNGHAM, Marquis of, of Ireland [22 Jan. 1816]. (Match with DENISON), 181 . ., Vol. XXX, fol. 119.

CONYNGHAM to DENISON [4 Sept. 1849], Lord Albert, K.C.H., of Denbies, co. Surrey, and co. York, 184 . ., Vol. XLIX, fol. 217. Supporters, fol. 295.

CONYNGHAM, Baron LONDESBOROUGH, Lord Albert DENISON. Supporters, as K.C.H., 184 . ., Vol. XLV, fol. 294 ; as Baron Londesborough, [4 Mar. 1850] Vol. XLIX, fol. 295.

COOCH, Charles and Octavius Tyndall (s. of Charles), of Dover, co. Kent, and Ryde, Isle of Wight, sometime Mayor of Ryde, 1876, Vol. LIX, fol. 260. (Berry's Suppl.)

COOK (*see* FLETCHER), PINXON *alias* PINXTON, of co. Derby. (Match with Fletcher), 17 . . ., Vol. VIII, fol. 139b.

   „ John, of Christchurch, Hampsh., 178 . ., Vol. XV, fol. 209.

COOK, widow of Capt. James Cook, of (Mile End), co. Middx., 3 Sept. 1785, Vol. XVI, fol. 79 (*see* British Encyclopædia, the Navigator).

„ William, of Holborn, London, and Enfield, co. Middx., 178 . ., Vol. XVI, fol. 341.

COOK (late GANE), John Howell, of South Brent, co. Devon, and Lympsham, co. Somerset, and his brother William, 182 . ., Vol. XXXII, fols. 245 and 247.

COOK, ..., of Camberwell, co. Surrey, 183 . ., Vol. XL, fol. 12.

COOK to ALTHAM (Major), William Surtees, of co. Somerset. Roy. Lic., 20 Feb. 1862, Vol. LIV, fol. 268.

COOK, (Sir) Francis, of Roydon Hall, co. Kent, and Doughty House, Richmond, co. Surrey [Bart. 1886], 186 . ., Vol. LVII, fol. 278.

„ Charles (s. of Thomas), and the descendants of Francis Cook of Kingsthorpe, co. Northampton (father of Sarah, Lady PRICHARD), of Hackney, co. Middx., 12 May 1711, Vol. V, fol. 423. (Misc. G. et H., New S., 1, p. 349.)

COOKE, Rev. . . . ., of Campsal, co. York, 16 . . ., Vol. III, fol. 198.

COOKE before YARBOROUGH, George, of Campsal, co. York. Quarterly Arms, 180 . ., Vol. XXI, fol. 403.

COOKE, Thomas, of Norwich, co. Norf., 16 May 1723, Vol. VII, fol. 190.

„ John, of Islington, co. Middx., 8 June 1725, Vol. VII, fol. 461.

COOKE to FREEMAN, John and brother Stephen, of Fawley, Bucks., 17 . ., Vol. IX, fol. 364.

COOKE, Francis, Vicar of Edmonton, co. Middx., 7 June 1760, Vol. X, fol. 239. (Berry.)

„ Thomas (s. of John), of Windsor, Berks., and Horncastle, co. Linc., 178 . ., Vol. XV, fol. 35.

„ . . . ., of Sible Hedingham, co. Essex. Quarterly to SNEYD. (*See* SNEYD.) 180 . ., Vol. XXIII, fol. 160.

„ . . . ., of Peterborough, co. Northampton. (*See* IMAGE.) 181 . ., Vol. XXVI, fol. 306.

„ William, of Worleston Rookery, co. Chester, and Chester Castle, Jamaica, May 1812, Vol. XXVIII, fol. 122. (Berry, Appx.)

COOKE to PIGGOTT, Simon Francis, of Lincoln's Inn, London, and Fitzhall, Iping, co. Sussex. (*See also* PIGGOTT.) 22 Aug. 1824, Vol. XXXV, fol. 5.

COOKE, John, of The Chase, co. Hereford, 17 Nov. 1843, Vol. XLVII, fol. 2.

COOKE, late MATHEWS, Rev. Thomas Alexander, of Wargrave, Berks., and Polstead Hall, co. Suff., 1850, Vol. XLIX, fol. 301.

COOKE, Thomas, of Pendleton, Eccles and Pendlebury, co. Lanc., 185 . ., Vol. L, fol. 113.

„ Joseph, of Brislington, co. Somerset, 185 . ., Vol. LI, fol. 464.

COOKE-HURLE, of Stourton, Wilts., and Clifton, Bristol, co. Glouc., 185 . ., Vol. LII, fol. 68.

COOKE, W. H., of The Green, Shelsley Kings, co. Worc., 1869. (Burke.)

COOKSON to CRACKANTHORPE, Christopher, of Penrith, co. Cumberland. Crest for Crackanthorpe, of Newbiggin Hall, co. Westmorland, 1792, Vol. XVIII, fol. 117.

„ to CRACKANTHORPE, Montagu H., Q.C., of London, 1890, Vol. LXV, fol. 333.

COOKSON, Col. George, R.A., of co. Chester and Durham, allusion to services ; also to brother Charles, 1814, Vol. XXVIII, fols. 159 and 160.

COOKSON to DOD, Rev. Joseph Yates, of Edge Hall, co. Chester, 1834, Vol. XL, fol. 286.

COOKSON, late EVANS-GORDON, Sarah, of Bon Accord Place, Guernsey, and Whitehill, Chester-le-Street, co. Durham, 18 . ., Vol. LIII, fol. 261.

COOKSON after FIFE, John Cookson, of Whitehill, co. Durham, 1878, Vol. LX, fol. 207. (Berry's Suppl.)

„ after REYNARD, George H., of Whitehill, co. Durham, 1864, Vol. LV, fol. 264.

COOKSON (SAWREY-), James, of Neasham Hall, co. Durham, 1882, Vol. LXI, fol. 390. (Berry's Suppl.)

„ *See* WORTHINGTON.

COOPE, Sarah Hannah (*see* DOORMAN), wife of, of Leytonstone, co. Essex. (Arms for wife), 181 . ., Vol. XXVII, fol. 74.

„ O. E., of Rochetts, Berechurch Hall, co. Essex, 1889, Vol. LXV, fol. 65.

COOPER, Thomas, of St. James', Garlickhithe, London, 1693, Vol. IV, fol. 150.

„ John, of Trowbridge, Wilts., 29 Mar. 1721, Vol. VII, fol. 59. (Berry.)

„ Samuel, D.D., of Norwich, co. Norf. (Baronets), 1765, Vol. XI, fol. 81. (Berry.)

COOPER to FISHER, Henry, of Soham, co. Leic., 1797, Vol. XX, fol. 66.

„ to FOURLE, of Arlington and Sandport, Lewes, co. Sussex, 180 . ., Vol. XXI, fol. 286.

COOPER, Robert Chester, Capt. of Militia, of Lewes, co. Sussex. (Match with TOMLINS), 181 . ., Vol. XXVI, fol. 160.

COOPER to PURNELL, Purnell B. [Bransby ?], (minor), of co. Glouc., 1801, Vol. XXI, fol. 286.

„ to REDE, Robert, of Ingoldsthorpe Barton, co. Norf., and Beccles and Barsham, co. Suff., 1822, Vol. XXXIII, fol. 338.

„ to GARDINER, of Thundridge Bury, co. Hertf., and Thurgarton Priory, co. Nottingham, 182 . ., Vol. XXXIV, fol. 47 ; 183 . ., Vol. XXXIX, fol. 342.

COOPER, formerly HEAP, William Dodge Cooper, of Toddington, co. Bedf., 182 . ., Vol. XXXV, fol. 303 and 304.

COOPER, Lieut.-Col. John Hutton, M.P., of Sleaford, co. Linc. (Bart.), (died 28 Dec. 1828), 1827, Vol. XXXVI, fol. 390.

„ Frederick, of Brighton, and Icclesham Place, co. Sussex, Solicitor to the Duke of Norfolk, Earl Marshal, 184 . ., Vol. XLVIII, fol. 373.

„ Samuel Thomas (and Barbara his wife), of The Hall, Bulwell, co. Nottingham, 186 . ., Vol. LV, fol. 278.

„ Samuel Joshua, of Mt. Vernon, Darfield, co. York, 186 . ., Vol. LV, fol. 318. (Berry's Suppl.)

„ George, F.R.C.S., of Hanwell, co. Middx., 186 . ., Vol. LVII, fol. 39.

„ Henry, of Forest Lodge, Shooters Hill, co. Kent, 1885,* Vol. LXIII, fol. 5.

„ John, of Hooley House, Purley, co. Surrey, 1885, Vol. LXIII, fol. 33.

COOPER-DEAN, J. E., of Littledown House, Holdenhurst, Hampsh., 1888, Vol. LXIV, fol. 215.

COOPER, Sir Daniel, Knt., Speaker, Legislative Assembly, New South Wales. [13 or 18 July 1857],* Vol. LII, fol. 288 [Bart. 26 Jan. 1863, K.C.M.G. 25 Oct. 1880].

„ Sir Daniel, G.C.M.G., of London. Supporters, 1888,* Vol. LXIV, fol. 286. Sir Daniel, G.C.M.G., of London. Supporters with the Baronetcy, 1889, Vol. LXV, fol. 45.

COOPEY, Rev. Samuel, M.A. (Oriel Coll., Oxf.), of Flax Bourton, co. Somerset, 16 Nov. 1734, Vol. VIII, fol. 190.

COORE to BLAGROVE, Henry John, of Bucks., and Jamaica, 184 . ., Vol. XLVI, fol. 191.

COOTE, Sir Charles, K.C.B. [16 Jan. 1764], of Coote Hall, co. Cavan, Ireland. Supporters, 176 . ., Vol. XI, fol. 45.

„ Maj.-Gen. Sir Eyre, K.B. [28 June 1770], of Ireland. Supporters, 177 . ., Vol. XII, fol. 98.

„ Maj.-Gen. Sir Eyre, K.B. [19 May 1802], of Ireland. Supporters, 180 . ., Vol. XXI, fol. 394.

COPE, Lieut.-Gen. Sir John, K.B. [12 July 1743], of Whitavie, co. Norf. Supporters, 17 . . ., Vol. IX, fol. 114.

„ Thomas (s. of Thomas), of Osbaston Hall, co. Leic., 1833, Vol. XXXIX, fol. 252.

COPE, late PINNIGER, John Alexander M., of Drumilly, co. Armagh, 1867, Vol. LVI, fol. 283 ; 184 . ., Vol. XLVIII, fol. 288.

COPELAND, William Taylor, of Longton, Stoke upon-Trent, co. Staff., and Lincoln's Inn Fields, London (Lord Mayor 1836), 1836, Vol. XXXI, fol. 238.

COPEMAN, ..., of Long Stratton, co. Norf., 186 . ., Vol. LIV, fol. 23.

„ . . . ., of Hemsby Hall, Hemsby, co. Norf., 186 . ., Vol. LV, fol. 194.

COPESTAKE after GOODALL, Thomas, of Langley, co. Derby, and Birmingham, co. Warw., 182 . ., Vol. XXXVI, fol. 190.

COPESTAKE, Sampson, of Sundridge, co. Kent (see George MOORE), 186 . ., Vol. LIV, fol. 144.

COPLEY, late alias NEWBY, Thomas, of Nether Hall, co. York, 1771, Vol. XII, fol. 111.

COPLEY, Lord LYNDHURST, Hampsh. Arms and Supporters, [1827], Vol. XXXVI, fols. 234 and 236.

COPPARD, William Hicks, of Hastings, co. Sussex, 28 Jan. 1769, Vol. XI, fol. 354. (Berry.)

COPPEN, John Maurice, of Bella Vista, Maidenhead, Berks., 1898, Vol. LXX, fol. 186.

COPPINGER to BURGH, Fysh, of Berks., 177 . ., Vol. XIV, fol. 121.

CORBET, late D'AVENANT, Sir Corbet, of Adderley, Shropsh. (bart. fil. [?]) [Bart.] 1786 (decd. s.p.), 178 . ., Vol. XV, fol. 144.

„ late MAURICE, Edward, of Petton, Shropsh.: Moreton Corbet and Ynysmaengwyn, co. Merioneth, Wales, 178 . ., Vol. XV, fol. 146.

„ late MAURICE, Athelstan, of co. Denbigh, and Ynys, co. Merioneth, Wales, 182 . ., Vol. XXXII, fol. 217.

„ late PIGOTT, Rev. John Dryden, of Sundorne Castle and Edgmond, Shropsh. (died s.p. 1889), 1865, Vol. LV, fol. 328.

CORBET, Rev. George W. (formerly PIGOTT), of Upper Magna Rectory, Shropsh., 1890, Vol. LXV, fol. 309.

CORBET, late SODEN, and WILLIAMES, his wife, of The Circus, Bath, and Ynys, co. Merioneth, Wales, 186 . ., Vol. LVI, fols. 27 and 29.

CORBETT after HOLLAND, Corbett, of Admington House, co. Glouc., 1839, Vol. XLIII, fol. 380.

CORBETT, Francis, of Admington House, co. Glouc., 1872, Vol. LVIII, fol. 123.

CORBETT, late FLINT, Robert, of Longnor and Micklewood, Shropsh., 5 Dec. 1774, Vol. XIII, fol. 44.

„ late PLYMLEY, Ven. Joseph, Archdeacon of Shropshire, 1804, Vol. XXIII, fol. 75.

CORBETT after THOMPSON, William, of Dennhall, co. Chester, and Elsham, co. Linc., 1810, Vol. XXVI, fol. 73.

CORBETT-WINDER, William (reputed son of LYON-WINDER ?), of Cotsbrook and Ashton Hall, Shropsh. (see LYON-WINDER), 186 . ., Vol. LVII, fol. 147.

CORBETT, John Impney, of Dodderhall, co. Worc., and Ynys-y-Maengwyn, Towyn, co. Merioneth, Wales, 1893,* Vol. LXVII, fol. 173.

„ Thomas, F.R.C.S., of Droitwich, co. Worc., 1894, Vol. LXVII, fol. 291.

CORBIN, ..., of Castlebury, co. Somerset, and St. Peter Port, Guernsey, 183 . .. Vol. XLII, fol. 73.

„ . . . ., M.R.C.S., of Castlebury, co. Somerset, and St. Peter Port, Guernsey, 183 . ., Vol. XLIV, fol. 117.

CORBOULD, ..., of Bracon Ash, and Tacolnestone, co. Norf., 185 . ., Vol. L, fols. 373 and 375.

CORDES (see HUGER), of Barbados. (Match), 177 . ., Vol. XII, fol. 110.

CORFIELD, Frederick Chamer, of Ormonde Field, Heanor, co. Derby, 1897, Vol. LXX, fol. 9.

CORMAC to LAWSON, of Feversham, co. Kent, Holme Shaw, Kirkpatrick, and Leith, Scotland. (Match), 180 . ., Vol. XXI, fol. 294.

CORNEWALL late AMYAND, Sir George, Bart., of co. Hereford, 5 July 1771, Vol. XII, fols. 93 and 94. (Berry.)

CORNEWALL after WALKER, Frederick, of Diddlebury, Shropsh., 17 . . ., Vol. XIV, fol. 342.

CORNFOOT, ..., of Ryde, Isle of Wight, and Petersham, co. Surrey, 183 . ., Vol. XLI, fol. 385.

CORNICK, Richard, of Allington, co. Dorset, 1881, Vol. LXI, fol. 150.

CORNISH, ..., of Exeter, co. Devon, 184 . ., Vol. XLVIII, fol. 347.

CORNISH to MOWBRAY, ..., of Exeter, co. Devon, co. Warw. and Sussex, 184 . ., Vol. XLVIII, fol. 385.

CORNISH-BROWN, Charles B., of Sandford, co. Devon, 186 . ., Vol. LV, fol. 134.

CORNWALL, Moses, Mayor of Kimberley, S. Africa, 2nd s. of William, 189 . ., Vol. LXXI, fol. . . . .

CORNWALLIS to MANN, James, 5th Earl, of co. Staff., s. of Bp. of Lichfield and Coventry [Roy. Lic., 9 April 1814], 181 . ., Vol. XXVIII, fol. 70.

CORNWALLIS, Adm. Sir William, G.C.B. [2 Jan. 1815]. Supporters, 181 . ., Vol. XXIX, fol. 41.

CORNWALLIS to MANN, Charles James, Viscount BROME, [16 Sept.] 1823, Vol. XXXIV, fol. 168.

CORNWALLIS, late MANN, Lady Julia, 1844, Vol. XLVII, fol. 253.

„ late WYKEHAM, Martin Fiennes, of Leeds Castle and Lidwells, co. Kent, 1859, Vol. LIII, fol. 255.

CORRIE, Daniel, LL.D., Bp. of Madras [1835-1837], of Colsterworth and Osbournby, co. Linc., and Morcott, co. Rutland, 183 . ., Vol. XLI, fol. 67.

„ John, of The Elms, Itchen Abbas, Hampsh., 1897, Vol. LXX, fol. 3.

CORTHINE, Josiah, of Kingston-upon-Hull, co. York, and Newchurch, Isle of Wight, 177 . ., Vol. XII, fol. 72.

CORY, late EADE, Henry COREY, of Redruth and St. Mawes, co. Cornw., and Plymouth, co. Devon (M.A., St. John's Coll., Camb.), 1864, Vol. LV, fol. 224.

COSBY (see JACKSON), of Barnsville Park, co. Glouc., 18 . . ., Vol. XXXI, fol. 252.

COSSERAT, Bernard, of Exeter, co. Devon, 9 Jan. 1729, Vol. VIII, fol. 54.

COSSHAM, John Nicholls, of Bristol, co. Glouc., 181 . ., Vol. XXVIII, fol. 236.

COSTER, ..., of Devonshire Lodge, London (naturalized British subject), 186 . ., Vol. LV, fol. 202.

COSTERTON, ..., of Great Yarmouth, co. Norf., 182 . ., Vol. XXXVI, fol. 50.

COSWAY to SOWDON (reputed s. of Sowdon), of Barnstaple, co. Devon, 185 . ., Vol. LI, fol. 286.

COTTAM, now MILNER, ... of Aylesford, co. Kent. [Surname and Arms of Milner only.] 24 May 1788, Vol. XVI, fol. 407. [Crisp, Fragm. Geneal., V, p. 67.]

COTTERELL, ..., Bart., and EVANS, his late wife, of Garnons, co Hereford, 182 . ., Vol. XXXV, fols. 382 and 384.

COTTIER, Charles Edward Ludlow, of Houndercombe, co. Devon, s. of Francis, of Plymouth, 1897, Vol. LXX, fol. 42.

COTTIN to MURRAY, Adolphus, of Ardlebury, co. Hertf. (see Murray of Clermont, in Baronets), 1834, Vol. XL, fol. 299.

COTTLE, Susannah, dau. of Sarah Lady HODGES, 1699, Vol. IV, fol. 315.

„ James, LL.D., Vicar of St. Mary Magdalene, Taunton, co. Somerset, and Marston Musgrave and Bemerton, Wilts., 184 . ., Vol. XLV, fol. 347.

COTTON, late SHEPPARD, William Thomas, of Littleton, Bucks., and Crakemarsh, co. Staff. (Match), 1800, Vol. XX, fol. 440.

COTTON before SHEPPARD, Thomas, of Littleton, Bucks., and Crakemarsh, co. Staff. Quarterly Arms, 180 . ., Vol. XXIII, fol. 370.

COTTON, Lieut.-Gen. Sir Stapleton, Bart., K.B. [21 Aug. 1812], of co. Chester. Supporters, 181 . ., Vol. XXVII, fol. 231. [See next.]

„ [Baron 17 May 1814, Viscount 8 Feb. 1827], of co. Chester. Supporters, 18 . ., Vol. XXXVIII, fol. 108.

COTTON after STAPLETON, Viscount COMBERMERE, of co. Chester, [1827], Vol. XXXVII, fol. 254.

COTTON, late GREEN, Elizabeth, widow of Joseph, of Dalbury and Etwall Hall, co. Derby, and Bellaport, Shropsh., 182 . ., Vol. XXXII, fol. 14.

COTTON, ..., of Letherhead and Clapham, co. Surrey (M.A. Oxf.), 18 . ., Vol. XXXVIII, fol. 212.

COTTON-JODRELL, E. J. D., of Reaseheath Hall, co. Chester, 1890, Vol. LXV, fol. 307.

COTTRELL-DORMER, Clement, s. of Charles, of Rousham, co. Oxf., 1877, Vol. LX, fol. 15.

COTTRELL to UPTON-COTTERELL-DORMER, Clement, of co. Oxf., and Ingmire Hall, Sedbergh, co. York, 1877, Vol. LX, fol. 17.

COTYGREAVE, late JOHNSON, Sir John, of co. Chester, 179 . .. Vol. XIX, fol. 67.

COULL after DIXON, Robert, of North Middleton, co. Northumberland (see FORSTER), 187 . ., Vol. LIX, fol. 143. (Berry's Suppl.)

COULSON, ... of Blenkinsop Castle and Jesmond, co. Northumberland, 180 . ., Vol. XXI, fol. 391.

COULTHART, John Ross, of Coulthart, co. Wigton ; Collyn, co. Dumfries, Scotland ; and Croft House, Ashton-under-Lyne, co. Lanc.. Nov. 1846, Vol. LIII, fol. 57 [and 17 Jan. 1859]. (Herald. and Geneal., III, p. 253.)

COUPLAND after BERGNE, Richard C., of Skellingthorpe, co. Linc., 186 . ., Vol. LVI,·fol. 337 (see Berry).

COURT, James, Sec. to the Corp^n. of the Trinity House, London, 181 . ., Vol. XXX, fol. 133.

COURTAIL, Charles, late BRADLEY (ALBERT, wife of), of Shropsh. and co. Sussex. ALBERT impaled (see ALBERT), 180 . ., Vol. XXIII, fol. 400.

COURTAULD, ..., of Folly House, Bocking, co. Essex, 184 . ., Vol. XLVII, fol. 128.

COURTENAY, Viscount, Earl of DEVON, of co. Devon. (Match with ARUNDEL), 17 . . ., Vol. X, fol. 426.

    „   (see JACKSON), of co. Devon.   Quarterly with BURGOYNE, 177 . ., Vol. XIV, fol. 271.

COURTENAY, late THROCKMORTON, George, of Weston Underwood, Bucks., and West Molland, co Devon, 17 . ., Vol. XVII, fol. 442.

    „   late THROCKMORTON, ..., of Weston Underwood, Bucks., and West Molland, co. Devon, 181 . ., Vol. XXXI, fol. 164.

COURTIN to ALLCARD, ..., of co. Devon, 186. ., Vol. LV, fol. 48.

COURTNEY to CURTIS, John, Lieut., R.N., of London, 181 . ., Vol. XXVIII, fol. 132.

COURTNEY (see STACKHOUSE), of Tregedllas, co. Cornw.   Match with WILLIAM and PENDARVES, 181 . ., Vol. XXVIII, fol. 282.

COUSINS, E.A., of Nash Court, Tenbury, co. Worc., 1887, Vol. LXIV, fol. 22.

COUSSMAKER, John Herman de, of Worplesden, co. Surrey, 17 . ., Vol. XIV, fol. 189 ; and Hockney, prov. of Brabant ; to grandfather John. Certified May 1779, Vol. XIV, fol. 189 (see Berry).

COUTTS. See MONEY, BARTLETT, &c.

COVENTON, ..., of Gray's Inn, London, 185 . ., Vol. LI, fol. 189.

COVENTRY after DARLEY, Thomas (minor), of Sargeants' Inn, London, and Henley-upon-Thames, co. Oxf.   Quarterly Arms, 17 . . ., Vol. XX, fol. 157.

COVENTRY-CAMPION, John William, of Oundle, co. Northampton, and Emanuel Coll., Camb., 183 . ., Vol. XLI, fol. 160.

COWAN to GREEN, Thomas, of London, 17 . . ., Vol. XX, fol. 327.

COWAN, Sir John, Bart. [1837], Lord Mayor of London [1837-38], 183 . ., Vol. XLII, fol. 228.

    „   Lieut.-Col. Phineas, of Lancaster Gate, London, Sheriff of London and Middx., 1883, Vol. LXII, fol. 134.

COWARD, Bridget (s. of Colonel William, M.P.), of Wells, co. Somerset.   Match with Hon. George HAMILTON, 17 . . ., Vol. XVII, fol. 103.

COWARD, ..., of co. Somerset. (Match with HASTINGS.) Augmentation to BECKFORD (M.P. ?), 18 . . ., Vol. XXV, fol. 388.

COWARD, ..., of Whitehall, and Islington, Jamaica, ? London, 18 . . ., Vol. XXXI, fol. 317.

COWBURN to SMITH-MASTERS, Rev. Allan, of Sydenham, co. Kent, 1862, Vol. LIV, fol. 308.

COWELL, Lieut.-Col. John Stepney. K.H., of Coleshill, Bucks., and Llanelly, co. Carmarthen, Wales, 1857, Vol. LII, fol. 318.

COWELL-STEPNEY, ..., Bart., of Coleshill, Bucks., and Llanelly, co. Carmarthen, Wales, 1857, Vol. LII, fol. 330.

COWNE to TUDOR-NELTHORPE, ..., of Sedgwick Park, co. Sussex, and Heathfield Lodge, Acton, 180 . ., Vol. XXIV, fol. 29.

COWPER, Baron [9 Nov. 1706], Lord Keeper of the Great Seal, of co. Hertf. and Kent. Supporters, 17 . . ., Vol. V, fol. 193.

,,　. . . ., of Nutbank, Skelton, co. Cumberland, 18 . . ., Vol. XXXI, fol. 364. (See COWPER-ESSEX), 188 . ., Vol. LXIV, fol. 288. (Crisp, VI, p. 13.)

COWPER-TEMPLE [17 Nov. 1869], William Francis, P.C., of Broadlands, Hampsh., [? afterwards] Baron MOUNT-TEMPLE [25 May 1880], (died s.p.). [1869], Vol. LVII, fol. 210.

COWPER-COLES, Cowper Phipps, C.B., of Wigmore Street, London, 1888, Vol. LXIV, fols. 207 and 211.

COWPER-ESSEX, J. C., of Yewfield Castle, Hawkshead, co. Lanc., .and Oldfields, Essex Park, Acton, co. Middx., 1888, Vol. LXIV, fol. 288. (Crisp, VI, pp. 9 and 13.)

COX (see TATEM), of Colchester, co. Essex. (Match), 17 . . ., Vol. VIII, fol. 135.

COX, Robert, s. of Joshua, of Quarley, Hampsh., and Clent, co. Worc., 1761, Vol. X, fol. 398. (Berry.)

,,　. . . ., of Charton, Farningham, co. Kent, and Limpsfield, co. Surrey, 182 . ., Vol. XXXIII, fol. 142.

,,　. . . ., of the Middle Temple, London ; Charton, Farningham, and Middleton Longfield, co. Kent, 18 . . ., Vol. XLIV, fols. 198 and 200.

COX-MURCHISSON, Capt., K.M.M., 1888, Vol. LXIV, fol. 297.

COXED, John, D.C.L., Warden of New Coll., Oxf., 14 Nov. 1737, Vol. VIII, fol. 224[b].

COXHEAD, Thomas, of Beckley, co. Oxf., and London, 17 . . ., Vol. XVII, fol. 73.

COXWELL-ROGERS, Richard Rogers, of Dowdeswell House and Charlton Kings, co. Glouc., [25 April] 1850, Vol. XLIX, fol. 307 ; 185 . ., Vol. LI, fol. 170. [Misc. G. et H., 1, p. 257.]

COYTMORE after BELASYSE (heretofore WYNN), of co. York, 181 . ., Vol. XXIX, fol. 319.

COZENS, William Hardy, of Letheringsett, co. Norf., 184 . ., Vol. XLVI, fol. 119.

COZENS-HARDY, W. H., of Letheringsett and Norwich, co. Norf., 184 . ., Vol. XLVI, fol. 130.

COZENS, James Brewster, of Woodham Mortimer, co. Essex, 18 . . ., Vol. XLIX, fol. 473.

COZENS to GRIMWOOD, ..., of Woodham Mortimer, co. Essex, and Cressing Temple, 18 . . ., Vol. XLIX, fol. 486.

CRABB to BOUCHER, ..., of Hampsh. and Jamaica, 183 . ., Vol. XLII, fol. 195.

CRABBE to BOULTON, Henry and brother Richard, of co. Warw. and London, 17 . . ., Vol. IX, fol. 182.

CRACKANTHORPE, late COOKSON, ..., of co. Cumberland, 179 . ., Vol. XVIII, fol. 117.

CRACKANTHORPE, M. H., of 65, Rutland Gate, London, 1890, Vol. LXV, fol. 333.

CRACROFT to AMCOTTS, ..., of Hackthorn, co. Linc., 185 . ., Vol. LI, fols. 104-6.

CRACROFT before AMCOTTS, . . ., of Kettlethorpe, co. Linc., 185 . ., Vol. LII, fol. 277.

CRADDOCK, Maj.-Gen. Sir John Francis, K.B. [16 Feb. 1803], (s. of Craddock, Archbp. of Dublin), 180 . ., Vol. XXII, fol. 90. Supporters, fol. 92.

CRADOCK-HARTOPP (late BUNNY), Sir Edmund, of co. Leic. Quarterly Arms and escutcheon of pretence HARLOCK, Bart., 1796, Vol. XIX, fol. 249.

CRADOCK, late GROVE [1849], Edward HARTOPP-, M.A., of Shenston Park, co. Staff., Canon of Worc., Rector of Tedstone Delamere, co. Hereford, 18 . ., Vol. XLIX, fol. 150.

CRADOCK-HARTOPP, Sir William Edmond, Bart., of co. Warw.. 18 . . ., Vol. XLIX, fol. 158.

CRADOCK, Christopher (rep. son), of Hartforth, co. York, 185 . ., Vol. L, fol. 199.

„ Edmund J. Woodburne, of Ryde, Isle of Wight (s. of C. C. Adderley), 1886, Vol. LXIII, fol. 251.

CRAGG to BARKER, of Ruddington, co. Nottingham, nat. and reputed son of Barker, 183 . ., Vol. XL, fol. 5.

CRAGGS, James, of Wysel alias Wyserley, par. of Wolsingham, co. Durham, and Newland, co. Dublin. Three daughters mar. TREFUSIS, ELERT and NEWSHAM, 18 Feb. 169⁹⁰, Vol. IV, fols. 73 and 74. (Berry.)

CRAGGS [before Eliot], Baron ELIOT. (Match with NUGENT [?]), [15 April 1789] Vol. XVII, fol. 123.

CRAGGS, Elizabeth BLENKEN, only issue of William, of Barstwick-in-Holderness, co. York, wife of Joseph EGLIN, of Kupen House, 2 June 1826, Vol. XXXVI, fol. 16.

„ Hariot (see Richard ELIOT), 1726, Vol. VII, fol. 519.

CRAIG, [Maj.-Gen.] Sir James Henry, K.B. [14 Jan. 1797]. Arms and Supporters, 17 . . ., Vol. XX, fol. 95.

CRAMER to ROBERTS, Martha, wife of Rev. John, of Cranbrooke, co. Kent; Sallymount, co. Kildare; and Brightfields, co. Cork, Ireland, 180 . ., Vol. XXI, fol. 280.

„ to COGHILL, Jonah, of Coghill Hall, co. York, and Belvedere House, Drumcondra, co. Dublin, Ireland, 1817, Vol. XXX, fol. 190.

CRAMPHORNE, James, of Albury; Joseph, of Sawbridgeworth, co. Hertf., 29 Jan. 170⁹⁰, Vol. V, fol. 24, and Add. MS. 14,830, fol. 66. (Berry.)

CRANBROOK, Viscount (GATHORNE-HARDY), of co. Sussex and York. Supporters, 1878, Vol. LX, fol. 111; quarterings, fol. 115.

CRANE to BLATHWAYT, ..., of co. Glouc. (Match), 181 . ., Vol. XXX, fol. 147.

CRANKE, Peter (J.P., Tower Hamlets), of Tower Hill, London, 3 Feb. 1727, Vol. VII, fol. 581, and Add. MS. 14,830, fol. 193.

CRANLEY, Lord [20 May 1776] (ONSLOW), of co. Surrey and Sussex. Supporters, 177 . ., Vol. XIII, fol. 209.

CRANMER, late WEBB, Ann, of Quendon House, co. Essex. (Match), 181 . ., Vol. XXVII, fol. 287.

„ late MOUNSEY, ..., of Quendon House, co. Essex, 181 . ., Vol. XXVIII, fol. 189.

„ late DIXON, Esther Maria (widow), of East Sheen, co. Surrey. Crest for MOHINNE?, 181 . ., Vol. XXVII, fols. 289 and 290.

CRANMER-BYNG, A. M., of Quendon Hall, co. Essex, 1882, Vol. LXI, fol. 323. (Berry's Suppl.)

CRANSTOUN (see BRENTON), Gov. of Rhode Island, N. America, 181 . ., Vol. XXVII, fol. 112.

CRANWORTH, Baron [1850] (ROLFE), of co. Norf. Arms and Supporters, 184 . ., Vol. XLIX, fols. 418-20.

CRASTER after WOOD, ..., of Craster, co. Northumberland, 183 . ., Vol. XLIII, fol. 46.

CRAVEN from DENHAM, Augustus, reputed son of Craven, of Benham, Berks., with consent of Earl Craven, 183 . ., Vol. XXXIX, fol. 180.

CRAVEN, John, of Waltham Abbey, co. Essex, and Wakefield, co. York, 17 . . ., Vol. IX, fol. 190.

CRAVEN, late GOODWIN, Capt., of Brockhampton Park, Sevenhampton, co. Glouc., 186 . ., Vol. LIV, fol. 96.

CRAWHALL, ..., of Nun Monkton, co. York, 18 . . ., Vol. LVII, fol. 236. (Berry's Suppl.)

CRAWLEY (-BOEVEY), ..., of Flaxley Abbey, co. Glouc. Arms of BOEVEY in chief of Crawley, 179 . ., Vol. XVII, fol. 127.

CRAWLEY, ... (Spr.), of Bridport, Rugby, co. Warw. and Stow-Nine-Churches. LLOYD quartering, 187 . ., Vol. LVIII, fol. 258.

CRAWSHAW, Baron (BROOKS), of co. Lanc., 1892, Vol. LXVII, fol. 69.

CRAWSHAY, ..., of Merthyr Tydvil, co. Glamorgan, Wales, 179 . ., Vol. XVIII, fol. 178.

CREALOCK, Col. Henry Hope, C.B., of Langerton, Littleham, co. Devon (Knt. 5th Class Medjedie), 186 . ., Vol. LV, fol. 238.

CREE (late MCMAHON), John, of Thornhill, co. Dorset, and Cullenswood, co. Dublin, 181 . ., Vol. XXIX, fol. 55.

CREE, John, of Marylebone, co. Middx., and Calcutta, 6 April, 1786. (Burke.)

CREED, James, of St. Dunstans in the East, London, 16 June, 1725, Vol. VII, fol. 400 ; Add. MS. 14,380, fol. 196.

   ,,   Richard (s. of Henry), of London. (Match with DODD), 18 . . ., Vol. XXV, fol. 75.

CREGOE-COLMORE, Capt., E.I.C.S., of Moor End, Charlton Kings, co. Glouc., 183 . ., Vol. XLI, fols. 180 and 182.

CREMER, late WOODROW, ..., of Beeston Regis, co. Norf., 178 . ., Vol. XVI, fol. 105.

CRESSETT before PELHAM, Henry, of Crowhurst, co. Sussex. Quarterly Arms, 179 . ., Vol. XVIII, fol. 129.

CRESSWELL, late EASTERBY, Francis, of Cresswell, co. Northumberland, an Elder Brother of the Trinity House, London, 181 . ., Vol. XXVI, fol. 32.

CRESSWELL-BAKER, Addison John, of Woodhorn, Northumberland, 18 . . ., Vol. XLIV, fols. 361-4 and 389.

CRESWELL, George, of Ocle Court, Ocle Prichard, co. Hereford, 1895, Vol. LXVIII, fol. 158.

CRESWICK, Henry, of Sheffield, co. York, and Hawthorne House, Melbourne, Victoria, 185 . ., Vol. LII, fol. 90.

CREW, Joseph of St. Paul, Shadwell, co. Middx., 18 . ., Vol. XXV, fol. 250.

CREWDSON, W. D., of Helme Lodge, Kendal, co. Westmorland, 5 Nov. 1888, Vol. LXIV, fol. 267.

CREWE, Baron [25 Feb. 1806], of co. Chester. Quarterly OFFLEY Arms, and Supporters, 180 . ., Vol. XXIII, fol. 328.

   ,,   (Bart.), late HARPUR, ..., of Calke Abbey, co. Derby. Quarterly Arms, 1808, Vol. XXIV, fol. 424.

CREWE-READ [John Offley Crewe-Read], of Pen-y-Bryn, co. Montgomery, Wales, and Muxton, co. Staff. [Roy. Lic., 25 Mar. 1836] Vol. XLI, fol. 260. [Exemplification 12 April 1836 (Powys-Land Club, XII, pp. 431-434).]

CRICHTON before STUART, ..., [26 Aug. 1805], of Scotland. Quarterly Arms, 180 . ., Vol. XXIII, fol. 196.

CRICHTON, Earl of DUMFRIES and STAIR, of Scotland. (Match with DUFF), 181 . ., Vol. XXVII, fol. 397.

CRICHTON before STUART, ..., of Scotland, 2nd s. of Lord MOUNTSTUART. (See Marquis of BUTE) [21 Mar. 1817], Vol. XXX, fol. 169.

CRIPPS-DAY, F. H., of Manchester Square, London, 1886, Vol. LXIII, fol. 306.

CRISP, William, of Hexton and Lilly, co. Hertf., [2nd June] 1774, Vol. XII, fol. 293 (see Family of Crisp, II, p. 2).

CRISP (MOLINEUX before MONTGOMERIE), of Garboldisham, co. Norf. Quarterly Arms, 181 . ., Vol. XXVII, fol. 392.

CRISP, Frederick A. P., of Hall, Playford, co. Suff., and Surrey, and Ingleden House, Grove Park, co. Middx., 1884,* Vol. LXII, fol. 292.

CRISP, Frederic, of White House, New So... 1898.
    fol. 127.
CROFT, Richard, of Blackburn, co. Lanc., Lon... 1772, Vol. XII, fol. 175.
CROFT (late WOODCOCK), James, of Berkhamps... Thatcham, Berks., 179 . ., Vol. XVIII, fol.
   ,, ..., of York, and Stillington, co. York, 180 .
CROFT to HUDDLESTONE, ..., of Wilts , 18 . . ., Vol.
CROFT, Eliza Ann, Francis M., Mary Anne, Charlotte L... co. Somerset, and Russell Place, St. Pancras, L... Arms of Croft, 182 . ., Vol. XXXIII, fol. 358.
CROFT, late MORGAN, ..., of Bedminster, co. Somerset, 18... fol. 210.
   ,, late MORGAN, ..., of Bedminster and Worle, co. S... Vol. XXX, fol. 356.
   ,, late MORGAN, ..., of Worle, co. Somerset, 182 . ., Vol. XX...
   ,, late PRITCHARD, ..., of Long Ashton and Worle, co. Som... Vol. XXXV, fol. 65.
CROFT, Sir John [Bart.], of Coaling Hall, co. York : Dodington, co. ... Oporto. Crest, 183 . ., Vol. XL, fol. 139. Supporters, K.B... Vol. XL, fol. 151 : [22 Mar. 1836], Vol. XLI, fol. 247. [... Geneal., 11, p. 87.]
CROFTS, Col. James, A.D.C. to Charles III of Spain, and sister Henrietta, of co. Kent (illeg. children of James, Duke of MONMOUTH), 25 July 1709, Vol. V, fol. 369 ; Add. MS. 14,831, fol. 3. (Berry.)
   ,, Robert, of Dumpton House, Isle of Thanet, co. Kent, and London ?, 1810, Vol. XXVI, fol. 8.
CROFTS after HUMBLE, William, of Dumpton House, Isle of Thanet, co. Kent, and Clayton, co. York, 1879, Vol. LX, fol. 291.
CROKER (or CROCKER), John, of Hook Norton, co. Oxf., 1556, Vol. I, fols. 37ᵇ and 38.
   ,, ..., of co. Oxf., Vol. XIII, fol. 72. *See* HEYWOOD.
CROLE-WYNDHAM, ... (illeg.), of Brighton, co. Sussex, and Rutland Gate, London, 1865, Vol. LVI, fol. 9.
CROMER, Baron (BARING), of Hampsh. Supporters, 1892, Vol. LXVII, fol. 71.
CROMPTON, Windmill, of par. of St. Mary le Bow, London (s. of Thomas, of St. Lawrence Jewry, London, Add. MS. 14,831, fol. 8), 16 June 1737, Vol. VIII, fol. 213ᵇ.
   ,, Samuel, s. of Samuel, of co. Derby, 17 . . ., Vol. X, fol. 100.
   ,, Elizabeth, dau. of Thomas, co. Derby, widow of COLTHURST, 1771, Vol. XII, fol. 87.
CROMPTON-STANSFIELD, William R., of Esholt Hall, co. York, 183 . ., Vol. XXXIX, fol. 40.
   ,, -STANSFIELD, William Henry, of Esholt Hall and Agerley Hall, co. York, 187 . ., Vol. LVIII, fol. 110.
CROMPTON, of Heaton Gate and Pilkington Old Hall, co. Lanc. (*see* ORMEROD), 184 . ., Vol. XLVIII, fol. 302.
CROMPTON-ROBERTS, Charles Henry, of London, 186 . ., Vol. LV, fols. 158 and 160.
CROMWELL to FRANKLAND [Henry], Rear-Adm. [1 Jan. 1801], of Muntham, co. Sussex [died 1814], 180 . ., Vol. XXIII, fol. 288.
CROOKES, John Farrer, of Harewell, Shedwick, co. Kent, and Grimthorpe Hadworth, co. York, 186 . ., Vol. LIV, fol. 266.
   ,, Sir William, of Kensington Park Gardens, London, 1898, Vol. LXX, fol. 80.
CROOKSHANKS before BAILLIE, Samuel, of Scotland. Quarterly Arms, 17 . ., Vol. XIV, fol. 213.
CROPPER, Edward (s. of James), of Fernhead, co. Lanc., 1872,* Vol. LVIII, fol. 278.

Edward Denman, of Chester Place, co. Lanc. ;
and San Francisco, 1874, Vol. LIX, fol. 230.

CROPPER after Ti Hodgkinson, of Lambeth, London, and Newcastle-
Swaylands humberland, 1821, Vol. XXXII, fol. 339 (see Berry).

CROSBY, late Wil., of Madras C. S., 182 . ., Vol. XXXIII, fol. 257.
upon-Ty Eaton Hastings, Faringdon, Berks., s. of Edward, of

CROSDILL, Lieut, co. York, 18 . . ., Vol. LXXI, fol. . . . .

CROSLAND, W Decimus, of Sunninghill, Berks., Sheriff of London and
Stainl, and died s.p.m.), 185 . ., Vol. LI, fol. 116.

CROSLEY, Sir Midd wife of), William, of Lincoln's Inn, London (1794), and Leith
Sussex. Escutcheon of pretence, 1807, Vol. XXIV, fol. 180.

CROSS (FA KEY, John, of Wrenbury Hall, co. Chester. 2 quarterings, 1813,
Va XI, fol. 360.

CROSS befo Yard sheton, of Red Scar, co. Lanc., 18 . . ., Vol. XLIX, fol. 250.

CROSS, Rich Assheton, G.C.B. [20 April 1880], Viscount, of co. Lanc.
Supp ers, 1886, Vol. LXIII, fol. 293.

    John, Hollybank, Portesbury, Shropsh., 186 . ., Vol. LV, fol. 322.

    Herbe of Kirkham, co. Lanc., 1884,[*] Vol. LXII, fol. 220.

    ,, SHE ERD-, Herbert, of co. Lanc., and Hamely Park, co. Hertf., 188 . .,
Vol. LXII, fol. 255.

    ,, T mas, of Ottawa, Canada, 1891,[*] Vol. LXVI, fol. 102.

    ,, William, of Leith Vale (s. of James, of Clifton), co. Sussex. FAWTRELL
escutcheon of pretence, co. Sussex. Of Lincoln's Inn, London, 1794 ;
called himself William CROSS-COOPER-SIMPSON, 1800, 180 . ., Vol. XXIV,
fol. 180.

CROSSE, Thomas, M.P. for Westminster [12 Dec. 1701 (Burke)], 23 Jan. 170½,
Vol. V, fol. 56.

    ,, Jane (Lady), Thomas, Bart., of Westminster, dau. of Patrick LAMBE.
Impaled with Lambe, of Stoke Pogis, Bucks., 14 April 1736, Vol. VIII,
fol. 197.

CROSSE, late DAY, Peter, of Baddow, co. Essex, 24 Dec. 1770, Vol. XII, fol. 40.
(Berry).

CROSSE after GODSALVE, John, of Baddow, co. Essex, 17 . ., Vol. XIV, fol. 235.

CROSSE to LEGH, Richard, of Adlington Hall, co. Chester ; Shall Hall and Crosse
Hall, co. Lanc., &c., 180 . ., Vol. XXIV, fol. 32 ; Crest, fol. 34.

    ,, to LEGH, Thomas, of Adlington Hall, co. Chester, co. Lanc. and York,
182 . ., Vol. XXXIV, fol. 108.

CROSSE, late IKIN (LEGH heretofore), of Adlington Hall, co. Chester ; Anna Mary,
wife of Thomas Bright Ikin, 182 . ., Vol. XXXVII, fol. 269.

CROSSE to HAMILTON, ..., of Howden, Tiverton, co. Devon ; Fyn Court,
Broomfield, co. Somerset ; and Garrison, co. Fermanagh, Ireland, 185 . .,
Vol. LIII, fol. 113.

CROSSE, Rev. Marlborough, of St. Clement's Vicarage, Ferrington, co. Norf., 1899,
Vol. LXX, fol. 312.

CROSSFIELD, Talbot King (s. of Abraham), of Stanningfield, co. Suff., 1898,
Vol. LXX, fol. 129.

CROSSLEY, John, of Scaitcliffe, co. Lanc., 182 . ., Vol. XXXII, fols. 267 and 268.

    ,, Sir Francis, Bart. [23 Jan. 1863], of Savile Lodge, Halifax, co. York,
18 . ., Vol. XLIX [? LV], fol. 461.

CROSSLEY (late KERSCHNER), Ernest Augustus John, of Greenwich, co. Kent,
and London, 1880, Vol. LX, fol. 385.

CROSSMAN, Col. Sir William, C.M.G., of Cheswick House, Ancroft, co. Northumberland, 1883,[*] Vol. LXII, fol. 151. (Berry's Suppl.)

CROW, Joseph, of Copgrove and Snape, co. York, 182 . ., Vol. XXXVI, fol. 319.

CROWDER, Major John, of Brotherton Hall, co. York, 182 . ., Vol. XXXII,
fol. 299.

    ,, John, of Wyrardisbury, Bucks., Alderman of London, Lord Mayor 1830,
182 . ., Vol. XXXV, fols. 240 and 241.

CROWE to MARLOWE, M. Sidney, of Leominster (co. Hereford), and London, 13 April 1776, Vol. XIII, fol. 179.
CROWFOOT, William John, M.D. (s. of William, s. of William), of Beccles, co. Suff., and to posterity of grandfather, 14 Feb. 1831, Vol. XXXVIII, fol. 195. (Misc. G. et II.. New S., IV, p. 40, and Crisp, I, p. 26, and Notes, Vol. I, p. 79.)
CROWLE, William, of Wiston, co. York, 6 Jan. 1725, Vol. VII, fol. 294.
„ . . . ., of Water Friston, co. York, 178 . ., Vol. XV, fol. 269. *See* UPPLEBY.
CROWLEY, Sir Ambrose, Knt., Sheriff of London and Middx., D. 14 (Berry) for ped., fol. 4, 14 June 1707, Vol. V, fol. 205 ; 17 . . ., Vol. XIV, fol. 831.
CROWTHER-BENYON, Rev. Samuel Bryan, Vicar of Ladsworth, Petworth, co. Sussex, 1879, Vol. LX, fol. 303.
CROWTHER-BEYNON, Capt. R. W. B., of Chelsham-in-Croydon, co. Sussex, 1874, Vol. LIX, fol. 69. Richard William Barnardiston-Crowther, Capt. Royal Scots, Roy. Lic., 21 Nov. 1874. (Berry's Suppl.)
CROXON, Henry F. (afterwards Henry FERRERS-FERRERS), of Penterheylin Hall, Oswestry, Shropsh., 1885,* Vol. LXIII, fols. 57 and 87.
CRUDGE, ..., of Gulvall, co. Cornw. (Match.) (*See* HAWKINS.) 179 . ., Vol. XVIII, fol. 243.
CRUGER to PEACH, ..., of Tockington, co. Glouc., 178 . ., Vol. XVI, fol. 411.
CRUMPE to BLAND, ... of Randalls Park, Leatherhead, co. Surrey, and Limerick, Ireland, 181 . ., Vol. XXVI, fol. 344.
CRUSE, Jonathan, of Sheering, co. Essex, and Ogbourne St. George, Wilts., 178 . ., Vol. XVII, fol. 143.
CRUSE to FEAKE, ..., of Durrington House, co. Essex. Arms of FEAKE, 180 . ., Vol. XXI, fol. 89.
CRUSO, ..., of Leek, co. Staff. (Match.) (*See* DAINTRY.) 181 . ., Vol. XXVI, fol. 281.
CRUTCHLEY, late DUFFIELD, ..., of Sunninghill Park, Berks., 180 . ., Vol. XXIII, fol. 321.
CRUTTWELL, ..., of Berrymead, Syncomb and Widcomb, co. Somerset, 183 . .. Vol. XXXIX, fol. 350.
CRUWYS after SHARLAND, ... of Cruwys-Morchard and South Molton, co. Devon, 18 . . ., Vol. XXXVIII, fol. 341.
CUBITT, ..., of London (? Baron ASHCOMBE), 184 . ., Vol. XLVI, fol. 209.
CUCHET to FLEMING, ..., of Farnham, co. Surrey, 18 . . ., Vol. XXV, fol. 238.
CUCTO to ELLERKER, Joseph Eulogio, of Hart, co. Durham, and Havannah, Island of Cuba, 181 . ., Vol. XXX, fol. 426.
CUFF to ADAMS (minors), Thomas, of co. Carmarthen, Wales, 184 . ., Vol. XLVI, fol. 132.
CULLEY, ..., (of Leather-Culley, 1896), of Fowberry Tower, co. Northumberland, 184 . ., Vol. XLV, fol. 313.
CULLINGTON, Daniel, of Exmouth, co. Devon, 1876, Vol. LIX, fol. 202.
CULLUM after MILNER-GIBSON, George Gery, of Hardwicke House and Thekerton House, co. Suff., 18 . . ., Vol. LX, fol. 241.
CULLUM, Dame Mary (*see* HANSON), [17 Aug.] 1793, Vol. XVIII, fol. . . . . (Misc. G. et II., 2nd S., V, p. 72.)
CUMBER, ..., of London, 186 . ., Vol. LIV, fol. 146.
CUMBERLEGE to WARE, ..., of Hendon Hall, co. Middx., 186 . ., Vol. LIV, fol. 330.
CUMMING, George, M.D., M.R.C.S., of Dothyfrydd, nr. Denbigh, Wales (Brownlow WYNNE), 1840, Vol. XLVI, fol. 251.
CUMMING to WYNNE, Brownlow Wynne, Bar.-at-Law, of Garthew, co. Denbigh, Wales (d. 1882), 184 . ., Vol. XLVI, fol. 253.
CUMMING-BRUCE after HOVELL-THURLOW, ..., of co. Suff., Lord THURLOW, 187 . ., Vol. LIX, fol. 53.
CUMMING-WHITTINGTON, E. J., of Eastbourne, co. Sussex, 1894, Vol. LXVIII, fol. 111.

CUNARD, Samuel, of Bush Hill, Edmonton, co. Middx., 18 . . ., Vol. LIII, fol. 80.

CUNLIFFE, Sir Ellis, Knt. and Bart., of Saighton Hall, co. Chester. Crest, 12 May 1760, Vol. X, fol. 236. (Misc. G. et H., II, p. 251).

CUNLIFFE-OFFLEY, of Madeley Manor, co. Staff., 182 . ., Vol. XXXVIII, fol. 85.

CUNLIFFE after PICKERSGILL, John, of Coulsdon, &c., co. Surrey, and Addingham, co. York, 1867, Vol. LVI, fol. 211.

CURRER, late ROUNDELL, Danson Richard, of Gledstone [? Clifton] House, &c., co. York, 1806, Vol. XXIV, fol. 18 [see Burke].

CURRER to ROUNDELL, Danson Richard, of Clifton House, co. York, 1851, Vol. L, fol. 68.

CURREY, Robert, of Herne Hill, co. Surrey, 184 . ., Vol. LXVII, fol. 85.

CURRIE, (Sir) Frederick (Bart.), of Poplar, co. Middx., Sec. to the Governor-Gen. of India, 184 . ., Vol. XLVIII, fol. 227.

CURRYER, John, of Broad Street, London, 19 July 1725, Vol. VII, fol. 473, and Add. MS. 14,881, fol. 40.

CURSON, late ROPER, ..., of Waterperry, co. Oxf., 178 . ., Vol. XVI, fol. 343.

CURSON, ..., of co. Oxf. Quarterly Arms, 181 . ., Vol. XXVII, fol. 349.

CURTIS, Richard Arthur F., of Lambeth and Peckham, co. Surrey (a ward of the Salters' Company), 182 . ., Vol. XXXVIII, fol. 123.

  ,, Matthew, Alderman and Mayor of Manchester, of Heaton Mersey, co. Lanc., 1877, Vol. LX, fol. 24. (Berry's Suppl.)

  ,, Rear-Adm. Sir Roger, Knt., of Gatcombe, Isle of Wight. Augmentation, 179 . ., Vol. XVIII, fol. 396.

  ., Adm. Sir Roger, G.C.B. [2 Jan. 1815], Knt. and Bart. Supporters, 181 . ., Vol. XXVIII, fol. 368.

  ,, (dau. of CONSTABLE), Anne, Lady, of Callands Grove, Southgate, co. Middx., 180 . ., Vol. XXII, fol. 48.

CURTIS, late COURTNEY, John, of London, 181 . ., Vol. XXVIII, fol. 132.

CURTLER, ..., of Droitwich and Bromsgrove, co. Worc., 188 . ., Vol. XLII, fol. 57.

CURWEN, late CHRISTIAN, ..., of co. Cumberland. Match, 17 . . ., Vol. XVII, fol. 207.

CURZON, Baron SCARSDALE. Supporters, [9 April 1761] Vol. X, fol. 298.

CURZON, Baron [13 Aug. 1794], [Assheton Curzon]. Supporters, 179 . ., Vol. XVIII, fol. 425.

CURZON, Baroness HOWE [5 Aug. 1799], [Sophia Charlotte]. Supporters, 17 . . ., Vol. XX, fol. 388.

CURZON after ROPER, Henry Francis, of Linsted Lodge, co. Kent, and Waterperry House, co. Oxf. (14th Lord ROPER), 178 . ., Vol. XVI, fol. 343. Quarterly Arms, 181 . ., Vol. XXVII, fol. 349.

CURZON-HOWE, Viscount, of co. Nottingham, [7 July 1821] Vol. XXXII, fol. 349.

CUSSANS, Thomas, of St. Thomas, Jamaica, 1767, Vol. XI, fol. 228. (Berry.)

CUST, Baron BROWNLOW, [20 May 1776] of co. Linc. and Hertf. (See BANKES.) Supporters, 177 . ., Vol. XIII, fols. 213 and 295.

CUST to EGERTON, Earl BROWNLOW, of co. Hertf. and Linc., [15 Mar. 1849] Vol. XLIX, fol. 134.

CUST [surname and Arms of EGERTON], of co. Hertf. and Linc., [5 Sept. 1853] Vol. L, fol. 390.

[CUST after BROWNLOW], of co. Hertf. and Linc., [6 July 1863] Vol. LV, fol. 70.

CUSTANCE, Hambleton, Sheriff of Norf., 17 . . ., Vol. IX, fol. 444.

CUTLER, ..., of co. Suff., 16 . . ., Vol. II, fol. 594ᵇ. Match, fol. 595.

  ,, Sir John, Knt. and Bart., 27 Mar. 1693, Vol. IV, fol. 132. (Berry.) (See Grantees of Arms, Vol. I.)

CUTTS, John, Baron of GOWRAN, of co. Kilkenny, Ireland. Supporters, 1692, Vol. IV, fol. 69.

CUYLER, Gen. Cornelius, of Welwyn, co. Hertf., Gov. of Kinsale, 181 . ., Vol. XXVI, fol. 173.

D

DACRE to ASSEY, Charles William, of Carlisle, 1723-24, Vol. XLI, fol. 337.

DE COSTA, Leonor, relict of Alvaro, of Highgate, co. Middx., 20 Feb., 172 . ., Vol. VII, fol. 233 (*see* De Costa).

„ Catherine, widow of Joseph, of Highgate, co. Middx., and Portugal, 8 April 1732, Vol. VIII, fol. 145ᵇ (*see* De Costa).

D'AETH, late HUGHES, George William, Lieut., R.N., of Knowlton, co. Kent, 1808, Vol. XXIV, fol. 440.

DAINTRY, ... of Macclesfield, co. Chester. (*See* RYLE.) (Match), 18 . . ., Vol. XXV, fol. 288.

„ John Smith, of Foden Bank, Prestbury, co. Chester, 10 July 1811, Vol. XXVI, fol. 281. Crest, 181 . ., Vol. XXVII, fol. 408.

D'ALBANI, A. J., of Newmarket, co. Camb., 1889, Vol. LXV, fol. 11.

DALBY-HUNT, Potte and Hutchinson, of Kirby Hall, Gretton, co. Northampton, and Brighton, co. Sussex, 184 . ., Vol. XLVIII, fol. 433.

DALBY, late BLUNT, Rev. Robert, of Castle Donnington, co. Leic., Vicar of Belton, co. Leic., 185 . ., Vol. L, fol. 309.

DALBY, Sir W. B., of Englefield Green, co. Surrey, and Savile Row, London, 1886, Vol. LXIII, fol. 239.

DALE, Robert, of Ashbourne, co. Derby, 22 Aug. 1816, Vol. XXX, fol. 3.

„ David, of Darlington, co. Durham, 1874, Vol. LIX, fol. 51.

„ John Brodrick, of Tynemouth, co. Northumberland, and Weston, co. Durham, s. of John, 1877, Vol. LIX, fol. 302. (Berry's Suppl.)

DALGAIRNS, Lieut., E.I.C., of Ingleston, co. Forfar, Scotland, 181 . ., Vol. XXXI, fols. 78 and 79.

DALGETY, ..., of Oakland Hall, East Tytherley, Hampsh., 186 . ., Vol. LVII, fol. 246.

DALLAS, George, Bart. [31 July 1798], of Petsall, co. Staff., and Upper Harley Street, London, 179 . ., Vol. XX, fol. 181.

„ Lieut.-Gen. Sir Thomas, G.C.B. [1 Aug. 1833], of London. Supporters, 183 . ., Vol. XL, fol. 86.

DALLAS before YORKE, Capt. of Dragoons, of Walmsgate Hall, co. Linc., 185 . .. Vol. LI, fol. 424.

DALLAWAY, Rev. James, F.S.A., of Stroud, co. Glouc. (Historian of Sussex), and Sec. to the Earl Marshal, 17 . . ., Vol. XVII, fol. 368.

DALMER, William, of St. Bartholomew Lane, London, 1772, Vol. XII, fol. 116. (Berry.)

DALRYMPLE to HAY, Sir John, Bart., of Park Place, Duneagit, Old Hall, co. Wigton, Scotland, [20 April 1798] Vol. XX, fol. 168.

DALTON to NORCLIFFE, Thomas, of Langton, co. York. [Aug. 1807] Vol. XXIV, fol. 312.

DALTON, after GRANT, Dalton, Robert Foster, of Shanks House, co. Somerset, 1826, Vol. XXXVI, fol. 131.

DALTON-FITZGERALD, Sir James Richard, [9th] Bart., of Bigods Hall, co. Essex; Thurnham Hall, co. Lanc.; and Ireland, 186 . ., Vol. LIV, fol. 142. [Arms exemplified and Roy. Lic., 4 April 1867 (Burke)], 186 . ., Vol. LVI, fol. 199.

DALTON after WADE, Col. H. C., C.B., of Hauxwell Hall, co. York, 18 . ., Vol. LX, fol. 356. (Berry's Suppl.)

DAMER after DAWSON, Henry and George, of co. Dorset, Earl of PORTARLINGTON, [14 Mar. 1829] Vol. XXXVII, fols. 400, 404, 409 and 411.

DANBY, George (formerly AFFLECK), of Swinton Park, Masham, co. York (died s.p.), 1880, Vol. LXI, fol. 21.

DANCE, now HOLLAND (Sir Nathaniel, Bart. [27 Nov. 1800]), M.P., of Wittenham, Berks., [4 July 1800] Vol. XXI, fol. 46.

DANCE, Lieut.-Col. Sir Charles Webb, Knt. (London), s. of George, R.A., Architect, City of London, 182 . ., Vol. XXXIII, fol. 51.

DANGAR, Henry, of Grantham, co. Cumberland ; Noetsville, co. Northumberland ; Turanville and Brisbane, New South Wales, 185 . ., Vol. LI, fol. 155.

D'ANGIBAN, ..., of Bath, co. Somerset, 186 . ., Vol. LV, fol. 252.

D'ANGLEBERMES to BERTRAND, ..., of the Island of Dominica, 182 . ., Vol. XXXII, fol. 179.

DANIEL before TYSSEN, William George, of Folley House, co. Kent, and Foulden Hall, co. Norf., 181 . ., Vol. XXVIII, fol. 66.

DANIELL, Thomas, of Truro, co. Cornw., 1761, Vol. X, fol. 373. (Berry.)

DANIEL(-TYSSEN-AMHURST), William George Tyssen, of co. Norf., &c., 186 . ., Vol. LVI, fol. 186.

  ,, C. TYSSEN-AMHERST, William George Tyssen, of co. Norf., 186 . ., Vol. LVI, fols. 27, 28, and 280.

  ,, -TYSSEN, ..., of co. Norf., 186 . ., Vol. LVI, fol. 273.

DANSON, late HAYWARD, Thomas, of London, 17 . . ., Vol. XX, fol. 255.

DANVERS, Mary, d. and h. of Sir John, Bart., and wife of [Hon. Augustus Richard] Butler, of Swithland, co. Leic., and Prescot Manor and Whitwood Forest, co. Oxf., 179 . ., Vol. XIX, fol. 373.

DANVERS after BUTLER, Hon. Augustus Richard, of London, 179 . ., Vol. XIX, fol. 375.

DARBISHIRE, H. A., of Pendyffryn, co. Carnarvon, Wales, and Rivington, Bolton-le-Moors, co. Lanc., 185 . ., Vol. LI, fol. 233. (Berry's Suppl.)

  ,, Samuel Dukinfield, of Pendyffryn, co. Carnarvon, Wales. Burke [no date].

DARBY, ..., of Sunniside, Coalbrookdale, Shropsh., 1835, Vol. XLI, fol. 375. (Crisp, IV, p. 48.)

DARBY after PAGE, John, of Clifton, Bristol, co. Somerset, and Hadley, co. Middx. (of Exeter Coll., Oxf.), 18 . . ., Vol. LX, fol. 120.

DARBY to ST. QUINTIN, William Thomas, of Sunbury, co. Middx., and co. York, 1795, Vol. XIX, fol. 145.

DARBY, Richard, of Battler's Green, Aldenham, co. Hertf., and Henley-on-Thames, co. Oxf., father of the next, 17 . . ., Vol. XX, fol. 155.

DARBY before COVENTRY, Thomas (minor), of Henley-on-Thames, co. Oxf., 17 . . ., Vol. XX, fol. 157.

  ,, before GRIFFITH, (Lieut.-Col.) Mathew C. of Padworth, Berks. Quarterly Arms, 180 . ., Vol. XXI, fol. 257.

D'ARCY, Sir Conyers, K.B. [1725], of co. York. Supporters, 172 . ., Vol. VII, fol. 541.

DARE after GRAFTON, John M., of Cranbrook House, and Theydon Bois, co. Essex. Quarterly Arms, 180 . ., Vol. XXIII, fol. 247.

  ,, after HALL, Robert Westley, of Wysfields, Cranbrook House, and Bantry Heath, co. Essex, 182 . ., Vol. XXXVI, fols. 96 and 100.

DARELL after ROKEWOOD, of Calehill, co. Kent, and Coldham Hall, co. Suff., 187 . ., Vol. LVIII, fol. 136.

DARELL-BLOUNT, J., of Calehill, co. Kent, and Mapledurham, co. Oxf., 1882, Vol. LXI, fol. 267.

[DARELL, formerly STEPHENS, Robert Darell Smythe, of Treworuan, co. Cornw., and Hillfield House, Stoke Fleming, co. Devon. Roy. Lic., 23 Nov. 1901, to take the surname of Darell in lieu of Stephens, and to bear the arms of Darell. Crisp, Visit. England and Wales, XIV, p. 135.]

DARK to BAYLY, ..., of Hampsh. and Wilts., 180 . ., Vol. XXV, fol. 240.

DARKER, John, of London, 2 Dec. 1768, Vol. XI, fol. 304. (Berry.)

DARLEY, late HARRYSON, Richard, of Aldby Park, co. York, 17 . . ., Vol. XX, fol. 177.

  ,, late WILKS, Henry, nat. s. of Henry BREWSTER-DARLEY, of Aldby, co. York, 180 . ., Vol. XXIV, fol. 409.

  ,, late WILKS, ... Quarterly Arms. Wilks quarterly. (Match with Darley), of Aldby, co. York, 180 . ., Vol. XXIV, fols. 25 and 264.

DARLING, Maj.-Gen. Ralph (afterwards G.C.H.), Allusion to services. Henry Charles, brother, William Lindsay, brother, and two sisters, one Mrs. KENDALL, all of co. Durham, 181 . ., Vol. XXVII, fol. 322.

DARLING to BAGSHAW, ..., Knt., M.D., of co. Derby, and London.   Arms for wife impaled, 181 . ., Vol. XXIX, fol. 79.

DARLING, ..., of Fowberry Tower, co. Northumberland : Halnaker House [? Sussex] and Boxgrove, co. Sussex, 186 . .. Vol. LIV, fol. 6.

DARLING-BARKER, James, 2nd s. of George, of Fowberry Tower, co. Northumberland, and Stockton-on-Tees, co. Durham ; Halnaker House and Boxgrove, co. Sussex, 186 . ., Vol. LIV, fol. 8.

DARLINGTON, [Charlotte Sophia] Countess of [1722].   Supporters, 172 . ., Vol. VII, fol. 171.

DARNELL, William Nicholas, B.D., Rector of Stanhope, co. Durham, &c., and Bow, his wife, [21 Dec. 1832] Vol. XXXIX, fol. 222 [Misc. G. et H., New S., IV, p. 144.]

D'ARTHENAY (see MORIN), of St. Lo, Normandy, 177 . ., Vol. XIV, fol. 108.

DARTINEQUINAVE, Charles (or DARTIQUENAVE), of Westminster, Paymaster H.M. Works, 27 Mar. 1720, Vol. V, fol. 402 ; Add. MS. 14,831, fol. 55.

DARTREY, Baron [18 May 1770] (DAWSON) Thomas, of [Dawson's Grove] co. Monaghan, Ireland, 177 . ., Vol. XII, fol. 27.

DARWIN, late RHODES, Francis, of Elston Hall, Elston, co. Nottingham, 184 . ., Vol. XLIX, fol. 345.

DARWIN, Reginald, of Fern, Hartington, nr. Derby (died 1892), 1890,* Vol. LXV, fol. 202.   (Crisp, IV, 116.)

DASH, Joseph, of St. Michael, Crooked Lane, London, 26 Sept. 1741, Vol. IX, fol. 41.   (Berry.)

DASHWOOD, Adm. Sir Charles, Knt., Capt., R.N., G.C.T. and S. of Portugal, of Vallow Wood, co. Somerset, 180 . ., Vol. XXV, fol. 183.

„   Sir Henry W., Bart., of Kirtlington, co. Oxf.   Supporters, and to his uncle Augustus.   Crest, a griffin's head erminois, erased gu., 1883, Vol. LXII, fols. 130 and 174.

DAUNTSEY, late BUCK, John, of Agecroft, co. Lanc., 1863, Vol. LV, fol. 132.

„   (late HULL), Robert, of Agecroft, co. Lanc., and Ambleside, co. Westmorland, s. of Robert PENNYMAN-HULL-BROWN, 1878, Vol. LX, fol. 137.

D'AUVERGNE, Maj.-Gen., Duc de BOUILLON, 178 . ., Vol. XVI, fol. 291.

[DAVAL, Elizabeth (wife of BURR), quartering, 13 June 1822 (Misc. G. et H., New S., III, 156).]

DAVENANT to CORBET (Bart.), Sir Corbet, of Shropsh., 178 . ., Vol. XV, fol. 144.

DAVENPORT, John, of Ball Hayes, Leek, co. Staff., 6 Feb. 1776, Vol. XIII, fol. 164.

DAVENPORT to TALBOT, Rev. William, of Bredon, co. Worc., 177 . ., Vol. XIV, fol. 23.

DAVENPORT-BROMLEY, Walter, of Ellaston, co. Staff., and Capesthorne, co. Chester, 182 . ., Vol. XXXIII, fol. 379.

DAVENPORT, late PRYCE-HUMPHREYS, Sir Salisbury, of Bramhall Hall, co. Cheshire; Maria his wife, nat. dau. of William Davenport, of Bramhall, 17 May 1838, Vol. XLIII, fol. 20.   (See Genealogist, Vol. VI, p. 34, and Berry's Suppl.)

DAVENPORT-BROMLEY to BROMLEY-DAVENPORT, William, of Capesthorne, co. Chester ; Baggington Hall, Baggington, co. Derby ; and Wootton Hall, Ellaston, co. Staff., 1867, Vol. LVI, fol. 324.   (Genealogist, VII, p. 23, and Berry's Suppl.)

DAVENPORT, Rev. G. H., Yazor Vicarage, Foxley, co. Hereford, 1891, Vol. LXVI, fol. 148.

DAVENPORT-HANDLEY, John William Hansley, of Clipsham Hall, co. Rutland, 7 Aug. 1881, Vol. LXI, fol. 173.

DAVEY, ..., of Redruth, co. Cornw., 182 . ., Vol. XXXV, fol. 179.

„   Baron [Horace, life Peer], of co. Sussex.   Supporters, 1894, Vol. LXVIII, fol. 110 ; Arms, fol. 108.

DAVID, *alias* LEWIS, ..., co. of Carnarvon, Wales (? not a grant), 1810,
    Vol. XXVI, fol. 156.

  ,, Rev. William, of St. Fagans, Cardiff, Wales, 1890,* Vol LXV, fol. 261.

  ,, Susannah, dau. of John James, of London, Merchant, wife of John Paul
    YVOUNET, of Isleworth, co. Middx., and Rochelle, France, 9 Feb. 173$\frac{1}{2}$,
    Vol. VIII, fol. 117^{b}.

DAVIDSON, David Meyer, of James' Street, Westminster, London, 18 . . ., Vol.
    XLIX, fol. 275.

DAVIE, John, of Bideford, Sheriff of Devon, 18 Jan. 1699-1700, Vol. IV, fol. 328.

  ,, ..., of Lyme, co. Dorset. (*See* TOWGOOD.) 17 . . ., Vol. XII, fol. 43.

  ,, Catherine, Elizabeth and Ann, daus. and co-heirs of James, of Bath
    Stamford, co. Linc., 178 . ., Vol. XVI, fol. 299.

DAVIE to BASSETT, of co. Devon. Quarterly Arms, 180 . ., Vol. XXII, fol. 173.

DAVIE, after FERGUSON, of Creedy, co. Devon, 184 . ., Vol. XLVIII, fol. 140.

DAVIES, Thomas, of New House, Stretton Grandison, co. Hereford, 21 Feb. 17$\frac{29}{30}$,
    Vol. VIII, fol. 69^{b}.

  ,, ..., of Combe Grove, co. Somerset. (*See* JENKINS.) Match, 180 . .,
    Vol. XXI, fol. 185.

DAVIES after TOUCHET, Henry, of Crickhowell, co. Brecon, and Ystrad, co.
    Cardigan, Wales, 1823, Vol. XXXIV, fol. 192.

  ,, after KEEVIL, Edward Hamond, of Croft Castle, co. Hereford, 183 . .,
    Vol. XLIII, fol. 143 ; William Trevelyan, of Croft Castle, co. Hereford,
    184 . ., Vol. XLVII, fol. 259.

DAVIES, John Evan (s. of John), of Bristol, and Cardiff, Wales, 18 . .,*
    Vol. XLV, fol. 136.

  ,, 1. John Birt, M.D., Coroner of Birmingham, co. Warw., Hampsh., &c.,
    of Nateley Scures, Hampsh. ; Tyglyn, co. Cardigan ; and Martley, co.
    Worc. ; 2. Alban Thomas, of Tyglyn ; 3. Rev. Edward Acton, D. of
    Martley, and sisters (brothers, *see* Landed Gentry), 184 . .,* Vol. XLVI,
    fol. 291.

  ,, ..., Capt. and Adj., Scots Fus. Guards, 184 . ., Vol. XLVII, fol. 56.

DAVIES to DAVIES-EVANS, Herbert, of Highmead, co. Carnarvon, Wales, 184 . .,
    Vol. XLVII, fol. 121.

DAVIES-LLOYD, Arthur Lloyd, of the Inner Temple, London, and Alltyr Oden,
    co. Cardigan, Wales, 1848, Vol. XLVIII, fol. 440.

DAVIES, John Lloyd, of Blaendyffryn, co. Cardigan, Wales. (*See* H. LLOYD-
    HARDWICKE.) 184 . ., Vol. XLVIII, fol. 415.

  ,, Robert, of Bodloudet, co. Carmarthen, Cardigan, and Llangefrin, Anglesey,
    Wales, 186 . ., Vol. LIV, fol. 242.

DAVIES after PRICE [Stafford Davies], of Marrington Hall and Brampton Hall,
    Shropsh., and Hendon House, Hendon, co. Middx. [together with his
    brothers and sister. Roy. Lic., 7 Jan. 1880 ; Grant and exemplification,
    28 Feb. 1880], 18 . . ., Vol. LX, fol. 350. [Powys-Land Club, XVI,
    pp. 409 to 412.]

DAVIES, Edmund, of Plas Dinam, Llandinam, co. Montgomery, Wales, 1893,
    Vol. LXVI, fol. 346.

  ,, Rev. E. W. L., of Tyisha and Glyn Rumney, co. Monmouth, 1889, Vol.
    LXV, fol. 112.

  ,, Major H. D., of Wateringbury Place, co. Kent (M.P., Lieut.-Col.), 1887,
    Vol. LXIV, fol. 55.

  ,, Theophilus H., of Hesketh Park, North Meols, co. Lanc., 1896,* Vol. LXIX,
    fol. 32.

  ,, W. Howell, of Chatford House, Clifton Down, co. Glouc., 1896, Vol. LXIX,
    fol. 53.

  ,, Thomas Henry (s. of Thomas Henry), Major, late 2nd W. I. Regt., 18 . . .,
    Vol. LXXI, fol. . . . . .

  ,, William David, s. of William David Davies, of Devynock, co. Brecon, Wales,
    18 . . ., Vol. LXXI, fol. . . . .

D'Avigdor, Mrs., of Princes Square, London, 1896, Vol. LXIX, fol. 88.

D'Avigdor-Goldsmid, O. E., of London, 189 . ., Vol. LXIX, fol. 103.

Davis to Batson (William), Thomas, 24 Dec. 1702, Vol. V, fol. 85 (see Berry).

Davis, Peter, s. of John, remainder to grandfather William (Recorder of Wells), of co. Somerset, and Bencher, Lincoln's Inn, London, 17 . . ., Vol. IX, fol. 145. [26 June 1745, Grant to Peter Davis (see Misc. G. et II., 4th S., I, p. 121).]

   „ . . . ., of Wells, co. Somerset. Arms to Sherston (see Sherston), 179 . ., Vol. XVIII, fol. 215.

   „ . . . ., of Little Ormond Street and Westminster, London, 1746, Vol. IX, fol. 164 (see Edmondson and Berry).

   „ Mark, of St. Augustine's, Bristol, co. Glouc., and North Wraxall, Wilts., 1772, Vol. XII, fol. 136. (Berry.)

   „ . . . ., of Bristol, co. Glouc., M.P. ? Bristol. (See Whittingham). Match. 181 . ., Vol. XXVIII, fol. 433.

Davis to Tresham, of Old or Wold, co. Northampton. Match, 181 . ., Vol. XXVII, fol. 187.

Davis, ..., of Bethnal House, Bethnal Green, co. Middx., 182 . ., Vol. XXXIII, fol. 295.

   „ . . . ., of Grimsend House, Suckley, co. Worc., and Worcester, 182 . ., Vol. XXXV, fol. 289.

   „ [Mary, wife of Burr. Arms, 13 June 1822. (Misc. G. et II., New S., III, p. 156.)].

   „ [William, of Grimsend House, par. of Suckley, co. Worc., s. and h. of William, late of the same. Arms used by his grandfather William and his grandmother Frances, dau. and at length sole heir of Thomas Mence, of the City of London; not registered. Arms, quarterly Davis and Mence, 12 Aug. 1825.]

   „ William, of Leytonstone, co. Essex; Montgomery, Wales; Wellclose, Brockworth, co. Glouc.; and Bishop's Castle, Shropsh., 183 . ., Vol. XL, fol. 17.

Davis-Protheroe, ..., of Turnworth, co. Dorset, and Cheltenham, co. Glouc., 184 . ., Vol. XLVII, fol. 301.

Davis, Sir Jno. Francis, Bart., of Henbury, co. Glouc., Governor and Com.-in-Chief, Hong Kong, 184 . ., Vol. XLVII, fol. 424.

   „ Lt.-Col. George Lenox, C.B., of Waterhouse, Wilts., 184 . ., Vol. XLVIII, fol. 360.

   „ John, of Greenhills, Tilford, Farnham, co. Surrey, and Ed. Mansions, Victoria Street, Westminster, 1884,* Vol. LXII, fol. 249.

   „ F., of Park Crescent, Portland Place, London, 1894, Vol. LXVIII, fol. 71.

   „ George Nullett (s. of John Davis), of Liverpool, 185 . ., Vol. LII, fol. 64.

   „ Henry Pelham, of co. Kent, June 1772 (see Edmondson and Berry).

Davis to Knight, Jane, of St. Marylebone, co. Middx., to take surname and Arms of Knight under the will of Robert, Earl of Catherlough. (See Knight.) [23 May] April 29 1772, Vol. XII, fol. 142. [Misc. G. et II., 2nd S., I, p. 173.]

   „ to Knight, ..., of Wootton-Wawen, co. Warw., nat. sons of Knight, Earl of Catherlough, 17 . . ., Vol. XVII, fol. 418.

Davis, James W., F.L.S., Alderman and late Mayor of Halifax, co. York, 18 . . ., Vol. LXXI, fol. . . . .

   „ . . . ., of Liverpool, 185 . ., Vol. LII, fol. . . . .

Davison (Stych), Samuel, of Brandhall, Norton, Shrophs., 5 Sept. 1737, Vol. VIII. fol. 217b. (Berry.)

Davison, late Eden, Morton John, of Beamish, and Windlestone, co. Durham, (died s.p.). Quarterly Arms, 181 . ., Vol. XXVII, fol. 127.

Davison after Wood, Thomas, of West Haddlesey, co. York, 181 . ., Vol. XXXI, fol. 56.

DAVISON, John, B.D., Fellow of Oriel Coll., Oxf., of Huntington, co. Derby, and Worthing, co. Sussex, Rector of Warlington, co. Durham, 180 . ., Vol. XXXI, fol. 227.

DAVISON to TYZACK, ..., of Tritlington, co. Northumberland, and Wheatfield House, nr. Edinburgh, 184 . ., Vol. XLVI, fols. 212 and 216.

DAVY, Sir Humphry, Bart., LL.D., F.R.S., ? Cornwall or London [Grosvenor Street, London, 1818 (Burke)], 181 . ., Vol. XXX, fol. 351.

   ,,   George Thomas, of Sussex Square, London, and Jamaica, 185 . ., Vol. L, fol. 39.

DAVY (see G. BARLEE), ..., 185 . ., Vol. L, fol. 133.

DAW, Thomas, s. of Thomas, of Westminster, London. (Match) with LE MOINE (see DAWES, in Berry's Suppl.), 28 Feb. 1781, Vol. XV, fols. 183 and 230.

DAWES, Matthew, of Colton, co. Staff., and Westbrooke, &c., co. Lanc., 184 . ., Vol. XLVII, fol. 139.

   ,, ..., of Colton, co. Staff., Westbrooke, &c., co. Lanc.   Alteration, 184 . ., Vol. XLVIII, fol. 65.

DAWES, late WILLOCK, Charles William, of Burton Hall, Barlavington, co. Sussex, and Woolwich, co. Kent, 1870, Vol. LVII, fol. 258.

DAWKINS, James, of Over-Norton, co. Oxf., &c., 31 Jan. 173¾, Vol. VIII, fol. 183ᵇ. (Berry.)

   ,,   Henry, of St. James', Westminster, Oxf., &c., 20 April 1761, Vol. X, fol. 352. (Berry.)

DAWKINS to PENNANT, George Hay, of Penrhyn, co. Carnarvon, Wales ; Standlynch, Wilts., and Jamaica, 180 . ., Vol. XXIV, fol. 414.

DAWKINS after COLYEAR, James, of co. Oxf., 183 . ., Vol. XLI, fol. 188.

DAWNAY, Viscount DOWNE [19 Feb. 1680], of Cowick, co. York.   Supporters, 16 . . ., Vol. IV, fol. 250.

DAWNAY to LANGLEY (Viscount DOWNE), Hon. Marmaduke, of co. York (died unm.), 182 . ., Vol. XXXIV, fol. 338.   [See Misc. G. et H., 2nd S., IV, p. 184.]

DAWNEY, Jonah (s. of Thomas), of Aylesbury, Bucks., 180 . ., Vol. XXI, fol. 174.

DAWSON, Thomas, of Penrith, co. Cumberland, and Bowran Church, Brough, co. Westmorland, 1761, Vol. X, fol. 356. (Berry.)

   ,,   Thomas, Baron DAWTREY, of London and Ireland, 15 Sept. 1770, Vol. XII, fol. 27. (Berry.)

   ,,   Betty Anne, Lady LOUGHBOROUGH, of co. York, d. and h. of John Dawson, of Morley, co. York.   Escutcheon of pretence, 177 . ., Vol. XIV, fol. 225.

   .,   Pudsey (s. of Ambrose, M.D.), of Liverpool, co. Lanc., and Langcliffe and Bolton Hall, co. York, 5 Nov. 1802, Vol. XXII, fol. 3.

DAWSON, late PERFECT, William Mosley, of Langcliffe Hall, &c., co. York, and Audley, Sidmouth, co. Devon, 1879 ?, Vol. LX, fol. 261 (see Berry's Suppl.).

DAWSON after KENNET, ..., of Manchester, co. Lanc. ; Wakefield, Bradford, and Daw Green, co. York.   Quarterly Arms, 180 . ., Vol. XXIV, fol. 133.

DAWSON before LAMBTON-, John Biddick, of co. Durham, 1815, Vol. XXVIII, fol. 212.

DAWSON, John, of the Node, Codicote, co. Hertf., and Broomfield, Northallerton, co. York, 188 . ., Vol. LXIII, fol. 47.

DAWSON after MASSY, ..., of Ballinacourty or New Forest, co. Tipperary, Ireland, and Sutterly, co. Linc., 182 . ., Vol. XXXVI, fol. 279.

DAWSON-DAMER, Henry and George, of co. Dorset (Earls of PORTARLINGTON), [14 Mar. 1829] Vol. XXXVII, fols. 400, 404 and 411.

DAWSON, Baker, of Mossley Hill, co. Lanc., 183 . ., Vol. XLIV, fol. 299.

   ,,   Thomas, s. of John, of Butterworth Hall, Rochdale, co. Lanc., and Thomas, of Leamington Priors, co. Warw., 184 . ., Vol. XLVII, fol. 309.

   ,,   (? Benjamin Franklin [Dawson]), of Horncastle, co. Linc., and New York, 185 . ., Vol. L, fol. 364.

DAWSON, Charles James, of the Inner Temple, London, and Melbourne, Victoria, 185 . ., Vol. LII, fol. 122.

„ Christopher Holdsworth, of Weston and Royds Hall, co. York, and wife Emma CARTER, 186 . ., Vol. LVI, fols. 65 and 162.

„ [Anne, of Carlton, co. York. Arms, quartering, *see* DUFFIELD].

DAWSON-LAMBTON, John, of Codicote, co. Hertf., and Broomfields, Northallerton, co. York, 180 . ., Vol. XXI, fol. . . . . .; 1885,* Vol. LXIII, fol. 47.

DAWTREY, ..., of Moorhouses, co. Sussex. (*See* GRATWICK.) Match, ..., 17 . . ., Vol. VI, fol. 332.

DAY to CROSSE, Peter, of Baddow, co. Essex, 24 Dec. 1770, Vol. XII, fol. 40.

„ to JACKSON, Jane, Frances and Catherine, of Betchton House, Sandbach, co. Chester, and Chester. Match, 1797, Vol. XX, fol. 10.

DAY-JACKSON after GALLEY, ..., of Congleton and Betchton House, co. Chester, 183 . ., Vol. XLII, fol. 261.

DAY, James Skurrey, of Burwell House and Hinton Charter House, co. Somerset, and Broughton and Westwood, Wilts., 181 . ., Vol. XXVI, fol. 12.

DAY after BRAXTON, ..., of Watford, co. Hertf., and Micklefield Green, Rickmansworth, co. Hertf., 182 . ., Vol. XXXVII. fol. 37.

DAY, Thomas, of Holly Hill, Snodland, co. Kent, and Stratton House, Stratton St. Margaret, co. Wilts., 187 . ., Vol. LX, fol. 20. (Berry's Suppl.)

„ Richard, M.D., of Trinity Coll., Dublin, now of Auckland, New Zealand : Robert, of Cork, Merchant ; William Tottenham, Rector of Rathclaren, Ireland ; sons of late Richard Day, of Youghal. Confirmed by Burke, Ulster, 8 Sept. 1875. (Misc. G. et II., New S., II, p. 372.)

DAZLEY-SMITH, Humphrey Smith, of Little Bardfield, co. Essex (B.A., St. John's Coll., Camb., M.A. 1848), 184 . ., Vol. XLVIII, fol. 49.

DEACLE, John (and brothers William and Edward), Woollen Drapers, of London (fined for Sheriff), 10 Aug. 1704,* Vol. V, fol. 161 ; Add. MS. 14,831, fol. 148 ; Proc. Soc. Antiq., 2nd S., XVI. p. 356. (Berry.)

DEACON (*see* CORTHINE), ..., of Upton, Isle of Wight, and Hampsh. Match, 177 . ., Vol. XII, fol. 72.

DEACON, Maj.-Gen. Sir Charles, K.C.B. [10 Mar. 1837], of Berkhampstead, co. Hertf., 18 . . ., Vol. XLIV, fol. 393.

DE AGUILAR, Ephraim (Baron H. R. E.), of Alderman's Walk, Bishopsgate, London, 17 . . ., Vol. X, fol. 52. (Berry.)

DEAKIN (*see* CAPPER), of Lichfield, co. Staff. Match, 17 . . . . Vol. XI, fol. 53.

„ C. F. N., of Moseley Hill, Cheadle, co. Chester, 1888, Vol. LXIV, fol. 144. (Berry's Suppl.)

DEALTRY [Henrietta] (SUTHERON), [wife of the Rev. William Dealtry], of Wigginton, co. York. Match, [6 May 1810] Vol. XXVI, fol. 6. (Misc. G. et II., New S., I, p. 222.)

DEALTRY to PROCTOR, Catherine, of Thorp-upon-the-Hill and Roothwell, co. York, &c., and Springfield House, Great Gransdon, co. Camb., 1847, Vol. XLVIII, fol. 283.

DEAN, now TYSSEN, ..., of co. Kent, 178 . ., Vol. XVI, fol. 391.

DEAN-PITT, Major (nat. s. of Baron RIVERS), 1818, Vol. XXXI, fol. 150.

DEANE, John, of Bengal, and Thomas, of Gray's Inn, London, and Bengal, 23 Feb. 172⅗, Vol. VII, fol. 501 ; Add. MS. 14,831, fol. 22.

DEANS to WHITLEY-DUNDAS, James William, Capt. R.N., of Barton, Berks. ; Aston, co. Flint ; and Fingask, co. Stirling. Match, 1808, Vol. XXIV, fol. 438.

DE BEAUVOIR after BENYON (late POWLETT-WRIGHTE), Rachel, of Englefield House, Berks., and Gidea Hall, co. Essex, 1822, Vol. XXXIII, fol. 261.

DE BEAUVOIR, late BROWNE and McDOUGALL (Bart)., of Dublin, 182 . ., Vol. XXXVI, fol. 270.

DEBENHAM, F., of Fitzjohn's Avenue, London, and Eastbourne, 1895,* Vol. LXVIII, fol. 214.

De Biandos, Remy Leon, Marquis de Castega, of Scarisbrick Hall, co. Lanc., 187 . ., Vol. LVIII, fol. 264.

De Bruhl, Count, Knight of the White Eagle, P.C. to Elector of Saxony, 181 . ., Vol. XXVI, fol. 404.

De Burgh, late Lill, ..., of West Drayton and Cobham, co. Middx., and Ireland. Escutcheon of pretence, 180 . ., Vol. XXI, fol. 52.

De Burgh-Canning, (Marquess of Clanricarde), Ireland, [9 July 1862] Vol. LIV, fol. 298.

De Butts to Burdon, ..., of Newcastle-upon-Tyne, co. Northumberland, 187 . ., Vol. LVIII, fol. 1.

De Capell (Brooke), late Supple, Richard, of Great Oakeley, co. Northampton, and Aghadoe, co. Cork, Ireland, 17 . ., Vol. XX, fol. 70.

De Cardonnel, late Dinevor, Cecil, Baroness Dynevor, of Wales. Supporters [Surname and Arms of Cardonnel], [21 May 1787] Vol. XVI, fol. 287.

   „   late Rice, Cecil, Baroness Dynevor, of Wales, 17 . ., Vol. XVIII, fol. 209. [? George Talbot, 3rd Baron Dynevor, 30 April, 1793.]

De Cardonnel to Rice, George [Talbot, 3rd] Baron Dynevor, of Wales, [4 Feb.] 1817, Vol. XXX, fol. 81.

De Cardonnel, Mansfeldt, of Chirton, co. Northumberland, and Caen, Normandy, 5 June 1773, Vol. XII, fol. 255 (see Berry).

De Carteret after Mallet, Edward Charles, 18 . . ., Vol. LIII, fol. 155 (see Authorized Arms, pp. 156 and 161).

De Cetto, Louis Charles, A. A., &c. (see Burke). [Confirmation, no date.]

Decie, now Prescott-Decie, Capt., R.E., of Bockleton, co. Essex, and Roehampton, co. Surrey, 18 . . ., Vol. LX, fol. 354.

Decker, Sir Matthew, Bart., s. of Direk, of Amsterdam and Haarlem, Holland, and Flanders. [Confirmation] 6 Aug. 1716, Vol. VI, fol. 267 (Misc. G. et H., 2nd S., IV, p. 289, and Berry).

De Costa, Leonor, relict of Alvaro, of Highgate, co. Middx., 20 Feb. 172$\frac{3}{4}$, Vol. VII, fol. 233.

   „   Catherine, widow of Joseph, of London, and dau. of Joseph De Costa, of London, Merchant (see Mendes), 8 April, 1732, Vol. VIII, fol. 145ᵇ.

De Coussmaker. See Coussmaker, [1799], Vol. XIV, fol. 189.

De Dunstanville. Baron [17 June 1796], Sir Francis Basset. Supporters, 179 . ., Vol. XIX, fol. 365.

De Eresby (Willoughby), Baron Gwydir, of co. Kent, [1829 ?] Vol. XXXVII, fol. 356.

De Ferrieres, Baron Charles, of Hardwicke Hall, co. Monmouth, naturalized British subject, 185 . ., Vol. L, fol. 432. (Authorized Arms, p. 27.)

De Gray [Sir William], Knt., Baron Walsingham [17 Oct. 1780]. Supporters, 17 . . ., Vol. XIV, fol. 255.

De Hochepied, late Porter, Lieut.-Gen. [George], M.P., of Stockbridge, Hampsh., and Haarlem, in Holland, 6 May, 1819, Vol. XXXI, fol. 334 (see Her. and Geneal., II, p. 538).

De Hochepied-Larpent, 1 John James, and 2 George Gerard, of E. Sheen and Putney, co. Surrey, and Haarlem, in Holland, 1 June 1819, Vol. XXXI, fol. 336 (see Her. and Geneal., II, p. 538).

De Hochepied, Daniel John, Baron. Letter Patent, Vienna, 8 April 1704 (see Her. and Geneal., II, p. 538).

De Hoghton [instead of Hoghton], Bart., of Hoghton Towers, co. Lanc. [6 Aug. 1862], Vol. LIV, fol. 306.

De Horsey, late Kilderbee, of Glemham, Frimley St. Martin, and Bury St. Edmunds, co. Suff., 183 . ., Vol. XXXIX, fol. 91.

De Jersey, ..., wife of Bowerbank, of Guernsey. Arms to self and descendants, 180 . ., Vol. XXI, fol. 271.

De Kewer, John, of Hackney, co. Middx., and Flanders, 25 Mar. 1742, Vol. IX, fol. 50. (Berry.)

DE KEYSER, Sir Polydore, Alderman of London, of co. Sussex, 1882, Vol. LXI, fol. 359 (*see* Berry's Suppl.).

DE KIERZKOWSKI- (STEUART), C. F., of Langley House, King's Langley, co. Hertf., 1888, Vol. LXIV, fol. 157.

DE KILLI KELBY, ... (*see* KELBY), [?] 17 . . ., Vol. XIV, fol. 282.

DE LA BERE (BAGHOT), late EDWARDS, Rev. John, of Prestbury, Bristol, and King's Stanley. co. Glouc., [3 May 1879] Vol. LX, fol. 277. (Berry's Suppl.)

DE LA FERTE, Charles Henry Joubert, of Harrington Street, Calcutta, 1898, Vol. LXX, fol. 158.

DE LA HAIZE, Philip, s. of Moses, of London, Spain, The Netherlands, and France, 1757, Vol. X, fol. 92. (Berry.)

DE LA MAGÈRE, ..., of L'Aigle, Normandy. (*See* SYMOND.) Match, 17 . . ., Vol. X, fol. 230.

DELAMERE, Arms to Mary Magdalen ALAVOINE, widow (impaled with ALAVOINE), 9 Oct. 1753, Vol. IX, fol. 460.

DE LA MOTTE, Maj.-Gen. Peter, of Weymouth, co. Dorset, 183 . ., Vol. XLIII, fols. 281 and 283.

DELANO, ..., of Enfield, and Edmonton, co. Middx., 183 . ., Vol. XXXIX, fol. 287.

DELANO-OSBORNE, ..., of Enfield and Edmonton, co. Middx., 183 . ., Vol. XXXIX, fol. 296. (Berry's Appx.)

DELAP, Capt. James Bogle, of Bow Brickhill, Bucks., and Stoke Park, Stoke-next-Guildford, co. Surrey, 1826, Vol. XXXV, fol. 320.

DELAPOLE after REEVE, Sir John George, Bart., of Hendens [?] House, Berks., and Shute House, co. Devon, 1838, Vol. XLIII, fol. 257.

DE LA RUE, Warren, of Portland Place, London, and Thomas, Lieut. King's Own, in remainder, 1883, Vol. LXII, fol. 35. (Berry's Suppl.)

DE LASAUX to AYERST, ..., of co. Kent, 181 . ., Vol. XXVII, fol. 153.

DELAVAL (BLAKE), Sir Francis, K.B. [23 Mar. 1761], of co. Northumberland. Supporters, 17 . ., Vol. X, fol. 333.

DELMAR, ..., of Canterbury, co. Kent, 181 . ., Vol. XXVII, fol. 228.

DELMÉ, Peter, Alderman of London, 17 Mar. 171¾, Vol. VI, fol. 141 ; Add. MS. 14,831, fol. 132, and 29,785, fol. 3ᵇ.

DELMÉ before RADCLIFFE, ..., of Hitchin Priory, co. Hertf. Escutcheon of pretence, quarterly, 180 . ., Vol. XXII, fol. 270.

DELPRATT, ..., of Bristol, co. Somerset ; Jamaica ; and Queen's Gardens, London, 186 . ., Vol. LVI, fol. 316.

DELVES-WALTHALL, E. W., of Winstanston Hall, co. Chester, 1888,* Vol. LXIV, fols. 291 and 146.

DE MORLAINCOURT to HALES, of Hales Place, co. Kent, and Bar le Duc, Lorraine, 182 . ., Vol. XXXVII, fol. 338.

DEMPSTER after SOPER, of Ashburton, Devon, and Pulrossie, co. Sutherland, nat. dau. of HAMILTON-DEMPSTER, impalement, 18 . ., Vol. XXIV, fol. 3.

DENDY, Richard Coffyn, s. of Richard, s. of Richard, of Horsham, co. Sussex, and London. Match, and to the descendants of his grandfather Richard, Sept. 1793, Vol. XVIII, fol. 259.

„ . . . ., of Dorking, co. Surrey, 183 . ., Vol. XXXIX, fol. 302.

DENHAM, now CRAVEN, Capt., of Berks., reputed s. of Craven, of Benham, Berks., 183 . ., Vol. XXXIX, fol. 180.

DENHAM-COOKES, Lieut.-Col. George, of 6, Princes Gate, London, 1891, Vol. LXVI, fol. 223.

DENISON, late WILKINSON, John, of Lothbury, London, 178 . ., Vol. XVI, fol. 25.

„ late BECKETT, Sir Edmund, co. Nottingham, [8 Sept. 1813] Vol. XXX, fol. 9.

DENISON, now BECKETT, Sir Edmond, Bart., of co. York, and Linc., [9 Dec. 1872] Vol. LVIII, fol. 164.

Denison, William Joseph, of Denbies, co. Surrey, and Seamer, co. York, with Butler quarterly, 181 . ., Vol. XXX, fol. 19.

Denison, late Conyngham, [4 Dec. 1849] Vol. XLIX, fol. 217. Lord Albert Conyngham, of co. Surrey, and York ; Baron Londesborough, [4 Mar. 1850]. Supporters, Vol. XLIX, fol. 295.

Denman, Baron, Thomas Denman, of co. Derby.   Arms and Supporters, [1834] Vol. XL, fols. 129 and 130.

Denmark, ..., M.D., Physician to the Fleet, &c., of Torquay, co. Devon, and Down, co. Down, Ireland, 18 . . ., Vol. XXXVIII, fol. 114.

Denne (heretofore Hollingberry), of Eldridge House, Littlebourne, co. Kent, 182 . ., Vol. XXXIV, fols. 33 and 35.

Dennett, ... (widow), of Alresford, Hampsh., and Ashurst, co. Sussex, 182 . ., Vol. XXXII, fol. 205.

Dennett (see Lister), of Wilton, Wilts. (See Agland.) 178 . ., Vol. XV, fol. 213.

Denning, ..., of Frome, co. Somerset, 180 . ., Vol. XXIV, fol. 94.

Denny, Rev. Richard, M.A., of Bugh Apton and Norton Subcourse, co. Norf., 182 . ., Vol. XXXVI, fol. 263.

Dent, late Hedley, ... of Newcastle-upon-Tyne and Shortflatt, Bolam, co. Northumberland, 183 . ., Vol. XXXIX, fol. 29.

,, late Tricket, Joseph, of Mattersen Hill, co. Nottingham ; Winterton, co. Linc. ; and Sheffield, co. York, 183 . ., Vol. XL, fol. 249.

Dent, John Coucher ?, of Sudeley Castle, co. Glouc. ; Walcot-cum-Membris, co. Worc. ; and Yarm, co. York, 184 . ., Vol. XLIX, fol. 116.

Dent after Hinrich, Henry Dent, of The Manor House, Hallaton, co. Leic. ; Covent Garden, London ; and Great Marlow, Bucks., s. of Sir Henry B. Hinrich, 1879, Vol. LX, fol. 299.

Denys, Peter, of Hamilton Place, London ; Fremington and Grinton, co. York, 180 . ., Vol. XXI, fol. 337.

Deramore. Baron, of co. York and Ireland. Supporters, 1886, Vol. LXIII, fol. 194.

,, Baron, of co. York and Ireland, 1892, Vol. LXVII, fol. 35 (Lloyd quartering, 1896, Vol. LXIX, fol. 115).

De Ramsey, Baron, Edward Fellowes, M.P., of co. Huntingdon and Norf. Supporters, 1887, Vol. LXIV, fol. 57.

Derbishire to Montagu, ..., of York Street, Baker Street, London, and Canada, 184 . ., Vol. XLV, fol. 125.

De Rhodes, late Gossip, ..., of Barlborough Hall, co. Derby, and St. John's Coll., Camb., 184 . ., Vol. XLVII, fol. 97.

De Rodes, Miss S. F. Sanders, of Barlborough Hall, co. Derby, 1884, Vol. LXII, fol. 176.

Derriman, Samuel Hoskins, Capt. R.N. (afterwards Adm., C.B.), 186 . ., Vol. LV, fol. 232.

Derville, Capt. Adolphus ?, Madras C. S., of London, 183 . ., Vol. XLI, fol. 319.

Derwent, Baron [1881], of co. York. Supporters, 1882°, Vol. LXI, fol. 251.

Derwentwater, Earl of [7 Mar. 168½], Sir Francis Radclyffe, Bart., of co. Northumberland. Supporters, 1696, Vol. IV, fol. 212 or 232.

De Salis after Fane, Count de Salis, ? of co. Surrey, 183 . ., Vol. XLI, fol. 154.

De Sauvournin, ... (see Prevost). (Match), 177 . ., Vol. XIII, fol. 125.

Desborough, ..., of Bugden, co. Huntingdon. (See Brickwood.) Match, 178 . ., Vol. XV, fol. 5.

Des Bouverie, William and Jacob, sons of Sir Edward, of London (? Radnor), 1695, Vol. IV, fol. 178.

Deschamps, John, s. of John, of St. Stephen, Walbrook, London, and Paris, [4 April, 1776] 177 . ., Vol. XIII, fol. 185.

De Tabley, ..., of co. Chester. Quarterings, 182 . ., Vol. XXXVI, fols. 57 and 87.

De Uphaugh, R. D., of Hollingbourne, co. Kent, 1888, Vol. LXIV, fol. 275.

DEVAS, ..., of Newgate Street, London, 1812, Vol. XXVI, fol. 412.
„ Thomas, s. of Thomas, of London and Maidenhead, Berks., 182 . ., Vol. XXXII, fol. 168.
DE VASSY, ..., of Flanders. (*See* COUSSMAKER.) Match with COUSSMAKER, 17 . ., Vol. XIV, fol. 189.
DE VELUZ, David Samuel Henry, of London, Merchant, impaling LEES, 14 July, 1775, Vol. XIII, fol. 112.
DE VILLE before O'KEEFFE, Gabriel Denis, of Romford, co. Essex, s. of Nicholas Gabriel, 180 . .. Vol. XXII, fol. 67. Escutcheon of pretence, wife of Nicholas Gabriel, fol. 70.
DE VITRE, ..., of Mill Hill, Hendon, co. Middx., 183 . ., Vol. XLI, fol. 172.
DEVON, Earl of (COURTNEY). Match, 181 . ., Vol. XXVIII, fol. 280.
DEVONPORT, Borough of, co. Devon, 1876, Vol. LIX, fol. 276.
DE WALLMODEN, Baroness and Countess of YARMOUTH, of co. Warw. Supporters, [24 March or 4 April 1750] Vol. VIII, fol. 266.
DEWAR, Thomas Robert, of Capel Lodge, Orleston, co. Kent, 1897, Vol. LXX, fol. 54.
DEWDNEY, ... *See* SWEETLAND.
DEWES, Count, of Mapleborough Green, par. of Studley, co. War., 5 July 1709, Vol. V, fol. 372^d; Add. MS. 14,831, fol. 44. (Berry.)
„ . . . ., Knt. and Bart, of Stowlangtoft, co. Suff. Arms, 1709, Vol. V, fol. 372.
D'EWES to GRANVILLE, ..., of Colwich, co. Staff., 178 . ., Vol. XVI, fol. 103.
DEWES to GRANVILLE, ..., of Buckland, co. Glouc., 182 . ., Vol. XXXVI, fol. 224; Colwich, co. Staff.; co. Surrey; and Wellesbourne, co. Warw., 178 . ., Vol. XVI, fol. 103.
DEWEY, Thomas Charles, of Cheshunt, co. Hertf., 18 . . ., Vol. LXXI, fol. . . . . .
DEWHURST, ..., of Dewhurst Houses, co. Lanc., and Isle of St. Croix, West Indies, 180 . ., Vol. XXIII, fol. 315.
„ J. Bonny, of Aireville, Skipton, co. York, 1883,* Vol. LXII, fol. 124. (Berry's Suppl.)
DE WINDT, late JENNYNS, Joseph Clayton, and Elizabeth Sarah JOHNSON, his wife, of London, and Paris, 184 . ., Vol. XLIX, fol. 448 (*see* Burke).
DE WINTON. Capt. R. H., of Graftonbury, Grafton, co. Hereford, 1894, Vol. LXVIII, fol. 35.
DE WINTON, from WILKINS, Cann, [of Clifton, J.P., D.L., with other branches of the family]. Roy. Lic., 1839 [*see* Burke].
D'EYNCOURT after TENNYSON, Charles, of Bayons Manor and Usselby, co. Linc., 1835, Vol. XLI, fol. 140.
DICCONSON, Edward, of Wrightington, co. Lanc., s. of Roger, s. of Hugh, of Wrightington, 1755, Vol. X, fol. 45.
DICCONSON, late ECCLESTON, Charles (minor), of co. Lanc., 1810, Vol. XXV, fol. 428.
DICCONSON to SCARISBRICK (heretofore ECCLESTON), Charles, of Wrightington, co. Lanc., 1833, Vol. XXXIX, fol. 372; Mary, of Wrightington, co. Lanc., 1834, Vol. XL, fol. 107.
DICK, Capt., E.I.C.S., of Edinburgh, Scotland, Member of the Bombay Council, 183 . ., Vol. XL, fol. 67.
DICK, late HUME, William W. F., of Hamewood, co. Wicklow, Ireland, 186 . ., Vol. LV, fol. 180.
DICK-DICK, Capt. O., 12, Grosvenor Crescent, London, 1893, Vol. LXVII, fol. 121.
DICKASON, Thomas, of London, 178 . ., Vol. XV, fol. 349.
DICKEN to TEMPLE, of Stonehouse, co. Devon, and Nash, co. Worc., [23 Sept. 1796] Vol. XIX, fol. 313.
DICKEN, Col. W. P., C.B., 1896,* Vol. LXIX, fol. 55.
„ F. R., of 8, Shorncliffe Road, Folkestone, co. Kent, 1896, Vol. LXIX, fol. 55.
„ C. G., of Glenrock, Surbiton, co. Surrey, 1896, Vol. LXIX, fol. 55.

DICKENS, C. S., C.M.G., of 33, Harrington Road, South Kensington, London, 1896, Vol. LXIX, fol. 55.

„ G. P., of Frazer's Island, Maryborough, Queensland, 1896, Vol. LXIX, fol. 55.

DICKENSON, John, of Birch Hall, co. Lanc., 181 . ., Vol. XXX, fol. 55.

DICKER, Philip (father of Samuel), of Exeter, co. Devon, and Walton-upon-Thames, co. Surrey, [17 Mar.] 1746, Vol. IX, fol. 171 . . (Misc. G. et H., 2nd S., IV, p. 290.)

DICKINS. . . . . (widow), of Southbridge House, Croydon, co. Surrey, 183 . ., Vol. XLIII, fol. 365.

„ . . . ., of King's Weston, co. Somerset, and Monks, Wilts., 178 . ., Vol. XVI, fol. 367.

„ . . . ., of Tiverton, co. Devon, 181 . ., Vol. XXVI, fol. 133.

DICKINSON to WALROND, now Bart., of co. Devon, 184 . ., Vol. XLVII, fol. 363.

DICKINSON, Maj.-Gen. Thomas, Bengal C.S., (? of Sussex), 185 . ., Vol. LII, fol. 214.

„ John, ? of the Middle Temple, London, and Abbots Hill, co. Hertf., 186 . ., Vol. LVII, fol. 173.

„ Francis and brother Marshe, of the par. of St. Thomas the Apostle, London, gent. (sons of John, late of the par. of St. Peter le Poor, drysalter, s. of John, of Gildersome, co. York, and to all the descendants of his said grandfather), 25 Nov. 1735,* Vol. VIII, fol. 193 ; and Add. MS. 14,831, fol. 48.

DICKS, John T., of Somerville, Speldhurst, co. Kent, 1884,* Vol. LXII, fol. 198.

DICKSON, Adm., Bart., of Hardingham Hall, co. Norf., 180 . ., Vol. XXI, fol. 422.

„ Richard (s. of John), of Stockton-on-Tees, co. Durham, and Great Ayton, co. York ; and to the descendants of his father, 183 . ., Vol. XXXVIII, fol. 60.

„ Maj.-Gen. Sir Alexander, G.C.B., of London. Supporters, [1838] Vol. XLIII, fol. 195.

„ James, of New Broad Street, London, 185 . ., Vol. LI, fol. 5.

„ R. W., of Domain Road, South Yarra, Melbourne, Victoria, 1892,* Vol. LXVI, fol. 243.

DICKSON-POYNDER, Sir J. P., Bart., of Wilts., and Scotland, 1881, Vol. LXI, fol. 169 ; 1888, Vol. LXIV, fol. 182.

DIGBY after WINGFIELD (s. of Bator), George, of Sherborne Castle, co. Dorset, and Orsett Hall, co. Essex, 185 . ., Vol. LII, fol. 54.

DIGGINS, Francis, s. of Richard, of Chichester, co. Sussex, 179 . ., Vol. XVII, fol. 400.

DIGGS, Dame Judith, [widow of Sir Maurice Diggs, Bart., now wife of Daniell SHELDON, of Ham Court, co. Surrey, and to Dame Margaret Sheldon, her sister, relict of Sir Joseph Sheldon, Kut., daus. and co-heirs of George ROSE, of Eastergate, co. Sussex], 16 Feb. 1681, Vol. III, fol. . . . . (Crisp, Notes, I, p. 103.)

DIGHT to BUTLER, ..., of Yeovil, co. Somerset, 179 . ., Vol. XVIII, fol. 199.

DIGHTON and JAMES, ... Escutcheon of pretence on GORDON, of Newmarket, co. Camb., 179 . ., Vol. XVII, fol. 77.

DILKE to FETHERSTON, John (F. s. of D.), of Packwood, co. Warw., 1833, Vol. XXXIX, fol. 325.

DILKE after FETHERSTON (s. F., s. of D.), Charles, on Arms, of Maxstoke Castle and Polesworth, co. Warw., 1858, Vol. LII, fol. 385.

DILLON before TRANT, Henry, of Easingwold, co. York ; Rathmile, co. Roscommon ; and Belgarde House, co. Dublin. Quarterly Arms, 181 . ., Vol. XXIX, fol. 364.

DILLON-TRENCHARD, ..., of Lytchett Matravers, co. Dorset, 184 . ., Vol. XLV, fol. 201.

„ -TRENCHARD, ..., of Lytchett Matravers, co. Dorset, 184 . ., Vol. XLVIII, fol. 214.

DILLON, Alfred, of Birkenhead, co. Chester, s. of Ralph C., of Manchester, co. Lanc., 18 . . ., Vol. LXXI, fol. . . . .

DILLWYN-LLEWELYN, Sir J. T., Bart., of Penllergare. Llangyfelach, co. Glamorgan, Wales, 1890, Vol. LXV, fol. 184.

DILLWYN-VENABLES-LLEWELYN, C. L., of Penllergare, Llangyfelach, co. Glamorgan, Wales, 1893, Vol. LXVII, fol. 211.

DIMES, ..., Lord of the Manor of Rickmansworth, co. Hertf., 183 . ., Vol. XLIII, fol. 347.

DIMSDALE, Baron [of the Russian Empire], Thomas Robert, of co. Essex and Hertf., 1829, Vol. XXXVIII, fol. 90.

  „   Baron, Joseph Cockfield, of co. Essex and Hertf., 1870, Vol. LVII, fol. 242.

  „   Joseph Cockfield, of Upton, West Ham, co. Essex (? 185 . ., Vol. LI, fol. . . . .) (see Burke).

DINEVOR, Baroness (RICE), of Wales.   Supporters, [1782] Vol. XV, fol. 277.'

DINEVOR to DE CARDONNEL, Baroness, of Wales.   (See also DE CARDONNELL and DYNEVOR.)   [21 May 1787] Vol. XVI, fol. 287.

DIPPLE, Mary, of co. Worc., wife of Everard BUCKWORTH, Esq., during her natural life, 21 June 1737, Vol. IV, fol. . . . .

DIROM after PASLEY, Major Thomas Alexander, of Mount Annan, co. Dumfries, Scotland, designated Dirom of Luce [co. Wigton] and Pasley, of Mount Annan, 1864, Vol. LV, fol. 168.

DIRS, ..., of Woodford, co. Essex, and London, 180 . ., Vol. XXI, fol. 183.

DISCIPLINE, Thomas, of Burnham Overy, co. Norf., and Bury St. Edmunds, co. Suff., 23 June 1731, Vol. VIII, fol. 109.   [Misc. G. et H., 4th S., II, p. 116.]

DISHER, William, of London, and Cheshunt, co. Hertf., 23 Nov. 1704, Vol. V, fol. 168.   (Berry.)

DISRAELI, of Beaconsfield, Bucks., 30 Nov. 1868, Vol. LVII, fol. . . . .

  „   The Right Hon. Mary Anne, Viscountess BEACONSFIELD, Countess, 1876, Vol. LIX, fols. 270 and 273.

  „   Benjamin, Earl of BEACONSFIELD, and the descendants of Isaac, his father, 21 Aug. 1876,* Vol. LIX, fol. 270.

DIXON, Thomas, of Hackney, co. Middx., 13 Oct. 1720, Vol. VII, fol. 17 ; Add. MS. 14,831, fol. 103.

DIXON to CRANMER, Esther Maria (widow), of East Sheen and Mitcham, co. Surrey.   Crest to male issue, 181 . ., Vol. XXVII, fols. 289 and 290.

DIXON, late BROWN, of Long Benton, co. Northumberland, 182 . ., Vol. XXXV, fol. 266.

DIXON, John, of The Knells, Stanwix and Whitehaven, co. Cumberland, 183 . ., Vol. XL, fol. 255.

  „   Thomas, J.P., of Liverpool, co. Lanc., and Littleton, co. Chester, 184 . ., Vol. XLVII, fol. 77.

  „   James, ? of Page Hall, Ecclesfield, co. York, 21 July 1849, Vol. XLIX, fol. 178.

DIXON-NUTTALL, ..., of Nutgrove, Burnley, and Colne, co. Lanc., 185 . ., Vol. LIII, fol. 368.

DIXON-COULL, Robert, s. of Ephraim, of North Middleton, Hartburn, and Morpeth, co. Northumberland, 1875, Vol. LIX, fol. 143.

DIXON, Thomas Rheda, of Arlecdon, co. Cumberland, and Anthony J. S., of Lorton Hall, Cockermouth, co. Cumberland, 1882, Vol. LXI, fol. 347. (Burke's Suppl.)

  „   Thomas, of Eastfield, Corbridge-on-Tyne, co. Durham (? Leadhill, Stockfield-on-Tyne), 1889,* Vol. LXV, fol. 24.

  „   Thomas, of Blythswood, Newcastle-upon-Tyne, co. Northumberland, 1889,° Vol. LXV, fol. 24.

DIXON-HARTLAND, Sir F. D., Bart., of Ashley Manor, nr. Cheltenham, co. Glouc., 1892, Vol. LXVII, fol. 37.

[DIXON, late GIBBONS, Rev. Thomas George, now of Holton Park, Holton-le-Moor, co. Linc. Dixon in lieu of Gibbons, Surname and Arms, Roy. Lic. 17 Jan., and Grant 19 Feb. 1907. Crisp, Visit. England and Wales, XIV, Add. and Corrections, p. xiv.]

DOBEDE, ..., of Soham Place, High Sheriff of Camb., 1830, Vol. XLII, fol. 54.

DOBIE-WILSON, ..., of Beith, co. Ayr, Scotland, 182 . ., Vol. XXXIII, fols. 362 and 364.

DOBINSON, ..., of Westminster, May 1816. (Burke.)

DOBRÉE, William, of London and Guernsey, to his brothers, John, Nicholas and Peter, 1726, Vol. VI, fol. 386.

„ . . . ., of Shern Hall, co. Essex, and Guernsey, 183 . ., Vol. XL, fol. 125.

DOBSON, Elizabeth, widow of William, of Gilnor, co. Lanc., 1897, Vol. LXIX, fol. 291.

DOD, late COOKSON, Rev. Joseph Yates, of Edge Hall, co. Chester (died s.p.), 1834, Vol. XL, fol. 286.

DOD after WOLLEY, Rev. Charles, and Frances [Lucy, dau. and heir of Pelly] PARKER, his wife, of co. Chester, 1868, Vol. LVII, fol. 7.

DODD, John, of The Hollies, Oldham, co. Lanc., 1890,* Vol. LXV, fol. 323.

DODDRELL, ..., of Bristol, and Glasgow, Scotland, 186 . ., Vol. LIV, fol. 77.

DODDS, Henry Luke (M.A., Oxf.), Vicar of Great Glentworth, co. Leic., 186 . ., Vol. LIV, fol. 244.

DODDS-PHILIPSON, R. H., of Newcastle-upon-Tyne, co. Northumberland, and Piccadilly, London, 1883, Vol. LXII, fols. 168 and 153.

DODINGTON, George, Lord MELCOMBE (formerly BUBB), of co. Dorset. Supporters and change of Crest, 1761, Vol. X, fol. 289.

DODINGTON after MARRIOTT, Rev. Thomas, of Bowden, Henstridge, Horsington, co. Somerset, 1853, Vol. L, fol. 377.

DODSON, R. B., of Denmark Terrace, Brighton, co. Sussex, 1888, Vol. LXIV, fol. 301.

„ John George (Baron MONK BRETTON), 1884, Vol. LXII, fol. 317. Supporters, fol. 319.

DODSWORTH, late SMITH, Sir Edward, Bart., of co. York, 1821, Vol. XXXIII, fol. 27.

„ late SMITH, Sir Charles, of co. York, 1846, Vol. XLVIII, fol. 103.

DOE, Thomas, [grandson ?] of Thomas, of Saughall, co. Chester, 1749, Vol. IX, fol. 343.

DOHERTY before WATERHOUSE, Capt. Daniel Henry (3rd Hussars), of Hope Hall, Halifax, co. York, 1872, Vol. LVIII, fol. 125 (see Burke).

DOLBEN, William Harcourt Isham Mackworth. Roy. Lic., 1835. (Burke.)

DOLLIFFE, alias D'OLIVEFF, James, Merchant and South Sea Director, of London, 22 Feb. 17¹³⁄₁₄, Vol. VI, fol. 137, and Add. MS. 14,381, fol. 161.

DOLPHIN, ... (see GRAVES), of Peckham, co. Surrey, 181 . ., Vol. XXX, fol. 85.

DOMENICHETTI, Rev. Richard Hippisley, M.A., Rector of Bleshford, co. Linc., and Richard, now Physician to H.M. the Queen, but rather [as] in Burke's Armory. [William Lewis Domenichetti, Esq., of Collingham, co. Nottingham. (Burke)], 18 . . ., Vol. LXXI, fol. . . . .

DOMETT, Rear-Adm., of Collyton, co. Devon, and Hawkchurch, co. Dorset, 180 . ., Vol. XXIII, fol. 103.

„ Adm. Sir William, G.C.B. [1820]. Supporters, 182 . ., Vol. XXXII, fol. 75.

DOMINICK, Andrew, of Great Marlow, Bucks., and Strathfieldsaye, co. Hertf., 9 July 1720, Vol. VI, fol. 436. (Genealogist, V, p. 124, and Berry.)

DOMVILLE, William, Lord Mayor of London [1813-14; Bart., June 1814], of St. Albans, co. Hertf. Arms and Augmentation, 181 . ., Vol. XXVIII, fol. 248.

DON, Lieut.-Gen. George, Lieut.-Governor of the Island of Jersey, and also of Jamaica ?, 1810, Vol. XXVI, fol. 48.

„ Gen. Sir George, [G.C.B., 1820] Lieut.-Governor of Gibraltar. Supporters, 182 . ., Vol. XXXVII, fol. 51.

DONALD to HARVEY, of Medmar. co. Aberdeen, Scotland, and Isle of Grenada. Match, 17 . . ., Vol. XVII, fol. 426.

DONALDSON-SELBY, Charles, of Cheswick. Alnwick and Swansfield, co. Northumberland, 183 . ., Vol. XLIII, fol. 375.

DONALDSON-HUDSON, Charles, of Cheswardine Hall, Shropsh.; Langholme, co. Dumfries; and Merton Coll., Oxf., 186 . ., Vol. LIV, fol. 238 (see Berry's Suppl.).

DONINGTON, Baron, 1887, Vol. LXIV, fol. 50. [cr. 4 May 1880 ?]

„ Baron, now Earl of LOUDOUN. Supporters, 1888, Vol. LXIV, fol. 232.

„ Baron, name and arms of RAWDON-HASTINGS in lieu of ABNEY-HASTINGS, 9 April 1887, Vol. LXIII, fol. 355.

DONKIN, Lieut.-Gen. Sir Rufane Shaw, K.C.B. [14 Oct. 1818], of Caversham, co. Oxf., 182 . ., Vol. XXXIII, fol. 232.

DONNISTHORPE. . . . . (Match), 182 . ., Vol. XXXV, fol. 312.

DONNITHORNE, Isaac, of St. Agnes. co. Cornw., and Hayne, co. Devon, 17 . ., Vol. XX, fol. 279.

DONNITHORNE before HARRIS, Isaac and Elizabeth, of co. Cornw., 17 . . ., Vol. XX, fol. 300.

DONSTON, Henry, of Worthrop, Sheriff of Nottingham, 17 . . ., Vol. IX, fol. 143.

DONSTON, late HUTHWAITE, George, s. of John, of co. Nottingham, 178 . ., Vol. XV, fol. 369.

DOORMAN after CAMMEYER, Charles, of co. Essex, 18 . . ., Vol. XXVII, fols. 296 and 298.

DOORMAN, Sarah Hannah, wife of the above, 17 Aug. 1812, fols. 296 and 298.

DORCHESTER, Countess of [20 Jan. 168⅔], of co. Dorset. Supporters, 16 . . ., Vol. III, fol. 288.

„ Baron [21 Aug. 1786] (Carlton, K.B.) [1776]. Supporters, 178 . ., Vol. XVI, fol. 177.

DORE, Thomas, of Wroughton, also Lydiard Tregoze, Wilts., 1765, Vol. XI, fol. 65. (Berry.)

DORINGTON, Sir John E., Bart., of Lypiatt Park, Stroud, co. Glouc., 1886, Vol. LXIII, fol. 182.

DORRIEN after SMITH, Robert Algernon, of Ashlyne Haresfoot, co. Hertf., 1845, Vol. XLVII, fols. 356 and 357.

DOTTIN, Samuel Rouse English, of Nuffield and Newnham Murren, co. Oxf., and Barbados, 17 Mar. 1817, Vol. XXXVI, fol. 107 (see Berry's Suppl.).

DOUGAL after RONEY [1871], Lieut.-Col. Richard at Jersey, of Ratho, co. Edinburgh, Scotland, 187 . ., Vol. LVIII, fol. 20.

DOUGHTY (late TICHBORNE), Sir Edward, Bart, of Hampsh., and co. Linc., 1826, Vol. XXXVI, fol. 65.

DOUGHTY-TICHBORNE, Sir James Francis, Bart., of Snarford Hall, co. Linc., 1853, Vol. L, fol. 329.

DOUGLAS, Andrew Snope, Capt., R.N. (Bart.), 178 . ., Vol. XV, fol. 227.

DOUGLAS and CLYDESDALE, Marquis of, s. of the Duke of HAMILTON, of co. Chester, 18 . . ., Vol. XXV, fol. 322.

DOUGLAS after SCOTT, Sir J. J., Bart., of Springfield, &c., Scotland, [10 July] 1822, Vol. XXXIII, fol. 278.

DOUGLAS-WILLAN, ..., of co. Middx., 182 . ., Vol. XXXVII, fol. 286.

DOUGLAS-GRESLEY, Robt. A., of High Park, Solways, co. Worc., and the Inner Temple, London, 1830, Vol. XXXVIII, fol. 37.

DOUGLAS after STODDART, Sir James, of co. Kent, and Edinb., 183 . ., Vol. XL, fol. 19.

DOUGLAS, Aretas, and see also AKERS-DOUGLAS, 24 May 1875, Vol. LIX, fol. 110.

DOUGLAS, late MACKENZIE, Lieut.-Gen. Sir Kenneth, Bart., of Glenbervie, Scotland, 1831, Vol. XL, fol. 21.

DOUGLAS OF BAADS after HOUSTON, Richard Alexander, of Hartley Mauditt, Hampsh., and Baads, co. Edinburgh, 183 . ., Vol XL, fol. 27.

DOUGLAS, Miss Elizabeth HOUSTON-, of Eaton Terrace, London, and Baads,
    co. Edinburgh, 185 . ., Vol. L, fol. 175.
    „   Sir HOWARD-, Bart., G.C.M.G. [18 Mar. 1835], of Ionian Islands. Sup-
        porters, 183 . .,* Vol. XL, fol. 374.
DOUGLAS-PENNANT, Hon. Edward Gordon, of Penrhyn Castle, co. Carnarvon,
    Wales, 184 . ., Vol. XLV, fols. 55 and 57.
DOUGLAS, Sir Joseph Abraham, Knt., of Whitehaven, co. Cumberland, and
    St. Peter's, Isle of Thanet, co. Kent, 1842, Vol. XLV, fol. 390.
DOUGLAS to IRVINE, Lord Douglas ? William, of Luddington House, co. Surrey, and
    H. B. M. Embassy, Constantinople, 184 . ., Vol. XLVII, fol. 418.
DOUGLAS after MONTEATH, Col. Thomas, C.B., of Kepp, co. Perth, Scotland, and
    Kingston, Jamaica. Arms, with design (Douglas suppor. and Monteath),
    1851, Vol. XLIX, fol. 442.
DOUGLAS, Sir Robert Percy, Bart., Governor of Jersey. Supporters of father,
    186 . .,* Vol. LIV, fol. 236.
DOULTON, Sir Henry, of Woolpits, Ewhurst, co. Surrey, 1890,* Vol. LXV,
    fol. 319.
DOVER, Baron [18 Sept. 1788] (Hon. Joseph YORKE, K.B.) [23 Mar. 1761].
    Supporters, 17 . . ., Vol. XVII, fol. 37.
DOVETON, Lieut.-Gen. Sir John. G.C.B. [1837], of Marylebone, London, and
    St. Helena, 17 . . ., Vol. XVII, fol. 404. Supporters, 183 . ., Vol. XLIII,
    fol. 173.
DOWIE, ..., of Kingston-upon-Thames, co. Surrey, 18 . . ., Vol. LVII, fol. 214.
DOWKER, Edmund, Vicar of Salton (?) and Willerby, co. York, 183 . ., Vol. XL.
    fol. 225.
DOWNE, Viscount Sir William (DUCIE), Bart. Supporters, 1676, Vol. III, fol. 19.
    „   Viscount Henry (DAWNAY). Supporters, 1678 [1687 ?], Vol. IV, fol. 250.
DOWNING to FULLERTON, George Alexander, of Wadham Coll., Oxf., and
    St. Anne's, Jamaica, 179 . ., Vol. XVIII, fol. 404.
DOWNES after PANTER, Edward Downes, of Rushford-with-Brettenham, co.
    Norf. ; Whitechurch, co. Hereford ; Shrigley, Worth and Rutley, co.
    Chester, 185 . ., Vol. LII, fol. 87.
DOWNES, Mrs., of Apsley House, Apsley Guise, co. Bedf., 1895, Vol. LXVIII,
    fol. 326.
    „   . . . . (see JACKSON), of East Meon, Hampsh., 182 . ., Vol. XXXVIII,
        fol. 152.
DOWNMAN to BERTIE (reputed s. of Mary Bertie), of Row Layton, co. Essex,
    182 . ., Vol. XXXIV, fol. 158.
DOWNSHIRE, Marchioness of (SANDYS) [cr. Baroness Sandys 19 June 1802],
    180 . .,* Vol. XXI, fol. 410.
DOWSON, ..., of Stratford, co. Essex, an Elder Brother of the Trinity House,
    182 . ., Vol. XXXIV, fol. 399.
DOWTEN, ...   See SWEETLAND.
DOYLE to NORTH, Lieut.-Col., of co. Surrey, 183 . ., Vol. XLIII, fol. 159.
D'OYLY, Thomas, Sergt.-at-Law, D.C.L. Oxf., of Buxted-cum-Uckfield, co.
    Sussex, 182 . ., Vol. XXXIII, fol. 63.
DOYLY, William, s. of George, D.D., 18 . ., Vol. LXXI, fol. . . . .
DRAGE, John, of Ely and Wicken, co. Camb., 1757, Vol. X, fol. 116. (Berry.)
DRAKE before TYRWHITT, William, of Shardiloes, Bucks., 26 Mar. 1776, Vol.
    XIII, fol. 168.
DRAKE after TYRWHITT, ..., of Shardiloes, Bucks. Quarterly Arms, 179 . .,
    Vol. XIX, fol. 344.
    „   after FULLER-ELIOTT, Thomas, of Trayton and Buckland Abbey, co. Devon,
        and Ashdown, co. Sussex, 181 . ., Vol. XXVII, fol. 277.
DRAKE, ..., of Havannah, Cuba (of Ashe, co. Devon), 181 . ., Vol. XXIX,
    fol. 224.
    „   . . . . (wife of YATES), of Rotherham, co. York, 182 . ., Vol. XXXVI,
        fols. 248 and 249.

DRAKE, ... (*see* WRIGHT-BEIGHTON), of co. Derby, 182 . ., Vol. XXXVIII, fol. 170.

DRAKE (ELLIOTT-) after FULLER, ..., Bart., of co. Devon and Sussex, [30 Oct. 1870] Vol. LVII, fol. 280.

DRAPER, Maj.-Gen. Sir William, K.B. [27 Dec. 1765], 17 . . ., Vol. XI, fol. 162.

DRAX (ERLE-) after SAWBRIDGE, John, of Charborough, co. Dorset, 1828, Vol. XXXVII, fol. 364.

DREW, Mrs. Beriah, of Leigham Manor, Streatham, co. Surrey, 1884, Vol. LXII, fol. 210.

DREWE-MERCER, A., of Elmhurst, Beadonwell, co. Essex [? Kent], 1889, Vol. LXV, fol. 126.

DREWETT, late BROWN, Thomas, of co. Durham and Wilts., 1867, Vol. LVI, fol. 311.

DRIFFIELD, late WADDINGTON, William, of Boston Spa, Bramham, co. York, 186 . ., Vol. LIV, fol. 20.

DRINKWATER, Sir William Lecce, Knt. (s. of John, decd.), of Kirby, Douglas, Isle of Man, 1879, Vol. LX, fol. 256. (Berry's Suppl.)

DRINKWATER before LAWE, John, of Kirby, Douglas, Isle of Man, and Trinity Coll., Camb., 1879, Vol. LX, fol. 269. (Berry's Suppl.)

DRIVER to WHITE, ..., of Godalming, co. Surrey, and Charlton Marshall, co. Dorset, 183 . ., Vol. XL, fol. 389.

DROUGHT to SAMWELL, Thomas Fuller, of Upton, co. Northampton (Baronets), 184 . ., Vol. XLVIII, fol. 287.

DRUMMOND, John, of Charing Cross, London. Quarterly Arms, with Augmentation, 178 . ., Vol. XVI, fol. 399.

   ,, Baron, Lord PERTH and, of Perth. Supporters, [26 Oct. 1797] Vol. XX, fol. 120.

DRUMMOND before BURRELL (Baron GWYDIR), of co. Kent and Suff. Quarterly Arms, [5 Nov. 1807] Vol. XXIV, fol. 310.

DRUMMOND, Lieut.-Col. Sir Gordon, G.C.B. [7 Jan. 1817], of Scotland. Supporters, 181 . ., Vol. XXX, fol. 210.

   ,, Lord PERTH, of co. Perth, [1868] Vol. LVII, fol. 28[b].

HEATHCOTE-DRUMMOND. *See* Baroness WILLOUGHBY, 1870.

DRURY to LOWE, William, of Denby and Locko, co. Derby, 17 . . ., Vol. XVII, fol. 334.

DRURY-LOWE, W. D. N., of Locko, co. Derby, 1884, Vol. LXII, fol. 283.

DRY, Henry (s. of William, of Milton, co. Northampton), Bencher of Lincoln's Inn, London, 7 July 1731, Vol. VIII, fol. 111.

   ,, Benjamin, of Ticehurst, co. Sussex, and his cousin-german John (B.C. of St. John's Coll., Oxford), 1 Dec. 1733, Vol. VIII, fol. 175[b].

DRYDEN, late TURNER, John, Bar.-at-Law, of Lincoln's Inn, London, and Canons Ashby, co. Northampton, afterwards [1795] a Bart., [1791] Vol. XVII, fol. 436.

DUBERLY, James, of Dingestow, co. Monmouth, 1766, Vol. XI, fol. 130. (Berry.)

DUCANE, Richard (Pedigree, 3 D., 14), of London, 16 Feb. 173?, Vol. VIII, fol. 93[b]; Add. MS. 14,831, fol. 82. (Berry's Appx.)

DUCIE, Baron (Matthew Ducie MORETON). Supporters, 1720, Vol. VI, fol. 426.

   ,, (MORETON, late REYNOLDS), [8 Mar. 1771] Vol. XII, fol. 168. Match and Supporters, ? fol. 63.

DUCKETT, late JACKSON, Bart., of Hartham Park, Wilts. Escutcheon of pretence, 179 . ., Vol. XIX, fol. 353.

DUCKWORTH, Rear-Adm. Sir John Thomas, K.C.B. [K.B., 6 June 1801; G.C.B., 2 Jan. 1815]. Arms, 180 . ., Vol. XXII, fol. 121. Supporters, fol. 124.

   ,, Vice-Adm. Augmentation, 180 . ., Vol. XXIV, fol. 359.

   ,, Adm. Sir John Thomas, K.B., Bart. [2 Nov. 1813.] Supporters. 181 . . ., Vol. XXVIII, fol. 23.

   ,, ..., of Over Darwen and Broughton Hall, co. Lanc., 182 . ., Vol. XXXV, fol. 51.

DUCKWORTH, Sir Dyce [Knt., M.D.], of Grafton Street, London, [8 May] 1886,* Vol. LXIII, fol. 319.

„   Canon, of Abbey Road, London, 1886, Vol. LXIII, fol. 319.

DUCKWORTH-KING, Adm. Sir George St. Vincent, K.C.B. [24 May 1873], of Wear House, Exeter, co. Devon, 1888, Vol. LXIV, fol. 191.

DUDER, R. J., of St. John's, Newfoundland, 1884, Vol. LXII, fol. 258.

DUDGEON to HARTLEY, . . ., of Settle and Sawley, co. York, 184 . ., Vol. XLV, fol. 315.

DUDLEY, Lord (LEA). Supporters [19 Nov. 1740], Vol. IX, fol. 283. [Her. and Geneal., V, pp. 214 *n* and 217.]

DUDLEY and WARD, Viscount. Quartering, 17 . ., Vol. XVII, fol. 81.

DUDLEY (BATE-), Henry, of Bradwell Lodge, co. Essex, and Kilscoran House, co. Wexford, Ireland, 180 . ., Vol. XXIII, fol. 318.

DUFF to LESLIE (relict of Duff), ..., of Wilcroft House, Lugwardine, co. Hereford, 180 . ., Vol. XXI, fol. 388.

DUFF before GORDON, William, Bart., M.P., of Scotland (grandson of the 2nd Earl of ABERDEEN); married with CRICHTON, Earl, of Dumfries. Quarterly Arms, [9 Oct.] 1813, Vol. XXVII, fol. 397.

DUFF-ASSHETON-SMITH, George William, of Tedworth, Hampsh.; Wellington Lodge, Isle of Wight; and Varnol, co. Carmarthen, Wales, 186 . ., Vol. LIV, fol. 190.

DUFFERIN, Marquess of. Addition to Supporters, 1889, Vol. LXV, fol. 114.

DUFFIELD to CRUTCHLEY, ..., of Berks., 180 . ., Vol. XXIII, fol. 321.

DUFFIELD, Thomas, of Ripon, co. York, confirmed by Betham, Ulster King of Arms, 12 Jan. 1848. [Misc. G. et II., II, pp. 49 and 50.]

DUFFIELD, Matthew Dawson, Canon of Middleham and Vicar of Stebbing, co. Essex, &c., &c. Dawson quartering, 21 Dec. 1858, by Sir J. B. Burke, Ulster King of Arms. (Misc. G. et II., II, p. 49, and Authorized Arms, pp. 195 and 196.)

DUFFIN, William, of St. George's, co. Middx., 31 Mar. 1739, Vol. VIII, fol. 251ᵇ; Add. MS. 14,831, fol. 64.

DUGDALE [Elizabeth, 1 Jan. 1683. Hamper's Life of Dugdale, p. 519].

„   Sir John, Knt., of Coventry, co. Warw. Augmentation, 22 June 1698 (Match), Vol. IV, fol. 19 (*see* Berry).

„   William, grandson to Sir William, Garter King of Arms, of co. Warw. [Augmentation, 22 July] 1698, Vol. IV, fol. 271. [Heraldic Exhib., 73.]

DUGDALE, late GEAST, Richard, of Blythe Hall, co. Warw., 1799, Vol. XX, fol. 295.

DUGDALE, Adam, s. of John, of Dovecot House and Great Harwood, co. Lanc., 181 . ., Vol. XXIX, fol. 329; to the descendants of his father, 5 June, 1833, Vol. XXIX, fol. 329. (Misc. G. et II., 3rd S., II, p. 7; Crisp, Vols. II and IV.)

DUKE, Sir James, Knt. [Bart. 1849], M.P., of Montrose, Scotland, Lord Mayor of London [1848-49], with limitations to the descendants of his father, but all died s.p., 18 . . .,* Vol. XLIX, fol. 236.

„   Major O. T., of Wimbledon, co. Surrey, 1891,* Vol. LXVI, fol. 49.

[DUKINFIELD, Borough of, co. Chester, 24 Mar. 1900, Geneal. Mag., IV, p. 41.]

DUMAS, Henry John Philip, of The Cedars, Clapham Common, co. Surrey (father naturalized), 186 . ., Vol. LV, fol. 170.

DUMBLETON, Thomas, of Norton Folgate, London, 1759, Vol. X, fol. 176. (Berry.)

DUMFRIES, Earl of (STUART after CRICHTON), of Scotland, 180 . ., Vol. XXIII, fol. 196.

DUMFRIES (CRICHTON), ..., of Scotland, 181 . ., Vol. XXX, fol. 169.

DUMMER, Edmund, of Swathling and Chickenhall, Hampsh., Deputy of the Great Wardrobe and Surveyor of the Navy [1692], London, 22 Oct. 1711, Vol. V, fol. 457. (Berry.)

„   Edmund, 5 April 1721, Vol. VII, fol. 62.

DU MOULIN-BROWNE, N. S., of Leamington, co. Warw., 1885, Vol. LXIII, fol. 157. (Crisp, I, p. 119.)

DUNBAR-BULLEN, C. W., of Toft Monks, co. Norf., and Woburn and Carrowdon, co. Down, Ireland, 1892, Vol. LXVI, fol. 255.

DUNCAN, Adm. Adam (Baron CAMPERDOWN), and Viscount, of Scotland. Supporters, [30 Oct. 1797] Vol. XX, fol. 162.

„ Viscount, Adm. Adam Duncan, of Scotland. Augmentation, 17 . . ., Vol. XX, fol. 159.

„ (BEVERIDGE-), James, of Blackheath [co. Kent?], and Damside, co. Perth, Scotland, 1813, Vol. XX, fol. 344.

DUNCOMBE, Baron FEVERSHAM [13 June 1747]. Supporters, 17 . . ., Vol. IX, fol. 294.

„ Baron FEVERSHAM, of co. York. Arms, 182 . .. Vol. XXXVI, fol. 43. Supporters, fol. 47.

DUNCOMBE-SHAFTO, Robert Eden, of Whitworth, co. Durham, and Barford, Wilts., &c. Match, 180 . ., Vol. XXIII, fol. 217.

DUNCOMBE before SHAFTO, Robert Eden, of Whitworth, co. Durham, and Duncombe Park, co. York. Quarterly Arms, 18 . . .. Vol. XXIII, fol. 226.

DUNCOMBE, (Pauncefort), of Great Brickhill Manor, Bucks., 18 . . ., Vol. LIII, fols. 134 and 233.

DUNDAS, Henry, Viscount MELVILLE [1802], of Scotland. Supporters, 180 . ., Vol. XXII, fol. 87.

„ Gen. Sir David, K.B. [28 April 1803], of Beechwood, co. Midlothian, Scotland. Supporters, 180 . ., Vol. XXII, fol. 171.

DUNDAS after WHITLEY, ... (see DEANS), of Scotland, 1808, Vol. XXIV, fol. 438.

DUNDAS, Vice-Adm. Sir James Whitley DEANS, G.C.B. [5 July 1855], of Scotland. Supporters, 185 . ., Vol. LI, fol. 313.

DUNDONALD, Earl of (Sir Thomas, K.B.), of Scotland, 181 . ., Vol. XXVI, fol. 431 ; grant to nat. sons, Scotland, 181 . ., Vol. XXVII, fols. 27 and 29. See COCHRANE.

DUNELL, . . .'., of Upper Hyde Park Gardens, London. 181 . ., Vol. XXVII, fols. 53 and 305.

DUNHAM, ..., of Clapham and Chelsea, co. Surrey, 186 . ., Vol. LV, fol. 344.

DUNLEATH, Baron (MULHOLLAND), of Ireland. Supporters, 1893, Vol. LXVII, fol. 125.

DUNMAN, ..., Assist. Councillor at Singapore, 186 . ., Vol. LVI, fol. 164.

DUNN, William John and Thomas, of Chatteris, Isle of Ely, co. Camb., 180 . ., Vol. XXIII, fol. 46.

DUNN before GARDNER, William, of Chatteris, Isle of Ely, co. Camb. Escutcheon of pretence, 180 . ., Vol. XXIII, fol. 50.

DUNN, ..., of Newcastle-upon-Tyne, co. Northumberland, 182 . ., Vol. XXXIV, fol. 200.

DUNN-GARDNER, late TOWNSHEND (John), of Chatteris, Isle of Ely, co. Camb., 1843, Vol. XLVI, fol. 365.

„ -GARDNER, William, of Fordham Abbey, co. Camb., 1843, Vol. XLVI, fol. 383.

„ -GARDNER, Cecil (Cornet, Light Dragoons), of co. Camb., and Magd. Coll., Oxf., 1847, Vol. XLVIII, fol. 290.

DUNN, Nicholas James, Capt. R.N., of Cheltenham, co. Glouc., 185 . ., Vol. LI, fol. 85.

„ F. W., of Park View House, Hackney, South Australia, 1895,° Vol. LXVIII, fol. 235.

„ W. A., F.R.C.S., of Millom, co. Cumberland, 1889,° Vol. LXV, fol. 47.

DUNNE to AMPHLETT, Rev. Charles, of Earls Croome, co. Worc., and Four Ashes, Enville, co. Staff., 185 . ., Vol. LI, fol. 255.

DUNNING, Baron ASHBURTON [8 April 1782], of co. Devon. Arms and Supporters, 178 . ., Vol. XV, fol. 47.

„ E. H., of Yewhirst, East Grinstead, co. Sussex, 1895, Vol. LXVIII, fol. 192.

DUNNINGTON-JEFFERSON, ..., of Thicket Priory, co. York, 184 . ., Vol. XLV, fol. 191.

DUNSTON, F. W., of Burltons, Donhead St. Mary, Wilts., 1888, Vol. LXIV, fol. 313.

DUPPA, late LLOYD, of Cheney Longueville, Shropsh., and Grove, Winstanton, 183 . ., Vol. XLII, fol. 251.

DUPRATT DU CHAURNAN, Magdalen, 2nd dau. and co-heir of Francis, of Maryle-bone, co. Middx., wife of Peter Abraham MASERES, of Westminster, Esq., 12 June 1736, Vol. VIII, fol. 202.

DUPRÉ, James, s. of Josias, of Wilton Park, Bucks., 1826, Vol. XXXVI, fol. 3.

DURAND, Sir E. L., Bart., of Ruckley Grange, Shropsh., 1892,* Vol. LXVI, fol. 285.

DURANT, ..., of High Cannons, co. Hertf., and Sharpham, co. Devon, 185 . ., Vol. L, fol. 17.

DURANTY, ..., of Liverpool, co. Lanc., 186 . ., Vol. LVI, fol. 42.

D'URBAN, Col. Sir Benjamin, K.C.B. [2 Jan. 1815], of Stratton, Wood Green, co. Norf., 181 . ., Vol. XXIX, fol. 202.

  ,,   Lieut.-Gen. Sir Benjamin, G.C.B. [20 June 1840], of co. Norf. Supporters, 184 . ., Vol. XLVI, fol. 14.

DURBIN, John, s. of Thomas, of Mainstone Court, co. Hereford, and Walton, co. Somerset, 17 . . ., Vol. XIV, fol. 16.

DURELL, late EVANS, Thomas, of St. James', Westminster, 10 Sept. 1771, Vol. XII, fol. 95. (Berry.)

DURELL-STABLES, J. L., of Ebury Street, London, 1895, Vol. LXVIII, fol. 238.

DURKIN, C. B., of Cambalt Road, Putney, co. Surrey, 1893, Vol. LXVII, fol. 136.

DURLEY, Henry (s. of Henry, Commander of an E. India ship), of London, 2 May 1709, Vol. V, fol. 353 ; Add. MS. 14,831, fol. 198. (Berry.)

DURRANT, Thomas, of Scottow, co. Norf., Sheriff, 5 Feb. 17$\frac{44}{45}$, Vol. VI, fol. 182. (Berry.)

  ,,   Samuel, of Lewes, co. Sussex, 17 . . ., Vol. IX, fol. 492.

DUSGATE (late BUSHBY), Richard Dusgate, of Halkin Street, London, s. of Joseph William Bushby, 1877, Vol. LX, fol. 54. (Berry's Suppl.)

DU STORRS, ..., 17 . . ., Vol. X, fol. 232.

DUTTON, late NAPER, James Lenox, Baron SHERBORNE [19 April 1784], of co. Glouc., 178 . ., Vol. XV, fol. 283. Supporters, fol. 313.

DUTTON, Frederick Hansbrow, of Cuxhaven, Hanover, and South Australia, 185 . ., Vol. LII, fol. 367. Authorised Arms, p. 91.

DUVELUZ or DE VELUZ, David Samuel Henry, of London, and Bournono, Morges, Berne. Impaling Lees, 14 July 1775, Vol. XIII, fol. 112.

DYALL, Thomas, of Berkswell, Coventry, co. Warw., and Mile End, London, 1758, Vol. X, fol. 165.

DYCE-SOMBRE, ... of Sirdhama, Province of Agra, 183 . ., Vol. XLIII, fol. 92.

DYER, ..., of Blackheath, co. Kent, 182 . ., Vol. XXXIII, fol. 42.

DYER after THISLETON, William Mathew, of London, 18 . . ., Vol. XLIV, fol. 248.

DYKE before POORE, Edward, of Syrencot, Devizes, Wilts., 1804, Vol. XXII, fols. 397 and 401.

DYKES to DYKES-BALLANTINE, Lawson, of Devizes [Dovenby], co. Cumberland, 24 June 1773, Vol. XII, fol. 251.

DYKES-BALLANTINE-DYKES, Joseph, of co. Cumberland, 1799, Vol. XX, fol. 450.

DYMOKE (see WILLAUME), of Ampthill, co. Bedf., 17 . . ., Vol. XI, fol. 194.

DYMOKE after WELLS, Edmund Lionel, of Shrubs Hill, Berks., and the Middle Temple, London, 1866, Vol. LVI, fol. 184.

DYNE-BRADLEY, Andrew Hawes, of Gore Court, co. Kent, 1800 (see Burke).

DYNELEY, late CHAMBERLAIN, Richard Dyneley, of Bramhope and Halton East, co. York, 186 . ., Vol. LIV, fol. 180.

DYNEVOR, George, 3rd Baron [CARDONNELL only, 30 April, 1793], of Wales, 179 . ., Vol. XVIII, fol. 209. [Resumed his patronymic, Rice, 4 Feb. 1817], of Wales, 181 . ., Vol. XXX, fol. 81.

Dyot-(Bucknoll, Thomas Stephen), of London, Augmentation, Dyot on a Canton, [1785] Vol. XVI, fol. 3.
Dyott, Maj.-Gen. Richard, of Freeford Hall, Lichfield, co. Staff., 1893, Vol. LXVII, fol. 274.
Dyson before Holland, of Rochdale, co. Lanc.; Heighington, co. Linc.; and Clay House, Halifax. co. York, 1817, Vol. XXX, fol. 248.
Dyson, Henry (B.A., Jesus Coll., 1825), of Stuat, co. Camb., 1824, Vol. XXXV, fol. 87.

E

Eade, ..., of Redruth, co. Cornw., 186 . ., Vol. LV, fol. 172.
Eade to Cory, Henry Cory, of Redruth, co. Cornw., M.A., St. John's, Camb., 186 . ., Vol. LV, fol. 224.
Eadon, late Mitton, ..., of Snaith and Salby, co. York, 183 . ., Vol. XLI, fol. 176.
Eales, Mrs., of Eastdon, Dawlish, co. Devon, 1889,* Vol. LXV, fol. 82 (see Crisp, I, p. 59).
[Ealing, Borough of, co. Middx., 22 Feb. 1902 (Geneal. Mag., V, fol. 549.]
Eamer, Sir John, Knt., Lord Mayor of London, Col. of Militia, 1808, Vol. XXV, fol. 157.
Eardley, late Gideon, of Spalding, co. Linc., 17 . . ., Vol. XVII, fol. 145.
Eardley, Fiennes [Gregory William] Twisleton [14 Feb. and 16 Mar. 1825], 11th Baron Saye and Sele. Quarterly Arms, 182 . ., Vol. XXXV, fol. 116.
Eardley, late Smith [14 May 1847], Sir Culling Eardley, Bart., of co. Hertf., 184 . .,.Vol. XLVIII, fol. 330.
Earl, ..., of Winchester, Hampsh., 181 . ., Vol. XXVIII, fol. 108.
Earle, ..., of Lacells, co. Cornw. Match with Medland (see Medland), 1 . . ., Vol. VIII, fol. 106.
„ [Anne] (widow), [dau. of Biscoe ?], of Swallowfield, Berks., and of Holton Park, co. Oxf., to Biscoe, 183 . ., Vol. XXXVIII, fols. 78, 79 and 80.
„ . . . ., of Ashton-under-Lyne, co. Lanc., 184 . ., Vol. XLVIII, fol. 181.
„ Hardman, Bart., of Allerton Tower, Woolton, co. Lanc., 4 Nov. 1869, Vol. LVII, fol. 171. (Hist. Soc. of Lanc. and Chesh., XLII, p. 64.)
Earle-Welby-Everard, E. E., of Gosberton, co. Linc., 1894, Vol. LXVIII, fol. 41.
[Earle, Sir Henry, of Allerton Tower, co. Lanc., Bart., eldest s. and h. of Sir Thomas Earle, late of the same. Confirmation, 6 Dec. 1904. Crisp, Notes, IX, p. 120.]
Earp, Mrs., of The Vinery, Dunstall Hill, co. Staff., 1886,* Vol. LXIII, fol. 287.
Eason, now Campion, ..., of Derby, 186 . ., Vol. LVI, fol. 230.
East, Sir Edward Hyde, Knt. (Bart. 1823), of London, Calcutta and Jamaica, 182 . ., Vol. XXXIV, fol. 29.
East after Clayton, ..., Bart., of East George, Bucks., and co. Surrey, 1829, Vol. XXXVIII, fol. 15.
East (Clayton to Gilbert East), ..., of Bucks. and co. Surrey, 184 . ., Vol. XLVIII, fol. 361.
East-East, Herbert Hinton (formerly Maclaverty), of Bourton House, Moreton-in the-Marsh, co. Glouc., 1879, Vol. LX, fol. 320. (Berry's Suppl.)
D'Este-East, Herbert (Roy. Lic.), 1895, Vol. LXVIII, fol. . . . .
Eastabrook to Rowlls, ... (widow), of Kingston-upon-Thames, co. Surrey, her husband, of Hampton Wick, 180 . ., Vol. XXIV, fol. 444.
Easterby to Cresswell, Francis, of co. Northumberland and London, 181 . ., Vol. XXVI, fol. 32.
Eastes, J. S., of Fairlawn, Ashford, co. Kent, 1884, Vol. LXII, fol. 281.
Easthope, ..., of Firgrove, co. Surrey, and Tewkesbury, co Glouc. (Bart., died 1866), 184 . ., Vol. XLV, fol. 254.

EASTMOND, ..., of Barbados, 17 . ., Vol. XVII, fol. 304.

EASTWICK, ..., of Hans Place, London, 183 . ., Vol. XLI, fol. 45.

EASTWOOD, George, and dau. Mary Thornhill, of Nether Flockton, co. York, 1747, Vol. IX, fol. 275. (Berry.)

„   F., of Buckden Mount, Huddersfield, co. York, 1895,* Vol. LXVIII, fol. 241. (Crisp, V, p. 157.)

„   Rev. John F., of Wokingham, co. Surrey, 1881,* Vol. LXI, fol. 105.

„   J. F., of Esher Lodge, Esher, co. Surrey, 1891,* Vol. LXVI, fol. 80.

EATON, late SELBY, Richard, of Great Budworth, co. Chester, 17 . . ., Vol. XIV, fol. 308.

„   late POTTER, ..., of Pole, co. Chester, 17 . . ., Vol. XVII, fol. 147.

EATON to BROWNE, ..., of Elsing, co. Norf., 17 . . ., Vol. XX, fol. 227.

„   to BROWNE, ..., of Elsing, co. Norf., 184 . ., Vol. XLVII, fol. 306.

„   to HAYWOOD, of Brownhills, par. of Burslem, co. Staff., 187 . ., Vol. LIX, fol. 112.

EBBESWORTHY (see FURSMAN), ..., of Bridestowe, co. Devon. (Match with Fursman), 17 . . ., Vol. IX, fol. 60.

EBBLEWHITE, Ernest Arthur, Bar.-at-Law, s. of John H., 189 . ., Vol. LXXI, fol. . . . .

EBDEN [Charles Hotson], of London, formerly Treasurer of the Colonies of Victoria, 186 . ., Vol. LV, fol. 204.

ECCLES, William, of Walton-le-Dale, Blackburn, co. Lanc., 1887,* Vol. LXIV, fol. 114.

[„   Borough of, co. Lanc., 7 Nov. 1893 (Geneal. Mag., VI, p. 160).]

ECCLESTON, Theodore, of Crowfield Hall, co. Suff., 17 . . ., Vol. IX, fol. 136.

ECCLESTON to SCARISBRICK, Basil Thomas, of Scarisbrick, co. Lanc., 18 . . ., Vol. XXV, fol. 426.

„   to DICCONSON, Charles, of Wrightington, co. Lanc.   Quarterly Arms, 18 . . ., Vol. XXV, fol. 428.

ECCLESTON after DICCONSON, now S. of S. [Scarisbrick of Scarisbrick], Charles, of Wrightington, co. Lanc., 183 . ., Vol. XXXIX, fol. 372.

ECCLESTON to DICCONSON, Mary (Spr.), of co. Lanc., 183 . ., Vol. XL, fol. 107.

ECKERSALL, George, of Drayton, co. Middx., and Lincoln's Inn Fields, London, 1765, Vol. XI, fol. 158. (Berry.)

ECKERSLEY, Nathaniel, of Standish Hall, co. Lanc. (died 1892), and his sons, Nathaniel H., of Ashfield, Wigan, co. Lanc. ; James C., of Carlton Manor, Yeadon, Leeds, co. York, 1887, Vol. LXIV, fol. 76.

ECROYD, William F., of Credenhill, co. Hereford, and Nelson, co. Lanc. (See also FARRER), 1890,* Vol. LXV, fol. 170.

EDEN, Sir Morton, K.B. [16 Dec. 1791], of co. Durham. [Afterwards (9 Nov. 1799) Baron HENLEY.]   Supporters, 17 . . ., Vol. XVII, fol. 432.

EDEN to DAVISON, Morton John, of Durham (died unm.), 181 . ., Vol. XXVII, fol. 127.

EDEN after JOHNSON [15 Feb. 1811], Sir Robert, Bart. (died unm.), of Durham, Windlestone and West Auckland, co. Durham. (Match), 181 . ., Vol. XXVIII, fol. 414.

EDEN, late METHOLD, John (died unm.), of Durham, Windlestone and Beamish, co. Durham, 1844 Vol. XLVII, fol. 224.

EDEN, Thomas Duncombe, of Beamish Park, co. Durham, 1885, Vol. LXIII, fol. 121.

EDGAR-WILLIAMS, John, of Appledore, co. Northampton. Williams and Edgar quarterly (fol. 128, Edgar, widow), 1875, Vol. LIX, fol. 129.

EDGE, late HURT, James Thomas, of Worksworth, co. Derby, and Strelley, co. Nottingham, 1848, Vol. XLIX, fol. 61.

EDGE, Richard (High Sheriff), of Strelley, co. Nottingham, 1709, Vol. V, fol. 356ᵇ; Add. MS. 14,830, fol. 4. (Berry.)

EDGE after WEBB, Thomas, of Strelley, co. Nottingham, and Sherborne, co. Warw., 9 May 1803, Vol. XXII, fols. 258 and 260. (Berry.)

EDGECOMBE, ... of co. Devon, 16 . . ., Vol. I. fol. 18.

EDGCUMBE, [Earl of Mount-Edgcumbe, 31 Aug. 1789], of co. Devon. Supporters, 17 . . ., Vol. IX, fol. 57.

EDGELL, Harry. of Standerwick, co. Somerset, 23 Nov. 1732, Vol. VIII, fol. 156[h].

EDGELL to VERNEY-CAVE, Baroness BRAVE (? of Berks.), [? the Hon. Frances Catherine Verney-Cave, sister of the 5th Baron Braye, 5 Feb. 1880], 18 . . ., Vol. LX, fol. 346.

EDGELL, Edgell WYOTT-, ..., of Milton Place, co. Surrey, 1813. (Burke.)

EDGER or EDGAR (widow of William), ..., of co. Devon, 1875, Vol. LIX, fol. 128.

EDLIN, Sir Peter Henry, Assist. Judge Middx. Sessions of (Plymouth), London, s. of Edward Colvill, and to brother, Rev. William James, and nephew Edward, M.R.C.S., of Holberton, Plymouth, co. Devon, 1875, Vol. LIX, fol. 169. (Burke's Suppl.)

EDLINGTON, ..., of Marylebone, London, 17 . . ., Vol. XVII, fol. 165.

EDMANDS, Charles Henry, of The Grange, Sutton, co. Surrey, 185 . ., Vol. LI, fol. 270.

EDMEADES, ..., of Owletts, Cobham, and Nurstead, co. Kent, 182 . ., Vol. XXXVI, fol. 138.

„ . . . ., of Owletts, Cobham, and Nurstead, co. Kent, 184 . ., Vol. XLVIII, fol. 231.

EDMONDS, Baroness DE SCHMIEDERN (widow), of Rye and Fairlight, co. Sussex, 185 . ., Vol. LI, fol. 267.

„ William (s. of William, decd.), of Birkdale, co. Lanc., 1879, Vol. LX, fol. 265. (Berry's Suppl.)

EDMONDSON, Joseph, Mowbray Herald Extraordinary, of London, 18 Mar. 1765, Vol. XI. fol. 69. (Berry.)

EDWARDES, William, [2nd] Baron KENSINGTON, of Wales. Arms of wife, [Dorothy Patricia] THOMAS. 180 . ., Vol. XXI. fol. 327.

EDWARDES to GWYNNE, ..., of Glantey and Monachty, co. Cardigan, Wales, 180 . ., Vol. XXIII, fol. 413.

EDWARDES (HOPE-), S. F., of Netley, Stapleton, Shropsh., Vicar of Greet, 186 . ., Vol. LVII, fol. 338.

„ Thomas, of St. Martin's-in-the-Fields, London, 6 May 1728, Vol. VIII, fol. 6.

„ Mary, d. and h. of Francis Edwards, of Welham Grove, co. Leic. Arms granted to Lord [Anne] HAMILTON, 15 Aug. 1733, Vol. VIII, fol. 170[h].

EDWARDS to NOEL, Gerard Noel, of Catmore Lodge, co. Rutland, 17 . ., Vol. XX, fol. 153.

EDWARDS, ..., of Long Parish, Hampsh., 178 . ., Vol. XVI, fol. 29.

EDWARDS, late RAYNSFORD, ..., of Henlow Grange, co. Bedf., and Lincoln's Inn, London, 1809, Vol. XXV, fol. 153.

EDWARDS after WILLIAMS, ..., M.A., Rector of St. George's, co. Denbigh, Wales ; Cerrig Llwydion, co. Denbigh : and Bodelwyddan, co. Flint (died s.p.), 182 . ., Vol. XXXI, fol. 359.

EDWARDS, late RICHARDS, Thomas William, of Llandaff and Cardiff, Wales, 1823, Vol. XXXIV, fol. 208.

EDWARDS, Joshua, of Ruthen, co. Denbigh, Wales, and Manchester, co. Lanc., 22 Jan. 1825, Vol. XXXV, fol. 95. (Berry's Appx.)

„ . . . .. of Ruthen, co. Denbigh, Wales, and Manchester and Liverpool, co. Lanc., 185 . ., Vol. XLIX, fol. 225.

EDWARDS after SMITH, ..., of Tarrington, co. Hereford, and The Bower, Ham Lacy [?], 182 . ., Vol. XXXV, fol. 102.

EDWARDS-VAUGHAN, John, Rheola, par. of Cadoxton juxta Neath, and Llanelly, co. Glamorgan, Wales, and Regent Street, Westminster [Vaughan and Edwards quarterly], 26 Feb. 1830, Vol. XXXVIII, fol. 45. [Crisp, Fragm. Geneal., VI, p. 13.]

EDWARDS, Thomas, of Sutton Green and Sutton Isacoed, co. Denbigh, Wales, 1832, Vol. XXXIX, fol. 309.

„ (Sir John, Bart.), M.P., of Garth, Llanidloes and Greenfields, Machynlleth, co. Montgomery, quartering OWEN, 2 July 1838, Vol. XLIII, fol. 62. (Powys-Land Club, X, p. 407.)

„ Richard, of Hampton Hall, Worthen, Shropsh., and Frimbley, Ellesmere, co. Lanc., 184 . ., Vol. XLVIII, fol. 234.

EDWARDS-MOSS [26 Mar. 1851], Sir Thomas, Bart. [23 Dec. 1868], of Roby Hall, co. Lanc., and Shropsh., 18 . ., Vol. XLIX, fol. 466.

EDWARDS to BRETTELL-VAUGHAN (Edwards), ..., of Burway, Bromfield and Ludlow, Shropsh., [1850] Vol. XLIX, fols. 341 and 343.

EDWARDS-WOOD, ..., of Stankhill, Budbrooke and Southam, co. Warw., 185 . ., Vol. L, fol. 66.

EDWARDS, ..., of Trematon Hall, co. Cornw., 186 . ., Vol. LV, fol. 23.

„ Sir Henry, Bart. [3 Aug. 1866], of Pye Nest, co. York, 186 . ., Vol. LVI, fol. 128.

„ John, Q.C., of Gray's Inn and the Inner Temple, London (from co. Lanc.), 1878, Vol. LX, fol. 186. (Berry's Suppl.)

„ John, s. of Thomas, of Prestbury and Bristol, co. Glouc., to the descendants of his father, 1879, Vol. LX, fol. 237.

EDWARDS to BAGHOT DE LA BERE, Rev. John, of Bristol, co. Glouc., 1879, Vol. LX, fol. 277.

EDWARDS, ..., of Pwllheli, co. Carmarthen, Wales, rather WILLIAMS-ELLIS or ELLIS to CLOUGH. Committee of Estates of John Parr Williams-Ellis. (See also CLOUGH), 18 . . ., Vol. LX, fol. 328.

„ . . . ., formerly BEDFORD, Capt. William, E.I.C.S., of Arlesey, Bury, co. Bedf., 1792. (Burke.)

„ Francis (s. of Edward), 111, Ashley Gardens, London, and of The Cottage, Knighton, co. Radnor, Wales, 1898, Vol. LXX, fol. 174.

„ Daniel, of Morfydd House, Morriston, Swansea, Wales, 1880, Vol. LXI, fol. 90.

„ Lieut.-Col. Sir F. F., K.C.B., of co. Kent, and St. James's Palace, London, 1890,* Vol. LXVI, fol. 27.

„ George F., of 6, Highbury Crescent, London, 1896, Vol. LXIX, fol. 86.

„ Rev. H. P., of St. Andrew's Rectory, Cardiff, Wales, 1895, Vol. LXVIII, fol. 312.

EDWIN, ..., of co. Linc. (Match with CORBETT), 181 . ., Vol. XXVI, fol. 73.

EGERTON, Baron GREY DE WILTON [1784]. Supporters, 178 . ., Vol. XV, fol. 297.

EGERTON, late HAYTER, of Roche Court, and Winterslow and Newton Toney, Wilts., 179 . ., Vol. XVIII, fol. 133.

„ late TATTON, ..., of Tatton Park, co. Chester, 180 . ., Vol. XXIII, fol. 415.

EGERTON to TATTON, ..., of Tatton Park, co. Chester, 180 . ., Vol. XXIII, fol. 417.

EGERTON, GREY-, ..., Bart., of Egerton and Oulton, co. Chester, 181 . ., Vol. XXVIII, fol. 180.

„ GREY-, [Sir John] [17 Oct. 1815, 8th Bart.], of Egerton and Oulton, co. Chester, 181 . ., Vol. XXIX, fol. 278.

EGERTON, ..., of Tatton Park, co. Chester, 181 . ., Vol. XXVIII, fol. 273.

EGERTON before WARBURTON, ... [? Rowland Egerton, 9 Aug. 1813], of Arley, co. Chester, 181 . ., Vol. XXIX, fol. 178.

EGERTON, GREY-, [21 July 1825], Sir Philip, [9th] Bart., of co. Chester. [Name and Arms of Grey.] Supporters, [23 July 1825] 182 . ., Vol. XXXV, fols. 235 and 237.

EGERTON, late LEVESON-GOWER, [24 Aug. 1833], Lord Francis, of co. Chester [Surname and Arms of Egerton only], Earl of ELLESMERE [1846], 183 . ., Vol. XXXIX, fol. 361.

EGERTON-CUST, Earl BROWNLOW, of co. Hertf. and Linc., 184 . ., Vol. XLIX, fol. 134. [? Viscount Alford, Surname and Arms of Egerton only, 15 Mar. 1849.]

„ -CUST [John William, 2nd Earl, 5 Sept. 1853], of co. Hertf., 185 . ., Vol. L, fol. 390.

„ -CUST [John William, 2nd Earl, 6 July 1863], of co. Hertf., 186 . ., Vol. LV, fol. 70.

EGERTON-GREEN, Claude Egerton, of King's Ford, Stanway All Saints, co. Essex, 1897, Vol. LXIX, fol. 219.

EGGINTON, Gardiner, of Kingston-upon-Hull, co. York, and Nottingham, to the descendants of his grandfather Robert, 20 Dec. 1800, Vol. XXI, fol. 107. (Berry's Appx. and Suppl.)

„ Rev. John Clement, of Bellrocke and Codsall, co. Staff., and Exeter Coll., Oxf., 182 . ., Vol. XXXVII, fol. 103.

EGGINTON-ERNLE, J. Lloyd (s. of Rev. John C.), of Charboro Park and Bere Regis, co. Dorset, and Elleston Abbey, co. York, 1887, Vol. LXIV, fol. 71.

„ -ERNLE-ERLE-DRAX, J. Lloyd, of co. Dorset, 1888, Vol. LXIV, fol. 193.

„ „ „ „ J. Lloyd, of co. Dorset, 1890, Vol. LXVI, fol. 17.

EGLIN, Joseph, and Elizabeth Craggs, his wife, of Kingston-upon-Hull, co. York, 2 June 1826, Vol. XXXVI, fol. 16. (Berry's Appx.)

EGREMONT, Earl of [1750] (WYNDHAM). Supporters, 17 . . ., Vol. IX, fol. 351.

EILLO, John Lamport, of Liverpool, 18 . . ., Vol. LXXI, fol. . . . .

ELDERFIELD, ..., of Sutton Courtney, Berks., 182 . ., Vol. XXXII, fol. 187.

ELDON, Baron [18 July 1799] (SCOTT, Knt.), of co. Dorset and Northumberland (L.C.J., Com. Pleas). Arms and Supporters, 17 . . ., Vol. XX, fol. 376.

ELERS, Carew Thomas, B.D., of Rishoughs, co. Suff., and Bickenhill, co. Warw., 183 . ., Vol. XLI, fol. 308.

„ William, of Oldbury Place, co. Kent, Suff. and Warw., brother of the next, 183 . ., Vol. XLI, fol. 308.

„ George E., of Crowcombe, co. Somerset, Suff. and Warw., brother of the last, and three sisters, 183 . ., Vol. XLI, fol. 308.

ELGOOD, E. J., Bar.-at-Law, of Lincoln's Inn, London, 1893, Vol. LXVII, fol. 233.

ELIOT, Hariot, wife of Richard, of St. Germans, co. Cornw., a Commissioner of Excise, 16 July 1726, Vol. VII, fol. 519. Arms "in lieu of those descended unto her from her father" (James CRAGGS). (Misc. G. et H., II, p. 43.)

„ Baron [30 Jan. 1784] [Eliot], of co. Cornw. Supporters, 178 . ., Vol. XV, fol. 273.

„ Baron (CRAGGS) [before Eliot, 15 April 1789], of co. Cornw., 17 . . ., Vol. XVII, fol. 123.

„ Sir John, of Peebles, Knt. and Bart., Doctor of Physick, by Ro. Boswell, Lyon Dep., 9 Oct. 1779. (Misc. G. et H., New S., IV, p. 179.)

„ Sir George Augustus, K.B. [8 Jan. 1783], of co. Sussex. Supporters, 178 . ., Vol. XV, fol. 138. Baron HEATHFIELD [6 July 1787], of co. Sussex. Supporters, 178 . ., Vol. XVI, fol. 303.

ELIOT-DRAKE after FULLER [Sir Thomas Trayton Fuller], of co. Devon and Sussex, 181 . ., Vol. XXVII, fol. 277.

„ -DRAKE after FULLER [30 Oct. 1870], [Sir Francis George Augustus], Bart., of co. Devon and Sussex, 18 . . ., Vol. LVII, fol. 280.

ELKIN, ..., of London, and Barbados, 183 . ., Vol. XLII, fol. 340.

ELLAMES, William BRADISH-, of Little Marlow, Bucks., s. of William Bradish, of Liverpool, co. Lanc., and Cheltenham, co. Glouc., 18 . . ., Vol. LXXI, fol. . . . .

ELLENBOROUGH, [3rd] Baron, of London. Coat and Supporters, 18 Feb. 1886. Vol. LXIII, fols. 184 and 187. Extended to descendants of 1st Baron, (? Supporters) 1886, Vol. LXIII, fol. 229. Extended to the descendants of the 1st Baron, 22 Mar. 1889 ?, Vol. LXV, fol. 227.

ELLERKER, late CUETO, Joseph Eulogio, of Hart, co. Durham, and Cuba, 181 . .,
    Vol. XXX, fol. 426.
  „ late SMITH, Thomas, of Hart, co. Durham, and Alnwick, co. Northumberland,
    182 . ., Vol. XXXV, fol. 394.
ELLERKER, Edward Onslow MAINWARING-, of co. Surrey, York and Hampsh.,
    1845, Vol. XLVII, fol. 391.
  „ Edward Mainwaring Onslow, of co. Surrey, 1848, Vol. XLVIII, fol. 427.
ELLERKER, MAINWARING-, G. I. H., of co. Surrey, 1861, Vol. LIV, fol. 192.
ELLERTON after LODGE, John, of Walburne and Ellerton, co. York, and Bod-
    silin, co. Carnarvon, Wales (see LODGE, 429, 9), 1838,* Vol. XLIII,
    fol. 72.
ELLEY, Col. Sir John, K.C.B. [2 Jan. 1815], 181 . ., Vol. XXIX, fol. 158.
ELLICOMBE, Hugh Myddelton, of Culverlands, par. of St. Sidwell, Exeter, co.
    Devon, eldest surviving son of William, Rector of Alplington, co. Devon,
    with remainder to the descendants of his father (decd.), 1 Oct. 1849. (See
    Misc. G. et H., II, p. 33.)
ELLIOT, Sir George, Bart. [15 May 1874], of co. Durham and York, 187 . .,
    Vol. LVIII, fol. 336.
  „ Lady (Margaret GREEN), his wife, of co. Durham and York, 1875, Vol. LIX,
    fol. 114.
ELLIOT-BATES, Rev. J. E., of (Whatton R[ectory ?]) Hampsh. (now decd.), 1880,
    Vol. LXI, fol. 96.
  „ -BATES, Col. Henry S., of Langton Alresford, Hampsh., 188 . ., Vol. LXI,
    fol. 96.
ELLIOT after FOGGE, 1827, John, of Bolton-le-Moors, co. Lanc., and Elvet Hill,
    co. Durham. (Burke.)
ELLIOT, James John, of Leigham, Egg Buckland, co. Devon, 1887, Vol. LXIII,
    fol. 346.
ELLIOTT, late OVENS, ..., of Binfield, Berks., and Lincoln's Inn, London,
    179 . ., Vol. XVIII, fol. 43.
  „ late GLASSE, Lieut.-Col. George Henry, of Binfield, Berks., 1811, Vol.
    XXVI, fol. 289.
ELLIOTT, ..., of Townend and Windy Bank, Rochdale, co. Lanc., 181 . .,
    Vol. XXX, fol. 328.
  „ . . . ., of Goldington House, co. Bedf., 184 . ., Vol. XLVII, fol. 35.
  „ John Lettsom, of Neath, co. Glamorgan, Wales, and Bath, co. Somerset, to
    the descendants of his father and of Philip, of Bath, 184 . ., Vol. XLIX,
    fol. 391.
ELLIS, ..., of Camborne, co. Cornw., 17 . ., Vol. XI, fol. 21.
ELLIS to RODBARD, ..., of London, 178 . ., Vol. XV, fol. 1.
ELLIS, wife of MATHEWS, of Much Marcle, co. Hereford.   Arms impaled, 178 . .,
    Vol. XV, fol. 329.
  „ Wellbore, Baron MENDIP [13 Aug. 1794], of Mendip, co. Somerset.
    Supporters, 179 . ., Vol. XVIII, fol. 422.
ELLIS, late AGAR, Baron MENDIP [7 Feb. 1802] and Viscount CLIFDEN.
    (Match with WELBORE), 180 . ., Vol. XXII, fol. 367.
ELLIS, ..., of Sunning Hill, Berks., and Jamaica, 180 . ., Vol. XXV,
    fol. 432.
  „ Baron HOWARD DE WALDEN (minor).   Supporters, [1810 ?] Vol. XXV,
    fol. 425.
  „ . . . ., of Minsterworth, co. Glouc.   (See SOUTHOUSE.)   Match, 181 . .,
    Vol. XXVI, fol. 285.
ELLIS before VINER, ..., of co. Glouc.   Quarterly Arms, 181 . ., Vol. XXVI,
    fol. 300.
ELLIS to LLOYD, John Ellis, of Trallwyn, co. Carnarvon, Wales, 181 . ., Vol.
    XXVIII, fol. 326.
  „ . . . ., of Westminster, Private Sec. to Earl of Buckinghamshire, 181 . .,
    Vol. XXVIII, fol. 406.

ELLIS after JOYNER, ..., of Berkeley, co. Glouc., uncle of Sir Henry Walton Ellis, K.C.B., Waterloo. [14 Feb. 1813 ?] Vol. XXX, fol. 74. Match with CARTWRIGHT and HOGG, 181 . ., Vol. XXX, fol. 305.

ELLIS, ? James, DAY (wid. SELBY), wife of, of Barming, co. Kent, and Burwash, co. Sussex, 1819, Vol. XXXI, fol. 399 (see Berry's Suppl.).

„ Sir Henry, Knt. (and FROSTE), of co. York, and London, Keeper of the MSS. in the Brit. Museum, 1825, Vol. XXXV, fol. 158.

ELLIS and SMITH, ..., of Ponsbourne Park, co. Hertf. ; Tankerton Tower, Whitstable, co. Kent; and Owndle, co. Northampton, 183 . ., Vol. XLI, fol. 192.

ELLIS-JERVOISE, Rev., M.A., of Britford, Wilts., and Shalston, Bucks., 184 . ., Vol. XLVIII, fol. 435.

ELLIS, William (s. of John), Commander, R.N., of Great Yarmouth, co. Norf., 186 . ., Vol. LIV, fol. 88.

„ . . . ., of Gloucester Gate, London ; Mount Gambier and Port Gawler, South Australia, 186 . ., Vol. LIV, fol. 204.

„ . . . ., of Monks, Balcombe, co. Sussex, and Eccleston Square, London, 186 . ., Vol. LV, fol. 234.

ELLIS after ISRAEL, ..., of London, and Hamburg, 186 . ., Vol. LVI, fol. 30.

ELLIS to CLOUGH, Thomas P. W., of Plas Clough, co. Denbigh, Wales, and Liverpool, 18 . . ., Vol. LX, fol. 328.

ELLIS, Sir John Whittaker, Bart. [Lord Mayor of London], of co. Surrey, 1882, Vol. LXI, fol. 284.

„ Sir John Whittaker, Bart., of co. Surrey, 1891, Vol. LXVI, fol. 133.

„ Richard Adam, s. of Edward, of Tottenham, co. Middx., 18 . . ., Vol. LXXI, fol. . . . .

ELLIS-NANNEY, Hugh John (Bart.) [1897], of Gwynfryn, Llanystumdy, co. Carnarvon, Wales, 1898, Vol. LXX, fol. 116.

ELLISON after CARR, Ralph, of Hedgeley, co. Durham. and co. Northumberland, 1871, Vol. LVII, fol. 320 ; and (1896), Vol. LXIX, fol. 42.

ELLWOOD. Quartering (see ROGERS), 7 Dec. 1774.

ELMHIRST, William and Richard, of Round Green, Elmhirst, co. York, and West Ashby, Boston, co. Linc., 8 July 1845, Vol. XLVIII, fol. 5.

ELMSALL after GREAVES, Joseph Edward, of Page Hall and Brierley Manor, co. York, 181 . ., Vol. XXX, fol. 153.

ELPHIN, Ireland [See of ?], TILSON, Bp. of, 181 . ., Vol. XXVI, fol. 402. [Henry Tilson, Bp. of Elphin, 1639, to his death in 1655.]

ELPHINSTONE, Rear-Adm. Sir George Keith, K.B. [30 May 1794], F.R.S., of Scotland. Supporters, 179 . ., Vol. XVIII, fol. 369.

„ Lieut.-Col., R.E., of Scotland, 181 . ., Vol. XXIX, fol. 282.

ELPHINSTONE to BULLER, Lieut.-Col., of Cornwall, 182 . ., Vol. XXXIV, fols. 286 and 287.

ELPHINSTONE before HOLLOWAY, Major, R.E., of Stoke Cottage, nr. Devonport, co. Devon ; Belair and Vineyard, Cape of Good Hope, 182 . ., Vol. XXXV, fol. 262.

„ before STONE, Webb Elphinstone, Capt., R.N., of Exmouth, co. Devon ; Bellair, Rozelle, co. Ayr, Scotland, 1879, Vol. LX, fol. 314. (Berry's Suppl.)

ELRINGTON (wife of PYGET), C. B., Capt., R.N. [? Peter, Adm., 1821], of Hampsh. Crest to brother and descendants, 182 . ., Vol. XXXII, fols. 151 and 152.

ELSEGOOD, William, of Norwich, co. Norf., 1774, Vol. XII, fol. 284.

ELSLEY, William, of co. York, 19 April 1736, Vol. VII, fol. 199.

ELSLEY to BAKER, Thomas Baker, of co. Camb., and Mayfield, co. Camb. [? Sussex], 179 . ., Vol. XVIII, fol. 285.

ELTON (Sir Edward Marwood, Bart. [1 Aug. 1838]), of Widworthey, co. Devon, and Grennay House, co. Somerset, 183 . ., Vol. XLIII, fol. 132.

ELVERSON, Capt. H. J., of Bushby, Thurnley, co. Leic., 1882,* Vol. LXI, fol. 381.

ELWES after HERVEY, late TIMMS, John, of Stoke by Clare, co. Suff., grand-nephew to Sir Harvey Elwes. Quarterly Arms, 179 . ., Vol. XVIII, fol 220.

ELWES, late PAYNE (reputed s. of Lieut.-Gen. Elwes), of Stoke College by Clare, co. Suff., 182 . ., Vol. XXXV, fol. 53.

ELWILL, Sir John, Knt., of Exeter, Devon, 12 Dec. 1701, Vol. V, fol. 54. (Berry.)

ELWIN after WOODYEARE, ..., of Crookhill Hall, co. York, 184 . ., Vol. XLVIII, fol. 75.

ELYOTT, Susannah, wife of THOMAS, of Cathanger, co. Somerset. Arms of THOMAS to self and sister, Elizabeth THOMAS, 1751, Vol. IX, fol. 393. (Berry.)

EMANUEL, ..., of Upper Wimpole Street, London, 186 . ., Vol. LV, fol. 254.

EMBLETON-FOX, ..., of Northoppe and Manchester, co. Lanc., 1860, Vol. LIV, fols. 276 and 288.

„ -Fox, William, of Northoppe, co. Lanc., and New Coll., Oxf., 1877, Vol. LIX, fol. 306.

EMBURY to TOLLET, ..., of Betley Hall, co. Staff., and Lincoln's Inn, London, 179 . ., Vol. XIX, fol. 309.

EMERIS, William Robert, M.A., Oxf., of Little Staughton, co. Bedf., and Louth, co. Linc., and Rev. John, of Southwood, co. Norf., 18 . ., Vol. LVII, fol. 288. (Crisp, I, p. 88.)

EMERSON to AMCOTTS, ..., of Wharton, co. Linc., and co. Nottingham, 177 . ., Vol. XIII, fol. 299.

„ to AMCOTTS, ..., of co. Linc. and York, 182 . ., Vol. XXXIII, fols. 130 and 132.

„ to AMCOTTS, ..., of co. Linc. and York, 183 . ., Vol. LI, fol. 104.

EMERSON, late GRANGE (reputed son), James, of Stokesley, co. York, 184 . ., Vol. XLVIII, fol. 31.

EMERSON, Peter Henry R., of Oulton, Lowestoft, co. Suff., 1897, Vol. LXX, fol. 5.

EMLY, ..., of Creeting, co. Suff., and Salisbury, Wilts., 181 . ., Vol. XXVIII, fol. 312.

EMMES, ..., of East Tisted, Hampsh. Match, 17 . . ., Vol. VIII, fol. 220.

EMMETT, ..., of London, and Deptford, co. Kent, 181 . ., Vol. XXVI, fol. 26.

EMMITT, late BAINES, ..., of Sausthorpe, co. Linc., 182 . ., Vol. XXXVI, fol. 135.

EMMOTT, late WAINHOUSE, Richard, of Emmott Hall, co. Lanc. Match, 17 . . ., Vol. XVII, fol. 41.

EMMOTT after OSWALD, Ellen, of Golding, co. Hertf., and Emmott Hall, co. Lanc., 182 . ., Vol. XXXIII, fol. 43.

EMMOTT, Thomas, of Brookfield, Oldham, co. Lanc. (decd.), and Charles, of co. Lanc., 1891, Vol. LXVI, fol. 217.

EMPEROR, William, of Norwich and Yarmouth, co. Norf., and Germany, 19 Nov. 1736, Vol. VIII, fol. 205.

ENDERBY, Samuel, of St. Paul's Wharf, London, 12 Aug. 1778, Vol. XIV, fol. 40. (Berry.)

ENGLAND, Thomas Hutchings, of East Sambrooke, co. Somerset, and Sevington, 182 . ., Vol. XXXVI, fol. 257.

„ Sir Richard, K.C.B., K.H., of co. Somerset, [1843 ?] Vol. XLVI, fol. 391.

ENGLEFIELD to SILVERTOP, Henry C., of Lartington Hall, co. York, and Minster Acres, co. Northumberland, 18 . . ., Vol. XLIX, fol. 126.

ENGLEHEART to ERSKINE, David, Bart., of Cambo House, co. Fife, Scotland, [1821] Vol. XXXII, fol. 169.

ENGLISH, Ellen (wife of John PENN), of Enfield, co. Middx. (See PENN-ENGLISH.) 185 . ., Vol. LI, fol. 438.

„ P. J., of 42, Egerton Gardens, London (decd.), and Mrs., of London, 1890,* Vol. LXV, fol. 181 or 81.

„ Richard, of Lower Berkeley Street, London, 1891,* Vol. LXVI, fol. 196,

ENTWISLE (late MARKLAND), John, of Leeds, co. York, 178 . ., Vol. XVI, fol. 289.

ENYS, late HUNT, ..., widow of, of Enys, co. Cornw., and Stratford-on-Avon, co. Warw., 181 . ., Vol. XXVIII, fol. 21.

ERICHSEN, Sir John Eric, Bart., of Cavendish Place, London, 1895, Vol. LXVIII, fol. 168.

ERLE-DRAX after SAWBRIDGE, J. G., of Charborough, co. Dorset, 1829, Vol. XXXVII, fol. 364.

ERNLE, ..., of Connock, Wilts., Rector of All Cannings, Wilts., 1816, Vol. XXX, fol. 72.

„ . . . ., of Wilts., 1809, Vol. XXV, fol. 197.

ERRINGTON, ... (see BIGLAND), of Benwell and Errington, co. Northumberland, 17 . . ., Vol. X, fol. 215.

ERRINGTON, alias STAPLETON, Thomas, of co. Northumberland, 10 June 1773, Vol. XII, fol. 247.

ERRINGTON after WARD, ..., of Newcastle-upon-Tyne, co. Northumberland, and Nether Stowey, co. Somerset, 17 . . ., Vol. XVII, fol. 310.

ERRINGTON, ..., wife of LOVELAND, late OLDERSHAW, of co. Northumberland, 186 . ., Vol. LIV, fol. 138.

ERRINGTON, late STANLEY, Sir Thomas, of Hooton, co. Chester ; Sandhoe, co. Northumberland ; and Red Rice, Hampsh., 1820, Vol. XXXII, fol. 84.

„ (late MASSEY-STANLEY), Sir John, Bart., of Hooton, co. Chester ; Sandhoe, co. Northumberland ; Red Rice, Hampsh. ; and Wickham Market, co. Suff., 1877, Vol. LX, fol. 22.

ERSKINE (ST. CLAIR-), Earl of ROSSLYN, of Scotland. Quarterly Arms, 180 . ., Vol. XXIII, fol. 171. Supporters, fol. 174.

„ Baron (Erskine), of Restormel Castle, co. Cornw. Supporters, 180 . ., Vol. XXIV, fol. 45.

ERSKINE, late ENGLEHEART, David, of Cambo House, co. Fife, Scotland, afterwards a Baronet, "at earnest wish of the Earl of Kellie," 182 . ., Vol. XXXII, fol. 169.

ESDAILE, Sir James, Knt., Alderman of London, 20 April 1775, Vol. XIII, fol. 96.

ESHELBY, Henry Douglas (and to uncle John Douglas Eshelby), of Birkenhead, co. Chester, 1898, Vol. LXX, fol. 188.

ESMEAD (Michell) after MOORE, of the Inner Temple, London, and Monkton House, Chippenham, Wilts., 184 . ., Vol. XLVII, fol. 315.

ESSINGTON, late WARD [William Webb], of The Nock, co. Warw. [Great Malvern, co. Worc.], and London, [4 Jan. 1828] Vol. XXXVII, fol. 16.

ESTCOURT to BUCKNALL, James Bucknall, of co. Glouc., Hertf., Wilts. and York, 182 . ., Vol. XXXIV, fol. 49.

ESTCOURT after BUCKNALL, James Bucknall, of co. Glouc., Hertf., Wilts. and York, 182 . ., Vol. XXXIV, fol. 106.

ESTCOURT-BUCKNALL to SOTHERON, Thomas Henry Sutton, of co. Glouc., Hertf., Wilts. and York, 1839, Vol. XLIV, fol. 48.

ESTCOURT after SOTHERON, Thomas Henry Sutton, of co. Glouc., Hertf., Wilts. and York, 1853, Vol. LI, fol. 323.

ESTCOURT (BUCKNALL) to SOTHERON-ESTCOURT, George Thomas John, 1876, Vol. LIX, fol. 198.

ESTLEN, ..., of Bristol, co. Glouc. Match, 180 . ., Vol. XXV, fol. 351.

ETHELSTON, Rev. C. W., of Wicksted Hall, co. Chester, Rector of Uplyme, co. Devon, 184 . ., Vol. XLVIII, fol. 129.

ETHELSTON, formerly PEEL-EDMUND, of co. Chester ; Wallington Hall, co. Norf. ; and Bryn-y-fys, co. Flint, Wales, 184 . ., Vol. XLIX, fol. 468.

ETHERIDGE, ..., of Kingsland, co. Middx., 184 . ., Vol. XLVIII, fol. 337.

EVANS to DURELL, Thomas, of St. James', Westminster, 10 Sept. 1771, Vol. XII, fol. 95.

EVANS, Thomas, of Bristol, co. Glouc. (of Norwich, in Edmondson), 1772, Vol. XII, fol. 119. (Berry.)

Evans, ..., of London, 180 . ., Vol. XXI, fol. 358.

„ Barrow, wife of, of High Grove, co. Glouc. Arms to wife and descendants, 180 . ., Vol. XXIII, fol. 131.

„ Walter, of Parwick and Darley Abbey, co. Derby. (*See* CARR, of Holbrooke?). Match, 181 . ., Vol. XXVIII, fol. 290.

Evans, late wife of COTTERELL, ..., of London, 182 . ., Vol. XXXV, fols. 382 and 384.

„ late CALCOTT, George, of Llanbeblig, co. Carnarvon, Wales. Evans arms, 1834, Vol. XL, fol. 268.

Evans, William Dimple Brooks (sheriff elect), of co. Surrey, and Llynon, co. Carnarvon, to descendants of his grandfather William, 1839,* Vol. XLIV, fol. 73.

Evans after DAVIES, Herbert (minor), s. of Adjutant Davies, of Highmead, co. Carnarvon, Wales, 184 . ., Vol. XLVII, fol. 121.

Evans, Thomas, and ROGER, his wife, Mayor of Hereford, of Bishopstone and Yazor, co. Hereford, 185 . ., Vol. L, fol. 49.

„ . . . ., of Pimlico, London, 185 . ., Vol. L, fol. 343.

„ Gen. Sir De Lacey, G.C.B. [1855]. Supporters, 185 . ., Vol. LI, fol. 309.

Evans-GORDON to COOKSON, Sarah, of Guernsey and co. Durham, 185 . ., Vol. LIII, fol. 261.

Evans to LOMBE, ..., of Great Melton and Bylaugh, co. Norf., 186 . ., Vol. LIV, fol. 83.

Evans, ..., of Great Melton and Bylaugh, co. Norf., and Criswell, co. Suff., 186 . ., Vol. LIV, fol. 336.

„ Lieut.-Col. William Edwgn, of Walthamstow, co. Essex, 186 . ., Vol. LIV, fol. 122.

„ Evan, of Towey Castle, co. Carmarthen, Wales, Canon of Glouc. (s. of David, of Picton Terrace, Carmarthen), 1861, Vol. LV, fol. 206.

„ Edward (s. of Thomas), of Oswestry, Shropsh., J.P. Worc., and Welshpool, co. Montgomery, Wales, 1864,* Vol. LVI, fol. 138.

„ . . . ., of Lovesgrove, co. Cardigan, Wales, 18 . . ., Vol. LVII, fol. 121.

Evans to PUGH, ..., M.A., of Lovesgrove and Aberystwith, co. Cardigan, Wales, and Albemarle [? co. Surrey], 18 . . ., Vol. LVII, fol. 125.

Evans, widow of Vernon (now VERNON-GORE), of Verville, co. Dublin, Ireland, 187 . ., Vol. LIX, fol. 220.

„ David Williams, of Clifton-cum-Glapton, co. Nottingham, s. of William, of Glascoed and Fownog, co. Montgomery, Wales [and descendants of his father]. Quartering DORSETT, [19 April] 1879, Vol. LX, fol. 253. (Berry's Suppl.) [Powys-Land Club, XII, p. 429.]

„ C. P., of Llanstephan, co. Radnor, Wales, 1890, Vol. LXV, fol. 287.

„ Alderman Sir David, K.C.M.G. [30 July 1892, Lord Mayor of London], of Ewell, co. Surrey, 1891, Vol. LXVI, fol. 209.

„ Josiah, of Hurst House, Prescot, co. Lanc., 1882,* Vol. LXI, fol. 368. (Berry's Suppl.)

„ Peter Fabyan Sparke, of Bristol, co. Glouc., 1883,* Vol. LXII, fol. 46. (Berry's Suppl.)

Evans-GWYNNE, Rev. G. F., of Potton, co. Bedf., 1883, Vol. LXII, fol. 52.

Evans, Edward, of the City of Worc., J.P., s. of Thomas, of Welshpool, co. Montgomery, and late of Oswestry, Shropsh., gent., decd., 17 Aug. 1866,* Vol. LVI, fol. 138. (Powys-Land Club, IX, p. 426 ; Crisp, IV, p. 92.)

„ David, of Grangetown, co. York, s. of Evan Evans, of Trecynow, co. Glamorgan, Wales, 18 . ., Vol. LXXI, fol. . . . .

„ William Gwynne, of Penlan Hall, Fordham, co. Essex, 189 . ., Vol. LXIX, fol. 265.

„ Franklin George, of Llwynarthen, Castleton, nr. Cardiff [? co. Monmouth], 1897, Vol. LXIX, fol. 261.

Evelyn, late HUME, Col. Alexander, of St. Clere, co. Kent, and Headley, co. Surrey (died s.p.), 17 . . ., Vol. XX, fol. 8.

[EVERARD, Raymond, by Gregory King, Rouge Dragon, 24 Mar. 168¾. Certificate of Nobility, Crisp, Fragm. Geneal., X, p. 81 ; R. C. Fam., III, p. 162.]

EVEREST, Lieut.-Col. George (s. of Tristram), E.I.C.S., of Gwernvale, co. Brecon, Wales, 184 . .,* Vol. XLVII, fol. 215.

EVERETT, ..., of Biddlesden and Heytesbury, Wilts., 179 . ., Vol. XVIII, fol. 49.

EVERETT, late BUTT, ..., reputed son (minor), of Wilts., 181 . ., Vol. XXVI, fol. 205.

EVERINGTON, Mitchell, of Herne Hill, co. Surrey, B.A., Trinity Coll., Camb. (s. of William), 1879, Vol. LX, fol. 330. (Berry's Suppl.)

EVERITT, now CALMADY, ..., late [?] wife of Charles Holmes Everitt, of Langdon, co. Devon, 178 . ., Vol. XVI, fol. 325.

EVERITT (late STIFFE), F. W. E., of Old Square, Lincoln's Inn, London, 186 . ., Vol. LIV, fol. 118.

EVERSFIELD, late MARKWICK, ..., of Catsfield, co. Sussex, 180 . ., Vol. XXIV, fol. 246.

EVERSHEAD [John of Evershed], of co. Surrey, [11 Mar. 1696] Vol. IV, fol. 222. [Misc. G. et H., II, p. 191.]

EVERY, [Sir Henry] Bart., of Egginton, co. Derby, and Chaffcombe, co. Somerset, 180 . ., Vol. XXIII, fol. 123.

EVERY-CLAYTON, [Edward] [21 Aug. 1835], of Rowley, nr. Burnley, co. Lanc., and Derby, 183 . ., Vol. XLI, fol. 107.

„ -CLAYTON, Mrs., of co. Essex, and Rowley, nr. Burnley, co. Lanc., 1886,* Vol. LXIII, fol. 282.

EVERY-HALSTEAD, Capt. Charles E., of co. Essex and York, 188 . ., Vol. LXIII, fol. 284.

EXETER, Countess of [5 April 1794] [see HOGGINS], of co. Linc., 179 . ., Vol. XVIII, fol. 304.

„ Marquis of, of co. Lincoln. Additional Crest, 1896, Vol. LXIX, fol. 123.

EXMOUTH, Baron [1 June 1814] (PELLEW, Bart.), of co. Devon. Supporters, 181 . ., Vol. XXVIII, fol. 196.

„ Viscount [10 Dec 1816], G.C.B. (PELLEW), of co. Devon. Augmentation and Supporters, 181 . ., Vol. XXX, fol. 94.

EXTON, ..., of Lyme Regis, co. Norf. Quartered by FOSTER (see PIGOTT), 182 . ., Vol. XXXVII, fol. 110.

EYCOTT, ..., of Bonds Mill. Stonehouse, co. Glouc., 180 . ., Vol. XXI, fol. 378.

EYLES, ..., MULLENS, wife of, of Bierley House, East Meon, Hampsh. Escutcheon of pretence, 181 . ., Vol. XXX, fol. 291.

EYRE (HARTLEY), Winchcombe Henry, of Weymouth Street, London, 179 . ., Vol. XIX, fol. 27.

EYRE before HARTLEY, Winchcombe Henry, of London, 179 . ., Vol. XIX, fol. 61.

EYRE, late PURVIS, William, of Newhouse, Wilts. (left a dau.), 179 . ., Vol. XIX, fol. 99.

„ late ARCHER-HOUBLON, Charles, of Berks., co. Essex and Derby, 18 . ., Vol. XXXVIII, fol. 336 ; 1831, Vol. XXXI, fols. 348 and 350.

EYRE, ..., of Berks., 183 . ., Vol. XXXIX, fol. 4.

EYRES (late KETTLEWELL), Henry William, of Armley, Leeds, co. York, and Trinity Coll., Camb., 1878, Vol. LX, fols. 155 and 157. (Berry's Suppl.)

F

FAIR, Thomas, of Lytham, co. Lanc., J.P. Lyon and H. Reg. [Thomas Fair, of Westwood, co. Lanc., Lyon Register, no date. John Fair, of London, Lyon Register, 1885.]

FAIRCLOUGH, Renell Anthony (s. of Thomas), of Craven Hill, Hyde Park, London, 1898, Vol. LXX, fol. 145.

FAIRFAX, late MARTIN, ..., of Denny, co. York, 1782, Vol. XV, fol. 83.

FALCON to HARRISON, ..., of Workington and Whitehaven, co. Cumberland, 184 . ., Vol. XLVII, fols. 181 and 194.

FALCON-STEWARD, Rev. R. S., of Newton Manor, co. Cumberland, Rector of Sulhampstead, Berks. (died 9 Nov. 1887), 1883, Vol. LXII, fol. 73. (Berry's Suppl.)

FALDER to RODDAM, ..., of Ballochshan, Isle of Man, and Roddam, co. Northumberland, 186 . ., Vol. LVI, fol. 3.

FALL after NICHOLSON, of Richmond and Rudd Hall, co. York, 181 . ., Vol. XXVI, fol. 398.

FALL, ..., of Herne Hill and Clapham Park, co. Surrey, 186 . ., Vol. LV, fol. 248.

FALLOWES, ..., of Fallowes Hall [co. Chester]. Match with COLTHURST. [Fallowes and Fallowes Hall are erased], 177 . ., Vol. XII, fol. 85.

FALMOUTH, Viscount [13 June 1720], of co. Cornw. Supporters, 172 . ., Vol. VII, fol. 3.

FANE after HOPKINS to CHOLMLEY, Henry, of co. York. Quartering, and escutcheon of pretence, 179 . ., Vol. XVIII, fol. 29.

FANE, Lieut.-Gen. Sir Henry, G.C.B. [K.C.B., 2 Jan. 1815, G.C.B., 24 Jan. 1826]. Supporters, 182 . .,* Vol. XXXVII, fol. 20.

FANE-DE SALIS, Count De Salis, of co. Sussex, 183 . ., Vol. XLI, fol. 154.

FANE to BENETT, ..., of Pytt House, Wilts., 185 . ., Vol. LII, fol. 221.

„   „   . . . ., of Pytt House, Wilts. Quarterly with Benett and STAN-FORD, 18 . ., Vol. LVII, fol. 74.

FANE after PONSONBY, Hon. Spencer, C.B., of co. Somerset (Earl of BESSBOROUGH), 187 . ., Vol. LIX, fol. 86.

FARDELL, John, of the Middle Temple, Bar. at-Law, F.S.A., of London, 180 . ., Vol. XXV, fol. 316 ; and co. Linc. Match with TUNNARD, impalement, 181 . ., Vol. XXVI, fol. 68. (Berry.)

FREKE-FAREWELL, Maj.-Gen. W. T., of Bath, co. Somerset, 1885, Vol. LXIII, fol. 119.

FARISH, Edward, of Elm Park Gardens, Chelsea, London, 1896, Vol. LXIX, fol. 170.

FARLEY, ..., of the Island of Antigua, 17 . . ., Vol. XVII, fol. 272.

„   William, M.A., Vicar of Effingham, co. Worc. ; Surrey : and Westbourne, co. Sussex. (See TURNER), 182 . ., Vol. XXXVII, fol. 200.

FARLEY after TURNER, Charles, Rector of Eastham, of Park Hall, Kidderminster, and Henwick Hallow, co. Worc., 1827, Vol. XXXVII, fol. 200.

„   after TURNER, Rev. Charles, of Park Hall, Kidderminster, and Henwick Hallow, co. Worc., 1848, Vol. XLIX, fol. 16.

„   after TURNER, Thomas McNaghten, now of Wartnaby Hall and Melton Mowbray, co. Leic., 1867, Vol. LVI, fol. 227.

„   after (TURNER-), ..., of Marnhull, co. Dorset, and Worthy Park, Hampsh., 1867, Vol. LVI, fol. 227.

FARMBOROUGH, Francis, of Denbigh Hall, Bucks., 186 . ., Vol. LIV, fol. 110.

FARMER, Sir William, Bart., cr. Baron LEMPSTER, of co. Northampton. Supporters, 1692, Vol. IV, fol. 115.

„   Joseph (HARLEY, [Caroline] his wife, quarterly), of Sydney, New South Wales ; St. John, Hampstead, and Finchley New Road, co. Middx., [4 Jan. 1855] Vol. LI, fol. 196 [see Crisp, Notes, X, p. 105].

FARMER-(HAYWOOD), Charles, of Comberford Hall, Tamworth, co. Staff., 1871, Vol. LVIII, fol. 121.

FARMER, Sir William, of Cowarth Park and Sunningdale Park, Berks., [24 Jan.] 1885,* Vol. LXIII, fol. 7. [Arms also to Martha Perkins, his wife, (Crisp, Notes, X, p. 106).]

FARNABY, ..., of Kippington, co. Kent [170¾, Charles, of Kippington, Gwillim, p. 171], 16 . . ., Vol. II, fol. 646.

„   Sir Charles, of Kippington, co. Kent, confirmed by Sir Henry ST. GEORGE, Clar., 30 Mar. 1703, Vol. V, fol. 98.

FARNABY to RADCLIFFE, [Sir Charles] Bart., of co. Kent, [1784] Vol. XV, fol. 265.
FARNAN, ..., of Old Ford, co. Middx., 187 . ., Vol. LVIII, fol. 267.
FARNCOMB, Thomas, of Castleham, Hollington, co. Sussex, Sheriff of London
    [1840-41], 18 . . ., Vol. XLIV, fol. 357.
FARNCOMBE-TANNER, W. T., of East Lenham, co. Kent ; Fishers, Wake-Colne,
    Halstead, co. Essex ; and Morehouse, Wivelsfield, Burgess Hall, co.
    Sussex, 1881, Vol. LXI, fol. 227. (Berry's Suppl.)
FARNWORTH, ..., Mayor of Liverpool, co. Lanc., 186 . ., Vol. LVI, fol. 67.
FARQUHAR, Capt. R.N., C.B., K.H., of Newhall, co. Kincardine, Scotland, 182 . .,
    Vol. XXXV, fol. 193.
  „   Horace, Lord. Supporters, 1898, Vol. LXX, fol. 178.
FARQUHARSON, late Ross, James, Capt. R.N., of Scotland, 180 . ., Vol. XXIII,
    fol. 293.
FARQUHARSON, ..., of Scotland. Match with BORTHWICK and GILCHRIST.
    Quartering 180 . ., Vol. XXXIV, fol. 9.
FARRAND, Robert, M.P., of Holme Hall, co. Norf., 182 . ., Vol. XXXIII, fol. 369.
FARRANT, late BINSTEAD, ... (Farrant, late wife), of co. Essex, 179 . ., Vol.
    XIX, fol. 97.
FARRANT, Sir George, Knt., of Northstead House, Chelsfield, co. Kent, and Great
    Hale, co. Linc., 184 . .. Vol. XLV, fol. 357.
FARRELL to SKEFFINGTON, William Charles, of Skeffington, co. Leic. (Bart.),
    13 June 1772, Vol. XII, fol. 197.
FARREN, Col., C.B., of Cork, Ireland, 18 . . ., Vol. LIII, fol. 319.
  „   George, of Trefenai, Llanbablig, co. Carnarvon, Wales, 1896,* Vol. LXIX,
    fol. 150.
FARRER to FAWKES, Francis, of Barnborough Grange, co. York (died s.p. 1818),
    178 . ., Vol. XVI, fol. 193.
FARRER, late SPURGEON, Farrer, George (minor), of Cold Brayfield, Bucks.,
    17 . . ., Vol. XX, fol. 338.
FARRER, William (late ECROYD), of Marton, co. York, 1896, Vol. LXIX, fol. 148.
  „   Baron, of Abinger Hall, Dorking, co. Surrey. Arms, 1893,* Vol. LXVII,
    fol. 205.
  „   Baron, of co. Surrey. Supporters, [1893] Vol. LXVII, fol. 215.
FARRINGTON, Gen. Anthony, Bart. [2 Dec. 1813], of Blackheath, co. Kent, 181 . .,
    Vol. XXX, fol. 338.
FARSYDE, late WATSON, George James, of Fylingdales and Bilton House,
    co. York, 182 . ., Vol. XXXVI, fol. 105.
  „   (late HULTON), William, of Fylingdales and Bilton House, co. York, 1877,
    Vol. LX, fol. 72. (Berry's Suppl.)
FARTHING-BEAUCHAMP, ..., of Tetton House, Kingston, co. Somerset, 182 . .,
    Vol. XXXII, fol. 88.
FASSETT, ..., (widow of HIGDEN), of Walworth, co. Surrey, wife of BYFIELD-
    HIGDEN, of Walworth, 181 . ., Vol. XXX, fol. 11.
FAUDEL-PHILLIPS, S. H., of co. Hertf., and Mapleton, Westerham, co. Kent, and
  „   „   (Sir) George F., Lord Mayor of London, of co. Kent, and Balls
    Pond, co. Hertf., [1896] Vol. LXIX, fol. 19. Supporters, to successors
    in the Baronetcy, 1896,* [? 1897] Vol. LXX, fols. 94 and 135.
FAULKNER, J., of Kempsford, co. Glouc., 1890*, Vol. LXV, fol. 223.
FAUNTLEROY (a Banker), Henry, of Berners Street, London, 180 . ., Vol. XXIV,
    fol. 308.
  „   Robert, of Potters's Fields, Southwark, and Wandsworth, co. Surrey, Merchant,
    Culversgrove, co. Essex, [12 Mar. 1823] Vol. XXXIV, fol. 24ʰ. [Crisp,
    Fragm. Geneal., VII, p. 48.]
FAVENC, Abraham, of Sizeham, &c., and London. 180 . ., Vol. XXII, fol. 268.
    (See Landed Gentry).
FAWCETT, [Lieut.-Gen.] Sir William, K.B. [20 Dec. 1786], of co. Middx. Sup-
    porters (Arms hitherto used were exemplified), 178 . ., Vol. XVI,
    fol. 265.

FAWCETT to PULTENEY (SUTTON, wife of), of Chiswick, co. Middx., 181 . ., Vol. XXVII, fol. 351.
FAWCETT (see HARGREAVES), of Heywood Hall, co. York. Match, 181 . ., Vol. XXIX, fol. 45.
FAWDINGTON, William (s. of William, of London), of Manchester, co. Lanc., and Thirsk, co. York, 183 . ., Vol. XXXIX, fol. 368.
FAWKES, late HAWKSWORTH, ..., of Farnley Hill, co. York, 178 . ., Vol. XVI, fol. 191 ; and late FARRER, fol. 193.
„ late HAWKSWORTH, of Hawkesworth, co. York, 179 . ., Vol. XVIII, fol. 131.
FAWSITT, late HORNBY, ..., of Hunsley, Leytham, Rowley and Kapen Hall. (Match), 180 . ., Vol. XXIII, fol. 194.
„ late WETHERELL, ..., of Drenston, Rowley, and Laythorne, co. York, 182 . ., Vol. XXXVIII, fol. 242.
FAWSITT after FERGUSON, John Daniel (Roy. Lic., 19 Dec. 1866), of Hunsley and Burton Constable, co. York, 1866, Vol. LVI, fol. 174.
FAYLE, ..., of London, 180 . ., Vol. XXV, fol. 121.
FAYRER, Sir Joseph, Bart., C.M.G., of 16, Devonshire Street, London. Supporters, 1896, Vol. LXIX, fol. 24.
FAZAKERLEY, late GILLIBRAND, Henry Hawarden (minor), of Gillibrand Hall, Fazakerley, co. Lanc., 181 . ., Vol. XXVIII, fol. 139.
„ late GILLIBRAND, Hawarden Thomas, of Chaley, Gillibrand Hall, Fazakerley, co. Lanc., 182 . ., Vol. XXXVIII, fol. 43.
FEAKE, Anne, of Durrington, co. Essex (sheriff [?]). Arms of HAMPDEN quarterly, 22 Nov. 1774, Vol. XIII, fol. 38.
FEAKE (late CRUSE), Jonathan, of co. Essex, by Roy. Lic., 180 . ., Vol. XXI, fol. 89.
FEARNLEY-WHITTINGSTALL, ..., of Watford, co. Hertf., 182 . ., Vol. XXXV, fol. 168.
FECTOR, ..., of Dover, co. Kent, 181 . ., Vol. XXVIII, fol. 276.
FECTOR to "LAURIE OF MAXWELTON," of Maxwelton House, co. Dumfries, Scotland, and Dover co. Kent, 18 . . ., Vol. XLIX, fol. 53.
FEILDEN, Joseph (and to grandfather Joseph), of Witton, co. Lanc., 23 Nov. 1856, Vol. XLII, fol. 3.
FEILDING to POWYS [Henry Wentworth], of Shropsh. [grandson of the 6th] (Earl of DENBIGH) (died s.p.), 183 . ., Vol. XXXIX, fol. 166.
FELL, Robert Edward, of Swarthmoor Hall, co. Lanc.; St. Martin's-in-the-Fields, London ; and Windsor, Berks., 9 Jan. 1722, Vol. XII, fol. 185 (see Berry).
FELLOWES, William, Master-in-Chancery, of Lincoln's Inn, London ; John, a director, South Sea Company ; Edward, of St. Paul's, Covent Garden ; brothers and sons of William, late Citizen and Deputy-Alderman of Vintry Ward, London, 28 July 1713, Vol. VI, fol. 118, and Add. MS. 14,830, fol. 100.
FELLOWES, late WALLOP, Hon. Newton, s. of the Earl of PORTSMOUTH, of co. Devon, 1794, Vol. XVIII, fol. 379.
FELLOWES to BENYON, Richard, of co. Huntingdon and Essex, 1854, Vol. LI, fol. 215.
FELLOWS, (Hon.) J. S., Attorney-General of New Brunswick, of London, 1890,° Vol. LXVI, fol. 7.
FENOUIKLET, Peter (or FENOUILLET), of London, 23 April 1761, Vol. X, fol. 345. (Berry.)
FENTHAM, ..., of West End, Hampstead, co. Middx., 180 . ., Vol. XXV, fol. 8.
FENTON, John, of Fenton Park, and Shelton, Stoke, co. Staff., 29 Jan. 172⅘, Vol. VII, fol. 527.
FENTON before SCOTT, William, of Ledstone, co. York, 178 . ., Vol. XVI, fol. 5.
FENTON, James, M.A., F.S.A., of Norton Hall, co. Glouc., and Bamford Hall and Crimble Hall, co. Lanc., 186 . ., Vol. LVI, fol. 219. (Berry's Suppl.)

FENWICK to CLENNELL, Thomas (died s.p.), of co. Northumberland.   Clennell
    Arms, 179 . ., Vol. XIX, fol. 295.
FENWICK(-CLENNELL), ..., of Harbottle Castle, co. Northumberland ; Thomas,
    s. of Christopher Fenwick, of Earsdon, co. Northumberland, 1882,*
    Vol. XLI, fols. 372 and 382.
FENWICK, Ann, wife of George HARRISON, Norroy King of Arms.   Crest to the
    descendants of her father Michael, 179 . ., Vol. XIX, fols. 331 and 332.
FENWICK (late Lambert), Thomas, s. of Robert, of Burrow Hall, Tunstall, co.
    Lanc., 180 . .. Vol. XXI, fol. 241.
FENWICK before STUART, ... (Spr.), of London, 180 . ., Vol. XXIX, fol. 250.
FENWICK, late REID, Edward Matthew, of Burrow Hall, co. Lanc., 185 . .,
    Vol. L, fols. 12 and 14.
FEREDAY, Dudley, Acting Governor of Sierra, Leone, &c., and co. Staff. (M.A.,
    Oxf.), 182 . ., Vol. XXXIV, fol. 350.
FERGUSON before TEPPER, Peter, Brit. Merchant, and resident at Warsaw.
    Quarterly Arms, 17 . . ., Vol. XIV, fol. 165.
FERGUSON, late BERRY, William, of Austin Friars, London, and Raith, Scotland,
    178 . ., Vol. XV, fol. 11.
FERGUSON-DAVIE, ..., of Creedy, co. Devon, 184 . ., Vol. XLVIII, fol. 140.
FERGUSON after OLIPHANT, ... of Broadfield House, Hesket, co. Cumberland,
    186 . ., Vol. LIV, fol. 85.
FERMANAGH, Baroness [13 June 1792 ?] (Mary VERNEY), of Bucks. (See
    WRIGHT [?].) 181 . ., Vol. XXVI, fol. 165.
FERMOR-HESKETH [Sir Thomas George, 8 Nov. 1867], Bart., of co. Lanc.
    Quarterly Arms, 186 . ., Vol. LVI, fol. 306.
FERNE, Robert Bonsall, s. of Henry, of Snitterton and Perewick, co. Derby,
    Receiver-General of H.M. Customs, 10 Oct. 1707, Vol. V, fol. 264 ;
    Add. MS. 14,381, fol. 6.
FFERAND, late WADDINGTON, Thomas, s. of Rev. Joshua, of co. Nottingham,
    178 . ., Vol. XVI, fol. 413.
FERRAND after BUSFIELD, William, of co. York, 1839, Vol. XLIV, fols. 123
    and 129.
FERRAND, William, of St. Ives and Harden Grange, co. York, 1890, Vol. LXV,
    fol. 207.
    „   Lieut.-Col. William (see BUSFIELD), of co. York, 188 . ., Vol. LXIII,
        fol. 299.
FERRAR, Michael Lloyd, of Little Gidding, co. Huntingdon, and Ealing [co.
    Middx. ?], 18 . ., Vol. LXXI, fol. . . . . .
FERRERS, Baron (SHIRLEY) [by Writ, 14 Dec. 1677].   Supporters, 16 . . .,
    Vol. III, fol. 70.
    „   Earl (SHIRLEY), [? Washington, 5th Earl].   Supporters, 17 . . ., Vol. XIV,
        fol. 96.
    „   Baroness.   Supporters. [1778] Vol. XIV, fol. 96.
    „   Henry F. (formerly CROXON), of Pentrabeyliu Hall, Shropsh., 1885, Vol.
        LXIII, fol. 57 or 87.
FERRIS, Rev. Thomas, of Great Stambridge, co. Essex, and Dallington, Battle,
    and Chichester, co. Sussex, 30 May 1812.   Match, Vol. XXXVII, fol. 149.
FETHERSTON, late DILKE, John, of co. Warw., 1833, Vol. XXIX, fol. 325.
FETHERSTON-DILKE, Charles and William (sons of John), 1858, Vol. LII, fol. 385.
FETHERSTONHAUGH, late SMALLWOOD, Charles, of Kirk Oswald, co. Cumberland.
    (Match), [1 Sept. 1797] Vol. XX, fol. 136.
FETHERSTONHAUGH, Alexander Stephenson, of Hopton Court, co. Worc., and
    Windy Hall, Kirkhaugh, Alston, co. Northumberland, 185 . ., Vol. LI,
    fol. 67.   (Berry's Suppl.)
FETTIPLACE, late GORGES, Richard, of Eye Court, co. Hereford, and Swinbrook,
    co. Oxf., &c., 180 . ., Vol. XXIII, fol. 254.
FEUILLETEAU, William, s. of Lewis, s. of Jacob, of St. Christopher's, 20 Sept. 1774,
    Vol. XIII, fol. 7.

FEVERSHAM, Earl of [8 April 1676] (SANDS). Supporters, 16 . . .,* Vol. III, fol. 53.

„ Lord [Fevesham, Baron, of Downton, Wilts., 23 June 1747] (DUNCOMBE). Supporters, 17 . . ., Vol. IX, fol. 294.

„ Baron [14 July 1826 (DUNCOMBE)], of co. York, 182 . ., Vol. XXXVI, fol. 43. Arms and Supporters, fol. 47.

FEWTRELL-WYLDE, ..., of Uplands, and the Manor House, Chelmarsh, Shropsh. ; and Claverdon and Norton Lindsey, co. Warw., 185 . ., Vol. L, fol. 193.

FICKLIN, P. B., of Downlands, Hordle, Hampsh. (See C. B. BROWN.) Ficklin Arms only, 1889, Vol. LXV, fol. 60.

FIDLER, ..., of Camberwell, co. Surrey, 182 . ., Vol. XXXIV, fol. 156.

FIELD to PARKER, ..., of Moorhouse Hill, co. Cumberland, 17 . ., Vol. XVII, fol. 266.

FIELD, ..., of Stroud, co. Gloue. Quarterly to PHELPS, 17 . ., Vol. XVII, fol. 346.

„ Jane Anne Elizabeth, of Euston Square, London, dau. of Lieut. Michael Field, R.N., and wife of Edmond LODGE, Norroy King of Arms, 1815, Vol. XXIX, fol. 298.

„ . . . ., of Heaton in Bradford Dale, co. York, 182 . ., Vol. XXXII, fol. 255.
„ . . . ., of Yaxley, co. Huntingdon, 182 . ., Vol. XXXIII, fol. 226.

FIELD-CHILD, ..., of Yaxley, co. Huntingdon, 182 . ., Vol. XXXIII, fol. 228.

FIELD, Edward, of Ipswich and Sedgrave, co. Suff., 183 . ., Vol. XLII, fol. 64.

„ Baron, [Sir] William Ventris [-Field], of co. Surrey and Sussex, 1890,* Vol. LXV, fols. 255 and 257.

FIELDEN, John, s. of John, of Dobroyd Castle, co. Lanc., and Grimston Park, co. York, 1879, Vol. LX, fol. 301. (Berry's Suppl.)

FIELDER, ..., of Shorfield, nr. Basing, Hampsh., 182 . ., Vol. XXXVIII, fol. 55.

FIENNES after TWISLETON, ... [11th Baron Saye and Sele, 14 Feb. 1825], 182 . ., Vol. XXXV, fol. 114.

FIENNES, EARDLEY and TWISTLETON [11th Baron Saye and Sele]. Arms quarterly, [16 Mar. 1825] Vol. XXXV, fol. 116.

„ (WYKEHAM-) after TWISLETON, ..., Baron SAYE AND SELE, 182 . ., Vol. XXXV, fol. 118. [? 13th Baron, 14 Feb. 1849.]

FIFE, John Cookson, s. of William Henry (deed.), Capt., 65th Foot, of Newcastle-upon-Tyne, co. Northumberland, and co. Durham, 1878, Vol. LX, fol. 203.

FIFE-COOKSON, John Cookson, of Whitehill, co. Northumberland, and co. Durham, 1878, Vol. LX, fol. 207. (Berry's Suppl.)

FILDER, ..., of Eastbourne, co. Sussex, 181 . ., Vol. XXXI, fol. 241.

FINCH, Baron [1640], of Fordwich, co. Kent, Lord Keeper of the Great Seal. Supporters, 16 . ., Vol. I, fol. 425.

„ Baron (DAVENTRY) [1673]. Supporters, 16 . . ., Vol. III, fol. 36.

„ [The Hon. Heneage], Baron GUERNSEY [15 Mar. 170⅔]. Supporters, 17 . . ., Vol. V, fol. 113.

FINCH, late INGLE, William, of Shelford, co. Camb., 178 . ., Vol. XV, fol. 159.

FINCH to GRIFFITH-WYNNE, Charles Wynn, of Wales (Earl of AYLESFORD), 180 . ., Vol. XXIV, fols. 40 and 42.

FINCH (WYNNE-), late GRIFFITH-WYNNE, Charles, M.P., 185 . ., Vol. L, fol. 82.

FINCH, late THOMSON, ..., nat. son and dau. of the Earl of WINCHILSEA AND NOTTINGHAM, 180 . ., Vol. XXV, fols. 208 and 210.

FINCH, ..., of Dolleys Hill, Willesden, co. Middx., 182 . ., Vol. XXXV, fol. 306.

FINCH to WYNNE, George Henry, of Voelas, co. Denbigh, Wales, 182 . ., Vol. XXXVII, fol. 142.

FINCH, John, of Watford, co. Hertf., 185 . ., Vol. L, fol. 49.

„ . . . ., of Blackheath Park, Kidbrooke and Greenwich, co. Kent, and Blaenavon, co. Monmouth, 186 . ., Vol. LVI, fol. 83.

FINCH-HATTON-BESLEY, W. D., of London, 1894, Vol. LXVIII, fol. 43.

FINCH, George Henry (George), of Burley-on-the-Hill, Oakham, co. Rutland, 18 . . ., Vol. LXXI, fol. . . . .

FINDEN, Rev. George Sketchley, M.A., Ph.D., of Newport Pagnell, Bucks., 186 . ., Vol. LV, fol. 116.

FINN-KELSEY, Francis, of Lyminge, co. Kent, 188 , ., Vol. LXI, fol. 158.

FINZELL, ..., of Frankfort Hall, Clevedon, co. Somerset, and Frankfort-on-Maine, 18 . ., Vol. LIII, fol. 239.

FIOTT, Nicholas John, of Jersey, 17 . ., Vol. XIV, fol. 346.

FIOTT to LEE, John, LL.D., of Doctors' Commons : Colworth House, co. Bedf. ; and Totteridge, co. Hertf., 181 . ., Vol. XXX, fol. 145.

FIRBANK, Joseph Thomas, M.P., s. of Joseph, of St. Julian's, Monmouth, High Sheriff, 1866, 18 . . ., Vol. LXXI, fol. . . . .

FIRTH, Thomas, of Hartford Lodge, Great Budworth, co. Chester, and Halifax, co. York, 1836, Vol. XLII, fol. 24. (Crisp, IV, p. 141.)

  ,,   Mark, of Sheffield, co. York, 18 . . ., Vol. LVII, fol. 78. (Berry's Suppl.)

FISH, John, Lord of the Manor of Kempton, co. Middx., and for his wife Ann, dau. of William WHAPSHOTT, 18¹⁰⁄₁₂, Vol. XXVI, fol. . . . . (Berry's Appx.)

FISHER, Edward Ruckcroft, of Ainstalle and Dale, co. Cumberland, 181 . ., Vol. XXIX, fol. 272 ; and Beaconsfield, co. Nottingham (now FISHER-ROWE), 188 . ., Vol. LXII, fol. 62.

  ,,   Elizabeth, d. and h. of John, late Citizen of London, wife of James or Jacob SAWBRIDGE, of London, Solicitor, 12 June, 1717, Vol. VI, fol. 299, and Add. MS. 14,830, fol. 103.

  ,,   John, of Foremonk, co. Derby, 15 Sept. 1730, Vol. VIII, fol. 95ᵇ.

  ,,   John, grandfather Montgomery, of Stoney Stanton, Cossington, co. Leic. Quartering with WARD, 17 . ., Vol. XIV, fol. 199.

  ,,   John, Bishop of Salisbury, Chancellor of the Order of the Garter, of Hampsh., s. of John, M.A., rector of Colborne, Isle of Wight. Remainder to the descendants of his brother, 22 June, 1812,* Vol. XXVII, fol. 56. (Misc. G. et H., 2nd S., V, p. 97.)

  ,,   Joseph (s. of James, of Londonderry), of St. Andrew's, Holborn, London, 12 Aug. 1730, Vol. VII, fol. 10 ; and Add. MS. 14,381, fol. 145.

  ,,   Thomas, of Foremark, co. Derby, and Ravenstone, co. Leic., 30 Nov. 1771, Vol. XII, fol. 103. (Berry.)

FISHER, late COOPER, Henry, of Soham, co. Camb., and town of Leicester, 17 . . ., Vol. XX, fol. 66.

FISHER, ..., of Laxfield, co. Suff., 180 . ., Vol. XXV, fol. 331.

FISHER to PONSONBY, of Hale Hall, co. Cumberland, 181 . ., Vol. XXIX, fol. 362.

FISHER, ..., of the Inner Temple, London, and Cockermouth, co. Cumberland, 182 . ., Vol. XXXV, fol. 39.

FISHER (HORMAN-), ..., of Englefield Green, co. Surrey, 18 . . ., Vol. XXXVIII, fols. 229 and 230.

FISHER to BROCKLEBANK, ..., of co. Cumberland, and Lanc., 184 . ., Vol. XLVIII, fol. 61.

FISHER, Rev. Isaac, of Bentley Hall, nr. Walsall, co. Staff., 184 . ., Vol. XLVIII, fol. 119.

  ,,   Major, Bo.S.C. [Bombay Staff Corps ?], 184 . ., Vol. XLVIII, fol. 192. To other descendants of his father, 184 . ., Vol. XLVIII, fol. 193.

  ,, ..., of Donnington-on-the-Heath and Cossington, Barrow-upon-Soar, co. Leic., 186 . ., Vol. LVI, fol. 103.

  ,,   Edward, s. of John, of Almondbury, co. York, 1876, Vol. LIX, fol. 250. (Berry's Suppl.)

FISHER to PHILIPPS, Charles Edward Gregg, of Picton Coyth, co. Pembroke. Wales, and the Inner Temple, London, 187 . ., Vol. LIX, fol. 262. (Berry's Suppl.)

FISHER, Henry, of Ladbroke Grove, London, 1881, Vol. LXI, fol. 187.

FISHER-ROWE, Capt. E. R., of Thornecombe, co. Surrey, and London, 1883, Vol. LXII, fol. 62, and 181 . ., Vol. XXIX, fol. 272.

FISHER, Charles Edward, of Distington Hall, Whitehaven, co. Cumberland (s. of Charles), 189 . ., Vol. LXXI, fol. . . . .

„ Frederick (2nd s. of Octavius), of Tulse Hill, co. Surrey, 189 . ., Vol. LXXI, fol. . . . .

FISKE to WILKES, Rev. Robert, M.A., of Wendon Lofts, co. Essex, Vicar of Elmdon [co. Essex ?], 185 . ., Vol. LII, fol. 346.

FISON, William, of Greenholme, Otley, co. York, 186 . ., Vol. LV, fol. 18. (Berry's Suppl.)

FITCH [FYTCHE], ..., Bart., (of Woodham Walter, co. Essex), confirmation of the Arms of Fitch of Essex, 5 Mar., $\frac{1699}{1700}$, Vol. IV, fols. 335, 336 and 337.

„ [Fytche], Sir Comport, Bart., of Eltham and Mount Mascall, co. Kent, 17 . . ., Vol. V, fols. 71 and 72.

FITCH, Thomas (? Frederick), 40, Highbury New Park, London, 1893,* Vol. LXVII, fol. 113.

FITCHES, ..., of co. Essex. (Match), 16 . . ., Vol. IV, fol. 336.

FITZALAN-HOWARD, Baron Howard, of Glossop, [9 Dec. 1869], of London. Supporters, 18 . . ., Vol. LVII, fols. 222 and 223.

FITZALAN (to TALBOT), ..., of London, 187 . ., Vol. LIX, fol. 254.

FITZCLARENCE to HUNLOKE, [19 Dec. 1863, Hon. Frederick Charles George Fitzclarence], [and the Hon. Adelaide Augusta Wilhelmina his wife, eldest dau. of Philip Charles Lord] (DE LISLE and DUDLEY), of Wingerworth Hall, co. Derby, 186 . ., Vol. LV, fol. 142.

FITZGERALD, Rev. Thomas, of Walton and Abinger, co. Surrey, 17 . . ., Vol. IX, fol. 111.

FITZGERALD, late PURCELL, of Boulge, co. Suff.; Naseby, co. Northampton; Pendleton, co. Lanc.; and Little Island, co. Waterford, 181 . ., Vol. XXXI, fol. 69.

FITZGERALD, ... [Three lines marked for other names (?), but nothing filled in.]

FITZGERALD after DALTON, Bart., of co. Lanc., Essex and Ireland, 186 . ., Vol. LIV, fol. 182.

„ after DALTON, ..., Bart., of co. Lanc., Essex and Ireland, 186 . ., Vol. LVI, fol. 199. [Sir Gerald Richard, Bart., assumed by Roy. Lic., 23 Mar. 1867, the additional surname and arms of Dalton and became Dalton-Fitzgerald].

„ after WILSON, Ann, widow of Richard CLIFFE, of co. York, and Adelphi, co. Clare, Ireland, 187 . ., Vol. LVIII, fol. 138.

FITZGERALD, Baron, of Ireland, 1882, Vol. LXI, fol. 370.

FITZGERALD (formerly HEALY), John Gerald, of Royal Farm, Peperharow, Godalming, co. Surrey, 1897, Vol. LXIX, fol. 257.

FITZGIBBON, [John 1st] Earl of CLARE, in Ireland. Supporters [Baron FitzGibbon, of Sidbury, co. Devon, 24 Sept. 1799], 17 . . ., Vol. XX, fol. 394.

FITZHERBERT before BROCKHOLES, William, of Claughton, co. Lanc., and Swinnerton, co. Staff., 1783, Vol. XV, fol. 186.

„ before BROCKHOLES, ..., of Claughton, co. Lanc.; Swinnerton, co. Staff.; and Norbury, co. Derby. (See TASBURGH), 181 . ., Vol. XXVI, fol. 1.

FITZHERBERT-BROCKHOLES, William Joseph, of Claughton, co. Lanc., and Swinnerton, co. Staff., 1875, Vol. LIX, fol. 158.

FITZ-HUGH, T. Llewellyn, of Plas Power, Wrexham, co. Denbigh, Wales, 1885,* Vol. LXIII, fol. 59.

FITZ-PATRICK, late WILSON, ..., reputed son of Fitz-Patrick, Earl of UPPER OSSORY, Ireland, 184 . ., Vol. XLV, fol. 380.

Fitz-Patrick (John Wilson), Baron Castl...
    Supporters, 18 . . ., Vol. LVII, fol. 198.
Fitz-Roy, [Charles], Baron Southampton [17 ... cc. 1869], of Ireland.
    Vol. XIV, fol. 263.
FitzWilliam, Earl [6 Sept. 1746], [William FitzW ... of London, 17 . . . ,"
    Vol. IX, fol. 64 ; Wentworth, 181 . ., Vol. X.
    „ . . . ., of Bolle, co. Nottingham. (See Lonsdale co. York, 17 . . . ."
    XXVI, fol. 244.   296.
    „ and Wentworth quarterly, ..., of co. York, 185. . . , 181 . . . Vol.
Fladgate, ..., of Lincoln's Inn, London, 182 . ., Vol. XX...., fol. 70.
Flamank after Phillipps, Rev. William, B.A., of Llaniv.... 28.
    co. Cornw., and Glympton, co. Oxf., 18 . . ., Vol. XLIX, ... Boscarne,
Flavell, Sidney, of Leamington, co. Warw., 1882, Vol. LXI, fol. 3...
    Suppl. ; Crisp, 1, p. 207.)   Berry's
Fleete, Sir John, Knt., Alderman of London, 13 May 1691, Vol. IV,
    (Berry.)   77.
Fleetwood after Hesketh, ..., of Berks., and Rossall Hall and Nort... Me
    co. Lanc , Vol. XXXVIII, fol. 258.
    „ after Hesketh, ..., reputed son of Sir Peter, of Berks. and co. Lanc.,
    185 . ., Vol. LI, fol. 327.
Fleming. See Hughes.
Fleming, late Worsley, ... (widow of [Sir Richard ?] Worsley, Bart.), of
    Appuldercombe, Isle of Wight, and Gornhey, co. Devon, 18 . . ., Vol.
    XXV, fol. 235.
    „ late Cuchet, ..., of Hale, Farnham, co. Surrey, 18 . . ., Vol. XXV,
    fol. 238.
Fletcher, John, of Stausbery House, Horsley, co. Derby, Sheriff, 8 Mar. 173½,
    Vol. VIII, fol. 139ᵇ.
    „ George, York Herald of Arms, of Chichester, co. Sussex, 15 Dec. 1767,
    Vol. XI, fol. 248. (Berry.)
[„ Sir Henry, K.G., C.B. Supporters, 23 Dec. 1831. (Crisp, Notes, V, p. 85.)]
    „ Thomas, s. of John, of Manchester, and London, 17 . . ., Vol. XIV, fol. 294.
Fletcher before Bradshawe, ..., of Halton Hall, co. Lanc., 17 . . ., Vol.
    XIV, fol. 358.
Fletcher, Thomas, of Newcastle-under-Lyme and Besley, co. Staff., 17 . . .,
    Vol. XX, fol. 175.
    „ Caleb, of Liverpool, co. Lanc. ; late of Broughton, co. Cumberland ; and
    Lancaster, [3 April 1802] Vol. XXI, fol. 332. [Crisp, Notes, XI,
    p 10.]
Fletcher to Boughey, ..., [16 May 1805, Sir John Fenton Fletcher, Bart.],
    co. Staff., 180 . . ., Vol. XXIII, fol. 167.
    „ to Powell, ..., of Sutton, Shropsh., 180 . . ., Vol. XXIII, fol. 382.
Fletcher, Sir Richard, Knt. and Bart., Lieut.-Col. of Engineers, of co. Kent ?
    [Carrow, co. Cork, Ireland], [14 Dec. 1812, Vol. XXVII ?, fol. 154],
    181 . . ., Vol. XXIX, fol. 154.
    „ Thomas William, of Handsworth, co. Staff., and Dudley, co. Worc., 183 . .,
    Vol. XLI, fol. 26. (Crisp, III, p. 79.)
    „ Thomas William, of Handsworth, co. Staff. Alteration, [4 Sept. 1838]
    Vol. XLIII, fol. 158. (Crisp, III, p. 79) [Notes, V, p. 15].
    „ Rev. William, of Brasenose Coll., Oxf., and The Elms, nr. Derby, [second s.
    of Thomas], of Handsworth, &c., co. Staff. [Arms of Keeling to be borne
    with those of Fletcher, 21 Jan. 1836], Vol. XLI, fol. 208. (Crisp, III,
    p. 79) [Notes, V, p. 14].
    „ [Thomas William, now a student in Trinity Coll., Dublin, eldest s. and h.
    of Thomas Fletcher, of Handsworth, co. Staff., &c. (See William, above.)
    Grant of a Crest, 27 Jan. 1846, Crisp, Notes, V, p. 16.]
    „ . . . ., of St. Michael's Mount, Liverpool, co. Lanc., and Kevan House,
    co. Monmouth, 183 . ., Vol. XLI, fol. 252.

FLETCHER to W ... of Christ Ch., Camb.: Penywern, co. Merioneth,
. Wales, 183 .., Vol. XLI, fol. 264.

FLETCHER, late 393. and Bank Hall, Denton, Clifton and Eccles, co. Lanc., 184 .., ... (reputed s. of Fletcher), of co. Lanc.; Bradbury,

FLETCHER, G l.) Vol. .) co. Hamilton, of Clapham, co. Surrey, 186 .., Vol. LV, fol. 186.

FLETCHER (Ber NE, Capt. Thomas Hanmer, of Nerquis Hall, Bangor, and . Flint, Wales. 186 .., Vol. LV, fol. 222.

FLETCHER Orange Hamilton, of West Ridge House, Woodchurch, co. Chester, WANSEY, his wife, 186 .., Vol. LVII, fol. 31.

.P.), of Farnbank, Brigham, co. Cumberland (s. of John Wilson),
   " 1875, Vol. LIX, fol. 315.

R., of Vale House, Kearsley, co. Lanc., and Sale, co. Chester, 1894,*
   " Vol. LXVII, fol. 285.

FL HER-TWEMLOW, Capt. G. F., of Pilmaston, co. Worc., 1895, Vol. LXVIII, fol. 269.

FLINT to CORBETT, Robert, of Shropsh., 5 Dec. 1774, Vol. XIII, fol. 44.

FLINT, Sir Charles William, Knt., [29 May 1812], ? of Westminster, 180 .., Vol. XXI, fol. 355.

" ...., of St. Dunstan's, Canterbury, co. Kent, 186 .., Vol. LV, fol. 306.

FLITCROFT, Henry, s. of Jeffry, of Westminster, and Hampton Court, co. Middx., 17 ..., Vol. IX, fol. 332.

FLORY, (Rev.) William, of Leamington, co. Warw., 1891, Vol. LXVI, fol. 186. (Crisp, I, p. 253.)

FLOWER, Sir Charles, Bart., Lord Mayor of London [1808-1809], (SQUIRE, late wife), to self and the descendants of his late wife, 180 .., Vol. XXV, fols. 161 and 162.

FLOWER to WALKER, [23 Nov. 1827, Henry], 1st s. of 4th Viscount ASHBROOKE, of Berks., and co. Oxf., 182 .., Vol. XXXVII, fol. 5.

FLOWER, late WALKER, [Henry (as above), 15 July 1847], Vol. XLVIII, fol. 365.

FLOWER, Philip William, of Park Hill, Croydon, co. Surrey, 184 .., Vol. XLVIII, fol. 55.

FLOYD, Lieut.-Gen. (Sir John, Bart.), ? of London. Allusion to service, 180 .., Vol. XXV, fol. 405.

FLOYER, late CAWLEY, of Gwerssylt, co. Denbigh, Wales; co. Staff.; and Derby ?, 1793, Vol. XVIII, fol. 287.

FLOYER, Col. Sir Augustus, K.C.B. [7 April 1815] (mar. with KEBLE), 181 .., Vol. XXX, fol. 411.

FLUDYER, Sir Samuel, Knt. [19 Sept. 1755] and Bart. [14 Nov. 1759], Alderman of London [of Lee Place, co. Kent], 1759, Vol. X, fol. 196.   (Berry.)

FLUX, William (s. of Thomas), of London and Cirencester, co. Glouc., 1880, Vol. LX, fol. 381. (Berry's Suppl.)

FOGGE-ELLIOT, John, of Bolton-le-Moors, co. Lanc., and Elvet Hill, co. Durham, 1827. (Burke.)

FOLEY, Baron [31 Dec. 1711], of co. Worc. [extinct 1776]. Supporters, 17 .., Vol. VI, fol. 75.

   „   Baron [20 May 1776]. Supporters, 177 .., Vol. XIII, fol. 205.

   „   Vice-Adm. Sir Thomas, G.C.B. [16 May 1820], of Abermarton Park, co. Carnarvon, Wales, 182 .., Vol. XXXII, fol. 143 ; and of Ridgeways, co. Pembroke, Wales, 182 .., Vol. XXXII, fol. 147.

FOLEY after HODGETTS, of Stoke, co. Hereford, and Prestwood, co. Suff., 182 .., Vol. XXXII, fol. 285.

FOLJAMBE (formerly MOORE), Francis John Savile, of Aldworth, co. York, 1876, Vol. LIX, fol. 232 ; and to the descendants of Francis Ferrand Foljambe ; and of Osberton, co. Nottingham, 18 .., Vol. LX, fol. 213. (Crisp, I, p. 45, and II, p. 50, formerly Moore.)

FOLKES, Martin, ..., of co. Norf., 11 Mar. 1685, Vol. III, fol. 292. (Berry.)

FOLKESTONE, Viscount [29 June 1747 (Bouverie)], of co. Kent. Supporters, 17 . ., Vol. IX, fol. 200.

FONNEREOU (Zachariah, 1674), for proof of Arms *see* Certificate from France entered in 3 D, 14, fol. 146[h], but no Crest, 21 July 1730 ; Add. MS. 14,831, fol. 139 [*see* Burke].

FOORD-BOWES, late BOWES-FOORD, Col. Bernard, of co. York 18 . ., Vol. XXV, fol. 128 ; and co. Linc. (*see* JOHNSON, Bart.), fol. 815.

FOORD before BOWES, Timothy Fysh, of co. York and Linc., 181 . ., Vol. XXVII, fol. 139.

FOORD-BOWES (Juliet TOPHAM, wife of), Barnard, of co. York, 182 . ., Vol. XXXII, fol. 211.

" -BOWES (late TROLLOPE), Barnard, of Sidmouth, co. Devon, and Beverley, co. York, 186 . ., Vol. LIV, fol. 210.

FOORD-KELCEY, G., of Margate, co. Kent, 1881, Vol. LXI, fol. 156.

" -KELCEY, F., of Prospect House, Lyminge, co. Kent, 188 . ., Vol. LXI, fol. 158.

FOOTE, Elizabeth, of Brentford, co. Middx., 14 Dec. 1769, Vol. XI, fol. 370. (Berry.)

" Benjamin Hatley, of Veryan, co. Cornw., and Debtling, co. Kent, 1 June, 1772, Vol. XII, fol. 159. (Berry.)

FOOTE, Henry Wells, of London, and Cheltenham, co. Glouc., 185 . ., Vol. LI, fol. 317.

FOOTNER, H., of Wilmslow, co. Chester, 1889, Vol. LXV, fol. 116.

FORBES-STUART, ..., of London, 182 . ., Vol. XXXIII, fols. 23 and 25.

" . . . ., of London ; Clifton, co. Glouc. ; and Aberdeen, Scotland, 182 . ., Vol. XXXIII, fol. 170.

FORBES-BENTLEY, late CALLAND, George, of Glyncollen, co. Glamorgan, Wales. John on behalf of his son George, 185 . ., Vol. LI, fol. 57.

FORBES-BENTLEY, Thomas, of Clifton, co. Glouc. Takes Name and Arms of BENTLEY (F. 170 [?]), 182 . ., Vol. XXXIII, fol. 172.

FORBES to GORDON, Maj.-Gen., of Skellater and Balbithan, Scotland, 182 . ., Vol. XXXIV, fol. 132.

FORBES (HEPBURN-STUART-) before TREFUSIS, Baron CLINTON [and his wife, 4 Sept. 1867], [Stuart and Forbes quarterly with Trefusis], 186 . ., Vol. LVI, fol. 303.

FORCE, ..., of Honiton, co. Devon. Match with TEMPLER, 181 . ., Vol. XXIX, fol. 59.

FORD, Francis, (Bart.) [22 Feb. 1793], of Thames Ditton, co. Surrey, and Lears, Isle of Barbados, 179 . ., Vol. XVIII, fol. 187.

FORD after JONES, Cecil Clare (Spr.), of Gelli Gynan, co. Denbigh, and Bodlondet, co. Carnarvon, Wales, only child by the first wife of John Carstairs Jones. (*See* JONES.) 1875, Vol. LIX, fol. 139.

FORD, William, of Kingston-upon-Hull, co. York, 8th s. of James, of Doncaster, co. York, 18 . . ., Vol. LXXI, fol. . . . . .

FOREST (and FULBROOK), Robert, of Lambeth, London, 185 . ., Vol. LI, fol. 249.

FORREST after FORSYTH, Thomas, of Durham, 185 . ., Vol. LI, fol. 432.

FORRESTER after WELD, Cecil, M.P., of Ross Hall, Shropsh., Dosthhill and Willey [co. Warw. ?], 181 . ., Vol. XXVI, fol. 375.

FORSTER (*see* BACON), ..., of co. Northumberland. (*See* EXTON.) 180 . ., Vol. XXI, fol. 313.

" (*see* CROWDER-THORNE), ..., of co. York, 182 . ., Vol. XXXII, fol. 299.

" Sir Charles, Bart. [17 Mar. 1874], M.P., of Lysways, Longdon, co. Staff., 187 . ., Vol. LVIII, fol. 300.

FORSTER-COULL, W. D., of North Middleton Hall, co. Northumberland, 1887, Vol. LXIV, fol. 116.

FORSYTH, Thomas (the elder), of South Shields, co. Durham, 185 . ., Vol. LI, fol. 430.

FORSYTH-FORREST, Thomas (the younger), of Marsden Cottage, Weston, co. Durham, 185 . ., Vol. LI, fol. 432.

FORT, ..., of Read Hall, Stone Hey, Whalley, co. Lanc., 181 . ., Vol. XXXI, fol. 100.

FORTESCUE, late INGLETT, Richard, of Dawlish, co. Devon, and Oxf., 177 . ., Vol. XIII, fol. 283.

„ late GIBBS, ... (reputed son), of Sheep Drove, Chipping Lamborne, Berks., 182 . ., Vol. XXXII, fol. 49.

FORTESCUE-BRICKDALE, ..., of Dawlish, co. Devon ; Newlands, co. Glouc. ; West Monckton and Flory Combe, co. Somerset, 186 . ., Vol. LIV, fol. 106.

FORTESCUE (PARKINSON-), Baron CARLINGFORD [28 Feb. 1874], of Ireland. Supporters, 187 . ., Vol. LIX, fol. 1.

FORTH [John Doddington], Portcullis Pursuivant of Arms, of London, 179 . ., Vol. XVIII. fol. 55.

FORTNUM, Charles Drury Edward, The Hill House, Great Stanmore, co. Middx. (died s.p. 1899), 1898, Vol. LXX, fol. 153.

FORTUNE, Joseph, of Lucston Castle and Walwins Castle, Haverfordwest, co. Pembroke, Wales, 17 . . ., Vol. XX, fol. 351.

FORWARD, late HOWARD, Hon. William, of Ireland, 2nd s. of Baron CLONMORE ([afterwards 3rd Earl of] WICKLOW). 1780, Vol. XIV, fol. 273.

FORWOOD, Thomas B., of Thornton Manor, co. Chester (father of the Baronet), 1884,* Vol. LXII, fol. 206.

FOSBERY, Col. George Vincent, V.C. (s. of Thomas Vincent Fosbery), of 20, Victoria Square, London, 1898, Vol. LXX, fol. 205.

FOSKETT, ..., of Mooreplace, London. Match with MOORE, 179 . ., Vol. XIX, fol. 338.

FOSTER, George, of par. of St. Joseph, Island of Barbados, 3 May 1703, Vol. V, fol. 101 ; Add. MS. 14,831, fol. 184 ; Harl. MS. 6834, fol. 112.

„ William (s. of Thomas), of Boston, New England. (See also HINDE.) 178 . ., Vol. XV, fol. 159.

FOSTER to PIGOTT (Fellow, Eton Coll.), John, D.D., of Abingdon-Pigotts, Royston, co. Camb., and Mereworth, co. Kent. Escutcheon of pretence, 180 . ., Vol. XXIV, fol. 112. (Berry.)

FOSTER, Richard, of Lostwithiel, co. Cornw. Match with BOLITHO, 181 . ., Vol. XXVII, fol. 22.

FOSTER (or FORSTER) to BAIRD, John, of Newcastle-upon-Tyne and Alnwick, co. Northumberland, 182 . ., Vol. XXXII, fols. 231 and 233 [?].

FOSTER, ..., of London, 182 . ., Vol. XXXIV, fol. 377.

FOSTER after HYATT, ..., of London, 182 . ., Vol. XXXIV, fol. 392.

FOSTER-PIGOTT after GRAHAM, Lieut.-Col. George Edward, M.P., 182 . ., Vol. XXXVI, fol. 299 ; of Abingdon-Pigotts, co. Camb., 182 . ., Vol. XXXVI, fol. 303 ; of Mereworth, co. Kent, 182 . ., Vol. XXXVI, fol. 303 ; of Clewer, Berks., 182 . ., Vol. XXXVI, fol. 305 ; of Clewer, Berks., 182 . ., Vol. XXXVII, fol. 309. EXTON quartering to wife, 182, Vol. XXXVII, fol. 310.

FOSTER, Edmund B., of Clewer Manor, Windsor, Berks., 1885, Vol. LXIII, fol. 71.

„ William (s. of William), of Norwich, co. Norf., (Bart.) [3 Aug. 1838], 183 . ., Vol. XLIII, fol. 80.

FOSTER-MELLIAR, Andrew, of Wells, co. Somerset. (See MELLIAR). 184 . ., Vol. XLV, fol. 11.

FOSTER, Ebenezor (s. of Richard), of Anstey Hall, co. Camb., 15 Oct. 1851, Vol. XLIX, fol. 228.

FOSTER, late SMITH (Capt.), George Foster, 185 . ., Vol. LII, fol. 11.

FOSTER, John (of Queensbery, Bradford), co. York, and Black Dikes, Halifax, co. York, 185 . ., Vol. LII, fol. 45.

„ Henry Seymour (M.P.), of 129, Ashley Gardens, London, 1893,* Vol. LXVI, fol. 336.

FOSTER, Robert, of Newcastle-upon-Tyne, co. Northumberland (decd. 16 Nov. 1898, aged 87), 1888,* Vol. LXIV, fol. 250.
„ Richard Andrews, of Tutshill House, Tidenham, co. Glouc., 1898, Vol. LXX, fol. 296.
„ Frederick Durham, of The Hall, Thorne, co. York, 18 . . ., Vol. LXXI, fol. . . . . .
FOTHERGILL, late GRAINGER, John, of co. York, 17 . . ., Vol. XIV, fol. 76.
FOULDS, Elise Josephine, of The Old Hall, Broomhall Park, Sheffield, co. York. Only dau. of the late Astley Cooper Foulds, of the same, 18 . . .. Vol. LXXI, fol. . . . . .
FOULIS after SIDNEY [16 June 1850] [Philip Sidney], of co. York. ([2nd Baron] DE LISLE and DUDLEY), 18 . . ., Vol. XLIX, fol. 350.
FOULKES, Theodore, of Port Clarendon, Jamaica, 17 . . ., Vol. XX, fol. 19.
FOULSTON after HUNT, ..., of Tything, Compton Gifford, co. Devon, and London, 187 . ., Vol. LIX, fol. 106.
FOUNDLING HOSPITAL, London, 17 . . ., Vol. IX, fol. 238.
FOUNTAIN (formerly PRICE), Andrew, of Narford Hall, co. Norf., grandson of BRIGG-FOUNTAINE-PRICE, by Act of Parliament, 1874, Vol. LVII, fols. 250, 259 and 238. (Berry's Suppl.)
FOUNTAINE, Sir Andrew (Knt.), K.B. Supporters, 3 Mar. 172¾, Vol. VII, fol. 437. (Bishop's MSS.)
FOUNTAINE after ADDISON, William, of co. Durham, 180 . . ., Vol. XXI, fol. 72.
FOUNTAYNE before WILSON, of Melton, co. York, 180 . ., Vol. XXII, fol. 347.
FOUNTAYNE-WILSON to MONTAGU, of Melton Hill, Follyfot, co. York, and Popplewicke, co. Nottingham, 182 . ., Vol. XXXV, fol. 375.
FOWLER, Edward, Bishop of Gloucester, 1693, Vol. IV, fol. 144.
„ Samuel, Rector of Bluham, co. Bedf. (? See HURDIS.) 1695, Vol. IV, fol. 204.
„ . . . ., of Stonehouse, co. Glouc. Match with PHELPS, 17 . . ., Vol. XVII, fol. 346.
FOWLER to LEEVES, ..., of Chichester, co. Sussex. Match TORTINGTON, alias WALBERTON, 180 . ., Vol. XXV, fol. 445.
„ to BUTLER, Richard, of Pendeford Hall, co. Staff., 1824, Vol. XXXIV, fol. 275.
FOWLER, John, of Clifton, co. Glouc., 184 . ., Vol. XLV, fol. 364.
„ . . . ., of Wadsley Hall, co. York, 186 . ., Vol. LVI, fol. 320.
„ Sir R. N., Bart., Lord Mayor of London, of Wilts. Remainder to his father Thomas and uncle John, 1885,* Vol. LXIII, fol. 85.
„ Thomas Webb (Mayor of Coventry), of Wycombe House, Coventry, co. Warw., 1898, Vol. LXX, fol. 249.
FOWNES to SOMERVILLE, of Kittery Court and Brixham, co. Devon, and Dinder House, co. Somerset, 182 . ., Vol. XXXVIII, fol. 203.
FOX, Sir Stephen, Knt. [1 July 1665], of co. Dorset and Somerset, 16 . . ., Vol. IV, fols. 15, 164 and 165.
„ [Stephen], Lord ILCHESTER [11 May 1741], of co. Dorset and Somerset. Supporters, 17 . . ., Vol. IX, fol. 26.
„ [Georgiana Caroline], Baroness HOLLAND [6 May 1762], of co. Dorset and Linc. Supporters, 17 . . ., Vol. X, fol. 422.
„ . . . ., of Newark-on-Trent, co. Nottingham ; Macclesfield, co. Chester ; Lower Brookfort, South Owram, co. York, 18 . . ., Vol. XXXI, fol. 256.
„ . . . ., of Woodton Hall, co. Norf., 182 . ., Vol. XXXII, fol. 241.
FOX to SUCKLING, of Woodton Hall, co. Norf., 182 . ., Vol. XXXII, fol. 243.
FOX, George Croker, of Grove Hill and Falmouth, co. Cornw., with remainder, 1836, Vol. XLII, fol. 46.
„ . . . ., of London, 184 . ., Vol. XLVII, fol. 38.
„ . . . ., of Stockbridge, Peniston, co. York, 186 . ., Vol. LIV, fol. 134.
FOX after EMBLETON, of Northorpe, co. Linc., 1860, Vol. LIV, fol. 288.
„ after EMBLETON, William, of Northorpe, co. Linc., New Coll., Oxf., 1874, Vol. LIX, fol. 306.

Fox to Byron [1870 ?], Edward, of Scarborough, co. York, 1871, Vol. LVII, fol. 326.

Fox, Marmaduke, of Mirfield, co. York, 187 . ., Vol. LVIII, fol. 340. (Berry's Suppl.)

  ,,   Mrs. Sarah, widow of late Thomas Fox, of Tomdale, Wellington, co. Somerset, 1880,* Vol. LXI, fol. 59. (Berry's Suppl.)

Fox-Powys, Hon. L. W. H., of Bewsey Hall, Warrington, co. Lanc. (died s.p., 1893), 1890, Vol. LXVI, fol. 13.

Fox, Samson, of Grove House, Harrogate, co. York, 1891, Vol. LXVI, fol. 94.

Fox-Pitt-Rivers, A. H. L., of Rushmore, Wilts., 1881, Vol. LXI, fol. 109. (Berry's Suppl.)

Fox, John Staveley Colton, J.P., of Todwick Grange, co. York, 18 . . ., Vol. LXXI, fol. . . . .

Foxlow to Murray, ..., of Banner Cross, co. York, and Staveley Hall, co. Derby, 178 . ., Vol. XV, fol. 41.

Foxwell, ... (see Upcher), of Rattlesden, co. Suff. Match, 177 . ., Vol. XIII, fol. 269.

Foy, William Lowndes Toller, of Clayhill, Enfield, co. Middx., 1898, Vol. LXX, fol. 255.

Foyster, Samuel, of St. Pancras and St. Giles, London, 28 June 1784, Vol. XV, fol. 333.

Fraigneau, William, of St. James', Westminster, London, 1757, Vol. X, fol. 82. (Berry.)

Frampton, Mathew, M.D., of co. Oxf., 30 Mar. 1720, Vol. VI, fol. 391.

France (late Hayhurst), Thomas, of co. Lanc., [? s. of the] late James France, of Everton and Liverpool, co. Lanc., 1796, Vol. XIX, fol. 143.

France after Wilson, ..., of co. Chester, and Norbreck, Preston and Rawcliffe Hall, co. Lanc., 181 . ., Vol. XXX, fol. 234.

France-Hayhurst, Col. Charles, of Davenham and Bostock Hall, co. Chester, and co. Montgomery, 1869, Vol. LVII, fol. 300. (Berry's Suppl.)

  ,,   -[Hayhurst, Thomas, B.D., Rector of Davenham, co. Chester, 1870.]

France (late Hayhurst), Wallace James Arthur, of Ystym Colwyn, co. Montgomery, Wales, 1876, Vol. LIX, fol. 200. (Berry's Suppl.)

Francis, Sir Philip, K.B., M.P. Supporters, [29 Oct.] 1806, Vol. XXIV, fol. 118.

  ,,   Clement, M.A., Trinity Hall, Camb., of Quy Hall, co. Camb., 185 . ., Vol. LII, fol. 349.

  ,,   George, Bencher of Gray's Inn, London (left an only dau.), 1889, Vol. LXV, fol. 78.

  ,,   Capt. Thomas John, 16th (the Queen's) Regt. of Light Dragoons, s. of Thomas, of co. Glamorgan, and Hammersmith, London [no date given] (see Burke).

Francklyn to Webbe, ..., of Tunbridge Wells, co. Kent, and the Island of Nevis and Court of Scindia, 185 . ., Vol. L, fol. 106.

Franco, Jacob (afterwards Lopez), of St. Catherine Coleman, London. [2nd s. of Moses Franco, late of the City of Leghorn, decd.] [10 April] 1760, Vol. X, fol. 227. (Berry.) [Trans. Jewish Hist. Soc., II, p. 166.]

Franco to Lopes, ... [4 May 1831], (Bart.), of co. Devon, 18 . ., Vol. XXXVIII, fol. 240.

Franey, Rev. J., of St. Mary's Vicarage, Ely, co. Camb., 1892,* Vol. LXVII, fol. 16.

Frank, Frederick Bacon, of Campsall, co. York ; Eastham and Skelton, co. Norf. ; and Gipping Hall and Alderton, co. Suff., 18 . ., Vol. XLIX, fol. 148.

Franke, William, of The New Works, Leicester, 16 . ., Vol. IV, fol. 57.

Frankland, late Cromwell [Vice-Adm. Henry], of co. Essex, [28 Jan. and 30 Mar. 1806], Vol. XXIII, fol. 288. [Her. and Geneal., VII, p. 269 n.]

Frankland-Russell [Feb. 1837], Sir Thomas [Sir Robert], Bart., of Bucks. and co. York, 183 . ., Vol. XLII, fol. 88.

FRANKLAND, ..., of Eshing House, Godalming, co. Surrey, 185 . ., Vol. LII, fol. 269.

FRANKLAND to GILL, ..., of co. Surrey, 186 . ., Vol. LVI, fols. 240 and 242.

FRANKLIN, ..., of Dean's Place, and Lawrence Waltham, Berks., 180 . ., Vol. XXIV, fol. 51.

FRANKLIN to LITTLEGREEN, ..., of Dean's Place and Lawrence Waltham, Berks., and Hall Place [Berks.], 180 . ., Vol. XXIV, fol. 55.

FRANKS, William, s. of Roger, of London, 17 . . ., Vol. XIV, fol. 193.

FRASER after MACKENZIE, Maj.-Gen. Alexander, M.P., of Inverallochy, Scotland. Quarterly Arms, 180 . ., Vol. XXII, fol. 365.

„ after ALLAN, ..., of Hawkesbury Hall, co. Warw., and Hospital Field, St. Vigeans, co. Forfar, Scotland, 185 . ., Vol. L, fol. 19.

FRASER-MACKINTOSH, ..., of co. Inverness, Scotland, and Calcutta, 186 . ., Vol. LVI, fol. 63.

FRASK, James J., of Fairmouth House, Westbury, Wilts., 1885,* Vol. LXIII, fol. 39.

FRAUNCEIS to GWYN, John, of Combe Flory, co. Somerset. Quarterings, 17 . . ., Vol. XIV, fol. 245.

FREAKE, Charles James, Bart., of London, 1878, Vol. LX, fol. 163.

„ Sir Charles James, Bart., of co. Devon. Impaling WRIGHT, [23 May] 1882, Vol. LXII, fol. 14.

FREAN, ..., of Granville Park, Lewisham, co. Kent, 186 . ., Vol. LVII, fol. 248.

FREDERICK, Sir Charles, K.B., of Hampsh. Supporters, [23 Mar.] 1761, Vol. X, fol. 330.

FREELAND, Robert, s. of John, and descendants, of Cornbrook Park, Hulme, co. Lanc., and Westermains, co. Dumbarton, Scotland, 185 . ., Vol. LIII, fol. 21.

FREELING, ..., of Heathfield, co. Sussex, Secretary and Resident Surveyor, G.P.O., 180 . ., Vol. XXV, fol. 262.

FREEMAN, late COOKE, ..., and his brother Stephen, of Fawley, Bucks., 17 . . ., Vol. IX, fol. 364.

FREEMAN after WILLIAMS, Adm., of Fawley Court, Bucks., and Hoddesdon, co. Hertf., 182 . ., Vol. XXXIII, fols. 146 and 148.

FREEMAN, ..., of Holton, co. Suff., 178 . ., Vol. XV, fols. 55 and 56.

FREEMAN, now THOMAS, Inigo, of Ratton, co. Sussex. Arms, 1786,* Vol. XV, fol. 161.

FREEMAN, ..., of Ratton, co. Sussex. Arms, 17 . . .,* Vol. XVII, fol. 440.

FREEMAN, late MACKERETH, Rev. John, of Ecclesfield, co. York, 178 . ., Vol. XVI, fol. 327.

FREEMAN before MITFORD [28 Jan. 1809, Sir John], Baron REDESDALE, of co. Northumberland, and Battesford, co. Glouc., 180 . ., Vol. XXV, fol. 112. Augmentation to Supporters, fol. 115.

FREEMAN-MITFORD (C.B.), A. B., of Batsford, co. Glouc., 1887,* Vol. LXIII, fol. 327.

„ after WALSH, ..., of Abbots Langley, co. Hertf., 182 . ., Vol. XXXIV, fol. 5.

FREEMAN, J. R., Bar.-at-Law, of Lincoln's Inn, London, and Staines, co. Middx., 1890,* Vol. XLV, fol. 190.

FREEMAN, Rev. John (s. of John), Vicar of Woodkirk, Dewsbury, co. York, 1897, Vol. LXIX, fol. 213.

FREESE, ..., of Madras, 182 . ., Vol. XXXVII, fol. 342.

FREETH, Col., R.E., 186 . ., Vol. LVI, fol. 205.

FREIND to ROBINSON, John, of Rokely, co. York, Archdeacon of Armagh, 1793, Vol. XVIII, fol. 281.

FREIND, Rev. William Maximilian, M.A., of Hitcham, Bucks., Rector of Chinnor, co. Oxf., 1800, Vol. XXI, fol. 381.

FREKE after HUSSEY, Ambrose Denis, of The Hall, Salisbury, and Hannington Hall, Wilts., 1835, Vol. XLI, fol. 128.   ? Hussey Arms (*see* Burke).
  „   after HUSSEY, Ambrose Denis, of Salisbury and Hannington Hall, Wilts. Hussey and Freke quarterly, [1 Sept.] 1863, LV, fol. 102.
FREMAN, late BUTTON, ..., of Stifford and East Horndon, co. Essex, 182 . ., Vol. XXXVIII, fol. 353.   (Berry.)
FREMANTLE, John, of Fruth Park, Hampsh., 4 May 1761, Vol. X, fol. 363. (Berry.)
FRESHFIELD, ..., of Moor Place, Betchworth, co. Surrey, 18 . . ., Vol. XLIX, fol. 279.
FRESTON, Thomas, of Westphaling, Prestwich, co. Lanc., 189 . ., Vol. LXXI, fol. . . . .
FRETWELL, ..., of Gainsborough, co. Linc. (*See* SWEETLAND.) (Match), 18 . ., Vol. XXV, fol. 46.
  „   . . . ., of Gainsborough, co. Linc. (*See* LONSDALE.) (Match), 181 . ., Vol. XXVI, fol. 244.
FREWEN, ..., of Tortworth, co. Glouc.   Match, 181 . ., Vol. XXX, fol. 51.
FRIEND, ..., of Magdalen Coll., Oxf.   Match, 1813, Vol. XXVIII, fol. 1.
  „   Matthew, F.R.S., of Greenwich and Ramsgate, co. Kent, and Tasmania, 18 . . ., Vol. LIII, fol. 326.
FRITH, ..., Capt., Bengal Army, 182 . ., Vol. XXXIII, fol. 78.
FROHOCK, William, of Hadenham, Isle of Ely, co. Camb., and London, 1764, Vol. XI, fol. 33.   (1761, Berry.)
FROOM, ..., of London, 18 . . ., Vol. XLIX, fol. 50.
FROST, Meadows, of Meadows Lea, Hope, co. Flint, Wales, 186 . ., Vol. LVII, fol. 143.
  „   Sir Thomas Gibbons, Knt. [1869], of Wales, 186 . ., Vol. LVII, fol. 314.
  „   Francis Aylmer, of Heaton Reddish, co. Lanc., and Wales, 186 . ., Vol. LVII. fol. 314.
  „   Robert, of Lime Grove, co. Chester, and Wales, 186 . ., LVII, fol. 314.
  „   Robert, of Lambeth, co. Surrey.   (Burke [no date]).
  „   Rev. William, of Thorpe, co. Norf.   (Burke [no date]).
  „   George, of Clovelly, Bournemouth, Hampsh., 189 . ., Vol. LXX, fol. 104.
FROUDE, James, of Kingston, Edmeston, co. Devon, 1765, Vol. XI, fol. 126. (Berry.)
FRUCTUOZO, John Anthony, of Langham Place, London, 182 . , Vol. XXXVIII, fols. 65 and 66.
FRY, Sir Theodore, Bart., of Darlington, co. Durham, 1894, Vol. LXVII, fol. 289.
FRYE, late NEWTON, ..., of Wallington, co. Surrey, 180 . ., Vol. XXI, fol. 152.
FRYER-(HARRISON, wife of), George, s. of Cornelius, of London, and Low Row, Swaledale, co. York.   Impaled Arms, 17 . . ., Vol. XX, fol. 222.
FRYER, Richard or William, of New Cross House, The Wergs, and Wednesfield, co. Staff., 183 . ., Vol. XLI, fol. 349 ; 183 . ., Vol. XLIII, fol. 32.
FULBROOK and FOREST, Catherine, 185 . ., Vol. LI, fol. 249.
FULCHER, Lieut., Bengal S.C., of Ipswich, co. Suff., 182 . ., Vol. XXXIV, fol. 86.
FULLER before ELIOTT-DRAKE, Thomas Teryton Fuller, of co. Devon and Sussex, 181 . . ., Vol. XXVII, fol. 277.
FULLER-MEYRICK, Augustus ?, of Bodorgan, co. Anglesey ; Ashdown, co. Sussex ; and Morden Park, co. Surrey, 1825, Vol. XXXV, fol. 403.
  „   -MEYRICK, Owen John A., of Bodorgan, co. Anglesey ; Ashdown, co. Sussex ; and Morden Park, co. Surrey, 1870, Vol. LVII, fol. 280.
MEYRICK, Lieut.-Gen. Sir Joseph, G.C.H. [1827], of London, 182 . ., Vol. XXXVI, fol. 171.
  „   Henry Peter, M.R.C.S., of London, 183 . . ., Vol. XL, fol. 79.
FULLER-PALMER-ACLAND, Sir Peregrine, Bart., of co. Somerset and Devon, [12 Aug.] 1834, Vol. XL, fol. 237.
FULLER-ACLAND-HOOD [14 July 1849], Sir Alexander, B.P. [Bart.], of co. Somerset, 18 . . ., Vol. XLIX, fol. 215.

FULLER [James Franklin, July 1874. (Right to bear Arms, by X)].
  „ Firman, of March, Isle of Ely, co. Camb., and Witham, co. Essex, 18 . . .,
    Vol. LVII, fol. 49.
FULLER-ELIOTT-DRAKE, Sir Francis George Augustus, Bart., of co. Devon and
    Linc., [?] [30 Oct.] 1870, Vol. LVII, fol. 280.
FULLERTON, late DOWNING, George Alexander, of Ireland, and St. Anne's,
    Jamaica (of Wadham Coll., Oxf.), 179 . ., Vol. XVIII, fol. 404.
FUNCK, ..., of Carlscron, Sweden, 179 . ., Vol. XVIII, fol. 291.
FURNELL, John, of Bristol, co. Glouc., 1 Mar. 173⁶⁄₉, Vol. VIII, fol. 207ᵇ.
FURNESS, Sir Christopher [Knt.], of West Hartlepool, co. Durham, [1895] Vol.
    LXXI, fol. . . . .
FURSMAN, John, M.A., Rector of Lawhitton, co. Cornw. ; Vicar of Lamerton,
    co. Devon ; Chancellor and Canon Residentiary of Exeter. (Match with
    WYAT), 1 or 31 May 1742, Vol. IX, fol. 60 (see Geneal., II, p. 65 ;
    Berry's Suppl.).
FURZE, Peregrine, s. of John Jacob, of Heidelberg and Strasburg, Germany,
    17 . . ., Vol. IX, fol. 131.
FUSSELL, J. Coldham, of St. Leonard's, Willoughby, co. Cumberland, and New
    South Wales, 1887, Vol. LXIV, fol. 20.
FUST after JENNER, Sir Herbert, Knt., LL.D., P.C., of Hill Court, co. Glouc.,
    184 . ., Vol. XLV, fol. 359.
FUST, ..., of co. Glouc., 182 . ., Vol. XXXVI, fol. 321.
FYDELL, Robert, of St. Andrew's, Holborn, London (s. of Symon, of Freeston,
    co. Linc., and to his cousin Joseph, s. of William, s. of Thomas, of Boston,
    co. Linc.), 19 Feb. 172⁵⁄₆, Vol. VII, fol. 481, and Add. MS. 14,831, fol. 151.
FYERS, Peter, Capt., R.A., of Scotland, 180 . ., Vol. XXIII, fol. 234.
  „ William, Col., R.A., of Gibraltar, 180 . ., Vol. XXIII, fol. 234.
  „ Thomas, Paymaster at Malta, of Gibraltar, 180 . ., Vol. XXIII, fol. 234.
FYSH, Philip Oakley, of Lynn, co. Norf., and Hobart Town, Tasmania, 187 . .,
    Vol. LVIII, fol. 357. (Berry's Suppl.)

G

GABBIT, late SPIERS, of Sparsholt, Berks., and Salt Hill, Bucks., 179 . .,
    Vol. XIX, fols. 48 and 50.
GABRIEL [Sir Thomas], Bart. [3 or 14 Aug. 1867], Lord Mayor of London
    [1866-67], 186 . ., Vol. LVI, fol. 256.
GADD, George W., of Withington, Manchester, co. Lanc., 1884,* Vol. LXII,
    fol. 202.
  „ Mrs., of 59, Wilbraham Road, Chorlton-cum-Hardy, co. Lanc., 188 . .,
    Vol. LXII, fol. 202.
  „ George, of 13, Green Lane, Tulbrook, Liverpool, co. Lanc., 188 . .,
    Vol. LXII, fol. 202.
GAGE-ROKEWODE [20 Nov. 1838], John, of Coldham Hall, co. Suff., 183 . .,
    Vol. XLIII, fol. 293.
GAGE, ROKEWODE- [1843], Sir Thomas Gage, of Coldham Hall and Hengrave,
    co. Suff. (See SKINNER.) 184 . ., Vol. XLVI, fol. 363.
GAGE, ROKEWODE-, Sir Edward, Bart., of co. Suff., [1866] Vol. LVI, fol. 191.
  „ Viscount. SKINNER and HALL quarterings, 27 Feb. 179½, Vol. XVIII,
    fol. 1.
GAITSKELL, ..., of Egremont, co. Cumberland, 180 . ., Vol. XXIII, fol. 339.
GALE, (1) John, (2) Ebenezer, of Newcastle-upon-Tyne, co. Northumberland ;
    Acomb, co. York ; and co. Cumberland, (3) Elisha, all of Whitehaven,
    co. Cumberland, Newcastle-upon-Tyne, and Tralee, co. Kerry, Ireland.
    Arms, 28 June 1712, Vol. VI, fols. 52 and 54. (Crisp, I, p. 277, and
    Notes, III, p. 93.)

GALE to BRADDYLL, Wilson, of co. Lanc., 20 Sept. 1776, Vol. XIII, fol. 231.

GALE, William, s. of John, of co. York, and Jamaica, 178 . ., Vol. XV, fol. 92.

GALE, late MORANT, Edward Gregory, of Brockenhurst, Hampsh., and co. York, and Jamaica, 179 . ., Vol. XIX, fol. 189.

GALE (RICHMUND-) BRADDYLL, of co. Lanc. and Cumberland, 18 . ., Vol. XXXI, fol. 352.

GALL, Laurence, s. of Matthew, of London, 178, Vol. XV, fol. 377.

GALLEY, ..., of Betchton House, Sandbach, co. Chester, 182 . ., Vol. XXXII, fol. 331.

GALLEY to JACKSON, ..., of Sandbach, co. Chester, 182 . ., Vol. XXXII, fol. 333.

GALLEY - DAY - JACKSON, ..., of Sandbach, co. Chester. (*See also* DAY), .183 . ., Vol. XLII, fol. 261.

GALLIMORE (*see* HAMILTON), ..., of St. Anne's, co. Middx., and Jamaica. Match, 177 . ., Vol. XIII, fol. 108.

GALLINI, J. B. G., of Winnal House, Cuckfield, co. Sussex, 1888, Vol. LXIV, fol. 234.

GALLWEY after PAYNE [2 Mar. 1814], Lieut.-Gen. [Sir William], Bart., of St. Christopher's, 181 . ., Vol. XXVIII, fol. 61.

GALLWEY, Lieut.-Gen. Sir Thomas Lionel John, K.C.M.G. [1889], (s. of Major John), 189 . ., Vol. LXXI, fol. . . . .

GALPIN, Francis William (s. of John), Vicar of Hatfield Regis, Harlow, co. Essex, 1899, Vol. LXX, fol. 314.

GALPINE to SAMPSON, ... (Spr.), of co. Dorset and Somerset. Match with WILMONT, 180 . ., Vol. XXII, fol. 318.

GALT, Sir Alexander Tillock (s. of John), [G.C.M.G., 25 May 1878], of Greenock, Scotland. Supporters, 18 . . ., Vol. LX, fol. 226.

  „ Sir Alexander Tillock, G.C.M.G., of Greenock, co. Renfrew, Scotland, s. of John. Arms, 1879, Vol. LX, fol. 222. (Berry's Suppl.)

GALTON, ..., of Hadzor House, co. Worc., and Duddeston, co. Warw., 183 . ., Vol. XLII, fol. 135.

GALWAY, [2nd] Viscount, [22 Dec. 1769, Roy. Lic. name of ARUNDEL], of co. Nottingham. Arms of ARUNDEL with Supporters, 17 . . ., Vol. XII, fol. 8.

  „ [5th] Viscount, to discontinue name of ARUNDEL before titles of honour, [15 Feb. 1826] Vol. XXXV, fol. 371.

GAMBIER, Baron [9 Nov. 1807], (James), of Iver House, Bucks., 180 . ., Vol. XXIV, fol. 463.

GAMBLE, Lieut.-Col. (David), of Windlehurst, St. Helens, co. Lanc., 1885, Vol. LXIII, fol. 55 ; Bart., fol. 97.

GAMON, (Sir) Richard, (Bart.), bro. to the Duchess of CHANDOS, of Datchworth, co. Hertf., and London, 1795, Vol. XVIII, fol. 341.

GANDOLFI to HORNYOLD, ..., of Blackmore Park and Hanley Castle, co. Worc., and East Sheen, co. Surrey, 18 . . ., Vol. LIII, fol. 99.

GANDY-GANDY, J. Heaver, of Heversham, co. Westmorland, 1891, Vol. LXVI, fol. 202.

GANE to COOK, John H. and William, of South Brent and Lympsham, co. Somerset, 182 . ., Vol. XXXII, fols. 245 and 247.

GAPPER to SOUTHBY, ..., of Bridgewater, co. Somerset, and Bulford, Wilts., 183 . ., Vol. XLI. fol. 351.

GARBRAND, Joshua, of St. Thomas, Jamaica. Quarterly to BARRITT, 28 Oct. 1768, Vol. XI, fol. 312. (Berry.)

GARBUTT after WALSHAM, John (Lieut.-Col. of Militia), of Knill, co. Hereford, 180 . ., Vol. XXI, fol. 22.

GARDINER after WHALLEY, John, of co. Lanc., 1779, Vol. XIV, fol. 181. (Certified to William Gardiner, Esq., May 1779, Berry and Burke.)

  „ after SMYTHE, late WHALLEY, ..., Bart., of co. Lanc., 1798, Vol. XX, fols. 11 and 12.

GARDINER, Bart., of Roche Court, Hampsh. [? Took the name of SMYTHE between WHALLEY and Gardiner], 1787, Vol. XVI, fol. 277.

,, Lieut.-Col., 181 . ., Vol. XXVIII, fol. 240.

,, ..., Student of Jesus Coll., Camb., 181 . ., Vol. XXIX, fol. 420.

GARDINER after COOPER, ... of Thundridge Bury, co. Hertf., and Thurgarton Priory, co. Nottingham, 182 . ., Vol. XXXIV, fol. 47..

,, after COOPER, of co. Hertf., and Nottingham, 183 . ., Vol. XXXIX, fol. 342.

GARDINER, Robert and Frederick, sons of (Robert Barlow), of Yardley, Hastings-cum-Denton, co. Northampton, Vicar of Wadhurst, co. Sussex, 1 Mar. 1841, Vol. XLV, fol. 83.

,, Gen. Sir Robert William, G.C.B. [21 June 1859], 18 . . ., Vol. LIII, fols. 229 and 251.

,, John (s. of John), of Brailsford, co. Derby, and co. Somerset, Capt. 5th Dragoons, and to descendants of his uncle Robert. (See WEBBER, 188 . ., Vol. LXI, fol. 14), 1877, Vol. LX, fol. 30.

GARDNER, John, of St. Olave's, Southwark, London, and Jamaica, 1 Mar. 1703/3, Vol. VII, fol. 176.

,, Rear-Adm. Alan, afterwards Baron Gardner, 179 . ., Vol. XIX, fol. 151.

GARDNER, late PANTING, Rev. Laurence, M.A. [D.D.], of Westbury, Wrock-wardine, and Sansaw, Shropsh., 180 . ., Vol. XXI, fol. 164.

GARDNER, DUNN-, William John and Thomas, of co. Camb., 180 . ., Vol. XXIII, fol. 50.

,, DUNN- (late TOWNSHEND), John, M.P., of Chatteris House, Isle of Ely, co. Camb., 184 . ., Vol. XLVI, fol. 365.

,, DUNN- (late TOWNSHEND), William, of Fordham Abbey, co. Camb., 184 . ., Vol. XLVI, fol. 383.

GARDNER, Cecil, Cornet of Light Dragoons (Magdalen Coll., Oxf.), of co. Camb., 184 . ., Vol. XLIX, fol. 290.

GARDNER (late PANTING), Robert Leighton, of Wellington, Shropsh. (See KYNNERSLEY [Match ?] and G. [? Grant]), 184 . ., Vol. XLVII, fol. 208.

GARDNER, Robert, of Chaseley Hall, Eccles, co. Lanc., 185 . ., Vol. L, fol. 36.

,, Richard Cardwell, of Fluke Hall, Pilling, co. Lanc., s. of Thomas Gardner ([Gardner] and SYKES quarterly), 1878, Vol. LX, fol. 122. (Berry's Suppl.)

,, Frank Medwin, of Cheriton Place, Folkestone, co. Kent, 1898, Vol. LXX, fol. 239.

GARFIT, John Henry, of Bromley, co. Kent, 1890,° Vol. LXV, fol. 178.

GARLAND. See JOHNSON, George.

GARLAND to LESTER, ..., of Poole, co. Dorset. Match, 180 . ., Vol. XXIII, fol. 136.

,, to COPE, [Anna], widow of [Nathaniel] Garland, of Michaelstowe, co. Essex, 184 . ., Vol. XLVIII, fol. 288.

,, to LESTER, ..., of Wimborne, Minster, co. Dorset, and Florence, Italy, 185 . ., Vol. L, fol. 426.

,, to LESTER, ..., of Downing Coll., Camb., 185 . ., Vol. LI. fol. 186.

GARMSTON, John, of the City of Lincoln, 1758, Vol. X, fol. 157. (Berry.)

GARNETT, ..., of Lark Hill and Bleasdale Tower, co. Lanc., H.M. Master Forester of Bleasdale Forest, 18 . . ., Vol. XLIV, fol. 145.

,, of Wyrende, Garstang, co. Lanc., and Kirkby Lonsdale, co. Westmorland, 185 . ., Vol. L, fol. 78.

GARNETT-BOTFIELD, Rev. [William Bishton], M.A., of co. Chester and Shropsh., [30 Oct. 1863, Burke], Vol. LV, fol. 130.

GARNETT-ORME-. See ORME.

GARNIER after CARPENTER, John, of Mount Tavy, co. Devon, 186 . ., Vol. LV, fol. 242.

GARRATT-, ..., of Thorpe Melsor, co. Northampton. (Match), 181 . ., Vol. XXVII, fol. 187.

,, Job, of Wassell Grove, Hagby, co. Worc., 1894, Vol. LXVIII, fol. 83.

GARRETT, ..., of Portsmouth and Southwick, Hampsh., 180 . ., Vol. XXI, fol. 25.

GARRIQUES, ..., of Yarmouth Estate, Vere, and Kingston, in Jamaica, 182 . ., Vol. XXXVII, fol. 268.

GARROD, Sir A. B., of 10, Harley Street, London, 1888, Vol. LXIV, fol. 265.

GARRY, ..., of London, and Riga, Russia, 180 . ., Vol. XXIII, fol. 426.

GARSIDE, ..., of Worksop, co. Nottingham, 186 . ., Vol. LVI, fol. 166.

GARSTIN, Maj.-Gen., Bengal S.C. [Staff Corps ?], of London, 18 . . ., Vol. XXXI, fol. 4.

GARSTON, ..., of Garston, co. Lanc., Knt. R. of Greece, 186 . ., Vol. LV, fol. 268.

GARTH to COLLETON, ..., of Berks. and Wilts., 180 . ., Vol. XXIII, fol. 177.

GARTH, late LOWNDES (Rev.), formerly LOWNDES-STONE, of Morden, co. Surrey, and Baldwin Brightwell, co. Oxf., 183 . ., Vol. XLII, fol. 86.

GARTHORNE, ..., of Roodford, co. Durham. Match, 16 . . ., Vol. IV, fol. 73.

GARTHWAITE, Edward, of Shakleford, co. Surrey, 27 May 1748, Vol. IX, fol. 227. (Misc. G. et H., New S., IV, p. 422.)

GASCOIGN, John, of Stratford, co. Essex, 17 . . ., Vol. IX, fol. 243.

GASCOIGNE, Joseph, M.P., of Weybridge, co. Surrey, 15 June 1725, Vol. VII, fol. 274.

GASCOIGNE after OLIVER, ..., of Parlington, co. York, 180 . ., Vol. XXV, fol. 451.

    ., after TRENCH, Frederick Charles, of Parlington and Aberford, co. York, 185 . ., Vol. L, fol. 44.

GASCOYNE CECIL, Marquess of SALISBURY, of co. Hertf., [22 Mar. 1821, K.G. 11 April 1842], 184 . ., Vol. XLVI, fol. 52.

GASCOYNE to CHANDLER, Rev. George, LL.D., of co. Kent, 179 . ., Vol. XVIII, fol. 237.

GASKARTH, John, s. of John, of Penrith, co. Cumberland, and Farnborough, co. Warw., 178 . ., Vol. XV, fol. 135.

GASKELL, Benjamin, of Clifton Hall, co. Lanc., and Thornes House, co. York, 180 . ., Vol. XXIII, fol. 158.

    „ . . . ., of Chalfont St. Peter, Bucks., 180 . ., Vol. XXXIII, fol. 235.

    „ Henry Lomax, of Beaumont Hall, co. Lanc., and Kiddington, co. Oxf., 186 . ., Vol. LVI, fol. 195.

    „ (PENN), ..., of Shanagary, co. Cork, &c., Ireland, and Philadelphia, U.S.A., 186 . ., Vol. LVI, fol. 344.

GATCHELL, Henry, s. of Thomas, of North Petherton, co. Somerset, to descendants of his father, 1 Feb. 170¾, Vol. V, fol. 135 ; Harl. MS. 6834, fols. 69 and 71. (Misc. G. et H., 3rd S., II, p. 101.)

GATEHOUSE, George, of North Street, Chichester, co. Sussex, 1883, Vol. LXII, fol. 48. (Berry's Suppl.)

GATER, ..., of Lapford and Exeter, co. Devon, 182 . ., Vol. XXXII, fol. 373.

GATHORNE-HARDY (CRANBROOK, Viscount [4 May 1878]), of co. York. Quarterly, Gathorne and Hardy, [11 May 1878] Vol. LX, fol. 111 ; Supporters, fol. 115.

GATTY, Alfred, D.D. (Robert Henry and Charles Henry), of Ecclesfield, co. York, and co. Cornw., s. of Robert, s. of Joseph, and to the descendants of Uncle William, 1876, Vol. LIX, fol. 180.

    „ Alfred SCOTT-SCOTT, York Herald of Arms. Crest, &c., 1892, Vol. LXVII, fol. 105. (Crisp, II, p. 152.)

GAULIS, Jean Abraham Rodolph, Certificate, 1793, Vol. XVIII, fol. 294.

GAWEN after ROBERTS, Rear-Adm. (retired), of Salisbury, Wilts., 18 . . ., Vol. XLIX, fol. 435.

GAWEN (ROBERTS), late BOROUGH, Charles, of Chetwynd Park, Shropsh., 187 . ., Vol. LIX, fol. 108.

GAWLER, John, of Ramridge, Hampsh., 180 . ., Vol. XXII, fol. 104.

GAWLER to KER BELLENDEN, John, of Hampsh. (*See* Duke of ROXBURGH.)
180 . ., Vol. XXIII, fol. 96.

GAY, William (s. of William), of Falmouth, co. Cornw., and Stirling, Scotland
(died s.p.m. 1868), 185 . ., Vol. LII, fol. 105. (Crisp, V, p. 165.)

GAYFORD, Frederick, of West Wretham, co. Norf., 1855. (Burke.)

GEARY, Francis (Bart. [17 Aug. 1782]), of Polesden, co. Surrey, 178 . ., Vol. XV,
fol. 105.

GEARY-SALTE, William Geary, of The Poultry, London, 1798, Vol. XX, fol. 145.

GEAST to DUGDALE, Richard, of co. Warw. [Roy. Lic. dated 16 Mar. 1799],
[1799] Vol. XX, fol. 295.

GEAST [Henry, of co. Worc., surname and quarter DUGDALE, Lic. 10 April 1822].

GEE to GIBB (reputed s. and dau.), of Craven Road, Paddington, and Oxford
Square, Hyde Park, London, 187 . .,* Vol. LVIII, fol. 202.

  ,, to GIBB, ..., of London. (*See* GIBB, of Greenford.) 184 . ., Vol. XLIX,
fol. 368.

  ,, to GIBB, Margaret, of London, 1875, Vol. LIX, fol. 141.

GELL, David, Principal Registrar of the Coll. Ch. of St. Peter, Westminster, and
the Diocese of Llandaff, London, and to the descendants of his father
Ralph and uncle Thomas, 6 Mar. 173½, Vol. VIII, fol. 122ᵇ, and Add.
MS. 14,831, fol. 78. (Berry.)

GELL after CHANDOS-POLE, ..., of co. Derby, 186 . ., Vol. LV, fol. 28.

GENNYS, late HENN, of Whitleigh House, co. Devon, and Paradise, co. Clare,
Ireland, 180 . ., Vol. XXI, fol. 346.

GENT after THARP, of Chipperton Park, co. Camb., and Moyers Park, Steeple
Bumpstead, co. Essex, 186 . ., Vol. LIV, fol. 184.

GEORGE, ..., of Statenborough, nr. Sandwich, co. Kent, 180 . ., Vol. XXV,
fol. 276.

  ,, John D., of New King Street, Bath, co. Somerset, 1895,* Vol. LXVIII, fol. 239.

GEPP [Thomas Frost], Attorney and Capt. of Militia, of Chelmsford, co. Essex
[23 July 1823], Vol. XXXIV, fol. 112. [Geneal., New S., XXVIII, p. 79.]

GERARD, Lieut.-Col., of Walkerside, co. Aberdeen, Scotland, 180 . ., Vol. XXIV,
fol. 129.

GERARD-DICCONSON, Hon. R. J., of Wrightington, co. Lanc., 2nd s. of Baron
Gerard, 1896, Vol. LXIX, fol. 44.

GERARD, Baron. Supporters, 1876, Vol. LIX, fol. 194.

GERMAN, ..., of Highfield House and Orrell House, Wigan, co. Lanc., and of
the Middle Temple, London, 18 . ., Vol. XLIX, fol. 80.

GERVIS after TAPPS, ... [3 Dec. 1835, 2nd] Bart., of Hampsh., and co.
Anglesey, Wales, 183 . ., Vol. XLI, fol. 174.

GERVIS, (TAPPS-), -Meyrick [16 Mar. 1876, 3rd] (Bart.), of Hampsh., and co.
Anglesey, Wales, 187 . ., Vol. LIX, fol. 208.

GERY after WADE, Rev. Hugh, M.A., of Bushmead Priory, co. Bedf., and
Newark, 179 . ., Vol. XVIII, fol. 123.

GIBB, ..., of Greenford, co. Middx., and Oxford Square, London, 18 . .,
Vol. XLIX, fol. 368.

GIBB to JONES-GIBB, ..., of Greenford, co. Middx., 18 . ., Vol. XLIX,
fol. 370.

GIBB, Margaret (formerly GEE). (*See* GEE.) 1875, Vol. LIX, fol. 141.

GIBB-ANDERTON, A. W., of Arbor Street, Southport, co. Lanc., 1893, Vol. LXVI,
fol. 334.

GIBBES, Sir Philip, Bart., of Barbados. Escutcheon of pretence, Agnes OSBORNE,
177 . ., Vol. XIV, fol. 71.

GIBBON after HOWARD, Edward, of London, York Herald and Earl Marshal's
Secretary, 184 . ., Vol. XLVI, fol. 224.

GIBBON, Matthew Charles HOWARD-, Richmond Herald, of co. Sussex, 185 . .,
Vol. L, fol. 384.

  ,, Matthew Samuel John, of Newton House and Great Howe, Bonvilstone,
co. Glamorgan, Wales (died 1893), 186 . ., Vol. LV, fol. 212.

GIBBONS, Rev. Bery John, of Hartlebury, co. Worc. (M.A., Wadham Coll., Oxf.), 187 . ., Vol. LVIII, fol. 16.
„   [Sills John], Bart. [Mar. 1872], Lord Mayor of London [1871-72], of Sittingbourne, co. Kent, 187 . ., Vol. LVIII, fol. 92.
„   Sir John, Bart., of Stanwell, co. Middx., 1761, Vol. X, fol. 307.
„   Sir John, Bart., K.B. [23 Mar. 1761]. Supporters, 17 . . ., Vol. X, fol. 318.
„   Robert Alexander, M.D., F.R.C.P., 2nd s. of David, of Alderney, 18 . . ., Vol. LXXI, fol. . . . .
GIBBS after HEAGREN, ..., of Quarles, co. Norf., 181 . ., Vol. XXXI, fol. 187.
GIBBS to FORTESCUE, ..., of Berks., 182 . ., Vol. XXXII, fol. 49.
„   to BRANDRETH, ..., of co. Bedf., 184 . ., Vol. XLVIII, fol. 209.
GIBBS, Charles Edward, of Icklingham, co. Suff., 18 . . ., Vol. LIII, fol. 273.
„   Henry Hucks, of Clist St. George, co. Devon, &c. ; Aldenham, co. Hertf. ; and Clifton Hamden, co. Oxf. And to descendants of his grandfather, Anthony, 1876, Vol. LIX, fol. 212.
GIRLIN, ..., of Swaffham, Bulbecks, co. Camb., 186 . ., Vol. LV, fol. 178.
GIBSON to KIRSOPP, ..., of Great Whittington and Spital, co. Northumberland, 182 . ., Vol. XXXIV, fol. 220.
GIBSON, Bradstone Brooke, of Shalford, co. Surrey, and Sandford Lodge, Sullington, co. Sussex, 183 . ., Vol. XL, fol. 170.
„   John, of Stratford, co. Essex, and Stratford, co. Middx., 183 . ., Vol. XL, fol. 222.
„   . . . ., of Saffron Walden, co. Essex, 184 . ., Vol. XLV, fol. 15.
„   James, of Doldowlod, Llangre, co. Radnor, Wales, and Edinburgh, 185 . ., Vol. LII, fol. 127.
GIBSON-WATT, James, of Doldowlod, Llangre, co. Radnor, Wales ; Edinburgh ; Heathfield, Handsworth, co. Staff. ; and Aston Hall, co. Warw., 185 . ., Vol. LII, fol. 129.
GIBSON-LEADBITTER, Thomas, of Newcastle-upon-Tyne and Lower Warden, co. Northumberland, 1875, Vol. LIX, fol. 88.
GIBSON-MILNER, Thomas (M.P.), of co. Suff. (See also MILNER-GIBSONE.) 18 . . ., Vol. LX, fol. 230.
GIBSON, Thomas G., Alderman, of Newcastle-on-Tyne and Lesbury, co. Northumberland, 1896, Vol. LXIX, fol. 140.
„   William, of "Scone," Launceston, Tasmania, 1898, Vol. LXX, fol. 265.
GIDDY, Edward, of St. Erth, co. Cornw., and Colenick, co. Sussex, 11 June 1770, Vol. XII, fol. 24. (Berry.)
„   . . . ., of St. Erth, co. Cornw., and Colenick, co. Sussex. Escutcheon of pretence, 17 . . ., Vol. XVII, fol. 232. (Berry.)
GIDDY to GILBERT, John, F.R.S., of Colenick and Eastbourne, co. Sussex, 1818, Vol. XXX, fols. 57 and 360. (Berry.)
GIDEON, Sampson, of Coneton, 17 . . ., Vol. IX, fol. 217.
GIDEON to EARDLEY, Sampson, of Spalding, co. Linc., 17 . . ., Vol. XVII, fol. 145.
GIFFORD, Baron [30 Jan. 1824], Lord Chief Justice, of co. Devon. Arms and Supporters, 182 . ., Vol. XXXIV, fols. 271 and 273.
GIGGER after MACE, James, of Reading, Berks., and Wareham, co. Dorset, 25 Mar. 1803. Match, Vol. XXII, fol. 95.
GILBERT, Thomas, s. of Thomas, of Colton, co. Staff., 26 Dec. 1759, Vol. X, fol. 208. (Berry.)
„   . . . ., of Chedgrave, co. Norf., 180 . ., Vol. XXIV, fol. 297.
GILBERT, late GIDDY, John Davies, of co. Cornw., and Eastbourne, co. Sussex, [and his two daughters, Roy. Lic. 7 Jan. 1818]. (Berry.) [Davies Giddy. Arms and name of Gilbert only, Roy. Lic. 10 Dec. 1817. (Berry.)], 1817-18, Vol. XXX, fols. 57 and 360.
GILBERT, Lieut.-Gen. Sir Walter Raleigh, Bart. [31 Dec. 1850], of co. Cornw., 185 . ., Vol. L, fol. 92.
„   . . . ., of co. Cornw. Supporters to descendants, 185 . ., Vol. L, fol. 274.

GILBERT-EAST, late CLAYTON-EAST, of Hall Place, Berks., &c., Bucks. and
co. Surrey, 183 . ., Vol. XLIII, fol. 361.

GILBEY, Sir Walter, Bart., of co. Essex, 1893, Vol. LXVII, fol. 209.

GILBY, ..., of Steynton, co. Linc., and Everton, co. Nottingham. (*See* LONS-
DALE.) (Match), 181 . ., Vol. XXVI, fol. 244.

GILCHRIST after BORTHWICK, ..., of London, 180 . ., Vol. XXIV, fol. 9.

GILCHRIST, P. C., of Frognal Bank, London, 1889,* Vol. LXV, fol. 74.

GILDART, ..., of Liverpool, co. Lanc., and Middleham, co. York, 20 Dec.
1759, Vol. X, fol. 204. (Berry.)

GILES-PULLER, ..., of Youngsbury, co. Hertf., 187 . ., Vol. LVIII, fols. 128
and 130.

GILKES, (Rev.) William, of London, (B.A. Pembroke Coll., Oxf.), 18 . . ., Vol.
XXXVIII, fol. 62.

GILL, William (Lord Mayor) [of London, 1788-9], of Yeoveney Hall, co. Middx.,
and Wyrardisbury, Bucks., [27 June 1803] Vol. XXII, fol. 283.

GILL to PRETOR, Samuel, of co. Dorset, 181 . ., Vol. XXVII, fol. 269.

GILL, ..., of Tavistock, co. Devon, 181 . ., Vol. XXIX, fol. 13.

„ C. B., Post-Capt., R.N., of Otterbourne, Hampsh., 181 . ., Vol. XXIX,
fol. 220.

GILL to VARENNE, ..., of Elm-cum-Emneth, co. Camb., M.A., Fellow of
St. John's Coll., Camb., of Westley Waterless, co. Camb., and Staplehurst, co. Kent, 181 . ., Vol. XXIX, fol. 436.

GILL, Joseph, M.A., Vicar of Scraptoft and Rector of Pickwell, co. Leic., 182 . .,
Vol. XXXIV, fol. 122.

„ Capt. Robert, of Hackney, London, and Madras S.C., 183 . ., Vol. XLII,
fol. 173.

GILL, late FRANKLAND [Mary Douglas, of Dover Street, London], of Godalming,
co. Surrey, 185 . ., Vol. LII, fol. 269.

„ late FRANKLAND, Hon. Agnes [Steuart KERR], of Godalming [of Eshing
House], co. Surrey, [15 June 1867], Vol. LVI, fols. 240 and 242.

GILL. *See* ANDERTON.

GILLETT, Frederick William Alfred Herbert (s. of Alfred), of Lombard Street,
London, 1899, Vol. LXX, fol. 328.

GILLIAT, John Saunders, of Liverpool, co. Lanc., and Fernhill, Berks., 186 . .,
Vol. LIV, fol. 65.

GILLIBRAND to FAZAKERLEY (minor), Henry Hawarden, 181 . ., Vol. XXVIII,
fol. 139.

„ to FAZAKERLEY, Hawarden Thomas, of co. Lanc., 18 . . ., Vol. XXXVIII,
fol. 43.

GILLOW, Richard, of Leighton Hall, Warton, co. Lanc., 184 . ., Vol. XLVIII,
fol. 184.

GILPIN-BROWN, ..., of co. Durham and York, 185 . ., Vol. LI, fol. 23.

GILPIN, Col. Richard Thomas, Bart., of Hockliffe, co. Bedf. (s. of Richard),
[19 Feb.] 1876, Vol. LIX, fol. 184. (Berry's Suppl.)

GILSON, ..., of Wing, co. Rutland. Arms, 182 . ., Vol. XXXV, fol. 85.

GILSON to SHIELD, ..., of co. Rutland. Change of name, 18 . . ., Vol. XLIX,
fol. 481.

GILSTRAP, ..., of Herringswell, Newark, co. Nottingham, and Fornham Park,
co. Suff., 186 . ., Vol. LV, fol. 186.

GIRDLESTONE, M. A., of Thorney Abbey, Isle of Ely, co. Camb., 18 . . ., Vol.
XXV, fol. 183.

„ Samuel, of Bodham and Baconsthorpe, co. Norf., 184 . ., Vol. XLVI, fol. 76.

GIRES, ..., of St. Lo, Normandy, 17 . . ., Vol. XIV, fol. 108.

GIRVIN, ..., of Everton, co. Lanc., 184 . ., Vol. XLVI, fol. 364.

GISBORNE, John, Sheriff, of Derby, 23 Mar. 174½, Vol. IX, fol. 47.

GIST, late SELLICK, of Bristol, co. Somerset, and London, 181 . ., Vol. XXX,
fol. 184.

GIST, heretofore SELLICK, of Bristol, co. Glouc., 182 . ., Vol. XXXV, fol. 59.

GITTON, Thomas Bridgnorth, of Clee St. Margaret and Bridgnorth, Shropsh., 18 Feb. 174⁹₁, Vol. IX, fol. 13.

GLADDISH, William, of Cliff Cottage and Chalk, co. Kent, [1825] Vol. XXXV, fol. 97.

GLADELL to VERNON, ..., of London, 178 . ., Vol. XV, fol. 321.

GLADSTONE, Sir John, Bart. [18 July 1846], of Fasque and Balfour, &c., Scotland, 184 . ., Vol. XLVIII, fol. 158.

GOODWIN-GLADWIN, Richard Henry, of Hinchley Wood House, Mappleton, co. Derby, 1889, Vol. LXV, fol. 149.

GLAISTER, Major Thomas, of Mill Hill House, Bolton-le-Moors, co. Lanc., 1883, Vol. LXII, fol. 153.

GLASSE to ELLIOTT, Lieut.-Col. George Henry, of London, and Binfield, Berks., 1811, Vol. XXVI, fol. 289.

GLAZEBROOK, Nicholas Smith, of Haymans Green, West Derby, co. Lanc. [and to his descendants and the other descendants of his father, Thomas Kirkland Glazebrook], [21 May] 1891,* Vol. LXVI, fol. 104. (Crisp, III, p. 59.)

GLEADOW, Rev. Thomas R., of Walsall and Kingston-upon-Hull, co. York, 182 . ., Vol. XXXIII, fol. 47.

GLENCROSS, James, M.A., of Luxstone, co. Cornw., 1876, Vol. LIX, fol. 229. (Berry's Suppl.)

GLENESK, Baron (Sir Algernon Borthwick, Bart.), of Scotland and London. Supporters, 1896, Vol. LXIX, fol. 13.

GLENNY, George, s. of William, of Sydenham, co. Kent, and Monymusk, co. Aberdeen, Scotland. Quarterly Arms, 178 . ., Vol. XV, fol. 163.

GLENORCHY, Viscount, Sir John CAMPBELL, of Scotland. Match with GREY, dau. of the Duke of Kent, 17 . . ., Vol. IX, fol. 480.

GLYN, Robert, of St. Andrew's, Holborn, s. of Robert, s. of Christopher, Rector of Burford, co. Oxf. (London), out of Flintshire, 25 June 1726, Vol. VII, fol. 516 ; Add. MS. 14,831, fol. 83.

GOBLE, James, of Petworth, co. Sussex, 17 . . ., Vol. IX, fol. 495.

GODDARD, ..., of Cliffe Pypard, Wilts. Match with BAYNTUN, 181 . ., Vol. XXIX, fol. 331.

„　Lieut. . . . ., of Croydon, co. Surrey, 181 . ., Vol. XXIX, fol. 427.

„　Mrs., of Oak Hill, Ipswich, co. Suff., 1889, Vol. LXV, fol. 9.

„　Anne, dau. and co-h. of Edmund, of Hartham, Wilts. (s. of Thomas, M.A., Canon of Windsor), and wife of Sir William JAMES, Bart., of Eltham, co. Kent, 1788, Vol. XVII, fol. . . . . .

GODFREY, Thomas, of Tamworth, co. Staff., 1765, Vol. XI, fol. 85. (Berry.)

GODFREY, late JULL, John, of Wingham, and Brook Street Ash, next Sandwich, co. Kent, 1810, Vol. XXVI, fol. 28.

GODFREY, Jane, wife of Henry Jermin Bond, of Bury St. Edmunds, co. Suff., 22 Nov. 1732, Vol. VIII, fol. 159.

GODOLPHIN [Viscount RIALTON and Earl of, 26 Dec. 1706], of co. Cornw. Supporters, 17 . . ., Vol. V, fol. 171.

„　. . . . [? Baron, 17 Jan. 1766], of co. Cornw. Supporters, 17 . . ., Vol. XI, fol. 134.

„　. . . ., of co. Cornw. Crest to Marquess of CARMARTHEN, 178 . ., Vol. XVI, fol. 71.

„　. . . ., of co. Cornw. Match with CRUDGE, 179 . ., Vol. XVIII, fol. 244.

GODSALVE before CROSSE, John, of co. Essex, 17 . . ., Vol. XIV, fol. 235.

GOETZ, Angelina (widow of Edward Ludwig Goetz, of London), of 18, Hyde Park Terrace, London, 1897, Vol. LXX, fol. 67.

GOFF to MALLARD, ..., of St. George's-in-the-East and Wapping, co. Middx., and Plaistow, co. Essex, 179 . ., Vol. XVIII, fol. 325.

GOLD, Henry, of 17, Cumberland (? Gloucester) Terrace, Regent's Park, London, 1897, Vol. LXIX, fol. 287.

GOLDFRAP, James, s. of James, of Dover, co. Kent, 1749, Vol. IX, fol. 346. (Berry.)

GOLDIE-TAUBMAN, ... of The Nunnery, Isle of Man, s. of Gen. Goldie.
Taubman Arms, 182 . ., Vol. XXXV, fol. 21.
GOLDING, late GRAVES, ..., of Kelsale, Thorington and Poslingford, co. Suff.,
180 . ., Vol. XXII, fol. 422.
GOLDING-PALMER, Rev. Henry, of Holme Park, Sonning, Berks., 1880, Vol. LXI,
fol. 85. A Crest, 1883 ; 188 . .. Vol. LXII, fol. 95.
GOLDNEY, Sir Gabriel, Bart. [11 May 1880], of Wilts., 18 . . .. Vol. LX, fol. 383.
GOLDSCHMIDT, ..., of Hamburgh and London, 182 . .. Vol. XXXV, fol. 176.
GOLDSMID, Aaron, s. of Aaron, of London, 17 . . .. Vol. XX, fol. 108.
GOLDSMID, late MOSES, ..., of London, 182 . ., Vol. XXXIV, fol. 346.
GOLDSMID, Sir Isaac Lyon, Bart., of London. Addition to Arms, 184 . ., Vol.
XLVIII, fol. 148.
GOLDSMID-MONTEFIORE, Claude Joseph, of London, 188 . ., Vol. LXII, fol. 170.
(Berry's Suppl.)
GOLDSMITH, ..., of London, 182 . ., Vol. XXXIV. fol. 383.
GOLDSWORTHY, Col. Philip, of London, and Down House, co. Dorset. Certified
(see Berry), May 1779, Vol. XIV, fol. 125.
GOLDTHORPE, William, of Brook House, Manchester, co. Lanc., 1898, Vol. LXX,
fol. 86.
GOLLOP, ..., of Strode, co. Dorset. 16 . . ., Vol. III, fol. 162.
„   Thomas, s. of Thomas, of Strode, co. Dorset.   Crest, 17 . . ., Vol. VI,
fol. 417.
GOMM, William, of Clerkenwell, London, 24 Jan. 1761, Vol. X, fol. 278. (Berry.)
GOMM after CARR, ..., of London, [1878] Vol. LX, fol. 130.
GOMM, Gen. Sir William Maynard, G.C.B., of London. Supporters, 10 Oct. 1859,
Vol. LIII, fol. 226. (Misc. G. et H., New S., II, p. 184.)
GONIN, Louisa Elizabeth, widow of Antonin Alphonse Gonin, Clerk, decd., of
Brighton and Hayward's Heath, co. Sussex, 18 . . ., Vol. LXXI, fol. . . . . .
GOOCH, ..., of Brixton, co. Surrey, 184 . ., Vol. XLVII, fol. 326.
„   Charles Cubitt (s. of Charles), of Porchester Gate, London, and Southwark,
co. Surrey, 1875, Vol. LIX, fol. 84. (Berry's Suppl.)
„   (Sir) Daniel (Bart. [15 Nov. 1866]), M.P., of Clewer Park, Berks., 186 . .,
Vol. LVI, fol. 152.
GOODALL-COPESTAKE, ..., of Langley, co. Derby, and Birmingham, co. Warw.,
182 . ., Vol. XXXVI, fol. 190.
GOODCHILD, Thomas, and SLOCOCK, his wife, of London and Malta. Impaled
Arms, 29 Sept. 1808, Vol. XXV, fol. 2.
GOODDEN, Robert, of Over Compton, co. Dorset, 17 . . .. Vol. IX, fol. 167.
GOODE to WYATT, ..., of Wennall House, Coventry, co. Warw., and London,
181 . ., Vol. XXVIII, fol. 155.
GOODENOUGH, [Samuel], Bp. of Carlisle [1808-27], of Berks., and co. Kent,
180 . ., Vol. XXIV, fol. 375.
GOODFELLOW, Col., Bo. C.S., 183 . ., Vol. XLII, fol. 296.
GOODFORD, John Ould, of Yeovil, co. Somerset, 1765, Vol. XI, fol. 73. (Berry.)
GOODHART, ..., of Great Ilford, co. Essex, 18 . . ., Vol. XXV, fol. 124.
GOODHEW, ..., of Sutton at Hone, co. Kent, 17 . . ., Vol. XVII, fol. 193.
GOODMAN before MUNKHOUSE. See MUNKHOUSE.
GOODMAN, ..., of Brixton Rise, co. Surrey, 187 . ., Vol. LVIII, fol. 182.
GOODRICK, Sir Henry, Knt. and Bart., of co. York. Crest altered, 1694, Vol. IV,
fol. 175.
„   John, brother of the above, of co. York.   Crest altered, 1698, Vol. IV, fol. 244.
GOODRICK-HARLAND, Anne (widow, died s.p.), of Sutton Hall, co. York.
Escutcheon of pretence. Crest to the descendants of grandfather, 180 . .,
Vol. XXI, fol. 367.
GOODSON, (Thomas ?), of Baltonsborough, co. Somerset (B.A., University Coll.,
Oxf. ?), 1852, Vol. LI, fol. 120.
GOODWIN, Nicholas, of Hammersmith, London (D.L.), 10 or 19 Dec. 1707, Vol. V,
fol. 276. (Add. MS. 14,831, fol. 136.)

GOODWIN (late MAXWELL), Hugh, M.A., of Farndon, co. Chester, and Alyn, nr. Wrexham, Wales, 181 . ., Vol. XXVIII, fol. 370.

„ late COLQUITT, G. C., of Farndon, co. Chester, Capt., Dragoon Guards, 184 . ., Vol. XLV, fol. 378.

GOODWIN to CRAVEN, G. C., of co. Glouc., 186 . ., Vol. LIV, fol. 96.

GOODWIN-GLADWIN, R. H., of Hincbley Wood House, co. Derby, 1889, Vol. LXV, fol. 149 (see Berry's Suppl.).

GOODWIN, Goodwin Charles (see Burke) [no date].

[GOOLD, Sir Henry. See GOULD.]

GORDON, Thomas, s. of Thomas, of All Hallows, Barking, London, and Scotland, 17 . . ., Vol. IX, fol. 190.

„ Sir William, K.B., of London, 1775, Vol. XIII, fol. 64. Supporters, Vol. XIII, fol. 68.

GORDON to BENTLEY, Bentley, of London, 177 . ., Vol. XIII, fol. 301.

GORDON (DIGHTON, late wife of), of Newmarket, co. Camb. Dighton and JAMES quarterly on escutcheon of pretence, 17 . . ., Vol. XVII, fol. 77.

GORDON, ..., of Braes, Trelawney, Jamaica, 179 . ., Vol. XVIII, fol. 308.

GORDON after DUFF, William (Bart.), M.P., of Scotland ; Rockville, co. Haddington ; and Crombie, co. Banff, Scotland, 1813, Vol. XXVII, fol. 397.

GORDON, late FORBES, Maj.-Gen., of Skellater and Ballotban, Scotland, grandson of the Earl of ABERDEEN, 182 . ., Vol. XXXIV, fol. 132.

GORDON, Sir James Alexander. R. H., K.C.B., of Scotland. Augmentation, 182 . ., Vol. XXXVII, fol. 180.

„ Lieut.-Gen. Sir James Willoughby, Bart., of co. Hertf. and Hampsh. Supporters, G.C.B. [1831], G.C.H., 18 . . ., Vol. XXXVIII, fol. 359.

„ James Willoughby. To descendants ?, 183 . ., Vol. XXXIX, fol. 23.

[GORDON to] GORDON-STUART, of Perth ; Keith, Inchuacap and Scanlan, co. Banff, Scotland, 183 . ., Vol. XL, fol. 370.

GORDON, late MATCHETT, William Pulham, of Home Lodge, co. Norf. ; and Madeira and Isle of Jersey, 183 . ., Vol. XLII, fol. 249.

[GORDON to] GORDON-CANNING, of Woodstock, co. Oxf. ; Foxcote, co. Warw. ; and Hartpury, co. Glouc., 18 . . ., Vol. XLIX, fol. 246.

GORDON (Evans) to COOKSON, Sampson, of Whitehill, co. Durham, and Bon Accord, Guernsey, 18 . . ., Vol. LIII, fol. 261.

GORDON after SMITH (Bart.), of co. Down, Ireland, [5 Feb. 1868] Vol. LVI, fol. 333.

GORE to LANGTON, William, of Newton Park, co. Somerset (now Earl TEMPLE), 178 . ., Vol. XV, fol. 205.

„ to [GORE-] BOOTH [30 Aug. 1804] (Bart.), of Salford, co. Lanc., and Lissadell, co. Sligo, 180 . ., Vol. XXIII, fol. 119.

GORE to ORMSBY-GORE, William, of Porkington, Shropsh., and Woodford, co. Leitrim, &c., Ireland, 1815, Vol. XXVIII, fol. 393.

„ after VERNON (widow), of co. Glouc., 187 . ., Vol. LIX, fol. 220.

GORGES to FETTIPLACE, ..., of co. Hereford, 180 . ., Vol. XXIII, fol. 254.

GORMAN, Edmond Sexton, of London. Match, 18 . . ., Vol. XXV, p. 398.

GORMAN to GORMAN-MUNKHOUSE, E. S., of London. Quarterly Arms, 18 . . ., Vol. XXV, fol. 421.

GORST, ..., of the Middle Temple, London, and Preston, co. Lanc., 183 . ., Vol. XLI, fol. 96.

GORST to LOWNDES, ..., of Preston, co. Lanc. ; Widdicombe, co. Somerset ; and Palterton, co. Derby, 184 . ., Vol. XLV, fol. 59.

„ to LOWNDES, ..., of Preston, co. Lanc. ; Widdicombe, co. Somerset ; and Palterton, co. Derby, 185 . ., Vol. L, fol. 350.

GORTON, ..., of Cuckney, co. Nottingham. Match, 181 . ., Vol. XXX, fol. 248.

„ Robert, of Gorton Hall and Salford, co. Lanc., and Cuckney, co. Nottingham. ATKINSON quartering, 183 . ., Vol. XLI, fol. 360.

GOSLING, ..., F.S.A., of Somerset Place, co. Middx., 1802, Vol. XXI, fol. 324.

GOSNALL after WALFORD (fol. 320), of Bentley Hall, co. Suff., 184 . ., Vol. XLVIII, fols. 318 and 320.

GOSSE, Henry, of Epsom, co. Surrey, 184 . ., Vol. XLVII, fol. 251.

GOSSELIN-LEFEBVRE, B. M. H., Lieut., Coldstream Guards, 1886, Vol. LXIII, fol. 227.

GOSSIP, Randall, of Boston and Thorp Arch Hall, co. York, 182 . ., Vol. XXXV, fol. 272.

GOSSIP to WILMER, Wilmer and Rev. Thomas George, of co. York, 183 . ., Vol. XXXIX, fol. 182.

„ to HATFIELD, Randall, of co. York, 184 . ., Vol. XLVII, fol. 242.

„ to DE RODES, ... (minor), of Barlborough, co. Derby (St. John's Coll., Camb.), 184 . ., Vol. XLVII, fol. 97.

GOSTWYCK-GOSTWYCK, William (formerly JARD), late of Culan Eileen, co. Inverness, Scotland, 1897, Vol. LXIX, fol. 259.

GOUGH, before CALTHORPE, Sir Henry, Bart., of co. Warw., 1788, Vol. XVI, fol. 406.

GOUGH to SEARE, ..., of Bradley, nr. Alton, Hampsh., and Grove Tring, co. Hertf., 180 . ., Vol. XXI, fol. 118.

GOUGH, late ASTLEY, Richard, of co. Leic., 181 . ., Vol. XXIX, fol. 200.

GOUGH, Lieut.-Col. Sir Hugh, C.B., of Ireland. Augmentation, 181 . ., Vol. XXIX, fol. 310.

„ Lieut.-Gen. Sir Hugh, Bart. [23 Dec. 1842], G.C.B. [14 Oct. 1841], of Ireland. Supporters and Augmentation, 184 . ., Vol. XLVI, fols. 234 and 237.

„ Viscount [Sir Hugh, Bart., G.C.B.], of Ireland. Augmentation, alteration and Supporters, [15 June 1849] Vol. XLIX, fols. 312 and 314.

GOUGH, late GOUGH-CALTHORPE, Hon. Frederick, 2nd surviving son of the 1st Baron Calthorpe, of co. Staff., [14 May 1845] Vol. XLVII, fol. 408.

GOUGH, Ralph, of Gorsebrook House, par. of Bushbury, co. Staff. (Ralph, of Wolverhampton), 14 Feb. 1854, Vol. LI, fol. 1.

GOUIN, Louisa Elizabeth, wid. of Rev. Anthony Alphonne, of Brighton, co. Sussex, 18 . ., Vol. LXXI, fol. . . . .

GOULD, Hon. Albert J., of Edgecliffe, Sydney, New South Wales, 18 . . ., Vol. LXXI, fol. . . . .

GOULD, Sir Henry, of London, and Sharpham Park, co. Somerset, [7 July 1699] Vol. IV, fol. 297.

„ Charles, s. of King Gould, of Streatham, co. Camb., 17 . . ., Vol. XIV, fol. 115 ; to MORGAN [16 Nov. 1792], Bart. [15 Nov. 1792], of Ruperra, co. Glamorgan, Wales, and co. Monmouth (Baron TREDEGAR). Quarterly, 179 . ., Vol. XVIII, fol. 141.

GOULD after BARING, ..., of co. Devon, 179 . ., Vol. XIX, fol. 121.

GOULD to YELVERTON, Baron GREY DE RUTHIN, of co. Nottingham. Arms of Yelverton. Grandson of the Earl of SUSSEX, [1800] Vol. XXI, fol. 48.

GOULD, Adm. Sir Davidge, G.C.B. [24 Jan. 1833]. Supporters, 183 . ., Vol. XXXIX, fol. 277.

GOULD, late JACKSON, ..., of Upway and Fleet House, co. Dorset, and Fanningstown, co. Limerick, Ireland, 18 . . ., Vol. LVII, fol. 336.

GOULTER, Thomas Morse, of Almondsbury, co. Glouc., 187 . ., Vol. LVIII, fol. 322. (Berry's Suppl.)

„ CYRUS-, ..., of Hawkesbury, New Zealand, 1878, Vol. LX, fol. 107. (Berry's Suppl.) [?]

GOUNTER-NICOLL, Sir Charles, K.B. [17 Jan. 1732], of Racton, co. Sussex. Supporters, 17 . . ., Vol. VIII, fol. 118^{b}.

GOVER, ..., of Ottery St. Mary, co. Devon, 183 . ., Vol. XLII, fol. 84.

GOVETT, ..., M.A., of Tiverton, co. Devon, Vicar of Staines, co. Middx., 182 . ., Vol. XXXVI, fol. 122.

GOVETT to GOVETT-ROMAINE, ..., of Castle Hill Lodge, Reading, Berks., 182 . ., Vol. XXXVI, fol. 266.

GOW, Philip BUTT-, of Lee, co. Kent, 18 . . ., Vol. LXXI, fol. . . . .

Gow-Steuart, Miss, of Fowler's Park, Hawkhurst, co. Kent, 1895, Vol. LXVIII, fol. 265.
Gowan to Mauleverer, William, of Arncliffe, co. York, 183 . ., Vol. XL, fol. 143.
Gowan, Col. C.B., Bo.C.S., A.D.C., 184 . ., Vol. XLVIII, fol. 356.
Gower, Baron [16 Mar. 1703], of Stittenham, co. York. Supporters, 17 . . ., Vol. V, fol. 110.
„ Viscount Granville [12 Aug. 1815]. Supporters, 181 . ., Vol. XXIX, fol. 128.
Gower, ..., of Morden, co. Surrey, 186 . ., Vol. LVI, fol. 17.
Gowland, Ralph, grandfather Ralph, of Little Eppleton, co. Durham, 1749, Vol. IX, fol. 339. (Berry.)
„ Thomas, s. of Edward, s. of Edward, of Sunderland, co. Durham, 180 . ., Vol. XXII, fol. 243.
Grabham, ..., F.R.C.S., of Rochford, co. Essex, 184 . ., Vol. XLVIII, fol. 123.
Graeme after Lloyd, of Yarburgh Graeme, co. York. (See also Greame.) 186 . ., Vol. LVI, fol. 254.
„ after Jones, Thomas Valentine, Capt., Dragoon Guards, of Oldbury Court, co. Glouc.; Bailbrooke, co. Somerset; and Island of Barbados, 182 . ., Vol. XXXIII, fol. 304.
„ after Hamond [3 April 1873] [Bart.], of Berks., and Scotland, 187 . ., Vol. LVIII, fol. 239.
Graeme or Greame to Yarburgh, of Yarburgh, co. Linc., 185 . ., Vol. L, fols. 215 and 307.
Grafton to Grafton-Dare, John Marmaduke, of co. Essex, 1805, Vol. XXIII, fol. 247.
Graham before Clarke, John A., of Newcastle-upon-Tyne, co. Northumberland, now of co. Glouc., and Wales, 178 . ., Vol. XVI, fol. 199.
Graham, late Vernon, Henry Charles E., of co. Staff., 18 . . .,* Vol. XXI, fol. 61.
Graham, ..., of Edmond Castle and Hayton, co. Cumberland, and Lincoln's Inn, London, M.P. (Kirkstall, co. York), 180 . ., Vol. XXV, fols. 92 and 95.
„ Lieut.-Gen. Sir Thomas, K.B. [22 Feb. 1812], [afterwards (1814) Baron Lynedoch]. Supporters, 181 . ., Vol. XXVII, fol. 44.
Graham to Webster, ..., of London, and co. Forfar. Match with Wedderburn, Meathie and Balmure, A. F., 181 . ., Vol. XXX, fol. 65.
Graham, now Wedderburn, of Pearsie and Meathie, co. Forfar, Scotland, 182 . „ Vol. XXXVII, fol. 348.
Graham-Foster-Piggott, George Edward, M.P., of co. Camb., Kent and Berks., 182 . ., Vol. XXXVI, fols. 299, 302, 305 and 310.
Graham (Vernon) to Vernon only, Col. Henry C. E., of Hilton Park, co. Staff., 183 . .,* Vol. XLIII, fol. 48.
Graham, John, Bishop of Chester, co. Chester, 184 . ., Vol. XLIX, fols. 28 and 29.
„ John Benjamin, of Prospect House, Adelaide, South Australia, 184 . ., Vol. XLIX, fol. 64.
Graham-Wigan, John Alfred [Wigan], of Oakwood, Maidstone, co. Kent, 1897, Vol. LXIX, fol. 221.
Graham, Robert Gore (s. of William), of Southmead, Westbury-on-Trym, co. Glouc., 18 . . ., Vol. LXXI, fol. . . . . .
Grainger, John, of St. Margaret's, Westminster, a Deputy-Teller of the Exchequer, 16 July 1716, Vol. VI, fol. 258; Add. MS. 14,831, fol. 53.
Grainger to Fothergill, John, of co. York, 17 . . ., Vol. XIV, fol. 76.
Grange, ..., of Chelsea, London, 181 . ., Vol. XXX, fol. 218.
Grange to Emerson, James, of Stokesley, co. York, reputed son of Emerson, 184 . ., Vol. XLVIII, fol. 31.

GRANGER, His Honour Judge Thomas Colpitts, C.C. Judge (3rd s. of Thomas, Q.C., M.P.), 18 . . ., Vol. LXXI, fol. . . . .
GRANT (Hon.), ..., of Jamaica, and London, 17 . . ., Vol. XVII, fol. 296.
  ,,   William, of Litchborough, co. Northampton, 181 . ., Vol. XXVII, fol. 418.
GRANT to POWELL, Capt. Wife's arms impaled, 181 . .. Vol. XXVIII, fol. 402.
GRANT after KEIR, Maj.-Gen., K.H., of Rossie, co. Fife, Scotland, 182 . ., Vol. XXXIII, fol. 158.
GRANT to PHILLIPS, ..., of Picton Castle, co. Pembroke, Wales, 182 . ., Vol. XXXIV, fol. 260.
GRANT-DALTON, Robert Foster, of co. Somerset, 182 . ., Vol. XXXVI, fol. 131.
GRANT, Charles, Col. of Horse, Jamaica, (s. of Ludovic Grant, Bart., of Dalvey, Scotland), of Hopewell Estate, Jamaica. Crest, 182 . ., Vol. XXXVIII, fol. 85.
GRANT-BROWNE-SHERIDAN, ..., of Frampton, co. Dorset, 183 . ., Vol. XLI, fol. 226.
GRANT, Capt. Edward Fitzherbert, R.A., of Woolwich and Portsmouth, 185 . ., Vol. L, fol. 53.
GRANT after McPHERSON . . . . (Spr.), of Garbity, co. Moray, Scotland, 185 . ., Vol. LI, fol. 108.
GRANT, Maj.-Gen. Sir Patrick, G.C.B. [1861], (afterwards Field-Marshal). Supporters, 186 . ., Vol. LIV, fol. 164.
  ,,   Maj.-Gen. Sir James Hope, G.C.B. [1860], 186 . ., Vol. LIV, fol. 194.
  ,,   Thorold, of Wellsby House, co. Linc., 186 . ., Vol. LV, fol. 262.
GRANT-IVES, W. D., of Bradden House, co. Northampton, 1892, Vol. LXVI, fol. 289.
GRANT, John, of Glenlochry, in the Island of Jamaica, by J. H. Campbell, Lyon King of Arms, 6 Nov. 1783. (Burke's Commoners, II, p. 613.)
GRANTHAM, Sir Thomas, Agent of the Privy Chamber, Esquire of the Body at the Queen's Coronation and also to King William and Queen Mary; a Director of Greenwich Hospital from its foundation (his father, Thomas, of Cirencester, was killed at the siege of Oxford, 1645, &c., &c., &c.), of Bicester, co. Oxf., and Sunbury, co. Middx., 7 or 27 July 1711, Vol. V, fol. 440; Stowe MS. 714, fols. 78 to 83; Add MS. 14,831, fol. 120. (Berry.)
  ,,   Baron (Thomas ROBINSON), [7 April 1761]. Supporters, 17 . . ., Vol. X, fol. 292.
  ,,   Baron (ROBINSON to WEDDELL), [7 May 1803] 180 . ., Vol. XXII, fol. 234.
  ,,   William (Judge), of Barkham Place, Barcombe, co. Sussex, 1880,* Vol. LXI, fol. 9. (Berry's Suppl.)
GRANTLEY, Lord [and Baron of MARKENFIELD, 9 April 1782] (NORTON), of co. York, 178 . ., Vol. XV, fol. 51.
  ,,   Lady. Arms of CHAPPLE, of co. York, 178 . ., Vol. XV, fol. 51.
GRANVILE, George, Baron LANSDOWNE [1 Jan. 171½]. Supporters, 17 . . ., Vol. VI, fols. 32 and 211.
GRANVILLE, late D'EWES, Rev. John, of Calwich, co. Staff., 1786, Vol. XVI, fol. 103.
  ,,   late DEWES, of Court Calwich, co. Staff.; Wellesborne, co. Warw.; and Buckland, co. Glouc., 1826, Vol. XXXVI, fol. 224.
GRANVILLE, Baron [Granville, 13 Mar. 170⅔ ?]. Supporters, 17 . . ., Vol. V, fol. 107.
  ,,   Countess (quartering CARTERET) [1 Jan. 171⅘ ?]. Supporters, 17 . . ., Vol. VI, fol. 211.
  ,,   Viscount [15 July or 12 Aug. 1815] (LEVESON-GOWER), 181 . ., Vol. XXIX, fol. 128.
  ,, ..., of Westminster, London, and Ceylon, 180 . ., Vol. XXIII, fol. 139.
GRAPE, Richard, of New Windsor, Berks., 1764, Vol. XI, fol. 6. (Berry.)
GRASETT, William, M.A., of Dawlish, co. Devon, and Barbados, 181 . ., Vol. XXX, fol. 389.
GRATWICK, William, of Ham, co. Sussex, 16 Oct. 1717, Vol. VI, fol. 332.

GREATWICKE after KINLESIDE, William, of Ham, co. Sussex, 1823, Vol. XXXIII, fol. 132 (see Berry's Suppl.).
„ after KINLESIDE, of Ham, co. Sussex, 186 . ., Vol. LV, fol. 44.
„ after ARCHDALE, George, D.D., of Ham, co. Sussex, 182 . ., Vol. XXXIII, fol. 132.
„ after ARCHDALE, ..., of Ham, co. Sussex, 186 . ., Vol. LV, fol. 44.
GRAVE, Rev. William Cecil, of Bishops Hatfield and Quickerwood, co. Hertf., and his brother, Thomas Cecil, 17 Feb. 1773, Vol. XII, fol. 228 (see Berry).
GRAVENOR to ST. ALBYN, of Alfoxton and Nether Stowey, co. Somerset, 180 . ., Vol. XXIII, fol. 432.
GRAVER to GRAVER-BROWNE, ... (minor), of Wymondham and Tacolnestone, co. Norf., 181 . ., Vol. XXVIII, fol. 320.
GRAVES, Richard, of Mickleton, co. Glouc., 4 July 1728, Vol. VII, fol. 588. [Geneal., IV, p. 103.]
„ Adm. [1779, Thomas], Baron of LIGHTHAUSEL, co. York, &c. ; Thanckes, co. Cornw. ; and Gravesend, co. Londonderry, Ireland, [1794] Vol. XVIII, fol. 412.
„ Rear-Adm. Sir Thomas, K.B. [1801], of Ireland (died s.p.), 180 . ., Vol. XXII, fol. 115. Supporters, Vol. XXII, fol. 118.
GRAVES to GOLDING, ..., of co. Suff., 180 . ., Vol. XXII, fol. 422.
„ to SAWLE, Joseph Sawle, of Penrice, co. Cornw. Match, 181 . ., Vol. XXVIII, fol. 304.
GRAVES-SAWLE, Joseph Sawle, of Barley House, co. Devon, and co. Cornw., Bart. [1836], 182 . ., Vol. XXXVI, fol. 375.
GRAVES, John, of Southwark and Camberwell, co. Surrey, 181 . ., Vol. XXX, fol. 85
GRAVES-KNYFTON, R. B., of Uphill Castle, co. Somerset, 1895, Vol. LXVIII, fol. 182.
GRAY, Sir James, [2nd] Bart., K.B. [23 Mar. 1761]. Supporters, 17 . . ., Vol. X, fol. 316.
GRAY, now ROSS, ..., of Westminster, London, 178 . ., Vol. XVI, fol. 125.
GRAY, Elizabeth (wife of John GREEN), dau. of William Gray, of co. Northampton. Arms to herself and descendants, 18 . . ., Vol. XXV, fol. 285.
GRAY to BERNARD (nat. dau. of Gen. Bernard), of Heton Lodge, nr. Leeds, co. York, 181 . ., Vol. XXXI, fol. 374.
GRAY, late HUNTER, ..., of Carse, co. Forfar, Scotland, 184 . ., Vol. XLIX, fol. 440.
GRAY, John, of Old Park, Riverham, co. Kent, and Finadon, co. Northampton, 18 . . ., Vol. LIII, fol. 223.
„ . . . ., of Brafferton and Cray's Court, co. York, 185 . ., Vol. LVI, fol. 327ᵈ.
„ W. M., of Sefton Lodge, Heaton, Bradford, co. York, 1894, Vol. LXVIII, fol. 140.
„ Herbert, of Frisby, co. Linc., s. of William T. Miers, of Seacroft Grange, nr. Leeds, co. York, 18 . . ., Vol. LXXI, fol. . . . .
GRAY (SMITH-), (see SMITH), Baroness Gray, 1897, Vol. LXX, fol. 13.
GRAYHURST, William, s. of William, of Farmington, co. Glouc., 17 . . ., Vol. IX, fol. 148.
GREAT CENTRAL RAILWAY COMPANY, 1898, Vol. LXX, fol. 114.
GREATHED-HARRIS, Edward Baillie, of co. Dorset, and Lincoln's Inn, London, 180 . ., Vol. XXIII, fol. 389.
GREATHED, late HARRIS, Capt. Edward, of co. Dorset, and Uddeys, Kingston-upon-Hull, co. York, 180 . ., Vol. XXIII, fol. 393.
GREATHEED, Ann Caroline, of Guy's Cliff, co. Warw., and St. Kitts, West Indies, 181 . ., Vol. XXXI, fol. 222.
GREATHEED after BERTIE, Anne Caroline, of Guy's Cliff, co. Warw., 181 . ., Vol. XXXI, fol. 224.
GREATHEED-BERTIE-PERCY, Hon. Charles [Percy], M.P., of Guy's Cliff, co. Warw., 1826, Vol. XXXV, fol. 392.

GREATOREX, ..., of Ealing, co. Middx., and Carsington, co. Derby, 186 . .,
Vol. LVI, fol. 101.
GREAVES before ELMSALL, Joseph Edward, of co. York, 181 . ., Vol. XXX, fol. 153.
GREAVES, George, of Attercliffe, Sheffield, co. York, 178 . ., Vol. XV, fol. 58.
GREAVES, now LEY, ..., of Ingleby, co. Derby, and Mayfield, co. Staff.,
182 . ., Vol. XXXII, fol. 207.
GREAVES, late BRADSHAW, ..., of Nettleworth Hall, co. Nottingham, 182 . .,
Vol. XXXV, fol. 92.
GREAVES, ..., of Irlam Hall, co. Lanc., 183 . ., Vol. XLI, fol. 370.
GREAVES-BANNING, Louisa Sophia, of co. Lanc., wife of C. B. Banning, 186 . .,
Vol. LVI, fol. 48.
GREAVES after BROWN, Richard Edward (late Lieut.), of Woodthorpe Hall, co.
York, 1877, Vol. LIX, fol. 346.
GREAVES, J. E., of Bron Eifion, Criccieth, Wales, 1887,* Vol. LXIV, fol. 78.
GREAVES-BAGSHAWE (see Crisp, I, p. 143).
GREEN, Sir Beryn, Knt., 2nd s. of Richard, of Abingdon, Berks., s. and h.
of Richard, also of Abingdon, Berks., and sometime of Marlborough,
Wilts., 16 Dec. 1709, Vol. V, fol. 395 ; Add. MS. 14,830, fol. 33.
Sir Beryn, Knt., late Sheriff, now Alderman, Ward of Queenhithe,
London, second s. of Richard, s. of Richard, &c., 1709.
  „ John, of Great King's Hill, Bucks., and Oundle, co. Northampton, 13 Dec.
1768, Vol. XI, fol. 338. (Berry.)
  „ John, s. of John, of Bentley, co. York, and London. Escutcheon of pretence,
for FISHER, 17 . . ., Vol. XIV, fol. 332.
  „ Maj.-Gen. William (s. of Farbridge Green), of co. Durham, 17 . . ., Vol.
XVI, fol. 145.
GREEN, late KENT, ..., of Poulton Lancelyn, co. Chester, 179 . ., Vol. XVIII,
fol. 164.
  „ late KENT, ..., 182 . ., Vol. XXXVII, fol. 417.
  „ late COWAN, Thomas, of London, 17 . . ., Vol. XX, fol. 327.
GREEN, Col. . . . ., Governor of Grenada, of London, 180 . ., Vol. XXII, fol. 81.
  „ . . . ., of Stanway, co. Essex, 180 . ., Vol. XXIII, fol. 262.
GREEN to WILKINSON, Joseph (minor), of London. Quarterly Arms, 1805, Vol.
XXIII, fol. 265.
  „ to ARMYTAGE, Joseph, of co. York, 180 . ., Vol. XXIV, fol. 400.
GREEN, ..., pat. by Le Neve, 1725 (see Berry).
  „ John (and Elizabeth Gray, only dau. of William [Green], and wife of John
GRAY), of London ; Ledstone, co. York ; and Linton Abbey, co. Notting-
ham. GRAY Arms, 180 . ., Vol. XXV, fols. 284 and 285.
GREEN to COTTON, widow of Green, of Bellaport, Shropsh., and Dalbury and
Etnall Hall, co. Derby, 182 . ., Vol. XXXII, fol. 14.
GREEN, Edward Humphrys, of Hinxton Hall, co. Camb., 182 . ., Vol. XXXVI,
fol. 145.
  „ Edward Henry, of Hinxton Hall, co. Camb., 1885, Vol. LXIII, fol. 75.
GREENE-DE FREVILLE, Edward Henry, of Hinxton Hall, co. Camb., 188 . .,
Vol. LXIII, fol. 153.
GREEN, late VERRAL, Araunah, of Ringmer and Chiddingley, co. Sussex, 183 . .,
Vol. XLI, fol. 87.
GREEN, A., of Launceston, Tasmania, 1890,* Vol. LXV, fol. 331.
  „ Sir Edward, Bart., of Wakefield, co. York, 1886,* Vol. LXIII, fol. 190.
  „ Everard, of Heralds' Coll., London, 1894,* Vol. LXVIII, fol. 20. (Crisp,
IV, p. 45.)
  „ Alderman Samuel, of Bickley, Bromley, co. Kent, 1897, Vol. LXX, fol. 48.
GREEN-EMMOTT, Walter Egerton John, of Emmott Hall, Colne, co. Lanc., 1897,
Vol. LXIX, fol. 323.
GREENALL, Sir Gilbert, Bart., of Walton Hall, co. Lanc. With remainder to the
descendants of his father, Edward, 16 Feb. 1876, Vol. LIX, fol. 186.
(Geneal., IV, p. 290.)

GREENAWAY, Giles, of Barrington Parva, co. Glouc., High Sheriff, Alderman of
    Glouc. City, 4 Feb. 1795, Vol. XIX, fol. 9. (Misc. G. et H., 2nd S.,
    V, Plate, p. 241.)
GREENE, ..., of Slyne, co. Lanc., 179 . ., Vol. XVIII, fol. 79.
GREENE, late THOMAS, Henny, of Rolleston, co. Leic. Match, 181 . ., Vol. XXIX,
    fol. 107.
GREENE, Lieut.-Col. Edward Wattes (s. of Edward), of Netherhall, Bury
    St. Edmunds, co. Suff., 1898, Vol. LXX, fol. 298.
   „   [John Joseph, 31 Dec. 1893 (Right to Bear Arms, by X)].
GREENFIELD (Benjamin Wyatt), of Byworth, Petworth, co. Sussex ; Bryndereven,
    Llandegar, co. Carmarthen ; and Rhyddgaer, co. Anglesey, Wales, 1839,
    Vol. XLIII, fol. 369.
GREENHILL, Thomas, Surgeon, of London, 1 Sept. 1698, Vol. IV, fol. 278,
    and Add. MS. 14,381, fol. 190.
GREENHILL-RUSSELL, of Chequers, Bucks., and Lincoln's Inn, London, 18 . .,
    Vol. XXXVIII, fol. 261.
GREENLAND, late HOOKER, ..., of Rottingdean, co. Sussex, 182 . ., Vol.
    XXXII, fol. 115.
GREENLAW, Alexander, of Isleworth, co. Middx., and Elgin, co. Moray, Scotland,
    LL.D. St. Alb. Hall, Oxford, 181 . ., Vol. XXVII, fol. 83.
GREENLY, ..., of Titley House, co. Hereford, 179 . ., Vol. XIX, fol. 268.
GREENLY after COFFIN, Vice-Adm. Sir Isaac Coffin, Bart., of co. Hereford,
    181 . ., Vol. XXVI, fol. 226.
GREENLY, late ALLEN, ..., of Titley Court, co. Hereford, 186 . ., Vol. LV,
    fol. 302.
GREENOUGH after BELLAS, ..., of co. Camb., 179 . ., Vol. XIX, fol. 11.
GREENSILL, Capt., R.A.   Match with SPENCER, 181 . ., Vol. XXVII, fol. 60.
GREENSMITH, Robert, of Steeple Grange, co. Derby, Sheriff of Derby, [14 or 18 Jan.
    171½] Vol. VI, fol. 179.
GREENTREE, Lieut.-Col., E.I.C.S., of Cheltenham, co. Glouc., and St. Helena,
    182 . ., Vol. XXXV, fol. 74.
GREENUP, ..., of Halifax, co. York, 180 . ., Vol. XXI, fol. 19.
GREENVILLE, Viscount COBHAM.   Supporters [Hester, Viscountess Cobham,
    13 Sept. 1749 ?], 17 . . ., Vol. IX, fol. 329.
GREENWICH, Baroness of (TOWNSHEND) [19 Aug. 1767].   Supporters, 17 . . .,
    Vol. XI, Vol. 252.
GREENWOOD to HOLDEN, ..., of Palace House, co. Lanc., 18 . . ., Vol. XLIV,
    fol. 374.
GREENWOOD-PENNY, ..., of Higher Nutwall House and Colaton Raleigh,
    co. Devon, 184 . ., Vol. XLV, fol. 138.
GREENWOOD (life in remainder), Charles Staniforth, of Swarcliffe Hall, co. York.
    (See STANYFORTH.) 1888, Vol. LXIV, fol. 165. (Crisp, V, p. 129.)
   „   Herbert John, of 28, Chapel Street, London, s. of John, 1897, Vol. LXIX,
    fol. 271.
GREETHAM, ..., Deputy-Judge Advocate of the Fleet, 180 . ., Vol. XXV,
    fol. 131.
GREGG, Thomas, of Lee Hall, Norton, and Ilkeston, co. Derby, and of the Middle
    Temple, London, 25 June 1725, Vol. VII, fol. 328, and Add. MS. 14,380,
    fol. 36. (Berry.)
   „   Foot (s. of Francis), of Derby Bradley, and to the descendants of his father,
    172 . ., Vol. VII, fol. 328 ; Add MS. 14,380 ; Pedigree D. 14. (Berry.)
GREGOR, late BOOKER, ..., of co. Cornw., 182 . ., Vol. XXXVI, fol. 19.
GREGORY, ..., of Woolhope, co. Hereford.   Match, 181 . ., Vol. XXVIII,
    fol. 246.
GREGORY, late WILLIAMS, ..., of Kempstone, co. Nottingham, and Harlaxton
    and Denton, co. Linc., 182 . ., Vol. XXXIV, fol. 130.
GREGORY after SHERWIN (formerly LONGDEN), ..., of Denton, co. Linc., and
    Bramcote, co. Nottingham, 186 . ., Vol. LIV, fol. 56.

GREGORY after WELBY, ..., Bart., of Denton and Harlaxton, co. Linc., 182 . .,
Vol. XXXIV, fol. 130.
„ after WELBY, ..., [5 July 1861, 3rd Bart.], of Denton, co. Linc., 186 . .,
Vol. LIV, fols. 56 and 178.
GREGORY-WELBY, Sir William Earle, Bart. [? Welby-Gregory, 4th Bart. ?],
of Denton and Harlaxton, co. Linc., 1875, Vol. LIX, fol. 163 ; 1876,
fol. 178.
„ . . . .. of Addison Road, London, 186 . ., Vol. LVII, fol. 86.
GREGORY, Capt. William Filmer (retired Commander, R.N.), of Swanswick Hall,
co. Somerset, and Hanbury, eo. Worc., 186 . ., Vol. LVII, fol. 220.
GREGSON, late KNIGHT, Henry, of Lowlyn and Ford, co. Northumberland, 184 . .,
Vol. XLVI, fol. 145.
GREGSON, Rev. William, M.A., Rector of Whinburgh-with-Westfield, co. Norf.
(Burke) [no date].
„ Col. Lancelot Allgood, of Burdon Hall, Sunderland, co. Durham, s. of John.
of Murton, 1898, Vol. LXX, fol. 261.
GRENVILLE, NUGENT-TEMPLE-, [George], [2 Dec. 1779] (late [? before]
Grenville), Earl TEMPLE. Supporters, 17 . . ., Vol. XIV, fol. 195.
„ TEMPLE-NUGENT to TEMPLE-NUGENT-BRYDGES-CHANDOS-GRENVILLE,
[Richard], [15 Nov. 1799] 180 . ., Vol. XXI, fol. 154.
GRENVILLE, Baron [25 Nov. 1790] (WYNDHAM). Supporters, 17 . . ., Vol. XVII,
fol. 282.
„ Baron GLASTONBURY [20 Oct. 1797]. Supporters, 17 . . ., Vol. XX,
fol. 28.
GRENVILLE after NEVILLE, [Hon. George], of Berks. and co. Essex. (See Baron
BRAYBROOKE.) [7 July 1825], Vol. XXXV, fol. 246.
GRESLEY after DOUGLAS, Robert A., of Salwarpe, co. Worc., 1830, Vol.
XXXVIII, fol. 37.
GRESWOLDE after MEYSEY-WIGLEY, Capt. Edmund, of eo. Warw. and Worc.,
182 . ., Vol. XXXVIII, fol. 13.
GRESWOLDE, late WIGLEY, Henry, of Malvern Hall, Solihull and Shakenhurst,
co. Worc., 1833, Vol. XXXIX, fol. 245.
GRETTON, John, of Stapleford Park, co. Leic., s. of John, of Barton, co. Derby,
18 . . ., Vol. LXXI, fol . . . .
GREVILLE, Earl of BROOKE and WARWICK. Crest, 17 . . ., Vol. X, fol. 223.
„ Baron, of Ireland, to discontinue the name and arms of NUGENT, [10 Mar.]
1883, Vol. LXII, fol. 128.
„ Baron, of Ireland. Supporters, 1884, Vol. LXII, fol. 242.
GREVIS before JAMES, ..., of Ightham Court, co. Kent, [1817] Vol. XXX,
fol. 347.
GREY, Baron [1676 ?] (YELVERTON) of eo. Northampton. Supporters, 16 . . .,
Vol. III, fol. 117.
„ Marchioness CAMPBELL, of co. Northampton. Supporters, 17 . . ., Vol. IX,
fol. 480.
„ Sir Charles, K.B. [8 Jan. 1783]. [See next name, Baron Grey, of Howick.]
Supporters, 178 . ., Vol. XV, fol. 189.
„ Baron [23 June 1801], [Charles Grey], of Howick, co. Northumberland.
Supporters, 180 . ., Vol. XXI, fol. 206.
GREY [Baron Grey] DE WILTON, [15 May 1784] (Egerton, Bart.), of co. North-
ampton. Supporters, 178 . ., Vol. XV, fol. 297.
„ DE WILTON, ..., of eo. Northampton, 181 . ., Vol. XXVIII, fol. 180.
„ . . . ., of co. Northampton, 181 . ., Vol. XXIX, fol. 278.
GREY, Baron (GOULD to YELVERTON) [21 Feb. 1800], of co. Northampton, 180 . .,
Vol. XXI, fol. 48.
GREY-EGERTON [21 July 1825], 9th Bart., of eo. Chester. Supporters, [23 July
1825] Vol. XXXV, fols. 235 and 237.
GREY, Gen. Sir Henry George, G.C.B. [13 Sept. 1831], of eo. Chester. Supporters,
182 . ., Vol. XXXVIII, fol. 324.

GREY to SCURFIELD, George John, of Stockton-on-Tees, co. Durham, and
Northumberland (of St. John's Coll., Camb.), 18 . . ., Vol. XXXVIII,
fol. 355.

,, to DE GREY, ... Quartering ROBINSON, of co. Bedf., 183 . ., Vol.
XXXIX, fol. 331.

,, to SMITH, John William, of Stockton-on-Tees, co. Durham (of St. John's
Coll., Camb.), 183 . ., Vol. XXXIX, fol. 374.

., to ROBINSON, William Robinson, of Silksworth, Norton and Sunderland,
co. Durham, 183 . ., Vol. XLIII, fol. 310.

GREY DE RUTHYN, Baroness, of co. Lanc., 18 . . ., Vol. XLIX, fols. 92 and 93.

GREY, Edward J., of Hermitage, Wanstead, co. Essex, 1888,* Vol. LXIV,
fol. 173.

GRIBBLE, George J., of Hans Place, London, 1886,* Vol. LXIII, fol. 203.

GRIESDALE, Arthur (grandfather Arthur), of London, 17 . . ., Vol. IX, fol. 296.

GRIEVE, Rear-Adm. William Samuel (formerly BROWN), of Southsea, Hampsh.,
1884, Vol. LXII, fol. 315.

GRIEVESON, Henry John, of Findon Hill, Witton Gilbert, co. Durham, and Nevill
Holt, Holt, co. Leic., 187 . ., Vol. LVIII, fol. 284.

GRIFFIES before WILLIAMS, ..., of Wales. Quarterly Arms, 181 . ., Vol.
XXVIII, fol. 330.

GRIFFIN, Lord [? 1 Feb. 172⅘]. Supporters, 17 . . ., Vol. VIII, fol. 132ᵇ.

,, Sir Lepel Henry, K.C.S.I. [24 May 1881], s. of Rev. Henry, of Stoke,
co. Suff., 18 . . ., Vol. LXXI, fol. . . . . [? Vol. LXI.]

,, Sir John, K.B. [23 Mar. 1761], of Audley End, co. Essex, 17 . . ., Vol. X,
fol. 327.

GRIFFIN to STONESTREET, ..., of Eaton Bray, co. Bedf., and London. Match,
179 . ., Vol. XVIII, fol. 292.

GRIFFIN, late NEVILLE, ... [27 July 1797, 2nd] Baron BRAYBROOKE, of
Billingbere, Berks. Quarterly Arms, 17 . . ., Vol. XX, fol. 52.

,, (late TYLER), George Griffin, of Wales, 1877, Vol. LIX, fol. 335.

GRIFFIN to PARNELL, Thomas, of Sheephouse, Easton in Gordano, Clevedon,
co. Somerset, 18 . . ., Vol. LX, fol. 70.

GRIFFIN, late PARKER, William, D.D., formerly WHITWELL, 179 . ., Vol. XIX,
fol. 432.

GRIFFITH after DARBY, Lieut.-Col., of Berks, 180 . ., Vol. XXI, fol. 257.

GRIFFITH-WYNNE, late FINCH, ..., of Wales. Quarterly Arms and Crest.
180 . ., Vol. XXIV, fols. 40 and 42.

GRIFFITH to BOOTH, Capt., R.N., of co. Chester, 179 . ., Vol. XVIII, fol. 17.

GRIFFITH, Thomas, of Whitchurch, Shropsh., and Wales. ? NICKLIN Escutcheon
of pretence, quarterly with GURTH MURHALL, 181 . ., Vol. XXVII,
fol. 318.

GRIFFITH after MURHALL, Thomas, of Shropsh. and Wales. Arms and Crest,
181 . ., Vol. XXVII, fols. 331 and 333.

GRIFFITH-COLPOYS, Rear-Adm., of Raheen, co. Waterford, Ireland, 182 . .,
Vol. XXXIII, fol. 31.

GRIFFITH, ... (widow), of co. Cardigan, Wales, her son John, 182 . ., Vol.
XXXIV, fols. 258 and 259.

GRIFFITH to POYER, ..., of London, 183 . ., Vol. XL, fol. 193.

GRIFFITH, late WATKINS, John and William, of Shrewsbury, Shropsh., and
Wales, 184 . ., Vol. XLV, fol. 343.

GRIFFITH-WYNNE to WYNNE-FINCH, ..., of London, 186 . ., Vol. LV,
fol. 82.

GRIFFITH, Sir S. W., K.C.M.G., of Brisbane, Queensland, 1892, Vol. LXVI,
fol. 304.

,, Rev. T. H., of Lawnswood, Burgess Hill, co. Sussex, 1891,* Vol. LXVI,
fol. 120.

,, Richard William Smith, of Eyeworth Lodge, Lyndhurst, Hampsh., 1898,
Vol. LXX, fol. 176.

GRIFFITHS. . . . ., of Feltham Hill, co. Middx., and Montagu Place, London, 181 . ., Vol. XXVI, fols. 104 and 108.

„ . . . ., of Broomhead, Shropsh., 181 . ., Vol. XXVII, fol. 403.

„ Thomas, of Catton, co. Norf., s. of Thomas, of Llanaeglor, co. Denbigh, Wales, 183 . .,* Vol. XLI, fol. 365.

„ Edward Pryce, and to the descendants of his father, Rees Griffiths, of Varchoel, co. Montgomery, 184 . ., Vol. XLV, fol. 40.

„ Col. E. St. John, of Upton House, Nursling, Hampsh. (See also under St. John.) 1891, Vol. LXVI, fol. 215.

GRIGBY, Joshua, of co. Suff., 9 April 1743, Vol. IX, fol. 84.

GRIGGS, Joseph, Alderman of Loughborough, co. Leic., 1889, Vol. LXV, fol. 58.

GRIGSON, William, M.A. (C. C., Camb.), of co. Linc., Rector of Whinburgh, co. Norf. [to the descendants of his father], [1872] Vol. LVIII, fol. 97. (Berry's Suppl.)

[GRIMANI, ..., Venetian Ambassador. Knighted and Augmentation, April 1714 (Topog. and Geneal., III. p. 509).]

GRIMES to CHOLMLEY, Robert, of Howsham, co. York, and Coton House, co. Warw., 185 . ., Vol. LII, fol. 327.

GRIMKÉ-DRAYTON, T. D., of Golborne Park, co. York, 1892, Vol. LXVI, fol. 291.

GRIMSHAW after ATKINSON, Richard, of Broadstairs, co. Kent, M.A., Oxf., Vicar of Cockerham, co. Lanc., 1877, Vol. LX, fol. 92.

GRIMSTON, Baroness (WALTER), of co. Hertf., [? 1790] Vol. XVII, fol. 286.

GRIMSTON to BUCKNALL, ..., of Oxhey, co. Hertf., and Ireland, [1797] Vol. XIX, fol. 361.

GRIMSTON, ..., of Oxhey, co. Hertf., and Ireland, 181 . ., Vol. XXVIII, fol. 134.

GRIMSTON, late WILMOT, John, of Neswick, co. York, and Chaddesden, co. Derby, 186 . ., Vol. LIV, fol. 38.

GRIMTHORPE, Baron [BECKETT, 5th Bart.] Supporters, 1886, Vol. LXIII, fol. 249.

GRIMWOOD, late COZENS, Jeffrey Grimwood, sic, of Woodham Mortimer and Cressing, co. Essex, 18 . . ., Vol. XLIX, fol. 486.

GRINDALL, Vice-Adm. Sir Richard, K.C.B. [1815, 1816], of Ware, co. Hertf. (Trafalgar allusion), Vol. XXX, fols. 276 and 284.

GRINLINTON, Sir J. J., of Colombo, Ceylon, 1895,* Vol. LXVIII, fol. 363.

GRISEWOOD, George, of London and Durham, 13 April 1741, Vol. IX, fol. 19.

GRISSELL, ..., of Norbury Park, co. Surrey, 185 . ., Vol. L, fol. 152.

GROOM, ..., of Lincoln's Inn, London, 182 . ., Vol. XXXV, fol. 233.

GROOME to CARLETON, ... (Spr.), of co. Sussex, 181 . ., Vol. XXVII, fol. 310.

GROSE, Francis, of Richmond, co. Surrey, Richmond Herald; and to the descendants of his father, Oct. 1756, Vol. X, fol. 64 (Misc. G. et H., New S., IV, p. 1). (Berry.)

GROSETT-MUIRHEAD after STEUART, ..., of Bredisholm, co. Lanark, Scotland, 186 . ., Vol. LV, fol. 86.

GROSVENOR, ..., of co. Chester. Crest, 16 . . ., Vol. I, fol. 423.

„ Baron [8 April 1761], of co. Chester. Supporters, 17 . . ., Vol. X, fol. 295.

GROSVENOR, ERLE-DRAX-, Richard, of co. Dorset. (See also DRAX), (decd. 1819), 182 . ., Vol. XXXVII, fol. 364 [? Vol. XXVII].

GROSVENOR, G. W. of Broome House, Broome, co. Worc., 1893, Vol. LXVII, fol. 216.

GROTE, George, of Long Bennington, co. Linc., and Badgeworth, co. Oxf., 1797, Vol. XIX, fol. 450. (Berry.)

GROUNDWATER, Major, Bombay Artillery, 183 . ., Vol. XLI, fol. 41.

GROUT, Joseph, of Buckeridge, Braughing, co. Hertf., 182 . ., Vol. XXXIV, fols. 176 and 224. (Berry.)

GROVE to HILLERSDON, ..., of Waddon, co. Surrey, and Woodford and Sewardstone, co. Essex. Match, 180 . ., Vol. XXIV, fol. 242.

„ to CRADOCK, ..., of co. Hereford and Staff., 18 . . ., Vol. XLIX, fol. 150.

GROVE, John William, 3rd. s. of Thomas, of Tasmania, 18 . . ., Vol. LXXI, fol. . . . .

GROVER, Charles E., of Hemel Hempstead, co. Hertf., 1882,* Vol. LXI, fol. 279. (Berry's Suppl.)

GRUBBE (see Crisp, I, p. 27, Grubbe and RADCLIFFE quarterly ; Irish grant ?).

GRUNING, ..., of London and Hamburgh, 184 . . ., Vol. XLVI, fol. 264.

GUARD, Lieut.-Gen., of Honiton, co. Devon, Governor of Kinsale and Charles Fort [Ireland], 182 . ., Vol. XXXVIII, fol. 11.

GUBBAY, Maurice Elias, of Poona, India, [1868] Vol. LVII, fol. 9.

GUEST, ..., of Bridgnorth, Shropsh. (See BAKER.) 181 . ., Vol. XXVII, fol. 235.

„ Lord Ivor, of Wales. Arms, [1838 ?] Vol. XLIII, fol. 88. [Josiah John Guest, cr. a Bart. 14 Aug. 1838, his son Sir Ivor Bertie Guest, 2nd Bart., cr. Baron Wimborne 1880.]

„ Edwin, Fellow and M.A., Caius Coll. Camb. (Master 1852), and of Lincoln's Inn, London, 18 . . ., Vol. XLIX, fol. 496.

„ Sarah, d. of Richard, of co. Bedf., wife of Samuel CLERKE, of co. Somerset, 20 May 1732, Vol. VIII, fol. 141.

GUILLEBAUD, Peter, M.A., Brasenose Coll., Oxf., of Clifton, co. Glouc., 184 . ., Vol. XLVIII, fol. 388.

GUINNESS, Sir Benjamin Lee, Bart. [15 Apr. 1867], of Ireland. Supporters, [18 May 1867] Vol. LVI, fol. 217.

GUISE, ..., of London. Arms to WILLIAMS, nat. dau. of Sir John Guise and wife of Sir George NAYLER (aftewards Garter King of Arms), 180 . ., Vol. XXV, fol. 56.

„ Lieut.-Gen. Sir John W., K.C.B., of co. Glouc. Crest, 1843, Vol. XLVI, fol. 351.

„ Lieut.-Gen. Sir John W., [3rd] Bart., K.C.B. Supporters (to descendants). Crest, a swan. Badge, a bean. (Beauchamp), 12 July 1863, Vol. LIV, fols. 340 and 350.

GULL, Sir William Withey, Bart., M.D., of London. Augmentation, 17 Sept. 1872, Vol. LVIII, fols. 70 and 146. (Misc. G. et H., New S., I, 453.)

GULLY after SLADE, Rev. Samuel Thomas, of Trevennean House, Gorran, co. Cornw., 185 . ., Vol. LI, fol. 34.

GULLY, Right Hon. William Court, Speaker of the House of Commons (s. of James, M.D.), 18 . ., Vol. LXXI, fol. . . . .

GULSTON (late BIGG), Frederick, of co. Hertf. and Surrey, 17 . . ., Vol. XX, fol. 189. (Berry.)

GULSTON-STEPNEY, ... (Spr.), of Wales, London, and Ealing Green, co. Middx., 185 . ., Vol. LI, fol. 263.

GUMBLETON, ..., wife of Capt. RICKETTS, R.N., of Glencairn Castle, alias Castle Richard, co. Waterford, Ireland, 182 . ., Vol. XXXVI, fol. 406.

GUMLEY, John, J.P., D.L., of Isleworth, co. Middx., 13 Dec. 1722, Vol. VII, fol. 124 ; Add. MS. 14,380, fol. 93.

GUNNING, Sir Robert, K.B. [2 June 1773]. Supporters, 1773, Vol. XII, fols. 278 and 280.

„ Lieut.-Col. John, 8 Feb. 1777, Vol. XIII, fol. 263.

„ John, of Swanswick, co. Somerset, 1765, Vol. XI, fol. 49. (Berry.)

„ Geo. (1st s. of George, decd.), of Frindsbury, co. Kent, with remainder to the descendants of his father George, 6 Dec. 1821, Vol. XXXIII, fol. 106 (see Berry's Suppl. and Documents of Gunning family).

GUNNING-SUTTON, Commander, R.N., of Blendworth, Hampsh. ; Horton, co. Northampton ; and West Retford, co. Nottingham, 18 . ., Vol. XLIX, fol. 322.

GURDON to PRICE, Benjamin, of Towcester, co. Northampton, 180 . ., Vol. XXIV, fol. 456.

GURDON-REBOW, ..., of Wyvenhoe Park, co. Essex, and Letton, co. Norf., 183 . ., Vol. XLI, fol. 113.

GURTEEN (Stephen Humphrey), of Jesus Coll., Camb., and Bleane, co. Kent, 185 . ., Vol. LIII, fol. 339.

GURWOOD, Capt., of Flaxton-in-the-Moor, co. York, 181 . ., Vol. XXVI, fol. 424.

GUSCOTTE, John, of Horslake, Cheriton Bishop, co. Devon, and 47, Onslow Square, London, 1896, Vol. LXIX, fol. 168.

GUSH, William F., Solicitor, of Sussex Gardens, London, 1882, Vol. LXI, fol. 284. (Berry's Suppl.)

GUTCH, John (s. of John J.), of York, 18 . . ., Vol. LXXI, fol. . . . .

GUY, Thomas, Executors of, with leave to put on any monument, 24 May 1725, Vol. VII, fol. 284.

GUYON, John, Commander, R.N., of Richmond, Surrey ; Portarlington, Ireland ; and Montpellier Languedoc, France, 18 . . ., Vol. XLIV, fol. 314.

GWATKIN, Frederick, of Lincoln's Inn Fields, London, 186 . ., Vol. LVI, fol. 119. (Crisp, II, p. 1.)
    „　J. R. G., of The Manor House, Potterne, Wilts., 1891, Vol. LXVI, fol. 65. (Crisp, II, p. 166.)
    „　S. B., of 10, Abbey Road, London, 1894, Vol. LXVIII, fol. 132. (Crisp, II, p. 168.)

GWILT, George and Joseph, of Westminster, 1826, Vol. XXXV, fol. 355.
    „　Joseph, F.S.A., Architect. Crest, different (additional ?), 1828, Vol. XXXVII, fol. 13. (Berry.)
    „　Daniel, Rector of Icklingham, co. Suff., 182 . ., Vol. XXXVI, fol. 109.

[„　Mary Ann. *See* APPLEGARTH.]

GWINNETT, late CATCHMAYD, William, of co. Monmouth, 178 . ., Vol. XV, fol. 94.
    „　. . . ., of co. Monmouth, 179 . .. Vol. XVIII, fol. 232.

GWINNETT (late HAYTON), William Chute, of Moreton Court, co. Hereford, and Penlleire Castle, co. Glamorgan, Wales, 184 . ., Vol. XLV, fol. 104.

GWYDIR, Baron (BURRELL), Baroness WILLOUGHBY D'ERESBY, of co. Sussex. Supporters and Crest [? 1796], Vol. XIX, fol. 307.

GWYN, late FRAUNCEIS, John, of Combe Flory, co. Somerset. Quarterings, 17 . . ., Vol. XIV, fol. 245.
    „　(late POWELL), Thomas Gabriel Leonard Carew, of Wales, 184 . ., Vol. XLV, fol. 95.

GWYN, Joseph Edward Moore-Dyffrin, s. of the Rev. Joseph MOORE, M.A., 18 . ., Vol. LXXI, fol. . . . .

GWYNNE after JONES, ..., of Wales, 180 . ., Vol. XXIII, fol. 410.

GWYNNE-VAUGHAN, late JONES, ..., of Wales, 185 . ., Vol. LI, fol. 329.

GWYNNE, late EDWARDS, ..., of Wales, 180 . ., Vol. XXIII, fol. 413.

GWYNNE (*see* WETLY-PARRY), ..., "a testator," of Wales, 181 . ., Vol. XXIX, fol. 198.

GWYNNE-HOLFORD, James Price, of Wales, 183 . ., Vol. XXXIX, fol. 34.

Evans William GWYNNE to EVANS, of Fordham, co. Essex, 1897, Vol. LXIX, fol. 265.

GWYTHER to LESLIE, Countess of ROTHES, of Leslie House, co. Fife, Scotland, [1817] Vol. XXX, fol. 206.
    „　to PHILIPPS, ..., M.A., Vicar of Madeley, Shropsh., of Picton Castle, co. Pembroke, Wales ; Yardley, co. Worc. ; and Abercover, co. Carmarthen, Wales, 185 . ., Vol. LII, fol. 151.

GYBBON-MONYPENNY, ..., of Hole, Rolvenden, co. Kent, 183 . ., Vol. XLII, fol. 144.

H

HACKBLOCK, ..., of London, 184 . ., Vol. XLVI, fol. 183.

HACKER after MARSHALL, ..., of Church Enstone, co. Oxf., 181 . ., Vol. XXXI, fol. 380.

HACKER, ..., of Churchill, co. Oxf., 182 . ., Vol. XXXVI, fol. 254.

HACKER (HEATHCOTE-), Rowland, of East Bridgford, co. Nottingham, 181 . ., Vol. XXXI, fol. 392.

„ HEATHCOTE-, John, of Chesterfield, co. Derby, 18 . . ., Vol. XLIV, fol. 295.

., HEATHCOTE- [Rowland], of Chesterfield, co. Derby, and Hotfield, co. York, [1871] Vol. LVIII, fol. 10.

HACKETT, ..., of Yapton and Somersdown, Chichester, co. Sussex, and Adelaide, South Australia, 18 . . ., Vol. LVII, fol. 154.

HADEN after BARRS, Alfred, of co. Staff. and Worc., 187 . ., Vol. LIX, fol. 304. (Burke's Suppl.)

HADEN-BEST, George Alfred Haden, of co. Staff., 1879, Vol. LX, fol. 322. (Berry's Suppl. [?])

HADLEY, Simeon Charles, Alderman of London, of Barking, co. Essex (s. of Charles), 1876, Vol. LIX, fol. 252. (Berry's Suppl.)

HADWEN, Sidney John Wilson, of Dean House, Sowerby, co. York, and Bal Blair, co. Sutherland. ? Sidney, s. of John. 187 . ., Vol. LIX, fol. 44.

HAFFENDEN (WILSON-), Rev. John, of Stillington Vicarage, co. York, 1872, Vol. LVIII, fol. 76.

HAGGERSTON, Mariana Sarah, wife of David MARJORIBANKS, now ROBERTSON (died s.p.), 183 . ., Vol. XL, fols. 264 and 265.

HAGGIS, Charles, of London, and sister Ann, wife of Richard S. WHITE. (See WHITE.)   179 . ., Vol. XIX, fol. 342.

HAGGITT to WEGG-PROSSER, Francis Richard, of Belmont, co. Hereford, and Nuncham Courtney, co. Oxf., 18 . . ., Vol. XLIX, fol. 200.

HAIGH, Arthur S., of Bahamas, and Charles T. E., of Bradley and Huddersfield, co. York (sons of Thomas), 18 . . ., Vol. LXXI, fol. . . . .

HAINES, Gen. Sir F. P., G.C.B., United Service Club. Supporters, 1878, Vol. LX, fol. 144.

„ Elizabeth (wife of William J. HARRISON), d. and h. of Thomas, of London, 179 . ., Vol. XVII, fol. 314.

HALDANE, CHINNERY-, Rt. Rev. J. R. A., of Greenhill House, Scotland, and Flintfield, co. Cork, Ireland, 18 . . ., Vol. LX, fol. 279. (Berry's Suppl.)

HALDANE-DUNCAN-MERCER-HENDERSON, Hon. H. A. D. H., of Fordell, co. Fife, Scotland, 1888, Vol. LXIV, fol. 277. (Berry's Suppl.)

HALDIMAND, [Lieut.-Gen.] Sir Frederick, K.B. [30 Sept. 1785], Gov. of Quebec, of Yverden, Berne, Switzerland. Arms and Supporters, 178 . ., Vol. XVI, fol. 159.

HALDON, Baron [Sir Laurence Palk], of co. Devon. Supporters, [29 April] 1880, Vol. LXI, fol. 53.

HALE, late BLAGDEN, John, of Alderley, co. Glouc., 178 . ., Vol. XV, fol. 387.

HALE to RIGBY, Francis, M.P., of Mistley Hall, co. Essex, 178 . ., Vol. XVII, fol. 29.

HALE, Thomas Jacob John, D.D., of Bath Easton, co. Somerset, [1827 ?] Vol. XXXVI, fol. 379.

HALE to HILDYARD, John R. W., of Horsley, co. Durham, and The Plantation and Stokesley, co. York, 185 . ., Vol. LI, fol. 280.

HALE, Joseph Eaton, of Tho Hall, Somerton, co. Suff., 186 . ., Vol. LV, fol. 108.

„ . . . ., M.A., Ven. Archd. of London and Canon of St. Paul's, 186 . ., Vol. LV, fol. 182.

HALES, late DE MORTAINCOURT, ..., (of Hales Place, co. Kent), and Bar le Duc, Lorraine, France, 182 . ., Vol. XXXVII, fol. 338.

HALES-TOOKE [Rev. James Tooke-], of Salhouse, Tompson, and Norwich, co. Norf., [1842] Vol. XLVI, fol. 134.

„ -TOOKE, Baseley, of Salhouse, co. Norf., and Washbrook, co. Suff., s. of James HALES, 1876, Vol. LIX, fol. 294. (Berry's Suppl.)

HALES, Eli George, of St. George's Place, Brighton, Lieut., 1st Sussex R.E. Vol. Regt., 1898, Vol. LXX, fol. 286.

„ Edward, of North Frith, Hadlow, co. Kent, 185 . ., Vol. LI, fol. 395.

HALEY, John, of Gutters Edge, Hendon, co. Middx., [1777] Vol. XIII, fol. 297.
„ . . . ., of Edwarebury, co. Middx., 16 . . ., Vol. III, fol. 99.
HALFORD, late VAUGHAN [24 Aug. 1809], Henry, M.D., of Leicester and Wistow,
    co. Leic., 180 . ., Vol. XXV, fol. 280.
HALFORD, Sir Henry, Bart., K.H., M.D., of co. Worc. Arms, Augmentation and
    Supporters, [19 May 1827] Vol. XXXVI, fols. 272 and 274.
„ . . . ., of Chertsey, co. Surrey, and Laleham, co. Middx., 181 . ., Vol.
    XXXI, fol. 376.
HALIBURTON, Baron, 1898, Vol. LXX, fol. 241 ; Supporters, fol. 243.
HALIFAX, Baron [13 Dec. 1700] (MOUNTAGUE), of co. York. Supporters, 17 . . .,
    Vol. V, fol. 27.
HALL, John, Mayor of Norwich, co. Norf., 30 April 1716, Vol. VI, fol. 249.
  „ John, of London, Haberdasher of Small Wares, and of Horton Hall, Bucks.
    (2 Nov.) 1720, Vol. VII, fol. 27 ; Add. MS. 14,830, fol. 149.
HALL, late SHEPPARD, William, of Longfield, co. Kent ; Chatwell and Hopton
    Wafers, Shropsh. ; and Ridlington, co. Rutland, nephew of William Hall,
    172 . ., Vol. VII, fol. 448.
HALL, Thomas, of Moundsmere and Preston Candover, Hampsh., 1767, Vol. XI,
    fol. 232. (Berry.)
  „ William, of Skirwith, co. Cumberland, and St. Stephen Coleman, London,
    18 May 1768, Vol. XI, fol. 280.
HALL to WHARTON, William, of Gilling and Skelton, co. York, and Ireland, son
    of [J. W.] HALL STEVENSON, 180 . ., Vol. XXIV, fol. 342.
  „ to WHARTON, Maj.-Gen. James, of Skelton Hall, co. York, son of [J. W.] HALL
    STEVENSON, 180 . ., Vol. XXIV, fol. 344. [See Burke's Landed Gentry.]
HALL, ..., wife of KING, of Bridgetown, Barbados. Arms for self and descen-
    dants. (See also HALL-DARE-.) 181 . ., Vol. XXIX, fols. 132 and 133.
  „ John, s. of Gen. Thomas, s. of Joseph, of City of Durham, and sister
    Elizabeth Anne [?], only dau. of Gen. Thomas Hall, of Weston Colville,
    co. Camb., and co. Durham, (Elizabeth, only sister of the grantee, was
    wife of John MORSE, of Mount Ida, co. Norf.) [and their respective
    descendants]. Match, [1815] Vol. XXIX, fol. 214.
  „ John, Charles, Elizabeth, Charlotte, Anne, Lydia, natural children of
    John Hall, 181 . ., Vol. XXIX, fols. 234 to 244. (See also 187 . .,
    Vol. LVIII, fol. 142 ; name (and Arms of) HALL in lieu of PARKER,
    and BULLOCK to HALL.)
  „ William, sable, two bars ermine and in chief a lion's head erased between
    2 chaplets or (Her. Coll.), 172 . ., Vol. VII, fol. 448.
  „ ? James, C.B., Post-Capt., R.N., 181 . ., Vol. XXIX, fol. 388.
  „ Jane, wife of Sir Edward CODRINGTON, of Sutton Park, co. Bedf., and
    Jamaica, 182 . ., Vol. XXXIII, fol. 102.
  „ Jasper Taylor, of Sutton Park, co. Bedf., and his aunt Jane, Lady
    CODRINGTON. (See last entry.) 182 . ., Vol. XXXIII, fol. 102.
  „ Sir Benjamin, of Abercarne, co. Monmouth, and Wales (afterwards Baron
    LLANOVER), 182 . . .* Vol. XXXIV, fol. 380. (Crisp, IV, p. 31.)
  „ . . . ., of Trinidad, 182 . ., Vol. XXXIII, fol. 333.
  „ Robert Westley, of Ilford Lodge, co. Essex, 182 . ., Vol. XXXIV, fol. 94.
  .„ „ „ of Ilford Lodge, co. Essex, 1823, Vol. XXXIV, fols. 96 and 100.
HALL-DARE, „ „ of Ilford Lodge, co. Essex, and Wyefield, Cranbrook, co. Kent,
    1823, Vol. XXXIV, fol. 100.
HALL, late O'TOOLE, ..., of Holly Bush, co. Staff., 183 . ., Vol. XL, fol. 153.
  „ late ADCOCK, Thomas, of Workington and Carlisle, co. Cumberland, 183 . .,
    Vol. XLI, fols. 343 and 344.
HALL, Thomas Dickinson, of Whatton Manor and Broughton, co. Nottingham,
    183 . ., Vol. XLIII, fol. 70. (Crisp, VI, p. 108.)
  „ John, of Northscough, Penn Whitton, co. Cumberland ; Rock House, Walton-
    on-the-Hill, co. Lanc. ; and Mollance, Stewarty of Kirkcudbright, Scotland,
    183 . ., Vol. XLIII, fol. 341.

HALL [William John], M.A., Rector of St. Benet, Paul's Wharf, London, 184 . .,
    Vol. XLVI, fol. 260.
   „   ? Capt. James, Surgeon, R.N., 185 . ., Vol. LI, fol. 14.
HALL-SAY, Richard, of West Derby and Pennington Hall, co. Lanc., and
    Swaffham, co. Norf., 185 . ., Vol. LI, fol. 274.
HALL, Sir John, K.C.B., M.D., Insp.-Gen. of Hospitals, 185 . ., Vol. LII, fol. 167.
HALL, late BULLOCK, William Henry, of Westley and Six Mile Bottom, co. Camb.,
    187 . ., Vol. LVIII, fol. 142.
HALL, Sir Charles, Knt. [12 Dec. 1873], Vice-Chanc. [11 Nov. 1873], of London,
    and Manchester, 187 . ., Vol. LVIII, fol. 306.
   „   George, of Elm Park Road, Chelsea, London, 1884, Vol. LXII, fol. 278.
   „   Sir John, Knt., of Hororata, New Zealand, 1884,* Vol. LXII, fol. 253.
   „   P. C., of Purston Hall, Fetherstone, co. York, 1889,* Vol. LXV, fol. 158.
HALL-HALL, Charles Alexander (s. of Alexander), of Hawkhurst, co. Sussex,
    18 . . ., Vol. LXXI, fol. . . . .
HALL, John (s. of John), of Hale Grange, Altrincham, co. Chester, 18 . . ., Vol.
    LXXI, fol. . . . .
HALLAM, ..., of Westminster, 178 . ., Vol. XVI, fol. 295 ; and Bedford Place,
    London, 181 . ., Vol. XXVII, fol. 191.
HALLAMSHIRE, The Cutlers of, 1875, Vol. LIX, fol. 153.
HALLETT, Sir James, Knt. (s. of Stephen), of Crewkerne, co. Somerset, and to
    the descendants of his father, 19 Oct. 1722, Vol. VII, fol. 117 ; Add.
    MS. 14,830, fol. 144. (Berry.)
HALLETT after HUGHES, Charles, M.A., of Heghnam, co. Kent, Vicar of
    Patrixbourne, co. Kent, 182 . ., Vol. XXXIV, fol. 56.
HALLETT, ..., of Brighton, co. Sussex, 185 . ., Vol. L, fol. 116.
   „   of Brighton, co. Sussex, 185 . ., Vol. L, fol. 116.
HALLIDAY to TOLLEMACHE, Rear-Adm., of Leasowes, Shropsh., and Castlemains,
    co. Kirkcudbright, Scotland, 182 . ., Vol. XXXII, fol. 351.
HALLIDAY, Sir Andrew, Knt., M.D., Physician to the Forces, of Bemgall, Defusdale,
    co. Dumfries, Scotland, 182 . ., Vol. XXXIV, fol. 147.
HALLIFAX, ..., of Kenilworth, co. Warw. ; Springthorpe, co. Linc. ; and
    Mansfield, co. Nottingham, 17 . . ., Vol. XVII, fol. 49.
HALLIWELL, James (s. of James), of Broomfield, Bury, co. Lanc., and Lincoln's
    Inn, London, 1817 (of Brasenose Coll., Oxf.), 181 . ., Vol. XXXI, fol. 52.
HALLIWELL to PHILLIPPS, James Orchard, of Broadway, &c., co. Worc., 2nd s. of
    Thomas, of Brixton Hill, co. Surrey, [1872] Vol. LVIII, fols. 94 to 96.
HALLOWELL-CAREW, Vice-Adm. Sir Benjamin, K.C.B., of co. Surrey, and
    Orpington, co. Kent, 182 . . ., Vol. XXXVII, fols. 169 and 176.
   „   -CAREW, ..., of Beddington Park, co. Surrey, and Boston, America,
    [Adm. Sir Benjamin, G.C.B. (extra), 6 June 1831]. Supporters, 182 . .,
    Vol. XXXVII, fol. 239. [See Berry's Suppl, no date given.]
   „   -CAREW, Charles, Capt., R.N., of co. Surrey, 183 . ., Vol. XL, fol. 305.
    Supporters, 183 . ., Vol. XL, fol. 330.
   „   -CAREW, ... (a minor), of co. Surrey, 1849, Vol. XLIX, fol. 160.
HALLOWES, Brabazon, s. of Thomas, of Dethick Hall, Ashover, co. Derby, [14 April
    1766] Vol. XI, fol. 154.
HALSBURY, Baron, of co. Devon. Supporters, 1886, Vol. LXIII, fol. 196.
HALSEY, ..., of Great Gaddesden Parsonage, co. Hertf., 16 . . ., Vol. II,
    fol. 655.
HALSEY, late WHATELY, Joseph T., of co. Hertf. Escutcheon of pretence, 180 . .,
    Vol. XXIII, fol. 190.
HALSEY, Edmund, J. P., of Deadmans Place, co. Surrey, 30 Oct. 1716, Vol. VI,
    fols. 277 and 286 ; (alteration 15 April 1717) Her. and Geneal., I, p. 118.
HALSEY after MOORE, Rev. John F., of Swinhoe, [?] Bucks., and Great Gaddesden,
    co. Hertf., 182 . ., Vol. XXXII, fol. 229.
HALSEY, T. F., of Great Gaddesden and Hempstead, co. Hertf. Quartering,
    . . . ., 1890, Vol. LXV, fol. 204.

HALSTED to POOLE, ..., of Lymm, co. Chester, 178 . ., Vol. XV, fol. 115.
HALSTED, late HOLGATE, ... (Spr.), of Habergham Eaves and Rowley, Burnley, co. Lanc., 184 . ., Vol. XLVIII, fol. 152.
HAMBLEDON, Viscountess, 1895, Vol. LXVIII, fols. 299 and 300.
HAMBRO, ..., of Roehampton, co. Surrey, 18 . . ., Vol. XLIX, fol. 489.
HAMBROUGH, HOLDEN, wife of, of Pipewell, co. Northampton. Impaled Arms, 181 . ., Vol. XXVI, fol. 252.
HAMILTON (see PATOUN), ..., of Cambuslang, Scotland, 177 . ., Vol. XII, fol. 162.
  „   George Robinson, of St. James, co. Cornwall, Jamaica, 13 July 1775, Vol. XIII, fol. 108.
  „   Lord [Anne]. Arms of EDWARDS assigned, [1733] Vol. VIII, fol. 170ᵇ.
  „   Sir William, K.B. [15 Jan. 1772]. Supporters, 177 . ., Vol. XII, fol. 130.
[„   Dame Emma, of Clarges Street, Piccadilly, co. Middx., widow of the Right Hon. Sir William Hamilton, K.B. Warrant dated 29 Sept. last. Grant 1806. (Geneal. Mag., I, p. 168.)]
HAMILTON, late KELSO, Alexander H., H.E.I.C.S., of Topsham, co. Devon, and Hallerhurst, co. Ayr, Scotland, 181 . ., Vol. XXVII, fol. 87.
HAMILTON, Lieut.-Gen. Sir John, Bart. [21 Dec. 1814], of Woodbroke, co. Tyrone, Ireland, Governor of Duncannon Fort. Augmentation, ... [1814], Vol. XXVIII, fol. 425.
  „   Major Sir James John, [2nd] Bart., of Woodbroke, co. Tyrone, Ireland, and co. Devon. Supporters, [1835 or 36], 183 . ., Vol. XLI, fol. 270.
HAMILTON, late WARD, ..., of Winston (co. Chester), co. Suff., 181 . ., Vol. XXXI, fols. 93, 95 and 97.
HAMILTON to CAMPBELL, Catherine Eleanor, widow of Hamilton, of Asknish, co. Argyll, Scotland (died s.p.), 181 . ., Vol. XXXI, fol. 162.
HAMILTON, ..., M.D., of London and Edinburgh, 182 . ., Vol. XXXV, fol. 142.
HAMILTON, late JOHNSON, Charles, of the City of Chester, 183 . ., Vol. XL, fol. 58.
HAMILTON-RUSSELL (Viscount BOYNE), of Durham, 18 . . ., Vol. XLIX, fol. 352.
HAMILTON, late CROSSE, . . . '., of Howden, Tiverton, co. Devon, and Tyne Court, Broomfield, co. Somerset, 182 . ., Vol. XXXIII, fol. 113.
HAMILTON-GRACE, S., of Knole House, Trent, co. Sussex, 1880, Vol. LXI, fol. 11.
HAMILTON-HOARE, H. N. (Banker), of London, 1882, Vol. LXII, fol. 18.
HAMLET [Thomas], of [co. Middx.], Denham Court, Bucks, and Bentley Hall, co. Essex [19 Jan. 1816], Vol. XXIX, fol. 182. [Crisp, Fragm. Geneal., XIII, p. 21.]
HAMLYN, late HAMMETT, Sir James, Bart. [7 July 1795] [of Clovelly, co. Devon, and Wales], 179 . ., Vol. XIX, fol. 65.
HAMLYN to [before ?] WILLIAMS, James [2 Mar. 1798], s. of James, 1st Bart., of Clovelly Court, co. Devon, and Edwinsford, co. Carnarvon, Wales, 17 . . ., Vol. XX, fol. 117.
HAMLYN, now PRUST, ..., of Wolfardisworthy, co. Devon, [1808] Vol. XXIV, fol. 426.
HAMLYN, F., of Manton House, Oakham, co. Rutland, 1889, Vol. LXV, fol. 84.
HAMLYN (see CALMADY), ..., 1898.
HAMMERSLEY, ..., of Roxby and Broughton, co. Linc., and Pall Mall, St. James', London, 180 . ., Vol. XXII, fol. 197. (See also 16 . . ., II, 522, and II, 89, Brooke's Chaos.)
HAMMERSLEY, late SPODE, of Fenton Hall, co. Staff., and Ash, co. Surrey, [1828] Vol. XXXVII, fol. 27.
HAMMERSMITH, Parish of, [23 Dec.] 1897, Vol. LXX, fol. 71. (Geneal. Mag., III, p. 501.)
HAMMET, ..., of Castle Malgwyn, Wales, and Wilton, co. Somerset, 1803, Vol. XXII, fol. 98.
HAMMETT, Richard (?), M.A., of Clovelly, co. Devon, 1790, Vol. XVII, fol. 390.
HAMMETT to HAMLYN, Sir James, 1st Bart., of Clovelly, co. Devon (see above), 1795, Vol. XIX, fol. 65.

HAMMICK, Stephen Love, M.R.C.S., of London, 183 . ., Vol. XL, fol. 204.

HAMMOND, now LUCY, Rev. John, of Charlecote, co. Warw., 1787, Vol. XVI, fol. 229.

HAMMOND-CHAMBERS, ..., of Great Marlow, Bucks., 185 . ., Vol. LIII, fol. 235.

HAMMOND before SAMPSON, ..., of Battle and Ninfield, co. Sussex, 181 . ., Vol. XXVI, fol. 292.

., before SPENCER, ..., of Richmond, co. Surrey, and London, 181 . ., Vol. XXX, fol. 303.

HAMMOND, Baron, Edmund Hammond, of Kirk Ella Hall, co. York. Arms and Supporters, [5 March] 1874, Vol. LIX, fol. 5.

„ Basil Edward, M.A., Camb., 18 . . . ., Vol. LXXI, fol. . . . .

HAMOND, Edward, M.A., Richard and Nicholas, of South Wotton, co. Norf., 5 July 1698, Vol. IV, fol. 269.

., Sir Andrew [Snape], Knt. [15 Jan. 1779], Capt., R.N., of Holly Grove, nr. Windsor, Berks. [Bart., 18 Dec. 1783], 178 . ., Vol. XV, fol. 227.

., [Adm.] Sir Graham Eden, [2nd] Bart., G.C.B. [5 July 1855], of Norton Lodge, Isle of Wight, and Hampsh., co. Middx. and Scotland, 1st s. of [Sir Andrew Snape], 185 . ., Vol. LI, fols. 297 and 337.

HAMOND to HAMOND-GRAEME, Vice-Adm. [Sir Andrew Snape, 3rd] Bart., of Hampsh., co. Middx. and Scotland [Surname and Arms of Graeme, 3 April 1873], Vol. LVIII, fol. 239.

HAMPDEN [Renn Dickson], Bp. of Hereford [1847 to 1868], of co. Hereford, 184 . ., Vol. XLIX, fols. 3 and 4.

HAMPDEN, late HOBART, [5th] Earl of Buckinghamshire, of Bucks. and co. Devon ?, [Roy. Lic., 5 Oct. 1824], Vol. XXXV, fol. 31.

HAMPDEN after HOBART, [6th Earl], of Bucks. and co. Devon, [Roy. Lic., 5 Aug. 1878] Vol. LX, fol. 149.

HAMPDEN or HAMPTON, ... Quartering to Anne FEAKE, 22 Nov. 1774, Vol. XIII, fol. 38.

HAMPDEN after CAMERON OF LOCHIEL, ..., of Scotland, and Bucks., 186 . ., Vol. LVI, fol. 142.

HAMPDEN, Viscount, of Bucks., 1895,* Vol. LXVIII, fol. 258.

HAMSTEAD, Capt., R.N., of Tring, co. Hertf., 18 . . ., Vol. XXV, fol. 410.

HANBEY, [Mary] CASLON, widow of, of London, 17 . . ., Vol. XVII, fol. 65.

HANBURY to LEIGH, ..., of Wales, [1797] Vol. XIX, fol. 430.

HANBURY before TRACY, ... [10 Dec. 1798], of Toddington, co. Glouc., and Pontypool, co. Monmouth, 17 . . ., Vol. XX, fol. 275.

HANBURY-TRACY, ..., Baron SUDELEY [12 July 1838], of co. Glouc., and Pontypool, co. Monmouth, 183 . ., Vol. XLIII, fol. 99.

„ -TRACY, late LEIGH, ... [30 Mar. 1839], of co. Glouc., and Pontypool, co. Monmouth, 183 . ., Vol. XLIII, fol. 349.

HANBURY after BATEMAN, ... [4 Feb. 1837], Baron BATEMAN [30 Jan. 1837], of Hereford, co. Northampton, 183 . ., Vol. XLIII, fol. 53. Quarterly, fol. 84 [? Vol. XLII].

HANBURY-BATEMAN-KINCAID-LENOX, ..., with designations "of Woodhead and Kincaid" [28 Jan. 1862], of Woodhead and Kincaid, co. Stirling, Scotland. [Surname and Arms], 186 . ., Vol. LIV, fol. 234.

HANBURY, Daniel Bell, of Clapham Common, co. Surrey ; Ware, co. Hertf. ; Stamford Hill and Mark Lane, London ; and Llanfihangel, Pontymoyle, co. Monmouth, 18 . . ., Vol. LVII, fol. 284.

HANCOCK, ..., C.B., Capt., R.N., 182 . ., Vol. XXXII, fol. 41.

HANCOCK to LIEBENROOD, [John], Capt., R.N., of Berks. (s. of Rear-Adm.), [14 Jan. 1865] Vol. LV, fol. 288.

HANCOCKS, ..., of Cookley House, Wolverley, co. Worc., 184 . ., Vol. XLVII, fol. 384.

HANCOX, George, M.A., of Wellesbourn, co. Warw., and Dusby, co. Worc., 1812, Vol. XXVII, fol. 306.

HAND, George, of Avalon, Green Lanes, Hornsey, London, 1893, Vol. LXVII, fol. 151.

HANDASYDE after SHARP, ..., of Morpeth and Long Horsley, co. Northumberland. Quarterly Arms, [1808] Vol. XXIV, fol. 368.

HANDY-CHURCH, ..., of Acton, co. Middx., and Chigwell, co. Essex, 183 . ., Vol. XXXIX, fol. 184.

HANFORD, Col. John Compton, of Woollas Hall, Eckington, co. Worc., 1893, Vol. LXVII, fol. 187.

HANKEY, Henry, of Hepden and Cherton, co. Chester, 26 Nov. 1723, Vol. VII, fol. 225 (? 220).

HANKEY after ALERS, William, of London, 181 . ., Vol. XXIX, fol. 216.

HANKIN-TURVIN, ..., of Stanstead Abbots, co. Hertf., 183 . ., Vol. XLIII, fol. 316.

HANKINSON, Robert C., of Red Lodge, Hampsh., 1882,* Vol. LXI, fol. 321. (Berry's Suppl.)

HANMER, ..., of Hanmer, Wales, 16 . . ., Vol. I, fol. 220.

HANMER to HERVEY, Thomas, of Wales, 1st Foot Guards, 1774, Vol. XII, fol. 286.

HANNEN, Sir James, Knt., Chief Justice of the Queen's Bench, London, [1868] Vol. LVII, fol. 66.

HANNING, ..., of Dillington House, co. Somerset, [1825] Vol. XXXV, fol. 186.

HANNING to LEE, ..., of Orleigh Court, co. Devon, 182 . ., Vol. XXXV, fol. 187.

HANSARD, ..., of Norwich, co. Norf., and Gower Street, London. Quarterly Arms, [1809] Vol. XXV, fol. 268.

  „   Victor Hansard (formerly YORKNEY), of Silverleys, Port Talbot, co. Glamorgan, Wales, 1898, Vol. LXX, fol. 257.

HANSON (see HORTON), of Toothill, co. York. (Match), 172 . ., Vol. VII, fol. 533.

  „   William Henry (Fellow of Caius Coll., Camb.), of Beothorpe, co. Nottingham, 182 . ., Vol. XXXVIII, fol. 333.

  „   Benjamin, of Holborn, London, and Monk Friston, co. York (s. of Thomas, s. of Benjamin, both of Wakefield), to take Name and Arms of INGLISH only, 1800, Vol. XXI, fol. 35.

HANSON-INGLISH, Benjamin, of St. Mary-le-Strand, London, 183 . ., Vol. XL, fol. 301.

HANSON, C. A., of 49, Holland Park, London, 1896,* Vol. LXIX, fol. 84.

  „   Sir Reginald, Bart., of London, (28 May) 1887, Vol. LXIV, fol. 27.

  „   Mary, only dau. of Robert Hanson, of Normanton, co. York, wife of Sir Thomas Gery CULLUM, Bath King of Arms and Bart., 17 Aug. 1793, Vol. XVIII, fol. . . . . (Misc. G. et H., 2nd S., V, p. 72, plate.)

HANWAY (late BALACK), Hanway, ..., of the Middle Temple, London, 7 Sept. 1775, Vol. XIII, fol. 123.

HARBEN, Henry, of Seaford Lodge, Hampstead, London, s. of Henry, of St. George's, Bloomsbury, London, 1877, Vol. LIX, fol. 317. (Berry's Suppl.)

HARBORD, Sir William Morden, K.B. [28 May 1744], of co. Norf. [Bart. 22 Mar. 174⅞], 17 . ., Vol. IX, fol. 119.

  „   Baron SUFFIELD, [21 Aug. 1786, Sir] Harbord, of co. Norf., 178 . ., Vol. XVI, fol. 185.

HARCOURT, ..., of co. Oxf. (Match) Arms, 16 . . ., Vol. II, fol. 686.

  „   . . . ., of Stanton-Harcourt, co. Oxf. (Match), 16 . . ., Vol. IV, fol. 171.

  „   Baron Harcourt [3 Sept. 1711], of co. Oxf. Supporters, 17 . ., Vol. V, fol. 451.

HARCOURT, late VENABLES-VERNON, Edward, of co. York and Derby, Archbp. of York, 2 Feb. 1831, Vol. XXXVIII, fol. 181. (Crisp, Fragm. Geneal., V, p. 65.)

HARDEN, ..., of Hadley, co. Middx., [1815] Vol. XXIX, fol. 9.

HARDING, ..., of South Molton and Torr Down, and Combe Martin, co. Devon, 185 . ., Vol. LII, fol. 158.
HARDING to NOTT, ..., of South Molton and Torr Down, and Combe Martin, co. Devon, 185 . ., Vol. LII, fol. 160.
HARDING, John (s. of Thomas), of Dowlais, co. Glamorgan, Wales, 186 . ., Vol. LIV, fol. 220.
  „ William, of Leamington, co. Warw., 1879, Vol. LX, fol. 251.
  „ Q. R., of St. Anne's Towers, Headingley, co. York, 1888, Vol. LXIV, fol. 323.
  „ Edward Colin (s. of Charles), of Salisbury, Mashonaland, South Africa, 1899, Vol. LXX, fol. 338.
  „ Rev. John Taylor (s. of John), of Pentwyn, co. Monmouth, 18 . . ., Vol. LXXI, fol. . . . .
  „ Capt., R.N. (s. of the Rector of Stanhope), Commander. Augmentation to descendants of grandfather, 180 . ., Vol. XXV, fol. 84.
  „ Capt., R.N., of the " San Florenzo " frigate [reference crossed through].
HARDINGE, 1. John, of King's Newton, par. of Melbourne, co. Derby, s. of Robert, s. of Sir Robert, Knt., s. of Nicholas, all of King's Newton aforesaid ; 2. Gideon, Vicar of Kingston, co. Surrey, brother of the said Robert ; and unto 3. Nicholas, of Hatton Garden, London, s. of Nicholas, lately decd., who was brother of Sir Robert aforesaid, 3 July 1711, Vol. V, fol. 428 ; Add. MS. 14,831, fol. 51. (Berry.)
HARDWICKE, Baron [28 Nov. 1733] (YORKE), of co. Camb. and Hertf. Supporters, Alteration, Arms, and Crest, 17 . . ., Vol. VIII, fol. 178.
  „ Hardwicke Lloyd, of Wales and The Grange, Tytherington, co. Glouc., 1880, Vol. LXI, fol. 63.
  „ Powell Lloyd, of Wales, and co. Glouc., 1880, Vol. LXI, fol. 63. (Berry's Suppl.)
HARDWIN, Capt. George Hardwin Gallenga, 18 . . ., Vol. LXXI, fol. . . . .
HARDY (after Sir Thomas MASTERMAN), Capt., H.M.S. " Victory," of Portisham, co. Dorset, 180 . ., Vol. XXIII, fol. 341.
  „ after COZENS, ..., of Letheringsett Hall, Norwich, co. Norf., 184 . ., Vol. XLVI, fol. 130.
HARDY, Edward, of Theakstone Hall, Bedale, co. York, and Huasco, in Chili, 184 . ., Vol. XLIX, fol. 329.
  „ Sir John, Bart. [23 Feb. 1876], s. of John, of Dunstall Hall, co. Staff., 1876, Vol. LIX, fol. 188.
  „ Col. E. A., of Oldfield Road, Clifton, Bristol, co. Glouc., 1894, Vol. LXVIII, fol. 55.
  „ Paul, gent., of 3, Serpentine Road, Regent's Park, London (? of Palace Gate), 1899, Vol. LXX, fol. 320.
HARE, late LEIGH, ... [1791], of Iver, Bucks. ; and Stow Hall and Stow Bardolph, co. Norf. [Bart., 14 Dec. 1818], 1814-15, Vol. XXVIII, fol. 5.
HARE, Nicholas, of Iver, Bucks. ; and Stow Hall and Stow Bardolph, co. Norf., 1545 [?], Vol. I, fol. 17.
  „ Nicholas, of Iver, Bucks. ; Stow Hall, and Stow Bardolph, co. Norf. ; and Homersfield, co. Suff., 1574 [?], Vol. II, fol. 498.
  „ Sir Ralph, 1613 [?], Vol. II [?], fol. 579.
HARE late HENLEY, John, of Docking, co. Norf. 17 . . ., Vol. XIV, fol. 63.
  „ late CHRISTIAN, Rev. Edward, B.D., of co. Norf. ; Workington and Ousby, co. Cumberland, 17 . . ., Vol. XX, fol. 259.
HARE-CLARGES, Maj.-Gen., C.B., of Coln St. Dennis, co. Glouc., 184 . ., Vol. XLVII, fol. 143.
HARE, Sir John [1st July 1840], Knt., of co. Glouc. ; London ; and Brislington and Springfield, co. Somerset, 184 . ., Vol. XLVII, fol. 184.
HARE, late NORMAN, reputed children of Hare, Bart., of Stow Bardolph, co. Norf., 186 . ., Vol. LV, fols. 200 and 201.

HARF, Charles John, M.D., of Beeston, Leeds, co. York : Etchingham, co. Sussex ; and London, 186 . ., Vol. LVI, fol. 318.

HAREWOOD, Baron of [9 July, 1790, Edwin Lascelles]. of co. York, 17 . .., Vol. XVII, fol. 254.

„ [Baron, 18 June 1796, Edward Lascelles]. of co. York, [1796] Vol. XIX, fol. 285.

HARFORD, ... of Bosbury, co. Hertf. Match, 180 . ., Vol. XXV, fol. 41.

HARFORD before BATTERSBY, ..., of co. Glouc., [1815] Vol. XXIX, fol. 97.

HARFORD to LYNE, ..., of Keynsham. co. Somerset, 182 . ., Vol. XXXII, fol. 121.

„ to LYNE, ..., of Lansdown Crescent, Bath, 182 . .. Vol. XXXVI. fol. 176.

HARGOOD, Vice-Adm. Sir William, K.C.B. [2 Jan. 1815], (G.C.B.) [13 Sept. 1831], of London, 181 . ., Vol. XXVIII, fol. 302. Supporters, 183 . ., Vol. XXXIX, fol. 138.

HARGRAVE after PAWSON, George, Morpeth, Newcastle, and Shawdon, co. Northumberland. Quarterly Arms, 181 . ., Vol. XXX, fol. 122.

HARGREAVES, Col. (Mil.) John, of Ormerod House and Bank Hall, co. Lanc., 1815, Vol. XXIX, fol. 45.

„ John, of Broad Oak, Blackburn, and Wheatley Lane, nr. Burnley, co. Lanc., 1833, Vol. XL, fol. 75.

„ John (Mayor), of Greensnook House, Bacup, co. Lanc., 1885, Vol. LXIII, fol. 51.

„ R. Tattersall, of Heap, Bury, co. Lanc., 1891,[c] Vol. LXVI, fol. 37.

HARINGTON to CHAMPERNOWNE, Arthur, of co. Devon. 20 Sept. 1774, Vol. XIII. fol. 9.

HARKER to ALDERSON, ..., of London, and co. York. (See Christopher Alderson and Burke's Armory.) [1811] Vol. XXVI. fol. 190.

HARKER, John, M.D., of co. Lanc., 187 . ., Vol. LVIII, fol. 244. (Berry's Suppl.)

HARLAND, Ann, widow of Rev. Henry GOODRICK, dau. and h. of Philip Harland, of co. York. Crest to the descendants of grandfather. Escutcheon of pretence, 180 . ., Vol. XXI, fols. 367 and 368.

HARLAND, late HOAR, William, of Middleton St. George, co. Durham, and Sutton Hall, co. York, 1824, Vol. XXXV, fol. 55.

„ late HOAR, Sir Charles, Bart., of Middleton St. George, co. Durham, 1827, Vol. XXXVI, fol. 226. (See Burke's Commoners, [I], 111, 194.)

HARLAND, Sir E. J., Bart., of Ireland (died s.p.), 1885,[*] Vol. LXIII, fol. 83.

HARLE, late ATKINSON, Thomas, of co. Northumberland, 180 . ., Vol. XXIV, fol. 387.

HARLECH, Baron [Ormsby-Gore]. Supporters, [14 Jan.] 1876, Vol. LIX, fol. 196.

HARLEY, ..., Earl of OXFORD and Earl MORTIMER [23 May 1711], of co. Hereford. Supporters, 17 . . ., Vol. VI, fol. 9.

HARLEY before RODNEY [4 Nov. 1805], Thomas James, of co. Hereford, s. of [the 3rd] Baron Rodney (4th Baron, died s.p.), 180 . ., Vol. XXIII, fol. 243.

HARLEY, late BICKERSTETH [14 Mar. 1853], Jane Elizabeth, Lady LANGDALE, widow [dau. of the 5th] Earl of OXFORD and MORTIMER. Arms impaled with Baron LANGDALE's Arms, [1853 ?] Vol. L, fol. 311.

„ late TELEKI, Count, H. R. Empire, naturalized Brit. subject, married Jane, dau. of Baron LANGDALE, 18 . . ., Vol. LIII, fol. 264.

HARLEY, Caroline, dau. of Edward, of Cleobury Mortimer, Shropsh., and wife of Joseph FARMER. (See FARMER.) 185 . ., Vol. LI, fol. 196.

HARMAN, David James, s. of Richard, decd., of The Paragon, Bath, co. Somerset, late Standard Bearer to the Hon. Corps of Gentlemen-at-Arms. To descendants of his father Richard, 1874, Vol. LIX, fol. 46. (Berry's Suppl.)

HARMER, F. W., of Cringleford, co. Norf., 1889, Vol. LXV, fol. 139.

HARNAGE, late BLACKMAN [13 Oct. 1821], Sir George, Bart. [8 Sept. 1821], of
Belswardyne, Shropsh., 182 . ., Vol. XXXIII, fol. 88.
HARPER (late) MAYOR, ..., of Stamford, co. Linc., 181 . ., Vol. XXVIII,
fol. 360.
HARPER after HOSKEN, Maj. (Mil.) John, of Davenham Lodge, co. Chester, and
Carines, co. Cornw., 181 . ., Vol. XXX, fol. 40.
HARPER, Thomas, of Plymouth, co. Devon, 1893,* Vol. LXVII, fol. 157.
HARPUR to CREWE, ..., of co. Derby, [1808] Vol. XXIV, fol. 424.
HARRATT, John James, of Green Bank House, Walton, co. Lanc., 18 . . ., Vol.
LVII, fol. 150.
HARRINGTON, Baron [20 Nov. 1729] (STANHOPE). Supporters, 17 . . ., Vol.
VIII, fol. 104.
　,, ..., of Rands [?], co. Leic. Match, 17 . . ., Vol. XI, fol. 150.
HARRIS, Charles, of the Middle Temple, and Oxford, 1699, Vol. IV, fol. 300.
HARRIS ROOPE to ROOPE, ..., of Bristol, co. Glouc., 22 July 1771, Vol. XII,
fol. 96.
HARRIS, Sir James, of the Close of Sarum, Wilts. Arms, 17 . . ., Vol. XIV,
fol. 88.
　,, Sir James, K.B. [24 Feb. 1779], of Wilts. Supporters, 17 . . ., Vol. XIV,
fol. 92.
　,, [Sir James, K.B.], Baron MALMESBURY [19 Sept. 1788], of Wilts.
Supporters, 17 . . ., Vol. XVII, fol. 135.
HARRIS after DONNITHORNE, of St. Agnes, co. Cornw., and Hayne, co. Devon.
Quarterly Arms, 17 . . ., Vol. XX, fol. 300.
HARRIS (GREATHED-), ..., of Baillie, co. Dorset, and co. York, 180 . ., Vol.
XXIII, fol. 389.
HARRIS to GREATHED, ..., of Uddens House and Baillie, co. Dorset, and
Kingston-upon-Hull, co York, 180 . ., Vol. XXIII, fol. 393.
　,, to NORRIS, ..., of Davy Hulme Hall, co. Lanc., 180 . ., Vol. XXV,
fol. 37.
HARRIS, Baron [11 Aug. 1815], (Gen. [George Harris]), of Belmont, co. Kent,
Seringapatam and Mysore, India. Augmentation, 181 . ., Vol. XXIX,
fol. 111 ; Supporters, Vol. XXIX, fol. 115.
　,, ..., (Spr.), of Rosewarne, co. Cornw., 181 . ., Vol. XXIX, fol. 323.
　,, ..., (Spr.), of Petham, co. Kent, 182 . ., Vol. XXXIII, fol. 282.
　,, ..., of Dursley, co. Glouc., 182 . ., Vol. XXXIV, fol. 331.
HARRIS-WILLIAMS, Orlando Harris, Sheriff of Pembroke, of Ivy Tower, 182 . .,
Vol. XXXIV, fol. 332.
HARRIS-ARUNDELL, William Arundell, of Lifton Park and Hayne, co. Devon,
Kenegie and Menadaroa, in Camborne, co. Cornw., 182 . ., Vol. XXXVII,
fols. 399 and 401.
HARRIS-BURLAND, ..., of co. Dorset and Glouc., 183 . ., Vol. XLI, fol. 77.
HARRIS, Sir William Cornwallis, Knt. [7 June 1844], Major, Bombay Engineers.
Arms with Canton, 184 . ., Vol. XLVII, fol. 219 ; to brother, without the
Canton, 184 . ., Vol. XLVII, fol. 220.
　,, ..., of Change Alley, London, and co. Surrey, 184 . ., Vol. XLVIII,
fol. 84.
　,, John Dove, M.P., J.P., of Leicester, 184 . ., Vol. XLIX, fol. 67 (see Burke).
　,, Joseph Westcotes, of St. Mary, Leicester, 185 . ., Vol. L, fol. 178.
　,, William George, of St. Mary, Leicester ; Middle Temple, London ; and
Melbourne, Victoria, 18 . . ., Vol. LIII, fol. 363.
　,, George David, of the Bahamas, Castlebar, Christchurch, for Bishopric of
Nassau, New Providence, Bahamas, 186 . ., Vol. LVII, fol. 123.
　,, Susanna, of Cusgarne in Gwennap, co. Cornw., wife of Sir F. M. WILLIAMS,
Bart., 1874, Vol. LIX, fol. 15.
　,, Alfred, of Oxton Hall, Tadcaster, co. York, and Welworth, co. Surrey. To
the descendants of Richard, his father, 1878, Vol. LX, fol. 4. (Berry's
Suppl.)

[HARRIS, Alfred, 23 May 1877 (descendants of Samuel Harris, of London, 1878).]
„ Capt. Claudius Shirley, 1892, Vol. LXVI, fol. 281.
„ H. J., of Bowden Hill House, Laycock, Wilts., 1891,* Vol. LXVI, fol. 155.
„ Nathaniel (s. of Abraham), of Pembridge Villas, London, 1892,* Vol. LXVII, fol. 77.
„ Walter H., C.M.G., of 12, Kensington Gore, London, 1889,* Vol. LXV, fol. 160.
HARRISON, George, Bluemantle Pursuivant of Arms, of St. John's, Westminster, 1768, Vol. XI, fol. 272. (Berry.)
HARRISON before ANDREW, Thomas, of co. Middx., 11 April 1796, Vol. XIX, fol. 221.
HARRISON to POWLES, ..., of Darlington and Cockerton, co. Durham. Match, [1808] Vol. XXIV, fol. 340.
„ to WAYNE, ... (minor), of Angrove Hall, co. York, 180 . ., Vol. XXV, fol. . . . . .
HARRISON, ..., of Denne Hill, co. Kent, 181 . ., Vol. XXVIII, fol. 274.
„ (see BECKETT), ..., of Leeds, co. York, 181 . ., Vol. XXX, fol. 9.
„ Robert, of Ripley, co. Surrey, 31 Mar. 1819, Vol. XXXI, fol. 190. (Berry's Appendix.)
HARRISON, late STEERE, Robert, of Ripley and Jayes, co. Surrey, 14 May 1819, Vol. XXXI, fol. 191. (Berry's Appendix.)
HARRISON, ..., of Weston Hall, Sheffield, co. York, 182 . ., Vol. XXXII, fol. 79.
HARRISON after ROGERS, Valentine, of London, O.M., 11th Foot (called Valentine LOTT), nephew of George Harrison, Clarenceux King of Arms, 182 . ., Vol. XXXII, fol. 301.
HARRISON, ..., of St. James', Westminster, [1825] Vol. XXXV, fol. 221.
HARRISON after SLATER, John Harrison, of Margate, co. Kent, and Shelswell, co. Oxf., 183 . ., Vol. XL, fol. 280.
HARRISON (ROGERS), formerly Rogers only, George, of Hendon, co. Middx.; Wrexham, co. Denbigh, Wales; and Linethwaite, St. Bees, co. Cumberland, 18 . . ., Vol. XLIV, fol. 54; 184 . ., Vol. XLVI, fol. 187.
HARRISON, late FALCON, John, of Whitehaven, co. Cumberland, 184 . ., Vol. XLVII, fol. 194.
HARRISON, ..., of Snelston Hall, co. Derby, 185 . ., Vol. L, fol. 338.
„ Joseph, of Galligreaves House, Blackburn, co. Lanc., 185 . ., Vol. LI, fol. 88.
„ William, F.S.A., of Green Bank, Grasmere, co. Westmorland, [1858] Vol. LIII, fol. 276.
„ . . . ., of Bellwood, Ripon, co. York, 186 . ., Vol. LV, fol. 290.
„ Gilbert, of Ingleton, co. York. Arms for his wife, Margaret BROOKE, 178 . ., Vol. XVI, fol. 322.
„ (see FRYER-HARRISON), 17 . . ., Vol. XX, fol. 222.
„ William John, of the Million Bank, London, s. of Samuel, of Eltham, co. Kent, and for Elizabeth HAINES, his wife, [1790] Vol. XVII, fol. 314.
„ Richardson, Remembrancer of First Fruits and Tenths, and Mary MOORE, his wife, [1809] Vol. XXV, fol. 175.
„ Thomas Moore, 180 . ., Vol. XXV, fol. 49.
„ . . . ., of Ripon and Welton House, co. York. (See BROADLEY.) 186 . ., Vol. LV, fol. 312.
„ James J. T., of Bury, co. Lanc., and Singleton Park, Kendal, co. Westmorland, 186 . ., Vol. LVI, fol. 130.
„ David, of Thompson's Cross, Stalybridge, co. Lanc., 18 . . ., Vol. LVII, fol. 254.
„ Isaac, of Belgrave, co. Leic., 187 . ., Vol. LVIII, fol. 180.
„ F. J. Hare, of Appletree, Quernmore, co. Lanc., 1892,* Vol. LXVII, fol. 8.
„ Thomas F., of King's Walden, co. Hertf., 1892,* Vol. LXVII, fol. 67.
HARRISON-BROADLEY, H. B., of Tickton Grange and Welton House, Brough, co. York, 1896, Vol. LXIX, fol. 172.

HARRISON-TOPHAM, Thomas, late of Weybridge, co. Surrey, 1896, Vol LXIX, fol. 51.

HARRISON, William Bealy, of Aldershawe, Lichfield, co. Staff., 189 . ., Vol. LXIX, fol. 28 ; and for his wife, Georgiana Charlotte, dau. of Peter BANCROFT, of Norbiton Park, Kingston-upon-Thames, 1899, Vol. LXIX, fol. 283.

„ Graeme, of Easthorpe House, Ruddington, co. Nottingham, and Peyton, V[a] [Victoria ?], 189 . ., Vol. LXXI, fol. 6.

HARROP after HULTON, ... [minor, 18 years], of Ashton-under-Lyne, co. Lanc. [8 Dec. 1866], Vol. LVI, fol. 158.

HARROWBY, Baron [20 May 1776] (RYDER), of co. Glouc. and Staff. Arms and Supporters, 177 . ., Vol. XIII, fol. 195.

HARRYSON to DARLEY, Richard, of co. York, 17 . . ., Vol. XX, fol. 177.

HART to THOROLD, ..., of Harmston, co. Linc., and Middle Temple, London, 182 . ., Vol. XXXII, fol. 16.

HART, late TULK, ...,of Hampstead, co. Middx., 183 . ., Vol. XXXIX, fol. 239.

HART, Lieut.-Col. Arthur Fitzroy, C.B., East Surrey Regiment, 1883,* Vol. LXII, fol. 145.

„ Sir Israel, of Ashleigh, Knighton, co. Leic., 1896, Vol. LXIX, fol. 40.

„ Sir Robert [K.C.M.G., 17 April 1882], G.C.M.G. [24 May 1889], [Bart.], 1893, Vol. LXVII, fol. 221 ; Supporters, fol. 247.

„ S. H., of Hillingdon House, Sutton, co. Surrey, 1890,* Vol. LXV, fol. 217.

HARTER to HATFIELD, ..., of Manchester, co. Lanc. ; Wakefield and Hatfield Hall, co. York, 181 . ., Vol. XXIX, fol. 404.

HARTER, James Collier, of Broughton House, Manchester, co. Lanc., 18 . . ., Vol. XLIV, fol. 246.

HARTHILL, John T., of The Manor House, Willenhall, co. Staff., 1896,* Vol. LXIX, fol. 164.

HARTHORNTHWAITE, late BRADSHAW, of Lower Lee, Over Wyresdale, co. Lanc., 18 . . ., Vol. LVII, fol. 152.

HARTLEY (EYRE), Winchcombe Henry, of London, 179 . ., Vol. XIX, fol. 27.

HARTLEY after EYRE, Winchcombe Henry, of Lincoln's Inn, London, 179 . ., Vol. XIX, fol. 61.

HARTLEY, ..., of Rose Hill, co. Cumberland. (See LEWTHWAITE impaling ARMISTEAD.) Match, 181 . ., Vol. XXIX, fol. 252.

„ John, of Catteral Hall, Giggleswick, co. York, 184 . ., Vol. XLV, fols. 303 and 315.

HARTLEY, late CAMPBELL, Leonard ?, of Middleton Lodge and Bedale, co. York, 184 . ., Vol. XLV, fol. 337.

HARTLEY, James, of Bishopwearmouth, co. Durham, and Smethwick, Harborne, co. Staff., 186 . ., Vol. LV, fol. 356.

HARTOPP, late BUNNEY, of co. Leic. Quarterly Arms, [1796] Vol. XIX, fol. 249.

HARTOPP (CRADOCK), ..., of Four Oaks Hall, co. Warw., 184 . ., Vol. XLIX, fols. 150 and 158.

HARTREE, ... of Lewisham, co. Kent, 1855, Vol. LI, fol. 239.

HARTSHORN, William, Capt. in the Army, 186 . ., Vol. LV, fol. 222.

HARTWELL (see MESSENGER), ..., of Tamworth, co. Staff., and Warw., 17 . . ., Vol. XI, fol. 25.

„ . . . ., of London, Exmouth and Plymouth, co. Devon, [1803] Vol. XXII, fol. 112.

HARVEY, Tobiah, of Womersley, co. York, 1688, Vol. IV, fol. 18. (Berry.)

„ John, of Womersley, co. York, 1690, Vol. IV, fol. 71. (Berry.)

„ Samuel, of Womersley, co. York, 1690, Vol. IV, fol. 71. (Berry.)

HARVEY before HAWKE, Edward, [eldest] s. of [the 2nd] Baron Hawke, of co. York. Quarterly Arms, 17 . . ., Vol. XX, fol. 218.

HARVEY, Robert, s. of John, of Bridgwater and Hinton St. George, co. Somerset, 178 . ., Vol. XV, fol. 197.

HARVEY after BATESON, (Sir) Robert, Bart., of co. Lanc., 1788, Vol. XVII, fol. 15.

HARVEY, ..., of London ; Midmar, co. Aberdeen, Scotland ; and Isle of Grenada, 179 . ., Vol. XVII, fol. 242.

HARVEY, late RAE, ..., of Grenada, 17 . . ., Vol. XVII, fol. 424.

„ late DONALD, ..., of Midmar, co. Aberdeen, Scotland, and Grenada, 17 . . ., Vol. XVII, fol. 426.

„ late ABERDEIN, John, 17 . . ., Vol. XVII, fol. 428.

HARVEY, Vice-Adm. Sir Henry, K.B. [8 Jan. 1800]. Arms and Supporters, 1800, Vol. 20 H., fol. 29.

„ Thomas, of Finchley, co. Middx., and Mullenan, co. Londonderry, Ireland, 1800, Vol. XXI, fol. 97. (Crisp, I, p. 6.)

„ John Springitt, of Eastry and Dene Court, co. Kent, 180 . ., Vol. XXI, fol. 349.

„ John Springett, of the Middle Temple, London, and Eastry and Dene Court, co. Kent. Augmentation, 1802, Vol. XXII [?], fol. 227.

„ . . . ., of Winipole, co. Camb., 181 . ., Vol. XXVI, fol. 169.

HARVEY to NORTON, ..., reputed s. of Lord GRANTLEY, of Wonersh, co. Surrey, 181 . ., Vol. XXVII, fol. 456.

HARVEY, ..., Post.-Capt., R.N., C.B., of Wordwell, co. Suff., 181 . ., Vol. XXIX, fol. 228.

„ Robert, of Catton and Norwich, co. Norf., 181 . ., Vol. XXX, fol. 358.

„ Lieut.-Col. Sir Robert John, Knt., of Thorpe Hall, co. Norf. Peninsula augmentation, 181 . ., Vol. XXX, fol. 374.

HARVEY, late LEE, Margaret, reputed dau. of Major Harvey, late RAE, his wife, of Castle Semple, co. Renfrew, Scotland, 182 . ., Vol. XXXII, fol. 235.

HARVEY, Charles, of Brandon Park, co. Norf., Recorder of Norwich, 182 . ., Vol. XXXIV, fol. 265.

HARVEY to SAVILL-ONLEY, Onley, of Brandon Park, co. Norf., and Stisted Hall, co. Essex, 182 . ., Vol. XXXIV, fol. 267.

HARVEY, Adm. Sir Eliab, G.C.B. [11 Jan. 1825], 182 . ., Vol. XXXV, fol. 132.

„ Richard, of St. Dye, Gwennap, co. Cornw., 183 . ., Vol. XLII, fol. 37.

HARVEY-BONNELL, ... (Spr.), of Pelling, par. of Old Windsor, Berks., 184 . ., Vol. XLV, fol. 146.

HARVEY, Sir Robert Bateson, Bart. [28 Nov. 1868], of Langley Park, Bucks., 18 . . ., Vol. LVII, fol. 60.

„ John, of Leigh Woods, Long Ashton, co. Somerset, and Clifton Villa, Clifton, Bristol, 1885,* Vol. LXIII, fol. 21.

„ Robert, ..., of Trenouth, co. Cornw., and 1, Palace Gate, London, 1890, Vol. LXV, fol. 230.

„ Charles Pigott (3rd s. of Charles), of Sudborough House and Guilsborough House, co. Northampton, 18 . ., Vol. LXXI, fol. . . . .

HARWARD, late BLAKE, Rev. Charles, of Wales (of Woodstock, co. Oxf., and Hayne, co. Devon), 1816, Vol. XXIX, fol. 366.

HARWOOD, Henry (s. of John), of Crowfield Hall, co. Suff., and Little Chelsea, co. Middx., 13 Aug. 1722, Vol. VII, fol. 84 ; Add. MS. 14,381, fol. 104.

„ . . . . Quarterly with HILL and NOEL [William, 2nd, and Richard, 3rd, son of the 1st Baron BERWICK], of Shropsh., [19 Mar. 1824] Vol. XXXIV, fols. 300 and 302.

„ Edward, of Bath, co. Somerset, and Shrewsbury, Shropsh., 18 . ., Vol. XLIX, fol. 348.

„ Henry Harwood, late PENNY, Bar. of the Middle Temple, London, and of Chiswick, co. Middx., 185 . ., Vol. L, fol. 313.

„ . . . ., of Gorsefield, Eccles, co. Lanc., Mayor of Salford, 187 . ., Vol. LVIII, fol. 353.

„ Edward Woodhouse, of Olveston, co. Glouc., 1884, Vol. LXII, fol. 305. (Berry's Suppl.)

„ Sir J. J., of Broughton, co. Lanc., 1891, Vol. LXVI, fol. 152.

„ Samuel, of Battisford Hall, Needham Market, co. Suff., 1889,* Vol. LXV, fol. 9.

HARWOOD, Henry, and to the descendants of his father John, late of the City of London, Merchant, by Catherine, dau. of John MIDLETON, of Twickenham, co. Middx., sometime Sergt.-at-Arms, House of Commons. 1772.

HASE to LOMBE, John, of Great Melton, co. Norf. Quarterly Arms, 1750, Vol. IX, fol. 367. (Berry.)

HASELFOOT after PASKE, Theophilus, of New Wandsworth, co. Surrey, and Bath, co. Somerset, 186 . ., Vol. LV, fol. 144.

HASELL, Edward, of co. Cumberland, 1699, Vol. IV, fol. 258.

HASKER, ..., of Woburn Place, London. Canton for services, 180 . ., Vol. XXV, fol. 102.

HASLAM, Sir A. S., of West Bank, co. Derby, 1891,* Vol. LXVI, fol. 71.

HASLEDINE, ..., of Shropsh., Mayor of Shrewsbury, 183 . ., Vol. XLIII, fol. 177.

HASLER, ..., of Bognor and Shripney, co. Sussex, 182 . ., Vol. XXXII, fol. 30.

HASSARD to SHORT (Lieut.-Col.), of Edlington, co. Linc., 179 . ., Vol. XVIII, fol. 283.

  ,, to SHORT, Richard Samuel, of Great Bealings, co. Suff., and Edlington, co. Linc., 180 . ., Vol. XXIV, fol. 259.

HASSELL, John (Robert PROUS, of Wragsby ; John, of St. G. W. F., added in pencil), of Cholesbury, Bucks., 181 . ., Vol. XXX, fol. 345.

  ,, Peter, of The Laurels, Iron Acton, co. Glouc., 186 . ., Vol. LVI, fol. 95.

  ,, to OGDEN, Peter, of The Laurels, Iron Acton, and Bristol, co. Glouc., 186 . ., Vol. LVI, fol. 105.

HASTINGS (Baron RAWDON), ..., of co. York [? Name and Arms of Hastings, 10 Feb. 1790], 17 . ., Vol. XVII, fol. 198.

  ,, Lieut.-Gen. Sir, nat. s. of Earl of HUNTINGDON, 180 . ., Vol. XXIII, fol. 296.

  ,, [Lieut.-Gen. Sir] Charles, Bart. [28 Feb. 1806], 180 . ., Vol. XXIV, fol. 107; 180 . ., Vol. XXV, fol. 388 ?.

  ,, [William, of Hinton, co. Northampton, 10 July 1685 (Misc. G. et H., I, p. 322)].

HASWELL, John (Solicitor), of Bishop Wearmouth, co. Durham, 1883,* Vol. LXII, fol. 81. (Berry's Suppl.)

HATCH, Gen. William Sparkes, of co. Sussex, 1882, Vol. LXII, fol. 31. (Berry's Suppl.)

HATFEILD (late HARTER), John, s. of John, of co. Lanc. and York, 180 . ., Vol. XXIX, fol. 404.

  ,, late MARSHALL, of Laughton-en-le-Morthen and Doncaster, co. York, [1833] Vol. XL, fol. 52.

  ,, late GOSSIP, Randall, of Thorp Arch Hill, co. York, 184 . ., Vol. XLVII, fol. 242.

HATHERELL, ..., of Ardwick, co. Lanc., and Hawkesbury, co. Glouc., 181 . ., Vol. XXX, fol. 325.

HATHERLY, ..., M.D., Surgeon, R.N., of Plymouth and Bideford, co. Devon, 18 . . ., Vol. LIII, fol. 171.

HATSELL, Sir Henry, Knt., Sergt.-at-Law, Baron of the Exch., of co. Devon, 28 April 1708, Vol. V, fol. 296. (Berry.)

HAUGHTON, late ARNOLD, Henry, of co. Kent, 17 . ., Vol. XX, fol. 84.

HAUSSONILLIER to FRIST, ..., of Totnes, co. Devon, and London, 17 . . ., Vol. XX, fol. 336.

HAVELOCK, ..., of Guisborough, co. York, and Izon House, Henbury, co. Glouc., 1815, [?] Vol. XXX, fol. 244.

HAVELOCK to HAVELOCK-ALLAN, Sir Henry M., Bart., of co. Durham, 1880, Vol. LX, fol. 377.

HAVERSHAM, Baron [4 May 1696] (Sir John THOMPSON), Bart., of Bucks. Supporters, 16 . . ., Vol. IV, fol. 215.

HAVILAND-BURKE, ..., of Berks., 18 . . ., Vol. XXXI, fol. 48.

  ,, -BURKE, ..., of Bridgwater and Gundenham, Langford Budville, co. Somerset, 186 . ., Vol. LVI, fol. 97.

HAWKE, Sir Edward, K.B. [17 Nov. 1747], s. of Edward, of co. York. Arms, 17 . . ., Vol. IX, fol. 253 ; Supporters, ..., 17 . . ., Vol. IX, fol. 257.
„ Baron, [20 May 1776] ([Adm.] Edward, K.B.), of co. York. Supporters, [1776] Vol. XIII, fol. 224.
HAWKE after HARVEY, Edward, of co. York, 17 . . ., Vol. XX, fol. 218.
HAWKER, ..., of Plymouth, co. Devon, 181 . ., Vol. XXVII, fol. 347.
„ Ann (Spr.), of Luppit, co. Devon. Quarterly with SAMPSON, 181 . ., Vol. XXVIII, fol. 347.
„ . . . ., Capt., R.N. Match with POORE, 181 . ., Vol. XXX, fol. 173.
„ Joseph, Richmond Herald, of London, 182 . ., Vol. XXXII, fol. 310.
HAWKESBURY, Baron [1786] (JENKINSON), of co. Glouc. Supporters, 178 . ., Vol. XVI, fol. 181.
„ Baron [George Savill] (FOLJAMBE). Crest of JENKINSON in the first place, [10 Oct. and 12 Sept.] 1893, Vol. LXVII, fol. 223 (Supporters, fol. 231). (Crisp, Notes, Visit. of Eng. and Wales, II, pp. 50 and 53.)
HAWKESWORTH to FAWKES, Walter R. D., of co. York, 17 . . ., Vol. XVI, fol. 191.
HAWKESWORTH, now FAWKES, Walter R., of co. York, 179 . ., Vol. XVIII, fol. 131.
HAWKINS, Sir Christopher, Bart. [28 July 1791], of Trewithan, co. Cornw. Quarterly Arms of BELLOT, his great-grandmother, 179 . ., Vol. XVIII, fol. 243.
„ . . . ., of Minsterworth, co. Glouc. Match with ELLIS, 181 . ., Vol. XXVI, fol. 285.
„ . . . ., of Greenbank, Preston, co. Lanc., 186 . ., Vol. LIV, fol. 224.
HAWKINS-BROWNE, Isaac Hawkins [of Badger, in Shropsh.]. [Exemplification and quartering Hawkins, in memory of his grandmother. To the descendants of his grandfather, William Browne, 14 May 1779], Vol. XIV, fol. 129. [Misc. G. et H., New S., III, p. 41.]
HAWKSHAW (and [Anne] JACKSON, his wife), Sir John, of Great George Street, Westminster, 185 . ., Vol. L, fol. 170.
HAWKSLEY, ..., of Wales, and Havering-atte-Bower, co. Essex, 187 . ., Vol. LVIII, fol. 106.
„ B. F., of Campden Hill, London, 1895, Vol. LXVIII, fol. 162.
HAWORTH to LESLIE [Martin Leslie Haworth], of Balham Wood, co. Hertf., and Shrub Hill, Dorking, co. Surrey, [17 Jan. 1865], Vol. LV, fol. 282.
HAWORTH-LESLIE, M. E., ? of Devon. (See Earl of ROTHES.) 1886, Vol. LXIII, fol. 225.
HAWORTH-BOOTH, Lieut.-Col. Benjamin [Blaydes Haworth], of co. York. By Roy. Lic. Name only. [Arms of Booth in the 1st quarter.] 1869.
HAY, late LEITH, ..., of Leith Hall and Raines, Scotland, 17 . . ., Vol. XVII, fol. 187.
HAY, late DALRYMPLE [4 April 1798], (Sir) John, Bart. [7 April 1798], of co. Wigton, Scotland, 179 . ., Vol. XX, fol. 168.
HAY, Baron, Viscount DUPPLIN [Earl of Kinnoull], ..., of Scotland, [1809] Vol. XXV, fol. 197.
HAYCOCK, ..., of Woodchester, co. Glouc., and Stamford, co. Linc., 181 . ., Vol. XXVI, fol. 236.
HAYDOCK, late BONDMAN, of Bucks., 181 . ., Vol. XXVIII, fol. 438.
HAYES, ..., of St. James', Westminster, London, 1793, Vol. XVIII, fols. 168 and 169.
„ John Macnamara, M.D., of Old Burlington, London, 1797, [?] Vol. XIX, fol. 245.
HAYHURST to FRANCE, Thomas, of Liverpool and Everton, co. Lanc., 179 . ., Vol. XIX, fol. 143.
HAYHURST after FRANCE, Rev. Thomas, s. of Thomas, of co. Chester, 18 . . ., Vol. LVII, fol. 300.
HAYHURST to FRANCE, Wallace James Arthur, of co. Chester, [1876] Vol. LIX, fol. 200.

HAYHURST-FRANCE, G. H. H., of Ystym Colwyn, co. Montgomery, Wales, 1887, Vol. LXIV, fol. 34. [Shropshire, in Burke.]

HAYLEY, William, of Cleobury Mortimer, Shropsh., 8 Dec. 1701, Vol. V, fol. 51.

HAYNE, John (s. of John), Merchant, of Dartmouth, co. Devon, to descendants of his father, 18 June 1702, Vol. V, fol. 75 (XX, fol. 300 ?), and Add. MS. 14,831, fol. 27. (Berry.)

     ,, John, of London, and Honiton, co. Devon, 185 . ., Vol. L, fol. 142.

HAYNES, John, Principal Registrar of the Diocese and Province of Canterbury, of Chelsea, co. Middx., 17 Oct. 1734, Vol. VIII, fol. 188b, and Add. MS. 14,831, fol. 16.

HAYS, Sir James, Knt., of Great Badgbury, co. Kent, [8 May] 1689, Vol. IV, fol. 33.

HAYTER to EGERTON, ..., of Wilts., 179 . ., Vol. XVIII, fol. 133.

HAYTER, Sir George, Knt. [1 June 1842], of London, Principal Portrait Painter to His Majesty, 134 . ., Vol. XLVI, fol. 247.

     ,, Sir A. D. [William Goodenough ?], Bart. [19 April 1858], M.P., of Southill Park, Berks., 185 . ., Vol. LII, fol. 341.

HAYTON to GWINNETT, William Chute, of Wales, and Morton Court, co. Hereford, 184 . ., Vol. XLV, fol. 104.

HAYWARD, Samuel, s. of John, s. of Samuel, of Wallsworth Hall and Hucklecourt, co. Glouc., 1750, Vol. IX, fol. 383 (see Berry). Alderman of Gloucester, of Wallsworth Hall and Hucklecourt [co. Glouc.]. (Berry [?].)

HAYWARD to DANSON, ..., of London, 17 . ., Vol. XX, fol. 255.

HAYWARD-SOUTHBY, late PERFECT, ..., of Carswell, Berks., and Withington, co. Glouc., 182 . ., Vol. XXXIII, fol. 366.

HAYWARD, ..., of Bourton-on-the-Hill, co. Glouc., [1824] Vol. XXXV, fol. 15.

HAYWARD-WILKINS, Walter (s. of Walter Wilkins, fol. 350), of Maeslough Castle, Hay, co. Radnor, Wales, [1835] Vol. XL, fol. 362.

HAYWARD, Augusta Catherine Margaret, d. of WILKINS, and widow of Joseph ARNO, to take the Name and Arms of Hayward for self and descendants, of co. Glouc. and Wales. (See WILKINS, dau. of Walter WILKINS.) 29 Aug. 1811, Vol. XXVI, fol. 294.

HAYWOOD to HAYWOOD-FARMER, ..., of Comberford Hall, Tamworth, co. Staff., 187 . ., Vol. LVIII, fol. 121.

HAYWOOD (late EATON), Charles, of Brownhills, Burslem, co. Staff., 1875, Vol. LIX, fol. 112.

HEACOCK, Thomas, s. of Thomas, of Stoke Newington, co. Middx., 1746, Vol. IX, fol. 186. (Berry.)

HEAD to JAMES, Sir Thomas, of Denford, Berks., 31 Aug. 1773, Vol. XII, fol. 263.

HEAD, Sir Thomas, Knt., of Denford, Langley and Hampstead Norris, Berks., 17 . ., Vol. XIV, fol. 18.

HEAGREN-GIBBS, ..., of Quarles, nr. Holkham ; Thorpland-in-Fakenham, and Crab's Castle, Wighton, co. Norf., 18 . ., Vol. XXXI, fols. 185 and 187.

HEALD, James, of Porlwood, Stockport, co. Chester ; Waterside and Parrs' Wood, Manchester, co. Lanc., 182 . ., Vol. XXXVII, fol. 337.

     „ . . . ., of Horncastle, co. Linc., 18 . . ., Vol. XLIX, fol. 187.

HEALY, Richard, LL.D., of Wells, co. Somerset, 1698, Vol. IV, fol. 262.

HEAP to COOPER, ..., of co. Middx. and Bedf., 182 . ., Vol. XXXV, fols. 303 and 304.

HEAP, John, of Tottington, Bury, co. Lanc., 1879, Vol. LX, fol. 228. (Berry's Suppl.)

HEARD with TEALE, ... See TEALE.

HEARD, Isaac, Lanc. Herald, of London, and Bridgwater, co. Somerset, 1762, Vol. X, fol. 445. (Berry). Norroy, [1776] Vol. XIII, fols. 30 and 33. MASEY quartering. Clarenceux, 17 . . ., Vol. XIII, fol. 200, seals. Garter King of Arms, [1784] Vol. XV, fol. 278 ; Knight, [2 June 1786] Vol. XVI, fol. 135, seals.

HEARN, ..., of Buckingham, Bucks., 186 . ., Vol. LV, fol. 286.
HEATH, Robert, of Newcastle-under-Lyme and Biddulph, co. Staff, 187 . ., Vol. LVIII, fol. 228.
" Thomas, of Mile End, co. Middx., and his brethren, sons of William, decd., 21 or 1 June, 1707, Vol. V, fol. 222 (see Guillim, p. 382 ; Add. MS. 14,831, fol. 14 ; and Berry).
HEATH to NICHOLAS, Nicholas, of Stapleford Abbot, co. Essex, and Boyeourt, co. Kent, 15 Feb. 1772, Vol. XII, fol. 127.
HEATH, ..., M.D., of Fakenham, co. Norf. : Inkberrow, co. Wore. ; and Hanley Hall, co. Staff., 181 . ., Vol. XXVII, fol. 302.
HEATHCOAT-AMORY, ..., M.P., of Knightshayes, co. Devon, [1824] Vol. XXXV, fol. 26.
" -AMORY, ..., of Knighthayes, co. Devon, 187 . ., Vol. LVIII, fol. 312.
HEATHCOTE, Sir Gilbert, Knt., Sheriff, of London, and Chesterfield, co. Derby, 2 or 20 Dec. 1709, Vol. V, fol. 311 (see Guillim, p. 367).
HEATHCOTE to RODES, Cornelius, of Barlborough, co. Derby, 1776, Vol. XIII, fol. 227 ; see also 182 . ., Vol. XXXV, fol. 315.
HEATHCOTE after UNWIN, ..., of Sheephall Bury, co. Hertf. : Sutton-in-Ashfield, co. Nottingham ; and London. Match, [1815] Vol. XXIX, fol. 105. (See FITZWYGRAM, in Baronets.)
HEATHCOTE, ..., of Bakewell, co. Derby, and Tottenham, co. Middx., 181 . ., Vol. XXXI, fol. 378.
HEATHCOTE-HACKER, Rowland, of Chesterfield, co. Derby, and East Bridgford, co. Nottingham, [1819 ?] Vol. XXXI, fol. 392.
" -HACKER, John, of Chesterfield, co. Derby ; East Bridgford, co. Nottingham ; and Leek, co. Staff., 18 . . ., Vol. XLIV, fol. 295.
" -HACKER, ..., of Hatfield, co. York, [1871] Vol. LVIII, fol. 10.
HEATHCOTE, late SHEPLEY, of Stancliffe Hall and Blackwall, Bakewell, co. Derby, 182 . ., Vol. XXXII, fol. 393.
HEATHCOTE-DRUMMOND, Clementina Elizabeth, Baroness WILLOUGHBY D'ERESBY, 1870.
HEATHFIELD, Baron [6 July 1787] (ELIOTT). Supporters, 178 . ., Vol. XVI, fol. 303.
HEATHORN, ..., of Charlton Park, co. Glouc., and Maidstone, co. Kent, [1842] Vol. XLVI, fol. 155.
HEATON, John (s. of John), of Hunslet, Leeds, co. York, [1842] Vol. XLVI, fol. 228.
HEAVISIDE to William SPICER, Capt. in the Army, of Courtlands, Wilby, Combe Raleigh, co. Devon, 185 . ., Vol. LI, fol. 102.
HEBBERT, ..., of Birmingham, co. Warw., 183 . ., Vol. XXXIX, fol. 99.
HEBER to SHERSON, of Stainton and Marton, co. York. Match, 17 . . ., Vol. XIV, fol. 203.
HEBER-PERCY [4 Feb. 1847], Algernon Charles, of Hodnet, Shropsh. (See Duke of NORTHUMBERLAND.) 184 . ., Vol. XLVIII, fol. 258.
HEBERDEN, William, F.R.S., F.R.C.P., s. of Richard, of St. James', Westminster, London (of St. John's Coll., Camb.), 1752, Vol. IX, fol. 408.
HECTOR, ..., of Petersfield, Hampsh. Match, 181 . ., Vol. XXX, fol. 291.
HEDLEY to DENT, ..., of co. Northumberland, 183 . ., Vol. XXXIX, fol. 29.
HEGAN, ..., of Liverpool and London, 183 . ., Vol. XLIII, fol. 141.
HELBERT, late ISRAEL, John, of Gloucester Place, Portman Square, London, [1833] Vol. XXXIX, fol. 370.
HELE after SELBY, ..., of Colmworth, co. Bedf. Quarterly Arms, [1790] Vol. XVII, fol. 342.
HELLIER, Sir Samuel, Knt., of Woodhouse, co. Staff., and Rushock, co. Wore., Sheriff, 2 Jan. 1764, Vol. XI, fol. 3. (Berry.)
HELLIER, late SHAW, Rev. Thomas, of Woodhouse, co. Staff., and Rushock, co. Wore. Quarterly Arms, 1786, Vol. XVI, p. 195. (Berry's Appx.)

HELLYAR or HELYAR, ..., of Coker Court, co. Somerset, 181 . ., Vol. XXVIII, fol. 299.

HELME, ..., of Warton, co. Lanc., and Walthamstow, co. Essex, [1827] Vol. XXXVI, fol. 341.

HELPS, Arthur, of Balham Hill, co. Surrey, and Gloucester [K.C.B. 18 July 1872] ("Friends in Council"), [1824] Vol. XXXIV, fol. 360.

HELSHAM-BROWN, Edward, of Ireland, and co. Somerset, [1826] Vol. XXXVI, fol. 63.

HELSHAM-CANDLER, William (bro. of Edward), in Burke's Landed Gentry, but a mistake ?

HELSHAM-JONES, Henry Helsham, of Redlands, co. Surrey, and A. Helsham-Jones, of Pinner Hill, Holmwood, co. Middx., 1892,* Vol. LXVII, fol. 79.

HEMMING, ..., of Haselor, co. Warw., and Fox Lydiate House, Tardebigg, co. Worc., 18 . ., Vol. XLIV, fol. 319.

HENEAGE after WALKER (late WYLD), ..., of Speen and Chieveley, Berks., and Compton House, Wilts., [1818] Vol. XXXI, fol. 102.

HENEAGE, Baron [1896] [Edward Heneage]. Supporters, [1896] Vol. LXIX, fol. 132.

HENDERSON after MERCER, ..., C.B., Lieut.-Gen., of Fordell House, Dalgetty, co. Fife, Scotland, 185 . ., Vol. L, fol. 405.

„　after CLELAND, &c., ..., of Hampsh. and Scotland, [1868] Vol. LVII, fol. 92.　(Berry's Suppl.)

HENDERSON, Christopher Hope, s. of Peter, of Upton Macclesfield, co. Chester, and Bankfort, Bradford, co. York, 1879, Vol. LX, fol. 281.

HENDERSON-ROE, Christopher Hope, s. of Peter, s. of George, 1879, Vol. LX, fol. 307 ?.

HENLEY, Baron [27 Mar. 1760, Robert Henley]. Supporters, 17 . . ., Vol. X, fol. 221.

HENLEY to HARE, John, of co. Norfolk, 17 . . ., Vol. XIV, fol. 63.

HENLEY, ..., of Putney, co. Surrey, and St. John's, Wapping, London, 180 . ., Vol. XXI, fol. 430.

HENN to GENNYS, ..., of co. Devon, and Ireland.　Quarterly Arms, 180 . ., Vol. XXI, fol. 346.

HENNESSY, J., of Lancaster Gate, London, 1893, Vol. LXVII, fol. 249.

HENNIKER, John, of Newton Hall, co. Essex, 1765, Vol. XI, fols. 102 and 103. (Berry.)

HENNIKER to MAJOR [10 Aug. 1792], Baron John, of Newton Hall, co. Essex, and Thornton Hall, co. Suff., 179 . ., Vol. XVIII, fol. 97.

HENNIKER, Lady PRESS, Mary (dau. of William Press), of Newton Hall, co. Essex, 8 Jan. 1814, Vol. XXVIII, fol. 1.

HENNIKER-MAJOR [27 May 1822], Baron John, of Newton Hall, co. Essex, 182 . ., Vol. XXXIII, fol. 236.

HENNIKER-WILSON after WRIGHT, Mary, of Crofton Hall, co. York, 183 . ., Vol. XLIII, fol. 377.

HENRY to YELVERTON, Hastings Reginald, Capt., R.N., [1849] Vol. XLIX, fols. 92, 93 and 94.

HENRY, Barbara, Baroness GREY DE RUTHYN, [1849] Vol. XLIX, fols. 92, 93 and 94.

HENSHAW, late SMITH, ..., of co. Essex, 184 . ., Vol. XLVI, fol. 293.

HENSHAW-ASHTON, T. W., 2nd s. of John H. NICKSON-WALFORD, of Royton Towers, nr. Shrewsbury, Shropsh., 1887, Vol. LXIII, fol. 348.

HENSLEY, ..., of Clapton, co. Middx., 182 . ., Vol. XXXIII, fol. 328.

HENSOL, Baron TALBOT OF [5 Dec. 1733], Charles.　Supporters, 17 . . ., Vol. VIII, fol. 179^b.

HENSTOCK, Jesse, s. of John, of Bonsall Winston, Youlgreave, co. Derby, 1877, Vol. LIX, fol. 324 (see Berry's Suppl.).

HENTY, ..., of Westgate, Chichester, and Ferring, co. Sussex, 186 . ., Vol. LVI, fol. 281.

HENZELL, ... *See* PIDCOCK.

HEPBURN-STUART-FORBES before TREFUSIS [4 Sept. 1867], Baron CLINTON, 186 . ., Vol. LVI, fol. 303.

HEPWORTH, Rev. W. H. F., of Shepshed Vicarage, co. Leic., 1895,* Vol. LXVIII, fol. 251.

HERBERT, ..., of London. Match with COOKE, 172 . ., Vol. VII, fol. 461.

  „ [Baron and] Earl of TORRINGTON [29 May 1689, Arthur Herbert]. Supporters, 16 . . ., Vol. IV, fol. 42.

  „ Baron, of Chirbury, [28 April] 1694, Henry [Herbert]. Supporters, 1694, Vol. IV, fol. 167.

  „ Baron, of Chirbury [21 Dec. 1743, Henry Arthur Herbert]. [Baron Herbert of Chirbury and of Ludlow, 16 Oct. 1749]. Supporters, 17 . . ., Vol. IX, fol. 96.

  „ Earl of POWIS [27 May 1748, Henry Arthur Herbert], 17 . . ., Vol. IX, fol. 282.

  „ Baron PORCHESTER [17 Oct. 1780, Henry Herbert], 17 . . ., Vol. XIV, fol. 207.

HERBERT, now CLIVE, Edward Viscount, s. of the Earl of POWIS. Name and Arms of Herbert, 20 Mar. 1807, Vol. XXIV, fol. 144. (Powys-Land Club, V, p. 167.)

HERBERT, late BEILBY, Samuel, D.D., of Kingston-upon-Hull, co. York, and Wales, 17 . . ., Vol. XX, fol. 92.

HERBERT after MORTON, ..., of the Island of Nevis, 182 . ., Vol. XXXIII, fol. 208.

HERBERT, R. H., of Lincoln's Inn Fields, London, 1889, Vol. LXV, fol. 166.

  „ S. G., of Pietermaritzburg, Natal, 1889, Vol. LXV, fol. 166.

  „ William, of Longford, co. Glouc., 1884,* Vol. LXII, fol. 247.

HERCY, late SMALLWOOD, ..., of Winkfield, Berks., 182 . ., Vol. XXXIII, fol. 128.

HERDE, ... (*see* HEARD), 17 . . ., Vol. X, fol. 445.

HEREFORD, Bp. of (HAMPDEN), 18 . . ., Vol. XLIX, fol 34.

HERMON, Edward, M.P., of Preston, co. Lanc., and Wyfold Court, Checkendon, co. Oxf., 187 . ., Vol. LVIII, fol. 274.

HERNE (BUCKWORTH-), Sir Everard], Bart., of Broxbourne, co. Hertf., 180 . ., Vol. XXIV, fol. 97.

  „ (BUCKWORTH) to SOAME [Sir Buckworth Herne-Soame], [12 Dec. 1806], of Heydon, co. Essex, 180 . ., Vol. XXIV, fol. 99.

HERON (CLARKE), ..., of Bockenfield and Ford Castle, co. Northumberland, and Newark, [co. Nottingham?]. Match, [1755] Vol. X, fol. 19.

HERRICK after PERRY, ..., of Eardisley Castle, co. Hereford ; Beau Manor Park, co. Linc. ; and Merridale and Wolverhampton, co. Staff., 185 . .. Vol. L, fol. 361.

HERRING, ..., wife of Sir Francis BARING, of Larkbeer, co. Devon, 179 . ., Vol. XVIII, fol. 230.

  „ . . . ., of London and Finchley, co. Middx., 182 . ., Vol. XXXIII, fol. 323.

  „ . . . ., of Norwich, co. Norf., [1826] Vol. XXXVI, fol. 13.

HERRING to BARNEWALL, ..., of co. Norf., [1826] Vol. XXXVI, fol. 17b.

HERSCHEL, Sir John F. W. [Bart., 17 July 1838], of Slough, Bucks., 183 . ., Vol. XLIII, fol. 163.

HERSCHELL, FARRER, of co. Durham. Arms, 1877, Vol. LX, fol. 60.

HERSCHELL, Baron [8 Feb. 1886], (FARRER HERSCHELL), of co. Durham. Supporters, [1886] 1887, Vol. LXIII, fol. 350 [?].

HERTFORD, Marquis of. INGRAM before SEYMOUR-CONWAY [18 Dec. 1807]. Crest, 18 . . .,* Vol. XXIV, fols. 352 and 354.

HERVEY, Baron [23 Mar. 170⅔, John], of co. Suff., 170 . ., Vol. V, fol. 122.

HERVEY-ELWES after TIMMS, ..., of co. Suff., 179 . ., Vol. XVIII, fol. 220.

HERVEY after BATHURST, ... of Clarendon Park, Wilts., and Englefield Green, co. Surrey, 180 . ., Vol. XXI, fol. 329.

HERVEY, ...   Match with Baron HOWARD DE WALDEN, 180 . ., Vol. XXV,
  fol. 435.
HERVEY-BATHURST, ..., of Wilts., 182 . ., Vol. XXXVII, fol. 197.
HERVEY, Thomas (formerly HANMER), H.M.'s 1st Foot Guards, 1774, Vol. XII,
  fol. 286.
HESELTINE, James, of Doctors' Commons, London, s. of John, of Burton, co.
  York, 178 . ., Vol. XVI, fol. 347.
HESILRIGE to MAYNARD, Thomas, of Noseley, co. Leic., 28 Mar. 1770, Vol. XII,
  fol. 15.
HESKETH to BAMFORD, Robert, of co. Chester, &c., 180 . ., Vol. XXIII, fol. 379.
  „   to JUXON, ... [1792], Bart., of Little Compton, co. Glouc., and Rufford
  Hall, co. Lanc., 179 . ., Vol. XVIII, fol. 45.
HESKETH after BAMFORD, Robert, of co. Chester ; Rufford Hall, co. Lanc. ; and
  Wales, 18 . . ., Vol. XXV, fol. 377 ; Robert, of co. Chester and Lanc.,
  and Wales, 18 . . ., Vol. XXV, fols. 381 and 382.
HESKETH, Charles Hesketh Bibby, of the Rookery, North Meols, Stockport, co.
  Chester, Bar.-at-Law, s. of John Bibby, of Hart Hill, Liverpool, co. Lanc.,
  18 . . ., Vol. LXXI, fol. . . . .
HESKETH-FLEETWOOD, Peter, of co. Lanc., 6 Aug. 1829, Vol. XXXVIII,
  fols. 2 and 258 ; reputed son, of co. Lanc. and Berks., 185 . ., Vol. LI,
  fol. 327.
HESKETH after FERMOR, Sir Thomas George, Bart., of co. Lanc., and 2nd son of
  Thomas George, [Fermor quarterly with Hesketh], 1867, Vol. LVI,
  fol. 306.
HESKETT, John (late Lancaster Herald), of Dover, co. Kent, co. Lanc., and
  co. Cork, Ireland, 21 July 1727, Vol. VIII, fol. 4.
HESSE, John Adam Frederick, of Paddington, London, and Germany, 12 June
  1772, Vol. XII, fol. 193.   (Berry.)
HESSE-CASSEL, Landgrave of, of London.   Supporters, 179 . ., Vol. XVIII,
  fol. 365.
HESSE, late LE GREW, . . ., of Bloomsbury, London, and Norton Folgate,
  co. Middx., 179 . ., Vol. XVIII, fol. 371.
HESSING, Col., in serv. of Mahratta States, East Indies, 182 . ., Vol. XXXII,
  fol. 201.
HETHERSETT, late BARKER, Lieut.-Gen., of co. Norf.   Match, 180 . ., Vol. XXII,
  fol. 393.
HEWARD, Sir Simon, M.D., of Trough Head, Stapleton, &c., co. Cumberland.
  Served in the Burmese War. 183 . ., Vol. XLIII, fol. 277.
HEWETT formerly ROBINSON, Dame Dorothea, wife of Sir George Robinson, Bart.,
  of Cranford, co. Northampton, and Great Stretton, co. Leic., 1773, Vol.
  XII, fol. 246.
HEWETT, Sir George [Bart. 6 Nov. 1813], Gen. and Com.-in-Chief, East Indies.
  Supporters, 181 . ., Vol. XXVII, fol. 370.
  „   G. E., of Leasower, Charlton Kings, co. Glouc., 1889, Vol. LXV, fol. 168.
  „   Sir Prescott G., Bart., of London, 1883, Vol. LXII, fol. 120.
HEWITT, James of Alveston, co. Warw., Lord Chancellor, 1767, Vol. XI, fol. 256.
  (Berry.)
HEWITT to SMALLWOOD, ..., of Drayton in Hales, Shropsh., 179 . ., Vol.
  XVIII, fol. 355.
HEWITT, George, Viscount of GOWRAN and Baron of JAMESTOWN, of Ireland,
  1689, Vol. IV, fol. 35.
HEWITT to HUGHES, ..., of Clapham Common, co. Surrey, [1825] Vol.
  XXXV, fol. 268.
HEWITT after LUDLOW, Thomas A., of Littleton-on-Severn, co. Glouc., and
  Clanacole, co. Cork, 185 . ., Vol. LII, fol. 263.
HEYSHAM, William, of East Greenwich, co. Kent, M.P. for Lancaster. To the
  descendants of his grandfather Giles, 9 or 3 Feb. 172⅔, Vol. VII, fol. 158
  (see Misc. G. et H., New S., IV, p. 375, and Berry's Suppl.).

HEYWARD, Thomas, of the Middle Temple, and Carolina, 1 Dec. 1768, Vol. XI, fol. 326. (Berry.)

HEYWOOD, Mary, d. of John, wid. of WILMOT, of co. Oxf. Arms of WILMOT, 1775, Vol. XIII, fol. 72.

„ . . . ., (Bart.) [9 Aug. 1838], of Wakefield, co. York; Ormskirk and Liverpool, co. Lanc.: and Drogheda, Ireland, 183 . ., Vol. XL [?], fol. 165.

HEYWOOD-LONSDALE, Arthur Pemberton, of co. Lanc., co. York, and Gredington, co. Flint, &c., 1877, Vol. LX, fol. 74. (Berry's Suppl.)

HEYWOOD, Henry, of Witlo Court, Rumney, co. Monmouth, 1895,* Vol. LXVIII, fol. 188.

HEYWOOD-JONES, R. H., of Badsworth Hall, co. York, 1892, Vol. LXVI, fol. 283.

HEYWORTH, Laurence, M.P. Derby, of Yewtree, par. of West Derby, co. Lanc., s. of Peter, of Greensnook, par. of Newchurch-in-Rossendale, co. Lanc. To his descendants and the descendants of his father, Peter, 12 Nov. 1856, Vol. LII, fol. 102. (Geneal., VII, p. 88.)

HIBBERT, ..., of Munden House, Mottram, co. Chester, 184 . ., Vol. XLVIII, fol. 35.

HIBBERT after HOLLAND, Arthur Henry, of Watford, co. Hertf., 1876, Vol. LIX, fol. 234 (see Berry's Suppl.).

HIBBINS, ..., of Rowton, Shropsh. Match, 172 . .. Vol. VII, fol. 55.

HICCOCKS, John, of Lincoln's Inn, London, Master in Chancery, 30 Nov. 1707, Vol. V, fol. 273; Add. MS. 14,831, fol. 34. (Berry.)

HICK, John, of Mytton Hall, Whalley, co. Lanc. (died 1894), 1884,* Vol. LXII, fol. 251.

HICKES, Henry, of St. Paul's, Covent Garden, London, [31 or] 21 Dec. 1722, Vol. VII, fol. 146; Add. MS. 14,830, fol. 106.

„ William (see COPPARD), of Salehurst, co. Sussex, 1769. Vol. XI, fol. 354.

HICKIE, Michael, of Billing, co. Northampton, 25 July 1712, Vol. VI, fol. 66; Add. MS. 14,831, fol. 192.

HICKMAN, ..., of Alesbury, co. Staff., 17 . . ., Vol. V, fol. 22.

„ Nathan, of Oken, co. Staff., to descendants of his grandfather Richard, of Oken, 1 Feb. 170⅚, Vol. V, fol. 332; Add. MS. 14,831, fol. 84.

HICKMAN after BACON, Henry, of Thorrock Hall, co. Linc. (died unm. 1862), [1826] Vol. XXXVI, fol. 29.

HICKMAN, Sir Alfred, of Goldtham Hall, co. Staff., 1891, Vol. LXVI, fol. 86.

HICKS, Thomas, s. of Thomas, of Deptford, co. Kent, and Beccles, co. Suff., 17 . . ., Vol. X, fol. 58.

HICKS before BEACH . . . . [23 June 1790], of co. Glouc. and Wilts., 17 . . ., Vol. XVII, fol. 264.

HICKS-BEACH to BEACH, ... [24 Jan. 1838], of co. Glouc. and Wilts., 183 . ., Vol. XLII, fol. 281.

HICKS, late SIMPSON, Edward, of Great Wilbraham, co. Camb.: Corpus C. Coll., Oxf.; and Inner Temple, London (M.P. Camb.), 183 . ., Vol. XLI, fol. 105.

HICKS, Maj.-Gen. George, C.B., of Alcirat House, Jersey, 186 . ., Vol. LVI, fol. 5.

„ Henry, of St. Paul's, Covent Garden, London, 3rd s. of Henry, of Stretton-upon-Foss, co. Warw.: 3rd s. of William, of Shipton-on-Stour, co. Worc; to descendants of his father, Henry, 31 Dec. 1722, Vol. VII, fol. 146; Add. MS. 14,830, fol. 106.

HIDE. See HYDE.

HIGDEN after BYFIELD, George, of St. Mary, Lambeth, co. Surrey, 181 . ., Vol. XXX, fol. 11.

HIGFORD, late PARSONS, ..., of Toddington and Alvington, co. Glouc., and Hedgeberrow, co. Worc., 182 . ., Vol. XXXV, fol. 293.

„ late BURR, ..., of Berks., [1860] Vol. LIV, fol. 1.

HIGGINBOTHAM to PRICE, James, of Wales; Stoke, nr. Guildford, co. Surrey; and Gray's Inn, London, 17 . . ., Vol. XIV, fol. 300.

HIGGINS (see DAVISON), 17 . . ., Vol. VIII, fol. 218. [See also PLATT-HIGGINS.]

HIGGINS, Rev. Joseph, Rector of Eastnor and Pixley, co. Hereford, 1833, Vol. XXXIX, fol. 174.

„ Henry (and MORLEY, his wife), s. of William, of Moreton Jeffreys, co. Hereford, and Thing Hill, Withington, and Salford, co. Lanc., 1874, Vol. LIX, fol. 18 (see Crisp, Notes, II, p. 106, and Berry's Suppl.).

HIGGINSON, Joseph, of Budge Row, London, and Mile End, co. Middx., 1764, Vol. XI, fol. 29. (Berry.)

HIGGINSON, late BARNEBY, Edmund, of Saltmarsh and Brockhampton, co. Hereford, [1825] Vol. XXXV, fol. 264.

HIGGINSON, ..., of Everton and Wavertree, co. Lanc., 187 . ., Vol. LVIII, fol. 90.

HIGGS, W. A., of Willenhall Park, Barnet, co. Middx., 1887, Vol. LXIV, fol. 53.

HILBORNE, George, of Kingston, co. Somerset, [28 ?] 30 April 1708, Vol. V, fol. 299. (Berry.)

HILDYARD, late THOROTON, ..., of Winestead, co. York, and Flentham, co. Nottingham, [1815] Vol. XXIX, fol. 29.

., late HALE, John R. W., of co. York and D[urham ?], [1855] Vol. LI, fol. 280.

HILL, Daniel, Preb. of Rochester, 1699, Vol. IV, fol. 295.

„ Baron BERWICKE [19 May 1784], of Shropsh. Supporters, 178 . ., Vol. XV, fol. 309.

„ . . . ., of Bristol, co. Glouc., and Shrewsbury, Shropsh., [1785] Vol. XVI, fol. 67.

HILL to MEDLYCOTT, ..., of Cockayne, Rowell and Cottingham, co. Northampton, 180 . ., Vol. XXI, fol. 275.

HILL, Lieut.-Gen. Sir Rowland, K.B. [22 Feb. 1812.] Supporters, 18 . . .,* Vol. XXVII, fol. 18.

„ [Rowland, Baron Hill. Supporters [28 May 1842 (Geneal., New S., XXII, p. 156)].

HILL after NOEL, ..., of co. Chester and Shropsh. (See Baron BERWICK.) [1824] Vol. XXXIV, fols. 300 and 302.

HILL, Henry, Capt. in the Army, of Knutsford, co. Chester, 18 . . ., Vol. XLIX, fol. 451.

., [Anne, 2nd Viscountess Hill. Arms of CLEGG, 16 Dec. 1844 (Geneal., New S., XXII, p. 156).]

„ . . . ., of Wood Hall, Reddish, co. Lanc., [1856] Vol. LII, fol. 60.

HILL to SANDYS [11 Feb. 1861, 3rd] Baron Sandys, of co. Glouc., 186 . ., Vol. LIV, fol. 112.

HILL, John Smith, M.A., Caius Coll., Camb., of Wooding, Wacton, Portway, and Orleton, co. Hereford ; and Dinton, Bucks ; and Edward Smith, of the same, 186 . ., Vol. LIV, fol. 128.

HILL-TREVOR, ... [9 Sept. 1862], of co. Nottingham and Ireland, 2nd s. of the Marquis of DOWNSHIRE, 186 . ., Vol. LIV, fol. 320.

HILL, Edward Smith, of Woollahra, co. Cumberland, and Sydney, New South Wales, [1863 ?] Vol. LV, fol. 3.

„ William, of Catherine Hill House, co. Worc. ; and Suckley and Stourport, co. Worc., [11 Aug. 1864] Vol. LV, fol. 210. (Crisp, IV, p. 107.)

HILL, late LOWE, Col. Arthur C., of Court Hill, Shropsh., and Bromsgrove, co. Worc., 186 . ., Vol. LVI, fol. 75.

HILL (CLIFTON and), of Druid Stoke House, Stoke Bishop, co. Glouc., 186 . ., Vol. LVI, fol. 99.

HILL, ..., of Ditton and Britford, Wilts. ; and Kingsdown House, Roath, co. Glamorgan, Wales, 18 . . . . Vol. LVII, fol. 129.

HILL after CLEGG, Viscount Hill, of Shropsh., [17 April 1875 ?] Vol. LIX, fol. 94. [See Geneal., New S., XXII, p. 157.]

HILL, Joseph, of Bradford, co. York, 1877, Vol. LX, fol. 6. (Berry's Suppl.)

„ Arthur, of Bruce Grove, Tottenham, London, 1881,* Vol. LXI, fol. 136.

„ Sidney, of Langford House, Churchill, co. Somerset, 1882,* Vol. LXI, fol. 385. (Berry's Suppl.)

HILL, Thomas, of The Park, Nottingham, 1888, Vol. LXIV, fol. 196.
„ John (s. of Charles), of Saltburn-by-the-Sea, co. York, 189 . ., Vol. LXXI, fol. . . . .
HILLARY, Sir William, Bart. [8 Nov. 1805], of Rigg House, Aysgarth, co. York, and Danbury Place, co. Essex, [1806 ?] Vol. XXIV, fol. 257.
„ Charles Ernest Richard (formerly Preston), of Park Lodge, Upper Richmond Road. Arms of Hillary, 1898, Vol. LXX, fol. 149.
HILLERSDON, late GROVE, ..., of co. Essex and S. [?], 180 . ., Vol. XXIV, fol. 242.
HILLIER, ..., of London, and Norton, Wilts., 180 . ., Vol. XXI, fol. 406.
„ Nathaniel, of Stoke Park, co. Suff., and London, 4 June 1810, Vol. XXVI, fol. 130.
„ Lieut.-Col. G. E., C.B., of Elgin, co. Dublin, Ireland, 1883,* Vol. LXII, fol. 130. (Berry's Suppl.)
HILLINGDON, Baron [MILLS]. Supporters, 1886, Vol. LXIII, fol. 211.
HILLS, Arnold F. (s. of Frank), of Monkham and Redleaf, co. Kent, 189 . ., Vol. LXXI, fol. . . . .
„ Maj.-Gen. Sir James, K.C.B., of Wales, 1883,* Vol. LXII, fol. 110.
HILLS-JOHNES, Sir J., K.C.B., V.C., of Wales, 1887, Vol. LXIV, fol. 16.
HILLS, Mary, 24 Aug. 1738, Vol. VIII, fol. 248.
„ . . . ., of Chelsea, co. Middx., and Isle of Sheppey, co. Kent, 1784.
HILLYAR, Rear-Adm. Sir James [? John], K.C.B., 183 . ., Vol. XLIV, fol. 333.
HILTON to JOHNSON, ..., of Temple Belwood, co. Linc., 187 . ., Vol. LVIII, fol. 190.
HILTON, James, of 60, Montagu Square, London, 1885, Vol. LXIII, fol. 99.
„ William HALE-, of Union Court, Old Broad Street, London, [1885] Vol. LXIII, fol. 101.
HILTON-SIMPSON, Rev. W., of Milsted Rectory, co. Kent, 1890, Vol. LXV, fol. 273.
HINCHLIFFE, Dorothea, of St. Bride's, London, 25 Aug. 1741, Vol. IX, fol. 38.
HINCKES, H. I., of Wood House, Tettenhall, co. Staff., 1891, Vol. LXVI, fol. 150.
„ Ralph I., of Foxley, Yazor, co. Hereford, 1896, Vol. LXIX, fol. 83.
HINCKS, ..., of Huntington (Chorlton, ? Cheshire), [1811] Vol. XXVI, fol. 255.
HIND, W. H. S., of Ovington, Ovingham, co. Northumberland, 1895,* Vol. LXVIII, fol. 249.
„ John, s. of Jacob. (See also William FOSTER.) 178 . ., Vol. XV, fol. 159.
HINDE to LLOYD, Jacob Youde William, of Clock Farm, co. Montgomery, Wales, and Langham Hall, co. Essex. [Roy. Lic., 12 Dec. ; Exemplification] 26 Dec. 1868, Vol. LVII, fol. 100. (Powys-Land Club, X, pp. 410 and 412.)
HINDLIP, Baron [Alsopp], of co. Worc. Supporters, 1886, Vol. LXIII, fol. 241.
HINDSON, Mathew (s. of John), of Penrith, co. Cumberland, and Sandwicke, Martindale, co. Westmorland, 1878, Vol. LX, fol. 86.
HINE, John, Com., E.I.C.S. Marine, of Dartmouth, co. Devon, 18 . . ., Vol. XLIV, fol. 192.
HINGLEY, Sir Benjamin, Bart., of co. Worc., 1893,* Vol. LXVII, fol. 201.
HINRICH to HINRICH-DENT, Henry Dent, of Bucks. and co. Leic., s. of Sir Henry Bromley Hinrich [Knt.], 1879, Vol. LX, fol. 299.
HIPPISLEY, ..., Bart. [10 May or 30 April 1796], LL.D. [? D.C.L.], of Warfield Grove, Berks., Recorder of Sudbury, [1797 ?] Vol. XIX, fol. 428. Ducal Supporters, [1797] Vol. XIX, fol. 446.
HIPPISLEY to TUCKFIELD, ..., of Fulford, co. Devon, Wick Hill and Stow-on-the-Wold, co. Glouc., 180 . ., Vol. XXIV, fol. 237.
HIRONS, late BREWERTON, ..., of North Arson and Wardington, co. Oxf., [1827 ?] Vol. XXXVI, fol. 268.
HIRST, late SHIRT, Henry John, of Clough, Rotherham, co. York, 28 Oct. 1820, Vol. XXXII, fol. 183.

HIRST, ..., of Great Ropers, South Weald, co. Essex, and Down Grange, Basingstoke, Hampsh., 186 . ., Vol. LVI, fol. 309.

„ Reginald, of York Place, Huddersfield, co. York, 1895, Vol. LXVIII, fol. 142.

„ Thomas Julius (s. of Thomas, of Hamburgh), of Meltham Hall, co. York, 18 . ., Vol. LXXI, fol. . . . .

HISLOP, Gen. Sir Thomas, G.C.B. [14 Oct. 1818]. Augmentation and Supporters, 1813, [?] Vol. XXXIII, fols. 160 and 164.

HITCHIN-KEMP, Frederick William, of Margate, co. Kent, and Hendon, co. Middx. [Exemplification, Arms of Kemp, Roy. Lic., 1868], Vol. LVII, fol. 29. [Geneal. Mag., VI, p. 410.]

HIVES, ..., of Gledhow Grove, Leeds, co. York, 184 . ., Vol. XLVII, fol. 222.

HOADLY, Benjamin, D.D., Bp. of Bangor, &c., &c., of Wales, to descendants of his grandfather, John, 20 Feb. 1715, Vol. VI, fol. 225 (see Misc. G. et H., New S., 1, p. 188).

HOAR, now BERTIE, Thomas, Capt., R.N., of co. Essex, 178 . ., Vol. XVI, fol. 409.

HOAR, George, of Middleton St. George, co. Durham, Keeper of the Regalia, [1802] Vol. XXI, fol. 453.

HOAR to HARLAND, William, of co. Durham and York, [1824] Vol. XXXV, fol. 55.

„ to HARLAND, Charles, Bart., 182 . ., Vol. XXXVI, fol. 226 [? wrong reference].

HOARE, Henry, ..., of Stourhead, Wilts., 17 Dec. 1776, Vol. XIII, fol. 251.

„ [Henry], of Staplehurst, co. Kent ; Mitcham Grove, co. Surrey ; and Bury St. Edmunds, co. Suff. Quarterly MALORTIE and CORNELISEN, [1833] Vol. XL, fol. 32.

HOBART, ..., of Knettishall, co. Suff. (See BUCKLE to BARLEE.) Match, 181 . ., Vol. XXVI, fols. 346 and 348.

„ Sir John, Bart., K.B. [27 May 1725], of Bucks. Supporters, 172 . ., Vol. VII, fol. 411.

HOBART to HAMPDEN [5th Oct. 1824, 5th] Earl of BUCKINGHAMSHIRE, of Bucks., 182 . ., Vol. XXXV, fol. 31.

„ to HAMPDEN, Augustus Edward, Earl of BUCKINGHAMSHIRE, 1878, Vol. LX, fol. 149.

HOBART, Baron, of Bucks. Supporters, 1886, Vol. LXIII, fol. 198.

HOBBS, ..., of the Isle of Wight, 181 . ., Vol. XXVIII, fol. 295.

HOBHOUSE, ..., M.P., of Westbury Coll., Glouc. ; Chantry House, Wilts. ; and Minehead and Hadspen, co. Somerset, 181 . ., Vol. XXVII, fol. 106.

HOBHOUSE, Baron. Supporters, 1885, Vol. LXIII, fol. 115.

HOBLYN after PETER, ..., of Liskeard, co. Cornw., 183 . ., Vol. XLII, fol. 127.

„ after PETER, ..., of Colquite St. Martyn, co. Cornw., 186 . ., Vol. LV, fol. 354.

HOBLYN, ..., of Liskeard, co. Cornw., 186 . ., Vol. LIV, fol. 150. (Crisp, I, 183.)

HOBSON, R., of Mirfords Bromborough and Green Halls, Bollers, co. Chester, 1895,* Vol. LXVIII, fol. 274.

„ John Falshaw, of South Bailey, co. Durham, s. of Peter, 1897, Vol. LXIX, fol. 255.

HOCART, ..., of Weymouth, co. Dorset, and the Isle of Alderney, 183 . ., Vol. XLI, fol. 148.

HOCKENHULL to MOLINEUX, of Lymm, co. Chester, and Hawkley Hall, Pemberton, co. Lanc., 180 . ., Vol. XXIII, fol. 372.

HOCKIN, Rev. John, s. of John, of Cadrescott and Godrevy, co. Cornw., Vicar of Oakhampton and Rector of Lydford, co. Devon, 1764, Vol. XI, fol. 21. (Berry.)

HOCKLY, William, of Wickwar, co. Glouc., 23 Oct. 1772, Vol. XII, fol. 213.

HODDER, R. E., of Norcott Villa, Reading, Berks., 1891, Vol. LXVI, fol. 221. (Berry.)

HODGE, formerly ADAMS, ... (widow), of co. Cornw. Crest to descendants, [1808] Vol. XXIV, fol. 364.

HODGE, E. Grose, of Highbury Place, Islington, London, 1887,* Vol. LXIV, fol. 12.

HODGES [Sir William], Bart. [31 Mar. 1697, of co. Middx.], residing at Cadiz, 16 . . ., Vol. IV, fol. 287.

,, Lady, of Cadiz, 16 . . ., Vol. IV, fol. 315.

HODGES before NUGENT, of Donore, Ireland, Assist.-Com.-Gen. of the Forces. Match, 181 . ., Vol. XXVIII, fol. 387.

HODGES, late HODSON, of Heskin Hall, co. Lanc. ; Boston Hall, Skipton, co. York ; Holland Grove, nr. Wigan, co. Lanc. ; and Henley-on-Thames, co. Oxf., 184 . ., Vol. XLVII, fol. 66.

HODGETTS, John, of Prestwood and Shut End, King's Swinford, co. Staff., Sheriff, 26 Oct. 1768, Vol. XI, fol. 308. (Berry.)

HODGETTS-FOLEY, ..., of Prestwood, co. Staff. ; co. Worc. ; and Stoke, co. Hereford, 182 . ., Vol. XXXII, fol. 285.

HODGETTS, late CHAMBERS, William Thomas, of co. Devon and Worc., [4 Mar.] 1867, Vol. LVI, fol. 248.

HODGKINSON to, or late BRENT, William, of co. Kent and Surrey, and sister Rossean, 180 . ., Vol. XXIV, fol. 269.

HODGSON, Joseph, of co. Chester, 3 Oct. 1717, Vol. VI, fol. 326. (Berry.)

,, William (2nd s. of Peter, of Bascodyke, co. Cumberland), of Six Clerks' Office, London, 29 June 1730, Vol. VIII, fol. 82b.

,, ..., of Bascodyke, co. Cumberland. (See HUCK.) 17 . . ., Vol. XI, fol. 122.

,, Sir Richard, Knt., Mayor of Carlisle, co. Cumberland, 1796, Vol. XIX, fol. 201.

,, ..., of Thorney Abbey and Island of Ely, co. Camb., [1811] Vol. XXVI, fol. 179.

HODGSON to PEMBERTON, ... of Trumpington, co. Camb., and Inner Temple, London, 185 . ., Vol. LI, fol. 364.

HODGSON-NICOLL, C. R. P., of Copt Hall, Hendon, co. Middx., 1884, Vol. LXII, fol. 192.

HODSON, John, of Waterloo House, Cambridge, 1896, Vol. LXIX, fol. 142.

HOFFMAN, James Rex, of London. (Burke.)

HOFFNUNG, Sigismund, of Queen's Gate, London, 1896, Vol. LXIX, fol. 38.

HOFFNUNG-GOLDSMID, Sir F., of Pont Street, London, 1896, Vol. LXIX, fol. 61.

HOGARTH, Major, C.B., [1843] Vol. XLVI, fol. 397.

HOGG to CARTWRIGHT, ELLIS, wife of, of co. Chester and Warw., [1817] Vol. XXX, fol. 305.

HOGG after McGARELL, ..., Bart., of co. Antrim, Ireland [Sir James Weir Hogg, Bart., 20 July 1846], 184 . ., Vol. XLVIII, fol. 165. Supporters, [1877] Vol. LIX, fol. 333. [Surname and Arms, 8 Feb. 1877, cr. Baron Mageramorne, 1887.]

HOGGE, Edith Eliza (wife of Lionel Neville, Frederick AMES-LYDE), only dau. and h. of Major Hogge, of Thornham, co. Norf. [no date or reference.]

HOGGE-ALLEN, Capt., 2nd Life Guards, of Lyndhurst, Hampsh., 185 . ., Vol. LII, fol. 243.

HOGGINS, Sarah, Countess of EXETER, of Shropsh. Arms and Crest to her father, Thomas Hoggins, of Great Bolas, Shropsh., [5 April 1794] Vol. XVIII, fol. 304.

HOGHTON to BOLD-HOGHTON [15 Feb. 1825, Sir Henry, 8th Bart.], of co. Lanc., [1825] Vol. XXXV, fol. 138.

,, to BOLD-HOGHTON, ..., of co. Lanc. Arms to wives HARVEY and SANDERS, [1842] Vol. XLVI, fol. 232.

HOLBERTON, William of Torr House, Newton Ferrers, co. Devon, 182 . ., Vol. XXXVII, fol. 359.

HOLBROW, John, of King's Stanley and Kingseite, co. Glouc., [8 Feb. 1787] Vol. XVI, fol. 219.   [Geneal. Mag., V, p. 495, plate, p. 516.]

HOLDEN, late SHUTTLEWORTH, Charles, LL.B., of Aston, co. Derby, and Forcett, co. York, 1791, Vol. XVII, fol. 336.

HOLDEN, William, of Birmingham, co. Warw., Camb., and Hampsh. (died 6 Mar. 1806).   (His son, the Rev. William Lucas Holden, assumed the surname of ROSE in 1785.) [Arms] 10 Feb. 1791, Vol. XVII, fol. 290. (Burke.)

„   Rev. William Rose, grandson of William, of Upminster, co. Essex, and Summer Hill, Birmingham, co. Warw. [Arms confirmed and] Crest granted, 19 July 1827, Vol. XXXVI, fol. 295. (Burke.)

HOLDEN, late GREENWOOD, Henry, of Palace House, co. Lanc., 1840, Vol. XLIV, fols. 374 and 375. [Elizabeth, his wife, dau of Henry ASPINALL, of Reedly House, co. Lanc., obtained a Roy. Lic., 28 July 1840, authorizing her and her children to take the Name and Arms of Holden. (Burke.)]

HOLDEN, William Drury, of Darley Abbey, co. Derby, and Nuttall Temple, co. Nottingham, 185 . ., Vol. L, fol. 354.

HOLDEN to LOWE, William Drury, of Locke Park, co. Derby, 185 . ., Vol. L, fol. 356.

HOLDEN, Isaac, Bart., M.P., of Oakworth House, Keighley, co. York, 186 . ., Vol. LVI, fol. 322.

„   E. J., of Glenaly, Great Barr, co. Staff., 1889, Vol. LXV, fol. 131.

„   J., Bart., of Cemetery Road, Bradford, co. York, and France, 1893, Vol. LXVII, fol. 255.

HOLDEN to RENDALL, Francis Shuttleworth, of Aston Hall, co. Derby, 1877, Vol. LIX, fol. 350.

HOLDER, John Charles (Bart.), of Pitmaston, Moxley, co. Worc., 1898, Vol. LXX, fol. 100 [?].

HOLDICH, Rev. Thomas, Rector of Maidwell, co. Northampton, 1824, Vol. XXXIV, fol. 324. (Berry's Appx.)

HOLDICH-HUNGERFORD, Henry Hungerford, of Dingley Hall, co. Northampton, 185 . ., Vol. L, fol. 191. (Berry.)

HOLDIP, Thomas, of the Middle Temple, London (Thomas, s. of James), of Kingsclere, Hampsh., to the descendants of his father James, 5 June 1725, Vol. VII, fol. 315 ; Add. MS. 14,830, fol. 122.

HOLE, ..., of Caunton, co. Nottingham, [1825] Vol. XXXV, fol. 253.

HOLE, late CARTER, ..., of co. Devon, [1852] Vol. L, fol. 225.

HOLFORD, Charles, of Hampstead, co. Middx., 1832, Vol. XXXIX, fol. 21.

HOLFORD to GWYNNE-HOLFORD, Major James Price, of Wales, 1832, Vol. XXXIX, fol. 34.

HOLFORD, John, of Regent's Park, London, and Manchester, co. Lanc., 1844, Vol. XLVII, fol. 275.

HOLKER, Lawrence, of London, and Gravesend, co. Kent, 1 Jan. 1770, Vol. XII, fol. 3. (Berry.)

HOLLAND, Baroness [6 May 1762], [Lady Georgiana] Fox.   Supporters, 17 . . ., Vol. X, fol. 422.

HOLLAND to BATEMAN-ROBSON, ..., of Hartford, co. Huntingdon, and London, [1792] Vol. XVIII, fol. 13.

HOLLAND, late DANCE, Sir Nathaniel, M.P., of Wittenham, Berks., Lord of the Manor of Wittenham, [1800] Vol. XXI, fol. 46.

HOLLAND after DYSON, ..., of Rochdale, co. Lanc. ; Heighington, co. Linc. ; and Clay House, Halifax, co. York, [1817] Vol. XXX, fol. 248.

HOLLAND-CORBETT, ..., of Admington, co. Glouc., [1839] Vol. XLIII, fol. 380.

HOLLAND to HOLLAND-CORBETT, of Admington, co. Glouc., 187 . ., Vol. LVIII, fol. 123.

HOLLAND, Thomas Lindsey, of Cornwall Terrace, Regent's Park, London, 184 . ., Vol. XLV, fol. 88.

„   Henry, M.D., &c., of Sandlebridge, co. Chester, Physician to the Queen, 185 . ., Vol. L, fol. 320.

HOLLAND-HIBBERT, Arthur Henry, of Munden, co. Hertf., s. of Sir Henry Thurstan Holland, 1876, Vol. LIX, fol. 234 (see Berry's Suppl.).

HOLLAND, S. L., of Great Otterspool House, Aldenham, co. Hertf., 1895,* Vol. LXVIII, fol. 320.

HOLLES, Baron PELHAM [4 May 1762]. Supporters, 17 . . ., Vol. XI [? X], fol. 346.

HOLLEST to WILLIAMS, ..., of Castle Hill, Farnham, co. Surrey, [1842] Vol. XLVI, fol. 126.

HOLLESTER, Luke, of Worthy, Admondbury, co. Glouc., and Birdcombe Court, Wraxall, co. Somerset, [1780 ?] Vol. XIV, fol. 304.

HOLLIGAN, James, of Barbados, 18 . . ., Vol. XLIV, fol. 113.

HOLLINGBURY to DENNE, ..., of co. Kent, [1823] Vol. XXXIV, fols. 33 and 35.

HOLLINS, ..., of Shelton, co. Staff., [1811] Vol. XXVI, fol. 281.

HOLLINSHEAD after BROCK, ..., of co. Lanc., 180 . ., Vol. XXII, fols. 21 and 359.

„ after BLUNDELL, of Liverpool and Chorley, co. Lanc., 180 . ., Vol. XXII, fol. 34.

HOLLIS, Thomas (s. of Thomas), of Mansel Street, Goodman's Fields, London, 10 April 1727, Vol. VII, fol. 559. Add. MS. 14,831, fol. 29, to descendants of his father.

HOLLIST, late CAPRON, Anthony, of Midhurst, co. Sussex, 1833, Vol. XXXIX, fol. 376.

HOLLOWAY, John, of Westham, co. Essex, May 1725, Vol. VII, fol. 487.

„ John, Vice-Adm. and Gov. of Newfoundland, [1808] Vol. XXIV, fol. 407.

HOLLOWAY after ELPHINSTONE, Major, R.E., of co. Devon, [1825] Vol. XXXV, fol. 262.

HOLLOWAY, late MARTELLI, Horatio F. K., of Hampsh., and London (Brasenose Coll., Oxf.), 182 . ., Vol. XXXVII, fol. 227.

HOLLOWAY, Maj.-Gen. Sir Charles, Knt., of Stoke Cottage, Devonport, co. Devon, [1825] Vol. XXXV, fol. 260.

HOLLWAY-CALTHORPE, Henry (s. of James Henry), of Stanhoe, co. Norf., 1878, Vol. LX, fol. 153. (Berry's Suppl.)

HOLMAN, late PEACOCK, ..., of Enfield, co. Middx., and Jamaica, 180 . ., Vol. XXIV, fol. 215.

HOLME to BANKES, Meyrick, of Winstanley and Upholland, co. Lanc., 180 . ., Vol. XXII, fol. 320.

HOLME, late TORRE, Rev. Nicholas, of Snydale, co. York, Rector of Rise and Vicar of Aldborough, [1811] Vol. XXVI, fol. 373.

„ late TORRE, Rev. Henry James, of Paull Holme, Snydale, and Wakefield, co. York, [1833] Vol. XL, fol. 63.

HOLME, Patrick, of London. Supporters, 1897, Vol. LXX, fol. 58.

HOLMES, John, s. of James Edward, of Garstang, co. Lanc.; Streatham, co. Surrey ; and Lombard Street, London, [1780] Vol. XIV, fol. 336.

HOLMES (see CALMADY), formerly EVERITT, ..., 178 . ., Vol. XVI, fol. 325.

HOLMES to HUNTER, Gubbins, of co. Hertf., and Beoley Hall, co. Worc., 180 . ., Vol. XXII, fol. 430.

HOLMES, ..., of Sedburgh, co. York, and West Barnes, Merton, co. Surrey, [1827] Vol. XXXVI, fol. 359.

HOLMES (late HOLT, reputed son), William Holmes, of West Barnes, Merton, co. Surrey, [1827] Vol. XXXVI, fol. 361.

HOLMES, John, of the Bombay C.S., s. of Maj.-Gen. Sir George, K.C.B., (? of Sussex), [1831 ?] Vol. XXXVIII, fol. 346.

HOLMES after A'COURT, William Henry Ashe, 2nd Baron HEYTESBURY, of the Isle of Wight, and Wilts., [14 Oct.] 1833, Vol. XL, fol. 13.

HOLMES-A'COURT, ..., of Wilts., children of 2nd Baron HEYTESBURY, [9 Aug. 1860] Vol. LIV, fols. 12, 14 and 15.

HOLMES, ..., of Brook Hall, Brook, co. Norf., 184 . ., Vol. XLV, fol. 319.

HOLT, late MILLS, William ?, of Booth Bank, co. Chester, and Bispham Hall, co. Lanc., 181 . ., Vol. XLV, fol. 174.

HOLT-NEEDHAM, O. N. [Holt], of Aigburth, co. Lanc., 1893, Vol. LXVII, fol. 276.

HOLT, Edward, of Prestwich, co. Lanc., and Blackwall, co. Westmorland, 189 . ., Vol. LXXI, fol. . . . .

HOLTE after ORFORD, Richard, B.A., Trin. Coll., Camb., only s. of John, of Manchester, by Elizabeth, only surviving dau. of Robert Holte, of Chamber House, Rochdale, co. Lanc. (died s.p.), [1 Aug.] 1825, Vol. XXXV, fol. 244 (*see* Geneal., VI, p. 33). (Berry's Suppl.)

HOLWELL, John Zephaniah, of Mount Felix, Walton-on-Thames, co. Surrey, and Bengal, 176 . ., Vol. X, fol. 455.

HOLWELL to CARR (William) [Charlotte ?], of Etal, co. Northumberland, and Menheniott, co. Cornw., [20 Nov. 1798] Vol. XX, fol. 257 [*see* Misc. G. et H., New S., II, p. 417].

HOLYOAKE, ..., of Tettenhall, co. Staff., and Morton Bagot, co. Warw., [1809] Vol. XXV, fol. 189.

HOLYOAKE-GOODRICH, Francis, of Morton Bagot, co. Warw., and co. York, 1833, Vol. XL, fol. 50.

HOME, Sir Everard, Bart., H.M. Sergt.-Surgeon, of Well Manor Farm, Hampsh. Augmentation, [1812] Vol. XXVII, fol. 137.

HOME after LOGAN, Capt., R.M.A., of Berwick, Broome House, and Edromes, Scotland, 18 . . ., Vol. XLIX, fol. 305.

HOMFRAY to ADDENBROOKE, ..., of co. Hereford and Worc., [1795 ?] Vol. XIX, fol. 34.

HONYWOOD, ..., of Evington, co. Kent, 16 . . . (Vol. IV, fol. 180 ?).

,, Sir Philip, K.B., of Evington, co. Kent. Supporters, 17 . . ., Vol. IX, fol. 105 [Lieut.-Gen. Philip Honywood, K.B., 12 July 1743].

HOOD, Vice-Adm. Sir Alexander, K.B. [7 May 1788]. Arms and Supporters, 178 . ., Vol. XVI, fols. 383 and 385.

,, Baroness and Viscountess [27 Mar. 1795] (LINDZEE), [1796 ?] Vol. XIX, fol. 279.

HOOD-TIBBITS [6 Feb. 1841], Viscount Hood, of Hampsh. and co. Northampton, 184 . ., Vol. XLV, fol. 97.

HOOD, Sir Samuel, K.B. [26 Sept. 1804], Commodore. Supporters, 180 . ., Vol. XXIII, fol. 115.

HOOD after JACOMB, Robert, of Bardon Park, co. Leic., and Inner Temple, London, 183 . ., Vol. XL, fol. 173.

,, after FULLER-ACLAND, ..., of co. Somerset. [Arms and Name of Fuller-Acland, 14 July 1849], 18 . . ., Vol. XLIX, fol. 215.

HOOD, Baron [Hood of Avalon]. Supporters, 1892, Vol. LXVI, fol. 322.

HOOK to HOOK-CHILD, Albert Theodore, of co. Pembroke, Wales, and Finchley New Road, London, 187 . ., Vol. LVIII, fol. 160.

HOOKER to GREENLAND, ..., of Rottingdean, co. Sussex, [1820] Vol. XXXII, fol. 115.

,, to OTTLEY, John B. (B.A., Oriel Coll., Oxf.), of Testwood, Hampsh. ; Hengrave, co. Suff. ; and Rottingdean, co. Sussex, [1820] Vol. XXXII, fol. 123.

HOOKES, ..., of Conway, Wales. (*See* CORBETT.) Match, 178 . ., Vol. XV, fol. 142.

HOOLE, Henry Elliott, of Crookmere House, Sheffield, co. York, 187 . ., Vol. LVIII, fol. 104. (Berry's Suppl.)

,, ..., of Bradford, Sheffield and Edgefield, co. York, 187 . ., Vol. LVIII, fol. 288. (Berry's Suppl.)

HOOLE-LOWSLEY-WILLIAMS, G. W. L., of Aston, Bucks., 1892, Vol. LXVII, fol. 84.

HOOPER-WATLINGTON, ..., of Reading, Berks., [1852] Vol. L, fol. 223.

HOOPER (Mary, widow of Webster F. Henry), of Withington, co. Lanc., and Tunbridge, co. Kent, and to her son, 186 . ., Vol. LV, fol. 324. (Crisp, I, p. 176.)

HOOPER, Walter F. (Bar.-at Law), of Aylesbury, Bucks., and of the High Court, Madras, 1880, Vol. LXI, fol. 37.

„ . . . . (*see* PURNELL), 182 . ., Vol. XXXVI, fol. 119.

„ George Glass, 2nd s. of Samuel, of Devon, 189 . ., Vol. LXXI, fol. . . . .

HOPE, Lieut.-Gen. [Hon.] Sir John, K.B. [21 April 1809]. Supporters, [1810 ?] Vol. XXVI, fol. 116.

„ Lieut.-Gen. [Hon.] Sir Alexander, K.B. [29 June 1813]. Supporters, [1814 ?] Vol. XXVIII, fol. 30.

HOPE after WILLIAMS, John, of Trevorrick, co. Cornw., 178 . ., Vol. XV, fol. 43. Quartering for Williams, [1826] Vol. XXXVI, fols. 33 and 35.

„ after WILLIAMS. William, s. of John, of Trevorrick, co. Cornw. Crest, [1826] Vol. XXXVI, fols. 33 and 35.

HOPE, late WILLIAMS, ..., of London. [1811] Vol. XXVI, fol. 195.

HOPE-WALLACE [3 April 1844]. Lieut.-Col., of Fetherstone Castle, co. Northumberland, [2nd s. of the 4th] Earl of HOPETOUN, 184 . ., Vol. XLVII, fol. 103.

HOPE, ..., of Netley, Shropsh., 185 . ., Vol. LI, fol. 180.

HOPE-EDWARDES, St. Leger Frederick, Vicar of Grete, Shropsh., and of Netley, [1871 ?] Vol. LVII, fol. 338.

HOPEWELL to SAMBOURNE, ... of Hatfield, co. Hertf., and Wilford, co. Nottingham, [1777] Vol. XIV, fol. 9.

HOPGOOD, John (s. of Thomas), of London, 189 . ., Vol. LXXI, fol. . . . .

HOPKINS, John (s. of William), of Newland, co. Glouc., and Lincoln's Inn, London, with remainder to the descendants of his father, 16 Sept. 1734, Vol. VIII, fol. 187. (*See* PROBYN.) (*See* Misc. G. et H., 2nd S., III, p. 308 ; Crisp, IV, p. 4 ; Berry.)

HOPKINS, late BOND, Benjamin, of Hackney, London. Quarterly Arms, 20 Jan. 1773, Vol. XII, fol. 220. (Berry.)

„ late FANE, to CHOLMLEY, Henry, of co. York, [1792] Vol. XVIII, fol. 29.

„ late NORTHEY, Lieut.-Col. Richard, of Oving, Bucks., and Ivey, Wilts., 17 . . ., Vol. XX, fol. 348.

HOPKINS, Lieut.-Col., of Oving, Bucks.. and Wilts., [Crest, 1800] Vol. XXI, fol. 65.

„ . . . ., of Burdthrop, co. Oxf. Match with DOORMER, [1812] Vol. XXVII, fol. 298.

HOPKINS, Joseph, of Maryland, 1764 (*see* Edmondson's Armory and Berry).

HOPKINSON, late Lieut.-Col., of Wotton Court House, co. Glouc., [1823] Vol. XXXIV, fol. 10.

HOPLEY, George Augustus, of Charlestown, South Carolina, and Liverpool, co. Lanc., s. of Joseph, Gov. of St. Vincent, [1863] Vol. LV, fol. 50.

„ F. H., of Eastmead and New Vale, Albert, Cape of Good Hope, 1888, Vol. LXIV, fol. 282.

HOPPER to WILLIAMSON, Robert, of Whickham, co. Durham, 18 . . ., Vol. XXXVIII, fol. 23.

„ to SHIPPERDSON, Rev. Edward Hector, of Pittington Hall, Garth, co. Durham, 1856, Vol. LI, fol. 459.

HOPSON, late ONGLEY, Capt. William, of St. Margaret, Rochester, and Minster, Sheppey, co. Kent, 1824, Vol. XXXV, fol. 277 [?]. (Berry's Appx.)

HOPTON, ..., of Stanton Lacy, Shropsh., and co. Worc., 17 . . ., Vol. XVII, fol. 368.

HOPTON, late PARSONS, William, of Kemerton, co. Glouc., and Stretton Grandison and Canon Frome, co. Hereford, 1817, Vol. XXX, fol. 262.

HOPTON, Sybil Maud (Spr.) (formerly MYNORS-BASKERVILLE), of Clyro Court, Hay, co. Radnor, Wales, 1898, Vol. LXX, fol. 147.

HOPWOOD, ..., of Blackburn, co. Lanc., 18 . . ., Vol. XLIX, fol. 132.

„ . . . ., of Chancery Lane, London, [1851] Vol. L, fol. 42.

HORDERN, ..., of Oxley House and Shareshill, co. Staff., 182 . ., Vol. XXXIII, fol. 382.

„ Joseph, M.A., of Prestbury, co. Chester, Vicar of Burton Agnes, co. York, and Shaw Chapelry, co. Lanc., 186 . ., Vol. LVI, fol. 13.

HORNBY to FAWSITT, ..., of Hemsby, Leytham, and Kingston-upon-Hull, co. York, [1805] Vol. XXIII, fol. 194.

HORNBY, Rev. Hugh, Vicar of St. Michael-upon-Wyre, and of Kirkham, co. Lanc., [1846 ?] Vol. XLVIII, fol. 168.

„ Rev. George, D.D., of Winwick, co. Lanc. (Senior Fellow of Brasenose Coll., Oxf.), [1863] Vol. LV, fol. 54.

HORNCASTLE, Walter Radcliffe, of Taymouth House, Hackney, co. Middx., 1897, Vol. LXIX, fol. 273.

HORNE, late WARREN, Edmund Thomas, of Butterley, co. Derby, [1784] Vol. XV, fol. 323.

HORNE, John, now of Gamroon, in Persia, E.I.C.S., and to his eldest sister, Mary, and younger sister, Culling, children of John, late of Exeter, co. Devon, and afterwards of London, Turkey Merchant, 21 Feb. 17$\frac{39}{40}$, Vol. VIII, fol. 60 ; Add. MS. 14,831, fol. 12.

„ Edward William, of Cranage Hall, co. Chester, 189 . ., Vol. LXXI, fol. . . . .

HORNECK, Charles, of St. Margaret's, Westminster, June, 1772, Vol. XII, fol. 156. (Berry.)

HORNER, ..., of Wakefield, co. York, 186 . ., Vol. LVI, fol. 134.

HORNYOLD, late GANDOLFI, ..., of co. Surrey and Worc., [1859 ?] Vol. LIII, fol. 99.

HORROCKS, Samuel, M.P., of Lark Hill and Edgworth, co. Lanc., [1804] Vol. XXIII, fol. 17.

HORSENAILE, Christopher, of Warvill, Berks., and London, Feb. 7 or 17, 174$\frac{9}{1}$, Vol. IX, fol. 17. (Berry.)

HORSFALL, ..., of Elmfield House, Warmsworth, co. York, 184 . ., Vol. XLVIII, fol. 198.

HORSFALL to JARRATT, ..., of Elmfield House, Warmsworth, co. York, [1846] Vol. XLVIII, fol. 200.

HORSFALL, James, of Small Heath House, Aston, co. Warw., 1861, Vol. LIV, fol. 150.

HORSFORD, ..., of Weymouth, co. Dorset, [1804] Vol. XXIII, fol. 27.

„ Maj.-Gen. Sir John, K.C.B. Alteration for services, and to his brother, James, [1816] Vol. XXX, fols. 29 and 31. (Berry's Suppl.)

„ Lieut.-Gen. George, of Falmouth Estate, Antigua, [1831] Vol. XXXVIII, fol. 199. (Berry's Suppl.)

„ Sir Alfred Hastings, G.C.B. [29 May 1875], of London. Supporters, 1875, Vol. LIX, fol. 147. (Berry's Suppl.)

HORTON, Anne, of Barkisland Hall and Horton, &c., co. York, 10 Aug. 1725, Vol. VII, fol. 533 [? 333]. (Watson's Halifax, 266 (153).) [Geneal., New S., XXVII, p. 167.]

„ Isaac, of Ystrad by Carmarthen, Wales, and West Bromwich, co. Staff., 185 . ., Vol. LIII, fol. 48.

„ Mary Anne (Spr.), of Middleton Cheney, co. Northampton, and Highbury Grove, co. Middx., [1867] Vol. LVI, fol. 293.

HORTON, late KOLLE, John Henry, of Streatham, co. Surrey, and Islington, co. Middx. [Arms of Horton only.] 186 . ., Vol. LVII, fol. 186.

HORTON after WILMOT [8 May 1823], Sir Robert [John, 3rd] Bart., of Osmaston and Catton, co. Derby, 182 . ., Vol. XXXIV, fol. 60 ?. [Sir Robert Edward, 4th Bart., 11 May 1871], 187 . ., Vol. LVIII, fol. 8.

HORWOOD, formerly GREEN, Charles, of Brasenose Coll., Oxf., [1861] Vol. LIV, fol. 104.

HOSE, ..., of Kentish Town, co. Middx., 3 Feb. 1805, Vol. XXIII, fol. 252.

HOSKEN, Joseph, of Ellenglaze and Carines, co. Cornw., [1816] Vol. XXX, fol. 23.

HOSKEN before HARPER, ..., of Ellenglaze and Carines, co. Cornw., and Davenham, co. Chester, [1816] Vol. XXX, fol. 40.

HOSKYNS after WREN, Chandos, of Wroxall Abbey, co. Hereford, and co. Warw., 1837, Vol. XLII, fol. 112.

HOSTE. . . . .. Bart.. Post-Capt., R.N. Augmentation, Knt., Maria T. of Spain, [1848] Vol. XLVIII, fol. 422. [? Rear-Adm. Sir William, 1st Bart., K.C.B., K.M.T., of Spain, died 6 Dec. 1828.]

HOTBLACK, John, of Rockland St. Mary, and Wislergate, Norwich, co. Norf., 1894, Vol. LXVIII, fol. 69.

HOTHAM, Sir Charles, Bart., K.B. [15 Jan. 1772]. Supporters, 177 . ., Vol. XII, fol. 121.

HOTHAM, late KNOTT, William, of Wimbledon, co. Surrey, and Bognor, co. Sussex, 17 . . ., Vol. XX, fol. 379.

HOTHAM, Lady Anne Jeynes and her sisters. (See YOUNG.) 181 . ., Vol. XXVIII, fol. 352.

HOTHFIELD, Baron [Sir Henry James TUFTON, Bart.]. Supporters, [11 Oct.] 1881, Vol. LXI, fol. 201.

HOUBLON, Sir John, Knt., Alderman of London, of London, and Berks., 169 . ., Vol. IV, fol. 176. [Sheriff of London, Knighted 29 Oct. 1689] (see ARCHER, [1819 ?] Vol. XXXI. fols. 318 and 350).

HOUBLON, ARCHER- to EYRE, Charles, of Welford, Berks.. Derby and Essex, [1831] Vol. XXXVIII, fol. 326.

HOUBLON, (ARCHER-) to EYRE, Charles, of Berks., 183 . ., Vol. XXXIX, fol. 4.

HOUBLON (see NEWTON), 181 . ., Vol. XXXI, fol. . . . .

HOUGHTON, Baron, of co. Chester and York. Name and Arms of CREWE, 1894, Vol. LXVIII, fol. 61.

HOULDSWORTH, ..., of Manchester, co. Lanc., and Gonalston, co. Nottingham, 181 . ., Vol. XXIX, fol. 254.

HOULTON, Rear-Adm. John, of Fairleigh Castle, co. Somerset, and Grittleton, Wilts., 30 Dec. 1791, Vol. XVII, fol. 446 (see Berry's Suppl.).

HOUSTOUN-BOSWALL [? 1847], Bart., of Blackadder, Scotland. [1847] Vol. XLVIII, fol. 281.

  „ -BOSWALL-PRESTON, T. A., of Eden Hall, Kelso, Scotland. Bart., 1888, Vol. LXIV, fol. 257.

HOUSTOUN-DOUGLAS, Rev. Alexander, of Baads, and Elizabeth, of Hampsh. and Scotland, [1833] Vol. XL, fol. 27 ; 185 . ., Vol. L, fol. 175.

[HOVE, co. Sussex, Borough of, 16 Dec. 1899. (Geneal. Mag., IV, p. 29.)]

HOVELL, alias SMITH, ..., of co. Suff. Crest to Baron THURLOW. [Assumed the name Hovell, 8 July 1814], 181 . ., Vol. XXVII, fol. 327.

HOVELL-THURLOW-CUMMING-BRUCE, Thomas John, of co. Suff. Baron THURLOW, of Kinnaird, &c., 1874, Vol. LIX, fol. 53.

How, Richard, s. of Sir Richard, of London, 1691, Vol. IV, fol. 97. (Berry.)

How, ... Lord CHEDWORTH [Baron of Chedworth, 12 May 1741]. Supporters, 17 . . ., Vol. IX, fol. 29.

HOWARD [Henry], Earl of BINDON [30 Dec. 1706]. Supporters, 170 . ., Vol. V, fol. 188.

  „ . . . ., Earl of STAFFORD. Supporters, 172 . . ., Vol. VII, fol. 69.

  „ [Lieut.-Gen., Hon.] Sir Charles, K.B. [2 May 1749]. Supporters, 17 . . ., Vol. IX, fol. 319.

  „ [Lieut.-Gen.] Sir George, [Bart.], K.B. [1774]. Supporters, 177 . ., Vol. XIII, fol. 16.

HOWARD DE WALDEN, Baron [1807]. Supporters, 18 . . ., Vol. XXV, fol. 435 [?].

  „ DE WALDEN, Lucy, Baroness SCOTT before ELLIS, 1889, Vol. LXV, fol. 164.

HOWARD, Matthew and Richard, Merchants (sons of Samuel, late of London, Merchant), 21 Dec. 1714, Vol. VI, fol. 171 ; Add. MS. 14,831, fol. 98.

  „ Charles, of St. Andrew, Holborn, London, 1756, Vol. X, fols. 37 and [1761] 386. (Berry.)

HOWARD, late STANDISH, Ralph, of London. Arms and Crest, 1730, Vol. VIII, fol. 88.

HOWARD, John, Commissioner of Land Tax, of Hackney, co. Middx., fined for Sheriff of London, 1734. 24 Nov. 1735, Vol. VIII, fol. 195b; Add. MS. 14,381, fol. 79.

HOWARD, Eden, of Rendlesham, co. Suff., 17 . . ., Vol. IX, fol. 288.

,, Richard, of Kupon, Hull, co. York, 1773, Vol. XII, fol. 231.

HOWARD to FORWARD, Hon. William, 2nd s. of Baron CLONMORE, Ireland. (*See* Earl of WICKLOW.) [1780] Vol. XIV, fol. 273.

HOWARD, late Upton [? 1807], Lieut.-Col. Fulke Greville (2nd s. of Baron TEMPLETOWN), 180 . ., Vol. XXIV, fol. 271.

HOWARD before MOLYNEUX, ..., of Glossop, co. Derby ; Thornbury Castle, co. Glouc. ; Teversal and Wellow, co. Nottingham, 181 . ., Vol. XXVII, fol. 66.

HOWARD-MOLYNEUX, ... [9 July 1812], bro. of the [12th] Duke of NORFOLK. Exemplification, 181 . ., Vol. XXIX, fol. 305. (Supporters, [1818] Vol. XXXI, fol. 1.)

,, -MOLYNEUX, ..., of co. Cumberland, [1825] Vol. XXXV, fol. 118.

HOWARD-BROOKE, ... [3 Jan. 1835, s. of 1st Bart.], of Ireland, 183 . ., Vol. XL, fol. 303.

HOWARD-GIBBON, Edward, of London, York Herald and Marshal's Secretary, [1842] Vol. XLVI, fol. 224 (*see* MATTHEW, 185 . ., Vol. L, fol. 384).

HOWARD-VYSE, Col., of Stoke Poges and Boughton, Bucks., and co. Northampton, 184 . ., Vol. XLV, fol. 340.

HOWARD, James Scott, of Toronto, co. York, Canada, 185 . ., Vol. LII, fol. 142.

,, William, of Wooburn, Bucks., and Kondrova, Government of Kalouga, Russia, 186 . ., Vol. LVI, fol. 201.

,, Edward Carrington, of Binnington Hall, co. Chester, 187 . ., Vol. LVIII, fol. 117. (Berry's Suppl.)

HOWARD (FITZALAN-) to TALBOT, of London, [19 July 1876] Vol. LIX, fol. 254.

HOWARD, James, of Clapham Park, co. Bedf., M.P. for Bedford, 1879, Vol. LX, fol. 233. (Berry's Suppl.)

,, William, of St. Mary, Colchester, co. Essex, 1880, Vol. LX, fol. 362. (Berry's Suppl.)

,, J. J., Maltravers Herald, of Blackheath, London, 1893, Vol. LXVII, fol. 281.

,, Sir R. N., of Green Hill House, Radipole, co. Dorset, 1886,* Vol. LXIII, fol. 268.

,, Thomas (and TAYLOR, his wife, of Oldfield, co. Lanc.), of Hyde, Stockport, co. Chester, 1833-35, Vol. XL, fol. 134.

HOWE, Viscount. Crest of SCROPE, 177 . ., Vol. XIV, fol. 60.

,, [Maj.-Gen., Hon.], William, K.B. [13 Oct. 1776]. Supporters, 17 . . ., Vol. XIV, fol 104.

,, Baroness, widow of CURZON. Supporters, [1799 ?] Vol. XX, fol. 388 (*see* 16 . . ., Vol. III, fol. 13).

,, Lieut.-Col. Stephens, A.D.C. to the King, of Mistley Thorne, co. Essex, 179 . ., Vol. XIX, fol. 23.

,, ... (*see* STEPHENS), of Mistley Thorne, co. Essex, 182 . ., Vol. XXXII, fol. 157.

HOWE after CURZON [1821], Viscount, of co. Northampton and Nottingham, 182 . ., Vol. XXXII, fol. 349.

HOWEL to HUGHES, Thomas, of Glasbury, co. Radnor, Wales, [1816] Vol. XXIX, fol. 453.

HOWES, ..., of Spixworth and Morningthorpe, co. Norf., 186 . ., Vol. LIV, fol. 200.

HOWITSON, ..., of the Cape of Good Hope, [1812] Vol. XXVII, fol. 246.

HOWLETT, Col. Arthur, C.B., of Foston, co. Leic., and other descendants of his father John Henry 1874,* Vol. LIX, fol. 56. (Berry's Suppl.)

,, ..., other descendants, of co. Leic. The chevron differenced, 1874, Vol. LIX, fol. 58. (Berry's Suppl.)

HOWLEY, William, D.D., Bp. of London (afterwards Archbp. of Canterbury), with remainder to his sister Mary, 25 Sept. 1813, Vol. XXVII, fol. 389. (Misc. G. et H., New S., IV, p. 6 ; 2nd S., II, p. 330 ; and V, p. 831.)

HOWMAN to LITTLE, George A. K., of Newbold Pacy, co. Warw., 1879, Vol. LX, fol. 293.

HOWSON, John, M.A., of Criggleswick, co. York, 18 . . ., Vol. XLIX, fol. 72.

HOY, late BARLOW, ..., of co. Lanc., Essex, Hampsh., and Ireland, 18 . . ., Vol. XXXVII, fol. 241.

HOY after BARLOW, ... Alteration, 182 . . ., Vol. XXXVII, fol. 318.

HOY, Isaac A., of Higham, co. Suff., [1833] Vol. XXXIX, fol. 345.

HOYLE after WHEELWRIGHT, ..., of co. York, 186 . ., Vol. LIII, fol. 354.

HOYLE, Isaac, of The How, Prestwich, co. Lanc., and Hurrichill, Wimbledon, co. Surrey, 26 April, 1886,* Vol. LXIII, fol. 235.

HOZIER, William Wallace, Baron NEWLANDS. Supporters, 1898, Vol. LXX, fol. 180.

HUBBALD, William, of Stoke-next-Guildford, co. Surrey, and Germany, 3 Jan. 170⅞, Vol. V, fol. 285 (see Misc. G. et H., 2nd S., IV, p. 177). (Berry.)

HUBBARD, Nicholas, s. of Nicholas, of Norwich, co. Norf., and Paris, [1827] Vol. XXXVI, fol. 354.

„ John, Baron ADDINGTON [1887], of London, 188 . ., Vol. LXIV, fols. 107 and 109. Match, [1768] Vol. XI, fol. 318.

HUBBUCK, Edward Arthur, of London, s. of Thomas, of Rochester, co. Kent, 1878, Vol. LXX, fol. 199.

HUCK, Richard, s. of Robert, of Knock Longmarton, co. Westmorland, 176 . ., Vol. XI, fol. 122.

HUCK to SAUNDERS, Richard, Ph.D., of Westminster, [1777] Vol. XIII, fol. 293.

HUDDLESTON, late CROFT, Rev. George James, of Wilts., co. Surrey and Upwell Hall, co. Camb., 1819, Vol. XXXI, fol. 245.

HUDSON, Roger (and bro. John), Goldsmith, of London, and sister Hester, wife of Thomas CARY, of London, Merchant, 23 Feb. 170⅔, Vol. V, fol. 95 ; Add. MS. 14,830, fol. 89.

„ Elizabeth, relict of Benjamin, s. of William, Merchant, of Burlington, co. York, to descendants of William (with WILSON quartering), wife, 10 April 1766, Vol. XI, fol. 149. [See Burke.]

„ John, s. of Joseph, D.D., Prebend. of Carlisle, of Caldbeck, co. Cumberland, 1786, Vol. XVI, fol. 189.

„ Sir Charles Grave, of Bouther Beck, co. Cumberland, and Wanlip, co. Leic., [1791] Vol. XVII, fol. 350.

HUDSON to PALMER [13 Nov. 1813], Sir Charles Thomas, Bart., of co. Cumberland, and Wanlip, co. Leic., 1813, Vol. XXVII, fol. 443.

„ to BATEMAN, ..., of the Middle Temple, London, co. Lanc. and York, [1818] Vol. XXXI, fol. 80.

HUDSON after DONALDSON, Charles, of Shropsh., 1862, Vol. LIV, fol. 238.

HUDSON, James, of Capiner, Nutfield, co. Surrey, 1891, Vol. LXVI, fol. 110.

„ William H., Judge of Bengal, 1886,* Vol. LXIII, fol. 303.

HUDSON-EARLE, T. G., of Rocklands, Torquay, co. Devon, 1894, Vol. LXVIII, fol. 116.

HUDSON-KINAHAN, Sir E. H., Bart., of Ireland. Arms [granted ?] in Dublin. Supporters, 1888, Vol. LXIV, fol. 203.

HUDSON, Rev. Joseph, of Carlisle. [No reference.]

HUGER, Daniel, of South Carolina, 1771, Vol. XII, fol. 110. (D, 18, fol. 59, and Berry.)

HUGESSEN, late SPRATT, of Stodmarsh Court, co. Kent, 180 . ., Vol. XXI, fol. 276.

HUGESSEN after KNATCHBULL [6 Aug. 1849], Bart., of co. Kent, 184 . ., Vol. XLIX, fols. 212 and 214.

HUGGETT, late POTTER, Samuel, of Broadstairs and Stone Farm, Isle of Thanet, co. Kent, 184 . ., Vol. XLVIII, fol. 240.

„ late TOWLE, ..., of co. Kent, [1851 ?] Vol. XLIX, fol. 475.

HUGGINS, John (Warden of the Fleet), of St. Martins-in-the-Fields, London, J.P., co. Middx., 15 June 1725, Vol. VII, fol. 465 ; Add. MS. 14,831, fol. 50.

Huggins, Edward, of Kentish Town, London, 185 . ., Vol. L, fol. 155.
Hughes [Rear-Adm.], Sir Edward, K.B. [9 Dec. 1778], of Hertingfordbury, co.
    Hertf., [1778] Vol. XIV, fol. 50. Supporters, [1778] Vol. XIV, fol. 53.
Hughes, Edward Ball-, formerly Edward Hughes-Ball, [1819] Vol. XXXI,
    fol. 239 (see Johnson, 181 . ., Vol. XXXI, fol. 160).
Hughes, John, of Guildford, co. Surrey, 179 . ., Vol. XVIII, fol. 83.
Hughes to Chamberlain, Thomas C., of Wardington, co. Oxf., [1793] Vol.
    XVIII (fol. 276ᶜ).
Hughes, late Whitelock, Hugh, of Hoddesden, co. Hertf., [1795 ?] Vol. XIX,
    fol. 95.
Hughes before D'Aeth, Lieut., R.N., of co. Kent, [1808] Vol. XXIV, fol. 440.
Hughes, late Howel, Thomas, of Wales, [1816] Vol. XXIX, fol. 453.
Hughes-Hallett, ..., of co. Essex and Kent, [1823] Vol. XXXIV, fol. 56.
Hughes, late Hewett, ..., of co. Surrey, [1825] Vol. XXXV, fol. 268.
Hughes, Rev. Hugh, of Hardwick, co. Northampton, and Nuneaton and Wolvey,
    co. Warw., 1837 [1829 ?], Vol. XXXVIII, fol. 42.
Hughes, late Pringle, ..., of Middleton Hall, Ilderton, co. Northumberland,
    183 . ., Vol. XL, fol. 338.
Hughes, ..., of Wales, 185 . ., Vol. L, fol. 422.
Hughes to Thomas, ..., of Wales, 185 . ., Vol. L, fol. 428.
Hughes, ..., of Southcote Lodge, Reading, Berks., and Darling Downs,
    Queensland, Australia, [1861] Vol. LIV, fol. 188.
Hughes-Le Fleming, George C., of Rydal Hall, co. Westmorland, 1861, Vol.
    LIV, fol. 258.
Hughes to Otway, ... (Capt., Dragoon Guards), of Ceom Elan, co. Radnor,
    Wales, [1873] Vol. LVIII, fol. 193.
    ,,   to Hughes-Bonsall, James Frederick, of Aberystwith, co. Cardigan ;
        Glanheidd, Capel Bangor, co. Carmarthen ; and Berrow, co. Worc., 1879,
        Vol. LX, fol. 239.
Hughes, Col. Edwin, of Oaklands, Plumstead, co. Kent, 1887, Vol. LXIV, fol. 90.
    ,,   Lieut.-Gen. W. Templer, C.B., of Woodhayes, co. Devon, 1884,* Vol. LXII,
        fol. 204.
Hughes-Buller, H. W., of Dunley, Bovey Tracey, co. Devon, 1884, Vol. LXII,
    fol. 212.
Hughes, William, of Palace Road, Tulse Hill, co. Surrey, President of the Institute
    of Actuaries, 1898, Vol. LXX, fol. 263.
Hull to Dauntesey, ..., of co. Lanc., and Westmorland, [1878] Vol. LX,
    fol. 137.
Hull-Brown (see Dauntesey), [1878] Vol. LX, fol. 137.
Hull to Jonson, William, of Dunkettle, co. Cork, Ireland, 1773, Vol. XII,
    fol. 282.
Hull, Edward and Edmund Charles, sons of John, Vicar of Wickhambrook,
    co. Suff., 189 . ., Vol. LXXI, fol. . . . .
Hulley, William Holland, of Rainow, Macclesfield, co. Chester, 1881,* Vol. LXI,
    fol. 231.
Hulse, ..., of Breamore, Hampsh., [1803 ?] Vol. XXII, fol. 237.
Hulton (? Hilton), ..., of Durham. (Match), [1690 ?] Vol. IV, fol. 73.
Hulton to Preston, ..., of Wroxham, co. Norf., [1805] Vol. XXIII, fol. 144.
Humber, William, of Preston. co. Lanc., [1858] Vol. LII, fol. 344.
    ,,   John, Mayor of Preston, co. Lanc., [1858] Vol. LII, fol. 344.
Humberstone, Mathew and others, of Humberston, co. Linc., and Hertf., 1707,
    Vol. V, fol. 281.
Humble to Humble-Crofts, William John, M.A., of Dumpton, Isle of Thanet,
    co. Kent, 1879, Vol. LX, fol. 291.
Humby, George, of Bedford Row, co. Middx., 183 . ., Vol. XL, fol. 149.
Hume, Baron [20 May 1776] (Campbell), Lord Polwarth, of Scotland.
    Supporters, 177 . ., Vol. XIII, fol. 273.   Earl of Marchmont.   Match,
    178 . ., Vol. XVI, fol. 371.

HUME to EVELYN, Alexander, of St. Clere, co. Kent, and Headley co. Surrey, [1797] Vol. XX, fol. 8.

HUME, late MACLEOD, ..., of Harris, co. Inverness, Scotland; South Carolina, and Madras, &c.   Match, [1802] Vol. XXI, fol. 383.

HUME, Joseph, M.P., of Montrose, Scotland, [1811] Vol. XXVI, fol. 408.

HUME to DICK, ..., of Ireland, [1864] Vol. LV, fol. 180.

HUME (late KENNEDY), John Hume, of Ireland ; East Melbourne Colony, Victoria ; Brocklesby and Collingwood Colony, New South Wales, 1877, Vol. LIX, fol. 348. (Berry's Suppl.)

HUME, Robert, of Willow Tree Road, Leeds, co. York, 1889, Vol. LXV, fol. 137.

HUME-COOKSON, J. C., of Willow Tree Road, Leeds, co. York, 1889, Vol. LXV, fol. 145.

HUMFREY-MASON (late BLAKE-HUMFREY), Robert Harvey, of Necton Hall and Heygart Hall, co. Norf., 1879, Vol. LX, fol. 258. (Berry's Suppl.)

HUMFREY after BLAKE, Robert, of Swafield and Wroxham, co. Norf., 184 . ., Vol. XLVIII, fol. 369.

HUMFREYS, Sir William, Knt. and Bart., of London, and Wales, 22 April 1717, Vol. VI, fol. 290. [Powys-Land Club, XIV, p. 17.]   (Berry.)

HUMPHERY, John, Sheriff [1832], afterwards Lord Mayor, of co. Surrey and Middx., [1832] Vol. XXXIX, fol. 164.

HUMPHREY, Alfred Paget (s. of Sir George Murray Humphrey), of Foxton House, Royston, co. Camb., 1898 [? 1897], Vol. LXX, fol. 106.

HUMPHREYS, ..., of Dunsdale, Westerham, co. Kent, 182 . ., Vol. XXXV, fol. 334.

HUMPHREYS (PRICE-) to DAVENPORT, Sir Salusbury, Knt., C.B. and C.H., of co. Chester (his wife nat. dau. of Davenport), [1838] Vol. XLIII, fol. 20.

HUMPHREYS-OWEN, Arthur Charles, of co. Montgomery, Wales, and Lincoln's Inn, London. [Roy. Lic., 24 Nov., Exemplification, 24 Nov.] 1876, Vol. LIX, fol. 284. (Powys-Land Club, X, pp. 418 and 421.)

HUNGERFORD, late WALKER, ..., of Studley Hall, Wilts., and London, [1788] Vol. XVII, fol. 121.

HUNGERFORD after HOLDICH, Henry H., of Dingley Hall, co. Northampton, 185 . ., Vol. L, fol. 191.

HUNLOKE, late FITZCLARENCE, The Hon., of co. Derby (dau. of [1st] Baron DE LISLE), 186 . ., Vol. LV, fol. 142.

HUNT, ...   See WOLLEY.

HUNT before PRINN, ..., of Charlton Kings, co. Glouc., 180 . ., Vol. XXII, fols. 449 and 451.

HUNT to ENYS, ..., of co. Cornw. and Warw., [1814] Vol. XXVIII, fol. 21.

LE HUNT after BAINBRIGGE, ..., of co. Derby, [1833] Vol. XXXIX, fol. 199.

HUNT to ANDREWS, Elizabeth Anne, widow of Henry Hunt, of Shaw Place, Berks., and Goldicote, co. Warw., [1822 ?] Vol. XXXIII, fol. 246.

HUNT, Maj. Richard Burges, of Plympton St. Mary, co. Devon (SNELLING), [1833] Vol. XXXIX, fol. 178.

HUNT (HUSEY), late SENIOR, ..., of Pauncefoot and Compton Castle, co. Somerset, [1833] Vol. XXXIX, fol. 337.

HUNT, Thomas Yate, of Brades, Rowley Regis, and West Bromwich, co. Staff., [1842] Vol. XLV, fol. 372.

HUNT after DALBY, Patrick and Hutchinson, of Kirkby Hall, co. Northampton, [1848 ?] Vol. XLVIII, fol. 433.

HUNT, Thomas Newman, of Dartmouth, co. Devon, and London (Director of the Bank of England), 18 . . ., Vol. XLIX, fol. 299.

HUNT-FOULSTON, John Foulston, of co. Devon, 1875, Vol. LIX, fol. 106.

HUNT, John Joseph (s. of Henry), of Aldwark, Easingwold, co. York, 1898, Vol. LXX, fol. 229.

    „   Arthur Roope (s. of Arthur), of Torquay, co. Devon, Vol. LXXI, fol. . . . . .

    „   Sir F. Seager, Bart., of Cromwell Road, London, 1892,* Vol. LXVII, fol. 33.

HUNTBACH, ..., of Featherstone, Wolverhampton, co. Staff. Match, [1764] Vol. XI, fol. 3.

HUNTE, ..., of Cliff Court, Frenchay and Winterbourne, co. Glouc., [1864] Vol. LV, fol. 208.

HUNTER, ..., of Crowland Abbey, co. Linc., [1803] Vol. XXII, fol. 176.

HUNTER, late HOLMES, Thomas Gubbins, of co. Hertf., and Beoley Hall, co. Worc., 180 . . ., Vol. XXII, fol. 430.

HUNTER, Richard, of Bowkerhead, Ravenstonedale, co. Westmorland (M.A., and Fellow of Queen's Coll., Oxf.), 180 . ., Vol. XXV, fol. 301.

HUNTER-ARUNDELL, ..., of co. Cornw., and Scotland, [1825] Vol. XXXV, fol. 98.

HUNTER to SPEARMAN, ..., of Eachwick Hall, co. Northumberland, [1827] Vol. XXXVI, fol. 238.

HUNTER, John William, of Trin. Coll., Oxf., and Madras, 1828, Vol. XXXVII, fol. 99.

„ Joseph, Assistant-Keeper of the Public Records, London, [1843] Vol. XLVI, fol. 357.

„ William, Alderman of London, and of Bury St. Edmunds, co. Suff., 184 . ., Vol. XLVII, fol. 173.

„ William Henry, of Elm Bank, Manchester, co. Lanc., [1851 ?] Vol. XLIX, fol. 423.

HUNTER to GRAY, ..., of Carse, co. Fife, Scotland, [1851 ?] Vol. XLIX, fol. 440.

HUNTER-WESTON, Lieut.-Col. G. R., of Humberston, co. Ayr, Scotland, 1880, Vol. LXI, fol. 16.

HUNTINGFORD, Edward, D.D., Warden of Winchester Coll., Hampsh., [1802] Vol. XXI, fol. 459.

HUNTINGTON, William Balle, of Woodlands, Darwen, co. Lanc., 1898, Vol. LXX, fol. 151.

HUNTLEY, ... (widow), dau. of WEBSTER, of Boxwell Court, co. Glouc., [1832] Vol. XXXIX, fol. 38.

„ . . . ., of Boxwell Court, co. Glouc., 185 . ., Vol. L, fol. 412.

HUNTON after RAPER, John, B.A., of Londonderry, par. of Barneston, co. York. Quarterly Arms, [1811] Vol. XXVI, fol. 420.

HUNTSMAN, Francis, of Attercliffe, co. York, 18 . . ., Vol. XLIX, fol. 291.

HURD, John (s. of Jacob), of Boston, New England, [1783 ?] Vol. XV, fol. 159.

HURDIS, Thomas, of Atherstone-upon-Stow, co. Warw., 1695, Vol. IV, fol. 204.

HURLE after COOKE, ..., of co. Somerset and Wilts., [1856] Vol. LII, fol. 68.

HURST, J. S., of Copt Hewick Hall, co. York, 1887, Vol. LXIV, fol. 25.

„ John, of Welbury, co. Hertf., 1 Mar. 171⅘, Vol. VI, fol. 222. (Berry.)

„ William, of Hinckley, co. Leic., 1763, Vol. X, fol. 481. (Berry.)

„ Palmer, of Walton-upon-Thames, co. Surrey, 31 Mar. 1788, Vol. XVII, fol. 93.

„ John, of Wakesfield Hold, Helmsley, co. York, and London, 181 . ., Vol. XXVIII, fol. 77.

„ Thomas Toller, M.A. (s. of Thomas Stamford, clerk), Rector of Braceborough and Carlby, co. Linc., 182 . ., Vol. XXXIII, fol. 269.

HURST-WHITWORTH, ..., of Stamford, co. Linc., and Buckden and Stilton, co. Huntingdon, 182 . ., Vol. XXXIII, fol. 270.

HURST, Richard, of Spring Hill, Rochdale, co. Lanc., 1887, Vol. LXIV, fol. 110.

HURT to SITWELL, Francis Renishaw, of co. Derby, [1777] Vol. XIII, fol. 289.

„ to WOLLEY, Rev. John F. T., of Allen Hall, Matlock, co. Derby, and Beeston, co. Nottingham, 1827, Vol. XXXVI, fol. 351.

„ to EDGE, of Wirksworth, co. Derby, and Strelley Hall, co. Nottingham, 184 . ., Vol. XLIX, fol. 61.

HURT quartering to Sir George Reresby SITWELL, [4th] Bart., 1898, Vol. LXX, fol. 118.

HUSE, ..., of Walkingham [? Wokingham], Berks., [1815] Vol. XXIX, fol. 91.

HUSEY-HUNT, late SENIOR, ..., of co. Somerset. (*See* next name.) 183 . .,
Vol. XXXIX, fol. 337.
HUSEY-HUNT, James Hubert (s. of Rev. James Husey-Hunt, formerly SENIOR),
of Compton Castle, co. Somerset, and 68, The Drive, Brighton, co. Sussex,
1898, Vol. LXX, fol. 235.
HUSKISSON after TILGHMAN, ..., of Eastham, co. Sussex, 185 . ., Vol. LII,
fol. 267.
„ after MILBANKE [Sir J. R.], [5 Jan. 1866, 8th] Bart., 186 . ., Vol. LVI,
fol. 93.
HUSSEY, late ROWE, ..., of Marnhull, co. Dorset, [1788] Vol. XVII, fol. 33.
HUSSEY, Maj.-Gen. Vere-Warner, of Wood Walton, co. Huntingdon. Augmenta-
tion, 180 . ., Vol. XXIV, fol. 176. Supporters (Omrah of the Mogul
Empire), 180 . ., Vol. XXIV, fol. 208.
HUSSEY-BICKERTON [1823]. Sir Richard, Bart., of co. Huntingdon, [1823]
Vol. XXXIV, fol. 64.
HUSSEY (TREMELLYN) to MORSHEAD, Capt., of Lavethan, co. Cornw., 18 . .,
Vol. XXXVIII, fol. 132.
HUSSEY, late MOWBRAY, Richard, C.B., afterwards K.C.B., Rear-Adm., of Wood
Walton, co. Huntingdon, and Cockairney House, co. Fife, Scotland, 1832,
Vol. XXXIX, fol. 101. Supporters, [1835 ?] Vol. XLI, fol. 156.
HUSSEY, ..., of Lyme, co. Dorset, [1861] Vol. LIV, fols. 160 and 161.
HUSSEY-FREKE, Ambrose Denis, of Wilts., 1863, Vol. LV, fol. 102.
HUSTLER, Sir William, of Acklam in Cleveland, co. York, 8 June 1726, Vol. VII,
fol. 510.
HUSTLER, late PIERCE, Thomas, of Acklam in Cleveland, co. York, 178 . ., Vol.
XV, fol. 285.
HUTCHINGS, now MEDLYCOTT, ..., Bart. [3 Oct. 1808], of Sherborne, co. Dorset,
and Milborne Park, co. Somerset, 18 . . ., Vol. XXV, fols. 163 and 166.
HUTCHINS, ..., of Wareham and Swyre, co. Dorset. Impalement and escutcheon
of pretence, 179 . ., Vol. XVIII, fol. 73.
„ James (M.A., Oxf.), Rector of Selscombe and Vicar of Piddinghoe, co.
Sussex, 183 . ., Vol. XXXVIII, fol. 136.
HUTCHINSON, ..., of Uckfield, co. Sussex. Match with WILSON, 178 . ., Vol.
XVI, fol. 133.
„ Lieut.-Gen. Sir John Hely, K.B. [28 May 1801], bro. to the Earl of
DONOUGHMORE. Supporters, 180 . ., Vol. XXI, fol. 203.
HUTCHINSON to STAVELEY, Thomas Kitchinman, Capt., R.E., 181 . ., Vol.
XXVIII, fol. 374.
HUTCHINSON, ..., of Bury, co. Lanc., [1818] Vol. XXXI, fol. 119.
HUTCHINSON to SUTTON, G. W., of Stockton, co. Durham, [1823] Vol. XXXIV,
fol. 134. (Berry.)
HUTCHINSON, ..., of Newbiggin Hall and Appleby, co. Westmorland, and
Wollaston, co. Nottingham, 183 . ., Vol. XLI, fol. 380.
„ Robert, Mayor of Liverpool, co. Lanc., [1861] Vol. LIV, fol. 256.
HUTH, C. F. (naturalized), of London, and Stade in Hanover, 182 . ., Vol.
XXXIII, fol. 116.
HUTHWAITE to DONSTON, George, s. of John, of Worksop, co. Nottingham,
178 . ., Vol. XV, fol. 369.
HUTTON, ... (M.A., Oxf.), Vicar of Leckford, Hampsh., 1857, Vol. LII, fol. 230.
HUTTON to FARSYDE, William, of co. York, [1877] Vol. LX, fol. 72.
HUTTON, Col. George Morland, s. of William, of Gate Burton, co. Linc., and to
his uncles, George, Thomas and Henry Frederick, [28 April] 1898, Vol.
LXX, fol. 160. (Hutton Family History, Appendix, 14.)
„ Rev. Charles Frederick, M.A., 189 . ., Vol. LXXI, fol. . . . .
HUXHAM, John, of London, and Plymouth, co. Devon, Nov. 1759, Vol. X, fol. 192.
(Berry.)
HYATT-FOSTER, ..., of London (of the Navy Office), [1824] Vol. XXXIV,
fol. 392.

HYDE, Viscount [24 April 1681]. Supporters, 16 . . ., Vol. III, fol. 142.
„   Baron [3 June 1756] (Villiers). Supporters, 17 . . ., Vol. X, fol. 55.
HIDE, William, of Whetstone, co. Middx., 9 June 1691, Vol. IV, fol. 85. (Berry.)
HYDE, John, of Hyde House, nr. Winchester, Hampsh., Nov. 1717, Vol. VI,
    fol. 337 ; Add. MS. 14,831, fol. 56, as of the City of London, Merchant.
HYDE, widow of . . . . PEARSON, of Tothwell, co. Linc. Arms for Hyde and
    Pearson, the latter during her widowhood, 182 . ., Vol. XXXVI, fol. . . . .
HYETT, late ADAMS, William Henry, of Painswick, co. Glouc., 5 Aug. 1813, Vol.
    XXVII, fol. 343 (see Misc. G. et H., New S., III, 88).

                                    I

I'ANSON, William Andrew, L.R.C.P. (s. of William Andrew), of Westgate Hill
    House, Newcastle-upon-Tyne, co. Northumberland, 1898, Vol. LXX,
    fol. 182.
IBBETSON, Sir Henry, s. of James, Bart., of Leeds, co. York, 1753, Vol. IX,
    fol. 432.
IBBETSON to SELWIN, Sir Charles, Bart., of Donn Hall, co. Essex, 1817, Vol.
    XXX, fol. 103.
IBBETSON, formerly SELWIN, Sir Charles (? Sir John Thomas), Bart., of Donn
    Hall, co. Essex, 1825, Vol. XXXV, fol. 291.
IBBOTSON, Charles, of Crofton Hall, Halifax, co. York, 18 . . ., Vol. XLIV,
    fol. 268.
ICEBY (ICELY ?), Thomas, J.P., of Plymouth and Sydney, New South Wales,
    21 Sept. 1840, Vol. XLV, fol. 3.
IDDESLEIGH, Earl of, of co. Devon. Supporters, 1885, Vol. LXIII, fol. 113.
IDLE . . . ., and STATON, his wife, of Penrith, co. Cumberland, and London,
    180 . ., Vol. XXI, fol. 223 ; of Penrith, co. Cumberland, and London,
    180 . ., Vol. XXII, fol. 390.
IGGULDEN, ..., of London, and Deal, co. Kent, 180 . ., Vol. XXII, fol. 14.
IKIN to CROSSE, Anne Mary, wife to Thomas BRIGHT, of co. Chester and Lanc.,
    182 . ., Vol. XXXVII, fol. 269 (see Lanc. peds.).
ILBERT, William, of co. Devon, 1692, Vol. IV, fol. 122.
ILCHESTER, Lord [and Baron STRANGWAYS, 11 May 1741]. Supporters, 17 . . .,
    Vol. IX, fol. 26.
ILLIDGE, John, of Brixton, co. Surrey, [1833] Vol. XL, fol. 61.
IMAGE, Thomas, of Stanningfield, co. Suff., Rector of Whepstead, co. Suff. (See
    COOKE.) Match, [1811] Vol. XXVI, fol. 306.
IMPEY to IMPEY-LOVIBOND, Col., R.E., of Ireton House, Cheltenham, co. Glouc.,
    and Old Windsor Lodge, Berks., 187 . ., Vol. LVIII, fol. 156.
INCE, Surg.-Maj. John, M.D., of Farningham, co. Kent, 1886, Vol. LXIII,
    fol. 221.
„   Rev. Edward J. C. WHITTINGTON-, M.A. (s. of Rev. Edward Ince, of
    Merrick, Scotland), 189 . ., Vol. LXXI, fol. . . . .
INDERWICK, Frederick Andrew, of Winchelsea, co. Sussex, 1897, Vol. LXX,
    fol. 56.
INGALL, ..., of Clapham, co. Surrey, 18 . . ., Vol. LIII, fol. 66.
INGHAM, ..., of Sugwas Court, co. Glouc., 187 . ., Vol. LVIII, fol. 286.
INGILBY after AMCOTTS (formerly EMERSON), ..., of Wharton, co. Linc., and
    co. York, 1822, Vol. XXXIII, fols. 180 and 182, [1854] (Vol. LI,
    fols. 104 and 106).
INGILBY, Henry John (afterwards Bart.), of Westkeal, co. Linc., and Ripley
    Castle and Kirkleatham, co. York, 1854, Vol. LI, fol. 98 (104, 106).
INGLE to FINCH, William, of co. Camb., 17 . . ., Vol. XIV, fol. 159.
INGLE, George, of Eaton Town, co. Bedf., 1896, Vol. LXIX, fol. 109.
INGLETT to FORTESCUE, Richard, of Dawlish, co. Devon, [1777] Vol. XIII, fol. 283.

INGLISH (late HANSON), Benjamin, of Holborn, London, s. of Thomas, s. of Benjamin, both of Wakefield, co. York, 1800, Vol. XXI, fol. 35.

INGLISH after Hanson, Benjamin, of St. Mary le Strand, London, 1835, Vol. XL, fol. 301.

INGRAM, [5th] Viscount Irvine. Supporters, 171 . ., Vol. VI, fol. 90.

„ Francis, of Liverpool, co. Lanc., and co. York, s. of William, of Wakefield, co. York, 178 . ., Vol. XVI, fol. 147.

INGRAM to CLOPTON, Edward, of Barnet, co. Hertf., and Chelsea, co. Middx., 180 . ., Vol. XXI, fol. 186.

„ to CLOPTON, John, of Barnet, co. Hertf., and Chelsea, co. Middx., [1818] Vol. XXXI, fol. 58.

INGRAM before SEYMOUR-CONWAY [18 Dec. 1807] (Marquis of HERTFORD). Crest and Quarterly Arms, [1808] Vol. XXIV, fols. 352 and 354.

INGRAM after WINNINGTON, of Ribbesford House, co. Worc., and Inner Temple, London, B.A., [1817] Vol. XXX, fol. 254.

„ after MEYNELL, Hugo C., of Temple Newsam, co. York, and Hoar Cross Hall, co. Staff., 184 . ., Vol. XLV, fol. 335.

INGRAM, Sir William James, Bart., M.P., of London (Ill. London News), 1893,* Vol. LXVII, fol. 197.

INMAN, William, of Harefield House, Upton, co. Chester, [1862] Vol. LIV, fol. 292.

„ George Talfourd (s. of Richard Westerton), of Highmore Hall, Henley-on-Thames, co. Oxf., 1899, Vol. LXX, fol. 316.

INSOLE, James Harvey, of Ely Court, Llandaff, co. Glamorgan, Wales, [1872 ?] Vol. LVIII, fol. 99. (Berry's Suppl.)

INWEN, Thomas, M.P., of St. Saviour's, Southwark, London, 6 Feb. 173?, Vol. VIII, fol. 93.

IRBY [Sir William], Baron BOSTON [10 April 1761], of co. Linc. Supporters, 17 . . ., Vol. X, fol. 301.

IREDELL, Arthur, M.A., of Newhaven, co. Sussex, [1792] Vol. XVIII, fol. 37.

IRELAND, James, of Beaminster, co. Dorset, and Brislington, co. Somerset, [1802] Vol. XXI, fol. 439.

IRELAND after CLAYFIELD, James, of Brislington, co. Somerset, [1827] Vol. XXXVI, fol. 230.

IRONMONGER, late SOLA, of Effingham, co. Surrey, and Brighton, co. Sussex (IRWIN, his wife, reputed dau. of Ironmonger), [1837] Vol. XLII, fol. 154.

IRONSIDE after BAX, John Henry, C.B., of co. Durham and Hertf., [1866] Vol. LVI, fol. 223.

IRTON, ..., of Irton, co. Cumberland. (Match), [1783] Vol. XV, fol. 148.

IRTON-IRTON, John, of Irton Hall, co. Cumberland, and Holly Bank, Pendleton, Manchester, 1885, Vol. LXIII, fol. . . . . .

IRVINE, late DOUGLAS (s. of Baron Douglas), of Luddington House, co. Surrey, [1845] Vol. XLVII, fol. 418.

IRVINE, Robert, of West Hartlepool, co. Durham, 1882,* Vol. LXI, fol. 305. (Berry's Suppl.)

IRVING, Clarke, of Kelsick House, Moss, Bromfield, co. Cumberland, and Clarence River and Casino, Richmond River, New South Wales, [1863] Vol. LV, fol. 12.

„ Miss J. E., of Victoria Street, Rochester, co. Kent, 1892, Vol. LXVI, fol. 324.

IRWINE, Lieut.-Gen. Sir John, K.B. [15 Dec. 1775]. Supporters, 1776, Vol. XIII, fol. 159.

IRWIN, R. H., Commander Joseph, R.N., of Witherall Plains, Carlisle, co. Cumberland, 1889, Vol. LXV, fol. 49.

ISAAC, Henry, of London, 175 . ., Vol. IX, fol. 456.

ISHERWOOD, Henry, of Windsor, Berks., 1764, Vol. XI, fol. 14. (Berry.)

[ISLINGTON, London, Borough of, 2 Mar. 1901. (Geneal. Mag., IV, p. 313.)]

ISMAY, Thomas Henry, of Liverpool, co. Lanc., 1875, Vol. LIX, fol. 104.
(Berry's Suppl.)
„   Thomas Henry, of Liverpool, co. Lanc., 1890, Vol. LXV, fol. 321. (Berry's
Suppl.)
ISRAEL-HELBERT, ..., of Gloucester Place, Portman Square, and St. Mary
Axe, London, [1833] Vol. XXXIX, fol. 370.
ISRAEL to ELLIS, ..., of St. Mary Axe and Keppel Street, London, [1865 ?]
Vol. LVI, fol. 30.
IVEAGH, Baron [GUINNESS], of Ireland.   Supporters, 1891, Vol. LXVI, fol. 129.
IVENS, ..., of Swinbrooke, co. Oxf., and the Azores, [1816] Vol. XXIX,
fol. 451.
IVES, Jeremiah, of Colton, and St. Catherine Hill, Norwich, co. Norf., [1827]
Vol. XXXVI, fol. 333.

J

JACKSON-SHEPHARD, Miss, of Hill House, Cradley, Great Malvern, co. Worc.,
1892, Vol. LXVII, fol. 99.
JACKSON, Thomas, of Duddington, co. Northampton, 1689, Vol. IV, fol. 53.
„   Henry, of Christchurch, co. Surrey, 16 Oct. 1700, Vol. V, fol. 13 ; Add.
MS. 14,831, fol. 13. (Berry.)
„   James, of Woodford, co. Essex, and Winksley, nr. Ripon, co. York, 8 Oct.
1722, Vol. VII, fol. 110.
„   Gregory (s. of William), of St. Mary Clist, co. Devon, [1780] Vol. XIV,
fol. 271.
„   Sir George, Bart. [28 July 1791], of Corsham, Wilts., and Richmond and
Thirsk, co. York, [1791] Vol. XVII, fol. 356.
JACKSON to DUCKETT [3 Feb. 1797], Sir George, Bart., of co. York and Wilts.,
179 . ., Vol. XIX, fol. 353.
JACKSON (late ORANGE), Samuel, of St. George's-in-the-East, London, [1793]
Vol. XVIII, fol. 268.
JACKSON, ..., of London, [1802] Vol. XXI, fol. 436.
JACKSON, late SHACKERLEY, ..., rep. s. of Jackson, of Cogshall Hall, co.
Chester, 180 . ., Vol. XXIV, fol. 105.
JACKSON, Charles, of Tweedmouth, co. Northumberland, 180 . ., Vol. XXV,
fol. 298.
JACKSON (see TAYLOR), late of Warth, co. York (decd.), mar. the nat. dau. of the
Earl of SALISBURY, 18 . . ., Vol. XXV, fol. 443.
JACKSON (Sir John, Bart. [1815]), of Jamaica, and Bury Arlsey, co. Bedf., "one
of the Barons in the Parliament for Dover," [1810] Vol. XXVI, fol. 44.
„   . . . ., of Beach Hill, co. Surrey, and Fork Hill, co. Armagh, Ireland, [1814]
Vol. XXVIII, fol. 58.
„   . . . ., of the City of Worcester. Match with JONES, 181 . ., Vol. XXVIII,
fol. 163.
„   . . . ., of Wood Plumpton, co. Lanc., 181 . ., Vol. XXX, fol. 383.
JACKSON to CALVERT, ..., B.D., of Preston, co. Lanc., and St. John's,
Canterbury, 181 . ., Vol. XXX, fol. 385.
JACKSON, Maj.-Gen. (decd.), widow, of co. Chester, [1819] Vol. XXXI, fols. 252
and 324.
JACKSON, late DAY, Jane, Frances and Catherine, of Chester and Sandbach, co.
Chester, [1797] Vol. XX, fol. 10.
JACKSON, formerly GALLEY, ... (Spr.), of co. Chester, [1821 ?] Vol. XXXII,
fol. 331, or 333.
JACKSON (DAY) after GALLEY, John, of co. Chester, 183 . ., Vol. XLII, fol. 261.
JACKSON, Lieut., R.N., of Poplar, co. Middx., [1824] Vol. XXXV, fol. 18.
„   Maj.-Gen. Sir Richard Downes, K.C.B., of East Meon and Petersfield,
Hampsh., and Howarths Old, co. Lanc., 183 . ., Vol. XXXVIII, fol. 152.

JACKSON, ..., of Hyde Park Gardens, London. and Warrington, co. Lanc.
[? Sir William, Bart., 1869], 184 . ., Vol. XLVIII, fol. 109.

„ Rev. John, M.A., of Henley-on-Thames, co. Oxf., Canon of Bristol, Rector
of St. James's, Westminster, Chaplain in Ordinary to the Queen, 185 . .,
Vol. L, fol. 297.

„ Charles, J.P., of Doncaster, co. York, and Lincoln's Inn, London, and to the
posterity of his father. James Jackson, late of Doncaster, decd., 3 June
1854, Vol. LI, fol. 76 (see Misc. G. et H., New S., IV, fol. 37).

„ Gen. Sir James, G.C.B. [28 Mar. 1865]. Supporters, 186 . ., Vol. LVI,
fol. 40.

JACKSON to GOULD, ... [1871, Hamilton Llewellyn Jackson], of co. Dorset
and Ireland, 18 . . . ., Vol. LVII, fol. 336.

JACKSON, William Lawies, of Allerton Hall, co. York, 1878, Vol. LX, fol. 139.
(Berry's Suppl.)

„ Capt. Edwin, of The Hawthorns, Gosforth, and Crosthwaite, co. Cumberland,
1888, Vol. LXIV, fol. 303.

„ John T., Mayor of Rochdale, co. Lanc., 1893, Vol. LXVII, fol. 235.

„ Capt. Randle, of Low Farm, Upwell, co. Norf., 1882,* Vol. LXI, fol. 341.
(Berry's Suppl.)

„ William H., of Toowonga, Brisbane, Queensland, 1890,* Vol. LXV, fol. 327.
(? Berry's Suppl.)

JACKSON-BARSTOW, John J., of Thornton, co. York, and Weston-super-Mare,
co. Somerset, 1896, Vol. LXIX, fol. 118.

JACOB, Maj.-Gen. Herbert, of Tunbridge Wells, Faversham, and Sextin's, nr.
Canterbury, co. Kent, and Guernsey, "Jacob's Horse," 185 . ., Vol. L,
fol. 125.

„ Col. John, C.B., and Gen. Sir George, "Jacob's Horse," [1852] Vol. L,
fol. 209.

JACOBS, ..., of Bristol, co. Glouc., [1811] Vol. XXVII, fol. 25.

JACOBY, James Alfred (s. of Moritz), of The Park, Nottingham, 1879, Vol. LX,
fol. 211. (Berry's Suppl.)

JACOMB-HOOD, Robert, of Bardon Park, co. Leic., 183 . ., Vol. XL, fol. 173.

JACSON to WIDDRINGTON, ..., of Newton Bank, co. Chester, and Newton
Hall and Hauxley, co. Northumberland, 185 . ., Vol. LI, fol. 446.

JAFFRAY, Sir John, Bart., of Skilts, Studley, co. Warw., 1892, Vol. LXVII,
fol. 41.

JAGO before ARUNDEL, ..., of co. Cornw., 181 . ., Vol. XXVIII, fol. 280.

JAGO, John, D.D. (s. of John), of Milton Abbot and Tavistock, co. Devon,
[1818] Vol. XXXI, fol. 88.

JAGO-TRELAWNY, Lieut.-Col. John, of Coldrenicke, co. Cornw.,1886, Vol. LXIII,
fol. 245.

JALFOU, Isaac, of The Triangle, St. John, Hackney, co. Middx., [1839 ?] Vol.
XLIV, fol. 127.

JAMES, Henry. D.D., President of Queen's Coll., co. Cambridge, and sometime
Vice-Chancellor of Cambridge, and to his nieces Mary and Martha, sole
issue of his elder brother Samuel, late of London, Merchant, 21 Mar. 17¾½,
Vol. VI, fol. 17 or 18 ; Add. MS. 14,831, fol. 31.

„ Frederick C. and Walter C., of London (sons of Robert), 189 . ., Vol. LXXI,
fol. . . . .

„ Sir William, Bart. [27 Aug. 1778], of Eltham, co. Kent, and Anne GODDARD,
his wife, 17 . . ., Vol. XVII [? XI], fol. . . . .

„ Montagu, of Haughton Hall, Hanover, Cornwall, Jamaica, 29 June 1772,
Vol. XII, fol. 201. (Berry.)

JAMES, late HEAD, William, of Denford, Berks., 31 Aug. 1773, Vol. XII, fol. 263.

„ late HEAD [1778], Sir Walter, Knt., of Denford, Berks., 177 . ., Vol. XIV,
fol. 18.

JAMES-WOODHOUSE after SECRETAN, of co. Monmouth. Quarterly Arms, 181 . .,
Vol. XXVII, fols. 378 and 382.

James, William, of Deckham's Hill, co. Durham, and the Shieldfield, Newcastle-upon-Tyne, co. Northumberland, 181 . ., Vol. XXX, fol. 63.

James after Grevis, Demetrius, of co. Kent and Suff., 1817, Vol. XXX, fol. 347.

James, ..., of The Close, Exeter, co. Devon, and Yarbury, Banwell, co. Somerset, [1828] Vol. XXXVII, fol. 123.

„ . . . ., of Presteign, co. Radnor, Wales, [1830] Vol. XXXVIII, fol. 105.

„ . . . ., of Trevenan, St. Columb, Truro and Trevalryn, co. Cornw., 184 . ., Vol. XLVII, fol. 299.

„ . . . ., of Highfield House, Chew Magna, co. Somerset, [1868] Vol. LVII, fol. 58.

„ J. C. Horsley, of Kitcott Barton, co. Devon, and Highfield, Lydney-on-Severn, co. Glouc., 1896,* Vol. LXIX, fol. 75.

„ Sir William Milbourne, Knt., Vice-Chancellor, London, [1869 ?] Vol. LVII, fol. 135.

„ John Arthur, of Beaconsfield, Much Woolton, co. Lanc. (s. of David, decd.), 1879, Vol. LX, fol. 263. (Berry's Suppl.)

„ Charles (Col.), of The Crescent, Bedford, 1883, Vol. LXII, fol. 106. (Berry's Suppl.)

„ Baron (Sir Henry), of co. Hereford. Arms, 1896, Vol. LXIX, fol. 57. Supporters, fol. 59.

„ J. G., of Tynrwydd, Blackwood, Bedwelty, and Blaen Nant, Nantyglo, co. Monmouth, 1894,* Vol. LXVIII, fol. 120.

„ Rev. John B., M.A., of Vanbrughfields, Blackheath, co. Kent, 1882,* Vol. LXI, fol. 315.

„ Rev. J. Burleigh, of Vanbrughfields, Blackheath, co. Kent, 1890,* Vol. LXV, fol. 238. (Berry's Suppl., and Crisp, I, p. 266.)

Jameson, William, s. of Hugh (? of Cork), 177 . ., Vol. XIV, fol. 84.

Jamieson after Young, James, of Shilbottle, Newcastle-upon-Tyne, co. Northumberland, and Glasgow, [1848 ?] Vol. XLIX, fol. 18.

Jarratt, Herbert Newton J., of Trelawny, Jamaica, [1793] Vol. XVIII, fol. 218.

Jarratt, late Horsfall, ..., of co. York, [1846] Vol. XLVIII, fol. 200.

Jarrett, James, of London, 19 May 1696, Vol. IV, fol. 236.

Jarvis, ..., of King's Lynn, co. Linc., 185 . ., Vol. LIII, fol. 180.

Jasper, Edward, of Tower Hill, London, 30 July 1729, Vol. VIII, fol. 39 ; Add. MS. 14,831, fol. 121.

Jeaffreson, heretofore Pigott, C. W. (a minor), of Dullingham, co. Camb., 1838, Vol. XLIII, fol. 332.

Jeaffreson to Robinson, Christopher William, of Dullingham, co. Camb., and Denston Hall, co. Suff., 1857, Vol. LII, fol. 279.

Jeakes, ..., of Winchester Hall, Highgate, London, [1861] Vol. LIV, fol. 148.

Jebb, Samuel, of Stratford-le-Bow, co. Essex, and Mansfield, co. Nottingham, 20 Dec. 1728, Vol. VIII, fol. 20.

Jebb after Bowker, Robert, of co. Lanc. (Match), 178 . ., Vol. XVI, fol. 308.

Jeffcoat, J. H., of Newlands, Rochester, co. Kent, 1890, Vol. LXV, fol. 246.

Jeffcock, Capt. Edward, of Wolverhampton, co. Staff., 1882,* Vol. LXI, fol. 289. (Berry's Suppl.)

Jeffcott, ..., of Ballymac Thomas House, co. Kerry, Ireland, Chief Justice, Vice-Admiralty Court, Sierra Leone, [1833] Vol. XXXIX, fol. 249.

Jefferson to Sergison, ..., of Cuckfield Place, co. Sussex, 1812, Vol. XXVII, fol. 171.

„ to Sergison, ..., of Cuckfield Place, co. Sussex, 1784, Vol. XV, fol. 383.

Jefferson, ... Match with Lax, co. Sussex, [1785] Vol. XVI, fol. 7.

Jefferson after Dunnington, ..., of Thicket Priory, Thorganby, co. York, [1841 ?] Vol. XLV, fol. 191.

Jejeebhoy, Sir Jamsetjee, Bart., J.P., of Bombay, 14 April 1842.

Jeffery, ..., of Marazion, co. Cornw., [1775] Vol. XIII, fol. 117.

„ . . . ., of Poole, co. Dorset, 179 . ., Vol. XIX, fol. 197.

Jeffreys-Powell, ..., of Wales, [1867] Vol. LVI, fol. 250.

JEFFREYS, Walter P., of Llwynfron Llandansaint, co. Carmarthen, Wales, 1885,* Vol. LXIII, fol. 3.

JEKEN, John (minor), of Dover, co. Kent, 16 July 1803, Vol. XXII, fol. 304. (Berry.)

JELF, ... (see BOTT), of Out Hamlet, St. Michael's, co. Glouc., and Bushley, co. Worc., [1809] Vol. XXV, fol. 180.

JELF-SHARP, Capt., of Oaklands, co. Glouc., and Kincarrochy, co. Perth, Scotland, [1831] Vol. XXXVIII, fol. 216.

JENKINS after VAUGHAN, ... (minor), of Combe Grove and Preston, co. Somerset. Quarterly Arms, 181 . ., Vol. XXVIII, fol. 185.

„ after VAUGHAN, ..., of Combe Grove, Monckton Grove, co. Somerset, [1876] Vol. LIX, fol. 296.

JENKINS to VERNON, Charles, D.D., Rector of Herringswell, co. Suff., and of Long Sutton, co. Linc., [1860] Vol. LIII, fol. 331.

JENKINS, Sir Richard, G.C.B. [20 July 1838], of Bicton Hall and Abbey House, Shropsh., 183 . ., Vol. XLIII, fol. 212 ; Supporters, fol. 217.

„ . . . ., of Caerleon, co. Monmouth, and Lincoln's Inn, London, [1863] Vol. LV, fol. 64.

„ Maj.-Gen. Charles Vanbrugh, of Cruckton Hall, Shropsh., 1880, Vol. LX, fol. 344. (Berry's Suppl.)

„ E., of The Grove, Presteign, co. Radnor, Wales, 1888,* Vol. LXIV, fol. 205.

„ George H. V., of Douglas Park, Sydney, New South Wales, 1883,* Vol. LXII, fol. 155.

„ Sir J. J., of The Grange, Swansea, Wales, 1891, Vol. LXVI, fol. 235.

JENKINSON, Sir Paul, Bart. [17 Dec. 1685], of Walton, co. Derby (Sheriff), 1687, Vol. III, fol. 310. Match, [1687] Vol. IV, fol. 9.

„ Baron HAWKESBURY [21 Aug. 1786], of co. Derby (? co. Glamorgan, see Earl of LIVERPOOL). Supporters, [1786] Vol. XVI, fol. 181 ; [23 July 1796], Vol. XIX, fol. 391. [Grant of Augmentation to the 1st Earl, 24 Mar. 1797 (Crisp, Notes, II, p. 48).]

JENKS to BROADHURST, ..., of Bucks. and co. Hertf., 181 . ., Vol. XXVII, fol. 366.

JENKYN, late OSBORN, John and James (minors), of St. Albans, co. Hertf., 1800, Vol. XX, fol. 443.

JENNER-TYRRELL, ... [5 May 1828] (son of Bart.), of Boreham House, Billericay, co. Essex (Oriel Coll., Oxford), [1828] Vol. XXXVII, fol. 140.

JENNER-FUST, Sir Herbert, Knt., LL.D., P.C., of Hill Court, co. Glouc., and Chislehurst, co. Kent, 184 . ., Vol. XLV, fol. 359.

JENNER [Sir William], Bart. [1868], Physician to the Queen, of Harley Street, London, 186 . ., Vol. LVI, fol. 331.

JENNINGS, Robert, s. of Thomas, of Hartwell, co. Northampton, 1760, Vol. X, fol. 266.

JENNINGS to STARKEY, ..., of Wenbury Hall, co. Chester, and Allwoodley, co. York. (Match), 1811, Vol. XXVI, fol. 320.

JENNINGS, ... (CROSS and STARKEY), of Allwoodley, co. York. (Match), 1813, Vol. XXVII, fol. 360.

„ . . . ., of The Shrubbery, Buckland, nr. Dover, co. Kent, 183 . ., Vol. XLII, fol. 40.

„ John (s. of John), of Llanrhusted, co. Cardigan, Wales, M.A., Preb. of Westminster (Bishop's MS.), 16 June 1837, Vol. XLII, fol. 139.

„ . . . ., Sheriff of York, [1847] Vol. XLVIII, fol. 363.

„ Anne (see LINGARD), 1871. (Geneal., V, p. 145.)

„ Robert, of St. John's, Westminster, co. Middx., 1760. (Edmondson's Armory, Berry, and Burke.)

JENNYNS, Lieut. J. C., of London, 185 . ., Vol. XLIX, fol. 446.

JENNYNS to DE WINDT, ..., of London, 185 . ., Vol. XLIX, fol. 448.

JENYNS to BLOOMEFIELD, ..., of Bottisham Hall, co. Camb., and Swaffham, co. Norf., [1871 ?] Vol. LVIII, fol. 48.

JEPSON, John Wilkins, Sheriff of City of Gloucester, [s. and h. of Arthur Jepson, late of the City of] Bristol, co. Glouc. [decd.]. Quartering, [20 Aug. 1782] Vol. XV, fol. 98. (Crisp's Fragm. Geneal., V, p. 64.)

„ . . . ., of Heaton Norris, co. Lanc, [1823] Vol. XXXIV, fol. 128.

JERMY, late PROBY, Henry Francis, of Leghorn, Italy, [1784] Vol. XV, fol. 363.

„ late PRESTON, Isaac, of Stanfield Hall, Norwich, co. Norf., [1838] Vol. XLIII, fol. 165.

JERNINGHAM after STAFFORD, ... [5 Oct. 1826], (Baron), of co. Norf., [1826] Vol. XXXVI, fol. 115.

JERVIS, [Capt.] Sir John, K.B. [29 May 1782], of co. Staff. Crest and Supporters, [1782] Vol. XV, fol. 73.

„ [Adm. Sir John Jervis, K.B.], Earl of St. VINCENT [23 June 1797], Adm. of the Blue, of co. Staff. Supporters, 179 . ., Vol. XIX, fol. 455.

JERVIS, late RICKETTS [10 June 1801, William Henry, Capt., R.N.], heir of Earl ST. VINCENT, of co. Staff., 180 . ., Vol. XXI, fol. 188.

„ late RICKETTS, [7 May 1823, 2nd] Viscount ST. VINCENT, of co. Staff., [1823] Vol. XXXIV, fol. 62.

JERVIS after WHITE, ..., of Darlaston, co. Staff., and Bally Ellis, co. Wexford, Ireland. Quarterly Arms, [1793] Vol. XVIII, fol. 279.

JERVIS, ..., of Meaford and Darlaston, co. Staff., and Netherseale, co. Derby, [1818] Vol. XXXI, fol. 67.

JERVIS after PARKER, Edward Swynford, of co. Staff., [1861] Vol. LIV, fol. 140.

JERVIS, late PEARSON, William Henley, of Rocketh, co. Essex, and Bath Eaton, co. Somerset (Viscount ST. VINCENT), 186 . ., Vol. LV, fol. 338.

JERVOISE, ..., of Herriard, co. Hertford, and Britford, Wilts., [1792 ?] Vol. XVIII, fol. 65 and [1793] fol. 211.

JERVOISE after PUREFOY, ..., of Shalstone, Bucks., and co. Hertf. and Wilts., [1792] Vol. XVIII, fol. 67.

„ after PUREFOY, ..., of Shalstone, Bucks., and Wilts. Quarterly Arms, [1793] Vol. XVIII, fol. 212.

„ after PUREFOY, ..., M.A., of Shalstone, Bucks., and Wilts., [1791] Vol. XVIII, fol. 435.

„ after CLARKE, ..., of co. Essex and Hampsh. Quarterly Arms, [1813] Vol. XXVII, fol. 395.

„ after ELLIS, ..., M.A., of Bucks. and Wilts., [1848] Vol. XLVIII, fol. 435.

JERVOISE, DRUMMOND-, [Maj.-Gen.] Sir William Francis, G.C.M.G. [25 May 1878], of co. Surrey. Supporters, 1889, Vol. LXV, fol. 22.

JESSE, ..., of Dowles, Shropsh.; West Bromwich, co. Staff.; Ribbesford, co. Worc.; Chilmark, Wilts.; and Compton, Bucks., 1811, Vol. XXVII, fol. 64.

JESSEL, Sir Charles James, Bart., of co. Kent, 1883,* Vol. LXII, fol. 87.

JESSON, Thomas, of Hill Park, Westerham, co. Kent; Cooper's Hill, West Bromwich, and Leveretts, Handsworth, co. Staff., [1854] Vol. LI, fol. 64.

JESSOP, E., of Ryde, Isle of Wight, 1894,* Vol. LXVIII, fol. 134.

JESSUP, ..., of Westminster, London, and Connecticut, North America. Quarterly Arms, 178 . ., Vol. XVI, fol. 350.

JETT, Thomas, Auditor of the Court of Exchequer, of Churchill, co. Oxf., and Saxony, 11 April, 1709, Vol. V, fol. 339.

JEUNE to SYMONS-JEUNE, ..., of London, and Axbridge, co. Somerset, 18 . . ., Vol. LX, fol. 305.

JEUNE, John Frederic, s. of Francis, Bp. of Peterborough (SYMON-JEUNE), 1878, Vol. LX, fol. 179 and 18 . . ., fol. 305.

JEX-BLAKE, ... [1837], of Swanton Abbots, co. Norf., and co. Suff., [1837] Vol. XLII, fol. 168.

JEYNES, Anne, Lady HOTHAM and her sisters (*see* YOUNG), wife of Adm. Sir William Jeynes [Anne, wife of Adm. Sir William Hotham, G.C.B., and dau. of Sir Edward (or Edwin) Jeynes (or Joynes), Knt., Banker, of Gloucester], 181 . ., Vol. XXVIII, fol. 352.

JODRELL, late BOWER, John, of Manchester, co. Lanc., 5 April 1775, Vol. XIII, fol. 39.

JODRELL after PHILLIPS, ..., of Yeardsley and Henbury, co. Chester, and Manchester, co. Lanc. [1868] Vol. LVII, fol. 68.

JODRELL, Mrs., of Sall Park, co. Norf. (HIGGINS to JODRELL), 1883,[a] Vol. LXII, fols. 56 and 75.

   „   Rev. Herbert Henry, of London (CHURCHILL to JODRELL), 1883, Vol. LXII, fol. 75. (Berry's Suppl.)

   „   Paul, of Yardley and Twemlow, co. Chester ; Duffield, co. Derby ; and Lichfield and Moore House, co. Staff., Clerk to the House of Commons. (Match, JARMAN), 10 July 1707, Vol. V, fol. 241 ; Ped. 3 D., 14, Her. Coll. ; Add. MS. 14,831, fol. 60 ; Crisp, II, p. 104 ; and Berry. [Crisp, Notes, I, p. 104.]

JOEL, Solomon Barnato, of 6, Marble Arch (2, Great Stanhope Street), London, 1898, Vol. LXX, fol. 302.

JOGGETT-CHAMPANTE, ..., of Taunton, co. Somerset, and London, [1820] Vol. XXXII, fols. 110 and 177.

JOHN to FREKE, Col. (C.B.), of Hannington, Wilts., [1835 ?] Vol. XLI, fol. 128.

JOHNS, Richard, of Helstone, co. Cornw., 28 Nov. 1775, Vol. XIII, fol. 140.

JOHNS (BELDAM-), late NASH-WOODHAM, Frederick Meadows, of co. Camb. and Hampsh., 1867, Vol. LVI, fol. 232.

JOHNSON, Matthew, of Witheote, co. Leic., 9 July 1707, Vol. V, fol. 237. (Berry.)

   „   George, of par. of St. Michaell Royall, London, s. of George, of Stokesley, co. York, and of London, s. of Christopher, of Boswell and Stokesley, co. York, to descendants of his grandfather, 10 July 1730, Vol. VIII, fol. 78 ; Add. MS. 14,831, fol. 95.

   „   Elizabeth, dau. of John, of Warrington, co. Lanc. (Edmondson's Armory) (wife of C. POLE), 12 Feb. 174½, Vol. XLIII [Vol. IX], fol. 45.

JOHNSON before KEMEYS-TYNTE, ..., of Burhill, co. Surrey, and Kevn [Cefn ?] Mably, co. Glamorgan. Quarterly Arms, 178 . ., Vol. XVI, fol. 97.

JOHNSON, ..., of Whitehaven, co. Cumberland, 178 . ., Vol. XVI, fol. 324.

JOHNSON to COTGREAVE, (Sir) John, of co. Chester. [? Mayor of Chester, knighted 1816.] [1795] Vol. XIX, fol. 67.

JOHNSON, Croxton, of Wilmslow, co. Chester. (Burke.)

JOHNSON to LYNN, George Francis, of Norton, Bucks., and Spalding, co. Linc., [1796] Vol. XIX, fol. 251.

   „   to LYNN, Walter, of Norton, Bucks. ; Southwick Hall, co. Northampton ; and Horsford, co. Norf., [1831] Vol. XXXVIII, fol. 281.

   „   to SHARPE, ..., of Elksley, co. Nottingham, 17 . . ., Vol. XX, fol. 172.

JOHNSON, William (and John, of Thurmaston, co. Leic.), of Stamford, co. Linc., 181 . ., Vol. XXVIII, fol. 129.

JOHNSON before EDEN [15 Feb. 1811], Sir Robert, [5th] Bart., of co. Durham, [1815] Vol. XXVIII, fol. 414. [1811, Vol. XXVI, fol. 414 ?]

JOHNSON, ..., formerly wife of Edward Hughes BALL, of London, [1818] Vol. XXXI, fol. 160 ; on behalf of her son, Edward Hughes Ball, to be E. BALL-HUGHES, [1819] Vol. XXXI, fol. 239.

   „   Gen. Sir Henry, Bart., G.C.B., Gov. of Ross Castle. Supporters, 182 . ., Vol. XXXIII, fol. 154. Supporters to descendants, Barts., [1833] Vol. XXXIX, fol. 352. [Bart. 1 Dec. 1818, G.C.B. 20 May 1820. Supporters, Roy. Lic., 1833 ?]

   „   Rev. Richard, M.A., of Statham, co. Norf., [1826] Vol. XXXV, fol. 367. (Berry's Suppl.)

JOHNSON (LUTTMAN), late MICHELL, Henry Robinson, of Petworth, co. Sussex (M.A., Fellow of Trin. Coll., Oxf.), [1832] Vol. XXXIX, fol. 31.

JOHNSON, late STEER, Roger Popplewell, of Temple Belwood, co. Linc.　Arms quarterly, both granted, [1832] Vol. XXXIX, fol. 152 [see Burke].

  ,, 　late HILTON, John William D., of Temple Belwood, co. Linc., 1872, Vol. LVIII, fol. 190.　(Berry's Suppl.)

JOHNSON to HAMILTON, ..., of co. Chester, [1833] Vol. XL, fol. 58.

JOHNSON, John, of Runcorn, co. Chester, [1835] Vol. XLI, fol. 4.

  ,, 　James, Capt., Bengal Artillery, of St. Mary, Rotherhithe, co. Surrey, 183 . ., Vol. XL, fol. 99.

  ,, 　William, B.D., of Scaleby, co. Cumberland, [1838] Vol. XLII, fol. 324.

  ,, 　John Edward, of Bolton-le-Moors, co. Lanc., and Lincoln's Inn, London, [1848] Vol. XLIX, fol. 6.

JOHNSON, late CLANCHY, Lieut.-Col. Cassius, and wife Rebecca, of Benleighfield, co. Leic., and Aston upon-Trent, co. Derby, [1851] Vol. L, fol. 10.

  ,, 　late LILLINGSTON, George William, of Worc. Coll., Oxf.; Benleighfield, co. Leic.; and Aston-upon-Trent, co. Derby, 1859, Vol. LIII, fol. 138.

JOHNSON, Francis, of Low Newton and Eglingham Hall, co. Northumberland, and the Deanery, Chester-le-Street, co. Durham, [1873] Vol. LVIII, fol. 210.　(Berry's Suppl.)

  ,, 　Sir George, M.D., of Savile Row, London, 1888, Vol. LXIV, fol. 161.

  ,, 　James, of Catchdall Moss, Eccleston, co. Lanc., 1891,* Vol. LXVI, fol. 47. (Crisp, VII, p. 87.)

  ,, 　J. H., of Albert Road, Southport, co. Lanc.. 1887,* Vol. LXIV, fol. 112.

  ,, 　Richard, of Chislehurst, co. Kent, 1881,* Vol. LXI, fol. 138.　(Berry's Suppl.)

  ,, 　William, of Broughton Hall, Hawarden, Wales, 1880, Vol. LXI, fol. 43.

  ,, 　Thomas, Lord Mayor, London, 1841.　(Burke.)

  ,, 　Arthur, of Woodlands, Bishop Stortford, co. Hertf., 1898, Vol. LXX, fol. 137.

  ,, 　Thomas Fielding, of Knighton, nr. Leicester, 189 . ., Vol. LXXI, fol. . . . .

JOHNSTON impaled by BORWICK.

JOHNSTONE to VANDEN-BEMPDE, ..., of Hackness Hall, co. York, and Westerhall, co. Dumfries, [1795] Vol. XIX, fol. 56.

JOHNSTONE, late VANDEN-BEMPDE, of Hackness Hall, co. York, and Westerhall, co. Dumfries, [1795] Vol. XIX, fol. 59.

JOHNSTONE-SCOTT, ..., of Hackness Hall, co. York, and Woodhall, Kirkby Overblow, co. York, [1860] Vol. LIII, fol. 333.

JOICEY, Sir James, Bart., of co. Northumberland, 1893, Vol. LXVII, fol. 183.

  ,, 　Major William J., of Sunningdale Park, Berks., [1893] Vol. LXVII, fol. 241.

JOICEY-CECIL, Lord John Pakenham, of Newton Hall, co. Northumberland, Lieut., Grenadier Guards, and Isabella Maud, his wife, d. and co-h. of John Joicey, of Newton aforesaid.　Joicey and Cecil quarterly, 1898, Vol. LXX, fol. 237.

JOLLIFF, late MILNER, ..., of co. York, nat. s. of Jolliff, of Nun Monkton, co. York, Capt. of Militia, [1807 ?] Vol. XXIV, fol. 198.

JOLLIFFE, alias JOLLEY.　See TUFNAILE.

JOLLIFFE, ..., of Hull, co. York. (Match with WICKSTED.)　181 . ., Vol. XXVIII, fol. 118.

  ,, 　Baron HYLTON, of Hylton, co. Durham, and of Petersfield, co. Southampton. Supporters, [1866] Vol. LVI, fol. 146.

  ,, 　Rev. William John, M.A., of Merstham, co. Surrey.　Quartering for PYTCHES and HORSALL quarterly, 1832-3, Vol. XXXIX, fol. . . . .

JOLLY, Robert, of Hatton Garden, London, 1692, Vol. IV, fol. 119.　(Berry.)

JONES, Earl of RANELAGH.　Match, 171 . ., Vol. VI, fol. 310.

JONES to SKELTON, Arnoldus, of Branthwaite, co. Cumberland, 19 Nov. 1774, Vol. XIII, fol. 29.

  ,, 　. . . ., of Mainstone Court, co. Hertf.　Match with DURBIN, 177 . ., Vol. XIV, fol. 16.

JONES, ..., of Frankley and Bradford, Wilts., 178 . ., Vol. XVI, fol. 331.

JONES, late TYRWHITT, ..., of Stanley Hall, Shropsh., 17 . . ., Vol. XVII, fol. 213 ; 184 . ., Vol. XLV, fol. 214.

JONES to SMITH, ..., of Castle Comb and Broad Somerford, Wilts., [1798 ?] Vol. XX, fol. 132.

JONES before GWYNNE, ..., of Wales, [1806] Vol. XXIII, fol. 407.

JONES, ..., of Wales, [1806] Vol. XXIII, fol. 410.

    „ . . . ., of Poulston Fawley and Clere, co. Hertf., [1807 ?] Vol. XXIV, fol. 161.

    „ . . . ., of Liverpool, co. Lanc., and Sunderland, co. Durham. (See JELF.) Match, [1809] Vol. XXV, fol. 180.

    „ Thomas, of Sunderland (Banker), of co. Worc., and London, and brothers John and James, [1814 ?] Vol. XXVIII, fol. 163.

    „ Thomas, of Gresford, co. Denbigh, Wales, and Leeds, co. York. Match, 1808, [1809 ?] Vol. XXV, fol. 195.

JONES to CALDECOT, William Lloyd, of co. Linc., [1811] Vol. XXVI, fol. 211.

    „ to CHAMBERS or CHAMBRES, Rev. Edward, M.A., of Wales. Match, [1813 ?] Vol. XXVII, fol. 405.

JONES before LONG, ..., of Whaddon, Bradford, and South Wraxhall, Wilts., [1814] Vol. XXVIII, fol 68.

JONES, Rev. Hugh, M.A., Vicar of Northop, co. Flint, Wales ; and to nephew John and brothers Henry, of Plasterbridge ; Rev. Ellis J., of Lymington, Hampsh., M.A., Jesus Coll., Oxf. ; and Evan, of Coed-y-Rhiwyst, co. Denbigh, Wales, and a sister, 1815,* Vol. XXIX, fol. 136.

    „ Lieut.-Gen. Sir Richard, K.C.B., of Wales. Quarterly for BROUGHTON and his mother, 1817, Vol. XXX, fol. 129.

    „ Rice (s. of Thomas), of New Hall, Rhuabon, co. Denbigh, and Brecon, Wales, Capt., M.P., 1817, Vol. XXX, fol. 280.

JONES-GRAEME, Valentine, Capt. of Dragoons, of Oldbury Court, co. Glouc. ; Bailbrook House, co. Somerset ; and Jamaica, 182 . ., Vol. XXXIII, fol. 304.

JONES to BROWNE, ..., of co. Montgomery, Wales, [1823] Vol. XXXIV, fol. 182.

JONES, ..., of co. Radnor, Wales, and co. Hereford. Match, [1824] Vol. XXV, fol. 41.

    „ Sir Harford, Bart., of Wales. Augmentation (JONES-BRYDGES), [1826] Vol. XXXVI, fols. 7 and 9.

JONES-BRYDGES [4 May 1826], Sir Harford, Bart., of Wales. Supporters (Jones-Brydges), 182 . ., Vol. XXXVI, fol. 133.

JONES after WHITMORE, John Henry, of Chastleton, co. Oxf., 182 . ., Vol. XXXVII, fol. 346.

JONES, Col. John Thomas, C.B., A.D.C., of Cranmer Hall, co. Norf. (afterwards [1831] Bart.), [1831] Vol. XXXVIII, fol. 299.

JONES, now HAMPTON-LEWIS, ..., of Wales, [1832] Vol. XXXIX, fols. 76 and 79.

JONES-PARRY to YALE, Maj., of Madryn, co. Carmarthen, and Llwynn Oun, co. Denbigh, Wales, [1832] Vol. XXXIX, fol. 109.

    „ -PARRY to YALE, ..., of co. Denbigh, Carmarthen, and Merioneth, Wales, [1867] Vol. LVI, fol. 264.

JONES to ATCHERLEY, ..., of Shropsh., and co. Flint, Wales, 183 . ., Vol. XL, fol. 105.

JONES, Morgan (s. of Jacob), of co. Pembroke, Wales, 1835, Vol. XLI, fol. 38.

    „ William, M.D. (Army), of Llanbeblig, Glanhelen, and Panteglas, co. Carmarthen, Wales, 1839, Vol. XLIV, fol. 63 ; 184 . ., Vol. XLV, fol. 77.

JONES to TYRWHITT, ..., widow of . . . . Jones, Bart., of Stanley Hall, Shropsh., 17 . . ., Vol. XVII, fol. 213 ; 184 . ., Vol. XLV, fol. 214.

    „ to NORBURY, Thomas, of Droitwich, Sherridge, and Leigh, co. Worc., 1840 [1841 ?], Vol. XLV, fol. 297.

JONES, Joseph, of Wallshaw House, Oldham, co. Lanc., and Severnstoke, co.
     Worc., [1847] Vol. XLVIII, fol. 279.
JONES to VEEL, David, s. of Edward, of Stanley, St. Leonards, co. Glouc. (of
     Brasenose Coll., Oxf.), 184 . ., Vol. XLIX, fol. 88.
JONES-GIBB, ..., of co. Middx., 18 . . ., Vol. XLIX, fol. 370.
JONES, Lieut.-Col., of Chobham Place, co. Surrey, [1854] Vol. LI, fol. 18.
     „   William, of Spring Hall, Walsall, co. Staff., 185 . ., Vol. LI, fol. 148.
JONES to GWYNNE, Vaughan, of Wales, [1855] Vol. LI, fol. 329.
JONES-MARSHAM, Rear-Adm. Henry Shovell (retired), of Loose, co. Kent, and
     Ballynamore, co. Leitrim, Ireland, [1857 ?] Vol. LII, fol. 290.
JONES, Samuel Thomas, of Glanmere House, Sydenham, and Forest Hill, co. Kent,
     [1861] Vol. LIV, fol. 250.
    „   Lieut.-Gen. Sir Harry David, G.C.B. [28 June 1861], of co. Norf. (Gov.
     of the Mil. Coll., Sandhurst). [? Supporters], [1861] Vol. LIV,
     fols. 252 and 254.
    „   Henry, of Shrewsbury, Shropsh., and Binnum Binnum, co. Macdonald,
     Karrato, Guichan Bay, South Australia, [1863] Vol. LV, fol. 24.
    „   Henry Cadman, of Bower Hill, Repton, co. Derby, [1871] Vol. LVIII,
     fol. 24. (Berry's Suppl.)
JONES to JONES-WILLIAMS, ..., of Grove Hill, Suckley, Kidderminster, and
     Langherne Hill, Wichenford, co. Worc., [1871] Vol. LVIII, fol. 36.
JONES, Adm. Sir Lewis Tobias, G.C.B. [24 May 1873]. Supporters, [1873]
     Vol. LVIII, fol. 254.
JONES, now VAUGHAN, John, of co. Brecon, Wales, 1875, Vol. LIX, fol. 100.
JONES, John Carstairs, of co. Denbigh and Flint, Wales, s. of Wilson, decd.,
     1875, Vol. LIX, fol. 129. (See JONES-FORD, also Berry's Suppl.)
    „   D., of Warborne, Boldre, Hampsh., 1888, Vol. LXIV, fol. 238.
    „   Rev. Harry, of Barton More, Pakenham, co. Suff., 1890,* Vol. LXV, fol. 340.
     (Crisp, I, p. 286.)
    „   Rev. Henry, of Barton More, Pakenham, co. Suff., 1892,* Vol. LXVI, fol.
     306. (Crisp, I, p. 286.)
    „   M. C., F.S.A., of Gungrog, Guilsfield, co. Montgomery, Wales, 1882,*
     Vol. LXI, fol. 343.
    „   O. G., of Llanforda-Isaf, Oswestry, Shropsh., 1891,* Vol. LXVI, fol. 45.
    „   Sir Pryce, Knt., of Dolerw, Llanllwchaiarn, co. Montgomery, Wales
     [Knighted 6 July 1887], 1888, Vol. LXIV, fol. 224.
    „   Thomas O., of Duke Street, St. James', London, 1889,* Vol. LXV, fol. 26.
    „   W. Brittain, C.S.I., of Knockholt, co. Kent, 1896,* Vol. LXIX, fol. 136.
JONES-PARRY, Love Thomas D. (Bart.), of Madryn Castle, co. Carnarvon, Wales,
     1886,* Vol. LXIII, fol. 274.
JONES, William Charles (s. of William Charles), of Preston Brook, co. Chester,
     189 . ., Vol. LXXI, fol. . . . .
    „   Henry H. HELSHAM-, of Holmwood, co. Surrey, [1892] Vol. LXVII, fol. 79.
    „   Richard Heywood HEYWOOD-, of Badsworth Hall, co. York, [1892] Vol.
     LXVI, fol. 283.
    „   William WILLDING-, of Hampton Hall, Malpas, co. Chester, [1895] Vol.
     LXVIII, fol. 174.
JORDAN, ..., of Manchester, co. Lanc., [1839] Vol. XLIV, fol. 43.
JOSEPH, Hyman A., of Rutland House, Highbury, London, 1885,* Vol. LXIII,
     fol. 37.
    „   Thomas, of Botrills, Merthyr Dovan, co. Glamorgan, Wales, 1886, Vol.
     LXIII, fol. 173.
JOSEPH-WATKIN, Thomas Morgan, [Portcullis] Pursuivant of Arms [1894. Roy.
     Lic., surname Watkin, 1894].
JOSLIN, Henry, of Gaynes Park, Upminster, co. Essex, 1894,* Vol. LXVIII,
     fol. 99. (Crisp, IV, p. 65.)
JOUENNE, Lewis, of Bishopsgate Street, London, s. of Garves, of France, [1785]
     Vol. XVI, fol. 23.

JOURDAIN, Sir Henry John, K.C.M.G. [1 Jan. 1900], [1900] Vol. LXXI, fol. . . . .

JOWITT, Edward, of Eltofts, Thornes and Leeds, co. York, [1836] Vol. XLI, fol. 279.

JOYE, James, of St. Dunstan's-in-the-East, London, and Bemfield, co. Northampton, Sheriff, 19 Aug. 1738, Vol. VIII, fol. 246. (Berry.)

JOYE (late SLATER), Mary, of Knightsbridge, co. Middx., 1774, Vol. XII, fol. 290.

JOYNER-ELLIS, ..., of Berkeley, co. Glouc., 181 . ., Vol. XXX, fol. 74.

JOYNSON, Thomas, of Liscard and Wallasey, co. Chester, [1863] Vol. LV, fol. 62. (Crisp, II, p. 48.)

JUBB, Robert, of co. York, [1755] Vol. X, fol. 29.

JUDD, John Philip, of Rickling, co. Essex, [1866] Vol. LVI, fol. 109.

JULL to GODFREY, John, of co. Kent, 1810, Vol. XXVI, fol. 28.

JUMP, Henry, of Liverpool and Woodlands, Wootton, co. Lanc., 1875, Vol. LIX, fol. 92. (Berry's Suppl.)

JUXON to HESKETH, ..., Bart., 5 May 1761, of co. Glouc. and Lanc., [1792] Vol. XVIII, fol. 45. [HESKETH to JUXON [1792]. Sir Robert, 2nd Bart., the surname Hesketh resumed on his death in 1796.]

Report for the Year 1915.

The Council have to report that at and since the Annual General Meeting, held on the 6th day of March, 1915, two new Subscribers have joined the Society, both of whom are Subscribers to the Register Section, and one Subscriber has joined the Register Section.

During the same period the Society has lost three Subscribers by death, one of whom belonged to the Register Section.

The number on the Roll on the 31st of December, 1915, is two hundred and fifty-three, of whom one hundred and sixty-six are Subscribers to the Register Section.

A Volume containing a list of "Grantees of Arms to the end of the Seventeenth Century," compiled by JOSEPH FOSTER, Hon. M.A., Oxon, Brit. Mus. Add. MS. 37,147, edited by W. H. RYLANDS, Esq., F.S.A., Vice-Chairman of the Council, forming the sixty-sixth volume of the Publications, has been issued to the Subscribers for 1915.

A second Volume of "Grantees of Arms," between the years 1687 and 1898, compiled by JOSEPH FOSTER, Hon. M.A., Oxon, Brit. Mus. Add. MS. 37,149, now being transcribed, to be edited by W. H. RYLANDS, Esq., F.S.A., will be issued to the Subscribers for 1916.

Part II of the Registers of St. Mary le Bow with Allhallows, Honey Lane, and St. Pancras, Soper Lane, E.C., containing the Marriages, with Indexes to both parts, edited by the SECRETARY, forming the forty-fifth volume of the Registers, has been issued to the Subscribers to the Register Section for 1915.

The Registers of St. Olave, Hart Street, E.C., containing Baptisms, Marriages and Burials, 1563—1700, to be edited by the SECRETARY, from a transcript presented to the Society by the Executors of the late Bryan Corcoran, Esq., C.C., a past church-warden of the Church, will be issued to the Subscribers for 1916.

Part I of the Marriage Registers of St. Mary le Bone, Middlesex, commencing in 1668, edited by the SECRETARY, is in the press.

The Balance Sheet for the year, duly audited, is appended to the Report.

By Order of the Council,

W. BRUCE BANNERMAN,

Secretary.

The Harleian Society.

FOUNDED 1869.   INCORPORATED 1902.

ACCOUNTS FOR THE YEAR ENDING 31ST DECEMBER, 1915.

ORDINARY ACCOUNT.

Dr.		£	s.	d.	Cr.		£	s.	d.
Balance to 31st December, 1914 ...	...	63	9	7	Messrs. Mitchell, Hughes & Clarke:—				
Subscriptions	...	137	9	6	For printing Grantees of Arms ...	...	166	17	10
Books purchased by Subscribers ...	...	17	10	8	Paid for Transcript	...	51	19	6
Dividend, 3 per cent. Stock, Lancashire and					Fire Insurance	...	6	5	0
Yorkshire Railway (£500)	...	13	10	3	Commission on Cheques ...	...		2	6
					Auditor's Fee	...	1	1	0
					Balance	...	5	14	2
		£232	0	0			£232	0	0

REGISTER SECTION.

Dr.		£	s.	d.
Balance to 31st December, 1914 ...	... ...	99	8	2
Subscriptions	... ...	95	11	0
Books purchased by Subscribers	...	1	17	10
		£196	17	0

Cr.		£	s.	d.
Messrs. Mitchell, Hughes & Clarke:—				
Balance of Account for printing Registers of St. Mary le Bow, Allhallows, Honey Lane, and St. Pancras, Soper Lane, E.C.,				
Part II	...	113	6	5
General Account	...	17	6	6
Secretary and Treasurer	...	30	0	0
Balance	...	36	4	1
		£196	17	0

GENERAL BALANCE.

1915.		£	s.	d.
To Balance, Ordinary Section ...	...	5	14	2
Register Section ...	...	36	4	1
		£41	18	3

1915.		£	s.	d.
Dec. 31. By Balance in the Bank	...	41	18	3
		£41	18	3

Examined and approved.

M. W. KER, Auditor.

14 January, 1916.

W. BRUCE BANNERMAN, Treasurer.

www.ingramcontent.com/pod-product-compliance
Lightning Source LLC
Chambersburg PA
CBHW060335100426
42812CB00003B/1006